Psychological Explanations of Crime

The International Library of Criminology, Criminal Justice and Penology
Series Editors: Gerald Mars and David Nelken

Titles in the Series:

Psychological Explanations of Crime

Edited by

David P. Farrington

Professor of Psychological Criminology
Cambridge University

Dartmouth

Aldershot · Brookfield USA · Hong Kong · Singapore · Sydney

Published by
Dartmouth Publishing Company Limited
Gower House
Croft Road
Aldershot
Hants GU11 3HR
England

Dartmouth Publishing Company
Old Post Road
Brookfield
Vermont 05036
USA

British Library Cataloguing in Publication Data
Psychological Explanations of Crime. –
(International Library of Criminology &
Criminal Justice)
 I. Farrington, D.P.   II. Series
 364.3

Library of Congress Cataloging-in-Publication Data
Psychological explanations of crime / edited by David P. Farrington.
        p. cm. — (The International library of criminology and
 criminal justice)
  Includes bibliographical references and index.
  ISBN 1-85521-447-4
  1. Criminal psychology. 2. Criminal behavior. I. Farrington,
David P. II. Series
HV6080.P826 1994
364.3—dc20   93-37292
                                                                                 CIP

ISBN 1 85521 447 4

Printed in Great Britain by Galliard (Printers) Ltd, Great Yarmouth

Contents

Acknowledgements

The editor and publishers wish to thank the following for permission to use copyright material.

American Association for the Advancement of Science for the essay: Cathy Spatz Widom (1989), 'The Cycle of Violence', *Science*, **244**, pp. 160–66.

American Psychological Association for the essays: R. Loeber and T. Dishion (1983), 'Early Predictors of Male Delinquency: A Review', *Psychological Bulletin*, **94**, pp. 68–99; Joan McCord (1979), 'Some Child-Rearing Antecedents of Criminal Behavior in Adult Men', *Journal of Personality and Social Psychology*, **37**, pp. 1477–86.

American Sociological Association for the essay: Travis Hirschi and Michael J. Hindelang (1977), 'Intelligence and Delinquency: A Revisionist Review', *American Sociological Review*, **42**, pp. 571–87.

The British Journal of Psychiatry for the essays: E.A. Taylor (1986), 'Childhood Hyperactivity', *British Journal of Psychiatry*, **149**, pp. 562–73; I. Kolvin, F.J.W. Miller, M. Fleeting and P.A. Kolvin (1988), 'Social and Parenting Factors Affecting Criminal-Offence Rates: Findings from the Newcastle Thousand Family Study 1947–1980', *British Journal of Psychiatry*, **152**, pp. 80–90; Marshall B. Jones, David R. Offord and Nola Abrams (1980), 'Brothers, Sisters and Antisocial Behavior', *British Journal of Psychiatry*, **136**, pp. 139–45.

Cambridge University Press for the essay: Terrie E. Moffitt and Bill Henry (1989), 'Neuropsychological Assessment of Executive Functions in Self-reported Delinquents', *Development and Psychopathology*, **1**, pp. 105–18.

Her Majesty's Stationery Office for the essay: H.J. Eysenck (1987), 'Personality Theory and the Problem of Criminality' in B.J. McGurk, D.M. Thornton and M. Williams (eds), *Applying Psychology To Imprisonment*, pp. 29–58. Crown Copyright. Reproduced with the permission of The Controller of HMSO.

International Journal of Mental Health for the essay: Lee Nelken Robins and Kathryn Strother Ratcliff (1978), 'Risk Factors in the Continuation of Childhood Antisocial Behavior into Adulthood', *International Journal of Mental Health*, **7**, pp. 96–116.

The Journal of Child Psychology and Psychiatry and Allied Disciplines for the essays: Lee N. Robins, Patricia A. West and Barbara L. Herjanic (1975), 'Arrests and Delinquency in Two Generations: A Study of Black Urban Families and Their Children', *Journal of Child Psychology and Psychiatry*, **16**, pp. 125–40; Michael Rutter (1985), 'Family and School Influences on Behavioural Development', *Journal of Child Psychology and Psychiatry*, **26**, pp. 349–68.

Series Preface

The International Library of Criminology, Criminal Justice and Penology, represents an important publishing initiative designed to bring together the most significant journal essays in contemporary criminology, criminal justice and penology. The series makes available to researchers, teachers and students an extensive range of essays which are indispensable for obtaining an overview of the latest theories and findings in this fast changing subject.

This series consists of volumes dealing with criminological schools and theories as well as with approaches to particular areas of crime, criminal justice and penology. Each volume is edited by a recognised authority who has selected twenty or so of the best journal articles in the field of their special competence and provided an informative introduction giving a summary of the field and the relevance of the articles chosen. The original pagination is retained for ease of reference.

The difficulties of keeping on top of the steadily growing literature in criminology are complicated by the many disciplines from which its theories and findings are drawn (sociology, law, sociology of law, psychology, psychiatry, philosophy and economics are the most obvious). The development of new specialisms with their own journals (policing, victimology, mediation) as well as the debates between rival schools of thought (feminist criminology, left realism, critical criminology, abolitionism etc.) that contribute overviews offering syntheses of the state of the art. These problems are addressed by the INTERNATIONAL LIBRARY in making available for research and teaching the key essays from specialist journals.

GERALD MARS
Visiting Professor of Risk Management, Cranfield University

DAVID NELKEN
Visiting Professor of Law (Criminology), University College London

Introduction

Psychology and Crime

More than other types of theories, psychological explanations of crime focus on individual difference factors such as personality, impulsivity and intelligence, and on internal inhibitions against offending. However, psychological explanations of crime usually also include environmental factors, especially family influences, but also peer, school and situational factors to a lesser extent. In this Introduction, I shall discuss all these various kinds of influences sequentially, since many psychological theories are essentially multiple-factor explanations which assume that offending depends on the sum total of all these different influences acting together. Also, I shall review empirical evidence, since it is important to establish how far that evidence and psychological theories are concordant. I will not review larger societal or community influences which are less commonly included in psychological theories.

Psychologists believe that, like other types of behaviour, criminal behaviour results from the interaction between a person (with a certain degree of criminal potential or antisocial tendency) and the environment (which provides criminal opportunities). Some people will be consistently more likely to commit offences than others in different environments; conversely, the same person will be more likely to commit offences in some environments than in others. A major problem in psychological theories is to explain the development of individual differences in criminal potential. It is often assumed that offences and other types of antisocial acts are behavioural manifestations of an underlying theoretical construct such as the antisocial personality.

Psychologists view offending as a type of behaviour similar in many respects to other types of antisocial or deviant behaviour. Hence, the theories, methods and knowledge of other types of antisocial behaviour can be applied to the study of crime. Generally, psychologists are committed to the scientific study of human behaviour (e.g. Farrington, 1984), with its emphasis on theories that can be tested and falsified using empirical, quantitative data, controlled experiments, systematic observation, valid and reliable measures, replications of empirical results, and so on.

Psychologists usually concentrate on the types of offences that dominate the official criminal statistics in Western countries, principally theft, burglary, robbery, violence, vandalism and drug abuse. There is less concern with 'white-collar' crime or with crimes by organizations. Most research has concentrated on offending by males, since this is generally more frequent and serious than offending by females (e.g. Farrington, 1987a). Psychologists are also interested in biological factors that may underlie psychological constructs.

In order to understand the causes of offending, it is important to study developmental processes such as onset, persistence, escalation and desistance. Psychologists are not just interested in offending when it is in full flow in the teenage years, but also in its childhood precursors and adult sequelae. Also, psychologists believe that it is important not only to focus narrowly on offending, because offending is part of a much wider phenomenon of childhood and adult antisocial behaviour. Generally, offenders are versatile, committing not only many different types of crimes, but also many different types of antisocial acts. Psychological theories aim to explain the development of more general antisocial behaviour, not just legally-defined offending.

An underlying antisocial personality may lead to offending in some circumstances and to other types of antisocial acts in other circumstances, forcing attention to the interactive effects of influencing factors. In particular, there will be different antisocial manifestations at different ages from birth to adulthood. For example, the antisocial child may be troublesome and disruptive in school, the antisocial teenager may steal cars and burgle houses, and the antisocial adult male may beat up his wife and neglect his children. The variation in antisocial behaviour with age is one of the key issues that any theory needs to explain.

Psychologists argue that officially recorded offenders and non-offenders (or, in self-report studies, more and less serious offenders) are significantly different in numerous respects – before, during and after their offending careers. This is basically because of consistent individual differences in underlying criminal potential or antisocial tendency. Generally, the worst offenders according to self-reports (taking account of frequency and seriousness) tend also to be the worst offenders according to official records (e.g. Farrington, 1973; Huizinga and Elliott, 1986). For example, in the Cambridge Study between ages 15 and 18, 11 per cent of the males admitted burglary, and 62 per cent of these males were convicted of burglary (West and Farrington, 1977). The correlates of official and self-reported delinquency were very similar (Farrington, 1992c). Hence, conclusions about individual characteristics of offenders can be drawn validly from both convictions and self-reports. In this chapter, 'offenders' will refer to officially recorded offenders, unless otherwise stated.

Psychologists have made many contributions to the explanation of offending, and it is only possible to mention a small number of these, without a great deal of detail, in this introductory chapter. The essays chosen for inclusion in this book provide more details, while Wilson and Herrnstein (1985), Hollin (1989) and Blackburn (1993) have published more extensive reviews of psychological research on crime. In discussing influences on offending, I will refer especially to knowledge gained in the Cambridge Study in Delinquent Development, which is a prospective longitudinal survey of over 400 London males from age 8 to age 32 (e.g. Farrington and West, 1990). Similar results have been obtained in similar studies elsewhere in England (e.g. Kolvin et al., 1988, 1990), in the United States (e.g. McCord, 1979; Robins, 1979), in the Scandinavian countries (e.g. Pulkkinen, 1988; Wikstrom, 1987), and in New Zealand (e.g. Moffitt and Silva, 1988a).

Natural History and Predictors of Offending

Developmental research shows that the prevalence of most types of offending increases with age to a peak in the teenage years, and then decreases in the twenties and thirties. This pattern is seen in cross-sectional and longitudinal research with self-reports and official records of offending. For example, in the Cambridge Study, the prevalence of convictions increased to a peak at age 17 and then declined (Farrington, 1992a). Self-reports showed that burglary, shoplifting, theft of and from vehicles, and vandalism all decreased from the teens to the twenties, but the same pattern was not seen for theft from work, fraud or drug abuse (Farrington, 1989).

Many theories have been proposed to explain why offending peaks in the teenage years (see Farrington, 1986a). For example, offending has been linked to testosterone levels in males, which increase during adolescence and early adulthood and decrease thereafter, and to changes in physical abilities or opportunities for crime. The most popular explanation focuses on social influence. From birth, children are under the influence of their parents, who generally discourage offending. However, during their teenage years, juveniles gradually break away from the control of their parents and become influenced by their peers, who may encourage offending in many cases. After age 20, offending declines again as peer influence gives way to a new set of family influences hostile to offending, originating in spouses and cohabitees.

While the absolute prevalence of offending varies with age, there is also considerable continuity in offending over time. In the Cambridge Study, nearly three-quarters of those convicted as juveniles (age 10–16) were reconvicted between ages 17 and 24, and nearly half of the juvenile offenders were reconvicted between ages 25 and 32 (Farrington, 1992a). The males first convicted at the earliest ages tended to become the most persistent offenders, committing large numbers of offences at high rates over long time periods. Furthermore, this continuity over time did not merely reflect continuity in police reaction to crime. Farrington (1989) showed that, for ten specified offences, the significant continuity between offending in one age range and offending in a later age range held for both self-reports and official convictions.

Psychological theories assume that there is a high degree of consistency in the relative ordering of any cohort of individuals on an underlying dimension of criminal potential or antisocial tendency over time (e.g. Loeber, 1982; Farrington, 1991a). In general, the antisocial child tends to become the antisocial teenager and the antisocial adult, just as the antisocial adult then tends to produce another antisocial child.

Loeber and Dishion (1983; reprinted here as Chapter 1) and Loeber and Stouthamer-Loeber (1987) extensively reviewed the predictors of male offending. The continuity in antisocial behaviour over time is shown by the fact that among the most important predictors of offending were earlier measures of childhood problem behaviour, including troublesome or disruptive classroom conduct, aggressiveness, lying and dishonesty.

The other important predictors of offending identified by Loeber and Dishion were poor parental child management techniques, offending by parents and siblings, low intelligence and educational attainment, and separation from parents. All of these influences will be reviewed below. In contrast, low socioeconomic status was a rather weak predictor, in agreement with other research casting doubt on the importance of this factor (e.g. Hindelang et al., 1981). Socioeconomic status typically is a central feature of sociological theories, but not of psychological ones.

Individual Influences

Personality

Robins' (1979) explanation of crime suggests that there is an 'antisocial personality' that arises in childhood and persists into adulthod, with numerous different behavioural manifestations, including offending; this idea is embodied in the DSM-3R diagnosis of antisocial personality disorder (American Psychiatric Association, 1987). According to Robins, the antisocial adult male generally fails to maintain close personal relationships with anyone else, tends to perform poorly in his jobs, tends to be involved in crime, fails to support himself and his dependants without outside aid, and tends to change his plans impulsively and to lose his temper in response to minor frustrations. As a child, he tended to be restless, impulsive and lacking in guilt, perfomed badly in school, truanted, ran away from home, was cruel to animals or people and committed delinquent acts. Robins and Ratcliff (1978; Chapter 2) have documented the continuity between childhood and adult antisocial behaviour.

Psychologists have carried out a great deal of research on the relationship between different personality factors and offending. However, the personality scales that correlate most reliably with offending (the psychopathic deviate scale of the Minnesota Multiphasic Personality Inventory and the socialization scale of the California Psychological Inventory: see Tennenbaum, 1977) are probably measuring much the same antisocial personality construct that underlies offending itself. Hence, these personality constructs could not be regarded as possible causes of offending.

One of the best known theories linking personality and offending is that proposed by Eysenck (1977; summarized in Eysenck, 1987; Chapter 3). He viewed offending as natural and even rational, on the assumption that human beings were hedonistic – seeking pleasure and avoiding pain. He assumed that delinquent acts such as theft, violence and vandalism were essentially pleasurable or beneficial to the offender. In order to explain why everyone was not a criminal, Eysenck suggested that the hedonistic tendency to commit crimes was opposed by the conscience, which was viewed as a conditioned fear response. The likelihood of people committing crimes depended on the strength of the conscience.

Eysenck proposed that the conscience was built up in childhood. Each time a child committed a disapproved act and was punished by a parent, the pain and fear aroused in the child tended to become associated with the act by a process of classical (automatic) conditioning. After children had been punished several times for the same act, they felt fear when they next contemplated it, and this fear tended to stop them committing it. According to the theory, this conditioned fear response was the conscience; it would be experienced subjectively as guilt if the child committed a disapproved act.

On the Eysenck theory, people who commit offences are those who have not built up strong consciences, mainly because they have inherently poor conditionability. Poor conditionability is linked to Eysenck's dimensions of personality. People who are high on extraversion (E) build up conditioned responses less well because they have low levels of cortical arousal. People who are high on neuroticism (N) also condition less well because their high resting level of anxiety interferes with the conditioning. In addition, since neuroticism acts as a drive – reinforcing existing behavioural tendencies – neurotic extraverts should be particularly criminal. Eysenck also predicts that people who are high on psychoticism (P) will tend to be offenders because the traits included in his definition of psychoticism (emotional coldness, low empathy, high hostility, inhumanity) are typical of criminals. It seems likely that psychopathy may be a more accurate label than psychoticism for Eysenck's P scale.

Farrington et al. (1982) reviewed studies relating Eysenck's personality dimensions to official and self-reported offending. They concluded that high N (but not E) was related to official offending, while high E (but not N) was related to self-reported offending. High P was related to both, but this could have been a tautological result, since many of the items on the P scale are connected with antisocial behaviour or were selected in the light of their ability to discriminate between prisoners and non-prisoners. In the Cambridge Study, those high on both E and N tended to be juvenile self-reported offenders, adult official offenders and adult self-reported offenders, but not juvenile official offenders. Furthermore, these relationships held independently of other variables such as low family income, low intelligence and poor parental child-rearing behaviour. However, when individual items of the personality questionnaire were studied, it was clear that the significant relationships were caused by the items measuring impulsivity (e.g. doing things quickly without stopping to think). Hence, it was concluded that research inspired by the Eysenck theory, like other projects, had identified a link between impulsivity and offending.

The extent to which personality is influenced by nature (as Eysenck argued) or nurture is controversial. Studies of twins and adopted children suggest that there is some kind of genetic influence on offending. (For reviews, see Wilson and Herrnstein, 1985; Eysenck and Gudjonsson, 1989.) This is indicated by the greater concordance (similarity) of monozygotic (identical) than dizygotic (fraternal) twins in offending. It might be argued that identical twins behave more identically because they are treated more similarly in their social environment, not because of their greater genetic similarity. Against this, however, identical twins reared apart are as similar in many respects (e.g. intelligence, personality, attitudes) as identical twins reared together (Bouchard et al., 1990). Similarly, the offending of adopted children is more similar to that of their biological parents than to that of their adoptive parents (e.g. Mednick et al., 1983; see also Cloninger et al., 1982), again suggesting some kind of genetic influence.

Hyperactivity and Impulsivity

Hyperactivity is an important psychological construct that predicts later delinquency (Taylor, 1986; Chapter 4). It is usually associated with restlessness, impulsivity and a short attention span, and for that reason has been termed the 'hyperactivity-impulsivity-attention deficit' or HIA syndrome (Loeber, 1987). Hyperactivity usually begins before age 5 and often before age 2, and tends to persist into adolescence.

HIA may be an early stage in a causal or developmental sequence leading to offending. For example, in the Cambridge Study, Farrington et al. (1990) showed that HIA at age 8-10 significantly predicted juvenile convictions independently of conduct problems at age 8-10. Hence, it might be concluded that HIA is not merely another measure of antisocial tendency. Other studies have also concluded that hyperactivity and conduct disorder are different constructs (e.g. Taylor et al., 1986; Blouin et al., 1989). Similar constructs to HIA, such as sensation seeking, are also related to offending (see White et al., 1985; Chapter 5). In the Cambridge Study, the rating by parents and peers of daring or risk-taking at age 8-10 significantly predicted convictions up to age 32 independently of all other variables (Farrington, 1990, 1993a); moreover, poor concentration or restlessness was the most important predictor of convictions for violence (Farrington, 1994).

It has been suggested that HIA might be a behavioural consequence of a low level of physiological arousal. Offenders have a low level of arousal according to their low alpha (brain) waves on the EEG, or according to autonomic nervous system indicators such as heart rate, blood pressure or skin conductance; also, they show low automatic reactivity (e.g. Venables and Raine, 1987). The causal links between low autonomic arousal, consequent sensation seeking and offending are brought out explicitly in Mawson's (1987) theory of transient criminality.

Heart rate was measured in the Cambridge Study at age 18. In agreement with the low arousal theory, a low heart rate correlated significantly with convictions for violence (Farrington, 1987b), although it was not significantly related to convictions in general. In addition, being tattooed was significantly related to offending. While the meaning of this result is not clear, tattooing may reflect risk taking, daring and excitement seeking.

In the Cambridge Study, being shy, nervous or withdrawn was the main factor that protected boys from criminogenic backgrounds from becoming offenders (Farrington et al., 1988a, 1988b). In Boston, Kagan et al. (1988) classified children as inhibited (shy, fearful, socially avoidant) or uninhibited at age 2 on the basis of observations of how they reacted to unfamiliar people or objects. This classification of inhibited or uninhibited children remained significantly stable up to age 7 and was independent of social class and intelligence. Furthermore, the inhibited children had a higher resting heart rate and a greater increase in their heart rate in the unfamiliar situation. Hence, just as low arousal may be conducive to impulsivity, sensation seeking and offending, high arousal may be conducive to shyness and may act as a protective factor against offending.

Intelligence and Neuropsychological Deficit

As Hirschi and Hindelang (1977; Chapter 6) showed in their review, intelligence is an important correlate of delinquency – at least as important as social class or race. Consequently, psychological theories of crime often include intelligence as an individual difference factor. In the Cambridge Study, West and Farrington (1973) found that many more of the boys scoring 90 or less on a non-verbal intelligence test (Raven's Progressive Matrices) at age 8-10 were convicted as juveniles than of the remainder. Low non-verbal intelligence was highly correlated with low verbal intelligence (vocabulary, word comprehension, verbal reasoning) and with low school attainment, all of which measures predicted juvenile convictions to much the same extent. In addition to their poor school performance, delinquents tended to be frequent truants, to leave school at the earliest possible age (which was then 15) and to take no school examinations.

Low non-verbal intelligence was especially characteristic of the juvenile recidivists and those first convicted at the earliest ages (10-13). Furthermore, low non-verbal intelligence predicted juvenile self-reported offending to almost exactly the same degree as juvenile convictions, suggesting that the link between low intelligence and delinquency was not caused by the less intelligent boys having a greater probability of being caught. Also, measures of intelligence predicted measures of offending independently of other variables such as family income and family size. Similar results have been obtained in other projects (e.g. Wilson and Herrnstein, 1985; Moffitt and Silva, 1988a; Lynam et al., 1993). It has also been argued that high intelligence is a protective factor against offending for children from high-risk backgrounds (Kandel et al., 1988; White et al., 1989).

Intelligence may lead to delinquency through the intervening factor of school failure, as Hirschi and Hindelang (1977) suggested. However, a more plausible explanatory factor underlying the link between intelligence and offending is the ability to manipulate abstract concepts. People who are poor at this tend to do badly in intelligence tests such as the Matrices and in school attainment; they also tend to commit offences, mainly because of their poor ability to foresee the consequences of their offending and to appreciate the feelings of victims (i.e. their low empathy). Certain family backgrounds are less conducive than others to the development of abstract reasoning. For example, lower class, poorer parents tend to live for the present and to have little thought for the future, and also tend to talk in terms of the concrete rather than the abstract, as Cohen (1955, p. 96) pointed out many years ago. A lack of concern for the future is also linked to the concept of impulsivity.

Modern research is studying not just intelligence but also detailed patterns of cognitive and neuropsychological deficit. For example, in a New Zealand longitudinal study of over 1,000 children from birth to age 15, Moffitt and Silva (1988b) found that self-reported offending was related to verbal, memory and visual-motor integration deficits, independently of low social class and family adversity. Neuropsychological research might lead to important advances in knowledge about the link between brain functioning and delinquency. For example, the 'executive functions' of the brain, located in the frontal lobes, include sustaining attention and concentration, abstract reasoning and concept formation, anticipation and planning, self-monitoring of behaviour, and inhibition of inappropriate or impulsive behaviour (Moffitt, 1990). Deficits in these executive functions are conducive to low measured intelligence and to offending. Moffitt and Henry (1989; Chapter 7) found deficits in these executive functions, especially for delinquents who were both antisocial and hyperactive.

The importance of abstract reasoning and thinking is also emphasized in other psychological theories of offending, for example in the moral development theory of Kohlberg (1976). According to Kohlberg, people progress through different stages of moral development as they get older: from the preconventional stage (where they are hedonistic and only obey the law because of fear of punishment) to the conventional stage (where they obey the law because it is the law) to the postconventional stage (where they obey the law if it coincides with higher moral principles such as justice, fairness and respect for individual rights). The preconventional stage corresponds to rather concrete thinking, whereas abstract thinking is required to progress to the postconventional stage. Clearly, developing moral reasoning is related to developing intelligence.

The key idea of moral reasoning theory is that moral actions depend on moral reasoning (Kohlberg and Candee, 1984). Specifically, it is argued that offenders have retarded powers of moral reasoning and are mainly stuck in the preconventional stage. There is a good deal of evidence that offenders indeed show lower levels of moral reasoning than non-offenders (Thornton, 1987; Smetana, 1990), and some institutional treatment programmes have been designed to improve moral reasoning ability (Scharf and Hickey, 1976; Duguid, 1981; Arbuthnot and Gordon, 1988). However, while moral reasoning is important independently of intelligence, it is unclear whether it is a cause of offending or merely another symptom of an underlying antisocial personality.

Recent Theories Focusing on Individual Difference Factors

Two important recent theories focusing on individual difference factors in offending were propounded by Wilson and Herrnstein (1985; Chapter 8) and Gottfredson and Hirschi (1990; Chapter 9). In many ways, Wilson and Herrnstein's theory is a typical psychological explanation of crime, incorporating propositions seen in several other psychological theories. They suggest that people differ in their underlying criminal tendency, and that whether a person chooses to commit a crime in any situation depends on whether the expected benefits of offending outweigh the expected costs.

The benefits of offending, including material gain, peer approval and sexual gratification, tend to be contemporaneous with the crime. In contrast, many of the costs of offending, such as the risk of being caught and punished and the possible loss of reputation or employment, are uncertain and long-delayed. Other costs, such as pangs of conscience (or guilt), disapproval by onlookers and retaliation by the victim, are more immediate. As in many other psychological theories, Wilson and Herrnstein emphasize the importance of conscience as an internal inhibitor of offending, and suggest that it is built up in a process of classical conditioning according to parental reinforcement or punishment of childhood transgressions.

Nevertheless, the key individual difference factor in the Wilson–Herrnstein theory is the extent to which people's behaviour is influenced by immediate as opposed to delayed consequences. As in other psychological theories, they suggest that individuals vary in their ability to think about or plan for the future, and that this is linked to intelligence. The major determinant of offending is a person's impulsivity. More impulsive people are less influenced by the likelihood of future consequences and hence are more likely to commit crimes.

In many respects, Gottfredson and Hirschi's (1990) theory is both similar to the Wilson–Herrnstein theory and typical of psychological explanations of crime. Gottfredson and Hirschi (p. 208) castigated criminological theorists for ignoring the fact that people differ in underlying criminal propensities and that these differences appeared early in life and remained stable over much of the life course. The key individual difference factor in their theory is low self-control, which refers to the extent to which individuals are vulnerable to the temptations of the moment. People with low self-control are impulsive, take risks, have low cognitive and academic skills, are self-centred, have low empathy and short time horizons. Hence, they find it hard to defer gratification and their decisions to offend are insufficiently influenced by the possible future painful consequences of offending.

Gottfredson and Hirschi argue that crimes are part of a larger category of deviant acts (including substance abuse, heavy smoking, heavy drinking, heavy gambling, sexual promiscuity, truanting and road accidents) which are all behavioural manifestations of the key underlying theoretical construct of low self-control. They concede (p. 186) that self-control, as an internal inhibitor, is similar to the conscience, but prefer the term self-control because the idea of the conscience is less applicable to some of the wider category of acts with which they are concerned (e.g. accidents). Their theory easily explains the considerable versatility of antisocial behaviour.

They argue that between-individual differences in self-control are present early in life (by age 6–8), are remarkably stable over time, and are essentially caused by differences in parental child-rearing practices. Much parenting is concerned with suppressing impulsive behaviour, with making children consider the long-range consequences of their acts, and with making them sensitive to the needs and feelings of others. Poor parental supervision contributes to low self-control; such poor parental supervision is more common in large families, with single parents or with criminal parents. Ambitiously, Gottfredson and Hirschi aim to present a theory that applies to all kinds of crimes in all kinds of cultures.

Environmental Influences

Family Influences

Even in psychological theories focusing on individual difference factors, there is a great deal of concern with family influences. Loeber and Stouthamer-Loeber (1986) completed an exhaustive review of family factors as correlates and predictors of juvenile conduct problems and delinquency. They found that poor parental supervision or monitoring, erratic or harsh parental discipline, marital disharmony, parental rejection of the child, low parental involvement with the child (as well as antisocial parents and large family size) were all important predictors of offending. Utting et al. (1993) have provided the most recent extensive review of the literature on family factors in offending.

In the Cambridge-Somerville study in Boston, McCord (1979; Chapter 10) reported that poor parental supervision was the best predictor of both violent and property crimes. Parental aggressiveness (which included harsh discipline, shading into child abuse at the extreme) and parental conflict were significant precursors of violent but not property crimes, while the mother's attitude (passive or rejecting) was a significant precursor of property but not violent crimes. Robins (1979), in her long-term follow-up studies in St Louis, also found that poor supervision and discipline were consistently related to later offending, while Shedler and Block (1990) in San Francisco reported that hostile and rejecting mothers when children were aged 5 predicted their children's frequent drug use at age 18.

Other studies also show the link between family factors and delinquency. In a Birmingham survey, Wilson (1980; Chapter 11) concluded that the most important correlate of convictions, cautions and self-reported delinquency was lax parental supervision. In their English national survey of juveniles aged 14–15 and their mothers, Riley and Shaw (1985) found that poor parental supervision was the most important correlate of self-reported delinquency for girls, and that it was the second most important for boys (after delinquent friends). Similarly, family dysfunctioning is related to conduct disorder (e.g. Offord et al., 1989).

In the Cambridge Study, West and Farrington (1973) found that harsh or erratic parental discipline, cruel, passive or neglectful parental attitudes, poor supervision and parental conflict – all measured at age 8 – all predicted later juvenile convictions. Furthermore, poor parental child-rearing behaviour (a combination of discipline, attitude and conflict) and poor parental supervision both predicted juvenile self-reported as well as official offending (Farrington, 1979); moreover, poor parental child-rearing behaviour predicted offending independently of other factors such as low family income and low intelligence. Poor parental child-rearing behaviour was related to early rather than later offending (Farrington, 1986b) and was not characteristic of those first convicted as adults (West and Farrington, 1977).

Offenders tend to have difficulties in their personal relationships. The Cambridge Study males who were in conflict with their parents at age 18 tended to be juvenile but not adult offenders. Both juvenile and adult offenders tended either to have a poor relationship with their wife or cohabitee at age 32 or had assaulted her; they also tended to be divorced and/or separated from their children (Farrington, 1992c).

Widom's (1989; Chapter 13) follow-up study of abused children in Indianapolis showed that there was intergenerational transmission of violence. Children who were physically abused up to age 11 were significantly likely to become violent offenders later on in life. Similarly, harsh parental discipline and attitudes at age 8 significantly predicted later violent as opposed to non-violent offenders in the Cambridge Study (Farrington, 1978). However, more recent research showed that they were equally predictive of violent and frequent offending (Farrington, 1991b).

Bowlby's (1951) theory suggested that broken homes caused offending. He argued that mother love in infancy and childhood was just as important for mental health as were vitamins and proteins for physical health. He thought that it was essential that a child should experience a warm, loving and continuous relationship with a mother figure. If a child suffered a prolonged period of maternal deprivation during the first five years of life, this would have irreversible deleterious effects, including delinquency. Such deprived children tended to become 'affectionless characters', failing to develop loving ties with other children or with adults, and hence having no close friendships and no deep emotional feelings in their relationships. However, modern theorists emphasize the importance of the child having a continuous loving relationship with one person, but do not argue that this person should necessarily be the biological mother.

Most studies of broken homes focus on the loss of the father rather than the mother. In the Newcastle Thousand Family Study, Kolvin et al. (1988; Chapter 12) reported that marital disruption (divorce or separation) up to a boy's age 5 predicted his later convictions up to age 33. McCord (1982) in Boston carried out an interesting study of the relationship between homes broken by loss of the natural father and later serious offending. She found that the prevalence of offending was high for boys reared in broken homes without affectionate mothers (62 per cent) and for those reared in united homes characterized by parental conflict (52 per cent), irrespective of whether they had affectionate mothers. The prevalence of offending was low for those reared in united homes without conflict (26 per cent) or in broken homes with affectionate mothers (22 per cent).

These results suggest that it is not so much the broken home (or a single-parent female-headed household) which is criminogenic, as the parental conflict which causes it. However, teenage childbearing combined with a single-parent female-headed household is conducive to offending (Morash and Rucker, 1989). Single-parent families tended to have conduct-disordered and substance-abusing children in the Ontario Child Health Study, although such families were difficult to disentangle from low-income families (Blum et al., 1988; Boyle and Offord, 1986).

The importance of the cause of the broken home is also shown in the English national longitudinal survey of over 5,000 children born in one week of 1946 (Wadsworth, 1979). Boys from homes broken by divorce or separation had an increased likelihood of being convicted or officially cautioned up to age 21 in comparison with those from homes broken by death or from unbroken homes. Remarriage (which happened more often after divorce or separation than after death) was also associated with an increased risk of offending. The meta-analysis by Wells and Rankin (1991) also shows that broken homes are more strongly related to delinquency when they are caused by parental separation or divorce rather than by death.

In the Cambridge Study, both permanent and temporary (more than one month) separations before age 10 (usually from the father) predicted convictions and self-reported delinquency, providing that they were not caused by death or hospitalization (Farrington, 1992c). However, homes broken at an early age (under age 5) were not unusually criminogenic (West and

Farrington, 1973). Separation before age 10 predicted both juvenile and adult convictions (Farrington, 1992b) and predicted convictions up to age 32 independently of all other variables (Farrington, 1990, 1993a).

Criminal, antisocial and alcoholic parents also tend to have delinquent sons, as Robins (1979) found. Robins et al. (1975; Chapter 14) followed up over 200 black males in St Louis and found that arrested parents (her subjects) tended to have arrested children, and that the juvenile records of the parents and children showed similar rates and types of offences. McCord (1977), in her 30-year follow-up of about 250 treated boys in the Cambridge-Somerville study, also reported that convicted sons (her subjects) tended to have convicted fathers. Whether there is a specific relationship in her study between types of convictions of parents and children is not clear. McCord found that 29 per cent of fathers convicted for violence had sons convicted for violence, in comparison with 12 per cent of other fathers; however, this may reflect the general tendency for convicted fathers to have convicted sons rather than any specific tendency for violent fathers to have violent sons.

In the Cambridge Study, the concentration of offending in a small number of families was remarkable. West and Farrington (1977) discovered that less than 5 per cent of families were responsible for about half of the criminal convictions of all family members (fathers, mothers, sons and daughters). West and Farrington (1973) showed that having convicted mothers, fathers and brothers by a boy's tenth birthday significantly predicted his own later convictions. Furthermore, convicted parents and delinquent siblings were related to self-reported as well as to official offending (Farrington, 1979). Unlike most early precursors, convicted parents were related less to offending of early onset (age 10–13) than to later offending (Farrington, 1986b). Also, convicted parents predicted which juvenile offenders went on to become adult criminals and which recidivists at age 19 continued offending (West and Farrington, 1977). They also predicted convictions up to age 32 independently of all other variables (Farrington, 1990, 1993a).

Just as early family factors predict the early onset or prevalence of offending, later family factors predict later desistance. For example, it is often believed that male offending decreases after marriage, and there is some evidence in favour of this (e.g. Bachman et al., 1978). In the Cambridge Study, there was a clear tendency for convicted males who got married at age 22 or earlier to be reconvicted less often in the next two years than comparable convicted males who did not get married (West, 1982). However, in the case of both the males and their fathers, convicted males tended to marry convicted females, and convicted males who married convicted females continued to offend at the same rate after marriage as matched unmarried males. Offenders who married convicted females incurred more convictions after marriage than those who married unconvicted females, independently of their conviction records before marriage. Hence, it was concluded that the reformative effect of marriage was lessened by the tendency of male offenders to marry females who were also offenders. Rutter (1989) has drawn attention to the importance of studying turning points in people's lives, such as marriage. These are rarely included in psychological theories.

Social Learning and Psychoanalytic Theories

Most of the modern psychological theories that aim to explain the link between child-rearing methods and criminal behaviour are social learning theories. They assume that children are naturally selfish and hedonistic, and hence that it is natural for them to steal or fight or be delinquent in order to get what they want. According to these theories, children learn to rein in their antisocial tendencies and build up internal inhibitions against offending in a social learning (socialization) process as a result of the way their parents react to their transgressions.

One of the most influential social learning theories was propounded by Trasler (1962; summarized in Trasler, 1965; Chapter 15). This suggests that, when a child behaves in a socially-disapproved way, the parent will punish the child. This punishment causes an anxiety reaction, or an unpleasant state of physiological arousal. After a number of pairings of the disapproved act and the punishment, the anxiety becomes classically conditioned to the act, and conditioned also to the sequence of events preceding the act. Consequently, when the child contemplates the disapproved act, the conditioned anxiety automatically arises and tends to block the tendency to commit the act, so the child becomes less likely to do it. Also, the anxiety generalizes to similar acts, so the child tends to feel anxious when contemplating similar acts. Hence, as Eysenck (1977) also argued, conscience is essentially a conditioned anxiety response.

However, whereas Eysenck emphasized individual, constitutional differences in condition-ability, Trasler emphasized differences in parental child-rearing behaviour as the major source of differences in criminal tendencies (conditioned anxiety). Children are unlikely to build up the link between disapproved behaviour and anxiety unless their parents supervise them closely, use punishment consistently and make punishment contingent on disapproved acts. Hence, poor supervision, erratic discipline and inconsistency between parents are all conducive to delinquency in children. It is also important for parents to explain to children why they are being punished, so that they can discriminate precisely the behaviour that is disapproved.

Trasler argued that middle-class parents, who were more likely to explain to children why they were being punished, are more likely to be concerned with long-term character-building and the inculcation of general moral principles. This was linked to to the greater facility of middle-class parents with language and abstract concepts. In contrast, lower-class parents supervised their children less closely and were more inconsistent in their use of discipline. Generally, middle-class parents used love-oriented discipline, relying on withdrawal of love as the main sanction, whereas lower-class parents used much more physical punishment. Trasler contended that lower-class children committed more crimes because lower-class parents used less effective methods of socialization.

Historically, psychoanalytic theories were important in explaining the link between child-rearing and criminal behaviour (Kline, 1987; McDaniel et al., 1990). These theories suggested that there were three major personality mechanisms: the id, ego and superego. The id contained the instinctual, unconscious desires (especially sexual and aggressive) with which a child was born. It was governed by the pleasure principle, seeking to achieve pleasure and avoid pain. The ego developed out of the id by about age 3. This was the seat of consciousness which tried to achieve the desires of the id while taking account of the reality of social conventions. Hence, the ego was governed by the reality principle; it could delay immediate gratification in favour of long-term goals, think ahead and reduce the desires of the id through fantasy. Children would develop a strong ego only if they had a close emotional relationship with their parents.

The superego developed out of the ego by about age 5 and contained two functions – the conscience and the ego-ideal. The conscience acted to suppress or divert instinctual desires that violated social rules, while the ego-ideal was the internal representation of the parents' standards. In the formation of the conscience, punishment of the child by the parent aroused the child's aggressive energy towards the parent. However, because the child was punished even more if the aggression was expressed against the parent, children became self-punitive and turned their aggression against themselves. The verbal prohibitions of the parents became the superego. In the formation of the ego-ideal, children incorporated into themselves the emotionally charged images of their parents – thinking, feeling and acting like them. This process was called introjection, and it also depended on children having loving relationships with their parents.

According to psychoanalytic theories, offending resulted from a weak ego or a weak superego. The weak ego meant that people had a poor ability to control their instinctual desires (to balance the demands of the id and the superego) and a poor ability to defer gratification. The weak superego meant that people had a weak conscience or an undesirable ego-ideal. Since both depended on children having loving relationships with their parents, it followed that cold, unloving, rejecting parents tended to have delinquent children. Also, since the conscience depended on consistent discipline, parents who were inconsistent tended to have children with weak consciences, and the ego-ideal was undesirable to the extent that children had criminal or deviant parents. Generally, both social learning and psychoanalytic theories can explain empirical relationships between family factors and crime.

Peer Influences

The reviews by Zimring (1981) and Reiss (1988) show that delinquent acts tend to be committed in small groups (of two or three people, usually) rather than alone. In the Cambridge Study, most officially recorded juvenile and young adult offences were committed with others, though the incidence of co-offending declined steadily with age from 10 onwards. Burglary, robbery and theft from vehicles were particularly likely to involve co-offenders, who tended to be similar in age and sex to the study males and lived close to the males' homes and to the locations of the offences. The study males were most likely to offend with brothers when they had brothers who were similar in age to themselves (Reiss and Farrington, 1991; Chapter 16). In Ontario, Jones et al. (1980; Chapter 18) discovered that male delinquents tended to have a pre-ponderance of brothers, and proposed that there was male potentiation (and conversely female suppression) of antisocial behaviour. However, this was not found in the Cambridge Study.

The major problem of interpretation is whether young people are more likely to commit offences while they are in groups than while they are alone, or whether the high prevalence of co-offending merely reflects the fact that, whenever young people go out, they tend to go out in groups. Do peers tend to encourage and facilitate offending, or is it just that most kinds of activities out of the home (both delinquent and non-delinquent) tend to be committed in groups? Another possibility is that the commission of offences encourages association with other delinquents, perhaps because 'birds of a feather flock together' or because of the stigmatizing and isolating effects of court appearances and institutionalization. It is surprisingly difficult to decide among these various possibilities, although most researchers argue that peer influence is an important factor. For example, the key construct in Sutherland and Cressey's (1974) theory is the number of persons in a child's social environment with norms and attitudes favouring delinquency.

There is clearly a close relationship between the delinquent activities of a young person and those of his friends. Both in the US (Hirschi, 1969) and in the UK (West and Farrington, 1973), it has been found that a boy's reports of his own offending are significantly correlated with his reports of his friends' delinquency. In the American National Youth Survey of Elliott et al. (1985), having delinquent peers was the best independent predictor of self-reported offending in a multivariate analysis. In the same study, Agnew (1991) showed that this relationship was greatest for teenagers who were most strongly attached to their peers and felt most peer pressure.

The major problem of interpretation is that if delinquency is a group activity, delinquents will almost inevitably have delinquent friends: this result does not necessarily show that delinquent friends cause delinquency. In other words, delinquent friends could be an indicator rather than a cause. In the National Youth Survey, Elliott and Menard (1988) concluded that having delinquent peers increased a person's own offending and that a person's own offending also increased his likelihood of having delinquent peers. Hence, both effects seemed to be operating.

In the Cambridge Study, association with delinquent friends at age 14 was a significant independent predictor of convictions at young adult ages (Farrington, 1986b). Also, the recidivists at age 19 who ceased offending differed from those who persisted in that the desisters were more likely to have stopped going round in a group of male friends. Furthermore, spontaneous comments by the youths indicated that withdrawal from the delinquent peer group was seen as an important influence on ceasing to offend (West and Farrington, 1977). Therefore, continuing to associate with delinquent friends may be a key factor in determining whether juvenile delinquents persist in offending as young adults or desist.

Delinquent peers are likely to be most influential where they have high status within the peer group and are popular. However, studies both in the US (Roff and Wirt, 1984; Chapter 17) and in the UK (West and Farrington, 1973) show that delinquents are usually unpopular with their peers. It seems paradoxical for offending to be a group phenomenon facilitated by peer influence, and yet for offenders to be largely rejected by other adolescents (Parker and Asher, 1987). However, it may be that offenders are popular in antisocial groups and unpopular in prosocial groups, or that rejected children band together to form adolescent delinquent groups (Hartup, 1983). More worrying is the suggestion that some people act as 'recruiters', constantly dragging more people into the net of offending (Reiss, 1988).

School Influences

It is clear that the prevalence of offending varies dramatically between different secondary schools, as Power et al. (1967) showed more than 20 years ago in London. However, what is far less clear is how much of this variation should be attributed to differences in school climates and practices, and how much to differences in the composition of the student body.

In the Cambridge Study, Farrington (1972) investigated the effects of secondary schools on offending by following boys from their primary schools to their secondary schools. The best primary school predictor of offending in this study was the rating of troublesomeness at age 8–10 by peers and teachers. The secondary schools differed dramatically in their official offending rates, from one school with 21 court appearances per 100 boys per year to another where the corresponding figure was only 0.3. However, it was very noticeable that the most troublesome boys tended to go to the high delinquency-rate schools, while the least troublesome tended to go to the low delinquency-rate schools. Furthermore, it was clear that most of the variation between schools in their delinquency rates could be explained by differences in their intakes of troublesome boys. The secondary schools themselves had only a very small effect on the boys' offending.

The most famous study of the effects of school on offending was also carried out in London, by Rutter et al. (1979). They studied 12 comprehensive schools and again found big differences in official delinquency rates among them. High delinquency-rate schools tended to have high truancy rates, low ability pupils and low social class parents. However, the differences between the schools in delinquency rates could not be entirely explained by differences in the social class and verbal reasoning scores of the pupils at intake (age 11). Therefore, they must have been caused by some aspect of the schools themselves or by other, unmeasured factors.

In trying to discover which aspects of schools might be encouraging or inhibiting offending, Rutter et al. (1979) developed a measure of 'school process' based on school structure, organization and functioning. This was related to school misbehaviour, academic achievement and truancy independently of intake factors. The main school factors that were related to delinquency were a high amount of punishment and a low amount of praise given by teachers in class. Unfortunately, it is difficult to know whether much punishment and little praise are causes or consequences of antisocial school behaviour, which in turn is probably linked to offending outside school. Consequently, it is not clear what school factors are conducive to delinquency.

In the Cambridge Study, going to a high delinquency-rate secondary school was a significant predictor of later conviction (Farrington, 1993a). The important review by Rutter (1985; Chapter 19) describes various ways in which families and schools might influence offending and conduct problems. More recently, Mortimore (1991) has reviewed studies of school effectiveness, arguing that some schools have important effects on children's progress, especially where the staff and headteacher agree on the clear mission of the school and where there is a systematic assessment of the school's strengths and weaknesses.

Situational Influences

While most psychologists have aimed to explain the development of offending people, some have tried to explain the occurrence of offending events. As already mentioned, offenders are predominantly versatile rather than specialized. The typical offender who commits violence, vandalism or drug abuse also tends to commit theft or burglary. For example, in the Cambridge Study, Farrington (1991b) reported that 86 per cent of convicted violent offenders (43 out of 50) also had convictions for non-violent offences. Hence, in studying offenders, it seems unnecessary to develop a different theory for each different type of offence. In contrast, in trying to explain why offences occur, the situations are so diverse and specific to particular crimes that it is probably necessary to have different explanations for different types of offences.

The most popular theory of offending events suggests that they occur in response to specific opportunities, when their expected benefits (e.g. stolen property, peer approval) outweigh their expected costs (e.g. legal punishment, parental disapproval). For example, Clarke and Cornish (1985; Chapter 20) outlined a theory of residential burglary which included such influencing factors as whether a house was occupied, whether it looked affluent, whether there were bushes to hide behind, whether there were nosy neighbours, whether the house had a burglar alarm and whether it contained a dog. Several other psychologists have also proposed that offending involves a decision in which expected benefits are weighed against expected costs (e.g. Wilson and Herrnstein, 1985).

In the Cambridge Study, the most common reasons given for offending were rational ones, suggesting that most property crimes were committed because the offenders wanted the items stolen (West and Farrington, 1977). In Montreal, LeBlanc and Frechette (1989) also reported that most offences were motivated by the utilitarian need for material goods. (For a more extensive review of criminal motivation, see Farrington, 1993c.) In addition, a number of cross-sectional surveys have shown that low estimates of the risk of being caught were correlated with high rates of self-reported offending (e.g. Erickson et al., 1977). Unfortunately, the direction of causal influence is not clear in cross-sectional research, since committing delinquent acts may lead to lower estimates of the probability of detection as well as the reverse. Farrington and Knight (1980) carried out a number of studies using experimental, survey and observational methods which suggested that stealing involved risky decision-making. Hence, it is plausible to propose that opportunities for delinquency, the immediate costs and benefits of delinquency, and the probabilities of these outcomes all influence whether people offend in any situation.

Integrated Theories

In explaining the development of offending, a major problem is that most risk factors tend to coincide and to be inter-related. For example, adolescents living in physically deteriorated and socially disorganized neighbourhoods disproportionally tend also to attend high delinquency-rate schools, to have delinquent friends, to come from families with poor parental supervision and erratic parental discipline, and to have high impulsivity and low intelligence. The concentration and co-occurrence of these kinds of adversities make it difficult to establish their independent, interactive and sequential influences on offending and antisocial behaviour. Hence, any theory of the development of offending is inevitably speculative in the present state of knowledge. However, it seems likely that an adequate theory would have to be wide-ranging, including all the major influences on offending reviewed above, and not be narrowly psychological or sociological.

While it is not within the scope of this Introduction to review sociological theories of offending in any detail, it is clear that they have become more wide-ranging and comprehensive over time. The classic sociological theories include Cohen's (1955) delinquent subculture theory, which emphasized the status frustration of lower-class boys who could not succeed in school; Cloward and Ohlin's (1960) strain-opportunity theory, which focused on the strain between the goals of lower-class people and what they could actually achieve; Hirschi's (1969) control theory, which suggested that offending occurred when people's bonding to society was weakened; and Sutherland and Cressey's (1974) differential association theory, which argued that offending depended on learning antisocial norms and values in deviant groups.

The modern trend is to try to achieve increased explanatory power by integrating propositions derived from several earlier theories. For example, Elliott et al. (1985) combined strain, control, social learning and differential association theories. They proposed that strain (the inability to achieve goals in socially-approved ways), poor socialization (exposure to ineffective social learning and reinforcement processes) and living in a socially disorganized community caused weak bonding to conventional society, which in turn led to strong bonding to antisocial peer groups and ultimately to delinquency.

The Hawkins social development model (Hawkins et al., 1986; Farrington and Hawkins, 1991) is one of the most comprehensive integrated theories. This suggests that offending occurs when social bonding to conventional others is weak. The strength of this bonding depends on interaction with conventional others, involvement in conventional behaviour, opportunities for conventional involvement, possessing skills for conventional involvement and reinforcements for conventional involvement. In turn, interaction with antisocial others, involvement in antisocial behaviour and opportunities for antisocial involvement weaken the bond to society and make offending more likely. This theory has inspired a successful prevention programme in schools that aimed to decrease aggressive behaviour, delinquency and substance abuse by promoting social bonding (Hawkins et al., 1991, 1992).

My own theory of offending and antisocial behaviour (Farrington, 1986b, 1992b, 1993c) is also integrative, but distinguishes explicitly between the development of antisocial tendency and the occurrence of antisocial acts. The theory suggests that offending is the end result of a four-stage process: energizing, directing, inhibiting and decision-making. It is generally true that many psychological theories include these four mechanisms (Farrington, 1993c).

According to my theory, the main long-term energizing factors that ultimately lead to variations in antisocial tendency are desires for material goods, status among intimates and excitement. The main short-term energizing factors that lead to variations in antisocial tendency are boredom, frustration, anger and alcohol consumption. The desire for excitement may be greater among children from poorer families, perhaps because excitement is more highly valued by lower-class people than by middle-class ones, perhaps because poorer children think they lead more boring lives, or because poorer children are less able to postpone immediate gratification in favour of long-term goals (which could be linked to the emphasis in lower-class culture on the concrete and present as opposed to the abstract and future).

In the directing stage, these motivations produce antisocial tendency if socially disapproved methods of satisfying them are habitually chosen. The methods chosen depend on maturation and behavioural skills; for example, a 5-year-old would have difficulty stealing a car. Some people (e.g. children from poorer families) are less able to satisfy their desires for material goods, excitement and social status by legal or socially approved methods, and so tend to choose illegal or socially disapproved methods. The relative inability of poorer children to achieve goals by legitimate methods could be because they tend to fail in school and to have erratic, low status employment histories. School failure in turn may often be a consequence of the unstimulating intellectual environment that lower-class parents tend to provide for their children, and their lack of emphasis on abstract concepts.

In the inhibiting stage, antisocial tendencies can be inhibited by internalized beliefs and attitudes that have been built up in a social learning process as a result of a history of rewards and punishments. The belief that offending is wrong, or a strong conscience, tends to be built up if parents are in favour of legal norms, if they exercise close supervision over their children, and if they punish socially disapproved behaviour using love-oriented discipline. Antisocial tendency can also be inhibited by empathy, which may develop as a result of parental warmth and loving relationships. The belief that offending is legitimate and the acceptance of anti-establishment attitudes generally tend to be built up if children have been exposed to attitudes and behaviour favouring offending (e.g. in a modelling process), especially by members of their family, by their friends and in their communities.

In the decision-making stage, which specifies the interaction between the individual and the environment, whether a person with a certain degree of antisocial tendency commits an antisocial act in a given situation depends on opportunities, costs and benefits, and on the subjective probabilities of the different outcomes. The costs and benefits include immediate situational factors such as the material goods that can be stolen and the likelihood and consequences of being caught by the police, as perceived by the individual. They also include social factors such as likely disapproval by parents or spouses, and encouragement or reinforcement from peers. In general, people tend to make rational decisions. However, more impulsive people are less likely to consider the possible consequences of their actions, especially consequences that are likely to be long delayed.

Applying the theory to explain some of the results reviewed here, children with low intelligence are more likely to offend because they tend to fail in school and hence cannot achieve their goals legally. Impulsive children, and those with a poor ability to manipulate abstract concepts, are more likely to offend because they do not give sufficient consideration and weight to the possible consequences of offending. Children who are exposed to poor parental child-rearing behaviour, disharmony or separation are likely to offend because they do not build up internal controls over socially disapproved behaviour, while children from criminal families and those with delinquent friends tend to build up anti-establishment attitudes and the belief that offending is justifiable. The whole process is self-perpetuating, in that low intelligence and early school failure lead to truancy and a lack of educational qualifications, which in turn lead to low status jobs and periods of unemployment, both of which make it harder to achieve goals legitimately.

The onset of offending might be caused by increasing long-term motivation (an increasing need for material goods, status and excitement), an increasing likelihood of choosing socially disapproved methods (possibly linked to a change in dominant social influences from parents to peers), increasing facilitating influences from peers, increasing opportunities (because of increasing freedom from parental control and increasing time spent with peers) or an increasing expected utility of offending (because of the greater importance of peer approval and lesser importance of parental disapproval). Desistance from offending could be linked to an increasing ability to satisfy desires by legal means (e.g. obtaining material goods through employment, obtaining sexual gratification through marriage), increasing inhibiting influences from spouses and cohabitees, decreasing opportunities (because of decreasing time spent with peers), and a decreasing expected utility of offending (because of the lesser importance of peer approval and the greater importance of disapproval from spouses and cohabitees).

The prevalence of offending may increase to a peak between ages 14 and 20 because boys (especially lower class school failures) have high impulsivity, high desires for excitement, material goods and social status between these ages, little chance of achieving their desires legally, and little to lose (since legal penalties are lenient and their intimates – male peers – often approve of offending). In contrast, after age 20, desires become attenuated or more realistic, there is more possibility of achieving these more limited goals legally, and the costs of offending are greater (since legal penalties are harsher and their intimates – wives or girlfriends – disapprove of offending).

Conclusions

Most theories aim to explain offending in full flow in the teenage years. They do not aim to explain why offending begins, why it continues or escalates, why it diversifies into different types, and why it diminishes or ceases. Future explanatory research needs a developmental focus. While we know a great deal about offending in the teenage years, we know less about antisocial behaviour in the pre-teenage years and less still about prenatal, perinatal and infancy factors that influence later offending. Also, few studies have tried to document the changes in adulthood that coincide with the decline in offending. It is important to establish developmental sequences. For example, impulsivity at age 2–5 may lead to conduct disorder at age 6–10, which may lead to shoplifting at age 12–15, burglary at age 16–19, violence in the twenties, and drunken driving and spouse assault in the thirties. Knowledge about such developmental sequences would help in determining when and how it was best to intervene to try to disrupt them.

There are many common features in existing psychological theories of offending. Most assume that there are consistent individual differences in an underlying construct such as criminal potential or antisocial personality. Most assume that hedonism or the pursuit of pleasure is the main energizing factor. Most assume that there is internal inhibition against offending through the conscience or some similar mechanism, and that methods of child-rearing used by parents are crucial in developing this in a socialization process. However, where parents provide antisocial models, there can also be learning of antisocial behaviour. Most assume that the commission of offences in any situation essentially involves a rational decision in which the likely costs are weighed against the likely benefits. And most assume that impulsivity, or a poor ability to take account of and be influenced by the possible future consequences of offending, is an important factor, often linked to a poor ability to manipulate abstract concepts and low intelligence.

Future theories of offending need to be wide-ranging, including individual, family, peer, school and neighbourhood factors, as well as energizing, directing, inhibiting and decision-making processes. It is plausible to propose sequential models in which, for example, neighbourhood factors such as social disorganization influence family factors such as child-rearing, which in turn influence individual factors such as impulsivity (Farrington, 1993b). Existing theories aim to explain all types of offenders, but different theories may be needed to explain occasional or situational offenders as opposed to persistent or chronic offenders with an antisocial life-style (LeBlanc and Frechette, 1989). However, it is important that theories do not become so complex that they can explain everything but predict nothing. Theories need to be carefully specified, so that they lead to testable empirical predictions. The emphasis in the past has been on explaining existing findings rather than on predicting new findings. Future theorists should plan a programme of theoretical development where theories and evidence advance together in a cumulative fashion, with the theories guiding the research and the findings leading to a better specification of the theories.

References

Agnew, R. (1991), 'The interactive effects of peer variables on delinquency', *Criminology*, **29**, 47–72.
American Psychiatric Association (1987), *Diagnostic and Statistical Manual of Mental Disorders* (3rd ed. revised), Washington, D.C.: APA.

Arbuthnot, J. and Gordon, D.A. (1988), 'Crime and cognition: Community applications of sociomoral reasoning development', *Criminal Justice and Behaviour*, **15**, 379–93.

Bachman, J.G., O'Malley, P.M. and Johnston, J. (1978), *Youth in Transition*, Vol. 6, Ann Arbor, MI: University of Michigan Institute for Social Research.

Blackburn, R. (1993), *The Psychology of Criminal Conduct*, Chichester: Wiley.

Blouin, A.G., Conners, C.K., Seidel, W.T. and Blouin, J. (1989), 'The independence of hyperactivity from conduct disorder: Methodological considerations', *Canadian Journal of Psychiatry*, **34**, 279–82.

Blum, H.M., Boyle, M.H. and Offord, D.R. (1988), 'Single-parent families: Child psychiatric disorder and school performance', *Journal of the American Academy of Child and Adolescent Psychiatry*, **27**, 214–19.

Bouchard, T.J., Lykken, D.T., McGue, M., Segal, N.L. and Tellegen, A. (1990), 'Sources of human psychological differences: The Minnesota study of twins reared apart', *Science*, **250**, 223–8.

Bowlby, J. (1951), *Maternal Care and Mental Health*, Geneva: World Health Organization.

Boyle, M.H. and Offord, D.R. (1986), 'Smoking, drinking and use of illicit drugs among adolescents in Ontario: Prevalence, patterns of use and socio-demographic correlates', *Canadian Medical Association Journal*, **135**, 1113–21.

*Clarke, R.V. and Cornish, D.B. (1985), 'Modeling offenders' decisions: A framework for research and policy', in M. Tonry and N. Morris (eds), *Crime and Justice*, Vol. 6, Chicago: University of Chicago Press, 147–85.

Cloninger, C.R., Sigvardsson, S., Bohman, M. and von Knorring, A. (1982), 'Predisposition to petty criminality in Swedish adoptees. II. Cross-fostering analysis of gene-environment interaction', *Archives of General Psychiatry*, **39**, 1242–7.

Cloward, R.A. and Ohlin, L.E. (1960), *Delinquency and Opportunity*, New York: Free Press.

Cohen, A.K. (1955), *Delinquent Boys*, Glencoe, Illinois: Free Press.

Duguid, S. (1981), 'Moral development, justice and democracy in the prison', *Canadian Journal of Criminology*, **23**, 147–62.

Elliott, D.S., Huizinga, D. and Ageton, S.S. (1985), *Explaining Delinquency and Drug Use*, Beverly Hills: Sage.

Elliott, D.S. and Menard, S. (1988), 'Delinquent behaviour and delinquent peers: Temporal and developmental patterns', unpublished manuscript.

Erickson, M., Gibbs, J.P. and Jensen, G.F. (1977), 'The deterrence doctrine and the perceived certainty of legal punishment' *American Sociological Review*, **42**, 305–17.

Eysenck, H.J. (1977), *Crime and Personality* (3rd ed.), London: Routledge and Kegan Paul.

*Eysenck, H.J. (1987), 'Personality theory and the problem of criminality' in B.J. McGurk, D.M. Thornton and M. Williams (eds), *Applying Psychology to Imprisonment*, London: HMSO, 29–58.

Eysenck, H.J. and Gudjonsson, G.H. (1989), *The Causes and Cures of Criminality*, New York: Plenum.

Farrington, D.P. (1972), 'Delinquency begins at home', *New Society*, **21**, 495–7.

Farrington, D.P. (1973), 'Self-reports of deviant behaviour: Predictive and stable?', *Journal of Criminal Law and Criminology*, **64**, 99–110.

Farrington, D.P. (1978), 'The family backgrounds of aggressive youths' in L. Hersov, M. Berger and D. Shaffer (eds), *Aggression and Antisocial Behaviour in Childhood and Adolescence*, Oxford: Pergamon, 73–93.

Farrington, D.P. (1979), 'Environmental stress, delinquent behaviour, and convictions' in I.G. Sarason and C.D. Spielberger (eds), *Stress and Anxiety*, Vol. 6, Washington, D.C.: Hemisphere, 93–107.

Farrington, D.P. (1984), 'Delinquent and criminal behaviour' in A. Gale and A.J. Chapman (eds), *Psychology and Social Problems*, Chichester: Wiley, 55–77.

Farrington, D.P. (1986a), 'Age and crime' in M. Tonry and N. Morris (eds), *Crime and Justice*, Vol. 7, Chicago: University of Chicago Press, 189–250.

Farrington, D.P. (1986b), 'Stepping stones to adult criminal careers' in D. Olweus, J. Block and M.R. Yarrow (eds), *Development of Antisocial and Prosocial Behaviour*, New York: Academic Press, 359–84.

Farrington, D.P. (1987a), 'Epidemiology' in H.C. Quay (ed.), *Handbook of Juvenile Delinquency*, New York: Wiley, 33–61.

Farrington, D.P. (1987b), 'Implications of biological findings for criminological research' in S.A. Mednick, T.E. Moffitt and S.A. Stack (eds), *The Causes of Crime: New Biological Approaches*, Cambridge: Cambridge University Press, 42–64.

Farrington, D.P. (1989), 'Self-reported and official offending from adolescence to adulthood' in M.W. Klein (ed.), *Cross-National Research in Self-Reported Crime and Delinquency*, Dordrecht, Netherlands: Kluwer, 399–423.

Farrington, D.P. (1990), 'Implications of criminal career research for the prevention of offending', *Journal of Adolescence*, **13**, 93–113.

Farrington, D.P. (1991a), 'Antisocial personality from childhood to adulthood', *The Psychologist*, **4**, 389–94.

Farrington, D.P. (1991b), 'Childhood aggression and adult violence: Early precursors and later life outcomes' in D.J. Pepler and K.H. Rubin (eds), *The Development and Treatment of Childhood Aggression*, Hillsdale, N.J.: Erlbaum, 5–29.

Farrington, D.P. (1992a), 'Criminal career research in the United Kingdom', *British Journal of Criminology*, **32**, 521–36.

Farrington, D.P. (1992b), 'Explaining the beginning, progress and ending of antisocial behaviour from birth to adulthood' in J. McCord (ed.), *Facts, Frameworks and Forecasts: Advances in Criminological Theory*, Vol. 3, New Brunswick, N.J.: Transaction, 253–86.

Farrington, D.P. (1992c), 'Juvenile delinquency' in J.C. Coleman (ed.), *The School Years* (2nd ed.), London: Routledge, 123–63.

Farrington, D.P. (1993a), 'Childhood origins of teenage antisocial behaviour and adult social dysfunction', *Journal of the Royal Society of Medicine*, **86**, 13–17.

Farrington, D.P. (1993b), 'Have any individual, family or neighbourhood influences on offending been demonstrated conclusively?' in D.P. Farrington, R.J. Sampson and P.O. Wikstrom (eds), *Integrating Individual and Ecological Aspects of Crime*, Stockholm: National Council for Crime Prevention, 3–37.

Farrington, D.P. (1993c), 'Motivations for conduct disorder and delinquency', *Development and Psychopathology*, **5**, 225–41.

Farrington, D.P. (1994), 'Childhood, adolescent and adult features of violent males' in L.R. Huesmann (ed.), *Aggressive Behaviour: Current Perspectives*, New York: Plenum, 215–40.

Farrington, D.P., Biron, L. and LeBlanc, M. (1982), 'Personality and delinquency in London and Montreal' in J. Gunn and D.P. Farrington (eds), *Abnormal Offenders, Delinquency, and the Criminal Justice System*, Chichester: Wiley, 153–201.

Farrington, D.P., Gallagher, B., Morley, L., St Ledger, R.J. and West, D.J. (1988a), 'A 24-year follow-up of men from vulnerable backgrounds' in R.L. Jenkins and W.K. Brown (eds), *The Abandonment of Delinquent Behaviour*, New York: Praeger, 155–73.

Farrington, D.P., Gallagher, B., Morley, L., St Ledger, R.J. and West, D.J. (1988b), 'Are there any successful men from criminogenic backgrounds?', *Psychiatry*, **51**, 116–30.

Farrington, D.P. and Hawkins, J.D. (1991), 'Predicting participation, early onset, and later persistence in officially recorded offending', *Criminal Behaviour and Mental Health*, **1**, 1–33.

Farrington, D.P. and Knight, B.J. (1980), 'Four studies of stealing as a risky decision' in P.D. Lipsitt and B.D. Sales (eds), *New Directions in Psycholegal Research*, New York: Van Nostrand Reinhold, 26–50.

Farrington, D.P., Loeber, R. and Van Kammen, W.B. (1990), 'Long-term criminal outcomes of hyperactivity-impulsivity-attention deficit and conduct problems in childhood' in L.N. Robins and M. Rutter (eds), *Straight and Devious Pathways from Childhood to Adulthood*, Cambridge: Cambridge University Press, 62–81.

Farrington, D.P. and West, D.J. (1990), 'The Cambridge study in delinquent development: A long-term follow-up of 411 London males' in H.J. Kerner and G. Kaiser (eds), *Criminality: Personality, Behaviour, Life History*, Berlin: Springer-Verlag, 115–38.

*Gottfredson, M. and Hirschi, T. (1990), *A General Theory of Crime*, Stanford, California: Stanford University Press.

Hartup, W.W. (1983), 'Peer relations' in P.H. Mussen (ed.), *Handbook of Child Psychology*, Vol. 4, Toronto: Wiley, 103–96.

Hawkins, J.D., Catalano, R.F., Morrison, D.M., O'Donnell, J., Abbott, R.D. and Day, L.E. (1992), 'The Seattle social development project: Effects of the first four years on protective factors and problem behaviours', in J. McCord and R. Tremblay (eds), *Preventing Antisocial Behaviour*, New York: Guilford, 139–61.

Hawkins, J.D., Lishner, D.M., Catalano, R.F. and Howard, M.O. (1986), 'Childhood predictors of adolescent substance use: Toward an empirically grounded theory', *Journal of Children in Contemporary Society*, **8**, 11–48.

Hawkins, J.D., Von Cleve, E. and Catalano, R.F. (1991), 'Reducing early childhood aggression: Results of a primary prevention programme', *Journal of the American Academy of Child and Adolescent Psychiatry*, **30**, 208–17.

Hindelang, M.J., Hirschi, T. and Weis, J.G. (1981), *Measuring Delinquency*, Beverly Hills: Sage.

Hirschi, T. (1969), *Causes of Delinquency*, Berkeley: University of California Press.

*Hirschi, T. and Hindelang, M.J. (1977), 'Intelligence and delinquency: A revisionist review', *American Sociological Review*, **42**, 571–87.

Hollin, C.R. (1989), *Psychology and Crime*, London: Routledge.

Huizinga, D. and Elliott, D.S. (1986), 'Reassessing the reliability and validity of self-report measures', *Journal of Quantitative Criminology*, **2**, 293–327.

*Jones, M.B., Offord, D.R. and Abrams, N. (1980), 'Brothers, sisters and antisocial behaviour', *British Journal of Psychiatry*, **136**, 139–45.

Kagan, J., Reznick, J.S. and Snidman, N. (1988), 'Biological bases of childhood shyness', *Science*, **240**, 167–71.

Kandel, E., Mednick, S.A., Kirkegaard-Sorenson, L., Hutchings, B., Knop, J., Rosenberg, R. and Schulsinger, F. (1988), 'IQ as a protective factor for subjects at high risk for antisocial behaviour', *Journal of Consulting and Clinical Psychology*, **56**, 224–6.

Kline, P. (1987), 'Psychoanalysis and crime' in B.J. McGurk, D.M. Thornton and M. Williams (eds), *Applying Psychology to Imprisonment*, London: HMSO, 59–75.

Kohlberg, L. (1976), 'Moral stages and moralization: The cognitive-developmental approach' in T. Lickona (ed.), *Moral Development and Behaviour*, New York: Holt, Rinehart and Winston, 31–53.

Kohlberg, L. and Candee, D. (1984), 'The relationship of moral judgment to moral action' in L. Kohlberg (ed.), *The Psychology of Moral Development*, San Francisco: Harper and Row, pp. 52–73.

*Kolvin, I., Miller, F.J.W., Fleeting, M. and Kolvin, P.A. (1988), 'Social and parenting factors affecting criminal-offence rates: Findings from the Newcastle Thousand Family Study (1947–1980)', *British Journal of Psychiatry*, **152**, 80–90.

Kolvin, I., Miller, F.J.W., Scott, D.M., Gatzanis, S.R.M. and Fleeting, M. (1990), *Continuities of Deprivation?*, Aldershot: Avebury.

LeBlanc, M. and Frechette, M. (1989), *Male Criminal Activity from Childhood through Youth*, New York: Springer-Verlag.

Loeber, R. (1982), 'The stability of antisocial and delinquent child behaviour: A review', *Child Development*, **53**, 1431–46.

Loeber, R. (1987), 'Behavioural precursors and accelerators of delinquency' in W. Buikhuisen and S.A. Mednick (eds), *Explaining Criminal Behaviour*, Leiden: Brill, 51–67.

*Loeber, R. and Dishion, T. (1983), 'Early predictors of male delinquency: A review', *Psychological Bulletin*, **94**, 68–99.

Leober, R. and Stouthamer-Loeber, M. (1986), 'Family factors as correlates and predictors of juvenile conduct problems and delinquency' in M. Tonry and N. Morris (eds), *Crime and Justice*, Vol. 7, Chicago: University of Chicago Press, 29–149.

Loeber, R. and Stouthamer-Loeber, M. (1987), 'Prediction' in H.C. Quay (ed.), *Handbook of Juvenile Delinquency*, New York: Wiley, 325–82.

Lynam, D., Moffitt, T. and Stouthamer-Loeber, M. (1993), 'Explaining the relation between IQ and delinquency: Class, race, test motivation, school failure or self-control?', *Journal of Abnormal Psychology*, **102**, 187–96.

Mawson, A.R. (1987), *Transient Criminality*, New York: Praeger.

McCord, J. (1977), 'A comparative study of two generations of native Americans' in R.F. Meier (ed.), *Theory in Criminology*, Beverly Hills: Sage, 83–92.

*McCord, J. (1979), 'Some child-rearing antecedents of criminal behavior in adult men', *Journal of Personality and Social Psychology*, **37**, 1477–86.

McCord, J. (1982), 'A longitudinal view of the relationship between paternal absence and crime' in J. Gunn and D.P. Farrington (eds), *Abnormal Offenders, Delinquency, and the Criminal Justice System*, Chichester, Wiley, 113–28.

McDaniel, E., Balis, G.U. and Strahan, S. (1990), 'Psychodynamic antecedents of violence' in L.J. Herzberg, G.F. Ostrum and J.R. Field (eds), *Violent Behaviour*, Vol. 1, Great Neck, N.Y.: PMA, 69–84.

Mednick, S.A., Gabrielli, W.F. and Hutchings, B. (1983), 'Genetic influences on criminal behaviour: Evidence from an adoption cohort' in K.T. Van Dusen and S.A. Mednick (eds), *Prospective Studies of Crime and Delinquency*, Boston: Kluwer-Nijhoff, 39–56.

Moffitt, T.E. (1990), 'The neuropsychology of juvenile delinquency: A critical review' in M. Tonry and N. Morris (eds), *Crime and Justice*, Vol. 12, Chicago: University of Chicago Press, 99–169.

*Moffitt, T.E. and Henry, B. (1989), 'Neuropsychological assessment of executive functions in self-reported delinquents', *Development and Psychopathology*, **1**, 105–18.

Moffitt, T.E. and Silva, P.A. (1988a), 'IQ and delinquency: A direct test of the differential detection hypothesis', *Journal of Abnormal Psychology*, **97**, 330–33.

Moffitt, T.E. and Silva, P.A. (1988b), Neuropsychological deficit and self-reported delinquency in an unselected birth cohort', *Journal of the American Academy of Child and Adolescent Psychiatry*, **27**, 233–40.

Morash, M. and Rucker, L. (1989), 'An explanatory study of the connection of mother's age at childbearing to her children's delinquency in four data sets', *Crime and Delinquency*, **35**, 45–93.

Mortimore, P. (1991), 'School effectiveness research: Which way at the crossroads?', *School Effectiveness and School Improvement*, **2**, 213–29.

Offord, D.R., Boyle, M.H. and Racine, Y. (1989), 'Ontario Child Health Study: Correlates of disorder', *Journal of the American Academy of Child and Adolescent Psychiatry*, **28**, 856–60.

Parker, J.G. and Asher, S.R. (1987), 'Peer relations and later personal adjustment: Are low accepted children at risk?', *Psychological Bulletin*, **102**, 357–89.

Power, M.J., Alderson, M.R., Phillipson, C.M., Shoenberg, E. and Morris, J.N. (1967), 'Delinquent schools?', *New Society*, **10**, 542–3.

Pulkkinen, L. (1988), 'Delinquent development: Theoretical and empirical considerations' in M. Rutter (ed.), *Studies of Psychosocial Risk*, Cambridge: Cambridge University Press, 184–99.

Reiss, A.J. (1988), 'Co-offending and criminal careers' in M. Tonry and N. Morris (eds), *Crime and Justice*, Vol. 10, Chicago: University of Chicago Press, 117–70.

*Reiss, A.J. and Farrington, D.P. (1991), 'Advancing knowledge about co-offending: Results from a prospective longitudinal survey of London males', *Journal of Criminal Law and Criminology*, **82**, 360–95.

Riley, D. and Shaw, M. (1985), *Parental Supervision and Juvenile Delinquency*, London: HMSO.

Robins, L.N. (1979), 'Sturdy childhood predictors of adult outcomes: Replications from longitudinal studies' in J.E. Barrett, R.M. Rose and G.L. Klerman (eds), *Stress and Mental Disorder*, New York: Raven Press, 219–35.

*Robins, L.N. and Ratcliff, K.S. (1978), 'Risk factors in the continuation of childhood antisocial behavior into adulthood', *International Journal of Mental Health*, **7**, 96–116.

*Robins, L.N., West, P.A. and Herjanic, B.L. (1975), 'Arrests and delinquency in two generations: A study of black urban families and their children', *Journal of Child Psychology and Psychiatry*, **16**, 125–40.

*Roff, J.D. and Wirt, R.D. (1984), 'Childhood aggression and social adjustment as antecedents of delinquency', *Journal of Abnormal Child Psychology*, **12**, 111–26.

*Rutter, M. (1985), 'Family and school influences on behavioural development', *Journal of Child Psychology and Psychiatry*, **26**, 349–68.

Rutter, M. (1989), 'Psychosocial risk trajectories and beneficial turning points' in S. Doxiadis (ed.), *Early Influences Shaping the Individual*, New York: Plenum, 229–39.

Rutter, M., Maughan, B., Mortimore, P. and Ouston, J. (1979), *Fifteen Thousand Hours*, London: Open Books.

Scharf, P. and Hickey, J. (1976), 'The prison and the inmate's conception of legal justice: An experiment in democratic education', *Criminal Justice and Behaviour*, **3**, 107–22.

Shedler, J. and Block, J. (1990), 'Adolescent drug use and psychological health', *American Psychologist*, **45**, 612–30.

Smetana, J.G. (1990), 'Morality and conduct disorders' in M. Lewis and S.M. Miller (eds), *Handbook of Developmental Psychopathology*, New York: Plenum, 157–79.

Sutherland, E.H. and Cressey, D.R. (1974), *Criminology* (9th ed.), Philadelphia: Lippincott.

*Taylor, E.A. (1986), 'Childhood hyperactivity', *British Journal of Psychiatry*, **149**, 562–73.

Taylor, E.A., Schachar, R., Thorley, G. and Wieselberg, M. (1986), 'Conduct disorder and hyperactivity. I. Separation of hyperactivity and antisocial conduct in British child psychiatric patients', *British Journal of Psychiatry*, **149**, 760–67.

Tennenbaum, D.J. (1977), 'Personality and criminality: A summary and implications of the literature', *Journal of Criminal Justice*, **5**, 225–35.

Thornton, D. (1987), 'Moral development theory' in B.J. McGurk, D.M. Thornton and M. Williams (eds), *Applying Psychology to Imprisonment*, London: HMSO, 129–50.

Trasler, G.B. (1962), *The Explanation of Criminality*, London: Routledge and Kegan Paul.

*Trasler, G.B. (1965), 'Criminality and the socialisation process', *Advancement of Science*, **21**, 545–50.

Utting, D., Bright, J. and Henricson, C. (1993), *Crime and the Family*, London: Family Policy Studies Centre.

Venables, P.H. and Raine, A. (1987), 'Biological theory' in B.J. McGurk, D.M. Thornton and M. Williams (eds), *Applying Psychology to Imprisonment*, London: HMSO, 3–27.

Wadsworth, M. (1979), *Roots of Delinquency*, London: Martin Robertson.

Wells, L.E. and Rankin, J.H. (1991), 'Families and delinquency: A meta-analysis of the impact of broken homes', *Social Problems*, **38**, 71–93.

West, D.J. (1982), *Delinquency: Its Roots, Careers and Prospects*, London: Heinemann.

West, D.J. and Farrington, D.P. (1973), *Who Becomes Delinquent?*, London: Heinemann.

West, D.J. and Farrington, D.P. (1977), *The Delinquent Way of Life*, London: Heinemann.

*White, H.R., Labouvie, E.W. and Bates, M.E. (1985), 'The relationship between sensation seeking and delinquency: A longitudinal analysis', *Journal of Research in Crime and Delinquency*, **22**, 197–211.

White, J.L., Moffitt, T.E. and Silva, P.A. (1989), 'A prospective replication of the protective effects of IQ in subjects at high risk for juvenile delinquency', *Journal of Consulting and Clinical Psychology*, **57**, 719–24.

*Widom, C.S. (1989), 'The cycle of violence', *Science*, **244**, 160–66.

Wikstrom, P.O. (1987), *Patterns of Crime in a Birth Cohort*, Stockholm: University of Stockholm Department of Sociology.

*Wilson, H. (1980), 'Parental supervision: A neglected aspect of delinquency', *British Journal of Criminology*, **20**, 203–35.

*Wilson, J.Q. and Herrnstein, R.J. (1985), *Crime and Human Nature*, New York: Simon and Schuster.

Zimring, F.E. (1981), 'Kids, groups and crime: Some implications of a well-known secret', *Journal of Criminal Law and Criminology*, **72**, 867–85.

*Reprinted in this volume.

Predicting Offending and Antisocial Behaviour

[1]

Psychological Bulletin
1983, Vol. 94, No. 1, 68–99

Early Predictors of Male Delinquency: A Review

R. Loeber and T. Dishion
Oregon Social Learning Center, Eugene, Oregon

A systematic review is presented of prediction studies on delinquency. The main aim is to identify etiological variables for delinquency that, in different studies and across different populations, show good predictive validity. To achieve this goal, a measure of predictive efficiency was chosen that could be applied to studies from the United States and from abroad. The principal predictors of delinquency were the parents' family management and techniques (supervision and discipline), the child's conduct problems, parental criminality, and the child's poor academic performance. Data are presented to show the earliest age of the child at which these predictors have been measured. Results of the prediction data are used to demonstrate utility functions in which false positive and false negative errors are minimized. Recommendations are put forward to improve prediction studies in criminality.

Claims about the early identification of youths at risk for delinquency have sometimes been extravagant. The Gluecks (Glueck & Glueck, 1950) claimed to be able to correctly identify 90% of all future delinquents. The psychiatrist Glover, testifying before the Royal Commission on Capital Punishment (1949, cited in Hakeem, 1957–1958), expressed the belief that psychometric tests could do wonders. He stated that "if sufficient trouble were taken, pathological cases liable to commit murder could be detected during early childhood" (p. 492). However, prediction research has not substantiated these claims (Hakeem, 1957–1958). Moreover, the research by Glueck and Glueck (1950, 1959), with substantial claims of predictability of delinquency, has been criticized on methodological grounds (Hirschi & Selvin, 1967; Prigmore, 1963; Reiss, 1951; Weis, 1974). On the more positive side, there is a large and rather scattered body of studies with encouraging results for the identification of youths at risk for later delinquency. These studies will be reviewed here.

Prediction in criminology serves two main purposes. More accurate prediction helps parents, teachers, court officials, and therapists to take adequate action when discovering early warning signs of a juvenile delinquent career. Second, known predictors can be used for the construction of theories of delinquency. Here some predictors are equated with causal and moderating factors that may interact and form constellations of factors likely to bring about delinquency.

Theory building and predictive assessment have a major common element: the selection and weighting of variables in terms of their explanatory power for delinquency. Some variables may only account for small differences between delinquents and nondelinquents, whereas other variables may account for much of the variance between delinquent and nondelinquent groups.

Prediction in delinquency is possible for two reasons: the first is that problem behaviors of children have a high degree of continuity over time. Problematic conduct early in life for certain groups of children tends to continue rather than abate (Gersten, Langner, Eisenberg, Simcha-Fagan, & McCarthy, 1976; Ghodsian, Fogelman, Lambert, & Tibbenham, 1980; Loeber, 1982; Olweus, 1979; Patterson, 1982; Robins, 1966; Werner & Smith, 1977; West & Farrington, 1973). The challenge is to identify conduct problems that precede delinquency and are ultimately predictive of its occurrence. This will make it

The authors are indebted to L. R. Goldberg, D. J. Farrington, J. C. Gersten, R. F. Sparks, and an anonymous reviewer for their helpful comments. The paper was the result of frequent and fruitful discussions with the staff of the Oregon Social Learning Center, especially G. R. Patterson, J. B. Reid, and P. Holleran.

Requests for reprints should be sent to R. Loeber, Oregon Social Learning Center, 207 East 5th Avenue, Suite 202, Eugene, Oregon 97401.

possible to identify on the basis of the conduct problem those children at highest risk for delinquency. Another challenge is to establish the earliest age at which such conduct problems become predictive, so that preventive efforts can take place while the conduct problems are not yet firmly stabilized. One more challenge is to detect the interrelationships between different conduct problems and to see whether this pattern is more predictive of delinquency than the individual components.

The second reason prediction in delinquency is feasible is that we know what situations or social variables tend to enhance children's eventual engagement in delinquent activities. Known circumstantial variables are, for example, the social class of the parents and the parents' child-rearing methods.

The present article has three main goals: (a) to establish a measure of predictive efficiency that can be applied to the delinquency prediction studies in our review, (b) to identify variables from the literature that predict delinquency in adolescence or in early adulthood, and (c) to use the results of the prediction data to demonstrate the utility functions of predictors and to minimize false positive or false negative errors. The article closes with methodological considerations and suggestions for improving prediction studies in criminality.

Predictive Efficiency

Researchers in criminology have used a variety of methods to assess the power or efficiency of particular variables to predict latent delinquency (Gottfredson, 1970; Simon, 1971). However, predictive methods useable on the same population are not necessarily useable on different populations, because differences in the base rates of delinquency between groups affect most measures of predictive efficiency. The following discussion outlines a method that is less sensitive to such variations and that makes it possible to compare the predictive efficiency of a wide variety of predictors over a wide range of studies. We will first explain how this method of prediction has been developed and then review studies by using this method.

The following example illustrates widely used means of assessing predictive efficiency

and their implicit limitations for clinical or prevention activities. It was selected because of the care taken by the investigators to provide complete data that permitted additional analyses. Robins and Hill (1966), in a well-designed investigation of theoretical importance, studied 296 nonwhite youths and postulated that delinquency would be highest for youths with parents from a low employment background. To begin with, they determined the employment status of the child's guardian using retrospective evidence from school records. The criterion of delinquency was defined as a police or court record by the age of 17. Ideally, the prediction of delinquency on the basis of employment status should have a high degree of accuracy. Those children with a guardian of low employment status should be more at risk for delinquency than those with a guardian of higher employment status. The results reported by Robins and Hill (1966) are shown in Figure 1: 46 out of the 148 boys with guardians of low employment status became delinquents. This was compared with 30 out of 148 boys with guardians of high employment status who also became delinquent. Robins and Hill (1966) concluded that "about a third of the boys with . . . a lower status guardian eventually became delinquent, compared with one-fifth of the remainder" (p. 331). These results provided support for the relationship between economic stress and delinquency hypothesized by Robins and Hill (1966). Whereas such an analysis is extremely useful for establishing theoretically useful relationships, its potential application to issues of prevention is limited (i.e., it would be useful only for clinical situations in which one is confronted with lower or higher class parents; the social class of the parent could then be used to predict the delinquency of the offspring).

Because it was not relevant to their theoretical hypotheses, the authors did not explicitly report on the total number of correct predictions in the table, that is, those youths who were assumed to be at risk (because of low employment background) who ultimately become delinquent, and those youths who were identified as not at risk (on the basis of higher employment background) who ultimately did not become delinquent. Robins and Hill's (1966) evaluation of predictive efficiency is not idiosyncratic, but very typical for delinquency studies in general (e.g., Glueck & Glueck, 1950; West & Farrington, 1973; Wadsworth, 1979). Moreover, the formulation of predictive efficiency given above does not discriminate between the types of errors that are made in the process, nor do conclusions about the prediction reflect chance and maximum limits in identification.

These points can best be illustrated by using prediction methods widely used in personnel selection (Wiggins, 1973). First, the method should optimally identify youths who eventually become delinquent and identify those who do not become delinquent. The first kind of correct identifications are called *valid positives,* the second kind *valid negatives* (see Figure 1). Errors in identification are of two kinds: youths who are predicted to be at risk for delinquency but who do not become delinquent, *false positives,* and youths who are not identified to be at risk for delinquency but later become delinquent, *false negatives.* Depending on one's priorities, the percentages of false positives and false negatives should be low. Monahan

(1981) has pointed out that for judicial decisions about guilt, typically the percentage of false negatives should be low; that is, the predictors should not miss youths who are actual delinquents. For clinical decisions about treatment or prevention, the emphasis is put on reducing false positives; that is, capturing only those youths truly at risk for delinquency and minimizing the identification of those seemingly at risk but who do not become delinquent. Implicit here is the relative cost of certain types of errors for certain types of decisions. Sometimes costs and benefits of decisions in predictions are weighted. The application of such utility values will be discussed in a later section. Until then, we will treat prediction without discriminating between the relative utility of false positive or false negative errors.

Figure 1 summarizes the results obtained by Robins and Hill (1966) in terms of valid versus false positives and negatives, which have been calculated on the basis of the total number of subjects ($N = 296$). The percentage of total correct predictions consists of the sum of valid positives (15.5%) and valid negatives (40%), which amounts to 55.4%. Thus, only about half of the youths were correctly

	Delinquent	Nondelinquent	
	Valid Positives	False Positives	
Guardian's Low Employment Status	46	102	148 (50%)
	(15.5%)	(34.5%)	
	False Negatives	Valid Negatives	
Guardian's High Employment Status	30	118	148
	(10.1%)	(39.9%)	
	76 (25.7%)	220	296 100%

Figure 1. The relationship between juvenile delinquency and guardian's employment status as shown by the frequency of each. (Adapted from "Assessing the contribution of family structure, class and peer groups to juvenile delinquency" by L. N. Robins and S. Y. Hill, *Journal of Criminal Law, Criminology, and Police Science,* 1966, 57, 325–334. Copyright 1966 by Northwestern University School of Law. Reprinted by permission.)

identified on the basis of the guardian's employment status. The delinquency outcome
of less than half of the subjects was not correctly predicted. Most of these errors in prediction were false positives (34.5%), and fewer
were false negatives (10.1%).

The simplistic logic of these computations
is deceptive; the values in the 2 × 2 prediction
tables are influenced by chance and by a
maximum ceiling in prediction. We will discuss each of these limiting factors.

Chance occurrence of frequencies within
a 2 × 2 table is a function of the marginal
values of the table. These marginal values
represent, on one side, the number of delinquents found in the population (called *base
rate*), and on the other side, the number of
individuals selected as delinquent by means
of the prediction method (called *selection ratio*). In Figure 1, the base rate and selection
ratio, respectively, amounted to 25.7% and
50%. These proportions determine the chance
occurrence of frequencies within the table
(Meehl & Rosen, 1955; Wiggins, 1973). Most
authors take chance occurrence into account
by the calculation of chi square. In the example, Robins and Hill (1966) found that chi
square equalled 3.98, which was significant
at the .05 level. However, this only means that
one or more cells in the 2 × 2 table had
frequencies that could not be expected by
chance alone. Although this knowledge is essential, it fails to clarify which cell frequencies deviate from what could be obtained by
chance alone. As Meehl and Rosen (1955)
have stated, a significance test in this case
does not clarify "the number of correct decisions for individuals within [delinquent and
nondelinquent] groups" (p. 194). Two cells
in prediction tables are most important for
assessing predictive efficiency—the valid positives and the valid negatives. For that reason,
the degree that observed values in these cells
deviate from random or chance values provides a more accurate assessment of predictive efficiency than is possible by means of
a chi-square measure. The calculation of random correct prediction for valid positives and
valid negatives has been outlined by Wiggins
(1973). In the example of Robins and Hill
(1966), the random correct values for valid
positives and valid negatives are $76/296 \times 148/296 = .128$, and $220/296 \times 148/296 =$

.372, respectively. Translated into frequencies, the numbers expected by chance alone
amount to 38 valid positives (12.8%) and 110
valid negatives (37.2%; see Figure 2). Taken
together, 148 (50%) of the subjects in these
two cells could be predicted by a random selection of subjects on the basis of the marginal values in the prediction table.

The random correct value can be compared with the observed correct prediction
(see Figure 2). The observed valid positives
and valid negatives together account for
55.4% of the correct predictions. The difference between the observed correct predictions and the random correct predictions reveals the extent to which low employment
status of the guardian improved the identification of youths who would later become
delinquent. In the given example, the percent
improvement over chance was 5.4%. This
measure, as far as we know, has been used
in only one delinquency study (McCord,
1980), despite its obvious advantages. However, such a measure has different meanings
from study to study. To control for this, an
index was devised to represent the improvement over chance as a function of the range
of its possible predictive efficiency. The range
is delimited by two values: the random correct and maximum correct percentages. As
has been described in detail by Loeber and
Dishion (Note 1), each identification table
has a maximum value for the highest correct
identifications possible within the table. This
maximum ceiling is determined by the base
rate and selection ratio. Figure 3 shows the
best possible identification given the base rate
and selection ratio used by Robins and Hill
(1966). The number of subjects in the cell of
valid positives can only maximally be 76 because of the base rate limitation of 76 out of
296. Once this maximum value is set, the
frequencies in all other cells are fixed (see
Figure 3). The resulting maximum percentages of valid positives and valid negatives are
25.7% and 50%, respectively. Taken together,
correct predictions in the study by Robins
and Hill can never be higher than 75.7%.
Thus, the percent improvement over chance
in a given study always falls between the random correct value and the maximum correct
value. As the difference between the latter two
measures varies from study to study, it is ap-

72   R. LOEBER AND T. DISHION

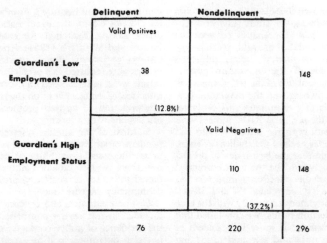

Figure 2. Frequencies of valid positives and valid negatives expected by chance. (Adapted from "Assessing the contribution of family structure, class and peer groups to juvenile delinquency" by L. N. Robins and S. Y. Hill, *Journal of Criminal Law, Criminology, and Police Science*, 1966, 57, 325–334. Copyright 1966 by Northwestern University School of Law. Reprinted by permission.)

propriate to express the improvement over chance (IOC) as a function of the difference between the random correct (RC) and maximum correct (MC) values in a given study. This value will be called relative improvement over chance (RIOC), and can be calculated as follows:

$$RIOC = \frac{\%IOC}{\%MC - \%RC} \times 100$$

A major problem in the evaluation of predictive efficiency is that it depends to a great

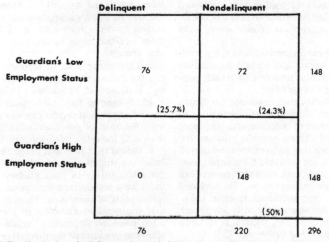

Figure 3. The distribution of cell frequencies maximizing correct predictions. (Adapted from "Assessing the contribution of family structure, class and peer groups to juvenile delinquency" by L. N. Robins and S. Y. Hill, *Journal of Criminal Law, Criminology, and Police Science*, 1966, 57, 325–334. Copyright 1966 by Northwestern University School of Law. Reprinted by permission.)

Psychological Explanations of Crime

extent on how well the selection ratio matches the base rate in a given study (Loeber & Dishion, Note 1). A discrepancy between the selection ratio and the base rate, which is very common in delinquency studies, influences the magnitude of the maximum correct value. The present use of the RIOC measure, which is partly based on the maximum correct value, largely eliminates this problem. To test this, the IOC and RIOC indices were correlated with both the selection ratio and the base rate for each of the studies reviewed. It was thought that the best index of predictive efficiency would be the least correlated with either of the selection parameters. As expected, the IOC correlated .54 and .38 and the RIOC correlated .13 and .22 with the base rates and selection ratios. We concluded that the RIOC measure is more independent of varying base rates and selection ratios and therefore superior as an overall evaluative index of predictive efficiency.

Inclusions and Exclusions in the Present Review

An extensive search of the delinquency literature resulted in a large number of studies with predictive data. A description of the studies included in this review follows:

1. The studies contained data that made it possible to reconstruct prediction tables as shown in Figure 1. Studies that contained only percentage information and did not allow the reconstruction of raw scores were excluded.

2. The review focused on males, but studies on mixed male and female populations were included. Studies solely on female populations were not included.

3. Only studies that contained predictors that had taken place at least a year prior to the measurement of outcome of delinquency were included. Thus, whereas studies concurrently measuring independent and dependent variables are valuable for identification of potential predictors, such studies were not included in the present review. We included only studies that predicted juvenile delinquency and delinquency in early adulthood; that is, we included only predictors and outcomes that occurred before age 22.

4. Only studies that used objective firsthand predictors were included. It was sometimes difficult to determine whether a study met this criterion because a number of studies did not clarify the exact nature of predictor scoring. Excluded, for example, was Powers and Witmer's (1951) report on the Cambridge-Somerville study, in which teacher ratings were reported as a predictor, but these ratings were, in fact, based on the researcher's interview of the teacher or on the researcher's interpretation of written protocols of such discussions with a teacher.

5. Most of the studies referred to independent variables that predicted acceleration or an increased probability of delinquency over time. We also included studies that predicted the offset or decreased probability of delinquency later in time.

6. The prediction and outcome variables included in this review comprised not only the incidence of police contacts youths had, but also outcomes such as arrest rates, reconviction rates, and high self-reported delinquency. Wherever possible, we did not include traffic violations in delinquency outcome measures. Studies on parole violations were excluded (see, e.g., Monahan, 1981; Ohlin & Duncan, 1949).

7. Both retrospective and prospective studies were included.

8. Whenever data were presented by authors in other than dichotomized fashion, we followed the cutting scores for predictor variables mentioned by authors. If the authors did not mention cutting scores, we set the cutting scores in such a way as to obtain the most optimal improvement in prediction over chance.

9. Personality tests to identify youths at risk for delinquency were not included (see, e.g., Hathaway & Monachesi, 1953, 1963).

10. Whenever recidivism studies were reviewed, the rate of recidivism was compared with the rate of one-time offenders rather than with the rate of delinquency in general.

It should be noted that the authors of the following studies do not all emphasize the predictive utility of their studies. Many of them have emphasized theoretical or empirical aspects of their data. However, the fact that independent variables in these studies often preceded dependent variables in time allows us to examine the predictive efficiency of a wide range of independent variables.

In the following review, Tables 1 through 10 supply information on the raw scores in

(*Text continues on page 78*)

Table 1
Outcome Statistics for Behavioral Predictors of Delinquency

Study predictor	Valid positives	False positives		Valid negatives	False negatives		N	PBR	PSR	Definition criterion of delinquency	Prediction interval	RIOC
		n	%		n	%						
West & Farrington (1973) Troublesomeness (teacher and peer ratings)[a]	41	51	12.4	276	43	10.5	411	20.4	22.4	One or more adjudicated offenses	8–10[b] to 17	34.1
Farrington (1979) Troublesomeness (teacher and peer ratings)	31	60	14.7	269	49	12.0	409	19.6	22.2	21 or more self-reported acts	8–10 to 14–16	21.1
Craig & Glick (1963) Problem behavior in Grades 1, 2, & 3 (teacher ratings)	35	70	23.3	187	9	3.0	301	14.6	34.9	"Serious and/or persistent"	6–9 to 16	66.3
Mitchell & Rosa (1981) Problem behavior (parent & teacher report)	30	71	22.9	179	30	9.7	310 "deviant group"	19.3	32.6	One or more adjudicated offenses	5–15 to 20+	25.7
Kirkegaard-Sørensen & Mednick (1977) Disciplinary problem (teacher rating)	10	15	5.3	236	21	7.4	282 (select sample)	11.0	8.9	Conviction	10–20 to 23–33	32.3
Robins (1966) Antisocial referral	185	27	7.7	75	63	18.0	350 (racially mixed)	70.9	60.6	Arrest	14 to 18	48.2
Stott & Wilson (1968) Marsh (1969) Delinquency Prediction scale (teacher rating)	29	53	6.5	683	53	6.5	818	10.0	10.0	Conviction	18 to 21	27.8
Scarpitti (1964) Potentially delinquent (teacher nomination)	27	43	24.9	99	4	2.3	173	17.9	40.5	Court contact	12 to 16	78.0
Reckless & Dinitz (1972) Likelihood of future delinquency (teacher nomination)	213	881	51.0	600	32	1.9	1726 (an experimental, control, & comparison group)	14.2	63.4	Police contact	13 to 16	64.4

Continued overleaf

Table 1 *(continued)*

Study predictor	Valid positives	False positives		Valid negatives	False negatives		N	PBR	PSR	Definition criterion of delinquency	Prediction interval	RIOC
		n	%		n	%						
Simcha-Fagan (1979) Mother-reported delinquency	32	54	13.5	581	62	11.7	729	12.9	11.8	Police contact	7 to 12 8 to 13 11 to 15 13 to 18 14 to 20 16 to 21	28.2
Roff, Sells, & Golden (1972) Who is liked best (peer choice)	20	76	5.5	1177	100	7.3	1373	8.75	7.0	Court contact	11–12 to 16	15.3
Havighurst, Bowman, Liddle, Matthews, & Pierce (1962) Aggressiveness (teacher and peer ratings)	32	40	19.1	122	15	7.2	209	22.5	34.4	Police contact	12–13° to 18–19	51.4
West & Farrington (1973) Aggressiveness (teacher rating)	23	59	15.1	264	45	11.5	391	17.4	21.0	One or more adjudicated offenses	8–10 to 17	16.4
Kirkegaard-Sørensen & Mednick (1977) Violence & aggressiveness (teacher rating)	7	20	7.1	231	24	8.5	282 (select sample)	11.0	9.6	Conviction	10–20 to 23–33	17.0
Easily angered (teacher rating)	13	50	17.7	201	18	6.4		11.0	22.3			25.2
Feldhusen, Thurston, & Benning (1973) Aggressiveness (teacher rating)	273	295	19.0	766	216	13.9	1550 (boys & girls)	31.6	36.7	Police record	9 to 17 12 to 20 15 to 23	30.3
Mulligan, Douglas, Hammond, & Tizard (1963) Aggressiveness (teacher rating)	54	189	9.2	1700	120	5.8	2063	8.4	11.8	Conviction	13 to 15	21.5

Table 1 (continued)

Study predictor	Valid positives	False positives		Valid negatives	False negatives		N	PBR	PSR	Definition criterion of delinquency	Prediction interval	RIOC
		n	%		n	%						
Mitchell & Rosa (1981) Destructiveness (parent reported)	12	14	4.4	244	51	15.9	321 "deviant group"	19.6	8.1	Court appearance for indictable offense	5–15 to 20+	31.8
Kirkegaard–Sørensen & Mednick (1977) Passivity (teacher rating)	13	50	17.7	201	18	6.4	282 (select sample)	11.0	22.3	Conviction	10–20 to 23–33	25.2
Farrington (Note 4) Truancy	16	23	5.6	304	68	16.5	411	20.4	9.5	One or more adjudicated offenses	8–10 to 17	26.3
Robins & Hill (1966) Truancy	44	83	28.0	137	32	10.8	296 (nonwhite)	25.7	42.9	Police or court record	6–12 to 17	26.2
Mitchell & Rosa (1981) Wandering (p. 25) (parent reported)	15	23	7.2	235	48	15.0	321 "deviant group"	19.6	11.9	Court appearance for indictable offense	5–15 to 20+	24.7
Stealing (p. 24) (parent reported)	12	6	1.9	252	51	15.9		19.6	5.6			57.8
Lying (p. 25) (parent reported)	22	37	11.5	221	41	12.8	321	19.6	18.4			22.0
Farrington (Note 4) Dishonest (peer rating)	33	55	13.4	272	51	12.4	411	20.4	21.4	One or more adjudicated offenses	10 to 17	22.7
Daring (peer rating)	38	62	15.1	265	46	11.2			24.3			27.5
Daring (p. 99) (peer and parent rating)	42	79	19.3	250	38	9.3	409	19.6	29.6	21 or more self-reported acts	8–10 to 14–16	32.6
Farrington (1979) Involved in fights after drinking	49	76	19.5	223	41	10.5	389	23.1	32.1	Conviction	18 to 21	49.3
Involved in antisocial groups	39	42	10.8	257	51	13.1			20.8			32.5
Unstable job	42	50	12.9	249	48	12.3			23.6			30.0
No money saved up	54	93	23.9	206	36	9.2			37.8			35.4
Drug user	45	77	19.8	222	45	11.6			31.4			27.0

Continued overleaf

Table 1 (continued)

Prediction: Recidivism

Study predictor	Valid positives	False positives		Valid negatives	False negatives		N	PBR	PSR	Definition criterion of delinquency	Prediction interval	RIOC
		n	%		n	%						
Mitchell & Rosa (1981)												
Problem behavior (p. 27, parent and teacher reported)	17	13	21.7	20	10	16.7	60	45.0	50.0	Two or more court appearances	5–15 to +20	26.0
Stealing (p. 29–30, parent and teacher reported)	11	3	5.3	28	15	26.3	57	45.6	24.6			60.5
Lying (pp. 29–30, parent and teacher reported)[d]	14	8	14.0	22	13	22.8	57	47.4	38.6			31.0
Osborn & West (1980)												
Unemployment over 5 weeks in last year	14	9	20.9	13	7	16.3	43	48.8	53.5	Persisting vs. temporary recidivism	18 to 23	28.1
Drug taking in past year	15	7	16.3	15	6	14.0			51.2			41.6
Self-reported aggression	15	8	18.6	14	6	14.0			53.5			38.5
Mulligan, Douglas, Hammond, & Tizard (1963)												
Aggressiveness (teacher rating)	22	31	17.8	94	27	15.5	174	66.7	30.5	Reconviction	13 to 15	38.3
Robins (1966)												
Antisocial referral	127	133	38.0	74	16	4.6	350 (racial mix)	40.9	74.3	Three or more arrests	14 to 18	56.2
Buikhuisen & Hoekstra (1974)												
Not moved after imprisonment	188	59	13.1	82	122	27.1	451 (inmates)	68.7	54.8	One reconviction	Juveniles to 5 yrs. later	23.7
Knight & West (1975)												
Offenses committed alone	16	3	3.9	27	31	40.2	77	61.0	24.7	Continued delinquent after age 17 vs. not cont.	17 to 18–19	59.2

Note. PBR = percent base rate; PSR = percent selection ratio; RIOC = relative improvement over chance.

[a] For teacher ratings and peer ratings of troublesomeness separately as predictors of delinquency, see West and Farrington (1973) and Farrington and West (1971).

[b] Average rating by different teachers at ages eight and ten.

[c] Excludes 356 boys with lowest SES for whom peer ratings did not discriminate.

[d] See Mitchell and Rosa (1981, p. 30) for combination of parent- and teacher-reported stealing or lying as predictor of delinquency.

the prediction table, the percentages of false positives and false negatives, and the percentages of base rate and selection ratio. The tables also indicate the brief definitions of the predictors, the criterion or outcome of delinquency, the time interval between measurements of the predictor (expressed in terms of the youth's age) and the criterion (also expressed in terms of the youth's age). Finally, as the principal evaluative index, the percentage of relative improvement over chance is provided. The first part of each table reports studies with delinquency in general as criterion, and the last part of each table reports on prediction studies of recidivists among populations of one-time offenders. The reader should keep in mind that samples in some studies were specially selected and matched with control groups (Buikhuisen & Hoekstra, 1974; McCord, 1979; Robins, 1966; Robins & Lewis, 1966; Robins, West, & Herjanic, 1975; Tait & Hodges, 1972; Trevvett, 1972; Voss, 1963) and consequently have much higher base rates than unselected populations of males.

We will first review predictors of delinquency that can be measured early in a person's life. This category has been separated into two subsets: (a) predictors that are extrapolative of the subject's own behavior, such as problematic or delinquent behavior as witnessed by parents, peers, or teachers; (b) predictors that are circumstantial—that is, representing the characteristics of the subject's family or social environment (Toby, 1961). Following the section on early predictors is a brief review of predictors of delinquency evident in late adolescence.

Early Youth Behavior as a Predictor of Later Delinquency

Table 1 lists a number of studies with extrapolative predictors based on a subject's behavior prior to the occurrence of delinquency. Among the earliest predictors was the child's problem behavior over ages 6 to 9 years (Craig & Glick, 1963) that improved predictability by about 66.3%. The prediction was based on teachers' ratings of children who presented problems in the first, second, and third grades. Another set of studies (West & Farrington, 1973) showed that the child's troublesomeness at the age of 8 to 10

was also predictive of delinquency, producing a relative increment of 34.1% for official delinquency and 21.1% for high self-reported delinquency. In these studies, the degree of troublesomeness was assessed by teachers on two occasions, and in addition, peer ratings were incorporated in the assessment.

In some studies, good predictors are based on multiple assessments and/or assessment by different respondents (e.g., Craig & Glick, 1963; Havighurst, Bowman, Liddle, Matthews, & Pierce, 1962; West & Farrington, 1973). Multiple assessment has the advantage of identifying a relatively high-risk group of youngsters with stable behavior, at least across the times of assessments, but most probably also through ensuing years (see Loeber, 1982; Olweus, 1979). The use of two or more respondents, such as teachers and peers or teachers and parents, has the additional advantage that the subject's behavior is observed in more than one setting, which improves the generalizability of the findings. In addition, if these individuals are nonprofessionals or service providers who can easily be contacted, then the assessment is cost efficient as compared with that done by mental health workers. It is assumed that when the problem behavior occurs across situations, as reported by different service providers, the stability of that behavior is higher than when it only occurs in only one setting (Loeber, 1982). Moreover, multiple assessments and/or multiple respondents tend to reduce measurement error. In general, it is difficult to assess which predictors are poor because of little association with a particular outcome or because of inadequate validity or reliability of measurement. The present review, however, by considering numerous studies, partly overcomes this problem because the recurrence of particular good predictors across studies may emerge. One such predictor seems to be antisocial or problematic predelinquent behavior at the age of 12 to 14 years (Mitchell & Rosa, 1981; Robins, 1966; Scarpitti, 1964), which improved the prediction of delinquency by about 51% and the prediction of recidivism by about 41%.

It is very likely that these problem categories include the child's aggressiveness. Aggression at the ages of 9 to 15 years produced improvements in prediction of 34% for delinquency in general and 38% for recidivism (Feldhusen, Thurston, & Benning, 1973; Mulligan, Douglas, Hammond, & Tizard, 1963; Havighurst et al., 1962).

Some of the specific problem behaviors in Table 1 are correlated and thus may predict the same group of individuals who eventually become delinquent. Ideally, predictors should not be highly correlated, so that the addition of each new predictor adds to the group of individuals at risk rather than confirming those individuals who already have been identified. In the context of the present review, children who are daring or disobedient are often also aggressive (DeBlois & Stewart, 1980; Robins, 1966; Loeber & Schmaling, Note 2).

The second specific problem behavior particularly predictive of recidivism is the subject's stealing as reported by teachers and parents. Mitchell and Rosa (1981) measured stealing in a sample of 5- to 15-year-olds, which improved the prediction of delinquency by 57.8% and of recidivism by 60.5%. Unfortunately, the authors do not specify at which of these ages stealing becomes not only prominent but also predictive. Moore, Chamberlain, and Mukai (1979) followed up samples of stealing, aggressive, and normal children. The first two groups had been referred for treatment between the ages of 4 and 14 years because of problem behavior. At intake, the mothers reported on the nature and frequency of the child's problematic behaviors. At follow-up 2 to 9 years later, 84% of the stealer sample had incurred a criminal record, compared with 24% of the children in the aggressive sample and 21% in the normative sample. Thus, the child's stealing as reported by a parent in the family home was highly indicative of later official delinquency.

A number of studies have shown that youths engaging in stealing are also likely to be involved in other, covert or more concealing antisocial acts such as lying, wandering, or truancy (Miller, Court, Knox, & Brandon, 1974; Patterson, 1982; Reid & Hendriks, 1973; Loeber & Schmaling, Note 2; Reid, Hinojosa-Rivero, & Lorber, Note 3). In the present review, Table 1 shows that dishonesty by the age of 10 is moderately predictive of later delinquency (Farrington, Note 4; see also Mitchell & Rosa, 1981), as is

truancy before age 12 and wandering between the ages of 5 and 15 (Mitchell & Rosa, 1981; Robins, 1966; Farrington, Note 4).

Unlike studies on older adolescents (Osborn & West, 1978, 1980), no studies on younger adolescents in our survey used composite predictors of more than one problem behavior such as, for example, high aggressiveness and theft. Considering the high improvements in prediction such composite measures have produced for the older age group (see Table 9), we anticipate sizeable improvements in prediction through the use of composite measures for the younger age group (see Loeber & Schmaling, Note 5, for some concurrent evidence). This has an added advantage because of the relative instability of problem behaviors in childhood and adolescence (Rutter, 1978). A number of longitudinal studies have shown that 30% to 43% of children who engage in maladaptive behavior at the ages of 4 to 11 years continue to show such behavior 4 to 9 years later (Farrington, 1978; Ghodsian et al., 1980; Glavin, 1972; Janes, Hesselbrock, Myers, & Penniman, 1979; Werner & Smith, 1977). Thus, 57% to 70% of the children ultimately improved and did not show the problem behavior years later. On the other hand, some who did not display problem behavior early in life revealed such behavior years later. Expressed in percentages, 12% to 27% of those who were initially free from the problem behavior, as defined by the investigators, joined the ranks of the chronic children over time (Farrington, 1978; Ghodsian et al., 1980; Janes et al., 1979). In absolute numbers, the percentages of newcomers given above refer to as large or larger numbers as the chronic risk group (Loeber & Dishion, Note 1). The presence of chronic and newcomer groups has an effect on the most profitable prediction strategy. The chronic group can be identified by means of, for example, aggressiveness. However, we assume that those who were not aggressive at the early assessment possibly showed other problem behaviors such as vandalism or lying that might eventually lead to delinquency. For that reason, we expect that composite measures of more than one precursor of delinquency will identify an optimal proportion of children at risk for delinquency.

Table 2
Outcome Statistics for the Prediction of Delinquency by Prior Delinquent Record and High Self-Reported Delinquency

Study predictor	Valid positives	False positives		Valid negatives	False negatives		N	PBR	PSR	Definition criterion of delinquency	Prediction interval	RIOC
		n	%		n	%						
McCord (1979)												
Juvenile delinquent records	19	18	11.8	92	23	15.1	152	27.6	24.3	Juvenile conviction for serious crimes	5–17 to 18–40	35.4
Wolfgang (Note 6)												
Offense before age 18	138	214	21.9	576	47	4.8	975	19.0	36.1	Re-arrest	Under 17 to 18–30	60.0
Osborn & West (1978)												
Prior convictions	37	15	14.1	30	24	22.6	106	57.6	49.1	Reconviction	8–18 to 19–23	32.0
Self-reported delinquency	31	17	16.0	37	21	19.8	106	49.1	45.3	Reconviction	14–16 to 19–23	30.4
Polk (1975)												
Delinquent at 15–16	31	19	7.5	157	45	17.9	252	30.1	19.9	Adult criminal record	15–16 to 28	45.5
Robins & Ratcliff (1979)												
Offense before age 15	25	23	11.7	125	23	11.7	196	24.5	24.5	Re-arrest	Under 15 to 30–35	36.5

Note. PBR = percent base rate; PSR = percent selection ratio; RIOC = relative improvement over chance.

Investigators have a choice of including various numbers of problem behaviors in the prediction exercises. Mitchell and Rosa (1981), for example, considered the total number of child problem behaviors reported by the mother between the ages of 5 and 15 years as a predictor of delinquency. A cutting score of five or more on the total deviation measure produced an improvement of 20.8% for delinquency in general and 16.4% for recidivism (not shown in Table 9). The inclusion of child problem behaviors in this index—such as anxieties—that are not predictive of delinquency, or correlate negatively, decreases the predictive power of such an index.

Delinquency is often said to be best predicted by taking into account prior delinquency (Monahan, 1981). Studies reviewed in Table 2 reinforce this idea, and produce increments averaging 40.0% (range 30.4% to 60.0%). Two points deserve attention. First, the rate of recidivism computed over a population of youths is often very small (usually below 15%). Normally, the prediction of such low base rate events is not feasible even when multiple gating or screening methods are used (Meehl & Rosen, 1955; Wiggins, 1973). This will be reviewed briefly in the discussion. Predicting recidivists among a population of one-time offenders on the basis of prior delinquency is more realistic (see Table 2). Second, for the studies shown in Table 2, prior delinquency as a predictor of continued delinquency was measured by age 15 to 17. Compared with aggressiveness or other nondelinquent problem behavior measured at an earlier age, prior delinquency appears to become a good predictor at a slightly later age. The statement, however, should be qualified in the sense that the age range is a function of the investigator's setting of the cutting score at that age. Koller and Gosden (1980), in a retrospective study on a prison population, found an average age of 14 years for the first officially recorded offense for inmate recidivists, whereas first-time prisoners were, on the average, 21 years old when they were arrested for their first officially recorded offenses.

The minimal age of measurement of predictors may seem arbitrary in the studies discussed above. For example, why not use criminal record at age 13, or perhaps even

Psychological Explanations of Crime

earlier? Perhaps with the exception of the study by Robins and Hill (1966), none of the studies systematically reviewed the predictability of measures taken over different age groups. On the one hand, problem behaviors including criminal activities need time to become recognizable as a stable phenomenon (Epstein, 1980). On the other hand, the stability of these phenomena at earlier ages than measured in the studies above may still prove sufficiently predictive of later delinquency. Clearly, only empirical research can demonstrate how much earlier predictors can be measured without losing predictive power. Such studies may make it possible to identify youngsters who are at risk for delinquency at an even earlier age than has been demonstrated up to now, especially if early precursors of delinquency are used.

Later Youth Behavior as a Predictor of Delinquency

Almost without exception, the early behaviors of the youths that are predictive of delinquency remain predictive at a later age. This is not to say that these acts occur in exactly the same form or situation when measured, for example, in early or late adolescence. What should be stressed here is the relative continuity of predictive categories, of behavior over time. For example, at age 18, involvement in fights after drinking improved predictability by 49.3%, while at that age high self-reported aggression improved the forecasting of recidivism by 38.5% (Farrington, 1979; Osborn & West, 1980). In prison populations, high aggressiveness or serious institutional misconduct is also known to be predictive of recidivism (Cowden & Pacht, 1967; Cymbalisty, Schuck, & Dubeck, 1975; Department of Corrections of the State of Michigan, 1978, cited in Monahan, 1981; Koller & Gosden, 1980). Thus aggressiveness from adolescence onward is a more or less continuous predictor of delinquency. In the same vein, unofficial theft predicts delinquency both at an early and at later ages. When property offenses are compared with offenses against people, the former seem to be more predictive of recidivism than the latter (Gendreau, Madden, & Leipciger, 1979; Koller & Gosden, 1980).

Not all predictors of delinquency measured in late adolescence necessarily occur in the earlier age groups. Bell and Pearl (1982) speak of age-specific manifestations of risk variables. For example, property offenses are often correlated with financial hardship caused by chronic unemployment, inability to hold jobs for extended periods of time, or expensive drug habits. The occurrence of these variables before the age of 12, as an obvious example, is rare, and because of that they do not sufficiently qualify as predictors in normal populations of young adolescents. Farrington (1979) and Osborn and West (1980) have shown that by the age of 18 unstable employment and extended unemployment are highly predictive of delinquency and recidivism (see Table 1). The same studies found that drug use at that age was also predictive of delinquency and recidivism, which is in line with studies on prison populations, especially for opiate users (Gendreau et al., 1979; Koller & Gosden, 1980; Pritchard, 1979).

Empirical research is necessary to make better use of peer involvement in the prediction of delinquency. Only the Farrington (1979) study considered a measure of involvement in antisocial groups at age 18. It will come as no surprise that involvement with antisocial or delinquent peers often occurs at a much earlier age and even then can still correlate highly with delinquency (Loeber, Dishion, & Patterson, Note 7). Thus, involvement with antisocial or delinquent peers is expected to become a more important early predictor for delinquency. It should be noted, though, that committing crimes alone discriminates between persisting offenders and offenders who cease delinquent activity in late adolescence (Knight & West, 1975).

Osborn and West (1978, 1980) have drawn up two profiles of behaviors that are, together, very predictive of recidivism. One profile, shown in Table 9, consists of six behaviors; the total score improves predictions by 68.3% (Osborn & West, 1978). The other profile lists 11 behaviors. A minimum cutoff score produces a relative increment of 30.6%. This study demonstrates a well-tried method in prediction in which not all, but a minimum number, of problem behaviors or adversities are associated with an improvement in prediction (Rutter, 1978; Simon, 1971). What is important is that the predictability of individual behaviors can be augmented by ag-

82   R. LOEBER AND T. DISHION

gregating these behaviors into a composite profile.

Educational Achievement as a Predictor of Delinquency

The school studies in the present review (Table 3) reinforce the image of delinquency-prone children who are underachievers in an educational sense. At the end of elementary school, low achievement, low vocabulary, and poor verbal reasoning improved the prediction of delinquency by 27% (Farrington, 1979; Rutter, Maugham, Mortimer, & Ouston, 1979; Wolfgang, Figlio, & Sellin, 1972). The best predictors during the high school years were low grade point average and school retardation by age 15, which improved predictability by 33.5% and 34.1%, respectively (Polk, 1975; Robins & Hill, 1966). Again, the same point can be made about educational achievement as has been made about prior criminal activity. The minimum age at which poor educational performance becomes recognizable, stable, and predictive still needs to be better established than has been possible up until now.

Early Circumstantial Predictors of Delinquency

The circumstances in which children grow up differ vastly from one family to another. Some children live in reasonably affluent families and have loving parents who are usually aware of what their children are doing and who are not reluctant to discipline when necessary; others do not. The following section reviews a variety of early circumstantial indicators of delinquency.

Table 4 shows the socioeconomic class of the parent as a predictor of the child's later delinquency. The studies recording socioeconomic class when the child was 4 to 12 years old improved predictions by a lesser fraction: $M = 19.8$.% (range = 10.5% to 30.9%; Farrington, 1979; Robins & Hill, 1966; Rutter et al., 1979; Wadsworth, 1979; Wolfgang et al., 1972). Only one study, by Knight and West (1975), showed a substantial improvement in prediction of 49.3% by considering social class as a predictor to distinguish those who continued their delinquent career after age 18 versus those who did not. Otherwise, socioeconomic class still proved a poor predictor for recidivism in large and less selected populations (Wolfgang et al., 1972).

Parents of a low socioeconomic status often have larger families. Farrington and West (1971) found that when a child had more than three siblings before the age of 10, the chance of delinquency for that child increased by 57.3% (see Table 5). Families are not necessarily intact all the time: family breaks or prolonged separations from parents, as shown in Table 6, led to little improvement in prediction ($M = 16.7$%; range = 7.4% to 30.2%). What seems to matter more is overall family functioning. Craig and Glick (1963) used teacher ratings when the child was about 6 years old, which improved predictions by an estimable 80.2%. Unfortunately, it is not clear from this study which family characteristics were taken into account by the teachers. One of these characteristics may be known criminal activity by family members. Table 7 shows that when one or more parent or a sibling has had police contacts, the prediction of the youth's delinquency or recidivism is improved by 50% (range = 28.4% to 100%; Knight & West, 1975; Osborn & West, 1979; Robins, West, & Herjanic, 1975). For these studies, the relative's delinquency occurred before the child was 8 to 19 years old. This does not mean that the subject engaged in delinquent activity with the family member, for that is uncommon (Farrington, Gundry, & West, 1975). According to those authors, even when the father's official delinquency occurred prior to the child's birth, this still can augment the chance that the child will eventually become delinquent. As is shown in Table 7, the improvement in prediction is often small, even when biological or adopted fathers are taken into account as a predictor of delinquency. Only in the case of two antisocial parents or grandparents when the child was 13 does the increment in prediction rise to 49.8% (Robins & Lewis, 1966).

It can be assumed that some parents, including those diagnosed as antisocial, are less skilled in rearing children than others. Thus, in some households, parents maintain few rules, do not exercise discipline when needed, or do not supervise youngsters (Patterson, 1982). Table 8 shows only a few studies taking such parenting skills into account as single predictors. The results are disappointing,

Table 3
Outcome Statistics for Educational Predictors of Delinquency

Study predictor	Valid positives	False positives n	False positives %	Valid negatives	False negatives n	False negatives %	N	PBR	PSR	Definition criterion of delinquency	Prediction interval	RIOC
Robins & Hill (1966, p. 329)												
School retardation before age 15	22	72	24.3	184	18	6.1	296 nonwhites	13.5	31.8	Police or court record	Under 15 to 17	34.1
Farrington (1979, p. 99)												
Low vocabulary at 10	40	87	21.3	242	40	9.8	409	14.7	31.0	21 or more self-reported acts	8–10 to 14–16	27.4
Poor school-leaving results	30	66	16.1	263	50	12.2	409	19.6	23.5		11 to 14–16	18.3
Polk (1975)												
Grade point average below C	30	26	10.3	105	46	15.9	252	30.2	10.3	One or more contacts with police–adult criminality	15 to 28–30	33.5
Rutter, Maugham, Mortimer, & Ouston (1979)												
Verbal reasoning	266	553	48.9	266	46	4.1	1131	27.6	72.4	Cautioned or found guilty	12 to 18	46.1
Wolfgang, Figlio, & Sellin (1972)												
Low achievement level in school	486	368	30.5	196	157	13.0	1207 nonwhites	53.3	70.7	Police arrest	6–12 to 18	16.4
	242	320	12.1	1632	448	17.0	2642 whites	26.0	21.3			22.9
Wadsworth (1979)												
Attitude toward school work (teacher rating)	68	262	14.6	1290	178	9.9	1798	13.7	18.3	Court appearance or caution by police	10 to 20	11.2

Note. PBR = percent base rate; PSR = percent selection ratio; RIOC = relative improvement over chance.

Table 4
Outcome Statistics for Socioeconomic Status of Parents in Predicting Delinquency

Study predictor	Valid positives	False positives n	False positives %	Valid negatives	False negatives n	False negatives %	N	PBR	PSR	Definition criterion of delinquency	Prediction interval	RIOC
Wadsworth (1979, p. 30) Lower manual socioeconomic status	197	704	32.1	1,156	134	6.1	2,191	15.1	41.1	All reported offenses		30.9
Wolfgang, Figlio & Sellin (1972, p. 54) Low socioeconomic status										Police record	4–5 to 18	
Sample 1	763	1,377	19.6	3,649	1,254	17.8	7,043 white	28.6	30.4			10.5
Sample 2	1,293	1,151	39.7	293	165	5.7	2,902 nonwhite	50.2	84.2			28.5
Robins & Hill (1966) Guardian's low occupational status	46	102	34.5	118	30	10.1	296 nonwhite (selected sample)	25.7	50.0	Police or court record	6–12 to 17	21.0
Farrington (1979) Low social class	24	55	13.4	274	56	13.7	409	19.6	19.3	21 or more self-reported acts	8–10 to 14–16	13.2
Rutter, Maughan Mortimer, & Ouston (1979) Parental occupational group	175	310	24.9	568	192	15.4	1,245	29.5	39.0	Cautioned or found guilty	12 to 18	14.4
Prediction: Recidivism												
Knight & West (1975) Low social class	23	6	7.4	27	25	30.9	81	59.3	35.8	Continuing delinquency vs. temporary delinquency	17 to 18–19	49.3
Wolfgang, Figlio, & Sellin (1972, p. 67) Low socioeconomic status										Recidivists vs. one-time offenders	4–5 to 18	
Sample 1	859	430	29.5	73	94	6.5	1,456 nonwhite	65.4	88.5			14.0
Sample 2	395	372	18.4	738	514	25.5	2,019 whites	45.0	38.0			11.7

Note. PER = percent base rate; PSR = percent selection ratio; RIOC = relative improvement over chance.

Table 5
Outcome Statistics for Family Size as a Predictor of Delinquency

Study predictor	Valid positives	False positives n	False positives %	Valid negatives	False negatives n	False negatives %	N	PBR	PSR	Definition criterion of delinquency	Prediction interval	RIOC
				Prediction: Delinquency in general								
Farrington & West (1971) Three or more siblings	33	130	31.6	230	18	4.4	411	12.4	39.7	Conviction	0–10 to 14	57.3
Wadsworth (1979) Less than two years of being only child	242	1,039	47.3	851	64	2.9	2,196	11.0	58.3	All reported offenses	2 to 21	50.0
				Prediction: Recidivism								
Osborn & West (1978) Six or more siblings	15	32	8.1	329	21	5.3	397	9.1	11.8	Two or more findings of guilt	8 to 24	33.6

Note. PBR = percent base rate; PSR = percent selection ratio; RIOC = relative improvement over chance.

partly due to the modest reliability of the measures used by psychiatric social workers assessing the parents (West, 1969, p. 125). More recent research on parents' child-rearing skills has demonstrated that considerable improvements can be made in the measurement of such skills and, possibly, in their ultimate predictive utility (Stouthamer-Loeber, Patterson, & Loeber, Note 8). The importance of the parents' child-rearing practices is most evident from composite measures in Table 9. In fact, some studies on parenting skills produced increments ranging from 77% (Trevvett, 1972) to 82% (Craig & Glick, 1968). At the time of the assessment, children were between 5 and 17 years old in the Trevvett study and 6 years old in the Craig and Glick study, but this is not fully clear from the published reports (see also Glick, 1972). The composite measure in these studies was an abridged version of the Glueck scale, consisting of ratings of the discipline and supervision of the boy by his mother, and a rating of the family's cohesiveness. The resulting scores were weighted for the frequency of delinquency associated with each rating, and then totalled. Voss (1963) also used a three-item version of the Glueck scale, but replaced family cohesiveness with discipline of the boy by the father, improving prediction by 48.3%, but thereby limiting the assessment to two-parent families.

The original Glueck and Glueck (1950, 1959) "prediction" study has not been included in Table 9 because it was retrospective in nature and relied heavily on the respondent's recall of the youth's behavior and family functioning of 7 years earlier. In the present review, replications of the original five-item Glueck scale (Tait & Hodges, 1972) did not perform as well as the three-item version usable for single-parent families. Two reports, not included in Table 9, have appeared that show very poor predictive performances of the original Glueck scale (Dootjes, 1972; Wahlen, 1954, cited in Lundman & Scarpitti, 1978).

McCord (1979) also used a composite score of family functioning leading to an increment of 45.7%, but the computation of the total score is not clear from the published report. In summary, among all circumstantial measures, composites of family functioning produced not only the highest improve-

Table 6
Outcome Statistics for Separation from Parents and Family Conflict as Predictors of Delinquency

Study predictor	Valid positives	False positives		Valid negatives	False negatives		N	PBR	PSR	Definition criterion of delinquency	Prediction interval	RIOC
		n	%		n	%						
Wadsworth (1980)												
Death or separation before 3 yr, 4 mo.	60	220	10.0	1,640	271	12.4	2,191	15.1	12.8	All reported offenses	8 to 21	7.4
Robins & Hill (1966)												
Father absent before age 15	26	129	43.6	128	13	4.4	296 nonwhite	9.8	52.4	Police or court record	6–15 to 17	30.2
Farrington & West (1971)												
Separation from parent through extended hospitalization	19	71	17.3	289	32	7.8	411	12.4	21.9	Conviction	0–10 to 14	19.6
Farrington (1979)												
Separated up to age 10	27	63	15.4	266	53	13.0	409	19.6	22.0	21 or more self-reported acts	0–10 to 14–16	15.0
Gregory (1965)												
Separation from parent by death or divorce	—	—	—	—	—	—	5,600	24.0	13.2	Police and court records; at least one minor offense	16 to 19	11.5
Farrington & West (1971)												
Parental disharmony	18	71	19.0	261	23	6.2	373	11.0	23.9	Conviction	8–9 to 14	26.4
Craig & Glick (1963)												
Family good/fair/poor (teacher rating)	37	21	7.0	236	7	2.3	301	14.6	19.3	"Serious and/or persistant"	6 to 16	80.2

Note. PBR = percent base rate; PSR = percent selection ratio; RIOC = relative improvement over chance.

Psychological Explanations of Crime

ments in prediction, but as in the Craig and Glick (1968) study, could probably be measured at a very early age. Moreover, composite predictors composed of family criminality, low income or socioeconomic status, family size, separation from parents, and so forth produced relative increments in prediction of 32% to 63% (May, 1981; West & Farrington, 1973; Wadsworth, 1979).

The importance of family functioning variables in the prediction of delinquency is also evident from studies showing the incidence of delinquency within families. For example, in the study samples of Farrington et al. (1975) and Wilson (1975), 47% to 62% of all offenses committed by youngsters in the sample were committed by children from 11% to 16% of all families. In fact, certain families were more at risk for delinquency than were other families. It is likely that parents' child-rearing practices set such families apart from less delinquent families (Wilson, 1975). Although the early identification of those families seems a promising avenue for delinquency prevention, such studies are still in their infancy.

Even when the object is the prediction of delinquency by youngsters rather than by members of a family, the Glueck method relies heavily on trained professionals to assess family functioning. Thus, such assessment, in sharp contrast with the teacher, parent, or peer assessment of the youngster's problem behavior, is relatively costly. Only in one study did teachers assess family functioning with good predictive success (Craig & Glick, 1963). There is an obvious need to replicate this study, as teachers are probably not usually as familiar with families as was the case in this study. Bell and Pearl (1982) have pointed out the necessity for using providers of services to children more systematically as assessors of children at risk for maladjusted behavior. They advocate a more systematic assessment of high-risk children as part of a community-based rather than a clinic-based identification program. Bell and Pearl (1982) rightly point out that such identification of high-risk children requires adequate intervention methods so that these children can be detoured from the anticipated undesirable outcome. In the process of a more widespread identification of high-risk children, the present repertoire of known predictors can probably be expanded. This would also be an important opportunity to improve the measurement quality of existing and forthcoming predictors.

Summary of the Results of the Prediction Studies

The preceding results have been summarized in Table 10 and have been ranked in terms of median percent relative improvement over chance. Composite measures of parental family management techniques tended to be most predictive of delinquency, followed by the child's problem behavior. Reports of the child's stealing, lying, or truancy come next, followed by criminality or antisocial behavior of family members, and the child's poor educational achievement. The lowest ranking predictors are socioeconomic status and separation from parents. This ranking should be accepted with caution, as the ranges of relative improvement over chance are considerable for some categories of predictors. Table 10 also shows the ranking for the predictors of recidivism. The best predictors were reports of the child's stealing, lying, or truancy, followed by the child's own problem behavior or prior delinquency. In comparison, socioeconomic status was the worst predictor. However, again the ranges in the percent of relative improvement over chance were large. The rankings of variables predicting delinquency in general and predicting recidivism are largely in the same direction. The two rankings are only partly comparable, however, due to the absence of studies reporting on the predictive efficiency of the following variables on the youth's recidivism: parental family management techniques, the child's poor academic achievement, and the child's separation from parents.

In summary, there is no doubt that certain extrapolative and circumstantial variables greatly improve predictability. However, none of the studies reviewed here attempted to combine extrapolative and circumstantial variables to further improve predictive efficiency. It is known from prediction studies in the field of mental health that such combinations can be very fruitful. For example, Rutter (1978) used a family adversity index

Table 7
Outcome Statistics for Delinquency in Other Family Members as a Predictor of Delinquency

Study predictor	Valid positives	False positives		Valid negatives	False negatives		N	PBR	PSR	Definition criterion of delinquency	Prediction interval	RIOC
		n	%		n	%						
Robins, West, & Herjanic (1975) One or both parents arrested	27	35	40.7	24	0	0	86 (nonwhite select sample)	31.4	72.1	Court or police contact before age 17 (nontraffic)	10–11 to 18+	100.0
One or both paternal grandparents antisocial	18	28	32.6	31	9	10.5	86 (nonwhite select sample)	31.4	53.5			28.4
Osborn & West (1979) One or more convictions for father	52	50	13.0	214	67	17.5	383	31.1	26.6	One or more convictions	8 to 24–25	29.1
One or more convictions for father or sibling	46	45	29.4	49	13	8.5	153	38.6	59.5			45.7
Farrington (1979) Criminal parent	35	69	16.9	260	45	11.0	409	19.6	25.4	21 or more self-reported acts	Under 10 to 14–16	24.4
Delinquent sibling	17	29	7.1	300	63	15.4	409	19.6	11.2			21.6
Hutchings & Mednick (1975) Criminal biological fathers (felony or misdemeanor)	21	79	7.0	914	106	9.5	1,120 (nonadopted adults)	11.3	8.9	Criminal record excluding minor offense	Unknown to 30–44	10.8
Criminal adoptive fathers (felony or misdemeanor)	39	105	9.4	834	141	12.6	1,119 (adults adopted as child)	16.1	12.9			13.0
Criminal biological fathers of adoptees (felony or misdemeanor)	80	273	28.1	534	84	8.7	971 (adults adopted as child)	16.9	36.4			19.5
Robins & Lewis (1966) Two antisocial parents or grandparents	9	17	25.4	37	4	6.0	67 (includes control group)	19.4	38.8	Arrest	13 to 18+	49.8

Continued overleaf

Table 7 (*continued*)

Study predictor	Valid positives	False positives		Valid negatives	False negatives		N	PBR	PSR	Definition criterion of delinquency	Prediction interval	RIOC
		n	%		n	%						
Kirkegaard-Sørensen & Mednick (1977) Criminal father & schizophrenic mother	16	63	31.3	102	20	10.0	201 (sons & daughters of schizophrenic mothers)	17.9	39.3	Conviction	Unknown to 23–33	8.3
Prediction: Recidivism												
Knight & West (1975) Parent or sibling convicted before S's age 10	31	9	11.1	24	17	21.0	81	59.3	49.4	Delinquency continued after age 17 vs. not cont.	9 to 18–19	44.8
Osborn & West (1979) Father with two or more convictions	56	34	18.4	61	34	18.4	185	48.6	48.6	Two or more convictions of son	8 to 24–25	26.4

Note. PBR = percent base rate; PSR = percent selection ratio; RIOC = relative improvement over chance.

Table 8
Outcome Statistics for Parenting Variables as Predictors of Delinquency

Study predictor	Valid positives	False positives n	False positives %	Valid negatives	False negatives n	False negatives %	N	PBR	PSR	Definition criterion of delinquency	Prediction interval	RIOC
Farrington (1979)												
Poor parental supervision (see West, 1969, pp. 73–74)	29	50	12.2	279	51	12.5	409	19.6	19.3	21 or more self-reported acts	8 to 14–16	21.2
Poor parental child rearing	27	71	17.3	258	53	13.0	409	19.6	24.0			13.1
West & Farrington (1973)												
Authoritarian mother (see West, 1969, pp. 178–180)	23	59	20.3	180	29	10.0	291	17.9	28.2	Conviction	9–10 to 17	22.6

Note. PBR = percent base rate; PSR = percent selection ratio; RIOC = relative improvement over chance.

containing both a measure of the subject's early behavior and measures derived from the subject's family environment. The resulting analysis showed that the risk of psychiatric disorders accelerated when four or more adversities were present. Similar combinations of circumstantial and extrapolative predictors have been used by Werner and Smith (1982) to predict which of those high-risk youths would be resilient and not show later maladjusted behavior. In the study of delinquency, we need to allow such examples, if only to make predictors as powerful as possible. Another important reason is that a better understanding of causal variables in delinquency is possible not only by identifying those variables predicting delinquency, but also by discovering the variables forecasting absence of criminal behavior. These in a sense negative predictions are most useful to better understand why certain youths do not engage in delinquent activities, even when their peers or relatives do so or even when they reside in a neighborhood characterized by antisocial lifestyles, unemployment, and ample opportunities for crime.

Figure 4 illustrates which early predictors of delinquency produced the best results. It shows the age of the child when various predictors were last measured, graphed against the measure of the percent relative improvement over chance. If we can be assured of the correctness of Craig and Glick's (1963) data, family characteristics when the child was 6 years old were both the earliest and among the best predictors. From 9 years onward, specific and generally problematic behaviors appear as predictors, with antisocial referrals, aggressiveness, and predelinquency being the best predictive triad. At age 10, parent criminality appears to be very predictive of later child delinquency, at least as measured retrospectively in Robins et al.'s (1975) study on a select sample. At age 15, grade point average becomes predictive, and a year later high self-reported delinquency and officially recorded delinquency come to the fore. These "minimum" ages for predictors are, as mentioned, not the result of systematic research. We anticipate that empirical studies will further decrease the age at which children can be reliably identified as at risk for delinquency.

The Evaluation of Delinquency Prediction Through Utility Estimation

The concern with simple accuracy in criminological prediction is the policy underlying our use of the measures of relative improvement over chance. These indices do not consider the errors concomitant with the valid predictions within a study. It is often the case, however, that investigators are not neutral to the two types of prediction errors (i.e., false positives and false negatives). One investigator may be primarily concerned with minimizing the false positive errors in a prediction strategy to reduce the economical cost of treating individuals not actually in need of treatment. Conversely, another investigator may be concerned with reducing false negative errors for the purpose of adequately covering the population of potential criminal offenders in a prevention program. A well-established component of personnel selection and decision theory involves the numerical estimation of the overall utility of selection or prediction procedures by attaching differential weights to false positive and false negative errors (Cronbach & Gleser, 1965; Rorer, Hoffman, Hsieh, 1965; Wiggins, 1973). The advantages of utility estimation in criminological prediction are (a) utility values assigned to each prediction outcome provide a representation of the institutional or personal values underlying a prediction procedure, (b) the overall utility of various prediction strategies may be evaluated diversely according to the idiosyncratic concerns of various institutions or social service settings, and (c) optimum cutting scores may be rationally selected that maximize the overall utility of a prediction procedure (Rorer et al., 1965).

The assignment of utility cost and gain values in criminological prediction is clearly a subjective process. One prediction strategy may be said to be superior to another only relative to a specific utility estimation policy. As examples three utility estimation policies are presented in Figure 5. The first policy consists of using our measure of relative improvement over chance, which assumes the same utility values for false positive and false negative errors. Policy 2 assigns a cost value to false negative errors (EU_1), and Pol-

icy 3 assigns a cost value to false positive errors (EU_2).

The computational formula for the expected utility (EU) of a prediction strategy recommended by Wiggins (1973) is

$$EU = U_1 \times p(VP) + U_2 \times p(FP)$$
$$+ U_3 \times p(FN) + U_4 \times p(VN),$$

where $p(VP)$ is the probability of a valid positive, $p(FP)$ is the probability of a false positive, $p(FN)$ is the probability of a false negative, $p(VN)$ is the probability of a valid negative, and U_i is the utility value of the outcome.

Wiggins (1973) further suggests that the cost of testing be estimated on the utility scale and incorporated into this formula. We have simplified the formula by eliminating the estimated cost of testing.

We will now reevaluate four of the prediction studies (Craig & Glick, 1963; Polk, 1975; Robins, 1966; Scarpitti, 1964) discussed above, using the three utility estimation policies (including the total percent correct and the relative improvement over chance as one). Table 11 provides the base rate, selection ratio, total percent correct, relative improvement over chance, and the expected utilities of the two alternative policies (EU_1 and EU_2).

Note that, depending on the evaluation index one adopts, the rank-ordered preference of the four studies radically varies. The Craig and Glick (1963) study is superior to the other three studies according to EU_1 because a cost is assigned to false negative errors. However, on EU_2, the Craig and Glick study is ranked third in terms of overall utility. Although the four studies are relatively equal according to the total percent correct, their rates of false positive and false negative errors determine their practical utility in the two hypothetical applications. The reader is invited to use these utility policies on further studies in our review, or apply other utility functions adjusted to needs to those studies.

Methodological Considerations and Recommendations in Prediction Studies

In this section we will consider prediction methodology in delinquency research and

Table 9
Outcome Statistics on Composite Measures as Delinquency Predictors

Study predictor	Valid positives	False positives		Valid negatives	False negatives		N	PBR	PSR	Definition criterion of delinquency	Prediction interval	RIOC
		n	%		n	%						
Tait & Hodges (1972) Glueck's Prediction Table (5 factors)	77	26	22.4	9	4	3.5	116 (selected sample)	69.8	88.8	Known to juvenile court	5 to 14	56.4
Trevett (1972) Modified Glueck's Prediction Table (3 factors)	119	15	9.3	23	5	3.1	162 (same as Tait & Hodges)	76.5	82.7			76.9
Craig & Glick (1968) Modified Glueck's Prediction Table (3 factors)	28	5	1.7	252	16	5.3	301	14.6	11.0	"Serious & persistent delinquents"	6 to 16	81.9
Voss (1963) Modified Glueck's Prediction Table (1 parent: 2 factors) (2 parents: 3 factors)	13	24	10.8	176	10	4.5	223 (whites, nonwhites, Puerto Ricans)	10.3	16.6	Police contact?	6 to 12	48.3
McCord (1979) Home atmosphere: 1. Mother affection 2. Supervision 3. Parental conflict 4. Parental aggress. 5. Mother's self-confidence 6. Father's deviance 7. Father's absence	27	19	9.5	133	21	10.5	200	24.0	23.0	One or more conviction for serious crime	5-13 to 21+	45.7
West & Farrington (1973) Combination of 1. parent criminality 2. low family income 3. poor parental behavior	10	4	1.0	323	74	18.0	411	20.4	3.4	Conviction	8-10 to 17	63.0

Continued overleaf

Table 9 *(continued)*

Study predictor	Valid positives	False positives n	False positives %	Valid negatives	False negatives n	False negatives %	N	PBR	PSR	Definition criterion of delinquency	Prediction interval	RIOC
Wadsworth (1979) 1. Birth order 2. Family size 3. Family growth 4. Parental divorce, separation, or death 5. Lengthy hospital stay 6. Social group	136	711	39.2	915	50	2.8	1,812	10.3	46.7	Court appearance or cautioned by police	0 to 21	49.5
Prediction: Recidivism												
Osborn & West (1980) 1. 9 wks. unemployed 2. Heavy smoking 3. Heavy drinking 4. Sexual intercourse with more than one partner 5. Drug use 6. Involved in fights	19	9	20.5	13	3	6.8	44	50.0	63.6	Persisting vs. temporary recidivism	18 to 23	68.3
Osborn & West (1978) Antisociality (score of 5 or more on 11 self-reported antisocial behaviors; see West & Farrington, 1977, p. 195)	33	19	18.6	33	7	16.7	102	49.0	50.1	Reconviction	18 to 19–23	30.6
May (1981) Social Disadvantage Score (score of 4 or more out of 16 items)	341	842	14.9	4082	389	6.9	5654	12.9	20.9	Police contact	11–16 to 13–18	32.4

Note. PBR percent base rate; PSR = percent selection ratio; RIOC = relative improvement over chance.

recommend ways in which prediction efficiency may be improved.

A formidable problem in criminology involves the use of police contact or court adjudication as prediction criteria. Hood and
Sparks (1970, p. 12) have specified two major
problems with the use of criminal justice statistics as a criterion variable in crime causation studies: (a) individuals engaging in
identical delinquent behavior who remain
undetected by law enforcement personnel are
virtually ignored; and (b) factors explaining
delinquent behavior are theoretically entan-
gled with factors responsible for official processing. Hood and Sparks suggest further that

we must start, not with known delinquents, but with
representative samples of the juvenile population drawn
without regard to their known or probable delinquent
histories. Then, on the basis of interviews, questionnaires, and tests we must differentiate these samples into
delinquents and nondelinquents of various degrees and
kinds. (1970, p. 46)

A majority of the prediction studies we have
reviewed here rely on court records as the
only criterion of juvenile delinquency. This
is quite reasonable given that juvenile delinquency is usually defined as a legal phenomenon, that is, juvenile delinquency refers to
youths having contact with police and court

officials for law-violating behavior. However,
criminological prediction research would
benefit from the use of multiple criteria for
juvenile delinquency. Some suggested criteria
of delinquency are self-reported delinquency,
parent-reported delinquency, teacher-reported school behavior problems, and peer
nominations of antisocial behavior.

Another consideration to be made when
developing a prediction procedure or evaluating past work in criminological prediction
is the base rate (i.e., violation rate) of the
principle criterion variable. As Meehl and
Rosen (1955) have discussed, the overall accuracy of prediction decreases as the incidence of the criterion variable decreases. This
phenomenon is evident in the prediction
studies reviewed here. For example, only 7
of the 71 delinquency prediction studies with
criterion base rates less than or equal to 30%
improve over the accuracy obtainable from
the base rate prediction alone. In contrast,
17 of the 32 prediction studies with criterion
base rates greater than 30% exceeded the
overall accuracy of the base rate prediction.
Meehl and Rosen (1955) argue that the utility
of low baserate prediction is severely limited
by the fact that the overall accuracy is likely
to be less for predictions based on an expen-

Table 10
*Rank Order of Predictors of Delinquency and Recidivism in Terms of Median Relative Improvement
Over Chance (Summarized from Tables 1–9)*

	RIOC	
Predictor	Mdn	Range
For delinquency		
1. Composite measures of parental family management techniques	.50	.31–.82
2. Child problem behavior	.32	.15–.78
3. Stealing, lying, or truancy	.26	.22–.58
4. Criminality or antisocial behavior of family members	.24	.08–1.0
5. Poor educational achievement	.23	.11–.46
6. Single measures of parental family management techniques	.23	.13–.23
7. Separation from parents	.20	.07–.80
8. Socioeconomic status	.18	.10–.31
For recidivism		
1. Stealing, lying, or truancy	.46	.31–.60
2. Child problem behavior	.38	.26–.56
3. Criminality or antisocial behavior of family members	.36	.26–.45
4. Prior delinquency	.36	.30–.60
5. Socioeconomic status	.14	.12–.49

Note. RIOC = relative improvement over chance.

sive test battery than for mere baserate predictions.

Obviously, one mode of attacking the low baserate problem in criminological prediction is to restrict prediction efforts to criteria with base rates approaching the optimal 50% level (Meehl & Rosen, 1955). Most recidivism studies based on samples of first-time offenders report recidivism rates of approx-

imately 50%. If an alternative criteria of delinquency is adopted—for example, self-reported delinquency—cutting scores may be established that provide an optimal base rate for prediction.

A recent development in the prediction of delinquency involves the systematic application of a multiple stage assessment battery to a successively reduced risk sample. This

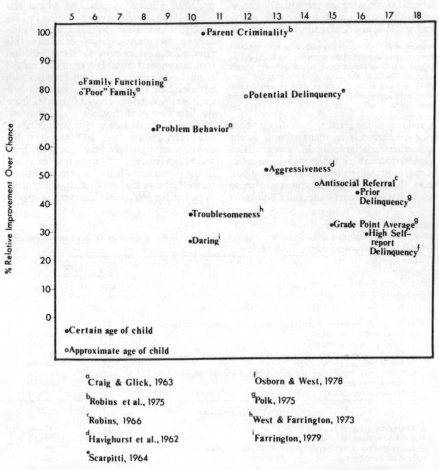

^aCraig & Glick, 1963

^bRobins et al., 1975

^cRobins, 1966

^dHavighurst et al., 1962

^eScarpitti, 1964

^fOsborn & West, 1978

^gPolk, 1975

^hWest & Farrington, 1973

ⁱFarrington, 1979

Figure 4. The accuracy of various predictors of delinquency in relation to the age of the child at the time of prediction.

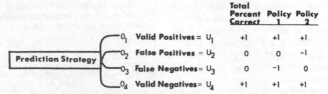

Figure 5. The utility values assumed for the total percent correct index compared with two alternative utility estimation policies.

procedure has been labeled *multiple gating* by Loeber, Dishion, and Patterson (Note 7) and is adapted from the field of personnel selection (Cronbach & Gleser, 1965; Wiggins, 1973). In the multiple gating procedure each assessment stage (i.e., predictor) is seen as a screening gate. The procedure being developed by the above investigators involves applying the first gate to a full sample of both risk and nonrisk subjects. On the basis of the first gate, a given proportion of subjects is temporarily defined as a risk group and is further assessed at the second gate. Based on the scores of the second gate, a smaller proportion of subjects is temporarily defined as a risk group and is retained for further assessment on the third gate. The final gate provides for the final formulation of a group predicted to be at high risk for future delinquency. The hypothesized result of each gate in the multiple gating procedure is the successive increase in base rates and the decrease in false positive errors, without a concomitant increase in false negative errors. The inclusion and order of predictor variables in the multiple-gating design involves two primary considerations: (a) the lowest economic cost of administering the predictor instruments, and (b) the correlations between the

predictor and criterion, and, further, the intercorrelations between the predictor variables. The best prediction battery would include predictors with relatively strong predictor–criterion correlations and low interpredictor correlations.

Finally, we will make three general comments concerning method and geographic factors in the cross-validation of identification studies. Regarding method factors, Farrington (1978) has compared various statistical prediction methods and found that the use of simple Burgess-type weights, unlike discriminant analysis and multiple regression, are less susceptible to shrinkage in cross-validation. Dawes and Corrigan (1974) also found that unit weightings perform satisfactorily in comparison to optimal weighting strategies and are most robust when the research is cross-validated. Duncan and Ohlin (1949) found that the predictive validity of prediction strategies diminished as the validation sample differed in sample parameters from the construction sample. Reiss (1951) concurs with these results and further demonstrates that inefficient and psychometrically unstable predictors have limited predictive validity. These authors' results suggest that to ensure optimal predictive validity in

Table 11

Evaluation of Six Delinquency Prediction Studies Using Diverse Utility Estimation Policies

Study	Base rate	Selection ratio	Total % correct	RIOC	EU_1	EU_2
Craig & Glick (1963) (Teacher ratings)	14.6	34.9	73.8	.66	.708	.505
Polk (1975) (School achievement)	30.2	10.3	71.4	.34	.532	.611
Robins (1966) (Antisocial referral)	70.9	60.6	74.3	.48	.563	.666
Scarpitti (1964) (Teacher rating of potentially delinquent)	17.9	40.5	72.8	.78	.705	.480

Note. RIOC = relative improvement over chance; EU_1 = Expected Utility Policy 1 (cost value attached to false positive errors); EU_2 = Expected Utility Policy 2 (cost value assigned to false negative errors).

cross-validation, one needs to include a small number of stable and efficient predictors with a high criterion–predictor correlation within the prediction battery. It is also advantageous to construct a prediction strategy from a sample homogeneous with the target population.

Second, there is a clear need to cross-validate screening measures to identify youths at risk for delinquency in different geographical areas to replicate promising criminological prediction results. As Rutter (1978) has shown in the field of child psychopathology, diverse geographical areas can be characterized by risk factors that only partly overlap. The present review indicates that many predictors from different locales operate in the same direction, although their predictive efficiency may vary from site to site. Such generality makes it possible to develop screening instruments that can be widely used.

These suggestions are provided in the conviction that improved methodology applied to criminological prediction will result in improved predictive efficiency. It is further reasonable to propose that through the systematic testing of objective predictors and a rigorous adherence to sound empirical procedures, our understanding of causal processes leading to criminal careers will be greatly enhanced.

Reference Notes

1. Loeber, R., & Dishion, T. J. *Strategies for identifying at-risk youths in the context of children's development.* Unpublished manuscript, 1981. (Available from the Oregon Social Learning Center, 207 East 5th, Suite 202, Eugene, Oregon).
2. Loeber, R., & Schmaling, K. B. *Empirical evidence for overt and covert patterns of antisocial conduct problems.* Unpublished manuscript, 1982.
3. Reid, J. B., Hinojosa-Rivero, G., & Lorber, R. *A social learning approach to the outpatient treatment of children who steal.* Unpublished manuscript, 1980. (Available from the Oregon Social Learning Center, 207 East 5th, Suite 202, Eugene, Oregon 97401.)
4. Farrington, D. P. Personal communication, 1981.
5. Loeber, R., & Schmaling, K. B. *The utility of differentiating between mixed and pure forms of antisocial child behavior.* Unpublished manuscript, 1982.
6. Wolfgang, M. E. *From boy to man—From delinquency to crime.* Paper presented at the National Symposium on the Serious Juvenile Offender, State of Minnesota, Minneapolis, Minnesota, September 19–20, 1977.
7. Loeber, R., Dishion, T. J., & Patterson, G. R. *Multiple gating: A multi-stage assessment procedure for identifying youths at risk for delinquency.* Unpublished manuscript, 1981.

8. Stouthamer-Loeber, M., Patterson, G. R., & Loeber, R. *Parental monitoring and antisocial child behavior.* Unpublished manuscript, 1981.

References

Bell, R. Q., & Pearl, D. Psychosocial change in risk groups: Implications for early identification. *Journal of Prevention in Human Services,* 1982, *1*(4).

Buikhuisen, W., & Hoekstra, H. A. Factors related to recidivism. *British Journal of Criminology,* 1974, *14,* 63–69.

Cowden, J. E., & Pacht, A. B. Predicting institutional and post release adjustment of delinquent boys. *Journal of Consulting Psychology,* 1967, *31,* 377–380.

Craig, M. M., & Glick, S. J. Ten years experience with the Glueck Social Prediction Table. *Crime and Delinquency,* 1963, *9,* 249–261.

Craig, M. M., & Glick, S. J. School behavior related to later delinquency and nondelinquency. *Criminologica,* 1968, *5,* 17–27.

Cronbach, L. J., & Gleser, G. C. *Psychological tests and personnel decisions.* Urbana: University of Illinois Press, 1965.

Cymbalisty, B. Y., Schuck, S. Z., & Dubeck, J. A. Achievement level, institutional adjustment, and recidivism among juvenile delinquents. *Journal of Community Psychology,* 1975, *3,* 289–294.

Dawes, R. M., & Corrigan, B. Linear models in decision making. *Psychological Bulletin,* 1974, *81,* 95–106.

DeBlois, C. S., & Stewart, M. Aggressiveness and antisocial behavior in children: Their relationships to other dimensions of behavior. *Research Communications in Psychology, Psychiatry, and Behavior,* 1980, *5,* 303–312.

Dootjes, I. Predicting juvenile delinquency. *Australian and New Zealand Journal of Criminology,* 1972, *5,* 157–171.

Duncan, O. D., & Ohlin, L. E. The efficiency of prediction in criminology. *American Journal of Sociology,* 1949, *54,* 441–452.

Epstein, S. The stability of behavior. I. Implications for psychological research. *American Psychologist,* 1980, *35,* 780–806.

Farrington, D. P. The family background of aggressive youths. In L. A. Hersov, M. Berger, & D. Shaffer (Eds.), *Aggression and antisocial behavior in childhood and adolescence.* Oxford: Pergamon Press, 1978.

Farrington, D. P. Environmental stress, delinquent behavior, and conviction. In I. G. Sarason & C. D. Spielberger (Eds.), *Stress and anxiety* (Vol. 6). Washington, D.C.: Hemisphere, 1979.

Farrington, D. P., Gundry, G., & West, D. J. The familial transmission of criminality. *Medicine, Science, and the Law,* 1975, *15,* 177–186.

Farrington, D. P., & West, D. J. A comparison between early delinquents and young aggressives. *British Journal of Criminology,* 1971, *11,* 341–358.

Feldhusen, J. F., Thurston, J. R., & Benning, J. J. A longitudinal study of delinquency and other aspects of children's behavior. *International Journal of Criminology and Penology,* 1973, *1,* 341–351.

Gendreau, P., Madden, P., & Leipciger, M. Norms and recidivism for first incarcerates: Implications for programming. *Canadian Journal of Criminology,* 1979, 1-26.

Gersten, J. C., Langner, T. S., Eisenberg, J. S., Simcha-Fagan, D., & McCarthy, E. D. Stability and change in types of behavioral disturbances of children and adolescents. *Journal of Abnormal Child Psychology,* 1976, *4,* 111-127.

Ghodsian, M., Fogelman, K., Lambert, L., & Tibbenham, A. Changes in behaviour ratings of a national sample of children. *British Journal of Social and Clinical Psychology,* 1980, *19,* 247-256.

Glavin, J. P. Persistence of behavior disorders in children. *Exceptional Children,* 1972, *38,* 367-376.

Glick, S. J. Identification of predelinquents among children with school behavior problems as a basis for multiservice program. In S. Glueck & E. Glueck (Eds.), *Identification of predelinquents.* New York: Intercontinental Medical Books, 1972.

Glueck, S., & Glueck, E. *Unraveling juvenile delinquency.* Cambridge, Mass.: Harvard University Press, 1950.

Glueck, S., & Glueck, E. *Predicting delinquency and crime.* Cambridge, Mass.: Harvard University Press, 1959.

Gottfredson, D. M. Assessment of predictive methods. In N. Johnston, L. Savitz, & M. E. Wolfgang (Eds.), *The sociology of punishment and aggression.* New York: Wiley, 1970.

Gregory, I. Interospective data following childhood loss of a parent: I. Delinquency and high school drop out. *Archives of General Psychiatry,* 1965, *13,* 99-109.

Hakeem, M. A critique of the psychiatric approach to the prevention of juvenile delinquency. *Social Problems,* 1957-1958, *5,* 194-205.

Hathaway, S. R., & Monachesi, E. D. (Eds.), *Analyzing and predicting juvenile delinquency with the MMPI.* Minneapolis: University of Minnesota Press, 1953.

Hathaway, S. R., & Monachesi, E. D. *Adolescent personality and behavior.* Minneapolis: University of Minnesota Press, 1963.

Havighurst, R. J., Bowman, P. H., Liddle, G. P., Matthews, C. V., & Pierce, J. V.. *Growing up in River City.* New York: Wiley, 1962.

Hirschi, T., & Selvin, H. C. *Delinquency research: An appraisal of analytic methods.* New York: Free Press, 1967.

Hood, R., & Sparks, R. *Key issues in criminology.* London: Weindenfeld & Nicholson, 1970.

Hutchings, B., & Mednick, S. A. Registered criminality in the adoptive and biological parents of registered male criminal adoptees. In R. R. Fieve, D. Rosenthal, & M. Brill (Eds.), *Genetic research in psychiatry.* Baltimore, Md.: Johns Hopkins University Press, 1975.

Janes, C. L., Hesselbrock, V. M., Myers, D. G., & Penniman, J. H. Problem boys in young adulthood: Teacher ratings and 12-year follow-up. *Journal of Youth and Adolescence,* 1979, *8,* 453-472.

Kirkegaard-Sorenson, L., & Mednick, S. A. A prospective study of predictors of criminality. In S. A. Mednick & K. O. Christiansen (Eds.), *Biosocial bases of criminal behavior.* New York: Gardner Press, 1977.

Knight, B. J., & West, D. J. Temporary and continuing delinquency. *British Journal of Criminology,* 1975, *15,* 43-50.

Koller, K. M., & Gosden, S. D. Recidivists: Their past and families compared with first time only prisoners.

Australian and New Zealand Journal of Criminology, 1980, *13,* 117-123.

Loeber, R. The stability of antisocial and delinquent child behavior: A review. *Child Development,* 1982, *53,* 1431-1446.

Lundman, R. J., & Scarpitti, F. R. Delinquency prevention: Recommendations for future projects. *Crime and Delinquency,* 1978, *24,* 207-220.

Marsh, R. W. The validity of the Bristol Social Adjustment Guides in delinquency prediction. *British Journal of Educational Psychology,* 1969, *39,* 278-282.

May, R. D. The Aberdeen delinquency study. In S. A. Mednick, A. E. Baert, & B. P. Bachmann (Eds.), *Prospective longitudinal research.* Oxford: Oxford University Press, 1981.

McCord, J. Some child-rearing antecedents of criminal behavior in adult men. *Journal of Personality and Social Psychology,* 1979, *9,* 1477-1486.

McCord, J. Patterns of deviance. In S. B. Sells, R. Crandall, M. Roff, J. S. Strauss, & W. Pollin (Eds.), *Human functioning in longitudinal perspective.* Baltimore, Md.: Williams & Wilkins, 1980.

Meehl, P. E., & Rosen, A. Antecedent probability and the efficiency of psychometric signs, patterns, or cutting scores. *Psychological Bulletin,* 1955, *52,* 194-216.

Miller, F. J. W., Court, S. D. M., Knox, E. G., & Brandon, S. *The school years in Newcastle upon Tyne.* London: Oxford University Press, 1974.

Mitchell, S., & Rosa, P. Boyhood behavior problems as precursors of criminality: A fifteen-year follow-up study. *Journal of Child Psychology and Psychiatry,* 1981, *22,* 19-33.

Monahan, J. *Predicting violent behavior: An assessment of clinical techniques.* Beverly Hills, Calif.: Sage Press, 1981.

Moore, D. R., Chamberlain, P., & Mukai, L. A follow-up comparison of stealing and aggression. *Journal of Abnormal Child Psychology,* 1979, *7,* 345-355.

Mulligan, G., Douglas, J. W. B., Hammond, W. H., & Tizard, J. Delinquency and symptoms of maladjustment. *Proceedings of the Royal Society of Medicine,* 1963, *56,* 1083-1086.

Ohlin, L. E., & Duncan, O. D. The efficiency of prediction in criminology. *American Journal of Sociology,* 1949, *54,* 441-452.

Olweus, D. Stability of aggressive reaction patterns in males: A review. *Psychological Bulletin,* 1979, *86,* 852-857.

Osborn, S. G., & West, D. J. The effectiveness of various predictors of criminal careers. *Journal of Adolescence,* 1978, *1,* 101-117.

Osborn, S. G., & West, D. J. Conviction records of fathers and sons compared. *British Journal of Criminology,* 1979, *19,* 120-133.

Osborn, S. G., & West, D. J. Do young delinquents really reform? *Journal of Adolescence,* 1980, *3,* 99-114.

Patterson, G. R. *A social learning approach, Vol. 3: Coercive family process.* Eugene, Oregon: Castalia Publishing Company, 1982.

Polk, K. Schools and the delinquency experience. *Criminal Justice and Behavior,* 1975, *2,* 315-338.

Powers, E., & Witmer, H. *An experiment in the prevention of delinquency: The Cambridge-Somerville youth study.* New York: Columbia University Press, 1951.

Prigmore, C. S. An analysis of rater reliability on the

Glueck scale for the prediction of juvenile delinquency. *Journal of Criminal Law, Criminology, and Police Science,* 1963, *54,* 30–41.

Pritchard, D. A. Stable predictors of recidivism: A summary. *Criminology,* 1979, *1,* 15–21.

Reckless, W. C., & Dinitz, S. *The prevention of juvenile delinquency.* Columbus: Ohio State University Press, 1972.

Reid, J. B., & Hendriks, A. F. C. J. A preliminary analysis of the effectiveness of direct home intervention for treatment of predelinquent boys who steal. In L. A. Hamerlynck, L. C. Handy, & E. J. Mash (Eds.), *Behavior therapy: Methodology, concepts, and practice.* Champaign, Ill.: Research Press, 1973.

Reiss, A. J. The accuracy, efficiency, and validity of a prediction instrument. *American Journal of Sociology,* 1951, *56,* 552–561.

Robins, L. N. *Deviant children grow up: A sociological and psychiatric study of sociopathic personality.* Baltimore, Md.: Williams & Wilkins, 1966.

Robins, L. N., & Hill, S. Y. Assessing the contribution of family structure, class and peer groups to juvenile delinquency. *Journal of Criminal Law, Criminology, and Police Science,* 1966, *57,* 325–334.

Robins, L. N., & Laws, R. G. The role of the antisocial family in school completion and delinquency: A three-generation study. *Sociological Quarterly,* 1966, *7,* 500–514.

Robins, L. N., & Ratcliff, K. S. Risk factors in the continuation of childhood antisocial behavior into adulthood. *International Journal of Mental Health,* 1979, *7,* 96–116.

Robins, L. N., West, P. A., & Herjanic, B. L. Arrests and delinquency in two generations: A study of black urban families and their children. *Journal of Child Psychology and Psychiatry,* 1975, *16,* 125–140.

Roff, M., Sells, S. B., & Golden, M. M. *Social adjustment and personality development in children.* Minneapolis: University of Minnesota Press, 1972.

Rorer, L. G., Hoffman, P. J., & Hsieh, K-C. Utilities as baserate multipliers in the determination of optimum cutting scores for the discrimination of groups of unequal size and variance. *Journal of Applied Psychology,* 1965, *50,* 364–368.

Rutter, M. Family, area, and school influences in the genesis of conduct disorders. In L. A. Hersov, M. Berger, & D. Shaffer (Eds.), *Aggression and antisocial behavior in childhood and adolescence.* Oxford: Pergamon Press, 1978.

Rutter, M., Maugham, G., Mortimer, P., & Ouston, J. *15,000 hours—Secondary schools and their effects on children.* Cambridge, Mass.: Harvard University Press, 1979.

Scarpitti, F. R. Can teachers predict delinquency? *The Elementary School Journal,* 1964, *65,* 130–136.

Simcha-Fagan, O. The prediction of delinquent behavior over time: Sex-specific patterns related to official and survey-reported delinquent behavior. In R. G. Simmons (Ed.), *Research in community and mental health: An annual compilation of research.* Greenwich, Conn.: JAI Publishing, 1979.

Simon, G. H. *Prediction methods in criminology.* London: Her Majesty's Stationery Office, 1971.

Stott, D. H., & Wilson, D. M. The prediction of early-adult criminality from school-age behaviour. *International Journal of Social Psychiatry,* 1968, *14,* 5–8.

Tait, C. D., & Hodges, E. F. Follow-up study of Glueck Table applied to a school population of problem boys and girls between the ages of five and fourteen. In S. Glueck & E. Glueck (Eds.), *Identification of predelinquents.* New York: Intercontinental Medical Books, 1972.

Toby, J. Early identification and intensive treatment of predelinquents: A negative view. *Social Work,* 1961, *6,* 3–13.

Trevvett, N. B. Identifying delinquency-prone children. In S. Glueck & E. Glueck (Eds.), *Identification of predelinquents.* New York: Intercontinental Medical Book, 1972.

Voss, H. T. The predictive efficiency of the Glueck Social Prediction Table. *Journal of Criminal Law and Criminology,* 1963, *54,* 421–430.

Wadsworth, M. E. J. *Roots of delinquency, infancy, adolescence, and crime.* Oxford, England: Robertson, 1979.

Wadsworth, M. E. J. Early life events and later behavioral outcomes in a British longitudinal study. In S. B. Sells, R. Crandall, M. Roff, J. S. Strauss, & W. Pollin (Eds.), *Human functioning in longitudinal perspective.* Baltimore, Md.: Williams & Wilkins, 1980.

Weis, K. The Glueck Social Prediction Table: An unfulfilled promise. *Journal of Criminal Law and Criminology,* 1974, *65,* 397–404.

Werner, E. E., & Smith, R. S. *Kauai's children come of age.* Honolulu: University Press of Hawaii, 1977.

Werner, E. E., & Smith, R. S. *Vulnerable, but inconvincible: A longitudinal study of resilient children and youth.* New York: McGraw-Hill, 1982.

West, D. J. *Present conduct and future delinquency.* London: Heinemann, 1969.

West, D. J., & Farrington, D. P. *Who becomes delinquent?* London: Heinemann, 1973.

Wiggins, J. S. *Personality and prediction: Principles of personality assessment.* Reading, Mass.: Addison-Wesley, 1973.

Wilson, H. Juvenile delinquency, parent criminality, and social handicap. *British Journal of Criminology,* 1975, *15,* 241–250.

Wolfgang, M. E., Figlio, R. M., & Sellin, T. *Delinquency in a birth cohort.* Chicago: University of Chicago Press, 1972.

Received March 12, 1982
Revision received December 27, 1982 ∎

Part I
Individual Influences

Antisocial Personality

[2]

In International Journal of Mental Health,
7 (3-4), Fall-Winter, 1978-79, pp. 96-116.

RISK FACTORS IN THE CONTINUATION
OF CHILDHOOD ANTISOCIAL BEHAVIOR
INTO ADULTHOOD

LEE NELKEN ROBINS
and KATHRYN STROTHER RATCLIFF

Antisocial patterns of behavior typically begin early in life, usually
before age 10 and sometimes in the preschool years. They are
characterized by resistance to parental and educational authority,
stealing, lying, fighting, and school achievement less than that predicted by IQ. Behaviors ordinarily reserved for late adolescence
or adulthood occur precociously, particularly drinking, use of illicit
drugs, sexual intercourse, and leaving home and school. In adolescence, such behaviors often lead to difficulty with the law, and thus
the antisocial child becomes a juvenile delinquent. These patterns
of behavior occur disproportionately, although not exclusively, in
males reared in homes disadvantaged by poverty and negligent parents who themselves have a history of antisocial behavior. Sibships
are often unusually large or unusually small (the latter sometimes
because the antisocial child is illegitimate), and homes are often
broken by parents' marital problems or failure to marry at all.

Antisocial behavior arising in childhood presents a remarkably
stable and ominous picture for the future (Clarizio, 1968; Glueck &
Glueck, 1968; Robins, 1966; Rutter, Tizard, Yule, Graham, & Whit-

---

The authors are associated with the Department of Psychiatry,
Washington University School of Medicine, 4940 Audubon Ave., St.
Louis, Mo. 63110.

The work reported here was supported in part by U. S. Public
Health Service Grants MH 14677, AA 00209, DA 00013, and MH
18864.

CONTINUATION OF ANTISOCIAL BEHAVIOR INTO ADULTHOOD

more, 1976). Although many disorders of early childhood are transient, severe antisocial behavior is not: it often worsens as the
child grows older (Gersten, Langner, Eisenberg, Simcha-Fagan, &
McCarthy, 1976), and frequently continues into adulthood. When the
childhood patterns persist into adulthood, their effects may extend
into virtually every aspect of adult life: marital, parental, occupational, legal, interpersonal, and substance abuse. People with such
pervasive patterns are diagnosed as having an "antisocial personality" or, under previous diagnostic nomenclatures, as being sociopathic or psychopathic. Almost all adults for whom this diagnosis
can be made evidenced conspicuously antisocial behavior in childhood. Similarly, most men with records of repetitive criminality
(Guze, 1976) have had such a childhood history, as have many alco-
holics (Jones, 1968; Rosenberg, 1969) and drug addicts (Robins,
Davis, & Wish, 1977). When adults with an antisocial childhood become parents, they are likely to neglect the supervision of their
children, fail to support them, and subject them to broken homes
when their own marriages fail, thus setting the scene for a renewal
of the same pattern in the next generation (Rutter & Madge, 1976).
It is therefore very important to try to discover ways of interrupt-
ing in childhood a pattern of antisocial behavior that may have dire
prognoses for the future, not only for the well-being of the affected
child but also for the benefit of future generations.

Although children who display antisocial behavior do have remarkably poor prognoses for adult adjustment, their outcomes are
by no means uniformly unfortunate. Even among the most highly
antisocial children, half or more will give up enough of their antisocial behavior in late adolescence so that they will not merit a
diagnosis of antisocial personality as adults, although they do tend
to have somewhat more antisocial behavior than the average person
(Robins, 1966). Few will be totally well-adjusted adults; still, it
would be valuable to be able to identify those antisocial children
most at risk of severe, long-term problems. Such identification
would be useful for testing new methods of intervention, because it
is easy in a group with a very high risk to demonstrate the advantages of effective treatment or preventive measures, since the effectiveness of such measures are not diluted by spontaneous improvement. From a clinical viewpoint, it would be valuable to be
able to identify the group at serious risk because it is both more

L. N. ROBINS & K. S. RATCLIFF

economical and less intrusive to treat only those children who one can be reasonably sure will have bad outcomes without treatment.

The problem is to find indices that will detect most of those who will have lasting problems and as few as possible of those who will not, i.e., a measure that is both as sensitive and as specific as possible. The information typically available for such identification would include the variety of antisocial behaviors that a child has shown, the particular types of antisocial behaviors, and the particular home environments to which the child was exposed prior to, or concurrent with, the expression of such behavior. We have noted that disadvantaged families are more likely to produce children with antisocial behavior. The question we have to ask is whether antisocial behavior that occurs in the homes most likely to produce it has a better or worse prognosis than that which occurs despite apparently reasonably good family background.

In our earlier study of the adult outcomes of white, child-guidance-clinic patients (Robins, 1966), we found that antisocial behavior in childhood predicted two adult diagnoses — antisocial personality (sociopathy) and alcoholism. We sought behavioral and family variables that predicted the continuity of childhood antisocial behavior into adulthood at a level consistent with a diagnosis of antisocial personality. We found that the greater the variety of symptoms, the greater the frequency with which antisocial behaviors occurred; and the greater their seriousness, as indicated by their being grounds for arrest, the more likely was the child to be diagnosable as having an antisocial personality as an adult. In addition, theft outside the family (e.g., from stores) and truancy were significantly predictive of antisocial personality even among highly antisocial children.

Among family predictors, we found that having antisocial parents influenced the likelihood that a person with moderate levels of childhood antisocial behavior would be highly antisocial as an adult, but did not significantly add to the risks for highly antisocial children. A child's exposure to strict or adequate discipline, on the other hand, appeared to decrease his chances of becoming a sociopath as an adult whether he was highly or moderately antisocial as a child. The advantages of good discipline were found even among those with antisocial fathers. Similarly, coming from unusually large or unusually small sibships was associated with adult sociopathy both among moderately and highly antisocial children, with or without an

CONTINUATION OF ANTISOCIAL BEHAVIOR INTO ADULTHOOD

antisocial father. Among nonfamilial factors, appearance in juvenile court and being sent to a correctional institution predicted sociopathy, even taking level of childhood antisocial behavior and family adequacy into account.

Other familial and environmental factors we examined seemed to
have no direct impact on the level of adult sociopathy. Thus, although broken homes, parental discord, low social status of the parental family, being on welfare, living in a slum, frequent moving,
being expelled from school, or being held back in school were all
related to adult sociopathy, when their impact was considered controlling on the child's own level of antisocial behavior and his father's antisocial behavior, there remained no independent effect of
any of these variables.

Subsequent to our study of white ex-patients of a child guidance
clinic, we initiated a study that would allow us to learn whether persistence of antisocial behavior was influenced by the same family
and environmental risk factors in a very different population. Our
second study utilized a cohort of black nonpatients who grew up almost a generation later. They were similar to our first sample in
two respects: they had normal IQs, and they had been reared in St.
Louis. The black men were identified through elementary-school
records and were further required to have been born in St. Louis,
to have attended St. Louis public schools for at least six years, and
to have resided in the St. Louis area for some time in the six years
preceding interview. Ninety-five percent of the sample selected
were found and interviewed when in their thirties.

In an earlier paper (Robins, Murphy, Woodruff, & King, 1971), we
explored to what extent the major findings from the first study were
replicated in this black, nonpatient, younger sample. Lacking clinic
records, we used as indicators of antisocial behavior before
age 18 a combination of elementary-school truancy and failure:
high-school truancy, expulsion, suspension, disciplinary transfers,
and being placed on probation; and police and juvenile court records.

For the young black men, as for the white child-guidance-clinic
patients, we found that antisocial behavior in childhood predicted
both antisocial personality and alcoholism in adulthood. In addition,
in the black sample it predicted drug addiction, which had been almost nonexistent in the white child-guidance-clinic sample, who
grew up before drug addiction became widespread among whites.

L. N. ROBINS & K. S. RATCLIFF

We again found virtually no cases of antisocial personality in the absence of antisocial behavior in childhood; and we also found for the new sample, as for the previous one, that antisocial fathers added to the risk of moderately antisocial children. For the young black men we had two new findings about predictors: antisocial fathers were associated with a worse prognosis for those severely as well as moderately antisocial in childhood; and, in addition, for moderately antisocial black schoolboys, those reared in white-collar families had lower rates of antisocial personality than did those reared in blue-collar families. We could not tell whether this was also true of the more severely antisocial, because so few of them came from white-collar homes. We found for the blacks, as we had for the whites, that even among the most highly antisocial children, fewer than half were diagnosable as having an antisocial personality as adults, and indeed only slightly over half (57%) had any of the three disorders predicted by an antisocial behavior pattern in childhood: antisocial personality, alcholism, or drug addiction.

Our purpose in the present paper is to reexamine the histories of these young black men, using more complete measures of both their early behaviors and their family environments in an effort to locate family descriptors that might have increased our prognostic precision.

Methods

We have improved our measurement of juvenile antisocial behavior in two ways: by increasing the variety of deviant behaviors considered, and by reducing the age span in which their occurrence was considered from before age 18 to before age 15. We have considered nine indicators of antisocial behavior: arrests, incarceration, excessive elementary-school absence (truancy), drinking, alcohol problems, sexual intercourse, marriage, drug use, and association with friends who were in trouble with school officials or the police. These data were drawn from several sources. Information on arrests and incarceration came from juvenile police and court records, and information on school attendance came from school records. All other information was reported retrospectively by the men in interview at ages 30-35. We chose these items for their similarity to the 26 antisocial behavior symptoms that had been abstracted from the records of the child guidance clinic in the previous study.

100

CONTINUATION OF ANTISOCIAL BEHAVIOR INTO ADULTHOOD

We have limited these measures of childhood antisocial behavior to events occurring before age 15 because male antisocial personality was found always to begin before 15. Further, from a treatment perspective, prognostic knowledge at an earlier time is advantageous, since the opportunities for intervention are greater before children leave home and school.

Our measure of adult antisocial behavior is a count of the number of ten possible behaviors that occurred in the five years before the interview, as evaluated by two psychiatrists: marital trouble, financial dependency (on the state or the family), poor work history, alcohol problems, drug problems (regular use of an illicit drug), crime (multiple arrests or felony conviction), impulsivity, vagrancy, physical aggression, and maintaining a deviant life-style (e.g., leisure time spent primarily on the street and in bars, gambling, etc.). These are the individual behaviors that have been considered by the psychiatrists in making the diagnosis of antisocial personality in these men. Most of the symptoms used to make a diagnosis of sociopathy in the follow-up of the guidance-clinic patients are included. Those excluded are school history (because we did not want to confound early and later behaviors), pathological lying and sexual promiscuity (because our information was inadequate), and suicide attempts (because they were not found in the earlier study to correlate with a diagnosis of antisocial personality). We shall be considering predictors both of the number of these symptoms and of particular symptoms.

The family variables that we shall consider as possible facilitators or inhibitors of the continuity between childhood antisocial behavior and adult antisocial behavior include the antisocial behavior of the father and the mother; the family's poverty level (as measured by reports in interview of the family's having a hard time providing clothes and food in childhood, the child's having had to work because the family needed the money, the family's receiving help from other relatives, the family's failing to aid other relatives because family members had no money themselves, and the family's receiving welfare); number of siblings; the guardian's occupation at the time the subject was in elementary school; discipline (as indicated by family insistence on changing clothes after school, playing in one's own yard, and playing only with approved other children); family breakup; the child's age at the time the family broke up; the

L. N. ROBINS & K. S. RATCLIFF

number of years in which there were both a male and a female parent figure in the home; the child's living with the mother only after a family breakup, compared with other patterns;[1] the number of changes in parent figures; whether the child himself was placed out of the home; whether the home broke up because of disagreement rather than death, illness, or job; whether either parent had achieved a high-school diploma; whether the parents were homeowners; and whether the child received adequate supervision after school if his mother was employed.

When selecting these men for follow-up from public elementary-school records, we oversampled those from high-status backgrounds and chose equal proportions with and without early school problems and broken homes. In presenting results, we have weighted proportions and numbers to make the sample representative of black men born in St. Louis between 1930 and 1934 with an IQ of 85 or higher in elementary school.

Results

Association Between Child and Adult Behaviors

Three of our measures of antisocial behavior before age 15 — incarceration, marriage, and alcohol problems — occurred too rarely to allow us to investigate their separate effects on the level of antisocial behavior in adulthood. Table 1 shows that the occurrence of each of the remaining six childhood behaviors was associated with an increased number of adult antisocial behaviors. The relationship was quite strong for all child behaviors except truancy, which was a barely significant predictor. The behavior with the most striking effect was drug use, which was almost always followed by a high level of adult behavior problems. Although about half of the sample eventually used an illicit drug, the average age at onset of initial drug use was 18; drug use before the age of 15 was clearly precocious use by local standards. We have shown elsewhere (Robins, Darvish, & Murphy, 1970) that illicit drug use starting after the teens had little or no prognostic significance.

102

CONTINUATION OF ANTISOCIAL BEHAVIOR INTO ADULTHOOD

Table 1

Childhood Behaviors Predicting Adult Antisocial Behaviors

Childhood behaviors* (before age 15)	Mean number of adult antisocial behaviors when childhood problem					
	Occurred		Did Not Occur			
	N	Mean	N	Mean	t	P <
Drug use	21	5.5	201	2.0	6.3	0.001
Sex	125	3.0	93	1.5	4.4	0.001
Arrest	48	3.5	175	2.1	3.3	0.001
Delinquent companions	101	2.9	109	1.8	3.2	0.001
Drinking problem	75	3.0	140	2.0	2.7	0.005
Truancy	95	2.8	125	2.1	1.9	0.05

*Omitted are marriage, alcohol problems, and incarceration because of the small numbers for each of these problems.

Having examined the effects of specific juvenile behaviors on the number of antisocial behaviors occurring in adulthood, we must next ask whether each of the adult antisocial behaviors was predictable from childhood behavior. In Table 2 we note that the number of different childhood behaviors was statistically associated with each type of adult antisocial behavior that we considered. The most accurately predicted behavior was criminality in adulthood, followed by financial dependence and deviant life-style. Divorce and vagrancy were the adult behaviors least well predicted by the variety of childhood deviant behaviors. Together, Tables 1 and 2 show the remarkable continuity between childhood and adult antisocial behaviors that has been noted so frequently in the literature. Each type of child antisocial behavior was associated with an increased risk of adult antisocial behavior, and having a large variety of deviant childhood behaviors increased the risk of each particular kind of adult antisocial behavior.

Although these results are striking, they could occur largely because there is continuity over time for certain specific behaviors. Childhood arrests are well known to forecast adult crime; early drinking, to forecast alcoholism; and early drug use, to forecast

L. N. ROBINS & K. S. RATCLIFF

later drug abuse. Of course, there are other, strictly adult behaviors that <u>cannot</u> be a mere continuation of behavior begun in childhood — e.g., marital problems, job problems, vagrancy.

Table 2

Prediction of Specific Adult Problems by
Number of Antisocial Behaviors in Childhood

	Number of antisocial behaviors in childhood			
	Low (0-1) (N = 84)	Moderate (2) (N = 53)	High (3+) (N = 86)	
Adult behaviors	%	%	%	P<
Crime	6	19	39	0.001
Financial dependence	18	32	52	0.001
Deviant life-style	2	9	22	0.001
Alcohol problems	21	35	45	0.001
Violence	11	15	30	0.001
Drugs	11	20	30	0.001
Poor work history	9	15	25	0.01
Impulsivity	4	15	14	0.01
Marital problems	12	15	23	0.05
Vagrancy	1	4	5	0.10

Table 3 shows that adult events that can begin in childhood can also occur in the <u>absence</u> of that behavior in childhood and are more likely to do so when there are high levels of other types of childhood antisocial behavior. There is a stronger likelihood of a specific problem's occurring in adulthood if it did begin in childhood, however. A second important observation from Table 3 is the frequency of <u>recovery</u> from childhood problems: only 45-58% of those with unusually early evidence for each problem continued to have it as an adult.

CONTINUATION OF ANTISOCIAL BEHAVIOR INTO ADULTHOOD

Table 3

Crime, Alcoholism, and Drug Use in Those Without
These Problems in Childhood as a Function of Level
of Childhood Antisocial Behavior

| | Adult problems | | | | | |
| | Alcoholism | | Crime | | Drug abuse | |
	Number	%	Number	%	Number	%
Child did have the relevant behavior*	75	45	48	52	21	58
Child did not have the relevant behavior; other antisocial behaviors						
None or one	48	24	54	4	57	14
Two	38	36	47	15	51	19
Three or more	30	37	47	30	66	22

*For alcoholism — drinking before age 15; for crime — arrest
before 15; for drug abuse — drug use before 15.

The evidence for frequent recovery appears again in Table 4,
which considers the number of antisocial behaviors in both time periods. As we expected, there is a strong association between the
number of childhood antisocial behaviors and the number of adult
antisocial behaviors, the correlation between the two being 0.45. But
even among very antisocial children, only 41% became very antisocial adults. Two-thirds (68%) of all highly antisocial adults, however, had been highly antisocial children — i.e., had displayed three
or more antisocial behaviors. Using a more stringent criterion —
e.g., four or more childhood antisocial behaviors — raises the proportion who became very antisocial adults to 51%, but sacrifices our
ability to identify ahead of time most of those who would be extremely antisocial adults: we would have identified only 36% of
them. A still more stringent criterion — five or more childhood
behaviors — yields no increase in specificity (again, 51% will be
antisocial adults) and suffers a serious loss in sensitivity (only 13%

L. N. ROBINS & K. S. RATCLIFF

of the very antisocial adults are identified).

Table 4

The Persistence of Antisocial Behavior

Number of adult antisocial behaviors	Number of childhood antisocial behaviors before age 15		
	None or one, %	Two, %	Three or more, %
None	45	31	14
One to three	47	48	45
Four or more	8	21	41
	100%	100%	100%
	(N = 84)	(N = 53)	(N = 86)

We find, then, that knowledge of childhood antisocial behavior alone enables us to do no better than to identify children with about a 50% risk of a high overall level of adult antisocial behavior or a specific adult behavior. On the other hand, absence of childhood antisocial behavior is a very powerful predictor, nearly ensuring (92%) the absence of severely antisocial behavior in adulthood for this sample. This finding parallels that from the white guidance-clinic patients.

Comparing Childhood Behavior
with Family Factors as Predictors

In our earlier study we had found that the degree of childhood antisocial behavior, whether measured by variety, frequency, or severity, was a more potent predictor of antisocial behavior than was any particular antisocial behavior, and was also more potent than any environmental factor. To see whether this was also the case in the current study, we entered all our childhood variables, including number of antisocial behaviors, individual behaviors, and family descriptors, into a stepwise multiple regression, with four or more adult antisocial behaviors as the dependent variable.

Four of the 24 childhood variables [2] explained 24% of the variance in adult behavior (Table 5), 78% of that explainable by all 24 vari-

CONTINUATION OF ANTISOCIAL BEHAVIOR INTO ADULTHOOD

ables taken together. The most efficient single predictor was the number of childhood antisocial behaviors, confirming the finding from our earlier study. The next best predictor was early drug use, which we previously noted as the most powerful of the individual childhood behaviors. No other specific childhood behavior was more powerful than family variables, the most important of which were the child's being placed away from both his natural parents and his growing up under conditions of severe poverty.

Table 5

Best Childhood Predictors of Having Four or More Adult
Antisocial Behaviors (By Stepwise Multiple Regression)

Childhood predictors	Additional variance explained, %
Number of antisocial behaviors	12
First used drug before 15	5
Placed away from both parents	5
Family poverty	2
	24
Total explained variance, 24 variables	30

The stepwise regression results confirm our earlier finding that a child's own antisocial behavior is the best predictor of his future antisocial behavior, but it also gives us hope that we may be able to improve our prediction based on behavior alone by considering family environments. From these results alone, however, we cannot be sure that the family variables of poverty and being placed away from parents are the best for detecting which highly antisocial children will be antisocial adults. These family variables could have appeared because they explain the rare emergence of adult antisocial behavior following a relatively conforming childhood.

To search for appropriate family predictors for children at high risk because of their antisocial behavior, we again performed a stepwise multiple regression — this time including only children who either had three or more antisocial behaviors or who had used drugs before age 15. Forty-two percent of these children became

107

L. N. ROBINS & K. S. RATCLIFF

highly antisocial adults, and they accounted for 71% of all children in our sample who would become highly antisocial adults. The challenge was to find family predictors that could distinguish those children with a substantially higher rate of adult antisocial behaviors than 42% while continuing to identify as many future antisocial adults as possible.

Family predictors for highly antisocial children

Three family variables accounted for 23% of the variance in the outcomes of highly antisocial children: the two variables found in our previous stepwise multiple regression, being placed out of the home and severe poverty in childhood, and a third, having few childhood years with parent figures of both sexes in the home. This last variable included years both before and after any family breakup that may have occurred (Table 6).

Table 6

Family Predictors of High Levels of Adult Antisocial Behavior in the 86 Highly Antisocial Children (Stepwise Multiple Regression)

Family predictors	Added explained variance, %
Placed away from both parents	12
Poverty	7
Few years with parent figures of both sexes	4
	23
Total explained variance, 17 variables	32

To learn how useful these family predictors might be in improving our ability to distinguish children at high risk, we looked at the adult behavior of children we could identify who had one, two, or three of these family predictors in addition to severely antisocial behavior in childhood. Table 7 shows us that the absence of all three family predictors in very antisocial children was an excellent indicator that the child would not be a very antisocial adult: 85% were not, a figure almost as high as that found for children who

108

CONTINUATION OF ANTISOCIAL BEHAVIOR INTO ADULTHOOD

were not very antisocial (88%). With all three family predictors, almost all very antisocial children were antisocial adults (89%). Although requiring all three family variables yielded a very high risk group, it identified only 14% of the antisocial adults in the total sample. Requiring two of these family variables seemed a better choice: two-thirds (66%) of the children could be expected to become antisocial adults, and half (50%) of all potentially antisocial adults would have been identified. (The best choice of criteria depends, of course, on the cost, efficacy, and acceptability of the intervention to be offered.) Selecting for intervention those antisocial boys with two or more family variables would have designated as eligible 18% of this urban black schoolboy population of average or better IQ, a more feasible target group than the 39% identifiable on the basis of behavior alone.

Table 7

Number of Family Variables as a Means of Selecting
Children at Especially High Risk Among Those Who
Use Drugs or Have Three or More Antisocial Symptoms

Number of family variables (out of placed out, poverty, & few years with parents of both sexes)	Highly antisocial adults Number	%	Percent of the 53 highly antisocial adults identified	Percent of whole sample (223) selected
Three	7	89	12	3
Two or more	39	66	50	18
One or more	64	52	63	29
None	23	15	7	11
All antisocial children	88	42	70	39

Family predictors for less antisocial children

Whereas two-thirds of all very antisocial adults had been very antisocial children, one-third had not. We applied the same method of stepwise multiple regression to the children without seriously antisocial behavior in childhood to learn whether there were any

109

L. N. ROBINS & K. S. RATCLIFF

family factors that could select a group at sufficiently high risk to make intervention practical.

The only family factor that made a substantial contribution to seriously antisocial behavior in adulthood was having an antisocial father. This confirmed the finding from our earlier study that having an antisocial father was an especially important predictor for children who were not very antisocial. Nonetheless, having an anti-social father explained only 2% of the variance. The next best variable was having an antisocial mother, which added another 1% to the explained variance.

We then looked to see whether these two variables could identify a group at significant risk (Table 8). Children both of whose parents were antisocial but who were without seriously antisocial behavior themselves became antisocial adults in 24% of cases. They accounted for only 5% of antisocial adults and made up only 5% of the child population. Requiring only one parent to be antisocial in the absence of seriously antisocial behavior in childhood would make eligible for intervention 23% of all black boys, and the group selected would have a 19% risk of being antisocial adults.

Table 8

Family Predictors for Less Antisocial Children

Antisocial parents	Children who became highly antisocial adults		Percent of the 53 highly antisocial adults identified	Percent of whole sample (223) distinguished
	Number	%		
Both	11	24	5	5
One or both	51	19	18	23
Neither	84	7	12	38
All children who are not highly antisocial	135	12	30	61

The risk rates for children without seriously antisocial behavior themselves appear to be too low to warrant intervention on the basis of family factors.

110

CONTINUATION OF ANTISOCIAL BEHAVIOR INTO ADULTHOOD

The role of social class

In the search for family predictors of the occurrence of adult antisocial behavior, five important childhood family predictors have been found: being placed away from both parents, serious poverty, lacking parent figures of both sexes, and having an antisocial father or mother. When given the opportunity to compete in multiple regression analysis, variables associated with class status — such as guardian's occupation, parent's education, and home ownership — were not found to play a significant role. Poverty did appear; and it is, of course, associated with lower class status; but it is an extreme measure. Only 35% of this predominantly lower-class sample qualified as meeting the poverty criteria. Guardian's occupation, the usual measure of social status, ranked 15th of 24 variables in the stepwise regression including the whole sample and contributed only 0.1% to the explained variance.

The absence of a role for lower class status as a predictor of severely antisocial behavior in adulthood again confirms a finding of the follow-up of white child-guidance-clinic patients. Since that early finding, we have been puzzled by the discrepancy between our results and the common observation that adult antisocial behavior is a class-related phenomenon. Indeed, one criticism of defining antisocial personality as a composite of antisocial behaviors has been that it is opprobrious labeling of patterns of behavior that are "normal," or at least beyond individual control, for lower-class males.

One possibility that occurred to us was that there might be a disjunction between antisocial behaviors of sufficient variety and severity to merit the diagnosis of antisocial personality and the antisocial behaviors common among adults disadvantaged by class and race. We may not have found social class to be a factor because we concentrated only on the extreme upper end of the range of antisocial behaviors, a range considered pathological at all class levels. Having a few kinds of adult antisocial behavior — such as multiple job changes and a few arrests — may indeed be normal in the lower class and abnormal in the middle class. If this were the case, it would explain the common observation of an association of lower class status with deviance, and would also validate the concept of antisocial personality as not being class-bound.

To test this possibility we set aside the highly antisocial adults

111

L. N. ROBINS & K. S. RATCLIFF

in our sample, those with four or more different forms of antisocial behavior, and subjected the remainder to a stepwise multiple regression analysis that included all childhood variables, both the child's own behavior and his family environment, to see which childhood factors distinguished those entirely free of antisocial behavior as adults from those with a moderate amount of antisocial behavior (one to three types). As Table 9 indicates, although less important than having an antisocial father, class of upbringing as measured by guardian's occupation does make an important contribution to explaining mildly antisocial behavior. It is also of interest that family factors matter more than childhood behaviors in explaining mildly antisocial behavior in adulthood, although we had found childhood behavior much the more important factor in explaining severely antisocial behavior. Furthermore, delinquency, rather than overall level of antisocial behavior, is the more important childhood behavioral predictor.

Table 9

Predictors of Moderately Antisocial Behavior in
170 Men Without Seriously Antisocial Behavior

Childhood factors	Addition to explained variance for one to three types of adult antisocial behavior vs. none, %
Father antisocial	9
Guardian's occupation	3
Arrested before 15	2
Placed away from both parents	2
	16
Total explained by all 24 variables	25

Table 10 shows that among men from lower-class backgrounds, antisocial adult behavior is by no means universal. One-third had none at all. Moreover, social status of rearing had a significant impact only for children whose fathers were not antisocial. Having an antisocial father was so powerful a factor that it alone was sufficient to account for few boys' being completely free of antisocial be-

CONTINUATION OF ANTISOCIAL BEHAVIOR INTO ADULTHOOD

havior as adults. When the father was not antisocial, lower class status did significantly account for the occurrence of a mild level of antisocial behavior ($P < 0.02$), even though it did not significantly predict a high level of antisocial behavior.

Table 10

Impact of Social Class of Rearing in Predicting Moderate Levels of Adult Antisocial Behavior Rather Than None

	Number	Percent with 1-3 adult antisocial behaviors	Percent with none	χ^2	C
Father antisocial	85	79	21	13.03	0.27
Father not antisocial	121	50	50		
Guardian's occupation low	152	66	34	3.84	0.15
Guardian's occupation skilled or white-collar	54	49	51		
Effect of guardian's occupation when:					
Father antisocial					
Low occupation	58	82	18	n.s.	—
Skilled or white-collar	26	73	27		
Father not antisocial					
Low occupation	93	57	43	5.04	0.22
Skilled or white-collar	28	31	69		

Summary and Discussion

We have tested and confirmed a number of findings of our earlier study of white child-guidance-clinic ex-patients in a sample from a very different population. It has been shown for black schoolboys, as for white child-guidance-clinic patients, that:

1. Seriously antisocial behavior in adults rarely occurs in the absence of a high level of childhood antisocial behavior.

2. Even very antisocial children become very antisocial adults

113

L. N. ROBINS & K. S. RATCLIFF

in only about half the cases.

3. The number of antisocial behaviors in childhood is nonetheless the best predictor of severely antisocial behavior in adulthood.

4. Among mildly antisocial children, having an antisocial father is the best predictor of severely antisocial behavior in adulthood.

5. Social class of rearing is not an important predictor of severely antisocial behavior in adults.

This study has gone beyond the earlier one to show that for black boys, early drug use is an important additional predictor. Further, it has identified three family factors that make a substantial contribution to predicting which highly antisocial children will be antisocial adults: being placed away from both parents, extreme poverty, and growing up in a family lacking parent figures of both sexes. In this sample, requiring two or three of these three family factors in addition to highly antisocial behavior in childhood would have identified 18% of the sample as at risk of seriously antisocial behavior in adulthood. Two-thirds of those so identified did become seriously antisocial adults, and these accounted for half the antisocial adults in the sample. Although we make no claim that any of the identified predictors are themselves causes of antisocial behavior in adults, they appear to be sufficiently sensitive and specific to be useful in selecting for intervention programs black schoolboys at very high risk.

The low rate of antisocial behavior in adulthood of highly antisocial boys who lacked all three family factors would seem to indicate that antisocial behavior in black boys from stable, intact homes is likely to be of little long-term significance, although, of course, intervention may be necessary to prevent its immediate consequences for the child, his family, and the community.

There appeared to be no family backgrounds so noxious that children growing up in them who were not very antisocial before age 15 could be predicted to develop seriously antisocial behavior at some later time.

The final contribution of this study is an attempt to resolve the controversy about whether antisocial behavior in people reared in lower-class environments is "normal." We found that some antisocial behavior was common in men who had been reared in low-status homes, but it was by no means universal. Mildly antisocial behavior in adults, unlike severely antisocial behavior, was found

114

CONTINUATION OF ANTISOCIAL BEHAVIOR INTO ADULTHOOD

to be more a function of the childhood environment than of childhood behavior. Moreover, an influential aspect of that childhood environment was social class.

We suggest that this finding, if replicated in other populations, may help to resolve the controversy between those who regard anti-social behavior in adults as the product of low status and racism and those who regard it as symptomatic of underlying psychopathology induced genetically or by pathological familial environments or by an interaction of the two. It may well be that mildly antisocial behavior in men reared in deprived environments is pathological only by middle-class standards, but that severely antisocial behavior, as indicated by failure to conform over a broad range of functioning — job failure, illegal activities, excessive drinking, heavy drug use, failure to maintain stable interpersonal relationships, and financial dependency — is pathological in every social stratum and has its origins chiefly within the person and his family.

NOTES

[1] Boys who grew up in households in which the mother was the only adult were found to have impaired educational success later (K. S. Ratcliff [1977] in their thirties: A study of adult outcomes. Unpublished doctoral dissertation, University of Wisconsin). Similarly, Kellam, Ensminger, & Turner (1977) found children from "mother only" households to have poor school adjustment in the first grade.

[2] The 24 variables included the 6 behavioral variables in Table 1, the number of childhood behaviors, and the 17 family variables described on page 101.

REFERENCES

Clarizio, H. (1968) Stability of deviant behavior through time. Ment. Hygiene, 52, 288.

Gersten, J. C., Langner, T. S., Eisenberg, J. G., Simcha-Fagan, O., and McCarthy, E. D. (1976) Stability and change in types of behavioral disturbance of children and adolescents. J. Abnorm. Child Psychol., 4(2), 111.

Glueck, S., & Glueck, E. (1968) Delinquents and nondelinquents in perspective. Cambridge, Mass.: Harvard University Press.

L. N. ROBINS & K. S. RATCLIFF

Guze, S. B. (1976) Criminality and psychiatric disorders. New York: Oxford University Press.

Jones, M. C. (1968) Personality correlates and antecedents of drinking patterns in adult males. J. Consult. Clin. Psychol.; 32(1), 2.

Kellam, S. G., Ensminger, M. E., & Turner, R. J. (1977) Family structure and the mental health of children. Arch. Gen. Psychiat. (Chicago). 34, 1012.

Robins, L. N. (1966) Deviant children grown up: A sociological and psychiatric study of sociopathic personality. Baltimore: Williams & Wilkins. Reprinted and published by Robert E. Krieger Publishing Co., Inc., Huntington, N.Y., 1974.

Robins, L. N., Darvish, H. S., & Murphy, G. E. (1970) The longterm outcome for adolescent drug users: A follow-up study of 76 users and 146 non-users. In J. Zubin & A. Freedman (Eds.), Psychopathology of adolescence. New York: Grune & Stratton.

Robins, L. N., Davis, D. H., & Wish, E. D. (1977) Detecting predictors of rare events: Demographic, family, and personal deviance as predictors of stages in the progression toward narcotic addiction. In J. Strauss, H. Babigian, & M. Roff (Eds.)., Origins and course of psychopathology: Methods of longitudinal research. New York and London: Plenum Press.

Robins, L. N., Murphy, G. E., Woodruff, R. A., Jr., & King, L. J. (1971) The adult psychiatric status of black school boys. Arch. Gen. Psychiat. (Chicago). 24, 338.

Rosenberg, C. M. (1969) Determinants of psychiatric illness in young people. Brit. J. Psychiat., 115, 907.

Rutter, M., & Madge, N. (1976) Cycles of disadvantage. London: Heinemann Educational Books Ltd.

Rutter, M., Tizard, J., Yule, W., Graham, P., & Whitmore, K. (1976) Research report: Isle of Wight studies, 1964-1974. Psychol. Med., 6, 313.

The Eysenck Personality Theory

[3]

2. PERSONALITY THEORY AND THE PROBLEM OF CRIMINALITY

H. J. EYSENCK

Introduction

In psychiatry generally, the diathesis—stress model is widely accepted; it postulates a *predisposition* to develop certain types of mental illness, such as neurosis or psychosis, which is activated by certain environmental stress factors. A similar conception can be applied to criminality; certain types of personality may be more prone to react with anti-social or criminal behaviour to environmental factors of one kind or another. To say this is not to accept the notion of 'crime as destiny', to quote Lange's famous monograph in which he showed that identical twins are much more alike with respect to criminal conducts than are fraternal twins. There is no predestination about the fact that heredity, mediated through personality, plays some part in predisposing some people to act in an anti-social manner. Environment is equally important, and, as we shall see, it is the interaction between the two which is perhaps the most crucial factor.

Much of the research in this field has been episodic and following the principles of benevolent eclecticism; in this chapter we will rather adopt the method of looking at a general theory of anti-social behaviour, which makes predictions as to the type of personality expected to indulge in such conduct, and summarise the evidence relating to the theory. Before turning to the evidence, it will therefore be necessary to present in brief outline the theory in question (Eysenck, 1960, 1977). The reason for singling out the theory is, in the first place, that it has attracted far more research than any other, and secondly, that it is the only one which has tried to link together genetic factors, a causal theory, and personality in one general theory.

Statement of theory

Briefly and concisely, the theory tries to explain the occurance of socialised behaviour suggesting that anti-social behaviour, being obviously egocentric and orientated towards immediate gratification, needs no explanation. It is suggested that the socialization process is essentially mediated by Pavlovian conditioning, in the sense that anti-social behaviour will be punished by parents, teachers, peers etc., and that such punishment constitutes the *unconditioned stimulus* (US), where the contemplation or execution of such behaviour constitutes the conditioned stimulus. The pain/anxiety properties of the US transfer through conditioning to the CS, and as a consequence the person will desist from committing anti-social acts, or even contemplating them, because of the painful CRs which inevitably follow. The theory is elaborated in Eysenck (1977), where supportive evidence will be found.

Individual differences in the speed and strength of formation of conditioned responses would, in terms of the theory, be fundamental in accounting for the observed relations between personality and criminality. As Eysenck (1967, 1980a) has shown, there is considerable evidence to suggest that introverts form conditioned responses more quickly and more strongly than extraverts, and accordingly one would expect extraversion to be positively correlated with anti-social conduct. Emotional instability or neuroticism would be expected to multiply with the habits of socialised or anti-social conduct, according to Hull's general theory in which performance is a multiplicative function of habit and drive, with anxiety in this case acting as a drive (Eysenck, 1973). The third major dimension of personality, psychoticism, comes into the picture because of the well-documented relationship between crime and psychosis (Eysenck and Eysenck, 1976), and because the general personality traits subsumed under psychoticism appear clearly related to anti-social and non-conformist conduct. The precise nature of these three major dimensions of personality will be discussed later on in this chapter; here we will only look at one particular problem which is closely related to the general theory of conditioning as a basis for anti-social conduct.

The theory suggests that conditioning produces socialised behaviour, and that introverts will show more socialised behaviour because they condition more readily. The same theory would also imply, however, that if the socialisation process were inverted, i.e. if parents, teachers, peers, etc. praised the child for anti-social conduct, and punished him for socialised behaviour, then introverts would be more likely to show anti-social behaviour. Raine and Venables (1981) have shown that this is indeed so; children who showed better conditioning in a laboratory situation than other children were remarkably socialised in their behaviour when brought up in a favourable type of environment, and remarkably anti-social in their behaviour when brought up in a non-favourable type of environment. This experiment shows more clearly than almost any other the inter relationship between genetic factors on the one hand, and environmental ones on the other.

Genetic factors in crime

Until the early 1970s there used to be still some controversy about the evidence implicating genetic factors in criminal behaviour; since then, however, the evidence has become so convincing that no one who has examined it doubts the insufficiency of environmentalist explanations to account for all the facts (Ellis, 1982). The most important support for the relevance of heredity to criminality are the so-called *concordance* studies, i.e. studies looking at concordance for criminality between monozygotic and dizygotic twins. MZ twins, being identical in heredity, should be more concordant than DZ twins, being on the average only 50 per cent identical with respect to heredity, provided that genetic factors play an important part. There are now 10 such studies, carried out in countries as different as Japan and Denmark, showing that concordance is about 4 times as high in MZ as compared with DZ twins (Eysenck, 1977). Some of these studies only have small numbers of twins in them, and the selection is not always above criticism; nevertheless, the best study of all, both from the point of view of number of twins and of selection methodology, by itself gives ample evidence for the importance of heredity. Cloninger *et al* (1978) found that the correlation for criminality among MZ twins (.70) was significantly higher than that among DZ twins (.41), and based on these findings they estimated the heritability as .59. There are various qualifications that lessen one's faith in the precision of this term, but it does suggest that at least half the total variance is accounted for by genetic factors.

Equally impressive is evidence from adoption studies, in which the relationships of delinquent and non-delinquent children to the delinquency or otherwise of biological and adoptive parents are investigated. Plomin *et al* (1980) have reviewed such adoption studies carried out in Denmark and the United States, including 321 first-degree biological relatives of adopted criminals or psychopathic probands and 316 controls (biological relatives of adoptees who have shown no criminality). Eighty-two of the biological relatives of criminal probands either had criminal records or were diagnosed as psychopaths. In the control group only 41 of the biological relatives were similarly diagnosed. The difference is between 25 per cent and 13 per cent, almost a doubling for the biological influences in the direction of criminality.

Of particular interest is a study by Mednick, Gabrielli and Hutchings (1984) in which the court convictions of 14,427 adoptees were compared with those of their biological and adoptive parents. A statistically significant correlation was found between the adoptees and their biological parents for convictions of property crime. This was not true with respect to violent crimes. There was no statistically significant correlation between adoptee and adoptive parent court convictions. Siblings adopted separately into different homes tended to be concordant for conditions, especially if their shared biological father also has a record of criminal behaviour. The authors conclude:

> **'That some factor transmitted by criminal parents increased the likelihood that their children will engage in criminal behaviour. This claim holds especially for chronic criminality. The findings imply that biological predispositions are involved in the etiology of at least some criminal behaviour'.**
> *(p. 893)*

Adoption study also enables us to look at the interaction between genetic and environmental factors. A very important study by Cadoret *et al* (1983) showed a powerful influence of such interaction, genetic factors only and environmental factors only, increasing the average number of anti-social behaviours, as compared with the situation in which both were absent. However, when both genetic and environmental factors were present, their combined action far out-performed the sum of the individual actions. As the authors conclude:

> **'The data in this paper suggest that, in the presence of a genetic fact, an adverse environmental factor might act as a catalyst in producing anti-social behaviour'.**
> *(p. 309)*

In genetic studies, the possibility of interaction factors should never be forgotten, and we now have statistical techniques and methodological facilities for measuring these effects.

We have dealt only very briefly with the general theory underlying our diathesis-stress model, the genetic and environmental factors involved, and their interaction; we must now turn to the evidence as far as it is concerned with personality as a mediating factor in anti-social and criminal conduct. It is clearly not sufficient to say that genetic factors are involved; they must be identified, and the precise mode of action must be clarified. Study of individual differences and personality is an important step on the way to achieving such knowledge, and the control which one would hope would follow from it.

32

Personality as related to anti-social activity and crime

Intelligence

There is a very large, complex and variegated literature on this topic which is difficult to review in the short compass of a chapter. The difficulty arises primarily from the problem of defining what is meant by 'personality', and what is meant by 'criminality'. Direct questionnaire studies of the major dimensions of personality, i.e. P (Psychoticism), E (Extraversion) and N (Neuroticism) are obviously relevant to our topic as are questionnaire studies of individual traits related to these major dimensions of personality. Should studies based on projective tests like the Rorschach or the TAT be included, in spite of the known unreliability and the lack of validity of these measures? Should we include studies based on experimental tests, such as the Porteus Q—score, which appears to be related to extraverted personality features, and has been shown to be related to criminality (Porteus, 1965), and psychopathy (Schalling and Rosen, 1970). Should the large body of psychophysiological data, relating to delinquency and psychopathy (Hare, 1975; Eysenck, 1980) be included? Should the enormous number of studies on psychopathy be included, seeing that while many psychopaths are criminals, and some criminals are psychopaths, the two terms are by no means synonymous? Should studies on the intelligence of criminals be included, seeing that while intelligence may certainly be subsumed under the general heading of personality, it is normally regarded as being rather different from the temperamental variables which more usually make up the field of personality study? In dealing with these problems we will have to proceed in a rather subjective manner, including and excluding studies depending on what appears to be their crucial relevance to the central issues involved.

It may be useful to dispose of the question of intelligence rather quickly, because there is little doubt about the general outcome of such studies. Summaries and large-scale studies by Sutherland (1931), Ellenberg (1961), Naar (1965), West (1967), Woodward (1955), Prentice and Kelly (1963), and Brown and Courtless (1968) are pretty well in agreement that while more offenders have an IQ below average than above, the mean IQ of offenders is within the average range, i.e. 90–109 IQ, with a mean probably around 92 or thereabouts. Less than 10 per cent of convicted criminals have an IQ below 70. Research, as Franks (1956) has pointed out, does not show any particular pattern of IQ scores.

While the fact of a correlation between delinquency and low IQ is undisputed, it is often argued that IQ is a spurious variable in the relationship between socio-economic status and delinquency, a lower rearing class status reflecting intellectual and emotional deprivation which motivates later illegal activity. Others have argued that intelligence, regardless of rearing status, is a chief determinant of criminal behaviour. Clearly only large-scale follow-up studies can settle this question, and the recent work of Moffitt, Gabrielli, Mednick and Schulsinger (1981) and McGarvey, Gabrielli, Bentler and Mednick (1981) appears to have settled the matter. They find that the negative correlation between IQ and level of delinquent involvement *remains* after SES effects were partialled out. They also found that rearing social class does relate to criminal behaviour, but indirectly. The model tested and supported in their research was that rearing-class status predicts educational performance, which in turn

33

preceeds the development of criminal activity. They posit that low IQ children may be likely to engage in delinquent behaviour because their poor verbal abilities limit their opportunities to obtain rewards in the school environment.

It should be added that all the data obtained refer of course to offenders and criminals who have been caught, and the possibility exists that more intelligent criminals, possibly engaging in white-collar crimes such as offences involving computers, may not be caught in equal proportions. There is probably some effect along these lines, but it should not be exaggerated. The number of white-collar offenders, particularly those involved with computers, is probably quite small compared with the large number of delinquents involved in stealing, burglaries, muggings, assaults etc., so that their inclusion would not materially affect the issue. However, it is a worth-while caution to remember that the published figures deal largely with some kinds of criminal activity only, although that activity is probably the most wide-spread of all.

Dimensions of Personality

We will now turn to personality factors as more narrowly defined. Our discussion will begin with the three major dimensions of personality, which emerge from hundreds of correlational and factor analytic studies in many different countries. Royce and Powell (1983) have summarised and reanalysed these data, and confirm the theory developed by Eysenck and Eysenck (1976) that these three factors deal essentially with social interactions (extraversion–introversion), emotional reactions and anxieties (neuroticism), and aggressive and egocentric impulses and their control (psychoticism). Many different terms are of course used for these dimensions but Eysenck and Eysenck (1984) discuss the experimental literature which suggests the relevance of the terms proposed above.

The nature of these three major dimensions of personality can best be discerned from the data shown in figure 2:1, 2:2 and 2:3. These list the various traits, correlations between which have generated at the empirical level the 3 major dimensions of P, E and N. In this section we will simply look at descriptive studies involving the relationship between anti-social and criminal behaviour, on the one hand, and these major dimensions, and the traits relating thereto, on the other. Causal questions, the relationship between criminality and constitutional factors, and the influence of genetic factors will be dealt with in later sections. Here let us mainly stress that the personality traits and dimensions dealt with here have a strong genetic component (Fulker, 1980); this does not prove, but it does suggest that genetic factors may also play an important part in the genesis of anti-social and criminal behaviour.

Much of the early literature has been summarised by Passingham (1972), who found that while a number of studies supported Eysenck's hypothesis of a positive correlation between criminality and P, E and N, there were many exceptions, and occasional reversals. There are of course many reasons why results have not always been positive. Criminals are not a homogenous group, and different investigators have studied different populations, specialising in different types of crime. Control groups have not always been carefully selected; some investigators, for instance, have used the usual students groups as controls, which is inadvisable. There has been a failure to control for dissimulation; there is evidence that high lie-scorers lower their neuroticism and psychoticism scores, and they seem to do the same for extraversion (McCue, Booth and Root, 1976). (This paper actually contains a calculation error,

Figure 2:1 Traits characterizing the psychoticism factor.

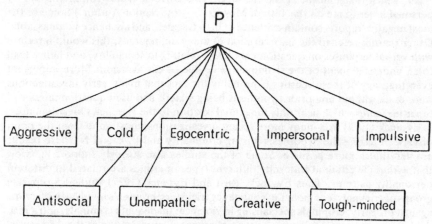

Figure 2:2 Traits characterizing the extraversion factor.

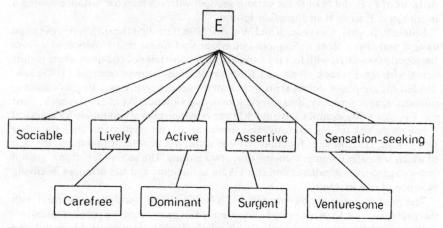

Figure 2:3 Traits characterizing the neuroticism factor.

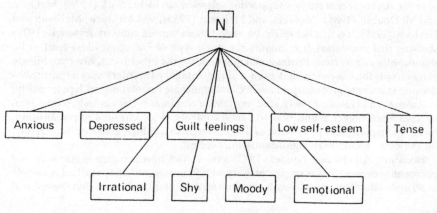

D

35

in that the correlation between E and L is stated to have been 0; in actual fact it was −.29, which is significant at the .02 level. This correction was communicated by personal letter to me on the 14th of May 1977 by the Senior Author.) Some of the most negative reports contain evidence of high L scales, and are hence inadmissable. Other reasons refer to the incarceration of many delinquents; this would interfere with verbal responses on questionnaire items relating to sociability, and hence lead to an understatement of the delinquent's degree of extraversion. More important even than any of these reasons is probably the fact that many early investigations were done without any prior hypothesis being stated, and used questionnaires and other measures which bear only tangential relation to the Eysenck Questionnaires.

Eysenck (1977) lists many more recent investigations, most done from the point of view of testing the hypothesis linking criminality and P, E and N; these results are very much more positive. Some of the studies also strongly support the view that within the criminal fraternity different types of crimes are related to different personality patterns. Thus Eysenck, Rust and Eysenck (1977) studied 5 separate groups of criminals (conmen, i.e. confidence tricksters; criminals involved with crime against property; criminals specialising in violence; inadequate criminals, and a residual group, not specialising in one type of crime). Figure 2:4 shows the differential patterns of P, E and N of these various groups, with conmen for instance having a much lower P score than the other groups.

Mitchell, Rogers, Cavanaugh and Wasyliw (1980) studied the difference between violent and non-violent delinquent behaviour and found that violence was more frequently associated with low trait anxiety than non-violent behaviour; their results agree with the Eysenck, Rust and Eysenck findings. Schwenkmezger (1983) subdivided his sample of delinquents into 3 major groups, corresponding to conmen, offences against property, and offences involving violence. As in the Eysenck, Rust and Eysenck study, conmen have much lower values on the various measures involved (impulsivity, risk taking, aggresiveness, dominance, and excitement) than the other two groups. Discriminant function analysis showed 2 significant functions, the first of which separates conmen from the other two groups. The second function involved mainly aggressive, dominant and risk taking behaviour, and has offences involving violence at one extreme.

The most recent study by Wardell and Yeudall (1980), specially concerned with this problem, used 10 personality factors derived from an extensive psychological test battery administered to 201 patients on criminal wards at a mental hospital and showed many important differences between patients involved with different types of crime. Other recent studies supporting this view are by McGurk (1978), McGurk and McDougall (1981), McGurk and McEwan (1983), and McGurk, McEwan and Graham (1981). To this list might be added some studies cited by Eysenck (1977) showing that murderers (i.e. mainly the usual type of family murder) tend to be significantly introverted. Professional gunmen, on the other hand, are exceedingly extraverted, thus showing that even a single category (murder) may require subdivision in order to give comprehensible and replicable correlations with personality.

Rahman and Hussain (1984), studying female criminals in Bangladesh, found them to have much higher P and N scores than controls; those engaged in prostitution, fraud, kidnapping and possession of illegal arms also had high E scores. Murderers, on the other hand, were significantly introverted.

Holcomb, Adams and Ponder (1985) have shown how complex motivation and personality even within a single category of crime may be. They studied a sample of 80 male offenders charged with premeditated murder, and found that these could

Figure 2:4 P, E and N scores of different types of criminals. From Eysenck, Rust and Eysenck (1977).

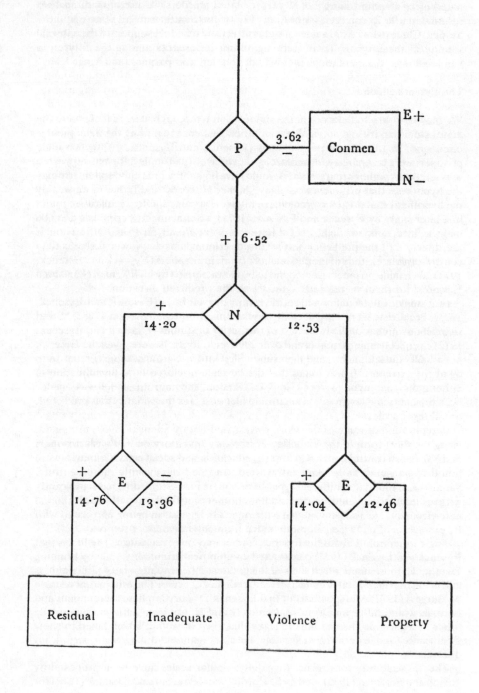

be divided into 5 personality types using MMPI scores. The results were cross validated using a second sample of 80 premeditated murders. A discriminant analysis
resulted in a 96.25 correct classification of subjects from the second sample into the
5 types. Clinical data from a mental status interview schedule supported the external
validity of these types. There were significant differences among the 5 types in
hallucinations, disorientation, hostility, depression and paranoid thinking.

The Eysenck Studies

We may now turn to the work of the Eysencks in temporal order, as these were the
major studies to try and obtain direct empirical evidence regarding the theory under
discussion. In the first of these studies (Eysenck and Eysenck, 1970), 603 male
prisoners were compared with a control group of over 1,000 males. Results supported
strongly the hypothesis that prisoners would have higher P scores, moderately strongly
the hypothesis that prisoners would have higher N scores, and rather more weakly
the hypothesis that prisoners would have higher E scores. Similar results were found
in a later study by Eysenck and Eysenck (1971), contrasting 518 criminals and 606
male trainee railmen. Significant differences were found on P and N, but on E
the direction of the prediction was reversed, criminals having lower E scores than
controls. In a later study of the personality of female prisoners (Eysenck and Eysenck,
1973) 264 female prisoners were found to be characterised by high P, high N and high
E scores; for them therefore E agreed with the predicted direction.

In a study of personality and recidivism in Borstal boys (Eysenck and Eysenck,
1974), recidivists were insignificantly higher than non-recidivists on P and N, but
significantly higher on E. In the last of this series of studies (Eysenck and Eysenck,
1977) over 2000 male prisoners and over 2400 male controls were given the Eysenck
personality questionnaire, and then subdivided into age groups, ranging from 16 to
69 at the extremes. It was found that the lie-scale disclosed little dissimulation in
either group. Scores on psychoticism, extraversion, and neuroticism fell with age for
both prisoners and controls. Prisoners had higher scores than controls, as predicted,
on all three scales.

A replication of some of this work was carried out by Sanocki (1969) in Poland,
using the short form of the Maudsley Personality Inventory on 84 Polish prisoners
and 337 Polish controls, matched for age, education and social class. Criminals were
found to be significantly more extraverted, and non-significantly more neurotic.
Sanocki also found that different types of prisoners in his study differed significantly
with respect to the inventory scores, adding another proof to the hypothesis of criminal
heterogeneity. He also showed that a prisoner's behaviour in prison correlated with
E, extraverts offending significantly more frequently against prison rules.

Two further points about the Eysenck studies may be of relevance. The first is that
Eysenck and Eysenck (1971) constructed an empirical criminality scale by bringing
together all those items which showed the greatest differentiation between criminals
and normals; this will later on be referred to as the 'C' scale. The other point is made
by Burgess (1972), who pointed out that Eysenck's theory implies that criminals and
normals would differ on a combination of N and E, not necessarily on one or the
other in separation; he was able to show that even in studies which failed to show
significance for one or the other variable, the combination did show highly significant
differences.

The 'C' scale was constructed for adults; similar scales have been proposed by
Allsop and Feldman (1975), and by Saklofske, McKerracher and Eysenck (1978) for

children. Like the adult scale they use selected items from the P, E and N scales. The scales have been found to be very useful in discriminating different groups of children. The data demonstrate clearly that delinquent boys have higher extraversion, psychoticism and neuroticism scores, and that the criminal propensity (C) scale discriminates even better between them and non-delinquent boys. Similar differences were also observed between well behaved and badly behaved non-delinquent boys.

Other recent studies

Barack and Widom (1978) studied American women awaiting trial. Compared to a heterogeneous control group, these women scored significantly higher on the neuroticism and psychoticism scales, and on Burgess's h scale ($h = E \times N$). Singh (1982) compared 100 Indian female delinquents with 100 female non-delinquents, matched in terms of socio-economic status, age and urban versus rural place of residence; he found that delinquents had higher scores on extraversion and neuroticism than did non-delinquents. Smith and Smith (1977) looked at the psychoticism variable in relation to reconviction, and found a very highly significant correlation between psychoticism and reconviction. Their finding supported the results obtained by Saunders and Davies (1976), who administered the Jesness Inventory to samples of young male offenders, and concluded that:

'one can . . . see a picture of the continuing delinquent as being unsocialised, aggressive, anti-authority and unempathic. This appears to present a somewhat similar pattern of characteristics to that described by Eysenck as "psychotic".'

Of particular interest are some results of a follow-up of an investigation carried out by West and Farrington (1973). (See also Farrington, 1982.) In the original study 411 boys, aged 8 to 9, attending 6 adjacent primary schools in a working class area of London, were given the Junior Maudsley Inventory at age 10 to 11, and again at age 14 to 15; they were also given the Eysenck Personality Inventory at age 16 to 17. The original data did not provide very strong support for the theory, but more interesting are new data relating to delinquency as a young adult, i.e. convictions in court for offences committed between a boy's 17th and 21st birthdays. Eighty four boys were classified as juvenile delinquents, 94 as young adult delinquents, and 127 as delinquents at any age (up to 21). This study is particularly important because the delinquents were almost all non-institutionalised at the time of testing. (The following data were communicated privately by D. P. Farrington on the 10th of June, 1976.)

Extraversion. As regards juvenile delinquency, E scores were dichotomised into roughly equal halves, and 24 per cent of those with above average scores became juvenile delinquents, in comparison with 16 per cent of those with below average scores; so the lowest quarter of E scores at age 16 included significantly few juvenile delinquents—12.6 per cent as opposed to 23.4 per cent. The tendency of above average E scorers at age 16 to become young adult delinquents was much clearer (30 per cent as opposed to 16 per cent). Farrington states that:

'Low E scores genuinely predicted a low likelihood of adult delinquency.'

The major burden of these and other significant relationships was born by the lowest quarter of E scorers; introverts were very unlikely to become delinquents.

Neuroticism. There was little overall relationship between neuroticism and criminality except that those on the lowest quarter of N scorers at age 10 tended not to become adult delinquents (12 per cent as opposed to 25 per cent), and not to be delinquents at any age (17 per cent as opposed to 34 per cent). Quadrant analysis, of the kind suggested by Burgess (1972) shows that neurotic extraverts at age 16 included significantly more adult delinquents, and significantly more delinquents at any age, than the remainder.

The data, as Farrington points out, suggest that the personality theory might apply to adult delinquency rather than to juvenile delinquency. It is notable that the adult offences included proportionately more aggressive crimes, more damaging offences and more drug offences than the juvenile offences.

For reasons to be discussed presently, this seems an unlikely hypothesis; in school-boys for instance very clear-cut relationships between personality and anti-social behaviour often of a not very serious kind, have been found. These studies are mainly based on self-reports (Gibson, 1971), a type of study which furnishes the child with a list of minor and not-so-minor misdemeanours frequently committed by school children, and asks him or her anonymously to endorse those items which they have been guilty of. There are 2 studies which have related self-reported offending to the 3 major dimensions of personality (Allsop and Feldman, 1975, 1976). In addition, these studies used an outside criterion (teacher's ratings) in order to check on the validity of self ratings; results were very similar for both types of measures. The ratings of the teachers were concerned with school behaviour ('naughtiness'). Scores on the anti-social behaviour scale (ASB) were positively and significantly related to P, E and N in descending order of significance, and 'naughtiness' (Na) scores to P and N, although only the former achieved statistical significance. The P, E and N scores were then divided at the median points and the mean ASB and Na scores plotted for those high (i.e. above the median) on all 3, 2 only, one only, or none out of P, E and N. The results, which are quite striking, are shown in Figure 2:5. They clearly suggest the usefulness of combining personality scores when analysing self-report data. These data come from the study of secondary schoolgirls (Allsop and Feldman, 1975); a similar study, done on schoolboys, has obtained very similar results (Allsop and Feldman, 1976).

The differential relationship between personality and type of offence has also been studied using self-reports. Hindelang and Weis (1972), using cluster analysis, formed 26 offences self-reported by 245 Los Angeles middle class high-school males into 7 groups, and then correlated the scores on each of the 7 clusters with the 4 possible combinations of E and N. They expected a descending order of frequency of offending—EN, either En or eN, and en; this was obtained for 'general deviance' and 'traffic truancy' and partially obtained for 2 other clusters, concerning 'drug-taking' and 'malicious destruction', respectively. No difference between the combinations of E and N was found for theft and the second of 2 clusters concerning drugs. For the 'aggressive' clusters the En combination was the highest. These data again show the need to break down criminality into more homogenous clusters, but of course the sample is a somewhat unusual one.

Allsop (1976) has reported one further study where he used 368 white boys between the ages of 13 and 16. Teachers were asked to rate the behaviour of the boys; on this basis they were divided into well and badly behaved. When these ratings were compared with the personality scale scores, the results indicated that:

40

Figure 2:5 Number of personality scales (P, E and N) on which subjects scored highly, as related to anti-social behaviour (ASB) score and naughtiness (Na) score. From Allsop and Feldman (1975).

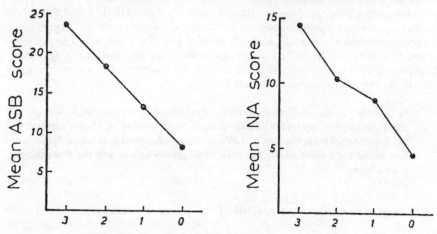

'badly-behaved boys predominate at the high level of P and at the low level of P where there is a combination of high E/high N scores; well-behaved boys predominate at the low level of P except where E and N are simultaneously high'.

Using the ASB, he subdivided the total scale into 10 sub-scales according to type of offence; this table sets out the correlations of P, E and N with each of the sub-scales as well as the total scale. It showed that all the correlations are positive, being highest with P and lowest with N.

Among non-incarcerated adolescents the pattern is much the same. R. Foggitt (1976) has studied a non-institutionalised sample of delinquent and non-delinquent adolescents. Factor analysis of the intercorrelations between the crimes and the personality scales of E and N showed that they were all positively intercorrelated and that a single general factor emerged from the analysis on which different crimes had loadings as follows. Truancy, 0.56; poor work history, 0.62; vagrancy, 0.71; attempted suicide, 0.56; frequency of violence, 0.74; destructiveness of violence, 0.72; heavy drinking, 0.45; excessive drugs, 0.52; theft, 0.71; fraud, 0.50; group-delinquency, 0.46; number of convictions, 0.59. For the personality variables the loadings were 0.44 for E and 0.42 for N.

Two interesting recent studies extend the scope of the work so far reviewed. Perez and Torrubia (1985) used Zuckerman's (1979) concept of sensation-seeking defined as the need for varied, novel and complex sensations and experiences, and willingness to take risks for the sake of such experiences. This scale, which is correlated with extraversion and defines one aspect of that dimension of personality (Eysenck and Eysenck, 1985) was measured in a Spanish translation of the scale published by Zuckerman, Eysenck and Eysenck (1978). Three hundred and forty-nine students were tested, using the sensation seeking scale as well as a 37-item Spanish version of a written self-report delinquency (SRD) scale. A correlation of 0.46 was obtained for the total of the sensation seeking scale, with the highest correlations going to the experience seeking (0.45) and disinhibition (0.43) scales. These are the values for males; for females they were 0.49 for the total scale, and 0.43 and 0.45 for the

41

experience seeking and disinhibition scales. Correlations for the other two scales were smaller (in the neighbourhood of 0.20) but still significant.

Also using a self-report format, Rushton and Chrisjohn (1981) tested 8 separate samples, obtaining significant positive correlations with extraversion, largely insignificant ones with neuroticism, and very positive and significant ones with psychoticism. Correlations with the lie scale were uniformly negative and mostly significant. Subjects of these experiments were high school and university students, totalling 410 in all. As the authors summarise their findings:

> 'The evidence showed clear support for a relationship between high delinquency scores and high scores on both extraversion and psychoticism. These relationships held up across diverse samples and different ways of analyzing the data. No support was found for a relationship between delinquency scores and the dimension of neuroticism.'
> *(p. 11)*

In another interesting study, Martin (1985) pointed out that:

> 'Attempts to verify Eysenck's theory of criminality have usually been concerned with the proportion by which delinquents differ from non-delinquents on the dimensions of extraversion, neuroticism and psychoticism. There are very few studies concerned with the proportion in which these dimensions are related to the acquisition of moral social rules, the real core of this theory. The current study examines the theory from a new approach, trying to show in what measures the value priorities of a group of 113 juvenile delinquents are related to the personality dimensions stated by Eysenck.'
> *(p. 549)*

It was found that extraversion and psychoticism showed the largest number of significant relationships. The youths who scored high and low on the E scale differed in 6 terminal values and 6 instrumental values out of a total of 36 values. Values concerned with morality, and those which imply an acceptance of the social norms, are considered the most important factors for the youths with low E scores.

Those who scored high on the psychoticism dimension consider the following values as the most important: 'An exciting life; pleasure; ability'; all these have clear personal significance. They gave less importance to values related to the social environment, such as 'world peace', 'equality' and 'social recognition'. As far as they go, these results are in good accord with the personality theory under discussion, and they also suggest a new approach to validating the theory.

Drug takers constitute a rather special sample of criminals, although the study just mentioned shows drug taking offences to be highly correlated with other types of criminality. Shanmugan (1979) compared 212 drug users and 222 non-drug users matched with respect to sex, age, educational qualification and socio-economic status, and found that drug users were high on extraversion and neuroticism; stimulant-depressant drug users were found to be high on psychoticism as well as on the 'C' (criminal propensity) scale. Gossop (1978) studied the personality correlates of female drug addicts convicted of drug-related violent and other offences. Convicted subjects were more extraverted than non-convicted subjects. Another study, Gossop and Kristjansson (1977), investigated 50 drug takers and found that subjects convicted of non-drug offences scored higher on extraversion than subjects not convicted of such offences. Drug-dependant subjects altogether scored extremely highly on the 'C' (criminal propensity) scale. This reflects to some extent their high scores on the P and N dimensions.

Specific traits and criminality

Before considering the large number of German-speaking studies using inventories derived from and similar to the Eysenck Questionnaires, it may be useful to consider quickly studies involving a number of specific traits which, as Figures 2:1, 2:2 and 2:3 show, are involved in the three major dimensions of personality. Most work has been done on such factors as anxiety and depression, sensation-seeking, impulsiveness, impulse control, hostility and aggression, and lack of conformity. Typical and relatively recent studies only will be quoted; these usually have bibliographies referring to earlier studies.

Sensation or stimulation-seeking has been studied by Farley and Sewell (1976) and Whitehill, De Myer-Gapin and Scott (1976), the former using a questionnaire, the latter a laboratory experimental technique. They found support for the hypothesis, which was formulated early by Quay (1965), that criminals would be sensation seekers. Robins (1972), can also be quoted in support.

Impulsiveness and lack of impulse-control has frequently been suggested as a major component of criminality. Hormuth *et al* (1977) using both questionnaires and experimental methods, were able to verify the prediction of less impulse control in delinquents with the former. The latter study also found positive results favouring the hypothesis. These data may be considered together with a related concept, namely that of risk-taking, which is often considered almost synonymous with impulsivity or lack of impulse control. A very thorough review of the literature is given by Losel (1975), who found risk-taking more prominent among delinquents. The best available study on risk-taking, also giving a good summary of the literature, is by Schwenkmezger (1983); his conclusion is that results obtained by various investigators can best be interpreted in the sense that delinquent behaviour is favoured by impulsive, risky decision strategies, influenced more by hope of luck and chance than by realistic estimates of ones own abilities and possibilities.

Hostility and aggression are other traits frequently associated with criminality, and the Foulds scales (Foulds, Cain and Creasay, 1960) have often been used as a measuring instrument. Data reported by Blackburn (1968, 1970), and Crawford (1977) suggest that positive relationships exist, with long term prisoners generally having higher total hostility scores than normals, and violent offenders being more extra-punitive than non-violent offenders. Megargee's (1966) hypothesis contrasting over- and under-control would distinguish between extremely assaultive offenders (over-controlled) who would be expected to express less hostility than only moderately assaultive offenders. This theory was supported by Blackburn (1968) but not by Crawford (1977). Berman and Paisley (1984) compared juveniles convicted of assaultive offences with others convicted of other types of offences, and found that the former exhibited significantly higher psychoticism, extraversion and neuroticism scores; sensation-seeking scores were also significantly lower for the non-assaultive group of property offenders.

A French Canadian group was studied by Cote and Leblanc (1982). Using the Jesness Inventory (Jesness, 1972) and the Eysenck Personality Inventory, they studied 825 adolescents from 14 to 19 years old, and correlated personality measures with self-reported indices of delinquency. They found the following traits very significantly correlated with delinquency; psychoticism (.36), manifest aggressiveness (.34), extraversion (.32), bad social adjustment (.32), alienation (.25), repression ($-.25$), and some traits showing even lower but still significant correlations.

The Jesness Inventory, just mentioned, consists of 155 items, scored on 10 sub-scales (social maladjustment, value orientation, immaturity, alienation, autism, withdrawal, manifest aggression, social anxiety, repression and denial), and a predictive score, the Anti-social index. The relationships between the Eysenck and Jesness Personality Inventories have been explored by Smith (1974). Some of the observed correlations are quite high, e.g. between social maladjustment, autism, manifest aggression, withdrawal, on the one hand, and N and P, on the other. Social anxiety is negatively correlated with E, and highly positively with N. Saunders and Davies (1976) found evidence for the validity of the Jesness Inventory, as did Mott (1969). The scales most diagnostic appeared to be social maladjustment, value orientation, alienation, manifest aggression, and denial. In addition, Davies (1967) found some evidence in his follow-up studies for the validity of the autism, withdrawal and repression scales.

There are many studies using MMPI profiles, such as those of Davies and Sines (1971), and Beck and McIntyre (1977). The scales usually involved are the psychopathic deviate and hysteria scales, hypochondriasis, masculinity/femininity interest patterns, and mania; these suggest neurotic extraversion in the main. A more detailed account of work with the MMPI will be found in Dahlstrom and Dahlstrom (1980). As regards anxiety, a typical report is that by Lidhoo (1971), who studied 200 delinquent and 200 non-delinquent adolescents, matched for age, sex and socio-economic status; all the subjects were Indian. The main and highly significant differences observed were with respect to emotionality, with the delinquents more tense, more depressed, and more easily provoked, and sexual maladjustment.

With only one or two exceptions, all the studies so far considered have been published in English and relate to English and American populations. It may be useful to summarize the major findings before going on to the large body of German-speaking studies investigating the major theories here considered. Replication is the life-blood of science, and here we would seem to have an ideal opportunity to compare 2 sets of data, not just collected by different investigators, but collected in different countries and by means of different inventories, although the German inventory used in all these studies was explicitly based on the Eysenck Personality Inventory. Thus we would here seem to have a cross-cultural replication, and if similar results are obtained, we could feel much more secure in regarding these conclusions as being firmly based.

The first conclusion which seems appropriate is that while the earlier studies summarized by Passingham were not theory centred, often used inappropriate questionnairies, and paid little attention to important methodological requirements, later studies summarized in Eysenck (1977), were methodologically much superior, and gave much more definitive and significant support to the personality theory in question. Studies carried out since then have maintained this improvement, and are nearly all equally positive in the outcome. Our first conclusion therefore must be that we now have good evidence for the implication of psychoticism, extraversion and neuroticism as predisposing factors in juvenile and adult criminality, and even in juvenile anti-social behaviour not amounting to legally criminal conduct. These correlations are based both on self-reported anti-social behaviour and criminal activity, and on legally defined criminality.

44

It would seem that different types of criminal activity may show differential relationships to personality, but too little has been done in that field to be very definitive to one's conclusions. Males and females seem to have similar personality patterns, as far as criminality is concerned, but little seems to have been done in making deliberate gender comparisons.

While P, E and N are related to criminality at all ages, there seem to be definite patterns suggesting that N is more important with older criminals, E with younger criminals. Why this should be so is not clear, but the data definitely tend in that direction. Possibly N, as a multiplicative drive variable, assumes greater importance with older people in whom habits have already been settled more clearly than is the case with younger persons. Another possibility is that the largely incarcerated adult samples cannot properly answer the social activity questions which make up a large part of the extraversion inventory. A study specifically directed to the solution of this problem would seem called for.

Summary of German studies

A summary of 15 empirical German studies, using altogether 3450 delinquents and a rather larger number of controls, has been reported by Steller and Hunze (1984). All these studies used the FPI (Freiburger Persönlichkeits Inventar) of Fahrenberg, Selg and Hampel (1978). In addition, Steller and Hunze report a study of their own, using a self-report device for the measurement of anti-social conduct. The FPI contains 9 traits and 3 dimensional scales, the latter being extraversion, emotional ability or neuroticism, and masculinity. The 9 trait scales relate to nervousness, aggressiveness, depression, excitability, sociability, stability, dominance, inhibition and openness. Typical of the general findings are those of the special study carried out by Steller and Hunze, where they found that delinquents showed higher scores on nervousness, depression, excitability, sociability, extraversion, and neuroticism. These results appeared separately on 2 alternative forms of the FPI.

In summarizing the results from all the other German studies, Steller and Hunze point out that for the trait scales there is a very clear picture. Delinquents are higher on depression, nervousness, excitability, and aggression. Regarding the major dimensions, a great majority show excessive degrees of neuroticism, and to a lesser extent extraversion. Sociability, as a major trait involved in extraversion, was significantly elevated in 25 per cent of all the comparisons, with criminals being more sociable. If we can use aggressiveness as an important part of psychoticism, then it is clear that these results agree very well with those of the English-speaking samples.

German studies show a similar differentiation between older and younger subjects, as far as neuroticism and extraversion are concerned. For the younger groups, delinquents are characterized much more clearly by greater sociability, dominance, and openness; extraversion is implicated in almost every comparison between young delinquents and non-delinquents. This agrees well with the English-speaking data.

The German data give evidence also for the fact that the different types of criminality may be related differentially to personality, but the data are not extensive enough to make any definitive summary possible. There is, however, an interesting summary of data relating personality to the duration of incarceration, suggesting an increase in emotional instability with incarceration. However, there is also evidence that prisoners on probation showed increases in emotional instability. Clearly a more detailed investigation of this question is in order, particularly as Bolton *et al* (1976) report discrepant findings.

It is sometimes suggested that possibly the differences between criminals and non-criminals might be due to the process of incarceration itself. This is unlikely, because several of the studies discussed compared the anti-social and criminal activites of children and juveniles none of whom were incarcerated at any time. Even more relevant and impressive is work showing that long before anti-social acts are committed, children who later on commit them are already differentiated from those who do not. Consider as an example the work of Burt (1965) who reported on the follow-up of children originally studied over 30 years previously. Seven hundred and sixty-three children of whom 15 per cent and 18 per cent respectively later became habitual criminals or neurotics, were rated by the teachers for N and for E. Of those who later became habitual offenders, 63 per cent had been rated as high on N; 54 per cent had been rated as high on E, but only 3 per cent as high on introversion. Of those who later became neurotics, 59 per cent had been rated as high on N, 44 per cent had been rated as high on introversion, but only 1 per cent as high on E. Similar data are reported by Michael (1956), and more recently Taylor and Watt (1977) and Fakouri and Gerse (1976) have published data showing that prediction of future criminal behaviour is possible from early school records. Thus the future criminal, like the future neurotic, is already recognisable in the young child.

Several of the studies summarized by Steller and Hunze used self-reported delinquency, and found, very much as did the English-speaking studies, that very similar personality correlates were observed here as in the case of legally defined delinquency. The authors conclude that:

> **'in agreement with Eysenck's hypothesis and findings, it was found that in many samples emotional instability ("neuroticism") and high extraversion were found (in delinquents). The corresponding increases in the FPI dimensional scales were found most clearly in juvenile samples, but for grown-up delinquents were found in the FPI trait scales which represent major components of dimensional scales emotional instability and extraversion.'**
> *(p. 107)*

We may thus conclude that this essay in replication has been eminently successful, in that identical findings are reported from the German literature as we have found to be representative of the English-speaking literature. There seems to be little doubt, therefore, that personality and anti-social and criminal behaviour are reasonably intimately correlated, and that these correlations can be found in cultures other than the Anglo-American. Eysenck (1977) has reported such confirmatory studies from widely different countries, including India, Hungary, Poland, and others, as well as the German and French-speaking samples mentioned in this chapter.

Constitutional factors in criminality

The notion that significant relationships exist between physical type and various morphological characteristics, on the one hand, and delinquency and criminality on the other, has a long history. It found a strong advocate in Lombrosco (1911) who studied morphological anomalies in criminals and founded the doctrine that the criminal, as found in prison, was an atavistic anomaly presenting morbid physical stigmata. The specific stigmata he listed were not found by later investigators to have any relationship to criminality, and this served for a long time to discredit the general hypothesis of the relationship between morphology and crime. However, negative results of this kind cannot be generalised. They discredit the specific hypotheses tested, but have no bearing on the possibility that other characteristics might show quite strong relationships. Later work has indeed found this to be so.

Interest in recent years has veered from the question of physical stigmata to other aspects of body build. Hooton (1939a, b) studied 17,000 prison and reformatory inmates and reported significant differences in various body measurements between persons convicted of different types of crime. Thus he found that both the shortest 6th and the heaviest 6th of the group headed the list of crimes for rape, sex offences, and assault, but were lowest in murder, whereas the contrasting group consisting of tall and slender criminals had the highest incidence of murder and robbery, but the lowest or the next lowest in crimes, such as burglary, assault, rape and other sex offences. These results should warn us that 'criminality' may not be a general trait uniquely associated with a certain type of body build, but that different types of crime may have to be distinguished. This is an ever-present difficulty, because most studies have concentrated on certain very common types of crime (burglary, stealing, assault, sex offences, etc.). Murder is seldom included, if only because of the very small number of murderers to be found, and white-collar crimes are also excluded, or only form a small portion of the total number of crime studied.

Most modern work on physique has used the methods of somatotyping introduced by Sheldon (1940), whose major descriptive hypotheses were borrowed from Kretschmer (1948). Detailed discussions of his and earlier work is given by Eysenck (1970) and Rees (1973), who also present a critical review of the Kretschmer, Sheldon and other systems. Here we will only give a brief description of Sheldon's system, and the terms used by him. He posits 3 major dimensions, called endomorphy, ectomorphy, and mesomorphy. These are regarded as *components* of total body build, each having a certain determinable influence which is rated by Sheldon on a 7-point scale, so that each body type may be represented by a set of 3 numbers denoting respectively the influence of each the 3 components.

Endomorphy, the first component, refers to the predominance of the digestive viscera, especially the gut; in these people the most manifest external characteristic is a conspicuous laying on of fat, which is indicative of predominance of the absorptive functions—the functions of the gut—over the energy-expending functions.

In a similar way, bones, muscles, connective tissue, and the heart and the blood vessels were seen to predominate overwhelmingly in the variants of type 2, the so-called mesomorphs. And as regards the 3rd type, the ectomorphs, the term refers to the predominance of the sense organs and the nervous systems, including the brain; relative to total bodily mass, all these organs are conspicuous in the bodily economy of the extreme variant of type 3.

Sheldon (1942) believed that these 3 bodily components were closely related to the major dimensions of personality, which he called viscerotonia, somatotonia, and cerebrotonia, as they seem to deal respectively with the functional predominance of the digestive viscera, the functional and anatomical predominance of the somatic structures and the prepotency of the higher centres of the nervous system. Thus viscerotonics are characterized by relaxation, love of physical comfort, love of eating, sociability, amiability, tolerance and easy communication of feeling. Somatotonics are characterized by assertiveness, love of physical adventure, enjoyment of exercise, dominance and lust for power, love of risk and chance, ruthlessness and freedom from squeamishness. Last, cerebrotonics are characterized by physiological over-response, love of privacy, mental over-intensity, lack of sociability, hypersensitivity to pain and need of solitude. In terms of the personality system here adopted, viscerotonia is very similar to extraversion, cerebrotonia to introversion, and somatotonia to psychoticism. In line with previous findings reported in this chapter, we would expect mesomorphs and somatotonics to be found significantly more frequently among criminals, ectomorphs and cerebrotonics much less frequently, and endomorphs and viscerotonics intermediate between the other 2 groups. What are the facts?

Sheldon (1949) carried out a study of 200 delinquent youths who were somatotyped according to his system, and were compared with 4000 college students. It was found that the sample of delinquents differed sharply from the college somatotype distribution, having a distinct and heavier massing in the endomorphic—mesomorphic sector. Ectomorphs were rare, as were ectomorphic mesomorphs in comparison with endomorphic mesomorphs. As a generalization they concluded that the 200 delinquent youths were decidely mesomorphic and decidely lacking in ectomorphy, but that there appeared to be no strongly defined tendency, either way, with regard to endomorphy.

Hartl, Monnelly and Elderkin (1984) carried out a 30-year follow-up of Sheldon's work, in which they characterized the now grown-up youths in terms of their future careers. Some of the youths had become criminals, some had turned into quite normal individuals, others still had psychological problems of one kind or another. The most important differentiation between normals and criminals in this sample was with respect to mesomorphy; criminals were very significantly more mesomorph than normals, even in this already excessively mesomorph group. Thus mesomorphy is a predictive characteristic, related to future conduct.

It is interesting to note that a psychiatric rating made 30 years before the follow-up proved quite highly predictive also; this related to 'affective exaggeration', i.e. what we would call neuroticism. This is important confirmation of the general finding that there is a relationship between neuroticism and criminality, which in this case has been shown to be predictive.

A well known study by Glueck and Glueck (1956) related to 500 juvenile delinquent boys and 500 carefully matched non-delinquent controls. The Gluecks found that 60 per cent of their delinquents were dominantly mesomorphic, compared with only 31 per cent of the non-delinquents. This was a major difference between the groups, in addition to a lower ectomorphic component in the delinquent group.

Gibbens (1963) carried out a study in which 58 young offenders were somatotyped according to Sheldon's rules; he found 29 men, i.e. exactly 50 per cent predominantly mesomorphic in physique, but only 11 predominantly endomorphic or ectomorphic; 12 had balanced physiques.

Epps and Parnell (1952), working like Gibbens in England, studied a group of 177 young women, between the ages of 16 and 21, undergoing Borstal training. Anthropometric measurements were carried out on the delinquent group and compared with a group of 123 university women. It was found that delinquents were heavier in body build and more muscular and fat; in other words they showed a predominance of mesomorphy and endomorphic mesomorphy. In temperament they showed a predominance of somatotonia and viscerotonia, i.e. high P and high E.

Cortes and Gatti (1972) also verified the predominance of mesomorphic physique in young delinquents. Using 100 delinquents and 100 matching controls, they found that 57 of the delinquents, but only 19 per cent of the controls were predominantly mesomorphic. The delinquent group also contained fewer endomorphs (14 per cent versus 37 per cent) and fewer ectomorphs (16 per cent versus 33 per cent) as compared with the non-delinquent groups.

One of the most compelling studies in this field is that by Seltzer (1950), who used many different types of anthropometric measurements to compare subjects in 2 juvenile groups of 496 delinquents and 486 non-delinquents. His conclusion was that he found delinquents to be

> 'absolutely and relatively more mesomorphic than the non-delinquents. The delinquents are also decidedly weaker in ectomorphy than the juveniles in the control group. The situation with regard to endomorphy, on the other hand, presents a more complicated picture. The data indicate that instances of extreme endomorphs are more common among the non-delinquents, but apart from these cases the relative endomorphic strength of the delinquents is by and large greater than that of the non-delinquents. Statistically significant differences in somatotype categories revealed the delinquents, relative to the non-delinquents, manifesting an excess of extreme mesomorphs, of mesomorphs, and endomorphic mesomorphs and a deficiency of extreme ectomorphs, of extreme andromorphs, of ectomorphs, and of mesomorphic ectomorphs.'
> (p. 350)

It should be noted that in the Sheldon system there are other rateable characteristics of body build which have also been found relevant. The most important of these are *andromorphy* and *gynemorphy*, i.e. the expression of masculine and feminine characteristics throughout the body. Sheldon (1949) and Hartl *et al* (1952) found that high andromorphy was another constitutional element highly correlated with criminality. They report a study of 283 inmates of the Duell State Penitentiary in California, where ratings were made of somatotype and the andric-gynic components of body build. They presented tables for the various components and conclude that:

> 'these data corroborate the association between criminality and the physique of high mesomorphy, low ectomorphy, and high andromorphy'.
> (p. 535)

A few words should be said in order to set these results in context. Eysenck (1970) and Rees (1973) have presented many criticisms of the Sheldon system. Statistically, 2 rather than 3 components are necessitated by the empirical data, referring to height and width of body build, respectively, i.e. the predominance of linear as opposed to transversal and circumferential factors. Again, the close association postulated by Sheldon between his temperamental and body-build variables has not been verified by later investigators, and is almost certainly due to poor experimental control; temperament judgements were made with full knowledge of the physique of the students involved. However, the literature does suggest that there is a modest correlation of about .4 between introversion and the linear measures (height; length of bones), and between extraversion and the width and circumferential measures (shoulder breadth; girth). Thus as far as they go, the data are in good agreement with the hypothesis that criminality is related to extraversion, and also to psychoticism; Sheldon's somatotonia, as defined by the scale of ratings which he uses, includes many items characteristic of P.

49

In looking at these data it should of course never be forgotten that the delinquents and criminals studied are only a non-random sample of all criminals. Murderers and white-collar workers are conspicuous by their absence, and as we have seen murderers tend to be introverted rather than extraverted. White-collar workers who turn to crime may be ectomorphs rather than mesomorphs, particularly when their crime involves complex manipulations of computers, etc. Thus there are certain qualifications to any generalization of the data. However, the characterisation would seem to fit the great majority of criminals in our society whose crimes consist of stealing, burglary, assault and the more frequent sexual crimes. These probably constitute something like 90 per cent or more of all crimes committed, and hence any generalization relating to them is of considerable importance, and deserves to be followed up.

It is unfortunate that in recent years there has been a lack of interest in constitutional factors, and that very little research has been done in order to verify, modify or disprove these intriguing results. As far as they go, they do fit into a larger picture of genetically determined personality traits, linked with hormonal, endocrine and other biochemical factors, and apparently also related to physique or body build. The relationships are closer than one might have expected at first sight, and they suggest interesting relationships between body build and hormones: e.g. the importance of the andromorphic component is almost certainly related to high testosterone levels, which in turn have been found to be characteristic of high P scores. Similarly the love of risk, freedom from squeamishness and sensation-seeking of mesomorphs almost certainly finds a ready explanation in low MAO platelet levels. (Zuckerman *et al*, 1984). Experimental studies of conditioning, of psychophysiological reactions, etc. should also be looked at in relation to body build. As Hartl *et al* (1984) point out:

> 'studies like these would benefit from using a constitutional scheme to classify the studied subjects, especially along the dimensions of mesomorphy and andromorphy'.
> *(p. 536)*

Claims for the importance of constitutional factors were pitched too high by Lambroso, but have been prematurely disregarded by many of his critics; a more balanced view would seem to be indicated.

Methods of treatment and rehabilitation

The theories here developed obviously have implications for treatment and rehabilitation of offenders, particularly youthful ones. In the first place, the stress on a *conditioning* model for the development of anti-social attitudes suggests that some form of *extinction* or *counter-conditioning* would be appropriate for rehabilitation. In the second place, the stress on individual differences suggests that it would not be possible to devise a uniform programme of rehabilitation, but that the form such a programme would take would depend very much on the personality of the offender.

In looking at the problem in this way, we must say a few words about certain misunderstandings that are likely to arise in connection with our insistence that anti-social behaviour is to a large extent determined by genetic causes. What is envisaged is a continuum from altruistic to anti-social behaviour, with the position of each given person determined to some extent at least by genetic factors which may or may not act through personality and constitutional variables of the kind considered. Most of the work, already reviewed, relates to anti-social and criminal behaviour but there is now evidence also at the other end. Using a three-part inventory measuring altruistic tendencies, Rushton, Fulker, Neale, Blizard and Eysenck (1984) obtained rough estimates of broad heritability of 56 per cent, 68 per cent, and 72 per cent respectively for the 3 inventories. Maximum-likelihood model fitting revealed about 50 per cent of the variance on each scale to be associated with genetic effects, virtually 0 per cent to be due to the twins' common environment, and the remaining 50 per cent to be due to each twin's specific environment and/or errors associated with the test. Heritability with measurement error eliminated would raise the genetic effects to over 60 per cent, and reduce the within family environmental effects to under 40 per cent.

There is of course a possibility that specific anti-social activities, such as rape, murder, etc., are caused in part by *specific* genetic factors. The situation is probably similar to that in the field of neurosis, where Torgersen (1979) and Rose and Ditto (1983) have demonstrated the importance of genetic factors for the development of phobic fears in general, but have also been able to show that *specific* phobic fears are to some extent inherited along specific genetic lines.

It is often thought that because a particular type of behaviour is to a large extent determined by genetic factors, therefore we must assume a policy of therapeutic nihilism, but nothing could be further from the truth. Even though obsessive-compulsive behaviour may be largely determined by genetic causes, the simple application of an animal model to the behavioural treatment of the disorder has been found to be extremely successful, in a very short period of time (Rachman and Hodgson, 1980). The advocates of therapeutic nihilism leave out of account the fact that estimates of heritability are population estimates which refer to a given population, at a given time; they have no absolute value or relevance. The introduction of novel techniques can alter the whole situation completely, and provide hope for environmental manipulation.

Methods of counter-conditioning and extinction have indeed been tried on a fairly large scale, using particularly the methods of operant conditioning, and 'token economies'. This work has been reviewed exhaustively by Stumphauzer (1973, 1979), and one can summarise the main conclusions rather briefly. Rehabilitation has not been successful with older subjects, but seems to give more positive results with young offenders. Treatment in prison or other large-scale aggregates is not on the whole successful, but treatment in small 'family' groups under a well trained house master can be more successful. It is easier to influence behaviour while the young offender is in custody, or under observation, than after he returns to his original environment; indeed, generalization of rules of conduct acquired during the period of conditioning to other environments seems to be the weakest point of these regimes. From the point of view of rehabilitation, these results are not too favourable, although it must be admitted that we simply do not know the best way of applying the principles of conditioning as yet, and better results may be obtained when suitable parameter studies have been carried out. Even as it is, conditioning methods of treatment give results at least as good as customary custodial methods, at one third the cost. From the financial point of view, therefore, these methods should certainly be adopted forthwith.

E

It will have been noted that the methods of treatment used have been those of operant conditioning; there is no record of Pavlovian extinction methods being used. It seems likely that generalization is easier when classical rather than instrumental conditioning is being applied, but of course it is always very difficult to say whether a particular method of social training is in fact more closely related to classical or instrumental conditioning, or indeed uses both sets of principles. There is much room here for careful research design and theoretical innovation.

One of the most important parameters to be taken into account in this type of work must be that of individual differences. Consider the suggestion that extraversion is one of the personality variables through which genetic factors predispose a person towards anti-social and criminal behaviour. Gray (1972, 1976, 1982) has suggested that signals of punishment, signals of non-reward, and signals related to novel stimuli, stimulate the behavioural inhibition system, which in turn activates behavioural inhibition, increments in arousal, and increased attention. He has also postulated, and brought forward evidence to show the truth of his contention, that introverts are more easily conditioned by stimuli of this kind, while extraverts are more easily conditioned through stimuli signalling reward, cessation of punishment, etc. Gupta (1976) and Gupta and Nagpal (1978) have also given experimental support for this contention. McCord and Wakefield (1981) have shown in a well designed experiment using classroom behaviour that extraverted children respond with better performance to praise and rewards, introverted children to blame and punishment.

It might therefore be suggested that in rehabilitation treatment using conditioning methods, the use of punishment and non-reward (aversion therapy) might be more fruitful for introverted offenders, the use of rewards and token economies generally for extraverted offenders. It is certainly possible that the relative failure of the methods described by Stumphauzer is due to the fact that they were not geared to the personality of the offenders. There is considerable interaction between method and personality, and when this is not taken into account this interaction effect ends up as part of the error variance. Such a disaster can only be avoided by carefully invoking personality theory in the design of the experiment, and relating type of reinforcement to type of personality in a proper experimental design.

As we have seen, extraversion is not the only factor involved in anti-social behaviour, and both neuroticism and psychoticism may require attention. As far as neuroticism is concerned, the methods of behaviour therapy are specifically geared to its behavioural consequences, and it is another fault of the experiments reported by Stumphauzer that little seems to have been done to decrease the neurotic behaviours of the offenders through orthodox behaviour therapy. It seems that doing so might improve the unsatisfactory set of outcomes reviewed above.

Psychoticism is a much more difficult variable to control or deal with. High P scorers are notoriously difficult to deal with by behaviour therapy, psychotherapy or any other non-drug method, and it may with confidence be suggested that in the conditioning trials mentioned above it is likely to have been the high P scorers who constituted the least successful group. The only suggestion that can be made is that during treatment high P scorers should be given anti-psychotic drugs, such as phenothiazines; this would make them more amenable to treatment, and once treatment was successfully concluded, the effects might be relatively lasting, without requiring the offenders to spend the rest of their lives on drugs. Unpublished work with neurotics having high P scores has tended to demonstrate the effectiveness of this technique, but of course the point at the moment is a purely theoretical one, and it would require empirical support before the efficacy of such methods can be asserted with any degree of certainty.

This section has been kept short on purpose because, in the first place, there is really not a great deal of direct evidence to refer to, and secondly because although theoretical considerations suggest some of the variables that require measurement and control, such experiments are obviously difficult to carry out, and often raise important ethical problems. It is not the purpose of this chapter to debate such questions. It seems to the writer that the problem of rehabilitation is one of very great importance to society as well as to the individual offender, and that vastly greater resources should be made available for a determination of the possibilities and limitations of psychological treatment along the lines suggested. Small-scale research in this field is in the nature of things not only difficult to carry out, but also not very persuasive; what is true of a small number of offenders may not generalise to others, and the personality of the 'house master', or the particular environment in which the experiment is carried out, may be impossible to replicate in another experiment. However, the theory does suggest to us some of the important variables in question, and in due course it is to be hoped that research will tell us to what extent action based on these theories can successfully deal with the problem of rehabilitation.

References

ALLSOP, J. F. (1975). 'Investigations into the applicability of Eysenck's theory of criminality to the anti-social behaviour of schoolchildren', London: Unpublished Ph.D. thesis, University of London.

ALLSOP, J. F. and FELDMAN, M. P. (1975). 'Extraversion, neuroticism and psychoticism and anti-social behaviour in school girls'. *Social Behaviour and Personality*, 2, 184–189.

ALLSOP, J. F. and FELDMAN, M. P. (1976). 'Item analyses of questionnaire measures of personality and anti-social behaviour in school girls'. *British Journal of Criminology*, 16, 337–351.

AMELANG, M. and RODEL, G. (1970). 'Persönlichkeits—und Einstellungskorrelate Krimineller Verhaltensweisen'. Psychologische, *Rundschau*, 21, 157–179.

BARACK, L. I. and WIDOM, C. S. (1978). 'Eysenck's theory of criminality applied to women awaiting trial'. *British Journal of Psychiatry*, 133, 452–456.

BECK, E. A. and McINTYRE, C. S. (1977).'MMPI patterns of shoplifters within a college population'. *Psychological Reports*, 41, 1035–1040.

BERMAN, T. and PAISLEY, T. (1984). 'Personality in assaultive and non-assaultive juvenile male offenders'. *Psychological Reports*, 54, 527–530.

BESHAI, J. A. (1971). 'Behaviour correlates of the EEG in delinquents'. *Journal of Psychology*, 79, 141–146.

BLACKBURN, R. (1968). 'Personality in relation to extreme aggression in psychiatric offenders'. *British Journal of Psychiatry*, 114, 821–828.

BLACKBURN, R. (1970). 'Personality types among abnormal homicides'. Special Hospital Research, No. 1. London.

BÖKER, W. and HAFNER, H. (1973). *Gewalttaten Geistesgestörter*. Berlin: Springer.

BOLTON, N., SMITH, F. V., HESKIN, K. J. and BARISTER, P. A. (1976). 'Psychological correlates of long-term imprisonment'. *British Journal of Criminology*, 16, pp. 38–47.

BROWN, B. S. and COURTLESS, T. F. (1967). 'The mentally retarded offender'. Reference document reproduced by the President's Commission on Law Enforcement and Administration of Justice.

BURGESS, P. K. (1972). 'Eysenck's theory of criminality: A new approach'. *British Journal of Criminology*, 12, 74–82.

BURT, C. (1965). 'Factorial studies of personality and their bearing in the work of the teacher'. *British Journal of Educational Psychology*, 35, 308–328.

CADORET, R. J., CAIN, C. A. and CROWE, R. R. (1983). 'Evidence for gene-environmental interaction in the development of adolescent anti-social behaviour'. *Behaviour Genetics*, 13, 301–310.

CLONINGER, C. R., CHRISTIANSEN, K. O., REICH, T. and GOTTESMAN, I. I. (1978). 'Implications of sex differences in the prevalence of antisocial personality, alcoholism and criminality for familial transmission'. *Archives of General Psychiatry*, 35, 941–951.

CORTES, J. B. and GATTI, F. M. (1972). *Delinquency and Crime: A Biosocial Approach*. New York: Seminar Press.

COTÉ, G. and LEBLANC, M. (1982). 'Aspects de personalité et comportement delinquent'. *Bulletin de Psychologique*, 36, 265–271.

CRAWFORD, D. A. (1977). 'The HDHQ results of long-term prisoners: Relationship with criminal and institutional behaviour'. *British Journal of Social and Clinical Psychology*, 16, 391–394.

DAHLSTROM, W. G. and DAHLSTROM, L. (Eds.) (1980). *Basic Readings on the MMPI*. Minneapolis: University of Minnerata Press.

DAVIES, M. B. (1967). *The use of the Jesness Inventory in a sample of British probationers*. London: HMSO.

DAVIES, K. R. and SINES, J. O. (1971).'An anti-social behaviour pattern associated with a specific MMPI profile'. *Journal of Consulting and Clinical Psychology*, 36, 229–234.

DETTENBORN, H. (1971). 'Beziehungen im psychologisch relevanten Determinationskomplex der Jugendkriminalität'. *Probleme und Ergebnisse der Psychologie*, 39, 27–79.

ELLENBERG, H. D. (1961). 'Remand home boys, 1930–1955'. *British Journal of Criminology*, 2, 111–131.

ELLIS, L. (1982). 'Genetics and criminal behaviour'. *Criminology*, 20, 45–66.

EPPS, P. and PARNELL, R. W. (1952). 'Physique and temperament of women delinquents compared with women undergraduates'. *British Journal of Medical Psychology*, 25, 249–255.

EYSENCK, H. J. (1960). Symposium:'The development of moral values in children. VII. The contribution of learning theory'. *British Journal of Educational Psychology*, 30, 11–21.

EYSENCK, H. J. (1967). *The Biological Basis of Personality*. Springfield: C. C. Thomas.

EYSENCK, H. J. (1970). *The Structures of Human Personality*, (3rd Ed.). London: Methuen.

EYSENCK, H. J. (1973). 'Personality, learning and "anxiety"'. In: H. J. Eysenck (Ed.), *Handbook of Abnormal Psychology*. 2nd Edition. London: Pitman, 390–419.

EYSENCK, H. J. (1976). 'The biology of morality'. In: T. Lickona (Ed.), *Moral Development and Behaviour*. New York: Holt, Rinehart & Winston, 108–123.

EYSENCK, H. J. (1977). *Crime and Personality*, (3rd Ed.) London: Routledge and Kegan Paul.

EYSENCK, H. J. (Ed.) (1980a). *A Model for Personality*. New York: Springer.

EYSENCK, H. J. (1980b). 'Psychopathie'. In: M. Baumann, H. Berbalk and G. Seidenstücker (Eds.), *Klinische Psychologie: Trends in Forschung Und Praxis*. Wien: H. Huber, 3, 323–360.

EYSENCK, H. J. and EYSENCK, M. W. (1985). *Personality and Individual Differences*. New York: Plenum.

EYSENCK, H. J. and EYSENCK, S. B. G. (1976). *Psychoticism as a Dimension of Personality*. London: Hodder and Stoughton.

EYSENCK, H. J. and EYSENCK, S. B. G. (1978). 'Psychopathy, personality and genetics'. In: R. D. Hare and D. Schalling (Eds.), *Psychopathic Behaviour*. London: John Wiley, 197–223.

EYSENCK, S. B. G. and EYSENCK, H. J. (1970). 'Crime and personality: An empirical study of the three-factor theory'. *British Journal of Criminology*, 10, 225–239.

EYSENCK, S. B. G. and EYSENCK, H. J. (1971). 'A comparative study of criminals and matched controls on three dimensions of personality'. *British Journal of Social and Clinical Psychology*, 10, 362–366.

EYSENCK, S. B. G. and EYSENCK, H. J. (1971). 'Crime and personality: item analysis of questionnaire responses'. *British Journal of Criminology*, 11, 49–62.

EYSENCK, S. B. G. and EYSENCK, H. J. (1973). 'The personality of female prisoners'. *British Journal of Psychiatry*, 122, 693–698.

EYSENCK, S. B. G. and EYSENCK, H. J. (1974). 'Personality and recidivism in Borstal boys'. *British Journal of Criminology*, 14, 285–287.

EYSENCK, S. B. G. and EYSENCK, H. J. (1977). 'Personality differences between prisoners and controls'. *Psychological Reports*, 40, 1023–1028.

EYSENCK, S. B. G., RUST, J. and EYSENCK, H. J. (1977). 'Personality and the classification of adult offenders'. *British Journal of Criminology*, 17, 169–179.

FAHRENBERG, J., SELG, H. and HAMPEL, R. (1978). *Das Freiburger Persönlichkeits–inventar*. Göttingen: Hogrefe.

FAKOURI, E. and JESSE, F. W. (1976). 'Unobtrusive detection of potential juvenile delinquency'. *Psychological Reports*, 39, 551–558.

FARLEY, F. H. and SEWELL, T. (1976). 'Test of an arousal theory of delinquency'. *Criminal Justice and Behaviour*, 3, 315–320.

FARRINGTON, P., BIRON, L. and LEBLANC, M. (1982). 'Personality and delinquency in London and Madrid'. In: J. Gunn and D. P. Farrington (Eds.), *Abnormal Offenders, Delinquency, and the Criminal Justice System*. New York: Wiley.

FOGGITT, R. (1974). 'Personality and delinquency'. London: Unpublished Ph.D. thesis, University of London.

FOULDS, G. A., CAINE, T. M. and CREASY, M. I. (1960). 'Aspects of extra- and intra-punitive expression in mental illness'. *Journal of Mental Science*, 106, 599–610.

FRANKS, C. M. (1956). 'Recidivism, psychopathy and personality'. *British Journal of Delinquency*, 6, 192–201.

FURNEAUX, W. D. and GIBSON, H. B. (1966). *Manual of the Junior Maudsley Inventory*. London: University of London Press.

GIBBENS, T. C. M. (1963). *Psychiatric Studies of Borstal Lads*. New York: Oxford University Press.

GIBSON, H. B. (1971). 'The factorial structure of juvenile delinquency: A study of self-reported acts'. *British Journal of Social and Clinical Psychology*, 10, 1–9.

GLUECK, S. and GLUEK, E. (1956). *Physique and Delinquency*. New York: Harper.

GOSSOP, M. (1978). 'Drug dependence, crime and personality among female addicts'. *Drug and Alcohol Dependence*, 3, 359–364.

GOSSOP, M. R. and KRISTJANSSON, I. (1977). 'Crime and personality'. *British Journal of Criminology*, 17, 264–273.

GRAY, J. A. (1972). 'Learning theory, the conceptual nervous system and personality'. In: V. D. Nebylitsyn and J. A. Gray (Eds.), *The Biological Basis of Individual Behaviour*. New York: Academic Press.

GRAY, J. A. (1976). 'Causal theories of personality'. In: J. R. Royce (Ed.), *Multivariate Analysis and Psychological Theories*. New York: Academic Press.

GRAY, J. A. (1982). 'The Neuropsychology of anxiety: An Enquiry into the Functions of the Septo-Hippocampal System'. Oxford: Oxford University Press.

GUPTA, B. S. (1976). 'Extraversion and reinforcement in verbal operant conditioning'. *British Journal of Psychology*, 67, 47–52.

GUPTA, B. S. and NAGPAL, M. (1978). 'Impulsivity-sociability and reinforcement in verbal operant conditioning'. *British Journal of Psychology*, 69, 203–206.

HARE, R. D. (1975). 'Psychopathy'. In: P. Venables and M. Christie (Eds.), *Research in Psychophysiology*. New York: Wiley, 325–348.

HARTL, E. M., MONELLY, E. P. and ELDERKIN, R. D. (1982). *Physique and Delinquent Behaviour*. New York: Academic Press.

HINDELANG, M. and WEIS, J. G. (1972) 'Personality and self-reported delinquency: an application of cluster analysis'. *Criminology*, 10, 268–276.

HOLCOMB, W. R., ADAM, N. A. and PONDER, H. N. (1985). 'The development and cross-validation up on MMPI typology of murderers'. *Journal of Personality Assessment*, 49, 240–244.

HOOTON, E. A. (1939a). *Crime and Man*. Cambridge, Mass.: Harvard University Press.

HOOTON, E. A. (1939b). *The American Criminal*. Cambridge, Mass.: Harvard University Press.

HORMUTH, S., LAMM, H., MICHELITSCH, I., SCHEUERMANN, H., TROMMSDORF, G. and VOGELE, I. (1977). 'Impulskontrolle und einige Persönlichkeitscharakteristika bei delinquenten und nicht-delinquenten Jugendlichen'. *Psychologische Beiträge*, 19, 340–359.

JESNESS, C. F. (1972). *The Jesness Inventory: Manual*. Palo Alto: Consulting Psychologist Press.

KALTSOUNIS, B. and HIGDON, G. (1977). 'School conformity and its relation to creativity'. *Psychological Reports*, 40, 715–718.

KRETSCHMER, E. (1948). *Korperbau und Charakter*. Berlin: Springer.

LANGE, J. (1929). *Verbrechen als Schicksal*. Leipzig: Thieme.

LIDHOO, M. L. (1971). 'An attempt to construct a psycho-diagnostic tool for the detection of potential delinquents among adolescents aged 14–19 years'. Panjab: Unpublished Ph.D. thesis, University of Panjab.

LOMBROSO, C. (1911). *Crime, its Causes and Remedies*. Boston: Little, Brown.

LÖSEL, F. (1975). *Handlungskontrolle und Jugend-delinquenz*. Stuttgart: Enke.

LÖSEL, F. and WÜSTENDORFER, W. (1976). 'Persönlichkeitskorrelate delinquenten Verhaltens oder offizieller Delinquenz?'. *Zeitschrift für Sozialpsychologie*, 7, 177–191.

McCORD, R. M. and WAKEFIELD, J. A. (1981). 'Arithmetic achievement as a function of introversion-extraversion and teacher—presented reward and punishment'. *Personality and Individual Differences*, 2, 145–152.

McCUE, P., BOOTH, S. and ROOT, J. (1976). 'Do young prisoners under-state their extraversion on personality inventories?'. *British Journal of Criminology*, 16, 282, 283.

McGARVEY, B., GABRIELLI, W., BENTLER, P. M. and MEDNICK, S. (1981). 'Rearing social class, education, and criminality: A multiple indicative model'. *Journal of Abnormal Psychology*, 90, 354–364.

McGURK, B. J. (1978). 'Personality types among "normal" homicides'. *British Journal of Criminology*, 18, 146–161.

McGURK, B. J. and McDOUGALL, C. (1981). 'A new approach to Eysenck's theory of criminality'. *Personality and Individual Differences*, 2, 338–340.

McGURK, B. J. and McEWAN, A. W. (1983). 'Personality types and recidivism among Borstal trainees'. *Personality and Individual Differences*, 4, 165–170.

McGURK, B. J., McEWAN, A. W. and GRAHAM, F. (1981). 'Personality types and recidivism among young delinquents'. *British Journals of Criminology*, 21, 159–165.

MARTIN, A. L. (1985). 'Values and personality: A survey of their relationship in the case of juvenile delinquence'. *Personality and Individual Differences*, 4, 519–522.

MEDNICK, S. A., GABRIELLI, W. F. and HUTCHINGS, B. (1984). Genetic influences in criminal convictions: Evidence from an adoption cohort. *Science*, 224, 841–894.

MEGARGEE, E. I. (1966). 'Undercontrolled and overcontrolled personality types in extreme anti-social aggression'. *Psychological Monographs*, 80, Whole Number 611.

MICHAEL, C. M. (1956). 'Follow-up studies of introverted children: IV. Relative incidence of criminal behaviour'. *Journal of Criminal Law and Criminality*, 47, 414–422.

MITCHELL, J., ROGERS, R., CAVANAUGH, J. and WASYLIW, O. (1980). 'The role of trait anxiety in violent and non-violent delinquent behaviour'. *American Journal of Forensic Psychiatry*.

MOFFITT, T. E., GABRIELLI, W. F., MEDNICK, S. and SCHULSINGER, F. (1981). 'Socioeconomic states, IQ, and delinquency'. *Journal of Abnormal Psychology*, 90, 152–156.

MOTT, J. (1969). *The Jesness Inventory: An Application to Approved School Boys*. London: HMSO.

NAAR, R. (1965). 'A note on the intelligence of delinquents in Richmond, Virginia'. *British Journal of Criminology*, 5, 82–85.

PASSINGHAM, R. E. (1972). 'Crime and personality: A review of Eysenck's theory'. In: V. D. Nebylitsyn and J. A. Gray (Eds.), *Biological Bases of Individual Behaviour*. London: Academic Press.

PEREZ, J. and TORRUBIA, R. (1985). 'Sensation seeking and anti-social behaviour in a student sample'. *Personality and Individual Differences*, 6, 401–403.

PLOMIN, R., DeFRIES, J. C. and McCLEARN, G. E. (1980). *Behavioural Genetics: A Primer*. San Francisco: Freeman.

PORTEUS, S. D. (1965). *Porteus Maze Test: Fifty Years of Application*. Palo Alto: Pacific Books.

QUAY, H. C. (1965). 'Psychopathic personality as pathological stimulation-seeking'. *American Journal of Psychiatry*, 122, 180–183.

RACHMAN, S. and HODGSON, R. (1980). *Obsessions and Compulsions*. Englewood Cliffs, N.J.: Prentice-Hall.

RAHMAN, A. and HUSAIN, A. (1984). 'Personality and female criminals in Bangladesh. *Personality and Individual Differences*, 5, 473–474.

RAINE, A. and VENABLES, P. (1981). 'Classical conditioning and socialization—a biosocial interaction'. *Personality and Individual Differences*, 2, 273–283.

REES, L. (1973). 'Constitutional factors and abnormal behaviour'. In: H. J. Eysenck (Ed.), *Handbook of Abnormal Psychology*. London: Pitman, 487–539.
ROBINS, L. N. (1972). 'Follow-up studies of behaviour disorders in children'. In: H. C. Quay and J. S. Werry (Eds.), *Psychopathological Disorders of Childhood*. New York: Wiley.
ROSE, R. J. and DITTO, W. B. (1983). 'A developmental-genetic analysis of common fears from early adolescence to early childhood'. *Child Development*, 54, 361–368.
ROTENBERG, M. and NACHSHON, I. (1979). 'Impulsiveness and aggression among Israeli delinquents'. *British Journal of Social and Clinical Psychology*, 18, 59–63.
ROYCE, J. P. and POWELL, A. (1983). *Theory of Personality and Individual Differences: Factors, Systems and Processes*. New Jersey: Prentice-Hall.
RUSHTON, J. F. and CHRISJOHN, R. D. (1981). 'Extraversion, neuroticism, psychoticism and self-reported delinquency: Evidence from eight separate samples'. *Personality and Individual Differences*, 2, 11–20.
RUSHTON, J. P., FULKER, D. W., NEALE, M. C., BLIZARD, R. A. and EYSENCK, H. J. (1984). 'Altruism and genetics'. *Acta Genetica Medicina Gemellol*, 33, 265–271.
SAKLOFSKE, D. H., McKERRACHER, D. W. and EYSENCK, S. B. G. (1969). 'Eysenck's theory of criminality: A scale of criminal propensity as a measure of anti-social behaviour'.
SANOCKI, W. (1969). 'The use of Eysenck's inventory for testing young prisoners'. *Przeglad Penitencjarny*, (Warszawa), 7, 53–68.
SAUNDERS, G. R. and DAVIES, M. B. (1976). 'The validity of the Jesness Inventory with British delinquents'. *British Journal of Social and Clinical Psychology*, 15, 33–39.
SCHALLING, D. and ROSEN, A-S. (1970). 'A note on Porteus Q-score and the construct of psychopathy'. Stockholm: *Reports from the Psychological Laboratories*, No. 307.
SCHWENKMEZGER, P. (1977). *Risikoverhalten und Risikobereitschaft*. Weinheim: Beltz.
SCHWENKMEZGER, P. (1983). 'Risikoverhalten, Rissikobereitschaft und Delinquenz: Theoretische Grundlagen und differentialdiagnostische Untersuchungen'. *Zeitschrift für Differentielle und Diagnostische Psychologie*, 4, 223–239.
SELTZER, C. C. (1950). 'A comparative study of the morphological characteristics of delinquents and non-delinquents'. In: S. Glueck and E. Glueck (Eds.), *Unravelling Juvenile Delinquency*. New York: Commonwealth Fund, 307–350.
SHANMUGAN, T. E. (1979). 'Personality factors underlying drug abuse among college students'. *Psychological Studies*, 24–35.
SHELDON, W. H. (1940). *The Varieties of Human Physique: An Introduction to Constitutional Psychology*. New York: Harper.
SHELDON, W. H. (1942). *The Varieties of Temperament: A Psychology of Constitutional Differences*. New York: Harper.
SHELDON, W. H. (1949). *Varieties of Delinquent Youth: An Introduction to Constitutional Psychiatry*. New York: Harper.
SINGH, A. (1980). 'A study of the personality and adjustments of female juvenile delinquents'. *Child Psychiatry Quarterly*, 13, 52–59.
SMITH, D. E. (1974). 'Relationships between the Eysenck and Jesness Personality Inventories'. *British Journal of Criminology*, 14, 376–384.
SMITH, D. E. and SMITH, D. D. (1977). 'Eysenck's psychoticism scale and reconvictions'. *British Journal of Criminology*, 17, 387–388.
STELLER, M. and HUNZE, D. (1984). 'Zur Selbstbeschreibung von Delinquenten im Freiburger Persönlichkeitsinventar (FPI)—Eine Sekundäranalyse empirischer Untersuchungen'. *Zeitschrift für Differentielle und Diagnostische Psychologie*, 5, 87–110.
STUMPHAUZER, J. S. (1973). *Behaviour Therapy with Delinquents*. Springfield: C. C. Thomas.
STUMPHAUZER, J. S. (1979). *Progress in Behaviour Therapy with Delinquents*. Springfield: C. C. Thomas.
SUTHERLAND, E. H. (1931). 'Mental efficiency and crime'. In: K. Young (Ed.), *Social Attitudes*. New York: Henry Holt, 357–375.
TAYLOR, T. and WATT, D. C. (1977). 'The relation of deviant symptoms and behaviour in a normal population to subsequent delinquency and maladjustment'. *Psychological Medicine*, 7, 163–169.
TORGERSEN, S. (1979). 'The nature and origin of common phobic fears'. *British Journal of Psychiatry*, 134, 343–351.
WARDELL, D. and YEUDALL, L. T. (1980). 'A multidimensional approach to criminal disorders: the assessment of impulsivity and its relation to crime'. *Advances in Behaviour Research and Therapy*, 2, 159–177.
WEST, D. J. (1967). *The Young Offender*. New York: International Universities Press.
WEST, D. and FARRINGTON, D. P. (1973). *Who becomes delinquent?* London: Heinemann.
WHITEHILL, M., De MYER-GAPIN, S. and SCOTT, T. J. (1976). 'Stimulation seeking in anti-social preadolescent children'. *Journal of Abnormal Psychology*, 85, 101–104.
WOODWARD, M. (1955). *Low Intelligence and Delinquency*. London: Institute for the Study and Treatment of Delinquency.

YOCHELSON, S. and SAMENOW, S. E. (1976). *The Criminal Personality*. 3 volumes. New York: J. Aronson.
ZUCKERMAN, M. (1979). *Sensation Seeking: Beyond the Optimal Level of Arousal*. Hillsdale: N.J.: Erlbaaum.
ZUCKERMAN, M., EYSENCK, S. B. G. and EYSENCK, H. J. (1978). 'Sensation seeking in England and America: cross-cultural, age and sex comparisons'. *J. Consulting and Clinical Psychology*, 1, 139–149.
ZUCKERMAN, M., BALLENGER, J. C. and PORT, R. M. (1984). 'The neurobiology of some dimensions of personality'. *International Review of Neurobiology*, 25, 391–436.

Hyperactivity, Impulsivity, Sensation Seeking

[4]

British Journal of Psychiatry (1986), **149**, 562–573

Review Article

Childhood Hyperactivity

E. A. TAYLOR

Severe degrees of inattentive and restless behaviour in childhood are a risk factor for later psychological disorders. They have many causes, but a pattern of severe and pervasive hyperactivity with poor concentration in the absence of affective or psychotic disorders should be recognised as a hyperkinetic syndrome. The syndrome is often associated with developmental delays in abilities such as language and motor control. Powerful short-term treatments are available, but long-term ways of promoting normal personality development need more research.

Hyperactivity means an enduring style of behaving in a restless, inattentive, and disorganised fashion. These are common complaints in children, and they have many different causes. When the problems are severe, they can handicap a child's learning and relationships with family and peers, and make him or her vulnerable to further psychiatric disability.

There has been a confusing debate about the existence of a psychiatric condition of hyperactivity. It has been argued that hyperactive behaviours are non-specific features of any psychopathology (e.g. Sandberg, 1981; Shaffer, 1980). Other authorities (e.g. Aman, 1984; Wender, 1971) recognise them as signs of a specific disorder. Most diagnostic schemes recognise a distinct category. DSM III (American Psychiatric Association, 1980) describes a condition of Attention Deficit Disorder that may be with or without hyperactivity. The former (ADDH) is defined by the presence of specified numbers of symptoms of developmentally excessive activity, attention deficit, and impulsiveness, especially at school, and affects about 3% of schoolchildren. ICD-9 (World Health Organisation, 1980) is less precise, but describes a condition of 'hyperkinetic syndrome' that is defined by short attention span and (in younger children) by 'extreme' overactivity not attributable to any other condition (Rutter *et al*, 1975). In practice, this has led to hyperkinesis being a rare diagnosis in the UK.

Historical sketch

Severe overactivity has been recognised as a symptom of disorder in handicapped children for at least a century (Ireland, 1877). A lecture series by the pioneer of paediatrics, Frederic Still, promoted the wider idea that organic disorder of the brain was a major cause of behavioural problems in childhood, through the induction of "defects of moral control" (Still, 1902). His description of affected children was strikingly similar to modern definitions of hyperactivity: it included "an abnormal incapacity for sustained attention", restlessness, fidgetiness, violent outbursts, destructiveness, non-compliance, choreiform movements, and minor congenital anomalies. Still's work helped to create an intellectual climate in which hyperkinesis and brain dysfunction became almost synonymous.

The next step in recognition came with the encephalitis pandemics in the wake of the First World War. Schachar (1986) studied contemporary reports, and commented that severe behavioural sequelae of encephalitis were uncommon and diverse. The cases did, however, emphasise that brain dysfunction is a possible cause of overactive and disinhibited behaviour. In this tradition, Kahn & Cohen (1934) described three cases of "organic drivenness"; their paper was influential in arguing that hyperactivity was the central behavioural abnormality, and that it resulted from disorganisation at the level of the brain stem.

The idea of hyperactivity soon became more widely applied. It was accelerated by the chance discovery of amphetamine's powerful action in reducing hyperactive and disruptive behaviour (Bradley, 1937). By 1938, Levin was able to identify more than two hundred restless children, compare them with normally active controls, and conclude that cerebral lesions caused severe restlessness (while milder degrees resulted from upbringing problems). Strauss's writings in the 1940s and 1950s broadened the idea further (Strauss & Lehtinen, 1947), to the point where hyperactivity—in the absence of a family history of subnormality—became sufficient evidence for a diagnosis of brain damage.

Laufer *et al* (1957) described "hyperkinetic impulse disorder" in children with emotional and conduct problems, most of whom did not have any overt evidence of brain damage. They reported a low threshold for induction of muscle jerks by metrazol and stroboscopic light; amphetamine restored the threshold to normal. The study was intended as a corrective to psychoanalytical views that strongly emphasised parents' contributions to children's problems. It was followed by an explosion of biological and pharmacological research, and by a great increase in the diagnosis of hyperactivity and the prescription of stimulants by American paediatricians.

A task force produced an influential document that regarded hyperactivity as a synonym for 'minimal brain dysfunction', and included an excessively wide range of children's psychological difficulties embracing most problems presented for psychiatric help (Clements, 1966). Hyperactivity, or ADDH, has remained the commonest psychiatric diagnosis for North American children. It has generated much good research, most notably into the cognitive deficits of affected children (reviewed by Douglas, 1983) and the nature of the action of stimulant drugs (reviewed by Cantwell & Carlson, 1978, and Rapoport, 1983).

In sharp contrast, British child psychiatry and paediatrics largely avoided the efflorescence of hyperactivity. Widely quoted papers by Ounsted (1955) and Ingram (1956) described series of severely disturbed children, all of whom were drawn from the authors' patients with overt neurological illnesses. The Isle of Wight surveys (Rutter *et al*, 1970) emphasised the infrequency of hyperkinetic syndrome in a whole population of nine year-olds. The diagnosis is still made sparingly, and around half of those receiving it are intellectually retarded or show signs of neurological illness (Thorley, 1984*a*). This narrow concept suffers, paradoxically, from vagueness of criteria, and has led to much less research than has stemmed from ADDH.

The attitudes of European nations have generally lain between these extremes, and rates of stimulant prescription vary enormously (World Health Organisation, 1985). Several different concepts of hyperactivity have evolved in different traditions, and taxonomic research is particularly necessary.

For clarity, I shall adopt arbitrary definitions to maintain some separation between concepts. 'Overactivity' will mean simply a quantitative excess of movement, without any necessary implication of inattention or disorganisation. 'Hyperactivity', as above, will refer to an excessively high level of inattentive and restless behaviour. 'ADDH' will refer to the DSM–III category and also to other, similar diagnoses used by North American, Australasian, and other workers; it is a relatively broad group, not only because there are few exclusion criteria, but also because impulsiveness and school misbehaviour can contribute to the diagnosis. 'Hyperkinetic syndrome' will be taken to mean the narrower style of diagnosis, often applied to severely disturbed children; criteria for a useful definition will be suggested below.

Taxonomy

Statistical studies make it clear that several symptoms of hyperactivity covary. Short attention span, distractibility, restlessness, constant fidgeting, and off-task activity are the most constant of these. They form a separate component in many independent factor-analytic studies of rating scales (e.g. Trites *et al*, 1982; Taylor & Sandberg, 1984). This 'hyperactivity factor' is distinct from one of defiantly or aggressively anti-social conduct. Nevertheless, some behaviours—such as disruptiveness, excitability, or impulsiveness—can appear as a part of either factor, and are probably non-specific.

The emergence of a factor of hyperactivity is only one step on the road to a rational classification. Most of the children referred for help because of their disruptive behaviour show both hyperactivity and antisocial conduct. Most hyperactive children are defiant or aggressive too; most antisocial children are somewhat hyperactive (Cantwell, 1980; Stewart *et al*, 1981; Taylor, 1986*b*). It is therefore crucial to determine whether the idea of hyperactivity has predictive and discriminative validity: does it predict anything that is different from conduct disorder? Shaffer & Greenhill (1979) demonstrated how resolutely this question had been ignored by investigators, and how little reason there was to base research or clinical practice on a widespread diagnosis such as ADDH. Researchers must therefore identify pure cases of hyperactivity that do not show conduct disorder, and pure cases of conduct disorder for comparison; otherwise, they must separately associate the two dimensions with other clinical features.

Distinction between hyperactivity and conduct disorder

Direct observations of children in playrooms or laboratories have provisionally confirmed that inattentive-restless behaviour (judged from case histories or from research interview techniques) predicts high observed levels of off-task activity, while defiance or aggression does not (Milich *et al*,

1982; Taylor *et al*, 1986*a*). Furthermore, the same groups of investigators have found that hyperactivity at home or at school correlates with the presence of developmental delays (such as motor clumsiness and low IQ) rather than with psychosocial factors. Conduct disorder, by contrast, is linked closely to indices of unsatisfactory family life, such as discord between family members, low levels of expressed warmth, and ineffective styles of coping (Loney *et al*, 1978; Taylor *et al*, 1986*a*). A comparison of pure hyperactivity with pure conduct disorder by Stewart *et al* (1981) also suggested that hyperactive children were symptomatically distinct; on the other hand, the two groups had equally high rates of antisocial relatives (Stewart *et al*, 1980).

These studies were based on clinical groups; McGee *et al* (1984) reported an epidemiologically based sample. Small numbers and missing data made conclusions uncertain, but the children with the single problem of conduct disorder had higher performance IQs than those with pervasive hyperactivity solely: socioeconomic status, perinatal history, and family relationships did not distinguish between the groups.

Existing studies of the taxonomic questions are too few to allow sharp and certain definitions. They suggest (but not conclusively) a valid separation of patterns of disorder. It is therefore worth considering the lessons from some less powerful studies, that have compared hyperactive children with other kinds of disorder, but have not included the requirement that the contrast group should be quite free of hyperactive behaviour.

Koriath *et al* (1985) have described a notable lack of differentiation between children referred to a paediatric psychiatry service in North Carolina who received different DSM–III diagnoses. Those with ADDH alone, ADDH plus other diagnoses, and other psychiatric diagnoses not combined with ADDH, were not even distinct in terms of ratings of symptoms—let alone in demographic factors or psychological test scores. Sandberg *et al* (1978) also found that different levels of severity of hyperactivity carried few implications for aetiology within a group of boys referred to a psychiatric clinic, when 'hyperactivity' was measured by a parental questionnaire, or a teacher rating scale, or a single period of direct observation at a clinic. Each of these measures was imperfect; when they were combined, a small group of children with pervasive hyperactivity across all measures could be separated from the others, and proved to have an earlier onset, more signs of motor clumsiness, and poorer performance on a psychometric test. Similarly, Schachar *et al* (1981) reanalysed the Isle of Wight survey to find that pervasively hyperactive children had poorer performance on a psychometric test, tended to come from lower social classes, and had a worse outcome than children with other kinds of disorder.

The distinction between pervasive and situational hyperactivity may not be very sharp, and some studies find the two groups to be similar (Firestone & Martin, 1979). The general point, however, is that hyperactivity can be validly distinguished from conduct disorder, but that good measures or severe degrees need to be taken if the separation is to be found.

Status of mixed cases

If the above argument is accepted, so that hyperactivity and conduct disorder are seen as separable patterns that overlap greatly in practice, what is the status of mixed cases? If they were clearly to resemble 'pure' conduct disorder or 'pure' hyperactivity, then their position in classification would be clear.

Stewart *et al* (1981) made just such a comparison on the basis of clinical features: children with unsocialised aggression and hyperactivity (identified mainly by parental accounts) resembled those with only unsocialised aggression more than those with only hyperactivity. On the other hand, August & Stewart (1982) presented another analysis of a closely similar series of children. When hyperactivity had to have been noted in several situations, there was little difference between the children with this problem only and those who combined it with unsocialised aggression.

McGee *et al's* (1984) epidemiological study seemed to show that the mixed group were particularly vulnerable. Their reading was worse than that of either pure group, and their short-term outcome was worse. Such a finding is in keeping with a dimensional approach to classification: children with both problems should be predicted to have the associations of both.

A separate class of hyperkinetic syndrome?

Hyperkinesis needs to be separated not only from conduct disorder but also from emotional disorders and specific disabilities of learning. Applications of cluster analysis to simple parent questionnaire ratings have given conflicting results about the presence of a discrete group of hyperactive children (Taylor *et al*, 1986*b*). Some workers find one, some do not. Halo effects and reliance on a single rater are serious problems in this research. A cluster analytical study reported by Taylor *et al* (1986*b*) was based on reliable, independent measures from several sources. The most robust feature of clustering procedures was the emergence of a small group of pervasively hyperactive and inattentive children with few emotional symptoms. This group also showed an early onset, a high rate of delays in cognitive development, and motor clumsiness. In addition, they had a much more marked response to a stimulant drug (methylphenidate).

Definition

Current evidence favours use of a rather restricted diagnostic concept of hyperkinetic syndrome, rather than the ADDH definition. Symptoms of overactivity alone are not sufficient for the diagnosis; it should be based on:

(a) A pattern of markedly inattentive, restless behaviour (not just antisocial, impulsive, or disruptive acts) that is excessive for the child's age and IQ, and a handicap to development

(b) presence of this pattern in two or more situations, such as home, school, and clinic

(c) evidence of inattention, restlessness, or social disinhibition, from direct observation or testing by the diagnostician (i.e. not solely by unconfirmed reports from a child's caretakers)

(d) absence of childhood autism, other pervasive developmental disorders, or affective disorders (including depression, anxiety states, and mania)

(e) onset before the age of six years and duration of at least six months.

Such a diagnosis is useful, though not very common (Taylor, 1986a). It should not be missed simply because an affected child has developed antisocial conduct as well.

Hyperactivity in special subject groups

The discussion of classification above has been based on studies of normally intelligent children in the first few years of their schooling. The behaviour problems of preschool children do not yet have a stable classification (Jablensky et al, 1983). In one investigation, pervasive hyperactivity in children at a day nursery predicted psychological disorder later (Campbell et al, 1977); in another, even pervasive hyperactivity was not a predictive variable among nursery children (Cohen & Minde, 1983). The behaviour matters, as will be shown later, but its classification is obscure, and clinicians should be correspondingly slow to diagnose. Overactivity is also common among intellectually retarded children, but its causes are not yet clarified. Affective disorder, autism, and atypical

pervasive developmental disorder are all important causes of overactivity in this group. I have argued elsewhere (Taylor, 1986a) that some individuals should be regarded as showing a distinct hyperkinetic syndrome, but more research is required.

Prevalence

No secure prevalence rate can be given, because of disputes about what constitutes a case. Hyperactivity is continuously distributed in the population, with smaller numbers at successively higher degrees (Taylor, 1986a). No validated cut-off yet exists, so no prevalence estimate has a scientific basis.

The numbers of schoolchildren who are in practice diagnosed vary wildly: a little over 1% in two US surveys (Lambert et al, 1978; Bosco & Robin, 1980), but only 0.1% in a London borough (data from the Camberwell Register)—half of the latter being intellectually retarded. By contrast, the rates derived from questionnaire surveys of teachers' ratings are much the same in the UK as in the USA and New Zealand, and range from 5% to 20% (Taylor & Sandberg, 1984). The low diagnostic rates in the UK are likely to be due to the diagnostic practice rather than the nature of the children (Prendergast et al, unpublished). Chinese populations are often said to be more docile and attentive, but a survey from Beijing, based on a combination of teacher ratings and medical diagnosis of ADDH, gave comparatively high rates (3–7% in different areas) (Shen et al, 1985). Hyperactivity, in some sense, evidently exists in many cultures; it remains to be seen whether it always takes the same form.

The prevalence of ADDH in boys is higher than in girls in the ratio of about 4:1 in American clinics (Ross & Ross, 1982). The ratio was similar for the narrower hyperkinetic syndrome at a London clinic, but fell to 1.6:1 for children with mental retardation (Taylor, 1986a). Girls with the diagnosis of hyperkinetic syndrome, or with the symptom of 'gross overactivity', were more likely than affected boys to show delays in cognitive development and neurological disorders such as epilepsy (Taylor, 1986a). The reason for the greater vulnerability of boys has not yet been explained. Several theories implicate damaged brain function. The greater vulnerability of male brains may well be a part of the explanation, but has not been shown to account for the whole of the enhanced risk. Adults are often more tolerant of hyperactivity in girls than in boys, at least before school age (Battle & Lacey, 1957).

Epidemiological studies in different cultures are needed to cast light on what is central to and universal about the conditions and what is peripheral and culturally determined.

Aetiology

In spite of much research, the causes of hyperkinesis remain uncertain. Most studies have compared children referred to clinics, because of mixed behaviour problems including hyperactivity, with controls drawn from the normal population. When positive findings appear in such a design, it is hard to know whether they are associated with hyperactivity, with behaviour problems generally, with the learning disorders that are often associated, or with the factors that lead to referral to clinics.

Brain damage

Brain disease with localising neurological signs is uncommon in children with ADDH, and is specifically excluded from most research series. The narrower hyperkinetic syndrome, by contrast, is often diagnosed in children with damaged brains. Table I summarises the findings in those investigations that have used an ICD-9 style of diagnosis and reported the range of diagnoses in various samples of children. Brain damage gives rise to a high rate of virtually all the psychiatric syndromes of childhood, rather than to any pathognomonic syndrome (Rutter *et al*, 1970). Accordingly, the best index for comparing groups is not the numbers with the diagnosis of hyperkinesis, but the rate of hyperkinesis as a percentage of all diagnoses made (Table I).

The relatively high rate in neurologically handicapped groups implies that there may be a specific vulnerability to hyperkinesis in brain-damaged children. This conclusion is not secure, for the diagnosis could in part be determined by judgements about neurological status. Explicit and independent criteria for case definition need to be developed. If there is a specific vulnerability, we do not know whether it resides in the brain damage itself or in the generalised intellectual retardation which can result. High rates of structural brain damage were reported by Reid (1980). Jenkins & Stable (1971) matched severely hyperkinetic cases (from a case register of intellectually subnormal people) with subnormal but not hyperkinetic controls: they found higher rates of cerebral palsy and other evidence of structural lesions in the hyperkinetic patients. However, the hyperkinetic patients were also more retarded on a global measure of development. Thorley (1984*a*), using the case records of severely hyperkinetic children, matched psychiatric controls individually for IQ level: no significant difference in rates of brain damage then appeared.

Severe hyperkinesis may have a specific neuropsychiatric predisposition; this should be investigated further. However, there is no reason to suppose that mild hyperactivity is therefore caused by mild brain dysfunction.

Perinatal trauma to the brain

This is not usually the cause of hyperactive behaviour. Case-control studies of children showing high levels of hyperactivity have usually shown little or no increase in rates of perinatal injury, retrospectively assessed (e.g. Minde *et al*, 1968; Gillberg *et al*, 1983). Cohort studies of children of low birth weight (Nelligan *et al*, 1976), or of children with complicated deliveries (Nichols & Chen, 1981), make it clear that

TABLE I
Prevalence of clinically diagnosed hyperkinetic syndrome (ICD-9) as a percentage of children with psychiatric diagnoses

Study	Type of study	Patient group		
		Neurologically normal children: %	Neurological disorders or epilepsy: %	Mental subnormality: %
Rutter *et al* (1970)	Epidemiological survey	~1	12	26[1]
Corbett (1979)	Case register	—	—	8
Reid (1980)	Clinic outpatients	—	—	15
Thorley (1984*a*)	Clinical records	0.9	—	2
Gillberg *et al* (1986)	Epidemiological survey	—	—	10

1. Severely handicapped children, not attending school.

hyperactivity is not particularly common in the later lives of such children. There is a small increase—as there is for other kinds of behaviour problem—but even this increase is partly attributable to coexisting family problems. Indeed, the Isle of Kauai study (Werner & Smith, 1977) suggested that perinatal damage only increased vulnerability in children with less advantaged backgrounds.

Minimal brain dysfunction

Minimal brain dysfunction has been intensively sought, so far largely in vain. Extensive reviews have concluded that there are few unequivocally positive findings of biological abnormalities in hyperactive children (Rie & Rie, 1980; Rutter, 1983*b*). When abnormalities have been found, their meaning is usually unclear. 'Soft' neurological signs (i.e. clumsiness and lack of coordination) are commoner in markedly hyperactive children than in other sorts of psychological disorder (Werry *et al*, 1972; Sandberg *et al*, 1978; Taylor *et al*, 1986*b*). However, they are not yet valid as a sign of cerebral or cerebellar pathology because of uncertainty about what causes them (Taylor, 1983*a*).

Neurophysiological unresponsiveness

Neurophysiological unresponsiveness to stimuli is another replicated finding. Hyperactive children, by comparison with controls, probably show normal resting levels of autonomic nervous system activity. However, peripheral autonomic responses and central averaged evoked EEG responses both suggest that a new or important stimulus produces a smaller change in hyperactive children (Taylor, 1985*a*). This lack of reaction may not be specific to hyperactive children: diminished physiological responsiveness also characterises children with learning disorders (e.g. Maxwell *et al*, 1974) and unsocialised aggression (Delamater & Lahey, 1983). Since these three clinical problems often coexist, which of them (or what other associated problem) is linked to unresponsiveness? We shall only know when further research untangles the various problems.

Attention deficit

Hyperactive children fail to sustain organised attention, and score poorly on psychological tests related to attention (Douglas, 1983). However, test performance can also be upset by many different sorts of psychopathology (Shaffer, 1980), and the impairment has not yet been shown to be specifically an attention problem. Although hyperactive children

behave impulsively, psychological tests of impulsiveness suggest that they respond too slowly, not too quickly (Sergeant, 1981; Sandberg *et al*, 1978; Firestone & Martin, 1979). Although they behave distractedly, the addition of distracting information does not particularly disrupt test performance (Douglas & Peters, 1979). The deficit is present in both short tests, such as the digit span, and long ones, such as continuous performance tests. It is even manifest in a downwards shift of IQ; indeed, when IQ is allowed for, hyperactivity shows much reduced (but still present) association with tests of concentration. There is as yet no sign of a structural deficit at any one stage of processing information—rather, there is a high-level failure to allocate resources sensibly to the task in hand and to maintain self-control in organising responses.

Animal models

Animal models of hyperactivity emphasise its heterogeneity. Prefrontal damage in monkeys, ventral tegmental lesions in rats, chemical damage to dopamine and noradrenaline synthesis, foetal exposure to lead, neonatal hypoxia, and social isolation can all produce a combination of overactivity and abnormal learning that is reversible by amphetamines (Robbins & Sahakian, 1979).

Genetic inheritance

No really persuasive study has yet been made on the effects of genetic inheritance. Full siblings of hyperactive children are more likely to be affected than are half-siblings (Safer, 1973), and hyperactive children, like antisocial children, have many relatives who themselves show sociopathy or alcoholism (Stewart *et al*, 1980). However, family interactions could explain these findings as well as genetic inheritance. The biological parents of hyperactive children living with their natural families were more likely to have had behaviour problems than the adoptive parents of adopted children (Cantwell, 1975), but this study could not compare biological with adopted parents of the same children. The adopted-away offspring of psychiatric patients were unusually likely to be hyperkinetic (Cunningham *et al*, 1975), but a transmission of hyperactivity itself was not demonstrated. Comparisons of dizygotic with monozygotic twins suggested that the latter were more concordant with regard to several temperamental dimensions, including overactivity (Torgersen & Kringlen, 1978); twin studies of children with diagnosable conditions have not yet been reported.

568

Chemical agents

The most controversial aspects of the aetiology of hyperactivity have come from theories implicating exogenous toxins, such as lead and food additives.

Severe lead poisoning causes brain damage, and its sequelae include hyperactivity. Lower levels of exposure can cause hyperactivity in animals, but their significance in children is still debated. High levels within the normal range are associated with small increases in problem behaviour and with lower IQ (Needleman *et al*, 1979; Yule *et al*, 1981). It is still uncertain whether these correlations reflect the damaging effect of lead at low levels of exposure, or an association with other kinds of social adversity (Rutter, 1983*a*). In any event, lead exposure is not the major cause of hyperactive behaviour.

In spite of the scientific uncertainties, there is a brisk trade in testing hair for lead and other minerals and in selling supposed therapies. The enterprise should not be encouraged: commercial hair measurement is unreliable (Barrett, 1985), and the proprietary treatments are unevaluated.

Food dyes and preservatives were implicated by Feingold (1975), with the suggestion that hyperactive children showed a genetically determined intolerance. Unfortunately, most trials involving elimination of food additives have given rather disappointing results: some children's behaviour improves for a while when a diet is started, but it does not usually worsen again if additives are given in a double-blind placebo-controlled fashion (Mattes & Gittelman, 1981). Occasionally, however, some children do seem to show a genuine improvement in behaviour due to the physical effect of removing additives (Weiss *et al*, 1980). The improvement is not confined to hyperactivity, but extends to 'difficult' behaviour generally. A recent trial involving exclusion of a wide range of different foods from the diet suggested that more children can be helped by a radical exclusion of many allergens; however, the trial was based on a selected sample with a high prevalence of physical allergies (Egger *et al*, 1985). Since some parents become preoccupied with diet to the exclusion of all else, more research is quite pressing.

Psychosocial factors

The psychological environment can determine the extent to which children are attentive (Taylor, 1980). It is therefore logical to seek evidence of psychosocial adversity in the hyperactive. Affected children, ascertained in a population survey of children with minimal brain dysfunction, can be distinguished from normal controls by signs of unsatisfactory family life

(Gillberg *et al*, 1983). Children who have grown up in institutions are particularly likely to be hyperactive in their classrooms, even after they have been adopted into a family home (Tizard & Hodges, 1978; Roy, unpublished). Children known to have been unwanted (because their mothers sought a termination of pregnancy unsuccessfully) are more likely to be excitable, unsociable, and hyperactive when they go to school (Matějcček *et al*, 1985).

Studies such as these are vulnerable to the same criticisms that have already been levelled at investigations of physical causes: they show correlations, not causes, and point the clinician only towards the need for comprehensive assessment.

Developmental course

Hyperactivity most commonly presents during the early years of schooling. Retrospective enquiry usually finds an onset before the age of five and often before the age of two.

Infants vary greatly in their activity levels, but the individual differences are not very stable over time. Indeed, one careful study suggested an inversion in the intensity of behaviour between the age of 3–4 days and that of $2\frac{1}{2}$ years (Bell *et al*, 1971): the neonates with highest magnitude, frequency, and speed of behaviours became the two year-olds with least vigour and lowest responsiveness.

In preschool children, overactivity is a common complaint made by parents, but sometimes reflects impaired parental tolerance rather than an abnormality of development. Although (as considered above) no clear hyperkinetic syndrome has been validated for this age-group, nevertheless, the complaint of overactivity should not be ignored: it predicts later antisocial disorder quite strongly (Richman *et al*, 1982).

From the age of about three years, the normal course of development involves a reduction of general level of activity in some settings but not in others (Routh, 1980). The appropriate modulation of activity can therefore be impaired by developmental delay, whatever the cause. The resulting restlessness becomes more of a problem as schooling proceeds and successively greater demands are made on children's powers of attention and self-control.

The continuities between the early years of schooling and outcome in adolescence have been examined by many follow-up studies, mostly of children referred to clinics with ADDH, contrasted with normal controls from the community (see reviews by Weiss, 1983, and Thorley, 1984*b*). The investigations are limited by design weaknesses (highlighted by

Shaffer & Greenhill, 1979), but taken as a whole, they suggest that the broad group of hyperactive children do not simply grow out of it. In adolescence, they tend to remain somewhat impulsive and inattentive, and to be characterised by high rates of academic failure, antisocial behaviour, and delinquency. An epidemiological study in England also found pervasive hyperactivity to be a strong predictor of persistence of psychiatric disorder between the ages of nine and 14 (Schachar *et al*, 1981).

There is even some evidence that severe overactivity remains a risk factor for adolescents when the controls themselves show antisocial conduct. Thorley (1984*b*) identified children with the hyperkinetic syndrome seen at a psychiatric hospital, followed them into adult life, and compared them with matched cases of conduct disorder from the same hospital. Their adolescent outcome was characterised by more episodes of psychiatric treatment, more epileptic fits, more accidental injuries, and more placements in special schools.

In adult life, most children with ADDH do not show diagnosable illness, but the rate of antisocial and impulsive personality disorder is high (Hechtman *et al*, 1984). It is probably no higher than that of less hyperactive children with conduct disorder (Thorley, 1984*b*); however, the degree of conduct disorder in childhood and the disturbance of family relationships are better predictors of an adult antisocial adjustment than is hyperactivity itself. It seems likely that pervasive hyperactivity has its major effect on development by increasing the risk that affected individuals will develop complicating problems such as educational failure or antisocial conduct disorder. It they can be protected from such complications, then a gradual improvement in adjustment in adult life can be expected.

Treatment

Multiple factors interact to cause hyperactivity; its course is largely determined by complicating adversity. Diagnosis is therefore not enough to dictate treatment; a wide assessment and a range of interventions are needed.

Drug treatment

Amphetamines and related central nervous system stimulants are the commonest treatment for ADDH in the USA, being given to more than 1 schoolchild in 100 (Bosco & Robin, 1980; Lambert *et al*, 1978). By contrast, they are so rarely used in the UK that the first-line drug, methylphenidate, has recently been withdrawn for lack of demand. Dogmatic guidelines are therefore inappropriate.

Scores of double-blind trials have shown that stimulants are more effective than placebo in suppressing hyperactive behaviour for children with ADDH (Taylor, 1985*b*). These trials are based on relatively short periods, from a few weeks to a few months; the long-term effect is less clear. Some children who have taken amphetamines for long periods are no longer getting any benefit (Charles *et al*, 1979). Others show worsened symptoms when their drug is removed (Sleator *et al*, 1974). Even if symptoms are controlled in the long term, it does not follow that long-term development will be improved. Follow-ups of treated and untreated groups leave it uncertain whether drug treatment is of any use over a period of years (Weiss, 1983). Accordingly, long-term treatment should only be embarked on when there is clear evidence of short-term benefit, and good supervision (including regular periods off-drug) can be provided to monitor the continuing need for therapy.

The short-term action of drugs is not paradoxical or unique to hyperkinetic children: the effects are qualitatively similar in hyperactive children, normal children (Rapoport *et al*, 1978), normal adults (Weiss & Laties, 1962), and conduct-disordered children (Taylor, 1983*b*). In all these groups, they act as stimulants, not sedatives; they reduce high-frequency and off-task behaviours, and they improve performance on a variety of psychometric tests. The mechanism probably involves catecholamine neurotransmitters (Rapoport & Zametkin, 1986). Though the action is similar in kind in different groups, it varies greatly in degree.

The best and clearest indication for stimulant medication is the uncommon nuclear hyperkinetic syndrome of pervasive and severe hyperactivity and cognitive impairment in the absence of overt emotional disorder, presenting in primary schoolchildren of normal or only mildly retarded intelligence. There are, however, other indications too. Sometimes it is desirable to induce a rapid reduction in restless, disruptive behaviour in order to bring about a change of attitude in the child's caretakers. Sometimes medication is necessary to allow a programme of learning to operate. In these circumstances, stimulants may be given to children with lesser degrees of hyperactivity. Whatever the indication, stimulants need to be planned as an adjunct to educational or psychological help.

Careful monitoring is needed, and the reader is referred to fuller accounts of drugs and their prescription (e.g. Barkley, 1981; Taylor, 1985*b*).

570   TAYLOR

Dietary treatments

Dietary treatments are very popular with parents, and present a dilemma because of the difficulty of recognising those few children who may be helped. The diets carry the hazards of poor nutrition and the neglect of other treatments. In present knowledge, they should only be prescribed with expert help, but it is reasonable to support parents who have themselves decided on a trial.

Psychological treatments

The techniques of behaviour modification can be applied in many different ways to the treatment of hyperactivity (Yule, 1986). Operant conditioning is of demonstrated value in the short-term reduction of off-task behaviour and increase of constructive activity in the classroom. Although it may sometimes be less potent than stimulant drugs (Gittelman *et al*, 1980), it is also more widely acceptable.

Reward-based schemes of learning can also be used to reduce gross motor activity and fidgetiness (Christensen & Sprague, 1973), but the mere lessening of activity is seldom enough to help children's adjustment. They also need to learn more positive skills of learning and social interaction.

Cognitive-behavioural therapy has promise as a tool for teaching techniques of self-control and problem-solving (Bornstein & Quevillon, 1976). Systematic evaluations have indicated that it can improve performance on laboratory tests, for instance of impulsiveness (Douglas, 1983). Its value in promoting longer-term adjustment and real-life performance is not yet established.

Considerations of developmental course emphasise the importance of helping wider aspects of a child's predicament than hyperactivity alone. Adverse and coercive styles of family interaction can readily develop, and may indicate behavioural techniques of modifying such interactions, or the training of parents in behavioural skills, or the approaches of conjoint family therapy. Educational failure is so common and important that a liaison with schools, and a consideration of special education needs, should be part of every psychiatric assessment. Many affected children acquire a very negative view of themselves as 'weird', 'rubbish', or 'stupid'; individual sessions therefore have a counselling purpose as well as that of instilling skills. If drug treatment is to be used, it needs full and repeated discussion with child and parents, lest it lead to scapegoating or to a glib alibi for bad behaviour.

Conclusions

Research continues, but provisional conclusions can be made. Severe degrees of inattentive and restless behaviour constitute a major problem for children's development, and are different from (but overlap with) conduct disorder. They probably need more recognition by psychiatrists and teachers in the UK, but may be over-diagnosed in the USA. Delays in motor and cognitive development are often associated, and may well be aetiologically important; however, they are not yet sufficiently specifically described to justify the view that affected children have a structural deficit in the processing of information from the environment. Powerful short-term treatments are available, in the shape of stimulant drugs and behaviour modification, but their long-term effect is inadequately known. Family, school, and peer relationships are usually more important than the core problem in determining eventual adult outcome. Clinical services therefore need to develop a range of treatments for affected children.

References

AMAN, M. G. (1984) Hyperactivity: nature of the syndrome and its natural history. *Journal of Autism and Developmental Disabilities*, 14, 39–56.

AMERICAN PSYCHIATRIC ASSOCIATION (1980) *Diagnostic and Statistical Manual of Mental Disorders* (3rd ed.) (DSM–III) Washington DC: APA.

AUGUST, G. J. & STEWART, M. A. (1982) Is there a syndrome of pure hyperactivity? *British Journal of Psychiatry*, 140, 305–311.

BARKLEY, R. A. (1981) *Hyperactive Children: A Handbook for Diagnosis and Treatment*. Chichester: John Wiley & Sons.

BATTLE, E. S. & LACEY, B. (1982) A context for hyperactivity in children over time. *Child Development*, 43, 757–773.

BARRETT, S. (1985) Commercial hair analysis: science or scam? *Journal of the American Medical Association*, 254, 1041–1045.

BELL, R. Q., WELLER, G. M. & WALDROP, M. R. (1971) Newborn and preschooler: organisation of behavior and relations between periods. *Monographs of the Society for Research in Child Development*, 36, 1–145 (Serial No. 142).

BORNSTEIN, P. H. & QUEVILLON, R. P. (1976) The effects of a self-instructional package on overactive preschool boys. *Journal of Applied Behavior Analysis*, 9, 179–188.

BOSCO, J. J. & ROBIN, S. S. (1980) Hyperkinesis: prevalence and treatment. In *Hyperactive Children: The Social Ecology of Identification and Treatment* (eds C. K. Whalen & B. Henker). New York: Academic Press.

BRADLEY, C. (1937) The behavior of children receiving benzedrine. *American Journal of Psychiatry*, 94, 557–585.

CAMPBELL, S. B., ENDMAN, M. W. & BERNFELD, G. (1977) A 3-year follow-up of hyperactive preschoolers into elementary school. *Journal of Child Psychology and Psychiatry*, 18, 239–249.

CHILDHOOD HYPERACTIVITY   571

CANTWELL, D. (1975) Genetic studies of hyperactive children: psychiatric illness in biologic and adopting parents. In *Genetic Research in Psychiatry* (eds R. Fieve, D. Rosenthal & H. Brill). Baltimore: Johns Hopkins University Press.

—— (1980) Hyperactivity and antisocial behavior revisted: a critical review of the literature. In *Biophysical Vulnerabilities to Delinquency* (ed. D. Lewis). New York: Spectrum.

—— & CARLSON, G. A. (1978) Stimulants. In *Pediatric Psychopharmacology: The Use of Behavior Modifying Drugs in Children* (ed. J. S. Werry). New York: Brunner/Mazel.

CHARLES, L., SCHAIN, R. J. & GUTHRIE, D. (1979) Long-term use and discontinuation of methylphenidate with hyperactive children. *Developmental Medicine and Child Neurology*, 6, 758–764.

CHRISTENSEN, D. & SPRAGUE, R. (1973) Reduction of hyperactive behavior by conditioning procedures alone and combined with methylphenidate (Ritalin). *Behaviour Research and Therapy*, 11, 331–334.

CLEMENTS, S. D. (1966) *Minimal Brain Dysfunction in Children: Terminology and Identification. Phase One of a Three-year Project.* (NINDB Monograph No. 3.) Washington DC: US Department of Health Education and Welfare.

COHEN, N. J. & MINDE, K. (1983) The 'hyperactive syndrome' in kindergarten children. Comparison of children with pervasive and situational syndromes. *Journal of Child Psychology and Psychiatry*, 24, 443–456.

CORBETT, J. A. (1979) Psychiatric morbidity and mental retardation. In *Psychiatric Illness and Mental Handicap* (eds F. E. James & R. P. Snaith). London: Gaskell.

CUNNINGHAM, L., CADORET, R., LOFTUS, R. & EDWARDS, J. E. (1975) Studies of adoptees from psychiatrically disturbed biological parents. *British Journal of Psychiatry*, 126, 534–539.

DELAMATER, A. M. & LAHEY, B. B. (1983) Physiological correlates of conduct problems and anxiety in hyperactive and learning-disabled children. *Journal of Abnormal Child Psychology*, 11, 85–100.

DOUGLAS, V. I. (1983) Attentional and cognitive problems. In *Developmental Neuropsychiatry* (ed. M. Rutter). New York: Guilford Press.

—— & Peters, K. G. (1979) Toward a clearer definition of the attentional deficit of hyperactive children. In *Attention and the Development of Cognitive Skills* (eds G. A. Hale & M. Lewis). New York: Plenum.

EGGER, J., CARTER, C. M., GRAHAM, P. J., GUMLEY, D. & SOOTHILL, J. F. (1985) Controlled trial of oligoantigenic treatment in the hyperkinetic syndrome. *The Lancet*, i, 540–545.

FEINGOLD, B. F. (1975) Hyperkinesis and learning disabilities linked to artificial food flavors and colors. *American Journal of Nursing*, 75, 797–803.

FIRESTONE, P. & MARTIN, J. E. (1979) An analysis of the hyperactive syndrome: a comparison of hyperactive, behavior problem, asthmatic and normal children. *Journal of Abnormal Child Psychology*, 7, 261–273.

GILLBERG, C., CARLSTRÖM, G. & RASMUSSEN, P. (1983) Hyperkinetic disorders in children with perceptual, motor and attentional deficits. *Journal of Child Psychology and Psychiatry*, 24, 233–246.

——, PERSSON, E., GRUFMAN, M. & THEMNER, U. (1986) Psychiatric disorders in mildly and severely mentally retarded urban children and adolescents; epidemiological aspects. *British Journal of Psychiatry*, 149, 68–74.

GITTELMAN, R., ABIKOFF, H., POLLACK, E., KLEIN, D. F., KATZ, S. & MATTES, J. (1980) A controlled trial of behavior modification and methylphenidate in hyperactive children. In *Hyperactive Children: The Social Ecology of Identification and Treatment* (eds C. K. Whalen & B. Henker). New York: Academic Press.

HECHTMAN, L., WEISS, G., PERLMAN, T. & AMSEL, R. (1984) Hyperactives as young adults: initial predictors of adult outcome. *Journal of the American Academy of Child Psychiatry*, 23, 250–260.

INGRAM, T. T. S. (1956) A characteristic form of overactive behaviour in brain damaged children. *Journal of Mental Science*, 102, 550–558.

IRELAND, W. H. (1877) *On Idiocy and Imbecility.* London: Churchill.

JABLENSKY, A., SARTORIUS, N., HIRSCHFELD, R. & PARDES, H. (1983) Diagnosis and classification of mental disorders and alcohol- and drug-related problems: a research agenda for the 1980s. *Psychological Medicine*, 13, 907–921.

JENKINS, R. L. & STABLE, G. (1971) Special characteristics of retarded children rated as severely hyperactive. *Child Psychiatry and Human Development*, 2, 26–31.

KAHN, E. & COHEN, L. H. (1934) Organic drivenness: a brain-stem syndrome and an experience with case reports. *New England Journal of Medicine*, 210, 748–756.

KORIATH, U., GUALTIERI, C. T., van BOURGONDIEN, M. E., QUADE, D. & WERRY, J. S. (1985) Construct validity of clinical diagnosis in pediatric psychiatry: relationship among measures. *Journal of the American Academy of Child Psychiatry*, 24, 429–436.

LAMBERT, N. M., SANDOVAL, J. & SASSONE, D. (1978) Prevalence of hyperactivity in elementary school children as a function of social system definers. *American Journal of Orthopsychiatry*, 48, 446–463.

LAUFER, M. DENHOFF, E. & SOLOMONS, G. (1957) Hyperkinetic impulse disorder in children's behavior problems. *Psychosomatic Medicine*, 19, 38–49.

LEVIN, P. M. (1983) Restlessness in children. *Archives of Neurology & Psychiatry*, 39, 764–770.

LONEY, J., LANGHORNE, J. & PATERNITE, C. (1978) An empirical basis for subgrouping the hyperkinetic/minimal brain dysfunction syndrome. *Journal of Abnormal Psychology*, 87, 431–441.

MCGEE, R., WILLIAMS, S. & SILVA, P. A. (1984) Behavioral and developmental characteristics of aggressive, hyperactive and aggressive-hyperactive boys. *Journal of the American Academy of Child Psychiatry*, 23, 270–279.

MATĚJCCEK, Z., DYTRYCH, Z. & SCHÜLLER, V. (1985) Follow-up study of children born to women denied abortion. In *Abortion: Medical Progress and Social Implications* (eds R. Porter & M. O'Connor). Ciba Foundation Symposium 115. London: Pitman.

MATTES, J. A. & GITTELMAN, R. (1981) Effects of artificial food colorings in children with hyperactive symptoms. *Archives of General Psychiatry*, 38, 714–718.

MAXWELL, A. E., FENWICK, P., FENTON, G. W. & DOLLIMORE, J. (1974) Reading ability and brain function: a simple statistical model. *Psychological Medicine*, 4, 274–280.

MILICH, R., LONEY, J. & LANDAU, S. (1982) The independent dimensions of hyperactivity and aggression: a validation with playroom observation data. *Journal of Abnormal Psychology*, 91, 183–198.

MINDE, K., WEBB, G. & SYKES, D. (1968) Studies on the hyperactive child: VI. Prenatal and paranatal factors associated with hyperactivity. *Developmental Medicine and Child Neurology*, 10, 355–363.

NEEDLEMAN, H., GUNNOE, C., LEVITON, A., REED, R. PERESIE, H., MAHER, C. & BARRETT, P. (1979) Deficits in psychologic and classroom performances of children with elevated dentine lead levels. *New England Journal of Medicine*, 300, 689–695.

572   TAYLOR

NELIGAN, G. A. KOLVIN, I., SCOTT, D. MCL. & GARSIDE, R. F. (1976) *Born Too Soon or Born Too Small.* Clinics in Developmental Medicine No. 61. London SIMP/Heinemann.

NICHOLS, P. L. & CHEN, T.-C. (1981) *Minimal Brain Dysfunction: A Prospective Study.* Hillsdale, NJ: Erlbaum.

OUNSTED, C. (1955) The hyperkinetic syndrome in epileptic children. *The Lancet, ii,* 303–311.

RAPOPORT, J. L. (1983) The use of drugs: trends in research. In *Developmental Neuropsychiatry* (ed. M. Rutter). New York: Guilford.

——, BUCHSBAUM, M., WEINGARTNER, H., ZAHN, T., LUDLOW, C. & MIKKELSEN, E. (1978) Dextroamphetamine: behavioral and cognitive effects in normal prepubertal boys. *Science,* 199, 560–563.

—— & ZAMETKIN, A. (1986) Critique of drug treatment of hyperactivity. In *Attention Deficit Disorder: 5th High Point Hospital Symposium* (eds J. Sergeant & L. Bloomingdale) (in press).

REID, A. H. (1980) Psychiatric disorders in mentally handicapped children: a clinical and follow-up study. *Journal of Mental Deficiency Research,* 24, 287–298.

RICHMAN, N., STEVENSON, J. & GRAHAM, P. J. (1982) *Preschool to School: A Behavioural Study.* London and New York: Academic Press.

RIE, H. E. & RIE, E. D. (1980) (eds) *Handbook of Minimal Brain Dysfunctions: A Critical View.* New York: Wiley.

ROBBINS, T. W. & SAHAKIAN, B. J. (1979) 'Paradoxical' effects of psychomotor stimulant drugs in hyperactive children from the standpoint of behavioural pharmacology. *Neuropharmacology,* 18, 931–950.

ROSS, D. M. & ROSS, S. A. (1982) *Hyperactivity: Current Issues, Research and Theory.* New York: Wiley.

ROUTH, D. K. (1980) Developmental and social aspects of hyperactivity. In *Hyperactive Children: The Social Ecology of Identification and Treatment* (eds C. K. Whalen & B. Henker). New York: Academic Press.

RUTTER, M. (1983a) Low level lead exposure: Source, effects and implications. In *Lead versus Health: Sources and Effects of Low Level Lead Exposure* (eds M. Rutter & R. Russell Jones). Chichester: John Wiley & Sons.

—— (ed.) (1983b) *Developmental Neuropsychiatry.* New York: Guilford Press.

——, GRAHAM, P. & YULE, W. (1970) *A Neuropsychiatric Study in Childhood.* London: Spastics International Medical Publications.

——, SHAFFER, D. & STURGE, C. (1975) *A Guide to a Multiaxial Classification Scheme for Psychiatric Disorders in Childhood and Adolescence.* London: Institute of Psychiatry.

SAFER, D. J. (1973) A familial factor in minimal brain dysfunction. *Behavior Genetics,* 3, 175–186.

SANDBERG, S. T. (1981) The overinclusiveness of the diagnosis of hyperkinetic syndrome. In *Strategic Interventions for Hyperactive Children* (ed. R. Gittelman). New York: M. E. Sharpe.

——, RUTTER, M. & TAYLOR, E. (1978) Hyperkinetic disorder in psychiatric clinic attenders. *Developmental Medicine and Child Neurology,* 20, 279–299.

SCHACHAR, R. J. (1986) Hyperkinetic syndrome: historical development of the concept. In *The Overactive Child* (ed. E. A. Taylor). Clinics in Developmental Medicine No. 97. London: MacKeith Press/Blackwell.

——, RUTTER, M. & SMITH, A. (1981) The characteristics of situationally and pervasively hyperactive children: implications for syndrome definition. *Journal of Child Psychology & Psychiatry,* 22, 375–392.

SERGEANT, J. A. (1981) *Attentional Studies in Hyperactivity.* Groningen: Rijksuniversiteit te Groningen.

SHAFFER, D. (1980) An approach to the validation of clinical syndromes in childhood. In *The Ecosystem of the 'Sick' Child* (eds S. Salzinger, J. Antrobus & J. Glick). London: Academic Press.

—— & Greenhill, L. (1979) A critical note on the predictive validity of 'The Hyperkinetic Syndrome'. *Journal of Child Psychology & Psychiatry,* 20, 61–72.

SHEN, Y.-C., WONG, Y.-F. & YANG, X.-L. (1985) An epidemiological investigation of minimal brain dysfunction in six elementary schools in Beijing. *Journal of Child Psychology & Psychiatry,* 26, 777–788.

SLEATOR, E., NEUMANN, H. & SPRAGUE, R. (1974) Hyperactive children: a continuous long-term placebo-controlled follow-up. *Journal of the American Medical Association,* 229, 316–317.

STEWART, M. A., DEBLOIS, C. S. & CUMMINGS, C. (1980) Psychiatric disorder in the parents of hyperactive boys and those with conduct disorder. *Journal of Child Psychology & Psychiatry,* 21, 283–292.

——, CUMMINGS, C., SINGER, S. & DEBLOIS, C. S. (1981) The overlap between hyperactive and unsocialized aggressive children. *Journal of Child Psychology & Psychiatry,* 22, 35–46.

STILL, G. F. (1902) The Coulstonian lectures on some abnormal psychical conditions in children. *The Lancet, i,* 1008–1012, 1077–1082, 1163–1168.

STRAUSS, A. & LEHTINEN, L. (1947) *Psychopathology and Education of the Brain-Injured Child.* New York: Grune & Stratton.

TAYLOR, E. (1980) Development of attention. In *Scientific Foundations of Developmental Psychiatry* (ed. M. Rutter). London: Heinemann.

—— (1983a) Measurement issues and approaches. In *Developmental Neuropsychiatry* (ed. M. Rutter). New York: Guilford Press.

—— (1983b) Drug response and diagnostic validation. In *Developmental Neuropsychiatry* (ed. M. Rutter). New York: Guilford Press.

—— (1985a) Syndromes of overactivity and attention deficit. In *Child and Adolescent Psychiatry: Modern Approaches* (2nd ed.) (eds M. Rutter & L. Hersov). Oxford: Blackwell.

—— (1985b) Drug Treatment. In *Child and Adolescent Psychiatry: Modern Approaches* (2nd ed.) (eds M. Rutter & L. Hersov). Oxford: Blackwell.

—— (ed.) (1986a) *The Overactive Child.* Clinics in Developmental Medicine No. 97. London: MacKeith Press/Blackwell.

—— (1986b) Nosology of attention deficit and conduct disorders. In *Assessment, Diagnosis and Classification in Child and Adolescent Psychopathology* (eds M. Rutter, H. Tuma & I. Lann). New York: Guilford Press (in press).

—— & SANDBERG, S. (1984) Hyperactive behavior in English schoolchildren: a questionnaire survey. *Journal of Abnormal Child Psychology,* 12, 143–156.

——, SCHACHAR, R., THORLEY, G. & WIESELBERG, M. (1986a) Conduct disorder and hyperactivity: I. Separation of hyperactivity and antisocial conduct in British child psychiatric patients. *British Journal of Psychiatry* (in press).

——, EVERITT, B., THORLEY, G., SCHACHAR, R., RUTTER, M. & WIESELBERG, M. (1986b) Conduct disorder and hyperactivity: II. A cluster analytic approach to the identification of a behavioural syndrome. *British Journal of Psychiatry* (in press).

THORLEY, G. (1984a) Hyperkinetic syndrome of childhood: clinical characteristics. *British Journal of Psychiatry,* 144, 16–24.

—— (1984b) *Clinical characteristics and outcome of hyperactive children.* PhD Thesis: University of London.

TIZARD, B. & HODGES, J. (1978) The effect of early institutional rearing on the development of eight year old children. *Journal of Child Psychology & Psychiatry,* 19, 99–118.

CHILDHOOD HYPERACTIVITY   573

TORGERSEN, A. M. & KRINGLEN, E. (1978) Genetic aspects of temperamental differences in infants: their cause as shown through twin studies. *Journal of the American Academy of Child Psychiatry*, 17, 433–444.

TRITES, R. L. BLOUIN, A. G. A. & LAPRADE, K. (1982) Factor Analysis of the Conners Teachers Rating Scale based on a large normative sample. *Journal of Consulting and Clinical Psychology*, 50, 615–623.

WEISS, B. & LATIES, V. (1962) Enhancement of human performance by caffeine and the amphetamines. *Pharmacological Review*, 14, 1–36.

—, WILLIAMS, J. H., MARGEN, S. ABRAMS, B. CAAN, B., CITRON, L., COX, C., MCKIBBEN, J., OGAR, D. & SCHULTZ, S. (1980) Behavioural response to artificial food colors. *Science*, 207, 1487–1489.

WEISS, G. (1983) Long-term outcome: findings, concepts and practical implications. In *Developmental Neuropsychiatry* (ed. M. Rutter). New York: Guilford Press.

WENDER, P. (1971) *Minimal Brain Dysfunction in Children*. New York: Wiley.

WERNER, E. & SMITH, R. (1977) *Kauai's Children Come of Age*. Honolulu: University of Hawaii Press.

WERRY, J. MINDE, K., GUZMAN, A., WEISS, G., DOGAN, K. & HOY, E. (1972) Studies on the hyperactive child. VII: Neurological status compared with neurotic and normal children. *American Journal of Orthopsychiatry*, 42, 441–450.

WORLD HEALTH ORGANIZATION (1980) *International Classification of Diseases* (9th revision) (ICD–9). Geneva: WHO.

—— (1985) *The Prescribing of Psychoactive Drugs for Children*. Copenhagen: WHO.

YULE, W. (1986) Behavioural treatments. In *The Overactive Child* (ed. E. Taylor). Clinics in Developmental Medicine No. 97. London: MacKeith Press/Blackwell.

——, LANSDOWN, R., MILLER, I. B. & URBANOWICZ, M. A. (1981) The relationship between lead concentration, intelligence and attainment in a school population: a pilot study. *Developmental Medicine and Child Neurology*, 23, 567–576.

Eric A. Taylor, FRCP, MRCPsych, *Reader in Developmental Neuropsychiatry, Institute of Psychiatry, De Crespigny Park, Denmark Hill, London SE5 8AF, and Honorary Consultant Psychiatrist, Bethlem Royal and Maudsley Hospitals, London*

(Accepted 14 May 1986)

[5]

THE RELATIONSHIP BETWEEN SENSATION SEEKING AND DELINQUENCY: A LONGITUDINAL ANALYSIS

HELENE RASKIN WHITE
ERICH W. LABOUVIE
MARSHA E. BATES

A sample of 584 male and female adolescents were studied at two points in time to determine the relationship between self-reported delinquency and sensation seeking. Analyses of variance and covariance were used to test the effect of delinquency status and frequency of minor delinquent activity on sensation seeking at Time 1 and on changes in sensation seeking from Time 1 to Time 2. The results indicated that delinquency and sensation seeking are related in adolescence regardless of sex; those adolescents who are delinquent score significantly higher on the Disinhibition scale. This finding was not obtained for experience seeking. One implication of the findings is that rates of minor delinquency could be lowered by providing high sensation seekers with socially approved opportunities for meeting their sensation-seeking needs.

The construct of sensation seeking is defined as an individual's "need for varied, novel and complex sensations and experiences and the willingness to take physical and social risks for the sake of such experience" (Zuckerman, 1979: 10). The construct is derived from optimal arousal theory that states that organisms are driven or motivated to obtain and maintain an optimal level of arousal (Zuckerman, 1978). Zuckerman (1979) and his colleagues (1964) have developed scales to measure individual differences in sensation-seeking needs. In general, individuals with high sensation-seeking scores have

The writing of this article was supported, in part, by grants from the National Institute on Alcohol Abuse and Alcoholism (AA-05823-02) and the National Institute on Drug Abuse (DA-03395-01). We would like to thank three anonymous reviewers for their suggestions on an earlier draft of this article.

JOURNAL OF RESEARCH IN CRIME AND DELINQUENCY, Vol. 22 No. 3, August 1985 197-211 been found to be more oriented to body sensation, more extraverted, more thrill seeking, more active, more impulsive, more antisocial and nonconformist, and less anxious (Zuckerman and Link, 1968).

In view of the definition of sensation seeking, it is not surprising that differences in this need have also been related to several types of adolescent "problem behaviors" such as drug use, premarital sexual activity, and delinquency (Zuckerman et al., 1972). As far as the latter is concerned, however, available empirical evidence does not consistently support the notion of a positive relationship between sensation-seeking needs and delinquent activity.

Farley (1973) postulated that delinquent behavior is a function of both stimulus-seeking needs and opportunities for obtaining and channeling stimulation. He stated that individuals who need higher levels of stimulation and come from environments with limited opportunities for the satisfaction of stimulus-seeking needs in a socially approved fashion are more likely to engage in delinquent behavior. Further, he suggested that regardless of environment, a low stimulation seeker would not be expected to become delinquent (Farley and Sewell, 1976).

Empirically, sensation seeking has been related to criminal behavior in both adolescent and adult samples. Almost all studies have been conducted on officially defined offenders, that is, those with police or court records. Identified offenders, however, are not necessarily representative of all offenders. In addition, both the stigma of being labeled and institutionalization may produce changes in personality characteristics that were not present before (Clinard and Meier, 1975).

Some of the studies conducted on identified delinquents have found a relationship between delinquency and sensation seeking. Farley and Farley (1972) studied delinquent girls in a correctional institution and found that delinquent behaviors during incarceration, such as escape attempts and disobedience, were related to the intensity of sensation-seeking needs. They suggested that even unsuccessful escape attempts satisfy high sensation seekers' stimulus input requirements not being met in the institution. Farley (1973) extended these findings to include male delinquents.

In a high school study, male and female adjudicated delinquents scored significantly higher than nondelinquents on the Sensation Seeking Scale (SSS; Farley and Sewell, 1976). Although the difference in sensation-seeking scores was statistically significant, the magnitude of the difference was not great. The authors suggested that the lack of a large difference might be due to the fact that the delinquency criterion was weak or that the sample was black. Other studies (e.g., Karoly, 1975; Kaestner et al., 1977) have suggested that the SSS may not be valid for nonwhites.

LeBlanc and Tolor (1972) also found that adult prison inmates seek more sensation than controls (prison staff). However, they raised the question as to whether the different personality characteristics of criminal offenders antecede their socially offensive behavior or represent a reaction to a criminal career and imprisonment.

Other studies have not found a significant relationship between delinquency and sensation seeking. Thorne (1971) studied sensation seeking among male and female juvenile delinquents (committed to state institutions) and adult prisoners. After controlling for age, he found no statistically significant differences in sensation seeking between the different groups of criminal offenders. Karoly (1975) also found no significant differences between black and white female delinquents (from a halfway house) and high school students on the SSS.

Very few studies have been conducted relating sensation seeking to self-reported delinquency. In a study of self-reported school violence, Wasson (1980) found that high sensation seekers tended to engage more often in school misbehavior. Hindelang (1972) found that male high school students who engaged in a wide range of delinquent behavior scored lower on the self-control scale of the California Personality Inventory (CPI). A low score on this scale parallels a high score on the SSS in indicating that an individual is impulsive, uninhibited, and pleasure seeking.

It should be obvious from this brief review that available empirical evidence concerning the relationship between sensation seeking and delinquency is limited and inconclusive. The present study was designed to provide a more reliable and valid assessment of the relationship between both constructs. Specifically, major improvements over existing studies include the following: (a) the use of a nonclinical, randomly selected sample of adolescents, and (b) the use of longitudinal observations permitting an investigation of this relationship over time; that is, changes in one measure can be compared with changes in the other.

METHODS

Design

The Rutgers Health and Human Development Project is a prospective longitudinal study that examines, primarily, the acquisition and maintenance of alcohol- and drug-using behaviors. A total of 1380 randomly chosen New Jersey adolescents are followed at three-year intervals. These adolescents were randomly selected by telephone survey. (More than 95% of New Jersey households have telephones.) After the telephone survey, field staff interviewed interested subjects and their parents in their homes. Following this contact, subjects came to the test site for a full day of testing.

The 698 males and 682 females were tested initially between 1979 and 1981 at the ages of 12, 15, and 18. Subjects originally tested in 1979 and 1980 returned three years later in 1982 and 1983 and were retested using essentially the same battery of instruments. The first retest of Wave 1 (1979) and Wave 2 (1980) yielded a 3-year follow-up rate of 94%. A comparison of Time 1 delinquency rates between those subjects who were retested and those who dropped out indicates high comparability. The retest of Wave 3 (1981) is in progress. (For greater detail on design and subject selection, see Lester et al., forthcoming; Pandina et al., 1984.)

Sample

The total sample for the present analyses consists of 584 adolescents grouped into two birth cohorts: 279 (m = 135, f = 144) born in 1961/1962 and 305 (m = 153, f = 152) born in 1964/1965. These subjects represent the ages of 18 and 15, respectively, at Time 1 (T1), and 21 and 18, respectively, at Time 2 (T2). The 12-year-olds were not included in this study because Zuckerman (1979) indicates that 14 is the minimum age level for which the scale should be used.

The sample is predominantly white (90%), a somewhat higher proportion than the 83% of whites in New Jersey (U.S. Bureau of Census, 1981). About half of the subjects are Catholic (50%); the others are as follows: Protestant (32%), Jewish (9%), and another or no religion (9%), analogous to the religious breakdown of New Jersey. The median

income of the sample, between $20,000 and $29,000, is also comparable
to that of the entire state ($24,510; U.S. Bureau of Census, 1981).

This sample differs from those used in previous studies in that it is not
obtained from an institutional or school population. The random
household survey provides a fairly representative sample of adolescents
living in New Jersey and includes subjects who are employed full time as
well as junior high, high school, and college students.

Data Collection and Instruments

Self-report questionnaires provide the data for this study. Self-report
is an accepted indicator of delinquency by most researchers in the field
(Hindelang et al., 1981) and provides a more direct measure of
delinquent behavior than do measures based upon official law enforcement records (Huizinga and Elliott, 1981). The level of delinquency
reported by our respondents parallels the amount of involvement found
in other surveys of predominantly middle-class adolescents (Linden,
1978; Levine and Kozak, 1979; Richards et al., 1979).

Variables

DELINQUENCY AT T1 AND T2

On each occasion, participants were asked to estimate the frequency
with which they had engaged in each of nine delinquent behaviors
during the three years prior to the time of testing (response scale: 0 times,
1-2 times, 3-5 times, 6-10 times, more than 10 times). The nine behaviors
were as follows: petty theft (stealing things worth less than $50.00),
evading payment (sneaking in or avoiding payment), vandalism (damaging others' property on purpose), grand theft (stealing things worth
more than $50.00), motor vehicle theft, breaking and entering, assault
(hurting someone badly enough to require medical attention), atrocious
assault (use of a weapon in a fight), and armed robbery.

The following indices were constructed for each occasion: (a)
delinquency status: nondelinquent if none of the behaviors had been
engaged in during the prior 3 years; delinquent if one or more were
reported for that time period; (b) minor delinquency: sum of the
frequencies (range: 0-12) reported for petty theft, evading payment, and

vandalism; (c) property crime: sum of the frequencies (range: 0-12) reported for grand theft, motor vehicle theft, and breaking and entering; and (d) violent behavior: sum of the frequencies (range: 0-12) reported for assault, atrocious assault, and armed robbery. As might be expected for this predominantly middle-class sample of adolescents, the measures of property crime and violent behavior displayed very small means and variances in both levels and changes over time. Consequently, only delinquency status and minor delinquency were employed as variables in subsequent analyses.

SENSATION SEEKING AT T1 AND T2

On each occasion, participants completed two truncated[1] subscales of Zuckerman's Sensation Seeking Scale (Form V, 1979), Disinhibition, and Experience Seeking. The Disinhibition (DIS) scale suggests a hedonistic pursuit of pleasure, an extraverted style, and an enjoyment of parties, social drinking, and a variety of sexual partners; the Experience Seeking (ES) scale measures a desire to expand experience through the mind and the senses, through music, art, travel, and an unconventional lifestyle with unconventional friends. Alpha coefficients of internal consistency were .64 and .66 for the DIS and .42 and .46 for the ES scale at T1 and T2, respectively. These estimates are approximately .10 (DIS) and .20 (ES) lower than those reported by Zuckerman et al. (1978) in their cross-cultural study of American and English samples. Zuckerman (1979) reported test-retest (3-week) reliabilities of approximately .90 for the DIS and ES scales. Our three-year stability coefficients were .54 for DIS and .49 for ES. The stability coefficients reflect less association between measurements, as was expected due to the longer length of intervening time. Note that there has been ample research over the past 20 years demonstrating the concurrent and predictive validity of the SSS (see Zuckerman, 1984 for a review).

Analyses

Analyses were designed to assess the relationship between delinquency and sensation-seeking needs, not only with regard to individual differences at a single point in time, but also in terms of differential changes over time. In view of the well-known phenomenon of regression toward the mean, it was decided to conceptualize actual or observed changes as the sum of the expected changes (as predicted from initial individual differences in the same variable at T1 via linear regression or analysis of covariance) and of residual changes (Labouvie, 1982). Such a strategy is, of course, based on the assumption that variation in expected or predicted changes (as defined above) is relatively uninformative when trying to assess empirical relationships to other variables.

The data were analyzed by carrying out several analyses of variance and analyses of covariance with unequal cell frequencies. For one set of analyses subjects were subdivided, on the basis of their delinquency status at both occasions, into four groups representing adoption of delinquency between T1 and T2 (ND-D), discontinuance of delinquency between test times (D-ND), continued nondelinquency from T1 and T2 (ND-ND), and continued delinquency from T1 to T2 (D-D). The following analyses were performed separately for males and females: (a) 4 (Delinquency status) × 2 (Age at T1) analyses of variance with DIS and ES scores at T1 as dependent variables; and (b) 4 (Delinquency status) × 2 (Age at T1) analyses of covariance with actual changes in DIS and ES as dependent variables and DIS and ES scores at T1, respectively, as covariates.

It is reasonable to assume that some minimal engagement in, rather than a total absence of, minor delinquency during middle and late adolescence is more normative even in a middle-class sample. Furthermore, if sensation-seeking needs are primarily related to deviations from such normative levels of delinquency, groupings on the basis of delinquency status as defined above may actually attenuate the empirical relationships that are observed. Thus linear regression analyses were carried out separately by sex to decompose actual changes in minor delinquency into predicted/expected and residual changes and the latter, together with deliniquency levels at T1, were used to define the following four groups: (1) group L-IL consists of subjects who score below the overall mean at T1 and who, due to negative residual changes, increase less than predicted in delinquency; (2) group L-IM includes subjects who score initially (at T1) below the overall mean and who, due to positive residual changes, increase more than predicted in minor delinquency; (3) group H-DM includes subjects who score initially above the overall mean and who, due to negative residual changes, decrease more than predicted in minor delinquency; and (4) group

H-DL consists of subjects who score initially above the overall mean and who, due to positive residual changes, decrease less than predicted in minor delinquency. The resulting analyses of variance and covariance performed on these groups were otherwise identical to the ones mentioned above.

RESULTS

Gender Differences

As expected, males displayed more delinquency than did females. That is, males were overrepresented in group D-D and underrepresented in group ND-ND (χ^2 = 47.17, df = 3, p < .01). In addition, males had a higher mean score on DIS at T1 than did females (t = 7.30, df = 582, p < .01). No significant sex differences were obtained for ES at T1.

Differences by Delinquency Status

Results of the least square means comparisons from the separate 4 (Delinquency Status) $\times$ 2 (Age) analyses of variance and covariance are shown in Table 1. No statistically significant (p > .01) main effects of age or age by status interactions were obtained. As can be seen, significant main effects for delinquency status were found for T1 levels (Males: F = 8.73, df = 3, p < .001; Females: F = 6.80, df = 3, p < .001) and residual changes (Males: F = 6.47, df = 3, p < .001; Females: F = 5.01, df = 3, p < .001) in DIS but not in ES. For comparison purposes, Table 1 also lists actual changes in both measures.

Although the main effect of delinquency status is only significant for DIS, results in Table 1 present a rather consistent picture. Specifically, both male and female adolescents who are initially nondelinquent (ND-ND and ND-D) tend to score lower on DIS and ES at T1. In addition, adolescents who remain nondelinquent (ND-ND) or become nondelinquent (D-ND) display negative residual changes suggesting that actual changes are reduced relative to predicted/expected changes. In comparison, adolescents who became delinquent (ND-D) or remain delinquent (D-D) exhibit generally positive residual changes, indicating that actual changes are inflated relative to predicted changes.

TABLE 1: Initial Level, Residual Change, and Actual Change in Disinhibition
and Experience Seeking by Sex and Delinquency Status

| Variable | Total | Delinquency Status | | | |
		ND-ND	ND-D	D-ND	D-D
MALES (N)	288	41	34	53	160
Disinhibition					
T1 level	4.51	3.35a	3.84ab	4.73bc	4.88c
Residual change	.00	−.60a	.04ab	−.66a	.37b
Actual change	−.01	.04	.40	−.80	.15
Experience Seeking					
T1 level	3.44	3.11a	3.20a	3.73a	3.50a
Residual change	.00	−.31a	.56a	−.23a	.05a
Actual change	.14	.01	.83	−.25	.16
FEMALES (N)	296	84	59	69	84
Disinhibition					
T1 level	3.32	2.68a	3.02ab	3.48bc	4.01c
Residual change	.00	−.48a	.51b	−.22ab	.30b
Actual change	.05	−.11	.72	.25	.00
Experience Seeking					
T1 level	3.38	3.11a	3.17a	3.33a	3.87a
Residual change	.00	−.22a	.33a	−.02a	.05a
Actual change	.13	.04	.57	.11	−.05

NOTE: Means followed by the different letters within a row differ significantly
$(p < .01)$.

Differences by Level and
Change in Minor Delinquency

Results of the least square means comparisons for the 4 (Delinquency group) $\times$ 2 (Age) analyses of variance and covariance are summarized in Table 2. Group differences in initial levels and changes in minor delinquency were included to validate the definition of each group.

Similar to the previous analyses, main effects of age and age by group interactions were not statistically significant. Not surprisingly, group differences in initial level (Males: $F = 7.09$, df = 3, $p < .001$; Females: $F = 8.86$, df = 3, $p < .001$) and residual changes (Males: $F = 6.53$; df = 3, $p < .001$; Females: $F = 3.89$, df = 3, $p < .01$) in DIS were significant and the patterns are consistent with those reported in Table 1. That is, adolescents who are initially low in minor delinquency (groups L-IL and

206   JOURNAL OF RESEARCH IN CRIME AND DELINQUENCY

TABLE 2: Initial Level, Residual Change, and Actual Change in Minor Delinquency, Disinhibition, and Experience Seeking by Sex and Delinquency Group

| | | | Delinquency Group | | |
Variable	Total	L-IL	L-IM	H-DM	H-DL
MALES (N)	288	98	80	76	34
Minor Delinquency					
T1 level	2.34	.55a	1.05a	4.54b	5.67c
Residual change	.00	−.88a	1.72b	−1.42c	1.41b
Actual change	−.67	−.34	1.93	−3.58	−1.53
Disinhibition					
T1 level	4.51	3.89a	4.46ab	5.18b	4.92b
Residual change	.00	−.38a	.57b	−.41a	.49ab
Actual change	−.01	−.06	.58	−.78	.26
Experience Seeking					
T1 level	3.44	3.39a	3.17a	3.83a	3.42a
Residual change	.00	−.29a	.19a	−.03a	.32a
Actual change	.14	−.12	.47	−.10	.48
FEMALES (N)	296	89	93	85	29
Minor Delinquency					
T1 level	1.25	.00a	.42a	2.39b	4.44c
Residual change	.00	−.73a	1.22b	−1.08c	1.37b
Actual change	−.23	.00	1.64	−2.16	−1.27
Disinhibition					
T1 level	3.32	2.63a	3.30ab	3.53b	4.77c
Residual change	.00	−.46a	.40b	−.06ab	.23ab
Actual change	.05	−.06	.47	−.12	−.46
Experience Seeking					
T1 level	3.38	3.15a	3.47a	3.80a	3.41a
Residual change	.00	−.21a	.18a	.07a	−.20a
Actual change	.13	.03	.27	.17	−.27

NOTE: Means followed by the different letters within a row differ significantly (p < .01).

L-IM) are also lower in DIS at T1. In addition, adolescents who remain low in minor delinquency (group L-IL) or decrease more than expected in delinquency (group H-DM) display negative residual changes in DIS, suggesting that actual changes in DIS are reduced relative to predicted changes. In comparison, adolescents who increase more than expected in delinquency (group L-IM) or remain high in delinquency (H-DL) exhibit positive residual changes in DIS, indicating that actual changes are inflated relative to the predicted changes. Trends in levels and changes in ES are again not significant. In addition, comparisons of T1 and residual change ES means do not reveal any consistent pattern for either sex.

DISCUSSION

The results of the present study are generally consistent with those reported earlier in the literature. As already observed by Zuckerman and his colleagues (1972), males tend to score higher than females on disinhibition but not on experience seeking. Males also tend to engage more often in delinquent behaviors than do females, confirming findings of earlier studies (e.g., Canter, 1982; Harris, 1977). Finally, the results also lend support to the notion that adolescents who are more delinquent are also more pleasure seeking and less concerned with adherence to social norms (Hindelang, 1972). In the present study, a positive relationship between delinquency and disinhibition was found for both males and females in terms of individual differences observed at a single point in time as well as when considering intraindividual changes across time. Obviously, the present findings are limited to adolescents who are primarily engaging in relatively low levels of minor delinquency. But in that sense, the results complement and extend findings by Farley (1973) and Farley and Farley (1972) for samples of officially identified delinquents.

That the relationshdip between delinquency and experience seeking, although sometimes consistent with that between delinquency and disinhibition, failed to reach statistical significance may be due to the lower internal consistency/reliability observed for that scale. On the other hand, it may also suggest that adolescents who are high in experience-seeking needs do not necessarily resort to delinquent activities to satisfy those needs.

Obviously, the present findings, although based on longitudinal observations, do not permit an unequivocal causal interpretation. Instead they suggest at least two possible causal pathways that may apply to the same or different individuals. On the one hand, it is conceivable that, at least for some adolescents, an involvement in delinquenct activities amply represents an overt expression of a high underlying level of disinhibition needs. According to Farley (1973), the overt expression of higher levels of disinhibition in the form of delinquent behavior is especially likely if there are relatively few opportunities to meet these needs in socially approved forms. This view suggests that if adolescents are presented with socially approved mechanisms for meeting sensation-seeking needs, they may be less likely to turn to minor delinquent behavior in order to fulfill these needs.[2] Perhaps if schools and community groups could develop alternative stimulating activities, rates of noninstrumental types of minor delinquency might be lowered. It should be noted, however, that according to the present findings high levels of disinhibition are no more likely to be maintained across time and are, thus, no more stable than low levels of disinhibition. Therefore, a consideration of possible prevention programs should address the question of how to modify levels of disinhibition more directly.

For other adolescents, however, engaging in delinquent activities may actually cause a more overt display and expression of needs that remained latent and inhibited until then. In that sense, the initiation of and involvement in minor delinquency may produce an increase in overt levels of disinhibition as experienced and reported by individuals. This latter interpretation is consistent with the fact that a consideration of delinquency status with its focus on transitions from nondelinquency to delinquency and vice versa (see Table 1) yielded essentially the same results in terms of increases and decreases in disinhibition needs. This interpretation also suggests that the design of potential prevention efforts does not have to be limited to the development of socially approved forms for the expression and gratification of disinhibition needs, but might also include attempts to modify levels of disinhibition more directly.

Besides evaluating potential prevention projects, further research should continue to examine longitudinally the relationship between delinquency and personality characteristics. It should also address the relationship between sensation seeking and the whole repertoire of adolescent behaviors such as drug use, sexual experience, and school performance over time.

NOTES

1. Two items were removed from each scale because they were similar to items asked elsewhere in the test battery.

2. Admittedly, this explanation does not consider the possibility that opportunities are available but not perceived as satisfying sensation-seeking needs. That is, the fact that delinquent activities are "forbidden" may be a critical feature of inducing the experience of excitement.

REFERENCES

Canter, R. J.
    1982 "Sex differences in self-report delinquency." Criminology 20: 373-393.
Clinard, M. B. and R. F. Meier
    1978 Sociology of Deviant Behavior. New York: Holt, Rinehart & Winston.
Farley, F. H.
    1973 "A theory of delinquency." Presented at the annual meeting of the American Psychological Association, Montreal.
Farley, F. H. and S. V. Farley
    1972 "Stimulus-seeking motivation and delinquent behavior among institutionalized delinquent girls." J. of Consulting and Clinical Psychology 39, 1: 94-97.
Farley, F. H. and T. Sewell
    1976 "Test of an arousal theory of delinquency." Criminal Justice and Behavior 3, 4: 315-320.
Harris, A. R.
    1977 "Sex and theories of deviance: toward a functional theory of deviant type-scripts." Amer. Soc. Rev. 42: 1-16.
Hindelang, M. J.
    1972 "The relationship of self-reported delinquency to scales of the CPI and MMPI." J. of Criminal Law, Criminology and Police Science 63, 1: 75-81.
Hindelang, M. J., T. Hirschi, and J. G. Weis
    1981 Measuring Delinquency. Beverly Hills, CA: Sage.
Huizinga, D. H. and D. S. Elliott
    1981 A Longitudinal Study of Drug Use and Delinquency in a National Sample of Youth: An Assessment of Causal Order (A Report of the National Youth Survey). Boulder, CO: Behavioral Research Institute.
Kaestner, E., L. Rosen, and P. Appel
    1977 "Patterns of drug abuse: relationships with ethnicity, sensation seeking and anxiety." J. of Consulting and Clinical Psychology 45, 3: 462-468.
Karoly, P.
    1975 "Comparison of 'psychological styles' in delinquent and nondelinquent females." Psych. Reports 36: 567-570.

Labouvie, E. W.
    1982   "The concept of change and regression toward the mean." Psych. Bull. 92:
           251-257.
LeBlanc, R. F. and A. Tolor
    1972   "Alienation, distancing, externalizing, and sensation seeking in prison in-
           mates." J. of Consulting and Clinical Psychology 39, 3: 514.
Lester, D., R. J. Pandina, H. R. White, and E. W. Labouvie
    forth- "The Rutgers health and human development project: a longitudinal study
    coming of alcohol and drug use," in S. Mednick and M. Harway (eds.) Longitudinal
           Studies in the United States. New York: Praeger.
Levine, E. M. and C. Kozak
    1979   "Drug and alcohol use, delinquency, and vandalism among upper middle class
           pre- and post adolescents." J. of Youth and Adolescence 8, 1: 91-101.
Linden, R
    1978   "Myths of middle-class delinquency: a test of the generalizability of social
           control theory." Youth and Society 9, 4: 407-431.
Pandina, R. J., E. W. Labouvie, and H. R. White
    1984   "Potential contributions of the life span developmental approach to the study
           of adolescent alcohol and drug use: the Rutgers Health and Human Develop-
           ment project, a working model." J. of Drug Issues 14, 2: 253-268.
Richards, P., R. A. Berk, and B. Forster
    1979   Crime As Play: Delinquency in a Middle Class Suburb. Cambridge, MA:
           Ballinger.
Thorne, G. L.
    1971   "Sensation seeking scale with deviant populations." J. of Consulting and
           Clinical Psychology 37, 1: 106-110.
U.S. Bureau of the Census
    1981   "Current population survey: money, income and poverty status of families in
           the United States: 1980." Current Population Reports Series P-60, No. 127.
Wasson, A. S.
    1980   "Stimulus-Seeking, perceived school environment and school misbehavior."
           Adolescence 15, 59: 603-608.
Zuckerman, M.
    1978   "Sensation seeking and psychopathy," pp. 165-185 in R. D. Hare and D.
           Schalling (eds.) Psychopathic Behavior: Approaches to Research. New York:
           John Wiley.
    1979   Sensation Seeking Beyond the Optimal Level of Arousal. Hillsdale, NJ:
           Lawrence Erlbaum.
    1984   "Sensation seeking: a comparative approach to a human trait. Behavioral and
           Brain Sciences 7: 413-471.
Zuckerman, M., R. N. Bone, R. Neary, D. Mangelsdorff, and B. Brustman
    1972   "What is the sensation seeker? Personality trait and experience correlates of the
           sensation-seeking scales." J. of Consulting and Clinical Psychology 39, 2:
           308-321.

Zuckerman, M., S. Eysenck, and H. J. Eysenck
  1978   "Sensation seeking in England and America: cross-cultural age and sex comparisons." J. of Consulting and Clinical Psychology 46: 139-149.
Zuckerman, M., E. A. Kolin, L. Price, and I. Zoob
  1964   "Development of a sensation-seeking scale." J. of Consulting and Clinical Psychology 28: 477-482.
Zuckerman, M. and K. Link
  1968   "Construct validity for the sensation seeking scale." J. of Consulting and Clinical Psychology 32: 420-426.

Low Intelligence, Low Attainment, Neuropsychological Deficit

[6]

INTELLIGENCE AND DELINQUENCY:
A REVISIONIST REVIEW

TRAVIS HIRSCHI AND MICHAEL J. HINDELANG

State University of New York, Albany

American Sociological Review 1977, Vol. 42 (August):571–587

Recent research on intelligence and delinquency suggests that (1) the relation is at least as strong as the relation of either class or race to official delinquency; (2) the relation is stronger than the relation of either class or race to self-reported delinquency. In an analysis of the history of the research on the IQ-delinquency relation, we trace the developments leading to the current textbook position that IQ is not an important factor in delinquency. This position, which came into vogue about forty years ago and is still held by many sociologists, has its roots in: (1) a medical to sociological paradigm shift in this century; (2) the failure of subsequent research to substantiate the early exorbitant claims that low IQ was a necessary and sufficient condition for illegal behavior; (3) early negative reviews of research on this question by Sutherland and others; (4) reservations about the validity of the measurement of both IQ and delinquency; (5) erroneous interpretation of research findings; (6) speculation regarding factors which might account for the relation. It is noted that many currently prominent sociological theories of delinquency implicitly or explicitly use IQ as a crucial theoretical element. We show that IQ has an effect on delinquency independent of class and race, and we argue that this effect is mediated through a host of school variables.

Few groups in American society have been defended more diligently by sociologists against allegations of difference than ordinary delinquents. From the beginning, the thrust of sociological theory has been to deny the relevance of individual differences to an explanation of delinquency, and the thrust of sociological criticism has been to discount research findings apparently to the contrary. "Devastating" reviews of the research literature typically meet with uncritical acceptance or even applause, and new theories and "new criminologies" are con-

572   AMERICAN SOCIOLOGICAL REVIEW

structed in a research vacuum, a vacuum that may itself claim research support.

A major source of this stance toward individual differences is the notion widely held in the field of deviance that "kinds of people" theories are non- or even anti-sociological. Most of the major theorists in the area (Sutherland, Merton, Cohen, Becker) have more or less explicitly argued this point, and efforts to bring criminology "up-to-date" with the rest of sociology frequently imply that interest in individual differences is an outmoded relic of the field's positivistic past (e.g., Matza, 1964; Taylor et al, 1973). Another source of this stance toward difference is frankly moral. According to Liazos (1972), who provides extensive documentation, sociologists repeatedly assert that deviants are "at least as good as anyone else." If Liazos' analysis is any guide, we may assume it is easy to confuse the moral-evaluative "as good as" with the empirical "the same as." For example, Liazos goes on to argue that the repeated assertion that " 'deviants' are *not different* may raise the very doubts we want to dispel." Sociologists have observed for some time that, "always and everywhere, *difference* is the occasion and excuse for ignoring the equal claims of others" (Ross, 1901:25). They therefore feel duty-bound, it seems, to protect delinquents from those who would justify abusing them on these grounds.

Among the many possible individual differences between delinquents and nondelinquents, none is apparently more threatening to the integrity of the field and to its moral commitments than IQ. To the standard list of scientific and moral arguments against IQ, the sociological student of crime and delinquency can add the weight of a half-century struggle against biological theories and the predatory social ethic they are alleged to foster. In fact, the single argument against IQ developed within criminology is sufficiently simple and persuasive that the standard list need not be invoked. At the time criminology became a subfield of sociology, marked differences in IQ between delinquents and nondelinquents were pretty much taken for granted, and a major task confronting those wishing to

claim the field for the sociological perspective was to call these alleged differences into question. This task was successfully accomplished. IQ, it was confidently suggested, doesn't matter (see Sutherland, 1924:108). Today, textbooks in crime and delinquency ignore IQ or impatiently explain to the reader that IQ is no longer taken seriously by knowledgeable students simply because no differences worth considering have been revealed by research.

As we shall show, the textbooks are wrong.[1] IQ is an important correlate of delinquency. It is at least as important as social class or race. This fact has straightforward implications for sociological theorizing and research, most of which has taken place within the context of official denial of IQ differences. Its implications for social policy are variably straightforward and are, in any event, strictly irrelevant to questions of the current impact of IQ on delinquency: the actual relation between IQ and delinquency must be the standard against which all arguments, including our own, are judged.

The Current Textbook View

Many textbooks do not even mention IQ (e.g., Gibbons, 1970; Bloch and Geis, 1962). Most, however, introduce the subject and then argue against its significance. The basic position is that there are no differences in IQ between delinquents and nondelinquents. The research and reviews most frequently cited in support of this conclusion are now over forty years old (e.g., Murchison, 1926; Sutherland, 1931; Zeleny, 1933). The tendency to rely on summaries provided by other textbooks, especially, in this case, those written by psychologists, is much in evidence.

Despite the selectivity of textbook summaries of the evidence, most of them leave the reader with the distinct impression that IQ may be a very important

[1] In a more general treatment of the measurement and correlates of delinquency, Gordon (1976) independently reaches conclusions about the importance of IQ that are very close to those reported here.

INTELLIGENCE AND DELINQUENCY 573

cause of delinquency after all. Few textbook writers seem able to resist additional arguments that have the effect of undercutting their basic position:

> It is now generally recognized that so-called intelligence tests tend to measure the degree to which the individual has assimilated and internalized middle-class values rather than intelligence.

> We could anticipate that a feeble-minded individual would be more readily incarcerated than other individuals. (Haskell and Yablonsky, 1974:216)

> It is not mental deficiency per se which results in crime; rather the inability of a mentally deficient person to make adequate social adjustments. . . . (Johnson, 1968:173)

> Although a higher percentage of delinquent children come from the ranks of the mental defective, particularly from those of borderline intelligence, it is not the mental deficiency per se but the inability of the child to make adequate school or social adjustments that usually results in delinquency. (Sutherland and Cressey, 1974:174, quoting Coleman, 1950)

> The great proportion of persons with low intelligence scores undoubtedly are nondeviants, whereas there are large numbers of persons with above normal intelligence who are. (Clinard, 1968:170)

All of these arguments take for granted a negative correlation between IQ and delinquency. The "middle-class values" interpretation of IQ tests suggests that scores on these tests may well be the strongest predictor of delinquency available. The "not per se" argument asserts that the relation is, in fact, causal in the usual meaning of the term—i.e., nonspurious. The "more readily incarcerated" view contradicts the "not per se" argument by suggesting a direct link between IQ and, at least, official delinquency. And the "great proportion" argument asserts only that the relation is not perfect. Still, the current view, simply stated, is that IQ makes no difference. This view is not supported by the results of research.

Recent Research on Official Delinquency

At least half a dozen recent studies permit examination of the effects of IQ on official delinquency. These studies have been conducted in diverse settings, they rely on a variety of measures of IQ and of delinquency, and they all employ some measure of control for the effects of such variables as social class and race. All of them show IQ to be an important predictor of official delinquency.[2]

How strong is this effect? Since social class and race are considered important correlates of official delinquency by almost everyone, they should provide a sufficiently stringent criterion and be available for comparison. Further, since both class and race are frequently used to discount the effects of IQ, this comparison will provide evidence relative to the common argument that IQ effects are merely a by-product of race and class effects.

IQ, Social Class and Official Delinquency

Reiss and Rhodes (1961) examined the juvenile court records of more than 9,200 in-school *white* boys in Davidson County, Tennessee. Using three-category divisions on occupational status of the head of household and on IQ, they found that the rate (per 100) of court adjudication ranged from 5.7 in the high to 9.6 in the low status groups, and from 4.8 in the high to 10.3 in the low IQ groups. In other words, the rate of adjudication in the lowest occupational group was 1.7 times that of the highest occupational group, while the rate of the adjudication in the lowest IQ group was 2.1 times that of the highest IQ group.[3] Since the distributions of occupational status and IQ were roughly comparable, in the Davidson County data IQ is more important than social class as a predictor of official delinquency among white boys.

Hirschi (1969) examined the police rec-

---

[2] Unless otherwise noted, all references to "the relation between IQ and delinquency" assume an inverse correlation.

[3] When father's occupational status was dichotomized and IQ trichotomized, the two variables were shown to have independent effects, with some tendency toward interaction: the effects of occupational status were more marked as IQ decreased, which also says that the effects of IQ were more marked for blue-collar than for white-collar boys.

ords of over 3,600 boys in Contra Costa County, California. Since previously published analyses do not directly compare the effects of social class and IQ, we have reanalyzed these data, with the results shown in Tables 1 and 2 (for details of data collection, see Hirschi, 1969:35–46).

In these data, the effect of IQ on official delinquency is stronger than that of father's education. Among whites, the gamma for the relationship between IQ and delinquency is −.31, while the comparable gamma for father's education is −.20; among blacks, the gammas are −.16 and −.05, respectively. Although the data are not shown, a composite measure of family status which includes employment and welfare status, presence of the father, and education and occupation of the parents shows results comparable to those for father's education in both racial categories. For whites, the gamma is −.18; for blacks, it is −.09. When the effects of this measure of family status and IQ are examined *simultaneously* within racial groups, the results are consistent with the zero-order relations. Both family status and IQ are independently related to official delinquency; the superiority of IQ in comparison with family status, however measured, is especially noticeable among blacks.

Wolfgang et al. (1972) obtained IQ scores on 8,700 of the 10,000 boys in their Philadelphia cohort. They do not present measures of association for these IQ scores and delinquency, nor do they show tabular material in which IQ is treated as an independent variable. They do, however, present average IQ scores by

Table 1. Percent Committing Two or More Official Delinquent Acts by IQ (Stanford Binet) and Race[a]

	IQ				
	0–19	20–39	40–59	60–79	80–99
White males	22.6 (204)	25.6 (282)	14.6 (309)	8.4 (341)	6.2 (403)
Black males	38.2 (429)	36.2 (273)	26.2 (153)	19.7 (71)	19.0 (42)

[a] IQ scores are shown as percentiles. Gammas, calculated on the entire range of delinquency scores (0–4), are −.31 for whites and −.16 for blacks.

number of contacts with the police in groups homogeneous on class and race. The differences in average scores between chronic offenders and nondelinquents range from nine IQ points among high socioeconomic status nonwhites to fourteen IQ points among low socioeconomic status whites (Wolfgang et al., 1972:62, 93). Again, although no direct comparison with social class is possible, the Philadelphia data reveal a strong relation between IQ and delinquency independent of class.[4]

West (1973:84) followed 411 London boys over a ten-year period and "compared the delinquent and non-delinquent groups on the prevalence of low IQ in just the same way [he] compared them on other factors such as poverty, large families, or criminal parents." The relation between IQ and delinquency in West's data is substantial. While one-quarter of those with IQ scores of 110 or more had a police record, the same was true of one-half of those with IQ scores of 90 or less. Even more impressively, while only one in fifty boys with an IQ of 110 or more was a recidivist, one in five of those with an IQ of 90 or less fell in this category. West (1973:84–5) concludes from his thorough analysis that "low IQ was a significant precursor of delinquency to much the same extent as other major factors." Although he reports a stronger relation between family income and delinquency than that typically reported in American studies, IQ was able to compete with it on equal terms and to survive when family income and several other measures of family culture were controlled by a matching procedure.

It should be noted that the striking differences in delinquency produced by IQ in West's data reflect a difference in IQ of about 12 points between nondelinquents and recidivists—a difference that falls within the range of the race- and SES-specific differences calculated from the Wolfgang et al. data. West's data agree with those of Wolfgang et al. that the IQ effect is largely attributable to multiple offenders (recidivists), which may explain

[4] Wolfgang et al. used the Philadelphia Verbal Ability Test. The typical IQ test has a standard deviation of 15.

INTELLIGENCE AND DELINQUENCY 575

Table 2. Percent Committing Two or More Official Delinquent Acts by Father's Education and Race[a]

| Race | Father's Education | | | | |
	Less than High School Grad.	High School Graduate	Trade or Business	Some College	College Graduate
White Males	17.7 (356)	14.3 (485)	13.4 (82)	8.0 (201)	7.8 (306)
Black Males	33.8 (343)	34.4 (209)	42.1 (57)	30.8 (123)	19.1 (84)

[a] Gammas, calculated on the entire range of delinquency scores (0–4), are –.20 for whites and –.05 for blacks.

the relatively weak performance of IQ in studies of self-reported delinquency.

IQ, Race and Official Delinquency

Comparison of the effects of race and IQ is more difficult than the class-IQ comparison because of a greater paucity of data or, at least, of appropriately analyzed data. There can be no doubt that IQ is related to delinquency within race categories. All of the studies mentioned are consistent on this point. The relative strength of the two variables is, however, open to question.

The multiple regression analysis using number of offenses as the dependent variable presented by Wolfgang et al. (1972:275–9) includes both race and IQ. Unfortunately for present purposes, it also includes highest grade completed and number of school moves, variables which account for the bulk of the explained variance in this measure of delinquency. Thus, the fact that race places third behind these school variables and IQ accounts for virtually nothing cannot be taken as direct evidence of their relative importance. We know that IQ is strongly related to delinquency in the Wolfgang

Table 3. Percent Committing Two or More Official Delinquent Acts by IQ and Race[a]

| Race | IQ | |
	Low	High
White males	24.3 (486)	9.4 (1053)
Black males	37.6 (702)	23.3 (266)

[a] IQ scores dichotomized at the 40th percentile.

data independent of race. We know, too, that IQ is strongly related to the school variables (r=.468 for highest grade completed) that, in variance terms, do most of the work. Therefore, we know that if these intervening variables were excluded from the analysis, the proportion of variance accounted for by IQ would increase substantially.

In the Contra Costa data, IQ and race have virtually identical effects on official delinquency. For illustration, we compare a dichotomous measure of IQ with the two categories of race in Table 3.

Measures of association between IQ and delinquency and between race and delinquency reflect the percentage differences in Table 3: race and IQ are virtually identical in their ability to predict delinquency. For race, r=.26; for IQ, r=.27.

The findings of McCord and McCord (1959:66, 203) from the Cambridge-Sommerville Youth Study are sometimes cited (e.g., West, 1973:91) as showing "no connection between low IQ and delinquency." Although in the McCords' data those in the lowest IQ group (80 or below) did have an intermediate rate of conviction during the follow-up period,[5] within the normal range of IQ scores (above 80) there was a monotonic decrease in rates of conviction from almost one-half in the 81–90 IQ group to one-quarter in the 110 or more IQ group. Because those in the lowest IQ group are only ten percent of

[5] Our figures are for the experimental and control groups combined (McCord and McCord, 1959:66, 203). Strictly speaking, the McCord data apply to adult criminality as well as juvenile delinquency, since the average age of their subjects was 27 at the time data on convictions were obtained.

the sample, the McCords' data, too, show an inverse relation between IQ and official misconduct.

Such problems of interpretation do not arise in Short and Strodtbeck's (1965) study of gang delinquency in Chicago. They report that gang boys scored lower on "all six intelligence measures" than non-gang boys in the same (lower) class; this difference held for white and black respondents alike.

Toby and Toby (1961) found "intellectual status" to be a significant forerunner of delinquency independent of socioeconomic status. And Reckless and Dinitz (1972) found that their teacher-nominated "good" boys had IQs from 8 to 12 points higher than their teacher-nominated "bad" boys in a class-homogeneous area.[6]

All in all, it seems reasonable to conclude on the basis of currently available data that IQ is related to official delinquency and that, in fact, it is as important in predicting official delinquency as social class or race. We know of no current research findings contrary to this conclusion.

Self-Reported Delinquency

A significant consequence of the no-IQ-difference position was that it helped set the stage for extensive use of self-report methods of measuring delinquent behavior. This position explicitly asserts that delinquents are as likely as others to possess the various skills reflected by IQ tests. If, however, the assumption of equal ability is unfounded, the measurement of delinquent behavior by the self-report method may be confounded with IQ, i.e., those most likely to commit delinquent acts may be least able to report adequately on their behavior. The self-report method, especially questionnaires,[7]

therefore does not provide an unambiguous test of the hypothesis that IQ is related to delinquent behavior.

In any event, most studies do find a relation between IQ and self-reported delinquency, but this relation is less robust than that found in official data. At one extreme, West (1973:158) found that 28.4 percent of the worst quarter of his sample on self-reported delinquency had low IQs, as compared to 16.6 percent in the remaining three-quarters—a difference only slightly smaller than his finding for official delinquency.

Weis (1973), too, found differences as strong as those typically reported when delinquency is measured by official data. In his study in a white upper-middle-class community near San Francisco, Weis collected Wechsler-Bellevue IQ scores and self-reports of delinquency for 255 male and female eleventh-grade students. One of the clusters emerging from his analysis was a property deviance scale that included items on theft, burglary, shoplifting and vandalism. When these scores were trichotomized, Weis found that 27 percent of those with IQ scores of less than 110, and 49 percent of those with IQ scores of 110 or more, had low scores on the property deviance scale. He found a similar difference (23% versus 41%) on a social deviance scale that included items on marijuana, alcohol and gambling.[8]

More typical of self-report studies, however, are the relations from the Contra Costa data shown in Table 4. Among white males, twice the proportion in the lowest as in the highest IQ group report involvement in two or more of a possible six delinquent acts; among black males the comparable ratio is 3:2.

Whatever the strength of the relations in Table 4, we believe they should be evaluated by comparison with social class and race. As Table 4 shows, race has no impact on self-reported delinquency—a finding consistent with much of the self-report literature (e.g., Williams and Gold, 1972). The same literature has consistently re-

---

[6] The Toby-Toby and Reckless-Dinitz studies may be marginal to the question of IQ effects. However, this concern would carry greater weight if their results were contrary to research focusing directly on the IQ question.

[7] Early warnings that the questionnaire method is especially limited by the high rates of illiteracy among delinquents (Erickson and Empey, 1963) have gone essentially unheeded.

[8] For details of data collection, see Weis (1973). The data reported in the text cannot be found in Weis dissertation. We are grateful to him for making them available to us.

INTELLIGENCE AND DELINQUENCY 577

Table 4. Percent Committing Two or More Self-Reported Delinquent Acts by IQ and Race [a]

Race	Low IQ				High IQ
White males	24 (196)	26 (270)	20 (302)	19 (336)	12 (396)
Black males	27 (393)	26 (257)	19 (149)	19 (68)	18 (39)

[a] IQ scores are grouped in percentiles as in Table 1. Gammas, calculated on the entire range of delinquency scores (0–6), are −.15 for whites and −.07 for blacks.

vealed a weaker relation of social class (e.g., Nye et al., 1958; Akers, 1964) to self-reported delinquency than that found in Table 4. The weight of the evidence is that IQ is more important than race and social class. The voluminous criticisms advanced against self-report delinquency research—with an eye to rescuing social class—presumably would have the same or even greater consequences for IQ. For example, the heavy reliance on in-school populations, the overabundance of minor offenders, and the dependence on subject cooperation may work to attenuate the relationship between social class and delinquency. If so, there is reason to believe that these factors would also depress the relation between self-reported delinquency and IQ. In fact, Hirschi (1969:46) reports that among those with the highest grades in English who had no police records, 79 percent cooperated with the self-report survey, while among those with the lowest grades in English who had police records, only 38 percent cooperated. More importantly, not only did grades in English and official delinquency substantially affect cooperation with the self-report survey, the two factors were found to interact: low ability boys with police records were disproportionately unlikely to appear in the self-report sample. Since official delinquents are likely to be "self-report" delinquents (if sampled), the number of self-reported delinquents in the sample is considerably depressed, especially at the low end of the ability scale.

In short, however delinquency is measured, IQ is able to compete on at least equal terms with class and race, the major

bases of most sociological theories of delinquency. At the same time, a relation between IQ and delinquency is routinely denied in sociological textbooks.

Implications for Theory

Our original purpose in introducing theory was frankly argumentive: we expected to find theorists struggling with a conflict between their own logic and the erroneous "results of research" on IQ. In short, we expected to find that they had often been led astray by the anti-IQ climate of criminology.

Actual examination of currently influential theories required revision of our plans. In most cases, theorists were not paying all that much attention to the "results of research." We had been led astray by the naive textbook assumption that theory organizes research and research tests and modifies theory. In the case of IQ, however, it would be more accurate to say that theory opposes research and research ignores theory.

Theories from the period (Merton, 1938; Sutherland and Cressey, 1974) when most researchers considered low IQ a strong correlate of delinquency ignore this variable,[9] while theories from the period when IQ was almost universally considered irrelevant predict either very strong negative (Cohen, 1955) or weak but important positive relations (Cloward and Ohlin, 1960) with delinquency. And a theoretical tradition (labeling) spanning both periods has managed to take a position opposite to research in both of them. Although all of these theories have been heavily researched, investigators have paid little or no attention to their views regarding IQ.

Since it is difficult to argue with those who agree, we will briefly show that resistence to consideration or inclusion of IQ does not characterize any current theory; that, on the contrary, several important theories require a relation between IQ and delinquency. Explicit recognition of this

---

[9] The Gluecks reported periodically throughout the thirties that their delinquents were "burdened with feeblemindedness" (e.g., Glueck and Glueck, 1934).

578   AMERICAN SOCIOLOGICAL REVIEW

fact would only increase their scope, the plausibility of their claims, and their consistency with research findings.

The best example is Cohen's (1955) effort to relate social class to delinquency by way of differential experience in the educational system. In Cohen's theory, children differentially prepared or qualified encounter a school system that treats all comers alike. Children inadequately "prepared" for success in school find the experience painful and are likely, as a consequence, to turn to delinquency. The place of IQ in this process would seem obvious and, in fact, Cohen (1955:102–3) could not be more explicit on this question:

> It may be taken as established that ability, as measured by performance in conventional tests of intelligence, varies directly with social class. . . . The conventional tests do test for abilities that are highly prized by middle-class people, that are fostered by middle-class socialization, and that are especially important for further achievement in the academic world and in middle-class society. In short, *the results of these tests are one important index of the ability of the child to meet middle-class expectations*, to do the kinds of things that bring rewards in the middle-class world. (emphasis added)

In Cohen's theory, intelligence intervenes between social class and delinquency or it is at least an important indicator of the social class of the *child*. In either case, IQ should be more strongly related to delinquency than such indirect measures of the ability of the child to meet middle-class expectations as *"father's* occupation."

Cohen's views on the interchangeability of IQ and class illustrate how the former could have been used to extend the scope of his theory beyond the confines of "lower-class delinquency." The situation facing the middle-class child with low IQ may not be all that different from the situation facing the lower-class child and, if such a situation explains the delinquency of one of them, it may explain the delinquency of the other as well. If both lower- and middle-class delinquency can be explained by the same mechanism, Cohen's reliance on a separate mechanism for middle-class boys (Cohen, 1955:162–9) is

inexplicable or is, at the very least, theoretically and empirically inelegant.

If a zero relation between IQ and delinquency would falsify Cohen's theory, it would virtually falsify the theory of Cloward and Ohlin (1960) as well, but for quite different reasons. Cloward and Ohlin (1960:111) suggest a positive relation between intelligence and delinquency:

> Some persons who have experienced a marked discrepancy between aspirations and achievements may look outward, attributing their failure to the existence of unjust or arbitrary institutional arrangements which keep men of ability and ambition from rising in the social structure. Such persons do not view their failure as a reflection of personal inadequacy but instead blame a cultural and social system that encourages everyone to reach for success while differentially restricting access to the success-goals. In contrast to this group there are individuals who attribute failure to their own inadequacies—to a lack of discipline, zeal, intelligence, persistence, or other personal quality.

In other words, the lower-class boy with a high IQ whose talents go unrecognized and unrewarded is a prime candidate for delinquency.

On the basis of available evidence, Cloward and Ohlin are wrong. For present purposes, however, the point is that their theory requires research on the IQ of juvenile offenders and is enduring testimony to the dangers in the view that IQ need be "no longer seriously considered" by criminologists.[10]

At first glance, labeling theory would seem to be an exception to our argument that IQ is important, since this theory puts no stock in the notion that individual differences may act as causes of delinquent behavior. In one of the first efforts by a labeling theorist to neutralize individual-difference research, Tannenbaum (1938:6) focused special attention on IQ, arguing that "whatever 'intelligence' is, it has no demonstrated relationship to crime." As labeling theory has "progressed," how-

---

[10] Although Merton (1938) ignores IQ and its "success" implications, IQ is obviously relevant to any opportunity theory.

INTELLIGENCE AND DELINQUENCY 579

ever, as it has become more closely associated with the conflict perspective according to which "society organizes itself for the protection of the ruling classes against the socially inferior" (Doleschal and Klapmuts, 1973:622), it has tended more and more to recognize that it too is dependent on individual differences. The generally low IQ of official delinquents is now accepted by labeling theorists and is used as evidence *for* their view that the system discriminates against or creates the disadvantaged (Doleschal and Klapmuts, 1973:612, 616; Polk and Schafer, 1972:34–54).

If labeling theorists argue that discrimination produces the relation between IQ and delinquency, then the mechanism that connects IQ to delinquency is the bone of contention between labeling and conventional theories—not the fact of a relation itself. We will return to the mechanism question.

Perhaps the only major theory strictly silent on the question of IQ is Sutherland's "differential association" (Sutherland and Cressey, 1974:75–7). Sutherland (1931) played a major role in constructing the current position of criminology on IQ. He rejoiced in its alleged failure to discriminate between delinquents and nondelinquents, and his influential text continues to belittle "mental testers" to the present day. Even so, differential association has nothing to fear from intelligence. This theory faintly suggests a positive association among those exposed to the delinquent culture (as does any theory that emphasizes the need to learn crime), but it really cannot be used to predict even the sign of the relation in the general population. If the theory cannot predict the sign of this relation, it is, nonetheless, capable of accounting for any relation between IQ and delinquency that might be revealed by research.

A final set of theories might be grouped under the heading of "social control" (for a convenient summary, see Nettler, 1974). These theories focus on a broad range of causal variables, and they are relatively open to individual differences, to the idea that "in learning to conduct ourselves, some of us need more lessons than others" (Nettler, 1974:232). Although none of them may now consider IQ of central importance, most suggest a negative association, and none would have difficulty absorbing this variable. In fact, for those sociologically-oriented control theories that emphasize "stakes in conformity" (e.g., Toby, 1957), IQ is of obvious importance.

Most sociological theories, then, have been saying for some time that IQ should be related to delinquency for the same reason that social class is, or should be related to it. Given the theoretical overlap of IQ and social class, the contrast in how the research community has reacted to their varying fates would be hard for an outsider to understand.

The finding that social class was unrelated to self-reported delinquency produced a large volume of follow-up research. The "finding" that IQ was unrelated to any measure of delinquency was, in contrast, accepted without so much as a murmur of protest. The literature on IQ contains none of the "what may have gone wrong" kinds of methodological critiques so often encountered in efforts to save social class. Instead, it is marked by considerable speculative ingenuity directed against an established relation. The extent to which this relation has been established may be revealed by a review of the history of IQ testing as it applies to delinquency and crime.

History

As a cause of delinquency, IQ got off to a very strong start in the first years of this century. The notion that "imbeciles" and "idiots" would be unable to resist criminal impulses or, for that matter, even to distinguish right from wrong, was a straightforward extension of Lombroso's then prestigious theory of the born or biologically defective criminal. Initial research did nothing to dampen enthusiasm for this idea. Goring (1972:255) in Great Britain reported that criminals "as a class, are highly differentiated mentally from the law abiding classes," and Goddard (1914:7) in the United States concluded that "probably from 25% to 50% of the

580   AMERICAN SOCIOLOGICAL REVIEW

people in our prisons are mentally defective and incapable of managing their affairs with ordinary prudence." In the period 1910–1914, the "percentage feebleminded" in fifty studies of institutionalized delinquents had a median value of 51 (Sutherland, 1931:358). Since it was then assumed that the proportion feebleminded in the general population was less than one percent (Goring used an estimate of .46 percent), the conclusion that faulty intelligence was the "single most important cause of crime" followed, or at least seemed to follow directly from the evidence.

If we follow the fate of IQ through mainstream criminology, we discover that its day was very brief. Less than two decades after Goring estimated .6553 as a "minimum value" for the correlation between mental defectiveness and crime, Sutherland (1931) was poking fun at the absurdities of the "mental testers."[11] His negative review of their research was so influential that the "modern" or "recent" position on IQ described by today's textbooks appears to have been firmly established at that time, i.e., forty-five years ago.

Sutherland's stance is not difficult to understand. As Savitz (1972:xviii) has reminded us, the medical profession seized power in criminology before the end of the nineteenth century and still maintained a preeminent position in the early days of intelligence testing—both Goring and Goddard were physicians. A short time later, however, criminology had become a subfield of sociology. Given this shift in disciplinary dominance, an equivalent

paradigm shift is now pretty much accepted as a logical necessity. "Intelligence" was a central element of the "old" paradigm. It just had to go. And go it did.

The history of IQ in research findings is not so quickly or easily told. The initial claims about the proportion of feebleminded delinquents were excessively high because—as Merrill (1947:159) has pointed out—researchers were basing their cutting point on children in institutions for the mentally deficient. The logic of this procedure went something like this: if no child in an institution for the feebleminded has a mental age in excess of twelve, then a mental age of twelve or less is sufficient to classify a person feebleminded. There was nothing especially silly about this procedure, it merely made the mistake of assuming that the same procedure would not also classify a large portion of the general population feebleminded. As it became apparent that a too-large portion of the general population would be classified feebleminded, the mental age requirement was first abruptly and then gradually lowered, with the result that the proportion feebleminded among delinquents also first abruptly and then gradually declined. Sutherland (1931) called attention to this twenty-year trend—which, in fact, continued for another 30 years (Woodward, 1955; Caplan, 1965)—and allowed his readers to conclude that it would continue until the initial claims of difference between delinquents and nondelinquents had no foundation in fact.

The most direct evidence against an IQ difference resulted from the extensive testing of the draft army in World War I. Murchison (1926) and Tulchin (1939) reported that the distribution of intelligence in the draft army was virtually identical to the distribution among adult prisoners. Without including details of the investigation, Murchison also reported that the prisoners in a certain midwestern institution were more intelligent than the guards, an anecdotal fact even now more widely quoted than the results of many carefully conducted studies showing important differences in favor of the intelligence hypothesis. Although Sutherland (1931:364) acknowledged that "serious questions

---

[11] Sutherland summarized about 350 studies conducted between 1910 and 1928 noting downward trends in the proportion feebleminded in delinquent and criminal groups, as well as inconsistencies in the results. "In those early days of mental testing the influence of Goddard was very great; he had asserted that the more expert the mental tester the larger the proportion of delinquents he would find to be feebleminded. Many of the testers attempted to demonstrate their superiority in that manner." "Consequently a report regarding the proportion of a delinquent group feebleminded is of primary significance in locating the mental tester upon a scale of mental testing methods. In this sense the psychometric tests of delinquents throw more light upon the intelligence of the mental testers than upon the intelligence of delinquents." (Sutherland, 1931:358–62).

INTELLIGENCE AND DELINQUENCY 581

have been raised regarding the validity of these tests and the validity of using the draft army as a sample of the general population," he carefully noted that "the consistency in results is a fact that cannot be overlooked."

By the late 1920s and early 1930s, the evidence was sufficiently mixed that summaries of the research literature were arriving at variant conclusions. Thomas and Thomas (1928:365) concluded from their review of the same literature examined by Sutherland that important differences between delinquents and nondelinquents on IQ were "beyond question." They reached this conclusion by focusing on the many studies reporting such differences and by discounting the draft-army research as being so clearly out of line as to be suspect. In 1935, Chassell published an extensive review of research on this question. Her general conclusion, based on nearly 300 studies:

> Undoubtedly the relation between morality and intellect in the general population is considerably higher than usually found in restricted groups. Nevertheless, it is hardly probable that this relation is high. Expressed in correlational terms, the relation in the general population may therefore be expected to fall below .70. (Chassell, 1935:470)[12]

As IQ tests improved, the average score of samples of delinquents also improved until, with the advent of the Revised Stanford Binet and the Wechsler-Bellevue scales in the late 1930s, they were obtaining an average IQ of about 92 (Merrill, 1947; Woodward, 1955; Caplan, 1965). With the advent of these improved tests about 35 years ago, the marked trends and occasional fluctuations of earlier research apparently came to an end. Since that time, it has been reasonable to expect that samples of delinquents would differ from the general population by about eight IQ points. This conclusion has been accepted by Woodward (1955) and Caplan (1965) in

major reviews of the literature and is generally consistent with the more recent research reviewed in this paper.

The question, then, is how a reliable eight IQ point difference was converted to the no-difference conclusion of the textbooks. One possibility is that an eight IQ point difference was not seen as theoretically or practically important. This possibility is easily disputed: no modern reviewer has questioned the importance of a difference of this magnitude.[13] Assuming that ten percent of the population is delinquent, this difference would produce a correlation (Yule's Q) between IQ and delinquency of about −.4.

The neglect of IQ after a reliable and important difference had been established may be traced to the initial plausibility of an unusual number of counter-arguments. These arguments are so numerous and diverse that we can hope to deal with them only generally and briefly.

The Spuriousness Argument

Scholarly reviews of the literature have made much of the hypothesis that the low IQs of delinquents are a spurious consequence of differences in class or culture. Against the estimated eight IQ point difference between delinquents and nondelinquents, Woodward (1955) assembles a good deal of material suggesting the possibility that cultural factors are at work: the children of professionals differ from those of unskilled manual workers by about 20 IQ points; average IQ scores are low in *areas* with high delinquency rates;[14] children in large families have low IQ scores and are more likely to be delinquent; overcrowding is related both to low IQ and to delinquency; finally, studies based on sib-sib comparisons (such as Healy and Bronner, 1936) and on other methods of control for cultural factors

---

[12] Present-day researchers would not be so modest about a correlation of .70! Chassell's caution may be indicative of the standards against which empirical relations were judged in the early days of quantitative research. These standards may account for the ease with which reviewers were able to reject IQ as a "significant" causal variable (see also footnote 1).

[13] Caplan (1965:104) refers to this eight-point difference as a "first class" relationship. As noted below, however, he cautions the reader that cultural factors be taken into account before it is accepted as genuine.

[14] This is an example of what might be called the reverse ecological fallacy: because IQ and delinquency are related at the ecological level, it is *unlikely* that they are related at the individual level.

"tend to support the contention that complete control *would* eliminate the difference between delinquents and nondelinquents" (Woodward, 1955:289; emphasis added).[15] As we have seen, the evidence says otherwise. Differences by class and race do not account for IQ differences between delinquents and nondelinquents. These differences remain pronounced within groups homogeneous on these variables. If there exists a cultural correlate of both IQ and delinquency strong enough to account for the relation between them, it has not yet been identified.

Ten years after Woodward's influential review (see Wootten, 1959:302), Caplan (1965) was unable to find additional research material bearing directly on her cultural hypothesis. His conclusions about the effects of IQ are, however, if anything, more skeptical than Woodward's, because he is able to cite an additional source of concern.

Arguments Focusing on the Measurement of Delinquency

The advent of the self-report method helped Caplan (1965:120–1) call into question the measures of delinquency upon which the original findings of IQ differences were based. Once again, the evidence against IQ was inferential rather than direct: if official data measure delinquency imperfectly, then imperfections in measurement rather than the phenomenon itself may account for the observed relation. And, indeed, few have been able to resist ascribing IQ differences between officially identified delinquents and nondelinquents to the ability of the bright delinquent to avoid detection or to differential response of officials to high and low IQ adolescents (e.g., Sutherland, 1931; Doleschal and Klapmuts, 1973; Stark, 1975).

Both the differential detection and differential reaction hypotheses require that IQ have a direct or independent effect on official delinquency.[16] Such direct effect hypotheses compete with intervening variable hypotheses and may be directly tested when the latter are available. A competing hypothesis widely mentioned in the literature (e.g., Short and Strodtbeck, 1965:238; West, 1973:44) is that IQ affects delinquency through school performance. If IQ has the direct effect suggested by the differential detection and reaction hypotheses, nothing consequent to IQ can explain the zero-order relation. Two studies bear on this question. When Wolfgang et al. removed by statistical adjustment the effects of such intervening variables as highest grade completed, the relation between IQ and such "detection" measures as number of offenses virtually vanished (Wolfgang et al., 1972:275–9). (We have replicated this finding with the Contra Costa County data.) Taking a somewhat different approach, West (1973:217) also was able to reduce the relation between IQ and official delinquency below the significant level by matching on peer and teacher ratings on "troublesomeness." These ratings were made at ages eight and ten, well before the delinquent acts recorded by officials. Once again, then, *the*

---

[15] Healy and Bronner (1936) controlled cultural factors by matching 105 delinquents with their same sex, nondelinquent sib nearest in age and then comparing IQ test scores. Although they found an IQ difference in favor of the nondelinquents, this difference was not statistically significant and was not interpreted as practically or theoretically significant by them. (Thirty-four percent of the delinquents and 26 percent of the nondelinquents had IQs under 90.)

The difficulty with this widely cited study (e.g., Wootton, 1959) is that its design makes the outcome a statistical necessity. Pushing the logic of Healy and Bronner's matching procedure one step further, we would compare identical twins raised together, only one of whom was delinquent. Since the correlation between the IQs of identical twins raised together is about .87, a figure "nearly as high . . . the correlation between two parallel tests for the same individual" (Eckland, 1967:177), we would be asking whether errors in IQ measurement are related to delinquency. By the same token, knowing that the "control" is a brother or sister reared in the same household tells us a good deal about what to expect in the way of IQ (in most studies the sib-sib correlation is in the neighborhood of .55), and there is little reason to expect the original relation to survive with anything like its "natural" magnitude.

[16] Contrary to the "intelligence per se is not a cause . . . " arguments with which it is often paired, the differential detection argument suggests that, in fact, intelligence per se *is* a cause of delinquency—when delinquency is measured by official records.

differential ability to avoid detection and the differential official reaction on the basis of IQ arguments are not supported by available evidence. (The tests of the official reaction hypothesis are limited by available data to reactions by the police.)

Tests of these and related direct effect hypotheses[17] at the same time identify the mechanism linking IQ to delinquency. This mechanism, the data suggest, is performance in and attitudes toward the school. That school variables are strong enough to account for the impact of IQ should come as no surprise. Their significance for delinquency is nowhere in dispute and is, in fact, one of the oldest and most consistent findings of delinquency research (e.g., Thrasher, 1963; Gold, 1970; Hindelang, 1973; Weis, 1973). What should come as a surprise is the easy acceptance of the no-difference-on-IQ conclusion, since the consequences of IQ differences are generally accepted as major predictors of delinquency. This brings us to the most troublesome of the arguments against IQ effects.

Arguments Focusing on the Measurement or Meaning of IQ

The facts we have presented compete with a wide variety of counter-arguments that focus on the meaning or measurement of IQ: "anybody can learn anything" (Eckland, 1967:174–5, quoting Faris, 1961:838), "it is impossible to make intelligence part of any respectable theory" (ASR referee, 1975), "so-called intelligence tests measure only 'test intelligence' and not innate intelligence" (Clinard, 1968:170), and "mainly they [IQ tests] measure the socioeconomic status of the respondent" (Chambliss and Ryther, 1975:373). Excellent discussions of many of these issues are available in the sociological literature (Eckland, 1967;

---

[17] Other very old direct effect hypotheses are that IQ differences stem from (1) the inability of the unintelligent to understand distinctions between right and wrong or (2) their inability to foresee and appreciate the consequences of their acts. These hypotheses assume that low IQ children are more likely to be delinquent, regardless of the social consequences (e.g., school difficulties) of their lack of IQ. Again, current data do not appear to support hypotheses of this form.

Gordon, 1975). We will deal only with those counter-hypotheses that have a direct bearing on the relation between IQ and delinquency and that can be addressed to some extent using data already presented.

The cultural bias of IQ tests. The argument against IQ tests most frequently encountered in the sociological literature is that these tests are biased against low-income and minority group children. Specific test items (e.g., "What color are rubies?") are often presented to show the obviousness of this bias (Chambliss and Ryther, 1975:373). Since the groups said to be discriminated against by IQ tests are the same groups with high rates of delinquency, the cultural bias hypothesis is certainly plausible. In form, it is identical to the traditional cultural hypothesis previously encountered and may be tested using the same data. These data show that the bias hypothesis is inadequate: important differences in IQ between delinquents and nondelinquents *within* race and class categories cannot be explained by argument or evidence that these tests are biased in favor of middle-class whites.

The stability of test scores. To the extent that IQ test scores are unstable and subject to subtle social influence, the meaning of a correlation between IQ and delinquency is open to question. It may be that reaction to the misbehavior of the child influences his IQ, that the low IQ child today may be the high IQ child tomorrow, and so on. These possibilities are summarized in assertions that "the scores are highly unstable through time" (Polk and Schafer, 1972:195). Unfortunately for such assertions, they are not consistent with the evidence: the IQs of children at four or five years of age have a correlation of about .7 with their IQs at age 17 (Bloom, 1964); after age ten, test-retest correlations (regardless of the number of years between the tests) fall between the test's reliability and the square of its reliability (Jensen, 1969:18). For that matter, the ability of IQ tests to predict delinquency at some period far removed from their administration is inconsistent with the gross implications of the instability argument.

A fall-back position for those who

584   AMERICAN SOCIOLOGICAL REVIEW

would argue instability is that these scores *could be* manipulated by simple and straightforward shifts in the environment of the child:

> We may treat people differently out of ignorance or prejudice, but the result is the same as if the supposed differences were real. Studies have shown that school children seen as liable to be educationally backward become educationally backward and that, vice versa, children seen as educationally capable become educationally capable. (Taylor et al., 1973:142; see also Polk and Schafer, 1972:46; Schur, 1973:164)

The study cited in support of such arguments is Rosenthal and Jacobson, *Pygmalion in the Classroom* (1968). In this study, students in grades K through 5 in one elementary school were given group-administered IQ tests at the end of the 1964 academic year. The following fall, a random 20 percent of the students were identified to their teachers as students expected to show unusual intellectual gains during the academic year. In May, 1965, all students were re-tested on the same IQ test. Although both the experimental and the control subjects showed IQ gains, the experimental group showed a 3.8 point greater gain, with the bulk of this gain coming in the first and second grades. On the basis of these results, Rosenthal and Jacobson (1968:98) conclude that favorable expectations of teachers "can be responsible for gains in their pupils' IQ's and, for the lower grades, that these gains can be quite dramatic."

Unfortunately, *Pygmalion* has problems. Snow (1969:197) asserts that the study "stands as a casebook example of many of Darrell Huff's (*How to Lie with Statistics*) admonitions to data analysts" and that it "fails to come close to providing an adequate demonstration of the phenomenon" (the effects of teacher expectations on IQ scores). Thorndike (1968:708) begins his similarly negative review with what has turned out to be a prophetic statement:

> In spite of anything I can say, I am sure it (*Pygmalion in the Classroom*) will become a classic—widely referred to and rarely examined critically. Alas, it is so defective technically that one can only regret that it ever

got beyond the eyes of the original investigators!

Thorndike concludes that "the basic data . . . are so untrustworthy that any conclusions based upon them must be suspect." And, indeed, this too was prophetic. Elashoff and Snow (1971) report that *none of nine attempts to replicate the effects of teacher expectations on IQ scores has been successful*. One would think that this would be enough to put an end to the "Rosenthal effect." However, Beeghley and Butler (1974:750) still maintain that the effects of teacher expectations on IQ "have been forcefully demonstrated by Rosenthal and Jacobson," and they muddy the waters by citing two "replications" of *Pygmalion*. In the first, "changes in intellectual functioning were not expected" by the investigators themselves (Meichenbaum et al., 1969:307) and in fact, as far as we can determine, IQ was not even a variable in the study. In the second, the author summarizes a variety of research results and concludes the findings do not "provide any direct proof that teacher expectations can influence pupil performance" (Pidgeon, 1970:126). Ironically—for a study which Beeghley and Butler purport to be a replication of *Pygmalion*—Pidgeon (1970:126) notes that the Rosenthal and Jacobson study "would bear repetition, providing conditions could be found for employing a more satisfactory research design." As of now, it is clear that no labeling or expectation effects of the sort alleged by Rosenthal and Jacobson (and widely cited in the crime and delinquency literature) have been established.

Conclusions

The assertion that IQ affects the likelihood of delinquent behavior through its effect on school performance is consistent with available data. The corollary descriptive assertion that delinquents have lower IQs than nondelinquents is firmly established. Both of these assertions are inconsistent with the "no-IQ-difference" view of the textbooks. They are clearly inconsistent with the image of the delinquent in much sociological writing on the subject, and those planning prevention and treat-

INTELLIGENCE AND DELINQUENCY 585

ment programs would do well to take them into account.[18]

Interestingly enough, most modern theories of delinquency assume (and some explicitly state) that IQ affects delinquency. That their views have been ignored by researchers testing them speaks to the depth of the concern that individual differences are both non-sociological and positively dangerous. In this sense, IQ is doubly significant in that it represents an entire class of variables traditionally ignored by sociological students of crime and delinquency. Variables in this large residual category (virtually everything beyond class, culture, and official processing) will not lose their status as alternative hypotheses simply by being ignored, and they will continue to restrict and even embarrass sociological theory until some effort is made to incorporate them.

For that matter, IQ is a poor example of a variable that may require modification of sociological perspectives. As of now, there is no evidence that IQ has a direct impact on delinquency. The police bias, differential ability to avoid detection, and inability to appreciate moral distinctions hypotheses are not consistent with current data. If the mechanism linking IQ to delinquency is school performance and adjustment, then IQ does not lead away from the arena in which sociological theories have focused their quest for the antecedents of delinquency; rather, it helps illuminate the social processes occurring there.

REFERENCES

Akers, Ronald L.
  1964 "Socio-economic status and delinquent behavior: a retest." Journal of Research on Crime and Delinquency 1:38–46.
Beeghley, Leonard and Edgar W. Butler
  1974 "The consequences of intelligence testing in public schools before and after desegregation." Social Problems 21:740–54.

[18] See Nettler (1974:162–5). The range of treatment programs affected by these differences is considerably broader than is usually imagined: "The frequent mental dullness . . . and reading and writing disabilities of a larger proportion of delinquents *make them poor risks for industrial training* (Shulman, 1951:781, emphasis added).

Bloch, Herbert A. and Gilbert Geis
  1962 Man, Crime and Society. New York: Random House.
Bloom, B.A.
  1964 Stability and Change in Human Characteristics. New York: Wiley.
Caplan, Nathan S.
  1965 "Intellectual functioning" Pp. 100–38 in Herbert C. Quay (ed.), Juvenile Delinquency. Princeton: Van Nostrand.
Chambliss, William J. and Thomas E. Ryther
  1975 Sociology: The Discipline and Its Direction. New York: McGraw-Hill.
Chassell, Clara F.
  1935 The Relation between Morality and Intellect. New York: Teachers College, Columbia University.
Clinard, Marshall B.
  1968 Sociology of Deviant Behavior. New York: Holt, Rinehart and Winston.
Cloward, Richard E. and Lloyd E. Ohlin
  1960 Delinquency and Opportunity. New York: Free Press.
Cohen, Albert K.
  1955 Delinquent Boys: The Culture of the Gang. New York: Free Press.
Coleman, James C.
  1950 Abnormal Psychology and Modern Life, Glenview, Il.: Scott, Foresman.
Doleschal, Eugene and Nora Klapmuts
  1973 "Toward a new criminology." Crime and Delinquency Literature: 607–26.
Eckland, Bruce K.
  1967 "Genetics and sociology: a reconsideration." American Sociological Review 32:193–4.
Elashoff, J. and R. Snow
  1971 Pygmalion Reconsidered. Worthington, Oh.: Jones
Erickson, Maynard L. and LaMar T. Empey
  1963 "Court records, undetected delinquency and decision-making." Journal of Criminal Law, Criminology and Police Science 54:456–69.
Faris, Robert E. L.
  1961 "The ability dimension in human society." American Sociological Review 26:835–43.
Gibbons, Don C.
  1970 Delinquent Behavior. Englewood Cliffs, N.J.: Prentice-Hall.
Glueck, Sheldon and Eleanor Glueck
  1934 Five Hundred Delinquent Women. New York: Knopf.
Goddard, Henry H.
  1914 Feeble-Mindedness: Its Causes and Consequences. New York: Macmillan.
Gold, Martin
  1970 Delinquent Behavior in an American City. Belmont, Ca.: Brooks/Cole.
Gordon, Robert A.
  1975 "Examining labeling theory: the case of mental retardation." Pp. 83–146 in Walter Gove (ed.), The Labelling of Deviance. New York: Wiley.
  1976 "Prevalence: the rare datum in delinquency measurement and its implications for the theory of delinquency." Pp. 201–84 in Mal-

586   AMERICAN SOCIOLOGICAL REVIEW

colm W. Klein (ed.), The Juvenile Justice
     System. Beverly Hills, Ca.: Sage.
Goring, Charles
  [1913] The English Convict. Montclair, N.J.: Pat-
  1972   terson Smith
Haskell, Martin R. and Lewis Yablonsky
  1974 Crime and Delinquency. Chicago: Rand
         McNally
Healy, William and Augusta F. Bronner
  1936 New Light on Delinquency and Its Treat-
         ment. New Haven: Yale University Press.
Hindelang, Michael J.
  1973 "Causes of delinquency: a partial replica-
         tion and extension." Social Problems
         20:471–87.
Hirschi, Travis
  1969 Causes of Delinquency. Berkeley: Univer-
         sity of California Press.
Jensen, A. R.
  1969 "How much can we boost I.Q. and scholas-
         tic achievement?" Harvard Educational
         Review 39:1–123.
Johnson, Elmer
  1968 Crime,   Correction   and   Society.
         Homewood, Il.: Dorsey Press.
Liazos, Alexander
  1972 "The poverty of the sociology of deviance:
         nuts, sluts, and preverts." Social Problems
         20:103–20.
McCord, William and Joan McCord
  1959 Origins of Crime: A New Evaluation of the
         Cambridge-Somerville Study. New York:
         Columbia Press.
Matza, David
  1964 Delinquency and Drift. New York: Wiley.
Meichanbaum, Donald H., Kenneth S. Bowers and
     Robert R. Ross
  1969 "A behavioral analysis of teacher expec-
         tancy effect." Journal of Personality and
         Social Psychology 13:306–16.
Merrill, Maud A.
  1947 Problems of Child Delinquency. Boston:
         Houghton Mifflin.
Merton, Robert K.
  1938 "Social structure and anomie." American
         Sociological Review 3:672–82.
Murchison, Carl
  1926 Criminal Intelligence. Worcester, Ma.:
         Clark University Press.
Nettler, Gwynn
  1974 Explaining Crime. New York: McGraw-
         Hill.
Nye, F. Ivan, James F. Short, Jr. and Virgil J. Olson
  1958 "Socio-economic status and delinquent be-
         havior." American Journal of Sociology
         63:381–9.
Pidgeon, Douglas
  1970 Expectation and Pupil Performance. Lon-
         don: National Foundation for Educational
         Research in England and Wales.
Polk, Kenneth and Walter E. Schafer
  1972 Schools and Delinquency. Englewood
         Cliffs, N.J.: Prentice-Hall.
Reckless, Walter C. and Simon Dinitz
  1972 The Prevention of Delinquency. Columbus:
         Ohio State University Press.

Reiss, Albert J. and Albert L. Rhodes
  1961 "The distribution of juvenile delinquency in
         the social class structure." American
         Sociological Review 26:720–32.
Rosenthal, R. and Lenore Jacobson
  1968 Pygmalion in the Classroom. New York:
         Holt, Rinehart and Winston.
Ross, Edward A.
  1901 Social Control. New York: Macmillan.
Savitz, Leonard D.
  1972 "Introduction."   Pp.   v–xx   in   Gina
         Lombroso-Ferrero, Criminal Man. Mont-
         clair, N.J.: Patterson Smith.
Schur, Edwin M.
  1973 Radical Non-Intervention: Rethinking the
         Delinquency Problem. Englewood Cliffs,
         N.J.: Prentice-Hall.
Short, James F., Jr. and Fred L. Strodtbeck
  1965 Group Process and Gang Delinquency.
         Chicago: University of Chicago Press.
Shulman, Harry M.
  1951 "Intelligence and delinquency." Journal of
         Criminal Law and Criminology 41:763–81.
Snow, R.
  1969 "Unfinished Pygmalion." Contemporary
         Psychology 14:197–9.
Stark, Rodney
  1975 Social Problems. New York: CRM/Random
         House.
Sutherland, Edwin H.
  1924 Criminology. Philadelphia: Lippincott.
  1931 "Mental deficiency and crime," Pp. 357–75
         in Kimball Young (ed.), Social Attitudes.
         New York: Holt, Rinehart and Winston.
Sutherland, Edwin H. and Donald R. Cressey
  [1939] Principles of Criminology. Philadelphia: Lip-
  1974   pincott
Tannenbaun., Frank
  1938 Crime and the Community. Boston: Ginn.
Taylor, Ian, Paul Walton and Jock Young
  1973 The New Criminology. New York: Harper.
Thomas, William I. and Dorothy Swaine Thomas
  1928 The Child in America. New York: Knopf.
Thorndike, R. L.
  1968 "Review of R. Rosenthal and L. Jacobson,
         'Pygmalion in the Classroom.' " American
         Educational Research Journal 5:708–11.
Thrasher, F.
  [1927] The Gang. Chicago: University of Chicago
  1963   press.
Toby, Jackson
  1957 "Social disorganization and stake in con-
         formity: complementary factors in the
         predatory behavior of hoodlums." Journal
         of Criminal Law, Criminology and Police
         Science 48:12–7.
Toby, Jackson and Marcia L. Toby
  1961 Low School Status as a Predisposing Factor
         in   Subcultural   Delinquency.   New
         Brunswick, N.J.: Rutgers University.
         Mimeo.
Tulchin, Simon H.
  1939 Intelligence and Crime. Chicago: Univer-
         sity of Chicago Press.
Weis, Joseph
  1973 Delinquency among the Well-to-Do. Un-

REDISCOVERING DELINQUENCY   587

published Ph.D. dissertation. University of California, Berkeley.

West, D. J.
1973 Who Becomes Delinquent? London: Heinemann.

Williams, Jay and Martin Gold
1972 "From delinquent behavior to official delinquency." Social Problems 20:209–29.

Wolfgang, Marvin, Robert M. Figlio and Thorsten Sellin
1972 Delinquency as a Birth Cohort. Chicago: University of Chicago Press.

Woodward, Mary
1955 "The role of low intelligence in delinquency." British Journal of Delinquency 5:281–303.

Wootton, Barbara
1959 Social Science and Social Pathology. New York: Macmillan.

Zeleny, Leslie D.
1933 "Feeblemindedness and criminal conduct." American Journal of Sociology 38:564–78.

[7]

Development and Psychopathology, 1 (1989), 105–118
Copyright © 1989 Cambridge University Press
Printed in the United States of America

Neuropsychological assessment of executive functions in self-reported delinquents

TERRIE E. MOFFITT AND BILL HENRY
University of Wisconsin, Madison

Abstract

Deficits in "executive" neuropsychological functions have been proposed to underlie the development of antisocial behavior such as juvenile delinquency. Results of research into the executive functions of delinquents have been mixed, and studies have been hampered by reliance on small samples of adjudicated subjects and questionable validity of the tests administered. This research examined the performance of a large unselected birth cohort of adolescent boys and girls on five tests of executive function that have documented reliability and validity. It is the first such study to use self-reports of antisocial behavior. Executive deficits were shown only by a subgroup of delinquent subjects with childhood comorbidity of antisocial behavior and attention deficit disorder; that subgroup's behavior was also rated as more aggressive and impulsive than comparison groups'. Group differences on executive measures remained significant after the effects of overall IQ were statistically controlled. Also, delinquents who had been detected by police did not show poorer executive functions than subjects with equivalent self-reports of delinquent behavior who had evaded official detection, suggesting that executive deficits are related to the development of antisocial behavior itself, and not simply to risk of detection.

The many normal functions of the frontal lobes of the brain include sustaining attention and concentration; abstract reasoning and concept formation; goal formulation; anticipation and planning; programming and initiation of purposive sequences of motor behavior; effective self-monitoring of behavior and self-awareness; and inhibition of unsuccessful, inappropriate or impulsive behaviors, with adaptive shifting to alternative behaviors. This group of functions is commonly referred to as the *executive functions*, and impairment of them holds consequent implications for the development of social judgment, self-control, responsiveness to punishment, and ethical behavior (see Fuster, 1980; Kolb & Whishaw, 1985; Milner & Petrides, 1984; Stuss & Benson, 1986, for reviews of clinical and experimental research).

Several theorists have postulated a developmental relationship between antisocial behavior and executive dysfunctions (Gorenstein, 1982; Pontius, 1972; Yeudall, 1980). They propose that executive dysfunctions that may be present or latent at birth may interfere with the ability to control behavior, producing inattentive, impulsive children who have difficulty considering the future implications of their acts. Such children may have trouble understanding the negative impact their behavior makes on others, may fail to hold in mind abstract ideas of ethical values and future contingencies while they attend to immediate rewards, and may be unable to inhibit inappropriate behavior or to adapt their behav-

This work was supported by USPHS Grant 1 RO1 MH-43746-01 from the Antisocial and Violent Behavior Branch of the National Institute of Mental Health. The Dunedin Multidisciplinary Health and Development Research Unit is supported by the Medical Research Council of New Zealand and directed by Dr. Phil A. Silva. The Dunedin Police Department generously provided advice, work space, and staff time. Appreciation is expressed for the methodological advice of Sarnoff A. Mednick, the critical eye of Jennifer White, and for the data collection efforts of Mrs. Pat Brasch, Mrs. Kathleen Campbell, Mr. Rich Poulton, and the psychometrists who administered the WISC-R.

ior readily to social feedback. Certain executive deficits may thus have serious developmental consequences (i.e., they may give rise to early childhood behavior problems that in turn set the stage for emerging delinquent behavior as the child grows chronologically older, but lags in social maturity (Buikhuisen, 1987)).

The neuropsychological study of executive functions can describe how psychopathology (such as antisocial behavior) relates to individual differences in the capacity to perform executive self-control functions in response to information from the social environment. This interactional relation between brain and environment is key. The brain does not produce behavior in a vacuum, but interacts dynamically with the environment as the developing child perceives social demands and experiences retribution for antisocial behaviors. Accordingly, one of the aims of neuropsychological research on delinquency is to be able to identify individuals whose neuropsychological dysfunctions place them at risk for maladaptive behavioral responses to social influences. In this way, a neuropsychological approach can guide inquiry into the complex relationships among the biological, social, and behavioral domains, and their implications for psychopathological development. Ideally, a neuropsychological approach to the development of delinquency and antisocial behavior can inform our understanding of the neuropsychological prerequisites for the acquisition of prosocial behavior, as well.

Pontius and Ruttiger (1976) tested Pontius's (1972) theory of "frontal lobe system maturational lag" by qualitatively rating stories told by school children between the ages of 9 and 16. Results showed that 70% of 67 normals, but only 47% of 36 delinquents, told stories that demonstrated their ability to switch the course of narrative action properly in response to new circumstances. (The authors assumed that the ability to adapt action in storytelling is related to analogous behavioral abilities.) Pontius (1972) suggested a number of neuropsychological tests that should be admin-istered to delinquents with the objective of assessing executive functions: the Wisconsin Card Sorting Test (WCST), tapping abstract concept formation and the ability to inhibit a previously rewarded, but now incorrect, response; the Stroop Color-Word Test, requiring inhibition of an over-learned automatic response; the Trail-Making Test, Form B, in which the child must sustain attention to two competing sequences, alternate between them, and inhibit out-of-turn responses; and Halstead's Category Test, wherein the child reasons from abstract categorical concepts. These tests operationalize a subset of the many executive functions; they allow quantitative measurement of samples of subjects' performance of executive-type tasks.

Two studies have applied batteries of executive function tests to delinquent subjects. Skoff and Libon (1987) compared the scores of 22 incarcerated delinquents to published test norms for the WCST, Porteus Mazes, Trails B, Verbal Fluency, and four additional executive tasks. They reported that one-third of their subjects scored in the impaired range on the battery as a whole. This study suffers from the absence of a nondelinquent comparison group; the test norms are of questionable relevance for delinquents in California, who might be expected to be low SES minority group members. In addition, examination of the data shows that the delinquents curiously scored more poorly on some of the simpler tasks that ostensibly required the same cognitive functions as tasks on which they performed adequately. Appellof and Augustine (1985, reported in abstract form) tested 30 male delinquents and 30 controls (selection criteria not described) on the WCST, Porteus Mazes, Verbal Fluency, and six other unnamed measures. They found no group differences and concluded that executive dysfunctions do not differentially characterize delinquents.

Other studies, while not focusing upon executive functions, have reported data from individual measures typically included in executive test batteries. These studies, taken together, provide some additional support for the association between delinquency and executive deficit. Berman and Siegal (1976) found that delinquents scored poorly on the Category Test and Trails B. Wolff, Waber, Bauermeister, Cohen, and Farber (1982) reported delinquency-related impairments on tests of selective attention and on the Stroop Color Word Test. Krynicki (1978) found that delinquent subjects performed similarly to subjects with documented organic brain damage on Verbal Fluency and on a test of motor perseveration from the Luria neuropsychological test battery. Four studies showed that delinquents scored poorly on various tests requiring sequencing of motor behavior (Brickman, McManus, Grapentine, & Alessi, 1984; Hurwitz, Bibace, Wolff, & Rowbotham, 1972; Karniski, Levine, Clarke, Palfrey, & Meltzer, 1982; Miller, Burdg, & Carpenter, 1980). Trails B and the WCST were administered by Yeudall and Fromm-Auch (1979), who concluded that the delinquent group's full-battery profile indicated anterior brain dysfunction, but they did not report group means for specific test scores. Riddle and Roberts (1977) reviewed 16 studies using the Porteus Maze Test Q score, which is thought to reflect an impulsive, poorly planned style of problem solving. They reported that, utilizing equal sized groups of delinquents and controls, 70% of subjects could be accurately classified using a specific cut-off point on the Q score distribution.

One possible element in the relation between executive function and delinquency that has not been explored to date is Attention Deficit Disorder (ADD). ADD embodies the impulsive, undercontrolled behavioral presentation associated with executive neuropsychological deficits, and it is a known risk factor for later delinquent outcome (Farrington, Loeber, & Van Kammen, 1987; Loney, Whaley-Klahn, Kosier, & Conboy, 1983; Offord, Sullivan, Allen, & Abrams, 1979; Satterfield, 1987). Moreover, there is emerging evidence that suboptimal metabolism in the prefrontal cortex (as measured by positron-emission tomography [PET] scanning) is associated with symptoms of ADD (Lou, Henriksen, & Bruhn, 1984) and with performance of executive function tests of sustained attention (Cohen, Semple, Gross, Holcomb, Dowling, & Nordahl, 1988).

Evidence that attentional mechanisms may be primary among delinquents' executive deficits comes from their especially poor performance on the WISC-R Arithmetic subtest. In many studies that reported data for subtests from the WISC-R, the subtest showing the largest delinquency group differences was Arithmetic (Berman & Siegal, 1976; Brickman et al., 1984; Moffitt & Silva, 1988a; Voorhees, 1981). In factor analytic studies of the WISC-R subtests, Arithmetic loads most heavily on factors taken to represent "sustained concentration" or "freedom from distraction" (Cohen, 1959). The high rates of comorbidity for delinquent conduct problems and ADD (see Hinshaw, 1987, for review), and the poor scores earned by some delinquents on attentional measures, suggest the hypothesis that the subgroup of delinquents with ADD may evidence particular deficits on executive function tests.

Our previous research using a sample of New Zealand children has identified subjects who demonstrate both ADD and delinquency as a subgroup that warrants closer neuropsychological study. When compared to other delinquents, these subjects exhibited earlier onset of antisocial behavior (Moffitt, in preparation) and their antisocial behaviors were more aggressive in nature (Moffitt & Silva, 1988b). They also showed greater neuropsychological deficits than did subjects exhibiting either delinquency or ADD, although they were indistinguishable from other ADD cases on the basis of behavioral ratings of inattention or motor hyperactivity (Moffitt & Silva, 1988b). Thus, the presentation of early aggressive conduct problems accompanied by neuropsychological deficits was unique to the subjects with ADD+delinquency comorbidity. Our earlier research reported analyses of composite neuropsychological variables, derived from a factor analysis (Moffitt & Heimer, 1988), in which each of the scores from the full neuropsychological test battery had loaded on factors representing modalities of information processing (i.e., verbal, visual–spatial, memory, visual–motor). These composites thus obscured fine-grained consideration of the subjects' scores from executive function tests, which spanned modalities. The research reported here examined individual executive test scores for delinquents with and without ADD, and for comparison groups of nondelinquents with and without ADD.

The present study assessed the relationship between executive functions and *self-reported* delinquency for the first time, using an unselected birth cohort of New Zealand children. Based on delinquency status and diagnoses drawn from the Diagnostic Interview Schedule for Children — Child version (DISC-C), members of the cohort were assigned to one of four groups: (1) the non-ADD/nondelinquent group; (2) the non-ADD/delinquent group; (3) the ADD/nondelinquent group; and (4) the ADD+delinquent group. The four groups were then compared on 14 scores obtained from five neuropsychological tasks thought to tap executive functions and on a self-report behavioral measure of impulsive behavior to test the hypotheses that delinquents with a history of ADD would show relatively greater executive deficits and that the deficits would be accompanied by a more impulsive behavioral style.

One problem for interpretation of previous findings of executive deficit in delinquents is that the studies have relied on incarcerated samples, raising the possibility that executive deficits (e.g., impulsivity, poor planning) are associated with increased risk of detection rather than with any tendency to engage in antisocial acts per se. The collection of police records and self-report data for this sample allowed us to address this possibility. The hypothesis that self-reported delinquents with police records would demonstrate more severe executive deficits than self-reported delinquents who had escaped detection was also tested for this report.

Methods

Subjects

Subjects were the members of an unselected New Zealand birth cohort, who have been studied extensively since their births as part of the Dunedin Multidisciplinary Health and Development Study. The history of the study and sample have been described in detail by McGee and Silva (1982). Briefly, the cohort consists of all children born at Queen Mary Hospital in Dunedin, New Zealand, between April 1, 1972, and March 31, 1973, who were still living in the province of Otago when the first follow-up of the sample began in 1975. At that time, 1,139 of the 1,649 live births met that criterion and thus were eligible for inclusion at age 3; 1,037 participated. The sample has been reassessed with a diverse battery of psychological, medical, and sociological measures every two years since then. Attrition has been low for the cohort: 82% (435 males, 415 females) of the original 1,037 were available for study at age 13 when the neuropsychological and delinquency data for this study were collected. McGee (1985) has compared the children who were lost to the study at each age with those who remained at age 11. He found no systematic differences between the groups, in terms of social class, IQ, or a variety of behavioral variables.

In comparison to the general population of New Zealand, the Dunedin sample is slightly socioeconomically advantaged. Also, Maoris and Polynesians are underrepresented: They are 10% of the general population, but only 2% of the sample. The predominantly European background of the sample suggests that it is comparable to those from other English-speaking Western cultures.

A *minimum* of 678 subjects had 100% present data on every neuropsychological and delinquency variable used in this report. Moffitt and Silva (1988b) reported that the 172 subjects with only partial data present did not differ significantly from the remainder of the cohort in terms of WISC-R Full Scale IQ or parental ratings of subject's antisocial behavior.

Measures

WISC-R Mazes. In this task, the child is presented with a series of increasingly more difficult mazes and is asked to draw the way out of each one. This test is an optional subtest of the WISC-R (Wechsler, 1974). Tow (1955) found that frontal leukotomy patients were slowed significantly and averaged more errors in their maze performance when compared to performance prior to the surgery. In addition to the number of errors, the "Q score," which reflects impulsive departures from the task instructions, was also taken from this measure (Riddle & Roberts, 1977).

Wisconsin Card Sorting Task. The WCST assesses ability of form abstract concepts, sustain attention, and to flexibly shift cognitive set in response to changing conceptual rules while inhibiting inappropriate perseverative responses. The subject is given a pack of cards on each of which are printed one to four of a single symbol (triangle, star, cross, or circle) in red, green, yellow, or blue. The subject's task is to place the cards one by one under four stimulus cards, according to a principle for matching (symbol, number, or color) that the subject must deduce from the pattern of the examiner's responses to the subject's placement of the cards. After ten consecutive correct placements, the examiner shifts the principle, indicating the shift only by the changed pattern of his or her "right" or "wrong" statements. (See Berg (1948) and Heaton (1981) for reports of reliability and validity.) Milner (1963, 1964) reported that patients with frontal lobe tumors achieved fewer sorting categories and made more perseverative errors than did patients with tumors localized in other brain regions. Resulting from time constraints, a shortened version of the WCST requiring three categories for completion was administered.

Measures taken from this task included number of responses to complete all three categories, number of perseverative responses, number of responses required to complete the first category, percentage of responses that were unique, percentage of responses that were errors, and percentage of responses that were perseverative errors.

Trail Making Test, Forms A and B (Trails). This task is a measure of ability to initiate, switch, and stop a sequence of complex purposive behavior, and of attention and concentration skills. The subject first must draw lines to connect consecutively numbered circles on a worksheet (A) and then must connect consecutively numbered and lettered circles on a second worksheet (B) by alternating between the two sequences. Lewinsohn (1973) and Reitan (1958) report validity and reliability for this test. Three measures were taken from the task: number of errors on Trails B, time required to complete Trails B, and the time required to complete Trails B minus the time required to complete Trails A (Reitan & Davison, 1974).

Rey-Osterreith Complex Figure Test (ROC). This task measures visual–spatial construction ability, visual nonverbal memory following an interpolated activity, and planning strategy in execution of a complex drawing task. The child copies a complex stimulus figure, and the examiner provides the child with successive colors of pencils for assessment of strategy. After 3 minutes delay, the child draws the figure from recall. See Rey (1941), Osterreith (1944), Milner (1975), and Waber and Holmes (1985) for reports of the reliability and validity of this test. Two measures were taken from this task for the purpose of this study: the copy accuracy score and the percentage of total time required for the child to complete the interior rectangle of the figure. The latter indicates how early in the drawing the child initiated a strategy of organizing his or her drawing in relation to the primary central element—a thoughtful planning approach to the task.

Rey Auditory Verbal Learning Test (RAVLT). This test measures immediate auditory verbal memory span, provides a learning curve over successive trials, reveals learning strategies, and measures free recall and recognition memory following an interpolated activity. The version used consisted of four presentations with recall of a 15-word list, one presentation of a second 15-word list, and a sixth recall trial, followed by a 15-minute delayed recall trial and finally a delayed recognition test with the stimulus words embedded in a paragraph. Rey (1964) and Taylor (1959) describe validity and reliability for the RAVLT. Lezak (1983) has suggested that evaluation of interference effects between trials four and six of the RAVLT is useful in assessment of impaired executive functioning.

The Diagnostic Interview Schedule for Children — Child Version. This measure was administered to all children in the cohort at age 11 by a child psychiatrist. The DISC-C (Costello, Edelbrock, Kalas, Kessler, & Klaric, 1982) is a structured diagnostic interview for children that was developed under the auspices of the National Institute of Mental Health (NIMH). It is based on the DSM-III diagnostic criteria for the various disorders of childhood and adolescence; all items refer to the child's functioning over the past year. The child's verbal responses are recorded as (0) *no*, (1) *sometimes*, and (2) *yes*. Additional comments from the child and extra clarification of symptoms when required were also recorded. The DISC-C data were used to diagnose ADD, as well as other childhood disorders. Interrater reliabilities (Cohen's kappa) for the individual diagnoses ranged from .69 to .84 (Anderson, Williams, McGee, & Silva, 1987).

An impulsivity scale calculated as the sum of eight items from the DISC-C was constructed for the purposes of this study. The items (e.g., "When you are playing games with other kids, do you have trouble waiting your turn?" "Do you often rush into things without thinking about what may happen?" "Does your teacher have to re-

mind you what to do again and again and again?") tapped four of six DSM-III criterion symptoms for the impulsivity portion of the diagnosis of ADD-H.

Rutter Child Scale A and B (RCSA&B). The Rutter Child Scales A and B (Rutter, Tizard, & Whitmore, 1970) are 31-item and 26-item questionnaires designed to be filled out by parents and teachers, respectively. The items inquire about the major areas of a child's behavioral and emotional functioning. The parent or teacher rates each item as (0) *does not apply*, (1) *applies somewhat*, or (2) *certainly applies*. The RCSA&B were supplemented with 16 items concerning inattention, impulsivity, and hyperactivity (see McGee, Williams, & Silva, 1985). These additional items were derived from the DSM-III diagnostic criteria for ADD and were rated in the same way as were the actual RCSA&B items. All items refer to the child's behavior during the past year.

Self-Reported Early Delinquency (SRED). This instrument, described fully in Moffitt & Silva (1988c), was administered to subjects by an examiner who was blind to their neuropsychological test scores. Briefly, this 58-item measure was designed specifically for use in New Zealand and includes validity checks between card-sort and interview protocols, as well as screening and assistance for poor readers. It also provides a score weighted for item seriousness. This score summarizes both variety and seriousness of a subject's delinquent behaviors; it was used to designate delinquent cases for this study. One-month test–retest reliability ($r = .85$), internal consistency (Kuder–Richardson Formula 20, $r = .90$), and concurrent validity (with parental report of subjects' socialized aggressive behaviors, $r = .43$, $p < .001$) have been found to be adequate for social science research. Thefts (especially shoplifting and burglary) accounted for 41.2% of acts reported by the subject, minor assault for 24.7%, and vandalism and substance abuse for 10.7% and 9.9%, respectively.

Group assignment

The subjects most heavily involved in delinquent activities were identified by exploiting the possibility for agreement between four available sources of information about antisocial behavior. The advantages of this "best estimate" approach have been described by Loeber and Dishion (1983). Subjects could report themselves delinquent by scoring above the 85th percentile on the SRED. (Use of the 85th percentile cut-off was suggested by an observed discontinuity in the skew at this point in the distribution.) Parents could report their children delinquent by providing scores above the 85th percentile on the Socialized Aggression subscale of the Quay and Peterson Behavior Problem Checklist — Revised (BPCR) (Quay & Peterson, 1983), which was completed at the time of the age 13 assessment. Teachers could report a child delinquent by giving him or her antisocial subscale scores beyond the 85th percentile on the RCSB (Rutter et al., 1970), also completed when the subjects were 13 years old. These parent and teacher scales are comprised of items assessing delinquent behaviors such as stealing, fighting, truancy, runaway, and drug use. All percentile ranks were calculated separately for boys and girls, so that group membership reflects serious delinquency *relative to same-sex peers*. A subject was assigned to the delinquent group if at least two reports met the above criteria, *or* if a file was found for him or her in the police district office. Thus, subjects could not name themselves delinquent without the consensus of at least one adult reporter. This reduced the chance of erroneous group assignment resulting from overzealous self-report. Likewise, a subject who underreported delinquent acts could nevertheless be designated delinquent by agreement between adult reporters. Seventy-one boys and 53 girls met these criteria. Mean scores for the SRED were 10.69 for delinquent girls; 2.19, nondelinquent girls; 15.73, delinquent boys; and 5.70, nondelinquent boys.

Diagnoses of the 53 ADD cases (described in detail by Anderson et al., 1987) were made at age 11 as follows. Three sources existed for report of symptoms meeting DSM-III criteria for ADD. The child reported symptoms during an interview with a child psychiatrist who used the DISC-C (Costello et al., 1982), and parents and teachers filled in the Inattention and Motor Hyperactivity subscales of the RCSA&B (Rutter et al., 1970). In 35 cases, two of the three possible reporters provided independent consensus report of all DSM-III criterion symptoms, and in 10 cases one reporter met the full criterion and another met some criteria, thereby ensuring pervasiveness of the symptoms (Schachar, Rutter, & Smith, 1981). In an additional 8 cases, one reporter alone provided enough symptoms to meet diagnostic criteria. Data concerning problem behavior collected from parents and teachers when the children were 5 and 7 years old confirmed onset of the disorder before age 7 for all 53 cases. At age 11 the prevalence of ADD so diagnosed was 6.7%, the sex ratio was 5.1 boys to 1 girl, and 85% of the cases had more than two symptoms of hyperactivity in addition to their attentional problems.

Table 1 presents the numbers of subjects, gender distributions, mean IQ scores, and mean SES for the four study groups: the delinquents with and without ADD, and the two comparison groups of nondelinquents with and without ADD.[1] Group

---

1. Forty-five subjects reported themselves as delinquent (above the 85th percentile on the SRED), but were not reported as delinquent by their parents or teachers and did not have a police record. Little is known about the characteristics of these subjects. Because no clear predictions could be made regarding their performance on the neuropsychological and behavioral measures, they were excluded from this study, but will be described elsewhere (Moffitt & Henry, in preparation).

Although, as previously mentioned, the minimum number of subjects with every neuropsychological and delinquency data point present was 678, the individual analyses here required only subsets of the total file of variables. The neuropsychological measure on which the largest number of subjects had complete data was present for 718 cases before the 45 uncorroborated reporters were excluded. Thus,

Table 1. *Gender distributions and means for IQ, SES, and impulsivity measures of nondelinquents and delinquents, with and without histories of attention deficit disorder*

Measure	Group[a]			
	Nondisordered	ADD/Nondelinquent	Non-ADD/delinquent	ADD+delinquent
Gender				
Girls	276 (51%)	1 (7%)	44 (49%)	2 (10%)
Boys	273 (49%)	13 (93%)	45 (51%)	19 (90%)
IQ[b]				
M	109.4	107.1	103.3	92.5
SD	14.3	12.5	16.5	12.8
SES[c]				
M	3.12	2.85	3.59	4.29
SD	1.31	1.23	1.36	0.91
Impulsivity z score[d]				
M	−0.15	0.72	0.06	2.04
SD	0.74	0.83	1.00	2.01

[a]Group *n*s were: nondisordered, 549; ADD/nondelinquent, 14; nonADD/delinquent, 89; ADD+delinquent, 21.
[b]WISC-R Full Scale IQ (Wechsler, 1974).
[c]A 6-point rating scale for parent's occupations in New Zealand; higher scores indicate lower social status (Elley & Irving, 1976).
[d]The Impulsivity scale was derived as a sum of the 6 items of the DISC-C that tap DSM-III impulsivity criteria for the diagnosis of ADD.

mean parent and teacher ratings of motor hyperactivity, inattention and aggression, and group means for reading achievement, a scale of family adversity and the SRED have been previously reported (Moffitt & Silva, 1988b).

Procedures

The subjects were seen within approximately two months of their 11th and 13th birthdays for a full day of testing at the Research Unit. All of the measures used in the present study were administered during the morning, in four 50-minute sessions that were counterbalanced in order and separated by 10-minute breaks. The five neuropsychological measures reported here were part of a larger test battery. Each examiner was blind to the subjects' performance on the other measures. The parent and teacher

that exclusion resulted in a maximum of 673 subjects and a minimum of 628 cases for any particular analysis. Degrees of freedom for individual analyses in the present study fluctuated slightly because of variations in the amount of data present for each task.

measures were filled in prior to the laboratory assessments.

Results

Because the prevalence of ADD was so low for girls (1.2%), statistical analysis of Gender × Group Differences would probably have been unreliable (e.g., only two girls had both ADD and delinquency). In a previous paper (Moffitt & Silva, 1988a), all neuropsychological measures in the data set had served as dependent measures into a 2×2 multivariate analysis of variance (MANOVA) with delinquent group (delinquent vs. nondelinquent) and gender as the independent variables. That analysis revealed no significant gender main effects for any of the 14 dependent measures (all univariate $ps < .05$). There was no significant Gender × Delinquency Group interaction for the linear combination of measures, nor for any individual measure, including those used for the present analyses. Therefore, the sexes were combined for the remaining analyses here.

The 14 neuropsychological measures of executive functions were entered into a

MANOVA with membership in one of the four ADD/delinquency groups as the independent variable. Significant differences were found among the four groups (Hotellings exact $F(42, 1838)=1.42$, $p=.04$). These differences remained when Full Scale IQ was entered into the MANOVA as a covariate (Hotellings exact $F(42, 1838)=1.44$, $p=.03$).

In order to attain a more fine-grained view of the differences among specific pairs of these four groups, the neuropsychological variables were tested in a series of one-way ANOVAs with group membership as the independent variable. Scheffe's test was used to control for the possibility of increased Type I error. Group mean scores are shown in Table 2; scores are presented in standardized (z) format to allow comparison of group differences across tests (data from the full sample were used to calculate z scores). The ADD+delinquent group's scores were lower than the nondisordered group's scores on 13 of the 14 measures, and lower than all three comparison groups' scores for 11 of the measures. The group comparisons indicated that the ADD+delinquent group scored significantly more poorly (at the .05 level) than the control group (non-ADD/nondelinquent) on 5 of the 14 dependent measures: the Mazes Q score, $F(3, 665)=5.37$; the Mazes raw score, $F(3, 667)=4.24$; Trails B minus Trails A time, $F(3, 658)=7.21$; Trails B total time, $F(3, 659)=6.67$; and the Rey-Osterreith copy score, $F(3, 669)=9.23$. Neither the delinquent-only group nor the ADD-only group differed significantly from controls on any measure. The ratios of boys to girls in the ADD+delinquent and ADD-only groups were similar (both=9:1), so that the finding of significant deficits for ADD+delinquents, but not for ADD-onlys, is not likely to have been confounded by gender ratio. Also, the group sizes were similar for the two ADD groups, so that same finding is not likely to be the result of differential statistical power for the Scheffe's comparisons with the nondisordered group.

The four groups were compared on a self-reported behavioral measure of impulsivity (taken from the DISC-C), using one-way ANOVA with Scheffe's test of differences between pairs of groups. The ADD+delinquent group was found to differ significantly from all other groups on self-reported impulsivity, $F(3, 641)=49.73$, $p<.001$; that is, a group average of 2.05 SD above the sample mean (see Table 1). The other three groups did not differ significantly from each other.

In order to examine whether the neuropsychological measures of executive deficit were associated with the behavioral impulsivity measure, the 5 neuropsychological variables on which the ADD+delinquent group differed from the control group were next entered into a multiple regression with self-reported impulsivity as the dependent measure. This analysis yielded a significant r value of .18 ($r^2=.03$), $F(5, 623)=4.34$ ($p<.001$).

Finally, differences between the 40 delinquents with a police record and the 70 without police records were assessed. Again, the 14 neuropsychological variables were entered into a MANOVA with the presence or absence of a police record as the independent variable. No significant difference was found between the delinquents who had come to police attention and those who had evaded police attention (Hotellings exact $F(14, 91)=.37$, $p=.98$). The prevalence of arrest was not significantly different for delinquent subjects with and without ADD, 36% of non-ADD delinquents and 32% of ADD+delinquents were known to police.

Discussion

This study was the first to examine executive deficits in delinquents identified by the self-report method, and several informative results were attained. First, executive deficits did not differentially characterize members of the cohort who were detected by law enforcement authorities. This finding suggests that executive deficits did not act as a mechanism for "differential detection" — that is, subjects with police records were not necessarily those who were perhaps less

Table 2. *Means and standard deviations of standardized (z) scores for tests of executive functions[a] of nondelinquents and delinquents, with and without histories of attention deficit disorder[b]*

Measure	Group			
	Non-disordered	ADD/non-delinquent	Non-ADD/delinquent	ADD+delinquent
Mazes "Q" score*				
M	0.06	−0.49	−0.07	−0.65
SD	0.95	0.99	1.08	0.99
Mazes attainment score*				
M	0.08	−0.04	−0.11	−0.57
SD	0.92	0.74	1.00	1.20
Trails B errors				
M	0.03	−0.23	0.03	−0.45
SD	0.93	1.17	0.71	1.48
Trails B time*				
M	0.04	−0.08	0.01	−0.98
SD	1.01	0.63	0.57	1.99
Trails B time − Trails A time*				
M	0.03	−0.05	−0.01	−1.02
SD	0.98	0.72	0.65	2.28
RAVLT recall interference				
M	−0.01	0.12	0.03	−0.26
SD	1.00	1.51	0.91	0.95
Rey–Osterreith copy accuracy*				
M	0.10	−0.20	−0.27	−0.68
SD	0.86	1.17	1.12	1.15
Rey–Osterreith copy strategy				
M	0.04	−0.29	0.04	−0.49
SD	0.98	1.10	1.05	0.96
WCST, total trials				
M	0.01	−0.24	−0.06	−0.28
SD	0.99	0.98	1.01	0.95
WCST, trials to complete first category				
M	0.01	0.01	−0.10	0.22
SD	0.98	0.55	1.15	0.19
WCST, number of perseverative errors				
M	0.06	−0.34	−0.18	−0.14
SD	0.85	1.17	1.31	0.81
WCST, percentage of errors that were perseverative				
M	0.04	−0.40	−0.24	−0.18
SD	0.90	1.23	1.44	0.89
WCST, percentage of responses that were unique				
M	−0.01	0.24	0.07	−0.40
SD	1.02	0.68	0.87	1.09
WCST, percentage of responses that were errors				
M	0.02	−0.22	−0.11	−0.34
SD	0.98	0.93	1.07	0.98

[a]To facilitate comparison, all variables were (1) standardized to a common z metric, and (2) recoded so that negative scores indicate poorer function.
[b]Group *ns* were: nondisordered, 549; ADD/nondelinquent, 14; non-ADD/delinquent, 89; ADD+delinquent, 21.
*Post hoc Scheffe test indicates difference between ADD+delinquents and nondisordered boys was significant ($p < .05$). No other disordered group was significantly different from the controls.

careful about concealing their delinquent behavior. The findings regarding executive deficits in this sample were not merely spurious effects of differential police detection of neuropsychologically impaired adolescents who behave antisocially.

Second, executive deficits did not discriminate "pure" cases of ADD or "pure" cases of delinquency from nondisordered controls. But, consistent with the hypothesis, relatively poor scores on some executive tests did discriminate ADD+delinquent cases from controls. Thus, there appears to be a special subgroup of delinquents who *do* evidence certain executive deficits upon neuropsychological testing even when the effect of general intellectual ability is controlled. It was found that delinquents with a history of ADD scored significantly below controls on five of the measures of executive function.

Executive cognitive deficits could be expected to manifest themselves clinically as an impulsive behavioral style, and, indeed, the delinquents with a history of ADD scored significantly higher on a self-report measure of impulsive behavior than did the other three groups. When the ability of a linear combination of the measures of executive function to predict impulsivity scores was tested, the regression equation attained statistical significance, but impulsivity explained only a very modest portion of the variance in the neuropsychological test scores. It is possible that the executive functions being measured in this study could influence social behavior through some medium in addition to impulsivity. For example, successful performance on all five of the measures on which significant group differences were found requires optimal visual–motor integration skills. Although programming of motor behavior is an acknowledged executive function of the frontal lobes of the brain, this would appear to be a qualitatively different mechanism from that proposed by Pontius (1972), who posited a developmental lag in ethical social judgement to account for the relationship between executive deficits and delinquent behavior. Perhaps the difficulties

with self-control of motor behavior shown by these boys on formal testing increases the odds that they will exhibit impulsive aggressive behavior in social interactions.

The ADD+delinquents came from more socioeconomically deprived homes than did the other subjects. It is possible that group differences in neuropsychological test performance are simply spurious differences resulting from a causal relation between socioeconomic status and performance on mental tests. However, although an index of adversity in the subjects' family environments did correlate significantly with parental ratings of the child's aggressiveness ($r=.30$), it was not a strong predictor of performance on the executive neuropsychological measures or of the self-report measure of impulsivity (maximum $r=-.18$). Social disadvantage tends to confound verbal tests more than nonverbal tests. Indeed, the sample correlations were lowest between family adversity and the nonverbal tasks showing significant group differences here (Mazes, Trails, and the Rey–Osterreith copy: maximum $r=-.10$). Previous research with this sample has shown that (1) the neuropsychological variables can explain a significant amount of variance in delinquency beyond that accounted for by SES (Moffitt & Silva, 1988a), and (2) significant differences among the four study groups' neuropsychological scores remain after the effects of family adversity are partialled out (Moffitt & Silva, 1988b).

Moffitt and Silva (1988b) have reported additional characteristics that differentiate delinquents with a history of ADD from cases of pure ADD, from pure delinquents, and from nondisordered boys. They reported that ADD+delinquent subjects scored significantly higher on parent and teacher ratings of aggressiveness than did the other three groups. However, ADD+delinquents did not differ significantly from pure ADD subjects on motor hyperactivity or inattention, nor from pure delinquents on types of delinquent behavior other than aggression; this would indicate that the ADD+delinquent subjects were not merely the most severely disordered cases on each pertinent clinical symptom dimension, but that they were specifically more aggressive on average than pure diagnostic groups. Early aggression has been found to be one of the best predictors of later criminality (Farrington, 1983; Moffitt, Mednick, & Gabrielli, 1989; Robins, 1966; Wolfgang, Figlio, & Sellin, 1972). Several researchers (Farrington et al., 1987; Loney et al., 1983; Offord et al., 1979; Satterfield, 1987) have shown that the early combination of ADD-H and aggressive conduct disorder indicates high risk for later serious recidivistic criminal offending. Therefore, the results reported here suggest that the neuropsychological characteristics of this group, including executive functions, warrant more detailed study.

One problem for the study of executive function and delinquency is the lack of sophisticated techniques for the measurement of executive deficit. Measures purported to tap executive functions often fail to correlate highly with each other (Cox & Evans, 1987; Hare, 1984). In this sample, the measures selected as executive measures did not load together on a unitary factor when the entire test battery was subjected to factor analysis (Moffitt & Heimer, 1988). Also,

executive tests are typically so complex in task requirements that they fail to reflect frontal dysfunction uniquely (Robinson, Heaton, Lehman, & Stilson, 1980), but rather, they require integrity of the brain as a whole. These measurement difficulties are especially problematic in regard to assessing executive functions in children. The present analyses employed a cross-sectional design at adolescence, and although the data documented an association between executive deficit and ADD+delinquency comorbidity, it did not show that the executive deficits were present prospectively when childhood forms of antisocial behavior were developing. Childhood measures are needed in order to support data collection in prospective designs before understanding of the relation of executive functions to the development of antisocial behavior can be attained. In addition, advances in childhood neuropsychological measurement are essential in order to make possible the application of a truly developmental neuropsychological approach to the study of both psychopathological and normal developmental processes.

References

Anderson, J., Williams, S., McGee, R., & Silva, P. A. (1987). The prevalence of DSM-III disorders in a large sample of preadolescent children from the general population. *Archives of General Psychiatry, 44,* 69–81.

Appellof, E. S., & Augustine, E. A. (1985). Prefrontal functions in juvenile delinquents. *Journal of Clinical and Experimental Neuropsychology, 7,* 79–109.

Berg, E. A. (1948). A simple objective test for measuring flexibility in thinking. *Journal of General Psychology, 39,* 15–22.

Berman A., & Siegal, A. (1976). Adaptive and learning skills in juvenile delinquents: A neuropsychological analysis. *Journal of Learning Disabilities, 9,* 51–58.

Brickman, A. S., McManus, M. M., Grapentine, W. L., & Alessi, N. (1984). Neuropsychological assessment of seriously delinquent adolescents. *Journal of the American Academy of Child Psychiatry, 23,* 453–457.

Buikhuisen, W. (1987). Cerebral dysfunctions and persistent juvenile delinquency. In S. A. Mednick & T. E. Moffitt (Eds.), *The causes of crime: New biological approaches* (pp. 168–184). New York: Cambridge University Press.

Cohen, J. (1959). The factorial structure of the WISC

at ages 7-6, 10-6, and 13-6. *Journal of Consulting Psychology, 26,* 285–299.

Cohen, R., Semple, W., Gross, M., Holcomb, H., Dowling, M., & Nordahl, T. (1988). Functional localization of sustained attention: Comparison to sensory stimulation in the absence of instruction. *Neuropsychiatry, Neuropsychology, and Behavioral Neurology, 1,* 3–20.

Costello, A., Edelbrock, C., Kalas, R., Kessler, M., & Klaric, S. (1982). *Diagnostic Interview Schedule for Children—Child Version.* Bethesda, MD: NIMH.

Cox, D. R., & Evans, R. W. (1987). Measures of frontal-lobe functioning in bright children. *Journal of Clinical and Experimental Neuropsychology, 9,* 28.

Elley, W. B., & Irving, J. C. (1976). Revised socioeconomic index for New Zealand. *New Zealand Journal of Educational Studies, 11,* 25–36.

Farrington, D. P. (1983). Offending from 10 to 25 years of age. In K. Van Dusen & S. A. Mednick, (Eds.), *Prospective studies of crime and delinquency* (pp. 17–38). Boston: Kluwer-Nijhoff.

Farrington, D. P., Loeber, R., & van Kammen, W. B. (1987, October). *Long-term criminal outcomes of hyperactivity-impulsivity-attention deficit and conduct problems in childhood.* Paper presented at the Meetings of the Society for Life History Research, St. Louis, MO.

Fuster, J. M. (1980). *The prefrontal cortex.* New York: Raven.

Gorenstein, E. E. (1982). Frontal lobe functions in psychopaths. *Journal of Abnormal Psychology, 91*, 368-379.

Hare, R. D. (1984). Performance of psychopaths on cognitive tasks related to frontal lobe function. *Journal of Abnormal Psychology, 93*, 133-140.

Heaton, R. K. (1981). *A Manual for the Wisconsin Card Sorting Test.* Odessa, FL: Psychological Assessment Resources.

Hinshaw, S. P. (1987). On the distinction between attentional deficits/hyperactivity and conduct problems/aggression in child psychopathology. *Psychological Bulletin, 101*, 443-463.

Hurwitz, I., Bibace, R., Wolff, P., & Rowbotham. B. (1972). Neurological function of normal boys, delinquent boys, and boys with learning problems. *Perceptual and Motor Skills, 35*, 387-394.

Karniski, W. M., Levine, M. D., Clarke, S., Palfrey, J. S., & Meltzer, L. J. (1982). A study of neurodevelopmental findings in early adolescent delinquents. *Journal of Adolescent Health Care, 3*, 151-159.

Kolb, B., & Whishaw, I. Q. (1985). *Fundamentals of Human Neuropsychology* (2nd ed.). New York: W. H. Freeman.

Krynicki, V. E. (1978). Cerebral dysfunction in repetitively assaultive offenders. *Journal of Nervous and Mental Disease, 166*, 59-67.

Lewinsohn, P. M. (1973). *Psychological assessments of patients with brain injury.* Unpublished manuscript, University of Oregon, Eugene, OR.

Lezak, M. D. (1983). *Neuropsychological assessment.* New York: Oxford University Press.

Loeber, R., & Dishion, T. (1983). Early predictors of male delinquency: A review. *Psychological Bulletin, 94*, 68-99.

Loney, J., Whaley-Klahn, M., Koiser, T., & Conboy, J. (1983). Hyperactive boys and their brothers at 21: Predictors of aggressive and antisocial outcome. In K. T. Van Dusen & S. A. Mednick (Eds.), *Prospective studies of crime and delinquency* (pp. 181-208). Dordrecht: Kluwer-Nijhoff.

Lou, H. C., Henriksen, L., & Bruhn, P. (1984). Focal cerebral hypoperfusion in children with dysphasia and/or attention deficit disorder. *Archives of Neurology, 41*, 825-829.

McGee, R. (1985). *Response Rates at Phase XI of the Dunedin Multidisciplinary Health and Development Study.* Unpublished report, Dunedin Multidisciplinary Health and Development Research Unit, Otago Medical School, Dunedin, New Zealand.

McGee, R., & Silva, P. A. (1982). *A thousand New Zealand children: Their health and development from birth to seven* (Special Report Series Number 8). Auckland: Medical Research Council of New Zealand.

McGee, R., Williams, S., & Silva, P. A. (1985). Factor structure and correlates of ratings of inattention, hyperactivity, and antisocial behavior in a large sample of 9-year-old children from the general population. *Journal of Consulting and Clinical Psychology, 53*, 480-490.

Miller, L. J., Burdg, N. B., & Carpenter, D. (1980). Application of recategorized WISC-R scores for adjudicated adolescents. *Perceptual and Motor Skills, 51*, 187-191.

Milner, B. (1963). Effects of different brain lesions on card sorting. *Archives of Neurology, 9*, 90-100.

Milner, B. (1964). Some effects of frontal lobectomy in man. In J. M. Warren & K. Akert (Eds.), *The frontal granular cortex and behavior* (pp. 313-334). New York: McGraw-Hill.

Milner, B. (1975). Psychological aspects of focal epilepsy and its neurological management. In D. P. Purpura, J. K. Penry, & R. D. Walter (Eds.), *Advances in neurology* (Vol. 8, pp. 75-89). New York: Raven.

Milner, B., & Petrides, M. (1984). Behavioural effects of frontal-lobe lesions in man. *Trends in Neurosciences,* November:403-407.

Moffitt, T. E. (in preparation). *Developmental trajectories of antisocial behavior in delinquents with and without ADD: Ages 3 to 15.* Unpublished manuscript, University of Wisconsin, Madison, WI.

Moffitt, T. E., & Heimer, K. (1988). *Factor analysis and construct validity of a research neuropsychological test battery.* Unpublished manuscript, University of Wisconsin, Madison, WI.

Moffitt, T. E., & Henry, B. (in preparation). Hidden delinquents: Correlates and predictors.

Moffitt, T. E., & Silva, P. A. (1988a). Neuropsychological deficit and self-reported delinquency in an unselected birth cohort. *Journal of the American Academy of Child and Adolescent Psychiatry, 27*, 233-240.

Moffitt, T. E., & Silva, P. (1988b). Self-reported delinquency, neuropsychological deficit, and history of attention deficit disorder. *Journal of Abnormal Child Psychology, 16*(5), 553-569.

Moffitt, T. E. & Silva, P. A. (1988c). Self-reported early delinquency: Results from an instrument for New Zealand. *Australian and New Zealand Journal of Criminology, 21*, 227-240.

Moffitt, T. E., Mednick, S. A., & Gabrielli, W. F. (1989). Predicting criminal violence: Descriptive data and predispositional factors. In D. Brizer & M. Crowner (Eds.), *Current approaches to the prediction of violence* (pp. 13-34). New York: American Psychiatric Association Press.

Offord, D. R., Sullivan, K., Allen, N., & Abrams, N. (1979). Delinquency and hyperactivity. *The Journal of Nervous and Mental Disease, 167*, 734-741.

Osterreith, P. A. (1944). Le test de copie d'une figure complex. *Archives de Psychologie, 30*, 206-356.

Pontius, A. A. (1972). Neurological aspects in some types of delinquency, especially among juveniles. Toward a neurological model of ethical action. *Adolescence, 7*, 289-308.

Pontius, A. A., & Ruttinger, K. F. (1976). Frontal lobe system maturational lag in juvenile delinquents shown in narratives test. *Adolescents, 11*, 509-518.

Quay, H. C., & Peterson, D. R. (1983). *Revised Behaviour Problem Checklist, Interim Manual.* Coral Gables, FL: University of Miami.

Reitan, R. M. (1958). Validity of the Trail Making Test as an indication of organic brain damage. *Perceptual and Motor Skills, 8*, 271-276.

Reitan, R., & Davison, L. A. (Eds.) (1974). *Clinical neuropsychology: Current status and applications.* New York: Halsted.

Rey, A. (1941). L'examen psychologique dans les cas

d'encephalopathie tramatique. *Archives de Psychologie, 28,* 286–340.

Rey, A. (1964). *L'examen clinique en psychologie.* Paris: Presses Universitaires de France.

Riddle, M., & Roberts, A. H. (1977). Delinquency, delay of gratification, recidivism and the Porteus Maze Tests. *Psychological Bulletin, 34,* 417–425.

Robins, L. N. (1966). *Deviant children grown up.* Baltimore: Williams & Wilkins.

Robinson, A. L., Heaton, R. K., Lehman, R. A. W., & Stilson, D. W. (1980). The utility of the Wisconsin Card Sorting Test in detecting and locating frontal lobe lesions. *Journal of Consulting and Clinical Psychology, 48,* 605–614.

Rutter, M., Tizard, J., & Whitmore, K. (1970). *Education, health, and behavior.* London: Longman.

Satterfield, J. H. (1987). Childhood diagnostic and neurophysiological predictors of teenage arrest rates: An eight-year prospective study. In S. A. Mednick & T. E. Moffitt (Eds.), *The causes of crime* (pp. 146–167). New York: Cambridge University Press.

Schachar, R., Rutter, M., & Smith, A. (1981). The characteristics of situationally and pervasively hyperactive children: Implications for syndrome definition. *Journal of Child Psychology and Psychiatry, 22,* 375–392.

Skoff, B. F., & Libon, D. J. (1987). Impaired executive functions in a sample of male juvenile delinquents. *Journal of Clinical and Experimental Neuropsychology, 9*(1), 60.

Stuss, D. T., & Benson, D. F. (1986). *The frontal lobes.* New York: Raven.

Taylor, E. M. (1959). *The appraisal of children with cerebral deficits.* Cambridge, MA: Harvard University Press.

Tow, P. M. (1955). *Personality changes following frontal leukotomy.* London: Oxford University Press.

Voorhees, J. (1981). Neuropsychological differences between juvenile delinquents and functional adolescents: A preliminary study. *Adolescence, 16,* 57–66.

Waber, D. P., & Holmes, J. M. (1985). Assessing children's copy productions of the Rey-Osterreith Complex Figure. *Journal of Clinical and Experimental Neuropsychology, 7,* 264–280.

Wechsler, D. (1974). *Manual of the Wechsler Intelligence Scale for Children – Revised.* New York: Psychological Corporation.

Wolff, P. H., Waber, D., Bauermeister, M., Cohen, C., & Ferber, R. (1982). The neuropsychological status of adolescent delinquent boys. *Journal of Child Psychology and Psychiatry, 23,* 267–279.

Wolfgang, M. E., Figlio, R. M., & Sellin T. (1972). *Delinquency in a birth cohort.* Chicago: The University of Chicago Press.

Yeudall, L. T. (1980). A neuropsychological perspective of persistent juvenile delinquency and criminal behavior. *Annals of the New York Academy of Science, 347,* 349–355.

Yeudall, L. T., & Fromm-Auch, D. (1979). Neuropsychological impairments in various psychopathological populations. In J. Gruzelier & P. Flor-Henry (Eds.), *Hemisphere asymmetries of function and psychopathology.* New York: Elsevier.

Recent Theories Focusing on Individual Difference Factors

8

2

A THEORY OF CRIMINAL BEHAVIOR

Theories of crime abound. The lay reader will wonder whether any theory can be an improvement on common sense, and the scholarly one will groan at the prospect of yet another theory. But what may be irrelevant to the former and redundant to the latter is, to us, important, for theories, whatever else they may do, direct our attention to some features of the situation and away from others. Much of the confusion about the sources of individual differences in criminality arise, we believe, from bad theories—that is, from views about how the world works that are incomplete and thus lead us to attend to some things but not to others.

For example, the theory that unemployment or economic want causes crime can lead us to look for increases in criminality during economic recessions but to overlook the possibility that crime may also be caused by prosperity (if it loosens the social bonds), by the distribution of income (if it causes social envy), or by some underlying factor that happens to cause both criminality and unemployment. More generally, theories that call attention to the social setting in which crime occurs (such as the attitudes of parents and peers, the perceived costs and benefits of crime, the influence of drugs and television) direct our attention away from preexisting individual traits that make people more or less susceptible to such social factors; by the same token, theories that emphasize the preferences of individuals tend to deemphasize the situational factors that determine how, or even whether, those preferences affect behavior. The quarrels among lay persons and scholars

42 EXPLAINING CRIME

about what causes crime are basically quarrels about the relative importance of those factors that occupy a central place in competing theories. These arguments are made more intense by the fact that sometimes people do not choose theories at random; very often, they choose them in part because the central factors in the theories—individual morality, social setting, economic circumstances, or the prospects of punishment—are ones, which for political or ideological reasons, the defenders of the theories *want* to believe are central.

We suggest that most of the common theories purporting to explain criminal behavior are but special cases of some more general theory. Specifying that larger theory is useful because, to the extent it is correct and comprehensive, it will keep before our eyes the full range of factors that cause individual differences in criminality. This, in turn, will restrain our tendency to give partial explanations of crime or to make partial interpretations of the empirical findings of criminologists. Ideally, of course, a theory should do much more than this. In principle, a theory is a testable statement of the relationships among two or more variables, so that, knowing the theory, we can say with some confidence that if we observe X, we will also observe Y. For instance: If we observe a left-handed, red-haired male, then we are 70 percent certain that we are observing a burglar. Unfortunately, theories about crime, even ours, often do not permit us to make such statements, but for the reasons already given, they are important nonetheless. If, given this state of affairs, "theory" sounds too grand a term for the systematic speculations we and others have produced, consider what we offer as an organized perspective on the causes of crime.

Our theory—or perspective—is a statement about the forces that control individual behavior. To most people, that is not a very interesting assertion, but to many scholars, it is a most controversial one. Some students of crime are suspicious of the view that explanations of criminality should be based on an analysis of individual psychology. Such a view, they argue, is "psychological reductionism" that neglects the setting in which crime occurs and the broad social forces that determine levels of crime. These suspicions, while understandable, are ill-founded. Whatever factors contribute to crime— the state of the economy, the competence of the police, the nurturance of the family, the availability of drugs, the quality of the schools—they must all affect the behavior of *individuals* if they are to affect crime. If people differ in their tendency to commit crime, we must express those differences in terms of how some array of factors affects their individual decisions. If crime rates differ among nations, it must be because individuals in those nations differ or are exposed to different arrays of factors. If crime rates rise or fall, it must be that changes have occurred in the variables governing individual behavior.

Our theory is eclectic, drawing from different, sometimes opposing, schools of thought. We incorporate both genetic predispositions and social learning and consider the influence of both delayed and immediate factors. An individual act is sometimes best understood as a reaction to immediate circumstances and at other times as an expression of enduring behavioral dispositions; both sorts of explanations have a place in our theory. Though eclectic, the theory is built upon modern behavioral psychology.*

Crime as Choice: The Theory in Brief

In this section, we give a brief overview of our theoretical perspective. Many lay readers may wish, after reading the material under this heading, to skip to page 61. Scholars and others interested in the derivation of the theory will probably want to read all of the chapter, as well as the Appendix (pages 531–535) to it.

Our theory rests on the assumption that people, when faced with a choice, choose the preferred course of action. This assumption is quite weak; it says nothing more than that whatever people choose to do, they choose it because they prefer it. In fact, it is more than weak; without further clarification, it is a tautology. When we say people "choose," we do not necessarily mean that they consciously deliberate about what to do. All we mean is that their behavior is determined by its consequences. A person will do that thing the consequences of which are perceived by him or her to be preferable to the consequences of doing something else. What can save such a statement from being a tautology is how plausibly we describe the gains and losses associated with alternative courses of action and the standards by which a person evaluates those gains and losses.

These assumptions are commonplace in philosophy and social science. Philosophers speak of hedonism or utilitarianism, economists of value or utility, and psychologists of reinforcement or reward. We will use the language of psychology, but it should not be hard to translate our terminology into that of other disciplines. Though social scientists differ as to how much behavior can reasonably be described as the result of a choice, all agree that at least some behavior is guided, or even precisely controlled, by things vari-

---

* The specialist will recognize the debt we owe to, and the liberties we have taken with, the work of Edward L. Thorndike, Albert Bandura, B. F. Skinner, R. B. Cattell, H. J. Eysenck, I. P. Pavlov, and E. C. Tolman, among others.

44   EXPLAINING CRIME

ously termed pleasure, pain, happiness, sorrow, desirability, or the like. Our object is to show how this simple and widely used idea can be used to explain behavior.

At any given moment, a person can choose between committing a crime and not committing it (all these alternatives to crime we lump together as "noncrime"). The consequences of committing the crime consist of rewards (what psychologists call "reinforcers") and punishments; the consequences of not committing the crime (i.e., engaging in noncrime) also entail gains and losses. The larger the ratio of the net rewards of crime to the net rewards of noncrime, the greater the tendency to commit the crime. The net rewards of crime include, obviously, the likely material gains from the crime, but they also include intangible benefits, such as obtaining emotional or sexual gratification, receiving the approval of peers, satisfying an old score against an enemy, or enhancing one's sense of justice. One must deduct from these rewards of crime any losses that accrue immediately—that are, so to speak, contemporaneous with the crime. They include the pangs of conscience, the disapproval of onlookers, and the retaliation of the victim.

The value of noncrime lies all in the future. It includes the benefits to the individual of avoiding the risk of being caught and punished and, in addition, the benefits of avoiding penalties not controlled by the criminal justice system, such as the loss of reputation or the sense of shame afflicting a person later discovered to have broken the law and the possibility that, being known as a criminal, one cannot get or keep a job.

The value of any reward or punishment associated with either crime or noncrime is, to some degree, uncertain. A would-be burglar can rarely know exactly how much loot he will take away or what its cash value will prove to be. The assaulter or rapist may exaggerate the satisfaction he thinks will follow the assault or the rape. Many people do not know how sharp the bite of conscience will be until they have done something that makes them feel the bite. The anticipated approval of one's buddies may or may not be forthcoming. Similarly, the benefits of noncrime are uncertain. One cannot know with confidence whether one will be caught, convicted, and punished, or whether one's friends will learn about the crime and as a result withhold valued esteem, or whether one will be able to find or hold a job.

Compounding these uncertainties is time. The opportunity to commit a crime may be ready at hand (an open, unattended cash register in a store) or well in the future (a bank that, with planning and preparation, can be robbed). And the rewards associated with noncrime are almost invariably more distant than those connected with crime, perhaps many weeks or months distant. The strength of reinforcers tends to decay over time at rates that differ among individuals. As a result, the extent to which people take into account distant possibilities—a crime that can be committed only tomorrow, or punishment that will be inflicted only in a year—will affect whether they choose crime or noncrime. All of these factors—the strength of rewards, the problems of uncertainty and delay, and the way in which our sense of justice affects how we value the rewards—will be examined in the remainder of this chapter.

Reinforcers

All human behavior is shaped by two kinds of reinforcers: primary and secondary. A primary reinforcer derives its strength from an innate drive, such as hunger or sexual appetite; a secondary reinforcer derives its strength from learning. The line dividing reinforcers that are innate from those that are learned is hard to draw, and people argue, often passionately, over where it ought to be drawn. When we disagree over whether people are innately altruistic, men are innately more aggressive than women, or mankind is innately warlike or competitive, we are disagreeing over whether behavior responds to primary or to secondary reinforcers.

In fact, most reinforcers combine primary and secondary elements. Part of the benefit that comes from eating either bread or spaghetti must derive from the fact that their common ingredient, wheat, satisfies an innate drive—hunger. In this sense, both are primary reinforcers. But bread and spaghetti differ in texture, flavor, and appearance, and the preferences we have for these qualities are in part learned. These qualities constitute secondary reinforcers. The diversity of the world's cuisines shows, to some extent, how extraordinarily varied are the secondary aspects of even a highly biological reinforcer such as food.

The distinction between primary and secondary reinforcers is important in part because it draws attention to the link between innate drives and social conventions. For example, in every society men and women adorn themselves to enhance their sexual appeal. At the same time, styles in clothing and cosmetics vary greatly among societies and throughout history. As we are all immersed in the fashions of our place and time, we may suppose that fashion is purely arbitrary. But we are probably wrong, for these conventions of personal beauty are dependent on primary sexual reinforcers. But what constitutes acceptable adornment changes within broad limits. Once, for a woman to appear nude in a motion picture meant that she was wanton and the film was trash. Today, female nudity, though it is still offensive to some, is not construed by most viewers as an indication of the moral worth of the woman.

Not only do innate primary reinforcers become blended with learned secondary ones, the strength of even primary reinforcers (and of course of secondary reinforcers) will vary. Bread that we eat hungrily at seven o'clock in the morning may have no appeal to us at one o'clock in the afternoon, right after lunch. In fact, many forms of food may appeal to us before breakfast even though none may appeal after lunch. A class of reinforcers whose strengths vary together allows us to speak of a "drive"—in this case, the hunger drive.

Drives vary in strength. The various food drives can be depended on to assert themselves several times a day, but the sexual drive may be felt much less frequently and then in ways powerfully affected by circumstances. The aggressive drive (to be discussed later in this chapter) may occur very rarely in some of us and frequently in others, and it may appear suddenly, in response to events, and blow over almost as quickly. We repeat these commonplace observations because we wish to emphasize that though much behavior, including criminal behavior, is affected by innate drives, this does not mean that crime is committed by "born criminals" with uncontrollable, antisocial drives. We can, in short, include innate drives (and thus genetic factors) in our theory without embracing a view of the criminal as an atavistic savage or any other sort of biological anomaly.

Secondary reinforcers change in strength along with the primary reinforcers with which they are associated. Those secondary reinforcers that change the least in strength are those associated with the largest variety of primary reinforcers. Money is an especially powerful reward, not because it is intrinsically valuable (paper currency has almost no intrinsic worth), but because it is associated with so many primary reinforcers that satisfy innate drives. Money can buy food, shelter, relief from pain, and even sexual gratification. (It can also buy status and power, but we will not discuss here the interesting question of whether the desire for these things is innate.) The reinforcing power of money is relatively steady because the many primary rewards with which it is connected make it somewhat impervious to fluctuations in the value of any one drive.

Because of the constant and universal reinforcing power of money, people are inclined to think of crimes for money gain as more natural, and thus more the product of voluntary choice and rational thought, than crimes involving "senseless" violence or sexual deviance. Stealing is an understandable, if not pardonable, crime; bestiality, "unprovoked" murder, and drug addiction seem much less understandable, and therefore, perhaps, less voluntary or deliberate. People sometimes carry this line of thought even further: These "senseless" crimes are the result of overpowering compulsions or irrational beliefs. But this is a false distinction. Certain reinforcers may have a steadier, more predictable effect, but all behavior, even the bizarre, responds to reinforcement. It is sometimes useful to distinguish between crimes that arise out of long-lasting, hard-to-change reinforcers (such as money) from those that stem from short-acting, (possibly) changeable drives (such as sexual deviance), but we must always bear in mind that these are distinctions of degree, not of kind.

Conditioning

Thus far, we have spoken of the "association" between primary and secondary reinforcers. Now we must ask how that association arises. The answer is the process known as conditioning. The simplest form of conditioning is the well-known experiment involving Pavlov's dog. The dog repeatedly heard a buzzer a few moments before receiving some dried meat powder in its mouth. Soon, the dog salivated at the mere sound of the buzzer. Two different stimuli—meat and buzzers—were associated. The meat elicited an innate tendency to salivate; the buzzer came to elicit salivation through learning. Pavlov's successors extended his discovery to much more complex responses than salivation and to many other species, including man. These Pavlovian experiments involved what psychologists now call "classical conditioning," which typically involves the autonomic nervous system (that part of our neural structure controlling reflexive behavior, such as heartbeats, salivation, and perspiration, and internal emotional states, such as fear, anxiety, and relaxation) and in which the behavior of the subject (the dog or the man) does not affect the stimulus being administered.

Classical (or Pavlovian) conditioning can make an arbitrary stimulus reinforce behavior by associating the stimulus with either a primary (i.e., innate) reinforcer or some already-learned secondary reinforcer. As we have seen, money is an arbitrary stimulus (a collection of scraps of paper and bits of metal) that has become one of the most universal and powerful secondary reinforcers. But there are many other examples. If a child is regularly praised for scrubbing his or her hands before dinner, then (provided that the praise is already felt to be rewarding), the child will in time scrub his hands without being told or praised. The satisfaction he feels in having scrubbed hands is now the internal feeling of reinforcement. In the same way, hand-scrubbing can be taught by scolding a child who does not wash up. If the scolding is

48   EXPLAINING CRIME

already felt by the child to be punishing, in time the child will feel uncomfortable whenever he has dirty hands.

Classical conditioning does not produce only secretions or muscle twitches. These external responses may be accompanied by a complex array of internalized dispositions. The child who learns to scrub his hands, because of either parental praise or parental disapproval, will have learned things on which his mind and his subsequent experience will come to work in elaborate ways. In time, the satisfaction he feels from having clean hands may merge with other similar satisfactions and become a general sense of cleanliness, which he may eventually believe is next to godliness. He imputes virtue to cleanliness and regards filth with great distaste, even when he finds it in the world at large rather than simply on his own hands. Of course, all this presupposes growing up in a society in which neighbors, friends, and even the government regularly praise cleanliness and condemn slovenliness.

Although it does not do justice to the subtlety and generality of the process or the way in which its outcome is linked to social settings, H. J. Eysenck's remark that "conscience is a conditioned reflex" is not far off the mark.[1] And it calls attention to the intriguing possibility that individuals may differ in their susceptibility to classical conditioning. As we will show in Chapter 7, people are not alike in how readily they internalize rules, and thus they are not alike in the value they attach to the costs in conscience of a prospective crime. For some people, the benefits of a crime are not reduced as much by a "conscience decrement" as they are for persons who have been more successfully subjected to classical conditioning.

Many people have a conscience strong enough to prevent them from committing a crime some of the time but not all of the time. In ways that will become clearer later in the chapter, a reasonably strong conscience is probably sufficient to prevent a person from committing a crime that would have only a modest yield *and* that could not take place for, say, two days. This would be true even if the person was confident he would not be caught. But now suppose the opportunity for committing the offense is immediately at hand—say, your poker-playing friends have left the room after the hand was dealt and you have a chance to peek at their cards, or the jewelry salesman has left the store with a tray of diamond rings open on the counter. Now, if the bite of conscience is not sufficient by itself to prevent the offense, the would-be offender will calculate, however roughly or inarticulately, the chances of being caught. He will know that if the friends suddenly return or the jewelry salesman is watching, he will lose things—in the first instance, reputation, and in the second, his freedom. People differ in how they calculate these risks. Some worry about any chance, however slight, of being caught and would be appalled at any loss of esteem, however small or fleeting; others will peek at the cards or grab a ring if they think they have any chance at all of getting away with it.

When present actions are governed by their consequences, "instrumental" (or operant) conditioning is at work. Unlike classically conditioned responses, instrumental conditioning involves behavior that affects the stimulus (e.g., not peeking at the cards or not taking the ring avoids the costs of the offense). Instrumental behavior affects the stimuli we receive and this, in turn, affects subsequent behavior.

The distinction between classical and instrumental conditioning is by no means as clear as our simple definitions may make it appear. But if we bear in mind that behavior cannot be neatly explained by one or the other process, we can use the distinction to help us understand individual differences in criminality. Persons deficient in conscience may turn out to be persons who for various reasons resist classical conditioning—they do not internalize rules as easily as do others. Persons who, even with a strong conscience, commit crimes anyway may be persons who have difficulty imagining the future consequences of present action or who are so impulsive as to discount very heavily even those consequences they can foresee, and hence will resist the instrumental conditioning that might lead them to choose noncrime over crime.

Delay and Uncertainty

Our argument so far is that behavior is controlled by its consequences. Those consequences—the primary and secondary reinforcers and punishers—may be immediate or postponed, certain or uncertain. Because not everyone has a conscience sufficiently strong to prevent every illegal act, the influence of delay and uncertainty on individual differences in criminality is great. Consequences gradually lose their ability to control behavior in proportion to how delayed or improbable they are. We have just observed that instrumental conditioning works best with persons who can conceive of future consequences and who attach a high value to even distant consequences. It can easily be shown that for many people, improbable or distant effects have very little influence on their behavior. For example, millions of cigarette smokers ignore the (possibly) fatal consequences of smoking because they are distant and uncertain. If smoking one cigarette caused certain death tomorrow, we would anticipate a rather sharp reduction in tobacco consumption.

50   EXPLAINING CRIME

The theft of $100 with eight chances in ten of getting away with it is worth more to a prospective thief than the theft of $100 with a one-in-two chance of success. A convenient, though somewhat fictitious, way of expressing these differences is with the concept of "expected value," which equals the product of the value of the gain times the probability of obtaining it ($100 × .8 = $80; $100 × .5 = $50). In fact, people may evaluate alternative gambles somewhat differently from what is implied by these objective expected values, but those differences can be ignored here. Other things being equal, a crime more certain of success will be valued more than one less certain; a more certain punishment will be feared more than a less certain one.

The increase in criminality resulting from the decreased probability of punishment occurs as a result of two processes—one involving instrumental conditioning, and the other, classical conditioning. If the threat of being punished oneself is reduced, the rewards for noncrime (i.e., the punishment that is not received) are weakened, making noncrime seem less profitable: This is an example of applying the principles of instrumental conditioning. If the spectacle of others being punished becomes less frequent, the rewards of crime may be strengthened because it now seems less wrong. The tendency for the punishment of others to affect the extent to which we feel guilty when we contemplate committing the same crime is an example of the use of classical conditioning.

Delay affects crime because there is almost always a lapse between when the crime may be committed and when the legal or social consequences, if any, will be felt. Put another way, the rewards of crime usually precede the costs of crime (except for such contemporaneous costs as those of conscience). Because of this, time discounting becomes extremely important in explaining criminal behavior. Figure 1 illustrates the effect of time on crime.* In each of the three cases, the rewards associated with noncrime are greater than the rewards arising from crime. Were it not for the effects of delay, no crime would be committed in any of the three examples. But as we shall see, the three cases, which involve little, some, or much time discounting, portray increasing susceptibility to crime.

In each graph, the vertical axis represents, for a given criminal opportunity, the net value of the two alternatives: committing a crime, or not committing it. By "net value" we mean the sum of all the reinforcements, positive and negative, less the punishments, associated with either crime or noncrime, as expressed in the strengths of the competing behaviors. In the

* The curves are not invented but are based on laboratory studies of animal and human behavior.[2] The relevant equations are reported in the Appendix.

FIGURE 1

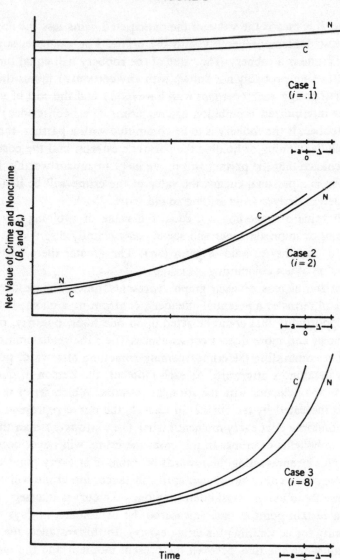

The value of crime (C) and noncrime (N) in relation to the time interval between each behavior and its reward. Noncrime is assumed to have a larger reward than crime, but the reward for noncrime is Δ time units more delayed than the reward for crime. The criminal act takes *a* time units to execute. In all three cases, Δ, *a*, and the rewards for noncrime and crime are the same. Only the time-discounting function varies from Case 1 to Case 3, as represented by the increasing value of *i*, the measure of impulsiveness. The more impulsive a person is, the more likely he or she is to find occasions when crime will seem to be more rewarding than noncrime, other things equal. In Case 2, the crossing curves imply that crime will seem more rewarding when a criminal opportunity is at hand, but not when it is remote. See Appendix for relevant equations.

52   EXPLAINING CRIME

case of crime, this means the value of the anticipated gains less the costs, if any, that occur contemporaneously with the crime. For example, suppose the potential crime is a robbery. The value of the robbery will equal the loot to be gained (a sum probably not known with any certainty) minus the risk of the victim's fighting back (perhaps with a weapon) and the cost of violating whatever internalized prohibition against crime (i.e., conscience) may exist in the robber. If the robbery is to be committed with a partner, the gain may also include winning or holding the partner's esteem, and the cost may include the chance that the partner will prove inept or untrustworthy. If the robbery victim is a personal enemy, the value of the crime will be increased by the satisfaction derived from settling an old score.

The net value of noncrime will equal the value of avoiding any legal penalties (fines or imprisonment) and social costs (family disgrace, lost social esteem, or inability to hold or get a job). The greater these costs, the greater the value of not committing the crime.

The horizontal axis of each graph represents time. The reader may think of time in terms of a potential offender's confronting a choice between a criminal opportunity that could be acted upon one hour, one day, or one week from now, and more distant consequences (i.e., the realization of the benefits of not committing the crime) coming sometime afterward, perhaps many weeks or months afterward. At each moment, the person in question will engage in the behavior with the stronger rewards. Which set of rewards is stronger is indicated by the curves. In Case 1, the curve representing the benefits of noncrime is at every moment higher (i.e., stronger) than the one measuring the benefits of crime. In this case, the crime will never occur. In Case 3, the curve representing the rewards of crime is at every point higher than the curve representing noncrime; in this instance, the crime will always occur. In Case 2—to us, the most interesting one—the curves intersect, crossing over at a certain point in time (measured, let us assume, in days before the opportunity for committing the crime exists). In this instance, the crime will not occur when the time between the present moment and the moment when the rewards of the crime are received is long enough to place the person on the left of the crossover point on the graph. But the crime will occur if the person is to the right of the crossover point—that is, if he is so close in time to the criminal opportunity that the rewards of crime seem stronger than the rewards of noncrime.

An example or two will make the significance of the crossover point easier to grasp. Consider a person on a diet. The benefits of not eating a rich dessert, such as chocolate cake, occur in the future and involve weight not gained and health hazards avoided. The benefits of the dessert—the marvelous taste of rich chocolate—are available immediately on eating the cake. Now, if the person on the diet thinks ahead to a meal he cannot eat for several hours or even a day, his thinking will be dominated by the (deferred) benefits of refusing the dessert. If asked, he will say, with absolute sincerity, that he will eat no dessert. But as the dinner hour approaches, his resolve may weaken. And when the cake is placed on the table, his resolve may collapse entirely as the benefits of eating it come to dominate the deferred benefits of refusing it. At some point, the dieter has passed through his crossover point. This example can readily be translated into a criminal opportunity. For many people, the benefits of noncrime exceed those of crime so long as the chance for committing the crime lies well in the future. These people would reject out of hand the suggestion that they might engage in shoplifting, because they are not now in a shop. But suppose later in the day they find themselves in a store with attractive merchandise casually displayed and no one watching. Now, some of these people will find the benefits of crime dominating the (deferred and uncertain) benefits of noncrime. They will grab something and stuff it under their coats.

The importance of the crossover point calls our attention to the importance of the shape of the curves that define it. These curves measure the rate at which individuals discount the future. All the curves in Figure 1 are hyperbolic for reasons well established in the scientific literature.[3] The steeper the curve, the more rapidly the individual discounts future rewards; the shallower the curve, the more the individual attaches value to future rewards.

In Figure 1, the horizontal axis, representing time, is marked off into two segments, a and Δ (delta). The period a is the time required to plan and execute a crime. Crimes that take a long time to devise and carry out—robbing the Brink's armored truck company, for example—will be engaged in only by persons either who expect gains that will substantially exceed the benefits of not committing the crime or who have a distant time horizon. We often refer to such persons as "professional" criminals, by which we mean that they attach little value to the benefits of noncrime, work to obtain a large amount of loot, or do not discount time very steeply, or some combination of all three. By contrast, crimes that can be committed on the spur of the moment—an unplanned assault, for example, or grabbing a woman's purse—appeal to persons to whom the prospect of even a small gain is appealing and for whom distant events are uninteresting. We call such persons "impulsive" or "opportunistic" offenders. For a given time-discounting curve, a crime that takes much planning must have a larger payoff than a crime that can be done on the spur of the moment. For a given payoff, a person with a steep time-discounting curve will be more likely to commit a crime than a person with a shallow discount curve. (The Appendix supplies the mathematics of these relationships.)

The period Δ represents the time between the crime and the delayed consequences of being caught for the crime (i.e., the value of noncrime). The length of this period depends on how swiftly a crime is detected and reported and on how quickly the perpetrator can be apprehended, convicted, and punished. The longer it takes for victims to report crimes and the criminal justice system to operate, the lower will be the rewards of noncrime as felt by a would-be criminal.

We can summarize the argument so far by noting that the three cases depicted in Figure 1 represent the effect of differing degrees of impulsiveness. In all three instances, the strength of the rewards of crime are the same, as are the rewards of noncrime. The time delays, a and Δ, are the same in all cases. All that changes is the steepness of the time-discounting curves. In Case 1, the value of noncrime exceeds the value of crime at all points in time because the absolute value of noncrime is greater than that of crime, and the person in question does not discount time very heavily. This person is not at all impulsive. In Case 3, the individual is very impulsive—that is, he discounts time very steeply. As a result, though the value of noncrime would be greater than the value of crime *if* they both occurred at the same moment, the delay in the criminal justice system (or in whatever other system, such as the marketplace, that rewards noncrime)—the magnitude of Δ—is sufficiently great so that the value of noncrime is discounted to a point below that of crime at all times shown. In Case 2, the individual is moderately impulsive, so that the value of noncrime exceeds the value of crime *provided* that the person is far enough in time from the chance to commit a crime—which is to say, he is to the left of the crossover point. But if the criminal opportunity is ready at hand (like the cake set before the weak-willed dieter), he will indulge.

Individuals differ in the degree to which they discount the future. These differences are often part of a personality trait that can be measured, and in Chapter 7 we will discuss efforts that have been made to measure it. They may also differ in their ability to conceive of the future or to plan for it. They may lack the imagination, experience, or intelligence to commit a crime that requires planning or to visualize what state of affairs may exist long in the future when the benefits of noncrime become available. This may help explain (as will be discussed in Chapter 6) why criminals tend to be less intelligent than noncriminals, though there are other possible explanations for this connection.

Individual differences in criminality may also exist because of the dif-

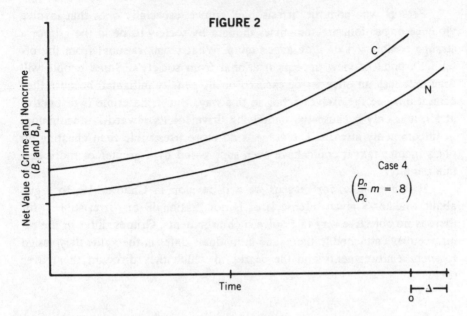

A Theory of Criminal Behavior 55

FIGURE 2

Same as Figure 1, except that the value of the reward for crime, adjusted for the probability of obtaining it, P_c, is here larger than that for noncrime, adjusted for the probability of obtaining it, P_n. Crime will seem more rewarding than noncrime at all delays of reward and for any degree of impulsiveness. See Appendix.

ferent values people assign to crime and noncrime. In Figure 2, we show a situation in which the perceived benefits of crime are greater than the perceived benefits of noncrime. At every point in time, rewards of crime are stronger than the rewards of noncrime. No matter how steeply the individual discounts the future, he will always find committing the crime preferable to not committing it. This is an illustration of a crime that from the offender's point of view is always rational though (paradoxically) society often supposes it is irrational. Circumstances that might create this situation are not hard to imagine. The value of the loot may be very large (millions are there for the taking) or the grievance against an individual may be very powerful (the victim is a political enemy or an unfaithful lover). The conscience of the offender may be especially weak and the support of peers participating in the crime especially strong. The value of noncrime may be low because the criminal justice system is ineffective, the perpetrator has no reputation to lose and no friends before whom to be disgraced, and there are no jobs or other sources of income worth what the crime will bring. The crime, in short, will be irresistible.

56   EXPLAINING CRIME

Persons who commit "irresistible" crimes, especially ones that involve violence or passion, are sometimes thought by society to be in the grip of a strange compulsion or a deranged mind. What seems rational from the offender's point of view appears irrational from society's. Some people will urge that such an offender be excused or his penalty mitigated because they cannot imagine themselves acting in this way. But if the crime is distinctive at all, it is only because the underlying drive for its reward is uncommon, or uncommonly intense. The crime is no more irresistible than cheating on one's income tax; it could have been suppressed by a greater or more certain penalty.

It is a mistake, for reasons we will develop in Chapter 19, to argue about whether a given offense is or is not "rational" or "irresistible," for there is no objective way to resolve such arguments. Crimes differ in the reinforcements attached to them, and individuals differ in the value they assign to such reinforcements and the degree to which they discount them over time.

Equity and Inequity

In assigning a value to the rewards of crime or noncrime, an individual often takes into account not only what he stands to gain but what others stand to gain from what he perceives as comparable efforts. The individual has some notion of what he is entitled to, and that notion is affected by what he sees other people getting.

This interaction between what one person thinks he deserves and what he sees other people getting is expressed by sociologists and social psychologists in terms of an "equity equation."[4] It is based on a much older notion of distributive justice, first elaborated by Aristotle in the *Nichomachean Ethics*. To Aristotle, an equitable allocation of goods or honors is one that gives to each person a share proportional to his or her merit.[5] In other words, the ratio of one person's share to another person's share will be the same as the ratio between one person's worth and the other's. The worth of the two parties will depend on their age, status, wealth, skill, effort, or virtue; which measure of worth is selected is influenced by the prior understandings of the parties or the nature of the political regime. For example, a sixteen-year-old boy lounging on a street corner may decide that what he and others ought to earn should be determined by how hard they work, their level of education, or by their racial or class status. The identity of the other person with whom one compares one's own merit will also vary. The sixteen-

A Theory of Criminal Behavior 57

year-old boy may compare his income to that of other sixteen-year-old boys, to that of all males in the city, or to that of all persons in the nation as a whole. What standard of comparison he uses and with whom he makes the comparison will obviously determine whether he thinks he has less or more money than he is entitled to have. For a given standard and a given reference group, he will feel he has what he is entitled to if the ratio between his income and his worth is the same as the ratio of the relevant other fellow's income to worth.

The equity equation can be expressed formally in the following terms. Let G stand for the gains a person receives from some transaction and C for the contributions (of time, skill, effort, or moral worth) in return for which he obtains these gains. The subscripts s and o stand for "self" and "other." A transaction is equitable when the ratio of one's own gains to one's own contributions $(\frac{G_s}{C_s})$ is the same as the ratio of the other person's gains to his contributions $(\frac{G_o}{C_o})$, that is, $\frac{G_s}{C_s} = \frac{G_o}{C_o}$. When $\frac{G_s}{C_s} \neq \frac{G_o}{C_o}$, the person with the lower ratio feels a sense of inequity.

This equity equation is the general case. Egalitarianism and humanitarianism are special instances of it, the former arising when both parties are assumed to have contributed equally $(C_o = C_s)$ and thus their shares must be equal $(G_o = G_s)$, the latter when what one person needs (as opposed to what he has actually contributed) is considered to be part of his contribution. The familiar concept of "relative deprivation" is also a special, albeit somewhat misleading, case of social inequity. Relative deprivation is usually defined as a state of affairs in which somebody is less well off than another person to whom he compares himself. This concept is often advanced as an explanation for why riots and revolutions may occur not when people are in utter misery but when they are becoming better off. They upgrade their sense of worth faster than their material gains, and so they feel justified in rebelling. The reason why relative deprivation is an incomplete and thus misleading statement of the problem is that it fails to take into account how one person evaluates the contributions (the worth) of another person. Individuals do not simply compare their gains to the gains of others; they compare the *ratio* of gains and contributions.

During their lives, most people change the way they evaluate a distribution of goods or honors. As infants, they are selfish, wanting everything without regard to the worth or contributions of others. As children, they may feel they are entitled to the same share as everybody else because, though they recognize that others are entitled to something, they do not recognize that others may deserve more than they.[6] As adults, they make finer distinctions regarding whom they should compare themselves with and on what grounds; some may even come to endorse altruistic standards.[7] A similar progression also occurs as people enter into more intimate and enduring relationships with each other, from the selfishness that often governs the relations of strangers to the altruism sometimes tying together husband and wife or parents and children.[8] A distribution that would be intolerably inequitable between strangers or business associates might be quite acceptable among friends or within a family. Changes in the way in which equity is defined, in short, may result from natural mental and moral development, from social learning,[9] from situational factors, or from all three. Moreover, individuals may differ in what they define as equitable because of differences in their level of understanding and, perhaps, their general intelligence.[10]

While much remains to be clarified, there can be little doubt that equity considerations influence all human transactions, including criminal ones. Every society recognizes this influence by incorporating some conception of equity or fairness into its legal code, criminal as well as civil.[11] The universal recognition of the importance of equity arises, we think, from the fact that a concern for equity is naturally expressed in all personal relationships. Take something from another person without his permission and he will feel angry; let the other person obtain a larger salary than you without having displayed any recognized superiority of skill, effort, or merit, and you will feel angry. Fail to return a favor when asked, and the person who asks will be upset; do a favor for someone who cannot reciprocate and he will feel uncomfortable.

People differ in how they respond to a situation in which another person has received something without appearing to deserve it. Some people may blame the other party and direct anger at him or even try to take, by stealth or force, some part of what he has obtained. Other persons may blame themselves for not having worked hard enough to earn the larger share now going to the other party. The other party may flaunt his good fortune or attempt, by soothing words, self-deprecation, or exaggerated friendliness, to make it up to the aggrieved party. For example, suppose you and your co-worker in an office receive salaries that seem justly to reflect your relative contributions of time, skill, and effort. Suddenly the other person receives a key to the executive lounge, but you do not. The resulting inequity can be handled in a variety of ways. He may go out of his way to be nice to you so as to increase your rewards, while you may go out of your way to be nasty to him so as to decrease his. Or he may upgrade the amount or quality of his work to justify the extra prize, while you may reduce your efforts to compensate for the (comparatively) lessened rewards. One or both

A Theory of Criminal Behavior 59

of you may make a show of belittling the value of the lounge or of having privileged access to it so as to minimize the deviation from equity.

Which equity-restoring tactic we adopt depends on the psychological costs of it and on our prior dispositions.[12] For most of us, certain ways of restoring equity—reducing our efforts, stealing the valued key, punching the holder of the key—would be too costly. Many of us keep the resentment or anger we feel to ourselves rather than express it overtly to the recipient of the unjustified benefit. But other persons may habitually express open anger at perceived inequities. Overtly aggressive reactions to inequity are more likely in an angry atmosphere, under the disinhibiting influence of drugs or alcohol, and among persons with a history of violence.[13]

Criminals and aggressive persons frequently defend their behavior by denigrating their victims.[14] They may not see themselves as modern-day Robin Hoods, but they are likely to think of their victims as somehow deserving their fate (they are "jerks," or "suckers," or "people who don't deserve what they have"). The injury and loss of property may, in the extreme case, be seen by the perpetrator as setting right, to some degree, inequitable social arrangements in general. To the extent that the criminal feels that his offense is justified by some perceived inequity, then the rewards of committing the crime, far from being reduced by the bite of conscience, are enhanced by the sense of restored equity.

Because of this, it is a mistake to explain crime (or its absence) on grounds of profit maximization narrowly defined.[15] Potential offenders do not, in many cases, simply evaluate the net tangible rewards of the crime and compare them to the time-discounted costs of the crime that may occur in the future; they also take into account the intangible rewards (a sense of rectified injustice) or penalties (a sense of guilt) that occur contemporaneously with the crime. A narrow economic explanation of crime is, to us, inadequate because it does not recognize that the value one person assigns to the outcome of a course of action depends in part on the outcomes of other persons' actions. At the other extreme, those who believe that crime is powerfully influenced by real or perceived injustice should bear in mind that individuals differ greatly in how they interpret and respond to a disproportionality between one's own ratio of gains to inputs and another person's ratio of gains to inputs. A sociological or political explanation of crime that is insensitive to individual differences is also inadequate.

The Context of Reinforcement

The effect of a reward or punishment is inversely proportional to the strength of all the reinforcements acting on a person at a given time. The

FIGURE 3

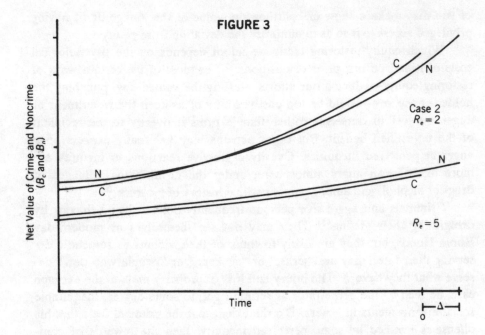

The upper pair of curves replots Case 2 from Figure 1. The lower pair of curves shows the same choice between crime and noncrime after an increase in the general context of reward, R_e. When the context increases, noncrime may rise above crime at all delays of reward. A crime that would have occurred, given the opportunity, is forestalled by a general improvement in the context of reinforcement. See Appendix.

more reinforcement a person is receiving, the less the value of any single reinforcement. The relativity of reinforcement has been demonstrated in the laboratory,[16] but it can be illustrated by everyday experience. Ten dollars received just after payday is less reinforcing than ten dollars received just before payday, when money is running low. The gentle pleasures of the elderly or the infirm, for whom rewards have become fewer, may be as reinforcing to them as the more boisterous pleasures of the young and vigorous.

When the amount of reinforcement acting on a person increases, the strength of a small reward decreases relatively more than that of a large one (see the Appendix). Since crime and noncrime usually have attached to them reinforcements of different magnitudes, changes in the context of reinforcement—that is, in the total amount of reinforcement operating—will affect the value of crime and noncrime differently. In Figure 3 we again show Case 2 (from Figure 1), but the context of reinforcement is expanded. The increase in the context of reinforcement reduces the rewards attached to both crime and noncrime, but the rewards attached to crime decrease more, with the result that now the person will not commit the crime. For example, a person who would commit a crime if the opportunity was sufficiently close in time and space (say, a boy who will grab a purse if he happens to come upon one being carried by a lone woman on the street) may not commit the crime if other reinforcers, having nothing to do with the value of crime or noncrime, start to operate (say, the boy has just fallen in love, is listening to some pleasant music on his portable stereo, and is enjoying a warm spring day).

There are other ways that a changed context of reinforcement might affect the probability of the commission of a crime. Suppose not only that our boy has fallen in love, but that his girl has agreed to marry him. Suddenly he has more to lose from crime—that is, the value of noncrime has increased because now it includes retaining the affection of the girl and the respect of her parents. In this and other ways, the richer the supply of reinforcements operating on a person, the less the chance he will commit a crime.

The Theory as a Whole

We began this chapter by asserting that the chief value of a comprehensive theory of crime is that it will bring to our attention all the factors that explain individual differences in criminality and thus prevent us from offering partial explanations or making incomplete interpretations of research findings.* The larger the ratio of the rewards (material and nonmaterial) of noncrime to the rewards (material and nonmaterial) of crime, the weaker the tendency to commit crimes. The bite of conscience, the approval of peers, and any sense of inequity will increase or decrease the total value of crime; the opinions of family, friends, and employers are important benefits of noncrime, as is the desire to avoid the penalties that can be imposed by the criminal justice system. The strength of any reward declines with time, but people differ in the rate at which they discount the future. The strength of a given reward is also affected by the total supply of reinforcers.

Some implications of the theory are obvious: Other things being equal, a reduction in the delay and uncertainty attached to the rewards of noncrime

---

* There is an advantage to stating the theory mathematically. We thereby make it easier in principle to deal simultaneously with the interaction of several variables, and thus we resist the tendency in thinking about crime to keep only two or three things in mind at one time and to treat those few things as either-or propositions. But the essence of the theory can be grasped without the mathematical notation, and so we have put that in the Appendix.

will reduce the probability of crime. But other implications are not so obvious. For instance, increasing the value of the rewards of noncrime (by increasing the severity of punishment) may not reduce a given individual's tendency to commit crime if he believes that these rewards are not commensurate with what he deserves. In this case, punishing him for preferring crime to noncrime may trigger hostility toward society in retaliation for the shortfall. The increased rewards for noncrime may be offset by an increased sense of inequity and hence an increased incentive for committing a crime. Or again: It may be easier to reduce crime by making penalties swifter or more certain, rather than more severe, if the persons committing crime are highly present-oriented (so that they discount even large rewards very sharply) or if they are likely to have their sense of inequity heightened by increases in the severity of punishment. Or yet again: An individual with an extroverted personality is more likely than one with an introverted one to externalize his feelings of inequity and act directly to correct them (see Chapter 7).

In laboratory settings involving both human and animal subjects, each element of the theory has received at least some confirmation and the major elements have been confirmed extensively.[17] Extrapolating these findings outside the laboratory, into real-world settings, is a matter on which opinions differ. In this book, we propose to bring together evidence from a variety of disciplines bearing on the connection between elements of the theory and the observed characteristics of crime and criminals.

The connection between crime and impulsiveness has been demonstrated (Chapter 7) as has the link between (low) intelligence and crime (Chapter 6). Those features of family life that produce stronger or weaker internalized inhibitions will be seen to have a connection to the presence or absence of aggressiveness and criminality (Chapters 8 and 9). Certain subcultures, such as street-corner gangs, appear to affect the value members attach to both crime and noncrime (Chapter 11). The mass media, and in particular television, may affect both aggressiveness directly and a viewer's sense of inequity that can affect crime indirectly (Chapter 13). Schooling may affect crime rates by bringing certain persons together into groups that reinforce either crime or noncrime and by determining the extent to which children believe that their skills will give them access to legitimate rewards (Chapter 10). The condition of the economy will have a complex effect on crime depending on whether the (possibly) restraint-weakening impact of affluence dominates the restraint-strengthening influence of employment opportunities (Chapter 12).

Though we will be using, for the most part, examples of rather com-

A Theory of Criminal Behavior   **63**

mon criminality to illustrate our argument, the theory is quite consistent with the more bizarre and unusual forms of crime. Psychopathic personalities lack to an unusual degree internalized inhibitions on crime (Chapter 7). Persons possessed by some obsessive interest—for example, pyromania—attach an inordinately high value to the rewards of certain crimes. If everyone loved fire too much, society would try hard to teach the moral evil of fire, as well as its practical danger. As it is, what society does teach is sufficient to overcome whatever slight tendency toward pyromania every average person may have, but it is insufficient to inhibit the rare pyromaniac. One reason society punishes arsonists is not only to make it more costly for persons to use fire for material gain but also to provide extra moral education to the occasional person who loves fire for its own sake.

In addition to pathological drives, there are ordinary ones that can, under certain conditions, become so strong as to lead to crime. History and literature abound with normal men and women in the grip of a too powerful reinforcement. Many people have broken the law for love, honor, family, and country, as well as for money, sex, vengeance, or delusion. Such criminals may be psychologically unremarkable; they transgressed because as they perceived the situation the reward for crime exceeded that for noncrime, and an opportunity presented itself. The legal system often tries to minimize the punishment inflicted on such people, raising issues that will be considered in Chapter 19.

Other Theories of Crime

Our approach to explaining individual differences in criminality is not meant to supplant but to encompass other theories. Following Travis Hirschi, we note that there are three main sociological perspectives on the causes of crime:

> According to *strain* or motivational theories, legitimate desires that conformity cannot satisfy force a person into deviance. According to *control* or bond theories, a person is free to commit delinquent acts because his ties to the conventional order have somehow been broken. According to *cultural deviance* theories, the deviant conforms to a set of standards not accepted by the larger or more powerful society.[18]

Strain theory assumes that people ordinarily obey society's rules but violate them when following those rules does not enable them to satisfy their legitimate aspirations. There is a strain between the goal they seek and the means at their disposal to reach that goal. Their opportunities are

64   EXPLAINING CRIME

blocked; thus, strain theory is sometimes called the theory of differential opportunity.[19] In some versions of strain theory, persons who are frustrated in their efforts to achieve middle-class goals abandon them and embrace antisocial values.[20] In other versions, they persist in seeking wealth, property, and status, but use criminal means to do so.

Advocates of strain theory are calling attention to the importance of certain reinforcers associated with noncrime, in particular the value of jobs and other sources of wealth and status, and suggesting that as these decline in strength (because they are not available or are of little value) the reinforcers associated with crime come to dominate the choices confronting the individual. This is a useful but partial observation. It properly reminds us of the importance to the individual of whatever alternatives to crime are available to him, but it neglects other components of the rewards of crime and noncrime and pays little attention to individual differences in impulsiveness and internalized inhibitions.

The reinforcers associated with noncrime include avoiding the penalties of the criminal justice system as well as obtaining the benefits of jobs; thus, the reinforcement supplied by noncrime can decline because *either* jobs become less available *or* sanctions decline in certainty or severity, or both. The theory also neglects the fact that the value of committing a crime is the sum not only of the money-supplying or status-conferring components of the crime but also of the costs (if any) of violating some internal inhibition and the benefits (if any) of rectifying a sense of inequity. Finally, strain theory ignores individual differences in time discounting (or impulsiveness).

Because of these limitations, strain theory cannot account for all of the observed facts about crime. It can offer no explanation, for example, of middle-class crime. If crime is disproportionately committed by lower-class persons because they find their lack of schooling and job opportunities a barrier to realizing their legitimate aspirations, then persons with adequate schooling and reasonable job prospects should not commit crimes, yet they do. If the people most likely to commit crimes are those in great need of legitimate rewards who find their access to those rewards blocked, then crime should be most common among men with families and heavy financial responsibilities, but in fact crime rates are highest among unattached males in the adolescent and young adult years.

Control theory directs our attention to the importance of learned inhibitions against crime. Unlike strain theory, which assumes that people naturally want to do the right thing but are prevented from doing it by circumstances, control theory suggests that it is first necessary to explain why anyone should want to do the right thing. This is an important suggestion

A Theory of Criminal Behavior 65

because it reminds us of the intangible components of the reinforcements associated with both crime (the bite, if any, of conscience) and noncrime (the value, if any, of the good opinion of decent folk). Control theory asks how the social bond is formed and maintained.[21] But important as this bonding may be, control theory does not explain all of the differences among individuals in criminality. In particular, it neglects differences in personality and orientation toward time: Some persons may commit crimes not because their attachment to legitimate norms is weak but because they are impulsive, unable to foresee the distant consequences of their actions, or confident that those consequences will not be costly. Moreover, control theory provides an incomplete account of the relationship between low intelligence and predatory criminality. The theory explains this connection largely by the claim that low-IQ individuals, frustrated by their inability to do well in their studies and jobs, fail to develop an attachment to school and work.[22] This may well occur, but it is also possible that cognitive deficits affect criminality more directly because they are associated with having a short time horizon.[23]

Cultural deviance theory also focuses on learning, but asserts that criminals have learned their values from deviant rather than law-abiding persons. Like control theory, this view directs our attention to the intangible reinforcers associated with crime and noncrime, suggesting that criminals are those who have learned that crime is worthwhile because it is reinforced by the good opinion of persons in whose company one commits the crime or who later learn of it. In some versions of this theory, deviant behavior is learned from other offenders by a process called "differential association";[24] in other versions, it is learned from a distinctive subculture composed of lower-class males who may not directly teach criminality but who value toughness, excitement, autonomy, and "street smarts," and who have a fatalistic attitude toward the future.[25] Useful as this perspective is, it cannot explain why some persons take their cues from street gangs while others take them from their families and other nondeviant individuals, nor is it consistent with the fact that high-rate delinquents seem to be boys who are *not* well integrated into gangs and who have few close or lasting friendships.[26] In short, cultural deviance theory provides no explanation for individual differences and thus cannot account for the fact that in a given neighborhood or social class some boys adopt deviant values and others adopt conventional ones. And the theory has no place for those tangible reinforcements associated with crime and noncrime that may lead persons with conventional values to commit crimes (because they are so profitable) or dissuade persons with deviant values from committing them (because they are so unprofitable).

66   EXPLAINING CRIME

The three kinds of theories discussed so far draw heavily or entirely on sociological thought; it is because of this that they have in common a disinterest in individual differences that arise out of psychological or biological predispositions. Other disciplines have sought to remedy this defect, but usually at the expense of any attention to the social setting in which crime occurs or to the complexity of internalized inhibitions. Criminals are more likely than noncriminals to have mesomorphic body types (Chapter 3), to have fathers who were criminals even in the case of adopted sons who could not have known their fathers (Chapter 3), to be of somewhat lower intelligence (Chapter 6), to be impulsive or extroverted (Chapter 7), and to have autonomic nervous systems that respond more slowly and less vigorously to stimuli (Chapter 7). These findings provide important clues to anyone seeking to explain individual differences, but taken alone they do not constitute a theory of crime, for they do not place the would-be offender in the full context of the reinforcements acting on his behavior. An impulsive person can be taught greater self-control, a low-IQ individual can engage in satisfying learning experiences, and extroverted mesomorphs with slow autonomic nervous system response rates may earn honest money in the National Football League instead of dishonest money robbing banks.

We believe that all of these views are implicit in our larger behavioral theory. The risk we run by attempting to state so general a theory is that a theory general enough to explain everything about crime will not provide many testable hypotheses explaining any one thing very precisely. At the least, however, our perspective allows us to put into some order the full array of particular findings about crime and human nature that one encounters in the literature. We turn to that task in the next chapter.

9

5

The Nature of Criminality:
Low Self-Control

Theories of crime lead naturally to interest in the propensities of individuals committing criminal acts. These propensities are often labeled "criminality." In pure classical theory, people committing criminal acts had no special propensities. They merely followed the universal tendency to enhance their own pleasure. If they differed from noncriminals, it was with respect to their location in or comprehension of relevant sanction systems. For example, the individual cut off from the community will suffer less than others from the ostracism that follows crime; the individual unaware of the natural or legal consequences of criminal behavior cannot be controlled by these consequences to the degree that people aware of them are controlled; the atheist will not be as concerned as the believer about penalties to be exacted in a life beyond death. Classical theories on the whole, then, are today called *control* theories, theories emphasizing the prevention of crime through consequences painful to the individual.

Although, for policy purposes, classical theorists emphasized legal consequences, the importance to them of moral sanctions is so obvious that their theories might well be called underdeveloped *social control* theories. In fact, Bentham's list of the major restraining motives—motives acting to prevent mischievous acts—begins with goodwill, love of reputation, and the desire for amity (1970: 134–36). He goes on to say that fear of detection prevents crime in large part because of detection's consequences for "reputation, and the desire for amity" (p. 138). Put another way, in Bentham's view, the restraining power of legal sanctions in large part stems from their connection to social sanctions.

86   CRIMINALITY

If crime is evidence of the weakness of social motives, it follows that criminals are less social than noncriminals and that the extent of their asociality may be determined by the nature and number of their crimes. Calculation of the extent of an individual's mischievousness is a complex affair, but in general the more mischievous or depraved the offenses, and the greater their number, the more mischievous or depraved the offender (Bentham 1970: 134–42). (Classical theorists thus had reason to be interested in the seriousness of the offense. The relevance of seriousness to current theories of crime is not so clear.)

Because classical or control theories infer that offenders are not restrained by social motives, it is common to think of them as emphasizing an asocial human nature. Actually, such theories make people only as asocial as their acts require. Pure or consistent control theories do not add criminality (i.e., personality concepts or attributes such as "aggressiveness" or "extraversion") to individuals beyond that found in their criminal acts. As a result, control theories are suspicious of images of an antisocial, psychopathic, or career offender, or of an offender whose motives to crime are somehow larger than those given in the crimes themselves. Indeed, control theories are compatible with the view that the balance of the total control structure favors conformity, even among offenders:

For in every man, be his disposition ever so depraved, the social motives are those which . . . regulate and determine the general tenor of his life. . . . The general and standing bias of every man's nature is, therefore, towards that side to which the force of the social motives would determine him to adhere. This being the case, the force of the social motives tends continually to put an end to that of the dissocial ones; as, in natural bodies, the force of friction tends to put an end to that which is generated by impulse. Time, then, which wears away the force of the dissocial motives, adds to that of the social. [Bentham 1970: 141]

Positivism brought with it the idea that criminals differ from noncriminals in ways more radical than this, the idea that criminals carry within themselves properties peculiarly and positively conducive to crime. In Chapters 3 and 4, we examined the efforts of the major disciplines to identify these properties. Being friendly to both the classical and positivist traditions, we expected to end up with a list of individual properties reliably identified by competent research as useful in the description of "criminality"—such properties as aggressiveness, body build, activity level, and intelligence. We further expected that we would be able to connect these individual-level correlates of criminality directly to the classical idea of crime. As our review progressed, however, we were forced to conclude that we had overestimated the success of positivism in establishing important differences between "criminals" and "noncriminals" beyond their tendency to commit criminal acts. Stable individual differences in the tendency to commit criminal acts were clearly evident, but many or even most of the other differences between offenders and nonoffenders were not as clear or pronounced as our reading of the literature had led us to expect.[1]

If individual differences in the tendency to commit criminal acts (within an overall tendency for crime to decline with age) are at least potentially explicable within classical theory by reference to the social location of individuals and their comprehension of how the world works, the fact remains that classical theory cannot shed much light on the positivistic finding (denied by most positivistic theories, as pointed out in Chapters 3 and 4) that these differences *remain reasonably stable with change in the social location of individuals and change in their knowledge of the operation of sanction systems*. This is the problem of self-control, the differential tendency of people to avoid criminal acts whatever the circumstances in which they find themselves. Since this difference among people has attracted a variety of names, we begin by arguing the merits of the concept of self-control.

Self-Control and Alternative Concepts

Our decision to ascribe stable individual differences in criminal behavior to self-control was made only after considering several alternatives, one of which (criminality) we had used before (Hirschi and Gottfredson 1986). A major consideration was consistency between the classical conception of crime and our conception of the criminal. It seemed unwise to try to integrate a choice theory of crime with a deterministic image of the offender, especially when such integration was unnecessary. In fact, the compatibility of the classical view of crime and the idea that people differ in self-control is, in our view, remarkable. As we have seen, classical theory is a theory of social or external control, a theory based on the idea that the costs of crime depend on the individual's current location in or bond to society. What classical theory lacks is an explicit idea of self-control, the idea that people also differ in the extent to which they are vulnerable to the temptations of the moment. Combining the two ideas thus

[1] We do not mean to imply that stable individual differences between offenders and nonoffenders are nonexistent. The fact of the matter is, however, that substantial evidence documenting individual differences is not as clear to us as it appears to be to others. The evidence on intelligence is an exception. Here differences favoring nonoffenders have been abundantly documented (cf. Wilson and Herrnstein 1985).

88   CRIMINALITY

merely recognizes the simultaneous existence of social and individual restraints on behavior.

An obvious alternative is the concept of criminality. The disadvantages of that concept, however, are numerous. First, it connotes causation or determinism, a positive tendency to crime that is contrary to the classical model and, in our view, contrary to the facts. Whereas self-control suggests that people differ in the extent to which they are restrained from criminal acts, criminality suggests that people differ in the extent to which they are compelled to crime. The concept of self-control is thus consistent with the observation that criminals do not require or need crime, and the concept of criminality is inconsistent with this observation. By the same token, the idea of low self-control is compatible with the observation that criminal acts require no special capabilities, needs, or motivation; they are, in this sense, available to everyone. In contrast, the idea of criminality as a special tendency suggests that criminal acts require special people for their performance and enjoyment. Finally, lack of restraint or low self-control allows almost any deviant, criminal, exciting, or dangerous act; in contrast, the idea of criminality covers only a narrow portion of the apparently diverse acts engaged in by people at one end of the dimension we are now discussing.

The concept of conscience comes closer than criminality to self-control, and is harder to distinguish from it. Unfortunately, that concept has connotations of compulsion (to conformity) not, strictly speaking, consistent with a choice model (or with the operation of conscience). It does not seem to cover the behaviors analogous to crime that appear to be controlled by natural sanctions rather than social or moral sanctions, and in the end it typically refers to how people feel about their acts rather than to the likelihood that they will or will not commit them. Thus accidents and employment instability are not usually seen as produced by failures of conscience, and writers in the conscience tradition do not typically make the connection between moral and prudent behavior. Finally, conscience is used primarily to summarize the results of learning via negative reinforcement, and even those favorably disposed to its use have little more to say about it (see, e.g., Eysenck 1977; Wilson and Herrnstein 1985).

We are now in position to describe the nature of self-control, the individual characteristic relevant to the commission of criminal acts. We assume that the nature of this characteristic can be derived directly from the nature of criminal acts. We thus infer from the nature of crime what people who refrain from criminal acts are like before they reach the age at which crime becomes a logical possibility. We then work back further to the factors producing their restraint, back to the causes of self-control. In our view, lack of self-control does not require crime and can be counteracted by situational conditions or other properties of the individual. At the same time, we suggest that high self-control effectively reduces the possibility of crime—that is, those possessing it will be substantially less likely at all periods of life to engage in criminal acts.

The Elements of Self-Control

Criminal acts provide *immediate* gratification of desires. A major characteristic of people with low self-control is therefore a tendency to respond to tangible stimuli in the immediate environment, to have a concrete "here and now" orientation. People with high self-control, in contrast, tend to defer gratification.

Criminal acts provide *easy or simple* gratification of desires. They provide money without work, sex without courtship, revenge without court delays. People lacking self-control also tend to lack diligence, tenacity, or persistence in a course of action.

Criminal acts are *exciting, risky, or thrilling*. They involve stealth, danger, speed, agility, deception, or power. People lacking self-control therefore tend to be adventuresome, active, and physical. Those with high levels of self-control tend to be cautious, cognitive, and verbal.

Crimes provide *few or meager long-term benefits*. They are not equivalent to a job or a career. On the contrary, crimes interfere with long-term commitments to jobs, marriages, family, or friends. People with low self-control thus tend to have unstable marriages, friendships, and job profiles. They tend to be little interested in and unprepared for long-term occupational pursuits.

Crimes require *little skill or planning*. The cognitive requirements for most crimes are minimal. It follows that people lacking self-control need not possess or value cognitive or academic skills. The manual skills required for most crimes are minimal. It follows that people lacking self-control need not possess manual skills that require training or apprenticeship.

Crimes often result in *pain or discomfort for the victim*. Property is lost, bodies are injured, privacy is violated, trust is broken. It follows that people with low self-control tend to be self-centered, indifferent, or insensitive to the suffering and needs of others. It does not follow, however, that people with low self-control are routinely unkind or antisocial. On the contrary, they may discover the immediate and easy rewards of charm and generosity.

Recall that crime involves the pursuit of immediate pleasure. It follows that people lacking self-control will also tend to pursue immediate pleasures that are *not* criminal: they will tend to smoke, drink, use drugs, gamble, have children out of wedlock, and engage in illicit sex.

Crimes require the interaction of an offender with people or their property. It does not follow that people lacking self-control will tend to be gregarious or social. However, it does follow that, other things being equal, gregarious or social people are more likely to be involved in criminal acts.

The major benefit of many crimes is not pleasure but relief from momentary irritation. The irritation caused by a crying child is often the stimulus for physical abuse. That caused by a taunting stranger in a bar is often the stimulus for aggravated assault. It follows that people with low self-control tend to have minimal tolerance for frustration and little ability to respond to conflict through verbal rather than physical means.

Crimes involve the risk of violence and physical injury, of pain and suffering on the part of the offender. It does not follow that people with low self-control will tend to be tolerant of physical pain or to be indifferent to physical discomfort. It does follow that people tolerant of physical pain or indifferent to physical discomfort will be more likely to engage in criminal acts whatever their level of self-control.

The risk of criminal penalty for any given criminal act is small, but this depends in part on the circumstances of the offense. Thus, for example, not all joyrides by teenagers are equally likely to result in arrest. A car stolen from a neighbor and returned unharmed before he notices its absence is less likely to result in official notice than is a car stolen from a shopping center parking lot and abandoned at the convenience of the offender. Drinking alcohol stolen from parents and consumed in the family garage is less likely to receive official notice than drinking in the parking lot outside a concert hall. It follows that offenses differ in their validity as measures of self-control: those offenses with large risk of public awareness are better measures than those with little risk.

In sum, people who lack self-control will tend to be impulsive, insensitive, physical (as opposed to mental), risk-taking, short-sighted, and nonverbal, and they will tend therefore to engage in criminal and analogous acts. Since these traits can be identified prior to the age of responsibility for crime, since there is considerable tendency for these traits to come together in the same people, and since the traits tend to persist through life, it seems reasonable to consider them as comprising a stable construct useful in the explanation of crime.

The Many Manifestations of Low Self-Control

Our image of the "offender" suggests that crime is not an automatic or necessary consequence of low self-control. It suggests that many noncriminal acts analogous to crime (such as accidents, smoking, and alcohol use) are also manifestations of low self-control. Our image therefore implies that no specific act, type of crime, or form of deviance is uniquely required by the absence of self-control.

Because both crime and analogous behaviors stem from low self-control (that is, both are manifestations of low self-control), they will all be engaged in at a relatively high rate by people with low self-control. Within the domain of crime, then, there will be much versatility among offenders in the criminal acts in which they engage.

Research on the versatility of deviant acts supports these predictions in the strongest possible way. The variety of manifestations of low self-control is immense. In spite of years of tireless research motivated by a belief in specialization, no credible evidence of specialization has been reported. In fact, the evidence of offender versatility is overwhelming (Hirschi 1969; Hindelang 1971; Wolfgang, Figlio, and Sellin 1972; Petersilia 1980; Hindelang, Hirschi, and Weis 1981; Rojek and Erickson 1982; Klein 1984).

By versatility we mean that offenders commit a wide variety of criminal acts, with no strong inclination to pursue a specific criminal act or a pattern of criminal acts to the exclusion of others. Most theories suggest that offenders tend to specialize, whereby such terms as robber, burglar, drug dealer, rapist, and murderer have predictive or descriptive import. In fact, some theories create offender specialization as part of their explanation of crime. For example, Cloward and Ohlin (1960) create distinctive subcultures of delinquency around particular forms of criminal behavior, identifying subcultures specializing in theft, violence, or drugs. In a related way, books are written about white-collar crime as though it were a clearly distinct specialty requiring a unique explanation. Research projects are undertaken for the study of drug use, or vandalism, or teen pregnancy (as though every study of delinquency were not a study of drug use and vandalism and teenage sexual behavior). Entire schools of criminology emerge to pursue patterning, sequencing, progression, escalation, onset, persistence, and desistance in the career of offenses or offenders. These efforts survive largely because their proponents fail to consider or acknowledge the clear evidence to the contrary. Other reasons for survival of such ideas may be found in the interest of politicians and members of the law enforcement community who see policy potential in criminal careers or "career criminals" (see, e.g., Blumstein et al. 1986).

Occasional reports of specialization seem to contradict this point, as do everyday observations of repetitive misbehavior by particular offenders. Some offenders rob the same store repeatedly over a period of years, or an offender commits several rapes over a (brief) period of time. Such offenders may be called "robbers" or "rapists." However, it should be noted that such labels are retrospective rather than predictive and that they typically ignore a large amount of delinquent or criminal behavior by the same offenders that is inconsistent with their alleged specialty. Thus, for example, the "rapist" will tend also to use drugs, to commit robberies and burglaries (often in concert with the rape), and to have a record for violent offenses other than rape. There is a perhaps natural tendency on the part of observers (and in official accounts) to focus on the most serious crimes in a series of events, but this tendency should not be confused with a tendency on the part of the offender to specialize in one kind of crime.

Recall that one of the defining features of crime is that it is simple and easy. Some apparent specialization will therefore occur because obvious opportunities for an easy score will tend to repeat themselves. An offender who lives next to a shopping area that is approached by pedestrians will have repeat opportunities for purse snatching, and this may show in his arrest record. But even here the specific "criminal career" will tend to quickly run its course and to be followed by offenses whose content and character is likewise determined by convenience and opportunity (which is the reason why some form of theft is always the best bet about what a person is likely to do next).

The evidence that offenders are likely to engage in noncriminal acts psychologically or theoretically equivalent to crime is, because of the relatively high rates of these "noncriminal" acts, even easier to document. Thieves are likely to smoke, drink, and skip school at considerably higher rates than nonthieves. Offenders are considerably more likely than nonoffenders to be involved in most types of accidents, including household fires, auto crashes, and unwanted pregnancies. They are also considerably more likely to die at an early age (see, e.g., Robins 1966; Eysenck 1977; Gottfredson 1984).

Good research on drug use and abuse routinely reveals that the correlates of delinquency and drug use are the same. As Akers (1984) has noted, "compared to the abstaining teenager, the drinking, smoking, and drug-taking teen is much more likely to be getting into fights, stealing, hurting other people, and committing other delinquencies." Akers goes on to say, "but the variation in the order in which they take up these things leaves little basis for proposing the causation of one by the other." In our view, the relation between drug use and delinquency is not a causal question. The correlates are the same because drug use and delinquency are both manifestations of an underlying tendency to pursue short-term, immediate pleasure. This underlying tendency (i.e., lack of self-control) has many manifestations, as listed by Harrison Gough (1948):

unconcern over the rights and privileges of others when recognizing them would interfere with personal satisfaction in any way; impulsive behavior, or apparent incongruity between the strength of the stimulus and the magnitude of the behavioral response; inability to form deep or persistent attachments to other persons or to identify in interpersonal relationships; poor judgment and planning in attaining defined goals; apparent lack of anxiety and distress over social maladjustment and unwillingness or inability to consider maladjustment qua maladjustment; a tendency to project blame onto others and to take no responsibility for failures; meaningless prevarication, often about trivial matters in situations where detection is inevitable; almost complete lack of dependability . . . and willingness to assume responsibility; and, finally, emotional poverty. [p. 362]

This combination of characteristics has been revealed in the life histories of the subjects in the famous studies by Lee Robins. Robins is one of the few researchers to focus on the varieties of deviance and the way they tend to go together in the lives of those she designates as having "antisocial personalities." In her words: "We refer to someone who fails to maintain close personal relationships with anyone else, [who] performs poorly on the job, who is involved in illegal behaviors (whether or not apprehended), who fails to support himself and his dependents without outside aid, and who is given to sudden changes of plan and loss of temper in response to what appear to others as minor frustrations" (1978: 255).

For 30 years Robins traced 524 children referred to a guidance clinic in St. Louis, Missouri, and she compared them to a control group matched on IQ, age, sex, and area of the city. She discovered that, in comparison to the control group, those people referred at an early age were more likely to be arrested as adults (for a wide variety of offenses), were less likely to get married, were more likely to be divorced, were more likely to marry a spouse with a behavior problem,

94   CRIMINALITY

were less likely to have children (but if they had children were likely to have more children), were more likely to have children with behavior problems, were more likely to be unemployed, had considerably more frequent job changes, were more likely to be on welfare, had fewer contacts with relatives, had fewer friends, were substantially less likely to attend church, were less likely to serve in the armed forces and more likely to be dishonorably discharged if they did serve, were more likely to exhibit physical evidence of excessive alcohol use, and were more likely to be hospitalized for psychiatric problems (1966: 42–73).

Note that these outcomes are consistent with four general elements of our notion of low self-control: basic stability of individual differences over a long period of time; great variability in the kinds of criminal acts engaged in; conceptual or causal equivalence of criminal and non-criminal acts; and inability to predict the specific forms of deviance engaged in, whether criminal or noncriminal. In our view, the idea of an antisocial personality defined by certain behavioral consequences is too positivistic or deterministic, suggesting that the offender must do certain things given his antisocial personality. Thus we would say only that the subjects in question are *more likely* to commit criminal acts (as the data indicate they are). We do not make commission of criminal acts part of the definition of the individual with low self-control.

Be this as it may, Robins's retrospective research shows that predictions derived from a concept of antisocial personality are highly consistent with the results of prospective longitudinal and cross-sectional research: offenders do not specialize; they tend to be involved in accidents, illness, and death at higher rates than the general population; they tend to have difficulty persisting in a job regardless of the particular characteristics of the job (no job will turn out to be a good job); they have difficulty acquiring and retaining friends; and they have difficulty meeting the demands of long-term financial commitments (such as mortgages or car payments) and the demands of parenting.

Seen in this light, the "costs" of low self-control for the individual may far exceed the costs of his criminal acts. In fact, it appears that crime is often among the least serious consequences of a lack of self-control in terms of the quality of life of those lacking it.

The Causes of Self-Control

We know better what deficiencies in self-control lead to than where they come from. One thing is, however, clear: low self-control is not

The Nature of Criminality 95

produced by training, tutelage, or socialization. As a matter of fact, all of the characteristics associated with low self-control tend to show themselves in the absence of nurturance, discipline, or training. Given the classical appreciation of the causes of human behavior, the implications of this fact are straightforward: the causes of low self-control are negative rather than positive; self-control is unlikely in the absence of effort, intended or unintended, to create it. (This assumption separates the present theory from most modern theories of crime, where the offender is automatically seen as a product of positive forces, a creature of learning, particular pressures, or specific defect. We will return to this comparison once our theory has been fully explicated.)

At this point it would be easy to construct a theory of crime causation, according to which characteristics of potential offenders lead them ineluctably to the commission of criminal acts. Our task at this point would simply be to identify the likely sources of impulsiveness, intelligence, risk-taking, and the like. But to do so would be to follow the path that has proven so unproductive in the past, the path according to which criminals commit crimes irrespective of the characteristics of the setting or situation.

We can avoid this pitfall by recalling the elements inherent in the decision to commit a criminal act. The object of the offense is clearly pleasurable, and universally so. Engaging in the act, however, entails some risk of social, legal, and/or natural sanctions. Whereas the pleasure attained by the act is direct, obvious, and immediate, the pains risked by it are not obvious, or direct, and are in any event at greater remove from it. It follows that, though there will be little variability among people in their ability to see the pleasures of crime, there will be considerable variability in their ability to calculate potential pains. But the problem goes further than this: whereas the pleasures of crime are reasonably equally distributed over the population, this is not true for the pains. Everyone appreciates money; not everyone dreads parental anger or disappointment upon learning that the money was stolen.

So, the dimensions of self-control are, in our view, factors affecting calculation of the consequences of one's acts. The impulsive or short-sighted person fails to consider the negative or painful consequences of his acts; the insensitive person has fewer negative consequences to consider; the less intelligent person also has fewer negative consequences to consider (has less to lose).

No known social group, whether criminal or noncriminal, actively or purposefully attempts to reduce the self-control of its members.

96   CRIMINALITY

Social life is not enhanced by low self-control and its consequences. On the contrary, the exhibition of these tendencies undermines harmonious group relations and the ability to achieve collective ends. These facts explicitly deny that a tendency to crime is a product of socialization, culture, or positive learning of any sort.

The traits composing low self-control are also not conducive to the achievement of long-term individual goals. On the contrary, they impede educational and occupational achievement, destroy interpersonal relations, and undermine physical health and economic well-being. Such facts explicitly deny the notion that criminality is an alternative route to the goals otherwise obtainable through legitimate avenues. It follows that people who care about the interpersonal skill, educational and occupational achievement, and physical and economic well-being of those in their care will seek to rid them of these traits.

Two general sources of variation are immediately apparent in this scheme. The first is the variation among children in the degree to which they manifest such traits to begin with. The second is the variation among caretakers in the degree to which they recognize low self-control and its consequences and the degree to which they are willing and able to correct it. Obviously, therefore, even at this threshold level the sources of low self-control are complex.

There is good evidence that some of the traits predicting subsequent involvement in crime appear as early as they can be reliably measured, including low intelligence, high activity level, physical strength, and adventuresomeness (Glueck and Glueck 1950; West and Farrington 1973). The evidence suggests that the connection between these traits and commission of criminal acts ranges from weak to moderate. Obviously, we do not suggest that people are born criminals, inherit a gene for criminality, or anything of the sort. In fact, we explicitly deny such notions (see Chapter 3). What we do suggest is that individual differences may have an impact on the prospects for effective socialization (or adequate control). Effective socialization is, however, always possible whatever the configuration of individual traits.

Other traits affecting crime appear later and seem to be largely products of ineffective or incomplete socialization. For example, differences in impulsivity and insensitivity become noticeable later in childhood when they are no longer common to all children. The ability and willingness to delay immediate gratification for some larger purpose may therefore be assumed to be a consequence of training. Much parental action is in fact geared toward suppression of impulsive behavior, toward making the child consider the long-range consequences of acts. Consistent sensitivity to the needs and feelings of others may also be assumed to be a consequence of training. Indeed, much parental behavior is directed toward teaching the child about the rights and feelings of others, and of how these rights and feelings ought to constrain the child's behavior. All of these points focus our attention on child-rearing.

Child-Rearing and Self-Control: The Family

The major "cause" of low self-control thus appears to be ineffective child-rearing. Put in positive terms, several conditions appear necessary to produce a socialized child. Perhaps the place to begin looking for these conditions is the research literature on the relation between family conditions and delinquency. This research (e.g., Glueck and Glueck 1950; McCord and McCord 1959) has examined the connection between many family factors and delinquency. It reports that discipline, supervision, and affection tend to be missing in the homes of delinquents, that the behavior of the parents is often "poor" (e.g., excessive drinking and poor supervision [Glueck and Glueck 1950: 110–11]); and that the parents of delinquents are unusually likely to have criminal records themselves. Indeed, according to Michael Rutter and Henri Giller, "of the parental characteristics associated with delinquency, criminality is the most striking and most consistent" 1984: 182).

Such information undermines the many explanations of crime that ignore the family, but in this form it does not represent much of an advance over the belief of the general public (and those who deal with offenders in the criminal justice system) that "defective upbringing" or "neglect" in the home is the primary cause of crime.

To put these standard research findings in perspective, we think it necessary to define the conditions necessary for adequate child-rearing to occur. The minimum conditions seem to be these: in order to teach the child self-control, someone must (1) monitor the child's behavior; (2) recognize deviant behavior when it occurs; and (3) punish such behavior. This seems simple and obvious enough. All that is required to activate the system is affection for or investment in the child. The person who cares for the child will watch his behavior, see him doing things he should not do, and correct him. The result may be a child more capable of delaying gratification, more sensitive to the interests and desires of others, more independent, more willing to accept restraints on his activity, and more unlikely to use force or violence to attain his ends.

When we seek the causes of low self-control, we ask where this system can go wrong. Obviously, parents do not prefer their children to be unsocialized in the terms described. We can therefore rule out in advance the possibility of positive socialization to unsocialized behavior (as cultural or subcultural deviance theories suggest). Still, the system can go wrong at any one of four places. First, the parents may not care for the child (in which case none of the other conditions would be met); second, the parents, even if they care, may not have the time or energy to monitor the child's behavior; third, the parents, even if they care *and* monitor, may not see anything wrong with the child's behavior; finally, even if everything else is in place, the parents may not have the inclination or the means to punish the child. So, what may appear at first glance to be nonproblematic turns out to be problematic indeed. Many things can go wrong. According to much research in crime and delinquency, in the homes of problem children many things have gone wrong: "Parents of stealers do not track ([they] do not interpret stealing . . . as 'deviant'); they do not punish; and they do not care" (Patterson 1980: 88–89; see also Glueck and Glueck 1950; McCord and McCord 1959; West and Farrington 1977).

Let us apply this scheme to some of the facts about the connection between child socialization and crime, beginning with the elements of the child-rearing model.

The Attachment of the Parent to the Child

Our model states that parental concern for the welfare or behavior of the child is a necessary condition for successful child-rearing. Because it is too often assumed that all parents are alike in their love for their children, the evidence directly on this point is not as good or extensive as it could be. However, what exists is clearly consistent with the model. Glueck and Glueck (1950: 125–28) report that, compared to the fathers of delinquents, fathers of nondelinquents were twice as likely to be warmly disposed toward their sons and one-fifth as likely to be hostile toward them. In the same sample, 28 percent of the mothers of delinquents were characterized as "indifferent or hostile" toward the child as compared to 4 percent of the mothers of nondelinquents. The evidence suggests that stepparents are especially unlikely to have feelings of affection toward their stepchildren (Burgess 1980), adding in contemporary society to the likelihood that children will be "reared" by people who do not especially care for them.

Parental Supervision

The connection between social control and self-control could not be more direct than in the case of parental supervision of the child. Such supervision presumably prevents criminal or analogous acts and at the same time trains the child to avoid them on his own. Consistent with this assumption, supervision tends to be a major predictor of delinquency, however supervision or delinquency is measured (Glueck and Glueck 1950; Hirschi 1969; West and Farrington 1977; Riley and Shaw 1985).

Our general theory in principle provides a method of separating supervision as external control from supervision as internal control. For one thing, offenses differ in the degree to which they can be prevented through monitoring; children at one age are monitored much more closely than children at other ages; girls are supervised more closely than boys. In some situations, monitoring is universal or nearly constant; in other situations monitoring for some offenses is virtually absent. In the present context, however, the concern is with the connection between supervision and self-control, a connection established by the stronger tendency of those poorly supervised when young to commit crimes as adults (McCord 1979).

Recognition of Deviant Behavior

In order for supervision to have an impact on self-control, the supervisor must perceive deviant behavior when it occurs. Remarkably, not all parents are adept at recognizing lack of self-control. Some parents allow the child to do pretty much as he pleases without interference. Extensive television-viewing is one modern example, as is the failure to require completion of homework, to prohibit smoking, to curtail the use of physical force, or to see to it that the child actually attends school. (As noted, truancy among second-graders presumably reflects on the adequacy of parental awareness of the child's misbehavior.) Again, the research is not as good as it should be, but evidence of "poor conduct standards" in the homes of delinquents is common.

Punishment of Deviant Acts

Control theories explicitly acknowledge the necessity of sanctions in preventing criminal behavior. They do not suggest that the major sanctions are legal or corporal. On the contrary, as we have seen, they suggest that disapproval by people one cares about is the most powerful of sanctions. Effective punishment by the parent or major care-taker therefore usually entails nothing more than explicit disapproval of unwanted behavior. The criticism of control theories that dwells on their alleged cruelty is therefore simply misguided or ill informed (see, e.g., Currie 1985).

Not all caretakers punish effectively. In fact, some are too harsh and some are too lenient (Glueck and Glueck 1950; McCord and Mc-Cord 1959; West and Farrington 1977; see generally Loeber and Stouthamer-Loeber 1986). Given our model, however, rewarding good behavior cannot compensate for failure to correct deviant be-havior. (Recall that, in our view, deviant acts carry with them their own rewards [see Chapter 2].)

Given the consistency of the child-rearing model with our general theory and with the research literature, it should be possible to use it to explain other family correlates of criminal and otherwise deviant behavior.

Parental Criminality

Our theory focuses on the connection between the self-control of the parent and the subsequent self-control of the child. There is good reason to expect, and the data confirm, that people lacking self-con-trol do not socialize their children well. According to Donald West and David Farrington, "the fact that delinquency is transmitted from one generation to the next is indisputable" (1977: 109; see also Robins 1966). Of course our theory does not allow transmission of criminal-ity, genetic or otherwise. However, it does allow us to predict that some people are more likely than others to fail to socialize their chil-dren and that this will be a consequence of their own inadequate socialization. The extent of this connection between parent and child socialization is revealed by the fact that in the West and Farrington study fewer than 5 percent of the families accounted for almost half of the criminal convictions in the entire sample. (In our view, this find-ing is more important for the theory of crime, and for public policy, than the much better-known finding of Wolfgang and his colleagues [1972] that something like 6 percent of *individual* offenders account for about half of all criminal acts.) In order to achieve such concentration of crime in a small number of families, it is necessary that the parents and the brothers and sisters of offenders also be unusually likely to commit criminal acts.[2]

[2] It is commonly observed (in an unsystematic way) that in an otherwise law-abiding family individual children are seriously delinquent. This observation is taken as evi-

Why should the children of offenders be unusually vulnerable to crime? Recall that our theory assumes that criminality is not something the parents have to work to produce; on the contrary, it assumes that criminality is something they have to work to avoid. Consistent with this view, parents with criminal records do *not* encourage crime in their children and are in fact as disapproving of it as parents with no record of criminal involvement (West and Farrington 1977). Of course, not wanting criminal behavior in one's children and being upset when it occurs do not necessarily imply that great effort has been expended to prevent it. If criminal behavior is oriented toward short-term rewards, and if child-rearing is oriented toward long-term rewards, there is little reason to expect parents themselves lacking self-control to be particularly adept at instilling self-control in their children.

Consistent with this expectation, research consistently indicates that the supervision of delinquents in families where parents have criminal records tends to be "lax," "inadequate," or "poor." Punishment in these families also tends to be easy, short-term, and insensitive—that is, yelling and screaming, slapping and hitting, with threats that are not carried out.

Such facts do not, however, completely account for the concentration of criminality among some families. A major reason for this failure is probably that the most subtle element of child-rearing is not included in the analysis. This is the element of *recognition* of deviant behavior. According to Gerald Patterson (1980), many parents do not even recognize *criminal* behavior in their children, let alone the minor forms of deviance whose punishment is necessary for effective child-rearing. For example, when children steal outside the home, some parents discount reports that they have done so on the grounds that the charges are unproved and cannot therefore be used to justify punishment. By the same token, when children are suspended for misbehavior at school, some parents side with the child and blame the episode on prejudicial mistreatment by teachers. Obviously, parents who cannot see the misbehavior of their children are in no position to correct it, even if they are inclined to do so.

Given that recognition of deviant acts is a necessary component of the child-rearing model, research is needed on the question of what

---

dence against family or child-rearing explanations of crime. (If the parents reared most of their children properly, how can their child-rearing practices be responsible for their delinquent children as well?) Such observations do not dispute the strong tendencies toward consistency within families mentioned in the text. They do suggest that family child-rearing practices are not the only causes of crime.

102   CRIMINALITY

parents should and should not recognize as deviant behavior if they
are to prevent criminality. To the extent our theory is correct, parents
need to know behaviors that reflect low self-control. That many parents are not now attentive to such behaviors should come as no
surprise. The idea that criminal behavior is the product of deprivation
or positive learning dominates modern theory. As a consequence,
most influential social scientific theories of crime and delinquency
ignore or deny the connection between crime and talking back, yelling, pushing and shoving, insisting on getting one's way, trouble in
school, and poor school performance. Little wonder, then, that some
parents do not see the significance of such acts. Research now makes
it clear that parents differ in their reaction to these behaviors, with
some parents attempting to correct behaviors that others ignore or
even defend (Patterson 1980). Because social science in general sees
little connection between these acts and crime, there has been little
systematic integration of the child development and criminological
literatures. Furthermore, because the conventional wisdom disputes
the connection between child training and crime, public policy has
not focused on it. We do not argue that crime is caused by these early
misbehaviors. Instead, we argue that such behaviors indicate the
presence of the major individual-level cause of crime, a cause that in
principle may be attacked by punishing these early manifestations.
Nor do we argue that criminal acts automatically follow early evidence of low self-control. Because crime requires more than low self-
control, some parents are lucky and have children with low self-
control who still manage to avoid acts that would bring them to the
attention of the criminal justice system. It is less likely (in fact unlikely), however, that such children will avoid altogether behavior
indicative of low self-control. Put another way, low self-control predicts low self-control better than it predicts any of its specific manifestations, such as crime.

Family Size

One of the most consistent findings of delinquency research is that
the larger the number of children in the family, the greater the likelihood that each of them will be delinquent. This finding, too, is
perfectly explicable from a child-rearing model. Affection for the individual child may be unaffected by numbers, and parents with large
families may be as able as anyone else to recognize deviant behavior,
but monitoring and punishment are probably more difficult the
greater the number of children in the family. Greater numbers strain

parental resources of time and energy. For this reason, the child in the large family is likely to spend more time with other children and less time with adults. Children are not as likely as adults to be effective trainers. They have less investment in the outcome, are more likely to be tolerant of deviant behavior, and do not have the power to enforce their edicts.

If the analysis of criminality of parents and size of family is sufficient to establish the plausibility of our child-rearing explanation, we can now attempt to apply it to some of the more problematic issues in the connection between the family and crime.

The Single-Parent Family

Such family measures as the percentage of the population divorced, the percentage of households headed by women, and the percentage of unattached individuals in the community are among the most powerful predictors of crime rates (Sampson 1987). Consistent with these findings, in most (but not all) studies that directly compare children living with both biological parents with children living in "broken" or reconstituted homes, the children from intact homes have lower rates of crime.

If the fact of a difference between single- and two-parent families is reasonably well established, the mechanisms by which it is produced are not adequately understood. It was once common in the delinquency literature to distinguish between homes broken by divorce and those broken by death. This distinction recognized the difficulty of separating the effects of the people involved in divorce from the effects of divorce itself. Indeed, it is common to find that involuntarily broken homes are less conducive to delinquency than homes in which the parent was a party to the decision to separate.

With the continued popularity of marriage, a possible complication enters the picture. The missing biological parent (in the overwhelming majority of cases, the father) is often replaced at some point by a stepparent. Is the child better or worse off as a result of the presence of an "unrelated" adult in the house?

The model we are using suggests that, *all else being equal*, one parent is sufficient. We could substitute "mother" or "father" for "parents" without any obvious loss in child-rearing ability. Husbands and wives tend to be sufficiently alike on such things as values, attitudes, and skills that for many purposes they may be treated as a unit. For that matter, our scheme does not even require that the adult involved in training the child be his or her guardian, let alone a

104   CRIMINALITY

biological parent. Proper training can be accomplished outside the confines of the two-parent home.

But all else is rarely equal. The single parent (usually a woman) must devote a good deal to support and maintenance activities that are at least to some extent shared in the two-parent family. Further, she must often do so in the absence of psychological or social support. As a result, she is less able to devote time to monitoring and punishment and is more likely to be involved in negative, abusive contacts with her children.

Remarriage is by no means a complete solution to these problems. As compared to natural parents, stepparents are likely to report that they have no "parental feelings" toward their stepchildren, and they are unusually likely to be involved in cases of child abuse (Burgess 1980). The other side of the coin is the affection of the child for the parent. Such affection is conducive to nondelinquency in its own right and clearly eases the task of child-rearing. Affection is, for obvious reasons, less likely to be felt toward the new parent in a reconstituted family than toward a biological parent in a continuously intact family

The Mother Who Works Outside the Home

The increase in the number of women in the labor force has several implications for the crime rate. To the extent this increase contributes to the instability of marriage, it will have the consequences for crime just discussed. Traditionally, however, the major concern was that the mother working outside the home would be unable to supervise or effectively rear her children. Sheldon and Eleanor Glueck (1950) found that the children of women who work, especially the children of those who work "occasionally" or "sporadically," were more likely to be delinquent. They also showed that the effect on delinquency of the mother's working was *completely* accounted for by the quality of supervision provided by the mother. (Such complete explanations of one factor by another are extremely rare in social science.) When the mother was able to arrange supervision for the child, her employment had no effect on the likelihood of delinquency. In fact, in this particular study, the children of regularly employed women were least likely to be delinquent when supervision was taken into account. This does not mean, however, that the employment of the mother had no effect. It did have an effect, at least among those in relatively deprived circumstances: the children of employed women were more likely to be delinquent.

More commonly, research reports a small effect of mother's employment that it is unable to explain. The advantage of the nonemployed mother over the employed mother in child-rearing remains when supervision and other characteristics of the mother, the family, and the child are taken into account. One possible implication of this explanatory failure is that the effects of employment influence children in ways not measurable except through their delinquency. One way of addressing this question would be to examine the effect of mother's employment on measures of inadequate self-control other than the commission of criminal acts—such as on accidents or school failure. If we are dealing with a social-control effect rather than a socialization effect, it should be possible to find a subset of deviant behaviors that are more affected than others by mother's employment. Although our scheme does not allow us *a priori* to separate the enduring effects of child "rearing" from the temporary effects of child "control," it alerts us to the fact that self-control and supervision can be the result of a single parental act.

Another consequence of female labor-force participation is that it leaves the house unguarded for large portions of the day. The unoccupied house is less attractive to adolescent members of the family and more attractive to other adolescents interested only in its contents. As we indicated earlier, research shows that the absence of guardians in the home is a good predictor of residential burglary.

Child Rearing and Self-Control: The School

Most people are sufficiently socialized by familial institutions to avoid involvement in criminal acts. Those not socialized sufficiently by the family may eventually learn self-control through the operation of other sanctioning systems or institutions. The institution given principal responsibility for this task in modern society is the school. As compared to the family, the school has several advantages as a socializing institution. First, it can more effectively monitor behavior than the family, with one teacher overseeing many children at a time. Second, as compared to most parents, teachers generally have no difficulty recognizing deviant or disruptive behavior. Third, as compared to the family, the school has such a clear interest in maintaining order and discipline that it can be expected to do what it can to control disruptive behavior. Finally, like the family, the school in theory has the authority and the means to punish lapses in self-control.

All else being equal, it would appear that the school could be an effective socializing agency. The evidence suggests, however, that in

106   CRIMINALITY

contemporary American society the school has a difficult time teaching self-control. A major reason for this limited success of the modern school appears to stem from the lack of cooperation and support it receives from families that have already failed in the socialization task. When the family does not see to it that the child is in school doing what he or she should be doing, the child's problems in school are often directly traceable to the parents. For example, according to Robins (1966), truancy begins in the first and second grades (and is not, as some assume, solely an adolescent problem). Truancy or absence in the first and second grades can hardly be attributed to the child alone. Whatever the source of such truancy, it is highly predictive of low self-control later in life.

The question, then, is whether inadequate socialization by the family could be corrected by the school if it were given the chance—that is, if the family were cooperative. Robins, whose analyses of the stability of the antisocial personality are not ordinarily optimistic, notes that the school could be used to locate preadolescents with low self-control and that it might be effective in doing what the family has failed to do: "Since truancy and poor school performance are nearly universally present in pre-sociopaths, it should be possible to identify children requiring treatment through their school records. . . . [T]he fact that a gross lack of discipline in the home predicted long-term difficulties suggests trying a program in which the schools attempt to substitute for the missing parental discipline in acting to prevent truancy and school failures" (1966: 306–7).[3]

Even without parental support, in our view, the net effect of the school must be positive. As a result of the school experience, some students learn better to appreciate the advantages and opportunities associated with self-control and are thus effectively socialized regardless of their familial experiences. One of the major school correlates of crime has always been the mundane homework. Those who do it are by definition thinking about tomorrow. Those who do not do it have a shorter time frame. One mark of socialization is considering the consequences of today's activities for tomorrow. Homework thus indexes and perhaps contributes to socialization.

Another major predictor of crime is not liking school. This connec-

[3]In subsequent chapters we emphasize the limited power of institutions to create self-control later in life when it has been theretofore lacking. Our theory clearly argues, however, that it is easier to develop self-control among people lacking it than to undermine or destroy self-control among those possessing it. Consistent with this position, the data routinely show that preadolescents without behavior problems rarely end up with significant problems as adults (see, e.g., Robins 1966; Glueck and Glueck 1968).

tion is so strong that the statement "delinquents do not like school" does not require much in the way of qualification (Glueck and Glueck 1950: 144). The connection speaks well for the school as a socializing institution. Socializing institutions impose restraints; they do not allow unfettered pursuit of self-interest; they require accomplishment. Lack of self-control activates external controls, controls that are not applied to or felt by everyone, thus resulting in differences in attitude toward the school.

School performance also strongly predicts involvement in delinquent and criminal activities. Those who do well in school are unlikely to get into trouble with the law. This, too, supports the view of the school as a potentially successful training ground for the development of self-control. Students who like school and do well in it are likely to perceive a successful future and are thus susceptible to school sanctions (Stinchcombe 1964).

The crime and low self-control perspective organizes and explains most facts about the relation between schooling and crime, one of the staples of delinquency research. We will have more to say about the school and crime in later chapters, especially Chapter 6. For now, suffice it to say that self-control differences seem primarily attributable to family socialization practices. It is difficult for subsequent institutions to make up for deficiencies, but socialization is a task that, once successfully accomplished, appears to be largely irreversible.

The Stability Problem

Competent research regularly shows that the best predictor of crime is prior criminal behavior. In other words, research shows that differences between people in the likelihood that they will commit criminal acts persist over time.[4] This fact is central to our conception of criminality. In the next chapter we show how it calls into question the many theories of crime that depend on social institutions to create criminals from previously law-abiding citizens. For now, we briefly reconcile the fact of stability with the idea that desocialization is rare.

Combining little or no movement from high self-control to low self-control with the fact that socialization continues to occur throughout life produces the conclusion that the proportion of the population in the potential offender pool should tend to decline as cohorts age. This conclusion is consistent with research. Even the most active offenders burn out with time, and the documented number of "late-

[4] We described the research documenting the stability of "aggression" in Chapter 3, and the research documenting the stability of "criminality" is discussed at length in Chapter 11 in reference to methodologies for studying crime and criminality.

comers" to crime, or "good boys gone bad," is sufficiently small to suggest that they may be accounted for in large part by misidentification or measurement error. (This result is also consistent with Bentham's theory in that all sanction systems work against the possibility of lengthy careers in crime.) Put another way, the low self-control group continues over time to exhibit low self-control. Its size, however, declines.

Such stability of criminality is a staple of pragmatic criminology. The criminal justice system uses this fact in much the same way that educational institutions use prior academic performance to sort students and select personnel—that is, without much concern for the meaning of the variable. (A variant of the pragmatic response seeks to identify career criminals or high-rate offenders and thereby refine selection decisions, but here too nothing is usually said about what it is that produces long-standing differences in the level of involvement in crime [Blumstein et al. 1986].)

The traditional theoretical response denies stability and constructs theories that do not deal with "individual-level" variables. These theories automatically suggest that the causes of the "onset" of crime are not the same as the causes of "persistence" in crime. They also suggest that "desistance" from crime has unique causes. On analysis, however, most criminological theories appear to deal with onset and remain agnostic or silent on the persistence and desistence issues.

Thus no currently popular criminological theory attends to the stability of differences in offending over the life course. We are left with a paradoxical situation: a major finding of criminological research is routinely ignored or denied by criminological theory. After a century of research, crime theories remain inattentive to the fact that people differ in the likelihood that they will commit crimes and that these differences appear early and remain stable over much of the life course. Perhaps a major reason for ignoring the stability of low self-control is the assumption that other individual traits are stable and thereby account for apparently stable differences in criminal behavior. These are the so-called personality explanations of crime.

Personality and Criminality

Sociological criminology takes the position that no trait of personality has been shown to characterize criminals more than noncriminals (Sutherland and Cressey 1978: ch. 8). Psychological criminology takes the position that many personality traits have been shown to characterize criminals more than noncriminals (Wilson and Herrnstein 1985: ch. 7). We take the position that both views are wrong. The level of self-control, or criminality, distinguishes offenders from nonoffenders, and the degree of its presence or absence can be established before (and after) criminal acts have been committed. This enduring tendency is well within the meaning of "personality trait" and is thus contrary to the sociological view. Contrary to the psychological view, the evidence for personality differences between offenders and nonoffenders beyond self-control is, at best, unimpressive. Most of this evidence is produced by attaching personality labels to differences in rates of offending between offenders and nonoffenders—that is, by turning one difference into many.

For example, Wilson and Herrnstein (1985: ch. 7) report that delinquents score higher than nondelinquents on the following dimensions of personality (see also Herrnstein 1983):

1. "Q" scores on the Porteus Maze Tests.
2. Assertiveness.
3. Fearlessness.
4. Aggressiveness.
5. Unconventionality.
6. Extroversion.
7. Poor socialization.
8. Psychopathy.
9. Schizophrenia.
10. Hypomania.
11. Hyperactivity.
12. Poor conditionability.
13. Impulsiveness.
14. Lefthandedness.

All of these "personality" traits can be explained without abandoning the conclusion that offenders differ from nonoffenders only in their tendency to offend. One problem that has historically plagued personality research is the failure of its practitioners to report the content of their measuring instruments. This failure may be justified by the fact that the tests have commercial value, but the scientific result is the reporting of what are rightly considered "empirical tautologies," the discovery that two measures of the same thing are correlated with each other. In the present case, it seems fair to say that no one has found an independently measured personality trait substantially correlated with criminality. For example, the Minnesota Multiphasic Personality Inventory has three subscales said to distinguish between delinquents and nondelinquents. The major discriminator is the Psychopathic Deviate subscale. As Wilson and Herrnstein note, this subscale includes "questions about a respondent's past criminal behavior" (1985: 187). But if this is so, then scale scores obviously cannot be used to establish the existence of a trait of personality independent of the tendency to commit criminal acts.

The situation is the same with the socialization subscale of the

California Personality Inventory. This subscale contains items indistinguishable from standard self-report delinquency items. That it is correlated with other measures of delinquency supports the unremarkable conclusion that measures of delinquency tend to correlate with one another. By the same token, a high score on the Q scale of the Porteus Maze Tests indicates subjects who frequently "break the rules by lifting his or her pencil from the paper, by cutting corners, or by allowing the pencil to drift out of the maze channels" (Wilson and Herrnstein 1985: 174). This measure is reminiscent of the measure of cheating developed by Hugh Hartshorne and Mark May (1928). That people who lie, cheat, and steal are more likely to cheat is not particularly instructive.

Earlier we examined the misleading suggestion that offenders can be usefully characterized as highly aggressive. Because measures of aggressiveness include many criminal acts, it is impossible to distinguish aggressiveness from criminality (see Chapter 3). And so on through the list above. The measures of personality are either direct indicators of crime or conceptually indistinguishable from low self-control. Some, of course, are simply not supported by credible research (such as lefthandedness), and their continual reappearance should by now begin to undermine the credibility of psychological positivism.

The limited life of personality-based theories of crime is illustrated by the work of Hans Eysenck. He concluded that "persons with strong antisocial inclinations [should] have high P, high E, and high N scores," where P is psychoticism, E is extraversion, and N is neuroticism (1964: 58). Eysenck provided detailed descriptions of persons scoring high on extraversion and psychoticism. For example, the extravert is "sociable, likes parties, has many friends, needs to have people to talk to, and does not like reading and studying by himself. . . . He prefers to keep moving and doing things, tends to be aggressive and loses his temper quickly; his feelings are not kept under tight control and he is not always a reliable person" (pp. 50–51). In contrast, the person scoring high on the P factor is "(1) solitary, not caring for other people; (2) troublesome, not fitting in; (3) cruel, inhumane; (4) lack of feeling, insensitive; (5) lacking in empathy; (6) sensation-seeking, avid for strong sensory stimuli; (7) hostile to others, aggressive; (8) [has a] liking for odd and unusual things; (9) disregard for dangers, foolhardy; (10) likes to make fools of other people and to upset them" (p. 58).

Although Eysenck is satisfied that research supports the existence of these dimensions and the tendency of offenders to score high on them (Eysenck 1989), many scholars (e.g., Rutter and Giller 1984) have not been convinced of the utility of Eysenck's personality scheme. (Wilson and Herrnstein do not include Eysenck's dimensions among the many personality traits they list.) In the current context, this scheme epitomizes the difficulties of the personality perspective (whatever the assumed source of personality differences) when applied to criminal behavior. In Eysenck's case, these difficulties are manifest in the obvious conceptual overlap of the personality dimensions and in the inability to measure them independently of the acts they are meant to produce.

The search for personality characteristics common to offenders has thus produced nothing contrary to the use of low self-control as the primary individual characteristic causing criminal behavior. People who develop strong self-control are unlikely to commit criminal acts throughout their lives, regardless of their other personality characteristics. In this sense, self-control is the only enduring personal characteristic predictive of criminal (and related) behavior. People who do not develop strong self-control are more likely to commit criminal acts, whatever the other dimensions of their personality. As people with low self-control age, they tend less and less to commit crimes; this decline is probably not entirely due to increasing self-control, but to age as well (see Chapter 6).

Although the facts about individual differences in crime are consistent with our theory, they are also consistent with theories designed explicitly to account for them. Differences between these theories and our own should therefore be specifically discussed.

Alternative Theories of Criminality

It is common to say that there are multitudes of theories of criminality. In fact, however, the number of truly distinct explanations is small. One reason the number is limited is that the assumptions underlying theories are themselves limited and tend to cluster logically. Some theories assume that humans are naturally inclined to law-abiding or social behavior; others assume that humans are naturally inclined to criminal or antisocial behavior; still others try to make neither of these assumptions. Some assume that the motivation to commit crime is different from the motivation for lawful activities; others make no such assumption. Some assume that human behavior is governed by forces in the immediate situation or environment; others assume that stable personality characteristics govern conduct. Some assume that each item of behavior has unique determinants;

others assume that many items of behavior may have causes in common. In subsequent chapters, our theory will be frequently distinguished from other theories by the position it produces on various empirical and policy issues. Here we want to locate the theory along methodological dimensions as a means of exposing in some systematic way opportunities for further development.

One way to look at theories of crime is in terms of their assumptions about human nature and society. Another is to examine their intended scope, the range of deviant acts they encompass. Still another is to contrast the empirical tests that may be derived from them. Finally, one may ask where the theories are located in the temporal sequence leading to a particular criminal act. Taking the last first, it is relatively easy to describe current theories in terms of the proximity of their causal forces to the actual behavior they attempt to explain.

The Temporal Position of Criminality vis-à-vis Crime

Some theories (e.g., Becker 1974; Wilson and Herrnstein 1985; Cornish and Clark 1986) focus on decisionmaking in the immediate situation in which the offense is or is not committed. At an intermediate remove, other theories (e.g., Merton 1938; Cloward and Ohlin 1960) focus on the forces in adolescence that produce offenders—that is, people embarked on a course of life that ultimately leads to the commission of criminal acts. Still other theories (e.g., Mednick 1977; Colvin and Pauly 1983) focus on hereditary or class factors present at or before birth, factors that operate at great distance from the events they cause.

Traditionally, the more distant the causes from the criminal act, the harder it is to construct a plausible theory using them. As a result, "distant" theories tend to exaggerate differences between offenders and nonoffenders, or to suggest causes that eventually *require* criminal acts. The model for such explanations is Lombroso's born criminal, a person destined to commit criminal acts from the point of conception. Only slightly less deterministic is the predispositional theory of the biologist or psychologist. These theories, too, suggest that once people have developed their respective dispositions the criminal behavior of some of them is a foregone conclusion.

Even temporally intermediate theories tend to divide the population into sharply distinct categories and to suggest that those in the potential offender category must go on to commit their quota of criminal acts. For example, once the lower-class boy has adapted to strain by giving up allegiance to the legitimate means to wealth, criminal acts ineluctably follow; once the person has learned an excess of definitions favorable to the violation of law, the outcome in criminal behavior is fixed. (The labeling theory saves itself from this problem by retaining the proviso that labels do not always "stick." Fair enough. But if they do stick, delinquency is inevitable.)

Theories that focus on the immediate decisionmaking situation are accordingly least concerned about differences between offenders and nonoffenders. In fact, since they do not require differential tendencies to commit crime, these theories are inclined to suggest that such differences are trivial or nonexistent. Theories that combine distant *and* proximate causes, such as our own, thus combine opposing tendencies, and risk inconsistency.

In principle, distant and proximate theories should be consistent. On inspection, however, they are usually inconsistent. The marked differences that in distant theories require crime do not permit unrestricted decisionmaking from moment to moment depending on the situation. For example, Wilson and Herrnstein advance a theory in which the offender chooses between crime and noncrime on the basis of the costs and benefits accruing to both lines of action:

The larger the ratio of the rewards (material and nonmaterial) of noncrime to the rewards (material and nonmaterial) of crime, the weaker the tendency to commit crimes. The bite of conscience, the approval of peers, and any sense of inequity will increase or decrease the total value of crime; the opinions of family, friends, and employers are important benefits of noncrime, as is the desire to avoid the penalties that can be imposed by the criminal justice system. The strength of any reward declines with time, but people differ in the rate at which they discount the future. The strength of a given reward is also affected by the total supply of reinforcers. [1985: 61]

The criminal described by Wilson and Herrnstein is a person without a conscience who cares about the approval of his friends and has a strong sense that he has not been treated fairly. Those knowledgeable about basic criminological theories will see the resemblance between these characteristics of the offender and those described by control theory, cultural deviance theory, and strain theory—in that order—and will be troubled by the contradictory images these theories have always projected (Kornhauser 1978). For present purposes, the problem is that cultural deviance theory and strain theory do not take approval of one's friends or a sense of inequity as momentary decisionmaking criteria. On the contrary, these theories suggest that such considerations override concerns for legitimate employment, the opinion of family and friends, and the desire to avoid the penalties of the criminal law. If so, the decision to commit a criminal act is no decision at all.

114   CRIMINALITY

Wilson and Herrnstein argue that delinquents discount future consequences more than nondelinquents do. This is inconsistent with
strain theory. In the Merton and the Cloward and Ohlin versions of
this theory, the potential delinquent looks into the future and sees
dismal prospects. As a consequence, he turns to a life of crime designed to brighten these prospects. In other words, in strain theory
the delinquent is especially future-oriented as compared to the non-
delinquent. (We believe Wilson and Herrnstein may be correct about
the decisionmaking [crime] portion of their theory. The point is that
the crime portion of their theory cannot be squared with its criminal
portion.) The idea that offenders are likely to be concerned with equity is also contrary to the notion that they more heavily discount
time: equity concerns, as described by Wilson and Herrnstein, require that the person compare his effort/reward ratio with the effort/
reward ratios of others. Such calculations obviously require rather
broad perspectives on the social order, but for present purposes the
important point is that people who feel inequitably treated must have
put forth the effort that justifies their feelings (otherwise we would be
talking about envy). But people who discount the future do not exert
themselves for uncertain future benefits, and the notion of inequity at
the point of crime is therefore incompatible with the image of the
offender at the point of criminality.

The problems encountered by Wilson and Herrnstein are endemic
to social learning theories, theories that also attempt to consider crime
and criminality simultaneously. Social learning theories suggest that
people learn to commit criminal acts because they provide benefits
from valued groups in excess of their costs from neutral or disvalued
groups (and apart from any benefits obtained from the criminal act
itself). To the extent this is so, the idea that criminals differ from
noncriminals in such things as time-discounting, aggressiveness, or
impulsiveness is hard to sustain. On the contrary, such theories suggest that if there are differences between criminals and noncriminals,
they are opposite to those usually suggested by theories of criminality. Such inconsistencies between the demands of theories of choice
and theories of criminality are hard to ignore. Since data bearing on
both theories are abundantly available, they are even harder to ignore. In our view, they survive only because of the disciplinary interests they appear to serve.

Our theory was in part devised by working back and forth between
an image of crime and an image of criminality. Because crimes tend to
combine immediate benefit and long-term cost, we are careful to
avoid the image of an offender pursuing distant goals. Because crimes

tend to be quick and easy to accomplish, we are careful to avoid the image of an offender driven by deep resentment or long-term social purposes. Because crimes tend to involve as victim and offender people with similar characteristics, we are careful to avoid the image of an offender striking *out* against class or race enemies.

Because lack of self-control is not conducive to hard work, delayed gratification, or persistence in a course of action, we are careful to avoid an image of crime as a long-term, difficult, or drawn-out endeavor. Because lack of self-control is conducive to unpredictability or unreliability in behavior, we are careful to avoid an image of crime as an organized activity. And, because lack of self-control shows itself in many noncriminal as well as in criminal acts, we are careful to avoid an image of deviance as exclusively illegal behavior.

Our theory applies across the life course, and it applies from the point of decisionmaking back to the origins of differences in degree of self-control. In infancy and preadolescence it is a theory of socialization and social control, accounting for a variety of deviant acts— defiance, truancy, school failure—and constructing people unlikely in future years to commit criminal acts. In adolescence and the early adult years, the socialization component declines and the theory focuses largely on social control, accounting for an even greater variety of deviant and criminal acts: truancy, dropout, drug use, theft, assault, accidents, pregnancy. As adulthood approaches, natural (i.e., biological and physical) controls play an increasingly larger part, and there is a tendency for the rate of deviant behavior to decline. As a result of declining rates, the diversity of offenses committed by individual offenders tends to decline, but differences established earlier continue to explain the whole set of offenses, along with other manifestations of low social control.

The Scope of Theory

In principle, theorists must choose between broad theories roughly applicable to a wide variety of vaguely defined conduct and narrow theories directly applicable to specific, precisely defined acts. This choice is often seen as being broad, important, and wrong versus being narrow, trivial, and correct. Positivists have historically chosen the latter position. Unfortunately, the positivist assumption that the correctness of their theories compensates for their limitations is called into question by the frequency with which positivistic research disputes the correctness of positivistic explanations.

Theories that focus on decisionmaking have traditionally sought to

116   CRIMINALITY

explain all behavior with a single principle. This principle tends to be complicated beyond recognition the moment it confronts individual differences that transcend properties of the immediate environment.

Previous efforts at compromise have not been particularly successful. Wilson and Herrnstein take the novel approach of using their general theory to explain a *narrowly* described set of acts:

The word "crime" can be applied to such varied behavior that it is not clear that it is a meaningful category of analysis. Stealing a comic book, punching a friend, cheating on a tax return, murdering a wife, robbing a bank, bribing a politician, hijacking an airplane—these and countless other acts are all crimes. Crime is as broad a category as disease, and perhaps as useless. [1985: 21]

These considerations lead Wilson and Herrnstein to concentrate on those persons who "commit serious crimes at a high rate." By doing so, they argue, they "escape the problem of comparing persons who park by a fire hydrant to persons who rob banks" (1985: 21). By "serious crimes," Wilson and Herrnstein mean "predatory street crimes," those acts "regarded as wrong by every society, preliterate as well as literate; . . . among these 'universal crimes' are murder, theft, robbery, and incest" (ibid., p. 22).

One question that arises is why Wilson and Herrnstein would wish to restrict the range of their dependent variable without clear evidence that such restriction is necessary. What evidence do they use to justify dividing the domain of crime into serious street crime and other crime? For one thing, they are skeptical of the view that a general theory can explain crime across cultures or that it can explain all of the myriad crimes within a given culture. Clearly, the *a priori* conclusion that a theory should set its boundaries narrowly need not be taken to mean that the boundaries have been accurately described. The boundaries of a theory require theoretical justification. In its absence, concern for boundaries rightly suggests the operation of nontheoretical criteria.

The seriousness of crime is, in our view, a nontheoretical criterion. It is of course no accident that theorists prefer to limit their interests to "serious" matters—in the mistaken belief that the importance of the phenomenon has something to say about the importance of the theory. The fact of the matter is that the importance or seriousness of a phenomenon is often hard to assess anyway. Individually, serious crimes may tend to produce more injury or loss, but collectively they may produce much less injury or loss than less serious crimes. By the same token, hard drugs such as heroin may produce less harm in the aggregate than drugs such as tobacco or alcohol. Arguably, reducing the rate of cigarette smoking would be a greater contribution to the resolution of a serious problem than would reducing the rate of drug addiction.

In any event, we do not share Wilson and Herrnstein's skepticism about the possibility of a general theory of crime, and we note that limits on the range of a theory should not be taken too seriously unless those stating the limits provide evidence that it will not work outside the narrow domain they specify. (Put another way, modesty per se is not a virtue of a theory.)

Tests of generality or scope are, in our view, easy to devise. In criminology it is often argued that special theories are required to explain female and male crime, crime in one culture rather than another, crime committed in the course of an occupation as distinct from street crime, or crime committed by children as distinct from crime committed by adults. As subsequent chapters will show, we intend our theory to apply to all of these cases, and more. It is meant to explain all crime, at all times, and, for that matter, many forms of behavior that are not sanctioned by the state.

Human Nature and Society

Useful theories of crime make assumptions about human nature. The range of possible assumptions is limited. A theory can assume, as ours does, that people naturally pursue their own interests and unless socialized to the contrary will use whatever means are available to them for such purposes. In this view, people are neither naturally "good" nor naturally "evil." They are, however, expected to behave in predictable ways. The standard social-contract assumption thus has useful properties, properties described throughout this book.

In contrast, a theory can assume, as nearly all sociological theories do, that people naturally tend to pursue group interests and will continue to do so unless forced to do otherwise—that is, that people are naturally good or social. Such theories also have useful properties. They make possible specific predictions about the causes or correlates of crime, predictions that tend to conflict with the predictions derived from theories that do not share their assumptions about human nature. Throughout the book we take advantage of this fact by comparing the adequacy of the hypotheses derived from these distinct perspectives.

Some theorists argue either explicitly (Elliott, Huizinga, and Ageton 1985) or implicitly (Wilson and Herrnstein 1985) that these various perspectives can be usefully combined without fear of contradiction or ambiguity. In fact, however, as is easily shown, theorists arguing for "integration" of these divergent views usually simply adopt one set of assumptions at the expense of the other or refuse to make assumptions and thus weaken what claims to theory they may have had. In the first case, most sociological integrationists simply adopt "social behavior" assumptions about crime and reject "individual interest" assumptions on the grounds that the assumptions favored by their discipline are correct (Johnson 1979; Elliott, Huizinga, and Ageton 1985; see also Hirschi 1979). In the second case, some psychologists think the assumption issue can be finessed by adopting an assumption-free psychological learning theory. Unfortunately, the idea that all views (strain, cultural deviance, social control, and rational choice) can be subsumed under a single learning theory abrogates the responsibility of the theorist to theorize about the sources of crime. For example, Wilson and Herrnstein advance the proposition that, in a situation of choice, people select the outcome they prefer (1985: 43). It is possible to make a theory from this statement by introducing bias into preference, by asserting or believing that some tendency acts on choice in the first instance; for example, one could say that, other things being equal, people will prefer outcomes that reduce their wealth and happiness (hard to believe, but at least testable). In the absence of such a bias, all preferences are possible and the theory asserts nothing. Evidence that it asserts nothing comes from the fact that it is said to *subsume* strain, cultural deviance, and social control theories, theories often used to illustrate conflicting assumptions and predictions. (In Chapter 4, we demonstrated the incompatibility of the strain and cultural deviance components in the Wilson-Herrnstein theory; see also Kornhauser 1978.)

Empirical Tests of the Crime and Criminality Perspective

Our stability postulate asserts that people with high self-control are less likely under all circumstances throughout life to commit crime. Our stability notion denies the ability of institutions to undo previously successful efforts at socialization, an ability other theories take as central to their position.

Similarly, our versatility construct suggests that one avenue available for the identification of persons with low self-control is via its noncriminal outlets. Other theories predict no correlation or even negative correlation between the various forms of deviance. Our conception of versatility also predicts that one can study crime by studying other noncriminal manifestations of low self-control without being misled by the results.

Our idea of crime asserts that complex, difficult crimes are so rare that they are an inadequate basis for theory and policy. Other perspectives suggest that exotic crimes are as theoretically useful as mundane crimes and just as likely to occur. Our idea of crime predicts that the vast majority of crimes will be characterized by simplicity, proximity of offender and target, and failure to gain the desired objective. Other theories make no room for failure, assuming that crime satisfies strong forces and desires and thus reinforces itself. Our perspective asserts that crime can be predicted from evidence of low self-control at any earlier stage of life. No sociological or economic theory allows such predictions. Our perspective also asserts that low self-control can be predicted from crime at any earlier stage of life; most sociological theories do not allow such a prediction.

Our perspective asserts that many of the traditional causes of crime are in fact consequences of low self-control—that is, people with low self-control sort themselves and are sorted into a variety of circumstances that are *as a result* correlated with crime. Our theory predicts that prevention of one form of deviant behavior will not lead to compensating forms of behavior, but will reduce the total amount of deviant behavior engaged in by the population in question. Other theories predict displacement and suggest constant levels of deviance in a constantly "predisposed" population. We address these and other differences between our theory and rival perspectives in the pages that follow.

Conclusions

Theories that cannot incorporate or account for the stability of differences in offending over time are seriously at variance with good evidence. Theories that assume specialization in particular forms of crime or deviant behavior are seriously at odds with good evidence. Theories that propose to examine the parameters of criminal careers (such as onset, persistence, and desistence) or the characteristics of career criminals are at odds with the nature of crime. Theories that assume that criminal acts are means to long-term or altruistic goals are at odds with the facts.

Our theory explicitly addresses the stability and versatility findings. It accounts for them with the concept of self-control: with deferred gratification at one extreme and immediate gratification at the other, with caution at one extreme and risk-taking at the other. The

120   CRIMINALITY

mechanism producing these differences has been described as differences in child-rearing practices, with close attention to the behavior of the child at one extreme and neglect of the behavior of the child at the other.

The theory incorporates individual properties insofar as they have an impact on crime or on self-control. These properties are elucidated in subsequent chapters, where we apply our model to the facts about crime and deviant behavior. For now, we note that the theory is a direct response to analysis of the concept of crime and to our analysis of the failings of the theories of the positivistic disciplines. It incorporates a classical view of the role of choice and a positivistic view of the role of causation in the explanation of behavior. It produces a general explanatory concept that can be measured independently of the phenomenon it is alleged to cause, and it is thus directly testable.

We turn now to application of the theory to various topics in crime causation, research methods, and public policy.

Part II
Environmental Influences

Parental Child-rearing Factors

Journal of Personality and Social Psychology
1979, Vol. 37, No. 9, 1477–1486

Some Child-Rearing Antecedents of Criminal Behavior in Adult Men

Joan McCord
Department of Psychology and Sociology, Drexel University

Records collected during childhood and coded prior to knowledge of adult behavior provided information about the childhood homes of 201 men. Thirty
years later, information about criminal behavior was collected from court
records. Multiple regression and discriminant function analyses indicate that
six variables describing family atmosphere during childhood—mother's self-
confidence, father's deviance, parental aggressiveness, maternal affection, parental conflict, and supervision—have an important impact on subsequent behavior.

Despite a massive literature emphasizing
the importance of child rearing, conscientious
critics (e.g., Clarke & Clarke, 1976; Yarrow,
Campbell, & Burton, 1968) have raised legitimate doubts regarding the impact of parental
behavior on personality development. Many
of the studies that link parental behavior
with personality development rely upon a
single source of information for both sets of
variables; systematic reporting biases could
thus cause obtained relationships. Most of the
remaining studies have depended upon concurrent measurements, leaving doubt as to the
direction of influence between parents' behavior and characteristics of the child. Questions about interpreting the results of both
types of studies serve to highlight the importance of longitudinal research.

A few researchers have gathered information through longitudinal studies, using independent sources for measuring child rearing
and for measuring personality. Robins (1966)
analyzed information from clinic records
gathered during childhood and related that
information to data gathered when the subjects were adults. Robins pioneered assessment of long-term effects of child rearing, and
her study raises doubts about the validity of
retrospective reports on family socialization.
Nevertheless, since predictor models combined
variables describing child rearing with other
types of variables (empirically linked with
outcome), the research fails to provide convincing evidence that child-rearing differences
affected adult behavior.

Block (1971) evaluated character development among subjects in the Berkeley longitudinal studies. Dividing 63 subjects into five
types and checking differences in their backgrounds, Block reached the conclusion: "What
comes through, for both sexes and without exception in viewing the various types, is an
unequivocal relationship between the family
atmosphere in which a child grew up and his
later character structure" (p. 258). Although
Block reports many statistically reliable differences, his analyses do not permit the reader
to evaluate the strength of relationships between family atmosphere and character structure.

In 1973–1974, Werner and Smith (1977)
retraced 88% of the children born on Kauai
Island in 1955. Interviews with the mothers
provided evidence about the family environ-

This study was supported by U.S. Public Health
Service Research Grant 2 RO1 MH26779, National
Institute of Mental Health (Center for Studies of
Crime and Delinquency). It was conducted jointly
with the Department of Probation of the Commonwealth of Massachusetts. The author wishes to express appreciation to the Division of Criminal Justice Services of the State of New York and to the
Maine State Bureau of Identification for supple-
mental data from criminal records, though they are
responsible neither for the statistical analyses nor
for the conclusions drawn from this research.

Requests for reprints should be sent to Joan Mc-
Cord, Department of Psychology and Sociology,
Drexel University, Philadelphia, Pennsylvania 19104.

ment of subjects when they were newborn infants, age 2, and age 10. Although combined measures tended to account for a relatively high proportion of variance in several problem areas, the authors did not assess specific child-rearing models as predictors of outcome behavior.

Lefkowitz, Eron, Walder, and Huesmann (1977) used a main effects model in stepwise multiple regression for their longitudinal study of aggression. Only two of the six variables that together accounted for about a quarter of the variance in male aggressiveness at age 18 were related to child rearing at age 8. Since the model included both redundant measures of child rearing and heterogeneous variables (e.g., child's preference for girls' games, parents' religiosity, and ethnicity of family), effects of differences in child rearing may have been masked by collinearity (Blalock, 1963; Gordon, 1968; Mosteller & Tukey, 1977).

The paucity of evidence to support a view that child rearing affects personality has led some authors (e.g., Clinard, 1974; Jessor & Jessor, 1977) to the conclusion that home atmosphere during childhood has a negligible effect upon personality development. Such authors present the challenge to which the present research is addressed: if parental behavior has an important impact upon personality development, differences in child rearing ought to contribute to variations in subsequent behavior.

Method

Subjects for this study were selected from a treatment program designed to prevent delinquency. The youths ranged in age, at the time of their introduction to the program, from 5 to 13 ($M = 10.5$, $SD = 1.6$).

Counselors visited 253 boys twice a month, for an average 5-year period between 1939 and 1945. With the exception of one who was a nurse, the counselors had been trained as social workers. After each visit, the counselor recorded observations about the family as well as the child.[1]

Case records from the treatment program described, in detail, whatever activities the counselors had observed on their visits to the homes. The records included reports of conversations with parents, friends, neighbors, and teachers as well as with the boys. Counselor turnover (a potential problem from a treatment perspective) produced a benefit for re-

search: most of the families were visited by more than one counselor.

To justify treatment of family backgrounds as independent units for analyses, only one subject from a family was included. Boys not reared by their natural mothers were also excluded. After eliminating brothers ($n = 21$) and those not reared by their natural mothers ($n = 36$), 201 cases remained for analysis.[2]

In 1957, coders read each case thoroughly in order to form judgments about the home and family interaction. These coders had no access to information about the subjects other than that contained in treatment records. A 10% random sample of the records was read independently by a second coder to yield an estimate of the reliability of the coding.[3] Variables from the coded case records were used in the present study.

The mother's attitude toward her son had been classified as actively affectionate (if there had been considerable interaction, without continual criticism, between mother and child, $n = 95$), passively affectionate (if there had been little interaction between mother and son, though the mother had shown concern for her child's welfare, $n = 51$), ambivalent or passively rejecting (if there had been marked alternations in the mother's attitude toward her son so that she had seemed sometimes to be actively affectionate and sometimes rejecting, or if the mother had seemed unconcerned about the child's welfare, $n = 43$), or actively rejecting (if the mother had appeared to be constantly critical of the boy, $n = 11$). Independent reading of 25 cases resulted in the same ratings for 80%.

Two ratings from the original codes were combined to evaluate effects of supervision. One described whether the child's activities outside of school were governed by an adult. This scale was divided to indicate whether supervision was generally present, occasionally present, or absent. Independent coding yielded identical ratings for 84% of the 25 randomly selected cases. The second rating described parental expectations regarding the boys' activities. Coders were instructed to rate expectations as "high" if the

---

[1] The project included a matched control group. Since records on family life, for the control group, were limited to information gathered during the intake interviews supplemented by information from secondary sources, the control group was not used in this study. Originally, 325 boys were included in both the treatment group and the control group. By January 1942, 253 boys remained in each group. (See Powers and Witmer, 1951, for details regarding selection of cases and a description of the treatment program.)

[2] The criteria are not mutually exclusive. Five men were eliminated through both of the selection criteria.

[3] See McCord and McCord (1960) for a complete description of the coding.

SOME CHILD-REARING ANTECEDENTS OF CRIMINAL BEHAVIOR 1479

child was given responsibility for care of his younger siblings, for preparation of meals, for contributing to the financial support of the family, or for doing "extremely well" in school. Independent ratings yielded agreement for 76% of 25 cases. The scales from the 1957 codes were combined to classify subjects into one of four categories: supervision generally present and high expectations for the child to accept responsibilities ($n = 40$), supervision generally present without evidence that high expectations were placed on the child ($n = 78$), occasional supervision ($n = 60$), and supervision absent ($n = 23$).[4]

A rating of parental conflict was based on counselors' reports of disagreements between the parents. Raters were instructed to look for conflicts about the child and conflicts about values, about money, about alcohol, and about religion. Parental conflict was coded into one of four categories: no indication, apparently none, some, or considerable. For the present research, cases were divided into those whose parents evidenced considerable conflict ($n = 68$) and those coded in alternative categories. Independent readers agreed, for this division, on 80% of the cases checked for reliability.

Three measures from the 1957 codes were combined to identify aggressive parents. Coders classified the aggressiveness of each parent by looking for evidence that the parent "used little restraint" when angry. Case records included reports on parents who threw things (e.g., one father threw a refrigerator down the stairs in the midst of an argument with his wife), hit people, broke windows, and shouted abuses. Independent coders agreed on 84% of the fathers and 92% of the mothers in classifying parents as aggressive. The coders described paternal discipline; the category "consistently punitive" identified fathers who regularly used physical force (e.g., beating a child) or very harsh verbal abuse. Independent coders agreed on 92% of the cases for ratings regarding this classification. If a parent was coded as aggressive or the father was coded as consistently punitive, the child was classified as having an aggressive parent ($n = 75$).[5]

The 1957 codes included a measure of the mother's self-confidence. A rating as self-confident was assigned if that mother showed signs of believing in her own abilities ($n = 55$). Other possibilities for this rating were "no indication of general attitude; evidence that mother saw herself as a victim or pawn in a world about which she could do nothing; and neutral, that is, generally seemed merely to accept things as they came." For this variable, independent raters agreed in classifying 84% of the 25 cases used to estimate reliability.

In 1957, coders rated a father as alcoholic if the case record indicated that he had lost jobs because of repeated drinking, if marital problems were attributed primarily to his excessive drinking, if welfare agencies had repeatedly pointed to the father's drinking as grounds for family problems, or if the father had received treatment specifically for alcoholism. Independent coders agreed for 96% of the ratings on this

variable. In 1948, after termination of the treatment program, criminal records on the family members of subjects were collected; these records were locked in a file separate from the case histories. In 1975, after names had been replaced by numerical identifiers, an assistant unfamiliar with the case records coded these criminal records. For the present study, a father was considered "deviant" if the case record indicated that he was an alcoholic, if the criminal record showed that he had been convicted at least three times for drunkenness, or if his criminal record showed that he had been convicted for a serious crime (i.e., theft, burglary, assault, rape, attempted murder, or murder). These criteria led to identification of 86 fathers as deviant.[6]

Case records included information about family structure. A father was considered "absent" if his residence was not with the subject's mother. Independent coding of 25 cases yielded agreement on 96% regarding whether or not the boy was living with both natural parents.[7] The 71 boys having absent fathers ranged in age, at the time when the loss occurred, from birth to 16 ($M = 7.01$, $SD = 5.03$). The father-absent subjects were subclassified to identify those whose natural fathers had been present during their first 5 years ($n = 48$) and those for whom the absence had occurred prior to the age of 5 ($n = 23$).

These seven variables (mother's affection, supervision, parental conflict, parental aggression, mother's self-confidence, father's deviance, and paternal absence) were used to depict the home atmosphere of subjects during childhood. The first three are regarded as directly related to child rearing. Relationships among these measures are shown in Table 1.

Subjects had been selected from congested urban neighborhoods. Nevertheless, differences in social status could contribute to subsequent differences in behavior. Two measures of social status were available. The case records supplied information about the father's occupation. Coders classified these occupations as white-collar (9.6%), skilled tradesmen (32.8%), or unskilled workers (57.6%). The reliability check yielded agreement on 96% of the ratings. A second measure of social status was provided by a rating of the neighborhoods in which the boys were raised. These ratings had been made, in 1938 and 1939, as part of the selection procedures. The ratings took into account delinquency rates, availability of recreational facilities, and proximity to bars, railroads, and junkyards. These ratings were coded on a 4-point scale from better to worst neighborhoods. The two measures tended to covary, Cramer's $V(6) = .218$, $p = .0044$.

---

[4] Only nine boys exposed to high expectations had not been rated as generally supervised.

[5] Fifty of the subjects were classified as having aggressive parents by the direct description of parental aggression.

[6] Forty-nine had been convicted for serious crimes.

[7] Of the 86 deviant fathers, 40 were also absent fathers.

1480   JOAN McCORD

Table 1
Relationships Among Variables Describing Home Atmosphere (Cramer's V)

	Supervision	Parent conflict	Parent aggression	Mother's self-confidence	Father's deviance	Father's absence
Mother's affection	.241***	.209*	.184*	.199*	.209*	.110
Supervision		.267**	.106	.308***	.230*	.187*
Parent conflict			.188**	.109	.381***	.375***
Parent aggression				.289***	.144*	.024
Mother's self-confidence					.125	.087
Father's deviance						.206*

* $p < .05$. ** $p < .01$. *** $p < .001$.

Between 1975 and 1978, the subjects were retraced. Among the 201 men included in the study, 153 (76%) were alive and in Massachusetts at least until the age of 40;[8] 16 (8%) had died prior to their 40th birthdays; 29 (14%) had migrated from Massachusetts; and 3 (1%) remained to be found.

During 1975 and 1976, the names (and pseudonyms) of all the men who had been in the program were checked through court records in Massachusetts.[9] These criminal records were traced and coded by different people from those who coded other records. Coders of the criminal records (and those who traced them) had no access to other information about the subjects. The court records showed the dates of court appearances and the crimes for which the subjects had been convicted. They were coded to show the type of crime and the age of the person when he was convicted. Convictions for serious property crimes (larceny, auto theft, breaking and entering, arson) and serious personal crimes (assault, attempted rape, rape, attempted murder, kidnapping, and murder) were used as dependent measures for this study.

Among the 201 men, 71 had been convicted for at least one serious crime; 53 had been convicted for property crimes and 34 for personal crimes (including 15 convicted for both types). Their ages when first convicted ranged from 8 to 38, with a mean of 18.7 ($SD = 8.7$) and a median of 20. Those convicted prior to their 18th birthdays were classified as juvenile delinquents ($n = 43$); those convicted after reaching the age of 18 were classified as adult criminals ($n = 48$, including 20 who had been juvenile delinquents).

After analyzing the relationship to crime of each of the childhood variables separately, multiple regression analyses (General Linear Model Procedure, Barr, Goodnight, Sall, & Helwig, 1976) were used to ascertain the contribution of child rearing to the variance in number of serious property and personal crimes. To test the degree to which knowledge of home atmosphere could enable accurate prediction of subsequent behavior, the six central variables describing home atmosphere were used in discriminant function analyses to identify criminals.

As a more stringent test of the contribution of home atmosphere to subsequent crime, the discriminant function analyses were also used to predict criminals among the subsample whose criminal records provided the most complete histories of convictions: those men living in Massachusetts at least until the age of 40. If this function identified criminality more accurately for the total group than for those living in Massachusetts, there would be grounds for suspecting an interaction effect between home background and unmeasured variables. If this function identified criminality at least as accurately for those alive in Massachusetts at the age of 40, there would be additional support for a conclusion that home atmosphere during childhood contributes to criminality.

Results

As a first step toward learning whether parental behavior contributes to subsequent differences in criminality, the seven scales describing home atmosphere and the two scales describing social status were individually analyzed for their contributions to the variance in number of serious crimes against property and persons. (See Table 2.)

With the exception of father's absence, each of the scales describing home atmosphere accounted for a statistically significant ($p < .05$) proportion of the variance in number of crimes against property, persons, or both.[10]

---

[8] Among them, 147 were in Massachusetts through their 45th birthdays.

[9] These records were supplemented by court records from the states of New York, Maine, Michigan, Nebraska, and Florida, where some of the men had resided.

[10] The Duncan multiple range test, modified for unequal groups (Kramer, 1956), indicated that boys without supervision, reliably ($p < .05$) more than boys in the other three categories, were convicted

SOME CHILD-REARING ANTECEDENTS OF CRIMINAL BEHAVIOR 1481

Table 2

Relationships Between Variables Describing Home Background and Crimes

		Property crimes			Personal crimes		
	DF	R^2	F	PR > F	R^2	F	PR > F
Mother's affection	3, 196	.092	6.60	.0003	.029	1.92	.1261
Supervision	3, 197	.152	11.77	.0001	.071	5.04	.0023
Parent conflict	1, 199	.008	1.76	.1866	.035	7.14	.0081
Parent aggression	1, 199	.012	2.38	.1242	.036	7.36	.0073
Mother's self-confidence	1, 199	.022	4.50	.0350	.024	4.98	.0268
Father's deviance	1, 199	.024	4.81	.0295	.000	0.00	.9569
Father's absence	2, 198	.005	0.47	.6286	.026	2.67	.0715
Neighborhood	3, 197	.028	1.87	.1335	.016	1.10	.3513
Father's occupation	2, 195	.008	0.74	.4798	.012	1.15	.3181

Neither of the measures of social status was significantly related to these types of crimes.

Supervision and mother's self-confidence were related to both crimes against property and crimes against persons; mother's affection and father's deviance were related to property crimes (though not to personal crimes); conflict and parental aggression were related to personal crimes (though not to property crimes). The boys who lacked maternal affection, who lacked supervision, whose mothers lacked self-confidence, and whose fathers were deviant were more often subsequently convicted for property crimes. The boys who lacked supervision, whose mothers lacked self-confidence, and who had been exposed to parental conflict and to aggression were subsequently more often convicted for personal crimes.

The relationships to criminality of individual variables describing home atmosphere, though statistically significant, each accounted for a relatively small proportion of the variance. More important, since "criminogenic" conditions tended to be related to one another, these relationships could not be taken as evidence that the differences in home background that they represented resulted in differences in subsequent behavior.

To evaluate the contribution of parental behavior to subsequent behavior, the six central variables describing home atmosphere were divided into two sets. The first set included those variables that described characteristics of the parents, characteristics that might be viewed as antecedent to child-rearing practices: parental aggressiveness, paternal deviance, and mother's self-confidence. The second set included the three variables that described interpersonal behavior: parental conflict, supervision, and mother's affection; these were considered to be direct measures of child rearing. The effect of this division was to classify families in two ways. The first classification took account of relationships among the variables describing the parents; the second took account of relationships among the variables describing child rearing.

Sequential multiple regression models were used. They introduced the measure of social status (the interaction of father's occupation and neighborhood) as the first variable. The regression procedure next evaluated the sequential contribution to explained variance of parental characteristics (the interaction of paternal deviance, maternal self-confidence, and parental aggression). After controlling effects of both social status and parental characteristics, the procedure evaluated effects of child rearing (i.e., the interaction of supervision, parental conflict, and the mother's affection).

Child rearing, as measured in this longitudinal study, clearly accounts for a signif-

for both property and personal crimes. This a posteriori test showed that boys rejected by their mothers were most likely to be convicted for property crimes, and boys who had affectionate mothers were least likely.

1482   JOAN McCORD

Table 3
Home Environment and Subsequent Criminality

Sequential contribution	DF	R^2	F	PR > F
Predicting property crimes[a]				
Social status	11	.0688	1.55	.1185
Parental characteristics	7	.0610	2.16	.0404
Child rearing	27	.2612	2.40	.0005
Predicting personal crimes[b]				
Social status	11	.0541	1.16	.3222
Parental characteristics	7	.0588	1.97	.0616
Child rearing	27	.2444	2.13	.0023
Predicting total crimes[c]				
Social status	11	.0620	1.40	.0620
Parental characteristics	7	.0691	2.45	.0209
Child rearing	27	.2601	2.39	.0005

[a] Model: R^2 = .391, $F(45, 151)$ = 2.15, p = .0003. [b] Model: R^2 = .3573, $F(45, 151)$ = 1.87, p = .0028.
[c] Model: R^2 = .3912, $F(45, 151)$ = 2.16, p = .0003.

icant proportion of the variance in subsequent criminality. Table 3 describes the decomposition of the regression models.

As predictors of property crimes, the model accounts for 39.1% of the variance, $F(45, 151)$ = 2.15, p = .0003. Parental aggression, paternal deviance, and maternal self-confidence account for 6.1% of the variance after controlling social status, $F(7, 151)$ = 2.16, p = .0404. Parental conflict, supervision, and maternal affection contribute significantly to the variance after effects of social status and parental characteristics have been controlled, R^2 = .261, $F(27, 151)$ = 2.40, p = .0003.

As predictors of personal crimes, the model accounts for 35.7% of the variance, $F(45, 151)$ = 1.87, p = .0028. The three more direct measures of child rearing contribute significantly to the variance after effects of social status and parental characteristics have been removed, R^2 = .244, $F(27, 151)$ = 2.13, p = .0023.

As predictors of the total number of serious crimes for which the men had been convicted, the model accounts for 39.1% of the variance, $F(45, 151)$ = 2.16, p = .0003. Parental characteristics account for 5.9% of the variance after effects of social status have been controlled, $F(7, 151)$ = 2.45, p = .0209. The child-rearing variables account for 26.0% of the variance, $F(27, 151)$ = 2.39, p = .0005, after removing effects of both social status and parent characteristics.

Adding information about whether or not a man had been reared in a home marked by paternal absence did not reliably increase the accuracy of any of the predictions.[11]

Within the (relatively restricted) range of social class represented in the study, the contribution of social status to the variance in crimes was not statistically reliable. On the other hand, both parental characteristics and child-rearing practices were reliably related to the number of crimes for which the subjects had been convicted.[12]

Approximately a third of the 200 men coded on all six variables describing home atmosphere had been convicted for at least one serious crime. A discriminant function based on the variables describing home atmosphere for these 200 men correctly identified 147

[11] R^2 was increased by .002 for property crimes, .007 for personal crimes, and .001 for total crimes.
[12] Without controlling for social status, parental characteristics and child-rearing variables accounted for 36.7% of the variance in property crimes, $F(34, 162)$ = 2.76, $p \leq .0001$, 30.8% of the variance in personal crimes, $F(34, 162)$ = 2.12, p = .0010, and 36.3% of the variance in total number of serious crimes, $F(34, 162)$ = 2.71, $p \leq .0001$.

SOME CHILD-REARING ANTECEDENTS OF CRIMINAL BEHAVIOR 1483

Table 4
Results of Discriminant Function Analyses

Dependent and independent variables	Correct as criminals		Correct as noncriminals		Overall accuracy		% improve- ment over chance	z > p
	n	%	n	%	n	%		
All subjects								
Ever criminal								
Home atmosphere	71	67.6	129	76.7	200	73.5	19.3	.0001
Adult criminal								
Home atmosphere	48	56.3	152	87.5	200	80.0	16.5	.0001
Men living in Massachusetts through the age of 40								
Ever criminal								
Home atmosphere	60	81.7	92	70.7	152	75.0	22.8	.0001
Adult criminal								
Home atmosphere	42	71.4	110	84.6	152	80.9	20.9	.0001
Juvenile delinquency record	42	45.2	110	83.6	152	73.0	13.0	.0011

(73.5%) as criminals or noncriminals; random predictions based on prior probabilities would be expected to identify only 54.2% correctly,[13] $z = 5.48$, $p < .0001$. The function based on parental aggression, maternal self-confidence, paternal deviance, supervision, maternal affection, and parental conflict correctly identified 76.7% of the noncriminals and 67.6% of the criminals. (See Table 4.)

Forty-eight men had been convicted for serious crimes after their 18th birthdays. The six variables describing home atmosphere provided a discriminant function which correctly identified 27 (56.3%) of the 48 adult criminals and 133 (87.5%) of the 152 men without records for convictions as adults. Predictions based on the descriptions of home atmosphere provided a 16.5% improvement over the 63.5% expected from random predictions based on prior probabilities, $z = 4.85$, $p < .0001$. (See Table 4.)

After discarding men who had died before the age of 40, migrated from Massachusetts, or who had not yet been found, 152 men who were living in Massachusetts at least until the age of 40 and whose case records had been coded for all six variables describing home atmosphere remained for discriminant function analyses. Among these men, the discriminant function correctly identified 75.0%, a slight improvement over the rate of correct identification among the total group of men and a 22.8% improvement over random procedures based on prior probabilities, $z = 5.63$, $p < .0001$. (See Table 4.) This discriminant function correctly identified 81.7% of the 60 criminals and 70.7% of the 92 noncriminals.

A breakdown of the results shows that the discriminant function had correctly classified as criminal 78.1% of those convicted only for property crimes, 78.6% of those convicted only for personal crimes, and 92.9% of those

---

[13] The model used to estimate predictions based on chance assumes that the number of predictions as criminal would be proportional to the actual distribution of criminals among subjects. Alternative models that might be considered range from assuming that each individual is as likely to be convicted as not (which would result in an expectation for correct predictions among half the noncriminals and half the criminals) to assuming that all or no individuals would be convicted. Although a "rational bet" would maximize correct predictions by predicting that all individuals would fall into the larger class, this model is inappropriate when the interest is in correct identification of those in the smaller class. An equiprobability model for the discriminant function analysis based on family atmosphere resulted in correct sorting of 68% of the men (62% of the noncriminals and 79% of the criminals) in terms of whether or not they had been convicted for serious crimes.

convicted for both property and personal crimes.

Among the 60 men convicted for serious crimes and still living in Massachusetts at the age of 40, 18 (30.0%) had been convicted only as juveniles, 23 (38.7%) had first been convicted after the age of 18, and 19 (31.7%) had been convicted both as juvenile and as adults. Were one to predict that only and all juvenile delinquents would be convicted as adults, the prediction would be correct for 73.0%, an improvement over an expectation of 60.0% from random procedures based on prior probabilities, $z = 3.27$, $p = .0011$. This prediction would be correct for 45.2% of the adult criminals and for 83.6% of the men not convicted as adults. Predictions based on juvenile records would, of course, be right for *none* of the men first convicted as adults (54.8% of the adult criminals) and for only 51.4% of the juvenile delinquents.

Among men living in Massachusetts at the age of 40, the discriminant function analysis based on home atmosphere during childhood correctly identified 80.9% as criminal or non-criminal after the age of 18. (See Table 4.) Use of the variables describing home atmosphere during childhood resulted in a 20.9% improvement over chance identification, $z = 5.26$, $p < .0001$, and a 7.9% improvement over predictions based on the subjects' juvenile criminal histories, $z = 2.19$, $p = .0282$. This function correctly identified 71.4% of the adult criminals and 84.6% of the noncriminals. The discriminant function based on home atmosphere correctly identified as criminals 65.2% of the men who had first been convicted as adults. In terms of their subsequent criminal records, this discriminant function correctly sorted 78.4% of the juvenile delinquents and 81.7% of those who had not been juvenile delinquents.[14]

Summary and Discussion

Recent criticism of the assumption that child-rearing practices have an important impact on personality development posed the issue addressed in this research. In order to evaluate the assumption, records describing home atmosphere during childhood, recorded during childhood, were linked with records of subsequent criminality, gathered when the subjects were middle-aged. The two sources of information were independent: data collection had been separated by several decades, the data had been coded by different people, and the coders had no access to information other than that which they were coding. Therefore, measures of home atmosphere were uncontaminated by retrospective biases and measures of subsequent behavior were uncontaminated by knowledge of home background.

Records describing home atmosphere had been written between 1939 and 1945. These records were case reports of counselors' repeated home visits to the 201 boys included in this study. The case records were coded, in 1957, to provide descriptions of home atmosphere.

Information about criminal behavior was gathered from court records, 30 years after termination of the program from which descriptions of home atmosphere had been collected. Subjects were considered criminals if they had been convicted for serious crimes (those indexed by the Federal Bureau of Investigation).

In preliminary analyses, six of seven variables describing home atmosphere were reliably related to criminal behavior. Only father's absence failed to distinguish criminals from noncriminals. Considering the emphasis given to broken homes as a source of subsequent criminality (e.g., Bacon, Child, & Barry, 1963; Glueck & Glueck, 1951; Wadsworth, 1979; Willie, 1967), this finding is worthy of note.

Multiple regression analyses indicated that six variables describing home atmosphere in childhood account for a significant proportion of the variance in number of convictions for serious crimes. After controlling effects of differences in social status, parental characteristics and child-rearing variables ac-

---

[14] The "rational bet" that men not convicted as juveniles would not be convicted as adults would be correct for 80% of the men not convicted as juveniles. Since this bet would be correct only for the noncriminals, the prediction would fail to identify correctly any of the critical group: men first convicted as adults.

SOME CHILD-REARING ANTECEDENTS OF CRIMINAL BEHAVIOR 1485

counted for 32.2% of the variance in number of convictions for property crimes and 30.3% of the variance in number of convictions for personal crimes. The three most direct measures of child rearing (supervision, mother's affection, and parental conflict) accounted for approximately a quarter of the variance in number of convictions for serious crimes—after effects of both social status and parental characteristics had been removed.

Discriminant function analyses based on the six variables describing home atmosphere correctly identified 73.5% of the men as either subsequently criminal or noncriminal; further, these six variables provided a function that for 80% of the men correctly discriminated between those convicted and those not convicted for serious crimes as adults.

As compared with analyses for the total sample, the discriminant function analyses were (slightly) more accurate when used to predict behavior among the men whose criminal records provided the most complete histories of convictions. Among men living in Massachusetts at least to the age of 40, these functions correctly identified 75% as ever criminal or as noncriminal and 80.9% as criminal or noncriminal after the age of 18. Limiting analyses to men living in Massachusetts controlled any differences contributing to migration or early death; therefore, the accuracy of discriminant functions among this subsample is interpreted as supporting the view that home atmosphere during childhood contributes to criminality.

When used to identify men convicted as adults, the discriminant function identified as criminals almost two-thirds of the men first convicted after the age of 18. This function also correctly sorted more than three-quarters of the juvenile delinquents, distinguishing between those who were and those who were not adult criminals.

Although the discriminant functions based on home atmosphere were surprisingly successful in identifying men who were to become criminals, it would be a mistake to conclude that the longitudinal design of this research has led to recognition of the causes of crime. This research is limited not only by its subjects (all of whom were reared in congested urban areas during the thirties and early forties) but also by the hypotheses considered. In this research, parental aggression, paternal deviance, maternal self-confidence, supervision, mother's affection, and parental conflict indexed home atmosphere; unconsidered variables might better describe the features in the child's home that affect his behavior. In this research, the possibly confounding variable of social status was considered; other conditions might account for the apparent link between home atmosphere and crime. Nevertheless, the evidence from this study suggests that parental behavior does have an important impact on subsequent behavior: predictions of adult criminality based on knowledge of home atmosphere were not only markedly more accurate than chance—they were also more accurate than predictions based on the individuals' juvenile criminal records.

References

Bacon, M. K., Child, I. L., & Barry, H. A Cross-cultural study of correlates of crime. *Journal of Abnormal and Social Psychology*, 1963, *66*, 291–300.

Barr, A. J., Goodnight, J. H., Sall, J. P., & Helwig, J. T. *A user's guide to SAS 76.* Raleigh, N.C.: SAS Institute, 1976.

Blalock, H. M. Correlated independent variables: The problem of multicollinearity. *Social Forces*, 1963, *42*, 233–237.

Block, J. *Lives through time.* Berkeley, Calif.: Bancroft Books, 1971.

Clarke, A. M., & Clarke, A. D. B. *Early experience: Myth and evidence.* New York: Free Press, 1976.

Clinard, M. B. *Sociology of deviant behavior.* (4th ed.) New York: Holt, Rinehart & Winston, 1974.

Glueck, S., & Glueck, E. *Unraveling juvenile delinquency.* Cambridge, Mass.: Harvard University Press, 1951.

Gordon, R. A. Issues in multiple regression. *American Journal of Sociology*, 1968, *73*, 592–616.

Jessor, R., & Jessor, S. L. *Problem behavior and psychosocial development.* New York: Academic Press, 1977.

Kramer, C. Y. Extension of multiple range tests to group means with unequal numbers of replication. *Biometrics*, 1956, *12*, 307–310.

Lefkowitz, M. M., Eron, L. D., Walder, L. O., & Huesmann, L. R. *Growing up to be violent: A longitudinal study of aggression.* New York: Pergamon Press, 1977.

McCord, W., & McCord, J. *Origins of alcoholism.* Stanford, Calif.: Stanford University Press, 1960.

1486   JOAN McCORD

Mosteller, F., & Tukey, J. W. *Data analysis and regression*. Reading, Mass.: Addison-Wesley, 1977.

Powers, E., & Witmer, H. *An experiment in the prevention of delinquency: The Cambridge-Somerville youth study*. New York: Columbia University Press, 1951.

Robins, L. N. *Deviant children grown up*. Baltimore, Md.: Williams & Wilkins, 1966.

Wadsworth, M. E. J. *Roots of delinquency*. New York: Barnes & Noble, 1979.

Werner, E. E., & Smith, R. S. *Kauai's children come of age*. Honolulu: University Press of Hawaii, 1977.

Willie, C. V. The relative contribution of family status and economic status to juvenile delinquency. *Social Problems*, 1967, *14*, 326–335.

Yarrow, M. R., Campbell, J. D., & Burton, R. V. *Child Rearing*. San Francisco: Jossey-Bass, 1968.

Received August 7, 1978 ∎

Supervision

[11]

THE BRITISH JOURNAL
OF
CRIMINOLOGY

| Vol. 20 | July 1980 | No. 3 |

PARENTAL SUPERVISION: A NEGLECTED
ASPECT OF DELINQUENCY

HARRIETT WILSON (Coventry)*

*While all humans are intrinsically human, the expression of their humanity
is affected by the manner of childhood they have experienced.*
Jerome Bruner

Background and Objectives

THE title of this paper suggests an approach in the manner of traditional
positivist criminology. The purpose of the research seems to aim at the
establishment of a causal relationship between specific methods of parenting
and resultant functioning of children. Indeed, the title suggests that parental
supervision assumes the status of an "explanation" of juvenile delinquency.
The reader may well expect that the study contains a predictive and a
correctional perspective: what types of parenting lead to delinquency, and
how to prevent such behaviour. It must be stated right away that this is
not the objective and, although the research concerned itself with a close
examination of different patterns of parenting and their associations with
the activities of children, the findings establish relationships which underlie
these associations and which may well have to be accorded primacy in an
attempt to explain them.

The study has its origins in an earlier research, commissioned by the Home
Office, which was concerned with families known to a social services department and, in particular, examined the personality development of two
children in each family and related this to the social and economic circumstances of their homes (Wilson and Herbert, 1978). The objectives were to

* Ph.D. Senior Research Fellow, University of Warwick. The school data, including the self-
report, were assembled by Ian Richards, B.Sc., now at the University of Aston. I am indebted to
Professor M. Stacey and her steering committee for providing guidance, and to my husband for
assistance on statistical matters. The research reported in this article was sponsored by the Home
Office and made possible by the generous help given by the Chief Constable of the W. Midlands
Police and by the City's Education and Housing Departments.

HARRIETT WILSON

ascertain environmental factors that have a critical effect on child development; among the criteria of behavioural functioning of children was delinquency (Wilson, 1975). In comparing delinquent and non-delinquent
families, a highly significant association was discovered between parental
supervision and absence of delinquency. The child-rearing methods typical of
non-delinquent families included a strict parental regime that limited the
children's freedom of movement. Thus, the practice of parental supervision
re-affirmed the importance of opportunity structures in the aetiology of
delinquency.

Parental supervision as a protective measure against delinquency appeared
to operate effectively among very disadvantaged families resident in deprived inner-city areas. One would wish to know whether less disadvantaged
families, and families resident in less hazardous environments, would employ
different methods. The new study, therefore, is composed of two sub-samples
—one resident in deprived inner-city areas, the other in suburban housing
estates containing " hard-to-let " dwellings. Each of the two sub-samples is
composed of families representing low, moderate, and severe degrees of
social handicap.

The measure of delinquent behaviour, previously confined to police
records, needed to be widened to include not only " known " delinquents,
but also anti-social and delinquent behaviour which does not reach the
attention of the police. The discrepancies between crimes " recorded " and
" cleared up " point at the problem of the " dark " offender, not included in
police records. Moreover, a possible bias in police decisions whether to caution
or to charge or to warn the youngster informally may result in obtaining a
sample of delinquents who would not be entirely representative of the sample
of families upon which the research is based. To overcome these problems
it was decided to include in the investigation a self-report measure which was
to ascertain a wide range of acts in the classroom and in the neighbourhood.
This would provide information about the activities of individual boys as
well as the data on the prevalence of certain misbehaviours in specific
neighbourhoods.

The importance of the neighbourhood with its constraints and hazards, as
perceived by parents and referred to spontaneously, had already become a
major feature in the interpretation of data in the earlier study. The location
of the new study in two dissimilar areas puts even greater emphasis on
parental perceptions and, for that reason, a more systematic approach than
in the earlier study was indicated. One would wish to know whether the
measures that parents take, often at great cost to themselves, to protect
their children from a " bad " environment are, in fact, explained in terms
of the crime situation. It was necessary also to explore the phenomenon of
dissimilar methods of parental supervision in shared neighbourhoods
resulting in a great deal of delinquent behaviour in some, and none in other,
families. Neighbourhoods needed to be seen from the point of view of the
families who raise children in them; for that reason it was decided to include
in the interview schedule a section on problems in the neighbourhood.

The earlier study had shown many parental practices to be closely linked

PARENTAL SUPERVISION: A NEGLECTED ASPECT OF DELINQUENCY

to the constraints of their environment. High population densities, over-crowding in the home and high fertility rates contribute to traditional working-class patterns of play in the streets, delegation of mothering to older siblings, and a tendency to withdraw from close supervision when other people's children are involved in play, so as to minimise tensions with neighbours. These adaptations to environmental constraints are not always cherished but are necessary to make life tolerable. The results, in terms of child development, are detrimental in many ways and parents, sensitive to these matters, do break away from traditional patterns if they are able to do so. Parental choices increase with improvements in living conditions, as amply documented in the Newson studies (Newson, J. and E., 1968, 1976, 1977). More space, more privacy, more resources make new styles of life possible in which different scales of family priorities can be developed. The new study would offer an opportunity to investigate how parents supervise their children in differing circumstances and in different neighbourhoods, and the effect this has on the children's behaviour, a topic which has been strangely neglected in empirical and analytical criminology.

The Plan of the Research

The research proposal required an investigation at two levels; first, a comparison of families resident in two dissimilar areas in terms of degree of social handicap, parental supervision and delinquency; and secondly, a behavioural study, based on teachers' ratings, which was to be augmented by a self-report measure of misbehaviour in school and in the neighbourhood of the 10–11 year-old " focus boys ".

1. *Choice of areas*

(a) *The inner city.* A study that concerns itself with the ascertainment of delinquency must be located in delinquency areas. The Sheffield study of crime (Baldwin and Bottoms, 1976) shows that crime rates vary with other measurable factors among which child density, socio-economic status, housing tenure, immigrant status and shared accommodation play a part. There was a strong tendency for council and rented areas with a relatively high percentage of classes IV and V to have higher offender rates. On the basis of our previous findings and of the longitudinal study by West and Farrington (1973), which show the significance of low family income, large family size and concomitant factors in relation to delinquency, a search for areas of high deprivation was indicated.

The problem of urban deprivation has received increasing attention in recent years. Various studies were undertaken to ascertain location and to formulate some general conclusions about the nature of area deprivation. The most frequently used methods are based on census data, as for instance the study of areas of deprivation in Britain undertaken by Holterman (1975). Census data soon become out of date in areas of slum clearance and other forms of housing action. By a fortunate coincidence the West Midlands County Council Planning Department had reassessed areas of deprivation in a 10 per cent. household survey which was completed in 1977. The

HARRIETT WILSON

results of the analysis made an exact location of the most deprived inner-city enumeration districts possible. The indicators of deprivation are (1) household lacking a fixed bath, (2) household overcrowded, (3) economically active males unemployed or sick, (4) heads of household unskilled manual workers, (5) population aged 0–14, (6) household not owning a car, and (7) new Commonwealth immigrants. The deprived areas consistently have more than a proportionate share of the " worst " enumeration districts as defined in terms of one per cent. cut-off values. These would form the catchment areas for the selection of the inner-city sub-sample of families.

(b) *Suburban housing estates.* The identification of suitable housing estates caused problems of a different kind. These estates do not rank high in a measurement of indicators of deprivation even though they are ranked by local authority officials in social services, housing and education departments in terms of " difficulties " which some of the estates present. We decided to be guided by the city's housing department as being the agency most familiar with the problem of " difficult housing estates " as manifested in terms of vandalism, rent arrears and high turnover of tenants. This approach is in substantial agreement with the concept of " problem estates " as described by Wilson and Burbridge (1978).

The West Midlands city in which the fieldwork took place has three categories of population density on its estates: (i) pre-war estates at 40 persons per acre, (ii) early post-war medium-rise estates at 120 persons per acre, and (iii) modern estates at 60–80 persons per acre. Child densities vary from an estimated average of one child per two houses, a density of five children to the acre, to 30 children per acre in early post-war medium-rise estates containing blocks of flats and maisonettes. Length of residence is also associated with type of housing. The average duration of a tenancy of a three-bedroom early post-war flat or maisonette is five years, and was said to be falling when our research started, whilst for a three-bedroom house it is several decades. The high turnover of tenants was explained by the housing department as manifesting the unpopularity of these early post-war buildings and by the fact that a considerable number of new council houses were built in their immediate vicinities, giving tenants an opportunity to be transferred. The blocks of flats and maisonettes form parts of post-war housing estates which have population densities of up to 120 persons per acre. They had been designed in the early 1950s to house larger families but lack lifts, play areas and storage or other facilities considered essential for families with young children.

Nine distinct areas, formed by groups of flats and maisonettes, were identified by the housing department. Some form part of larger estates, others are surrounded by mixed development containing privately owned houses which were built in the inter-war and post-war periods. These nine areas were to be the " target areas " for the selection of the suburban sub-sample families.

2. *The school surveys*

With the aid of records of the education department, primary schools were

PARENTAL SUPERVISION: A NEGLECTED ASPECT OF DELINQUENCY

selected which were either situated in, or adjacent to, the deprived areas of the inner city and the suburban " target " areas. Accurate information was required on the distribution of social handicap in these schools to estimate the parameters of the population from which to draw the two samples of families. This information was obtained by a method which had been developed in the earlier study (Wilson and Herbert, 1974).

The definition of social handicap is expressed in terms of a scoring system recording father's social class, size of family, adequacy of school clothing, school attendance over two terms and parental contact with school. The degree of social handicap thus recognises the existence of factors in the child's environment which are known to be associated with performance in psychological tests and ratings, and which were shown to be significantly associated with these in the earlier study. The selection of items for the social handicap instrument was determined by the intention that it should be used in schools. The instrument is made up of weighted scores. Maximum weight of three points is given to poor attendance at school for suspect reasons and for inadequate school clothing, two factors that indicate clearly that the child is socially handicapped. Two points were given to social class V (unskilled) and to a family with five or more children. One point was given to families with four children and to parents who were seen at school only in moments of crisis, if at all. Class teachers were given written instructions defining rating details for school clothing, reasons for absence and parental contact. The research team ascertained class and family size, and percentage attendance over two terms. Total scores ranged from 0 to 11. Among the higher scores are more children with poor clothing, much absence for suspect reasons, from large families, and with unskilled fathers. The weighting system is designed in such a way that scores of five or more points will always include children scoring heavily on items which show the *severe* effects of material and social deprivation. Children who score adversely only on size of family and social class are most likely in the three-four range of scores, which we have called *moderate* social handicap. One or two points, or none at all, classify the child as having a *low* social handicap.

The school surveys included all indigenous boys aged 10–11. Numbers and percentages of ethnic minority groups were also recorded. In all, the survey covers 12 suburban and 25 inner-city schools. This is largely a result of the high proportion of ethnic minority groups in the inner-city schools; whilst the number of boys in these groups was insignificant in the suburban schools, it comprised 58 per cent. of the inner-city boys aged 10–11 in the schools visited.

Further significant differences were observed between the schools in the inner-city and the suburban target areas: there were more moderately and severely socially handicapped families in the inner city ($P < 0.001$), more unskilled and unemployed heads of families ($P < 0.001$) and a greater proportion of families with four or more children ($P < 0.001$). The overall differences between the two main samples indicate a social handicap distribution—low: moderate: severe—of 52: 30: 18 in the inner-city schools and of 77: 16: 7 in the suburban schools. In summary, it can be seen that, on a

HARRIETT WILSON

number of indicators of deprivation, the indigenous 10–11-year-old boys in 25 inner-city schools are more socially handicapped than similar boys in 12 schools situated in suburban estates which contain " hard-to-let " dwellings. However, the latter include varying percentages of pupils from less deprived neighbourhoods.

It was found that large families are not untypical of the more deprived areas both in the inner city and in the suburbs. The range of indigenous families with four or more children in 25 inner-city schools was considerable, but was nowhere less than one-fifth and in some schools as high as two-thirds. In the 12 suburban schools large families formed between 22 and 44 per cent. Nationally, the proportion of completed families with four or more children shows considerable variation with social class, from 10–15 per cent. of women with husbands in non-manual occupations to about 20 per cent. for skilled and semi-skilled occupations, and approaching 30 per cent. for unskilled occupations (Pearce and Britton, 1977).

3. *Selection of families*

(a) *The two sub-samples.* There are two samples, each containing 60 families, one resident in the inner city and the other on suburban housing estates. Each sub-sample contains equal proportions of families in the three social handicap categories, so that comparisons can be made within each sub-sample and across the two sub-samples with reference to degree of social handicap. The total number of families in both is thus 120, composed of 40 families severely, 40 moderately and 40 mildly socially handicapped.

(b) *The families.* The criteria for inclusion in the sample are as nearly as possible like the criteria by which the main sample had been selected in the previous study. This required the families to be indigenous (including Irish) so as to hold cultural factors constant; to be intact, that is with father and mother irrespective of marital status; and to be a " large " family. In the earlier research " large " was defined as having five or more children, but in the current study the number had to be reduced to four or more because of changes in average family size. In addition, each family in the current study has one boy aged 10–11, the " focus boy ", and a second one older than the focus boy.

(c) *Method of selection.* The families were selected from the social handicap lists obtained in the school surveys. In the first place, the required numbers of families who satisfied all criteria were identified; these families were then approached by letter asking if they would like to take part in the survey, and this was followed by a visit. Families were offered a fee of £2 for the interviews to bring in women who might otherwise have declined as being too busy.

The occupational distribution in the two sub-samples does not differ substantially. The relative absence of non-manual occupations (only six men gave managerial or supervisory positions as their occupation) was counterbalanced by a large contingent of non-skilled workers (classes IV

PARENTAL SUPERVISION: A NEGLECTED ASPECT OF DELINQUENCY

and V) in both samples—42 per cent. in the inner city and 35 per cent. in the suburban estates. A comparison of the two sub-samples with a national sample of primary school parents (Plowden Report, 1967) shows that the study families are not representative in that there is a heavy over-representation of the non-skilled occupations and an almost complete absence of middle-class families. This is not unexpected and is due to the sampling criteria. The distribution of social classes is largely explained by the scoring system in the three social handicap groups.

There is a remarkable similarity in the composition of families. The total number of children in the inner-city sample was 356, an average of 5·9 per family, and in the suburban sample it was 347, an average of 5·8 per family. Because of the research demands for at least two boys in each family the samples are strongly biased towards boys; of the total of 703 children only 254 are girls. The degree of social handicap is, by definition, related to the size of the family, and for that reason 80 per cent. of inner-city families (and 70 per cent. in the suburbs) in the " low " SH group have no more than five children. In contrast, only seven inner-city and eight suburban families in the " severe " SH group have no more than five children.

The suburban families had a substantially larger contingent of parents born in the West Midlands, whereas the inner-city families had a majority of parents from a distance; among these the Irish formed the largest sub-group. Educational experiences of both sub-samples were, however, very similar. None of the parents had education beyond secondary schooling, and almost all had left school at the earliest opportunity. The two samples differ in that there were twice as many men who had served apprenticeships in the suburbs than in the inner city. Again, the women in the inner city had a larger contingent who had been unskilled workers before marriage than in the suburban sample where there was more variety of skills. About 45 per cent. in both samples were at work, mostly part-time, at the time of interview.

4. *The interviews*

Two interview schedules were used, both semi-structured to allow for speedy coding of certain information and expressions of opinion qualifying set responses. The first interview covered details of family composition, parental occupations, education and geographical origin; there was also a section on perceptions of the neighbourhood (adapted from Baldwin, 1974). The second interview was an adapted version of the Newson interview schedule designed for 10-year-olds, which had also been used in the earlier study and thus provided opportunities for cross-comparisons (J. and E. Newson, unpublished).

The interviews were planned to be given on separate occasions, but the excessive amount of time spent in travelling eventually resulted in a combination of the two. On average, the time spent with each family was one-and-a-half to two hours. The majority of interviews took place in the day time, but some had to be arranged for the evening. The interviewer in all cases was HW.

HARRIETT WILSON

5. *A self-report measure of misbehaviour and delinquency*

(a) *Structure.* The research design and age of the sample necessitated the individual testing of boys which would allow the researcher to overcome any problems of comprehension. Of the three techniques employed to date—questionnaire, card-sort and interview—Farrington (1973) notes that the questionnaire, whilst being the most objective in administration to groups of subjects under anonymous conditions, is subject to errors through misinterpretation, carelessness and poor reading ability. Heal and Perry (Home Office Research Unit, unpublished) and McDonald (1969) found it necessary to read questions aloud to some subjects. The possibilities of concealment and exaggeration might also be expected to be greatest in this method although, as Hood and Sparks (1970) note, there is no evidence of consistent exaggeration in self-report studies. The card-sort technique (*e.g.* Belson, 1968; Gibson, 1967) requires the subject to sort cards on which are written descriptions of delinquent or "fringe-delinquent" acts according to commission and frequency. Once again, however, the expected poor reading and comprehension levels of the present sample argued against the use of this technique. The most reliable method of data collection for the study therefore appeared to be a structured interview in which the researcher could aid the respondent in problems of recall and interpretation, probe for details of offences, and question possible exaggerations and fantasies.

(b) *Content.* The majority of self-report studies have focused upon the 13–18 age range and have, consequently, employed measures comprising "under age" and "aggressive" acts such as "going to X films" and "attacking or fighting a policeman who is trying to arrest someone else" (Gibson, 1967), the majority of which would be inappropriate for the present sample. In addition, little attention has been paid to the question of "differential access/opportunity", a potentially important source of bias, particularly in studies comparing reported delinquency rates in different areas. With these considerations in mind, items were selected—partly from existing scales (Belson, 1968; Clark and Wenninger, 1962; Gibson, 1967; Gladstone, 1978; Heal and Perry, unpublished; McDonald, 1969) and partly from discussions with three classes of 10-year-olds from primary schools in the suburban area under study. The children were questioned about misbehaviour at school and in the community, their leisure activities and attitudes towards school. None of these children took any further part in the research.

The remaining sections of the interview cover attitudes to school (three items), leisure activities (11 items), parental strictness (nine items) and exposure to differential association (five items)—that is, how much time is spent out of the home and with whom. The majority of these questions correspond to items contained in the interview for parents and could thus be used to assess the validity of the subjects' reports.

The question of the reliability of information is central to the self-report method and, whereas some researchers (*e.g.* Gladstone) have attempted no check whatsoever, accepting "some concealment" as "probably inevitable", others have assessed validity by correlation of self-reported

PARENTAL SUPERVISION: A NEGLECTED ASPECT OF DELINQUENCY

delinquency scores with official records and with teachers' reports (West and Farrington, 1973). These two checks have been adopted in the present study, teachers' reports being obtained by means of a checklist of eight items extracted from the " Within school misbehaviour " section.

The average time for completion of the final version of the self-report measure was 30-minutes. The interviewer was in all cases IR.

6. *Criminal records*

With the co-operation of the Chief Constable, the following information was obtained: (i) records of delinquent acts committed by any child of the sample families while under the age of 10; (ii) official cautions; (iii) records of children found guilty of an offence; (iv) records of father/mother found guilty of a criminal offence.

It was thus possible to obtain four measures of delinquency rates: the rate of convictions as a function of age; the rate of offenders as a function of age; the percentage of boys so far unconvicted who become delinquent at each year of age; and the percentage of boys at each age who had become delinquent before the year in which they attained that age.

The objective in obtaining these measures was to compare families in three social handicap groups, resident in two dissimilar areas of the city, so as to ascertain the distribution of rates of delinquency among them and to relate these rates to parental supervision. In particular, the following hypotheses were to be tested:

A. There is a significant increase of delinquency with increasing degree of social handicap in both sub-samples.

B. There is a significant increase of delinquency wtih increasing parental laxness in both sub-samples.

C. The increase of delinquency with increasing parental laxness is greater than with increasing social handicap.

Parental Supervision

1. *The index of supervision*

The central focus of interest lies in the parental interviews which provided information about supervision. The interview schedule used for the purpose of ascertaining degree of supervision is a modified version of the instrument designed by J. and E. Newson which had also been used in the previous study. A further modification was made to incorporate some relevant questions contained in the schedule which focuses on six–seven year-old boys. At the time of writing the Newson study of 10-year-olds has not been published and comparisons with a general population cannot be made. In this section only those aspects of parenting which are relevant to supervision are discussed.

The interview is focused on the 10–11 year-old boy. Mothers are asked a series of questions which provide information on which the index of supervision is based. The following items were scored:

HARRIETT WILSON

Score

(i)   Mother describes the boy as " mainly outdoors "   1

(ii) Independent activities: goes to town, on bus, to the park on
      his own
          1–2 activities   1
          3 or more activities   2

(iii) No rules about coming in at a set time or about telling mother
      where he goes   2

(iv) Allowed to roam the streets:
          mother says she cannot always find him   1
          mother says she often cannot find him   2

                                                    Maximum score   7

As shown in Table 1, the distribution of total scores shows that there is
remarkably little difference between the inner-city and suburban families.

TABLE 1

Parental supervision: inner-city and suburban families

Total scores:	0	1	2	3	4	5	6	7	Totals
	Strict		Intermed.		Lax				
Inner city	2	8	17	13	5	3	7	5	60
Suburbs	5	9	18	12	6	6	1	3	60
Totals	7	17	35	25	11	9	8	8	120

The strict families, scoring zero or one point, consist of 10 in the inner city
and 14 in the suburbs. They do not allow unsupervised play outside their
own gardens or yards unless in the company of an older sibling. The boy
may be described as " mainly indoors " (score 0) or as " mainly outdoors "
(score 1) and, if " mainly indoors ", this type of boy is sometimes allowed
one or two independent activities for specific purposes (score 1) as he is
considered to be a responsible boy.

There are 30 families in each sub-sample scoring two or three points.
This group is neither very strict nor very lax and they form the largest
single group. In these families there are rules about coming in and about
telling mothers where the boys go. However, almost all of them score one
point for describing their focus boy as being " mainly outdoors " and a
second point for " one or two activities on his own ". Alternatively, some
parents would allow the boy to roam the streets as long as they say they
can usually (but not always) find him when they want him.

At the other end of the scale are the lax families who score four or more
points; the number in the inner city is 20 and in the suburbs 16. These
families allow a range of independent activities, and there may be no rules
about coming in or about telling mothers where they are going. These boys
roam the streets and their mothers often cannot find them.

PARENTAL SUPERVISION: A NEGLECTED ASPECT OF DELINQUENCY

2. *Parental supervision and social handicap*

Table 2 shows the overall distribution of parental supervision scores for each social handicap group. The close association of social handicap with parental supervision is clearly shown. There is a trend for laxness to increase with social handicap: in the low SH group only two inner-city and one suburban family are lax; in the moderate SH group six inner-city and six suburban families are lax; and in the severe SH group the respective numbers are 12 and nine. Conversely, only four out of 40 severe SH families manage to be strict, in contrast to 10 out of 40 low SH families.

TABLE 2

Parental supervision and social handicap: inner-city and suburban families

Parental supervision index	0 Strict	1	2 Intermed.	3	4 Lax	5	6	7	Totals
Low SH									
Inner city	1	2	10	5	2	0	0	0	20
Suburbs	2	5	8	4	1	0	0	0	20
Totals	3	7	18	9	3	0	0	0	40
Moderate SH									
Inner city	1	4	4	5	2	2	2	0	20
Suburbs	2	3	7	2	2	2	1	1	20
Totals	3	7	11	7	4	4	3	1	40
Severe SH									
Inner city	0	2	3	3	1	1	5	5	20
Suburbs	1	1	3	6	3	4	0	2	20
Totals	1	3	6	9	4	5	5	7	40

Chi-squared on Low SH/Severe SH/Strict PS/Lax PS gives 11·15 with 1 d.f., $p < 0.001$.

3. *Differences between the inner-city and suburban samples*

An examination of the four items making up the Parental Supervision Index shows differences between the two sub-samples which reach statistical significance but, as one of these works in a direction opposite to the two others, overall differences are undetectable. In the inner city there is a widespread custom for most boys to be " mainly outdoors ", and there is no difference between the three social handicap groups. Only 10 out of 60 boys are described as being mainly indoors. In the suburbs, in contrast, more than half the boys in the " low " and " moderate " SH groups are described as mainly indoors; and this was found to be associated with a wider range of resources and more adequate housing. The exceptions are the boys in the " severe " SH group; with only four boys described as mainly indoors their distribution is identical with the " severes " in the inner city. The difference in direction of stricter parental supervision on this item is significant overall ($p < 0.005$).

On independent activities the suburban families again tend to be stricter, and this is most apparent among the low social handicap group with 12 not allowing their boys to undertake an expedition by themselves, in contrast to only three out of 20 inner-city families. Once more the latter show no significant differences in the three social handicap groups, and the boys who are not allowed independent activities are a small minority. The difference,

HARRIETT WILSON

overall, is in the direction of stricter suburban families ($p < 0.006$). It appears that inner-city boys often need to take a bus to get to school playing fields or swimming baths, or to attend denominational schools some distance from home. They would be seen as able to shop for their mothers in the large shopping centres. In contrast the suburban boys have sports facilities and open spaces closer at hand, and they are not usually sent to the larger shopping centres by themselves. None of the boys had to travel to school.

Rules about play and when to come in are observed strictly by families in the "low" SH groups in both the inner city and the suburbs. The "moderates" tend to be laxer. It is the inner-city "severes" who show the greatest degree of laxness with fewer than half imposing rules; the suburban "severes" do not show the same degree of laxness with two-thirds imposing rules. There is no significant difference overall between the two sub-samples.

In contrast to the first two items indicating stricter parental supervision in the suburbs, the item measuring roaming indicates greater strictness overall among inter-city families, where 21 families allow no roaming. In the suburbs the number is only eight ($p < 0.02$). In the inner city the "low" SH families are strictest, with 11 not allowing roaming in contrast to two families in the "severe" SH group. In the suburbs, however, parents appeared to be more relaxed about roaming, and only four families in the "low" SH group, and one family in the "severe" SH group did not allow this activity. Once again, the inner-city severely socially handicapped families show a greater degree of laxness than the suburban ones in that nine parents admitted they often could not find their boys when needed, in contrast to only four suburban parents.

4. *Parental motivation*

Who are the supervising parents and what are their motives? The parents in the deprived inner-city areas expressed their feelings clearly; the environment was generally seen as a "bad" one in which to bring up children—it was not pleasant, not safe, there were unruly children, rough or criminal elements, inadequate amenities and, for those who still lived in old housing, the additional burdens of discomfort in their homes. The families in the suburban estates saw their neighbourhoods in a less sombre light but, even so, a substantial number expressed anxiety about vandalism, thieving and other undesirable behaviour of the youngsters with whom their children had contact. But the awareness of dangers and risks does not necessarily lead to parental measures of protection. What, for some parents, becomes the "reason" for strict supervision is turned into the "reason" for their children's misbehaviour by other parents whose methods are lax. The problem for the researcher consists in providing verbalised motives which typically explain actions. The method chosen was to select two pairs of families resident in the same neighbourhood and representing the same degree of social handicap, but having different parenting methods. Since the two extreme forms of parenting—strictness and laxness—present the differences in approach most clearly, the pairs have been chosen from these two categories only.

PARENTAL SUPERVISION: A NEGLECTED ASPECT OF DELINQUENCY

The first set consists of two severely socially handicapped families resident in " Large Heath " in the inner city:

The strict family: " The ones that have a bad influence, we keep them away from them, we have them in by half [past] seven . . . In Red Lane Park the big fellows take his football away, the other park is better but the same thing is happening. They were all Altar Boys, but they used to come home at nine at night, I had to stop it . . . I won't let him go off on his own—it worries me, he might get mugged. Two boys got mugged on Saturday for 75 pence—they got the money for a wedding—they are Altar Boys."

The lax family: " I've never been in trouble with him, I'm not worried. He comes out to you early in the morning before he goes and sometimes he don't come in—I don't see him till seven that night. He'll say, I'm just with me mates—I say, you should come in for your meals—he says, yes, Mum, I will."

The second set consists of two moderately socially handicapped families in " Southfields " in the suburbs:

The strict family: " Two boys I stopped him going with—it turned out to be right, they were both expelled from school. I let them play together in the garden where I could see them. I said to Mark I don't like these boys, they shout a lot, and I stopped Mark from bringing them into the garden. The family was dirty, a girl died from taking tablets, I felt sorry for the boys . . . You can't trust anybody today, anything could happen to him. They get mixed up in this shoplifting or break windows, they do—they have cheek!"

The lax family: " He's not bothered, he always mixes with the wrong children, there's a lot of boys around here—the one he calls his best friend I don't like. He's a daredevil if another boy says anything . . . You don't always know where they are—you can't always see what they're up to. I don't like it. I always think some people are funny with little lads—if a car pulled up, he'd be the one to get in, he's very vulnerable."

Self-reported Misbehaviour and Delinquency

The construction of the instrument was described in section 5 on page 210 above. The schedule included questions about leisure activities, school attitudes and parental strictness, as well as about misbehaviour and delinquency. The " neutral " questions were included partly to give the boys confidence before the possibly embarrassing questions about misbehaviour were reached, and partly to give an indication of the reliability of the boys' responses, which could be checked against information given by the parents and teachers. The present section gives a broad picture of self-reported misbehaviour.

1. *Seriousness of offences*

Previous self-report investigations in Britain were mainly concerned with older boys: West and Farrington (1973) used the groups aged 14–15 and 16–17, Shapland (1978) the groups aged 11–12 and 13–14, and Gladstone (1978) the wide range aged 11–15. The boys in the present investigation were 10–11 years-old, and some behaviour that would be taken seriously for

HARRIETT WILSON

older age groups can be regarded only as mischievous for boys who have barely reached the age of criminal responsibility. With these considerations in mind the seriousness of misbehaviour was judged by members of the West Midlands Criminal Records Office, taking into account that the sample consisted of boys aged 10 to 11 years. This resulted in a broad threefold classification of acts as " trivial ", " intermediate " or " serious ".

2. *Scoring of misbehaviour*

Comparisons given in this section are all made on the basis of a simple counting of the number of different items of misbehaviour reported. It may be argued that a truer picture would be given if the items were weighted by (a) the frequency of commission, and (b) the seriousness of the misbehaviour. Such weighting was tried but was found to make no appreciable difference to the general picture. This result is in accordance with the experience of Shapland (1978) and others.

TABLE 3

The prevalence of misbehaviour outside school: inner city and suburban samples

	Serious-ness	INNER CITY SOCIAL HANDICAP					SUBURBAN ESTATES SOCIAL HANDICAP						
		Low	Mod	Sev.	Total	%	Low	Mod	Sev.	Total	%	Totals	%
Playing " knock and run "	T	15	15	14	44	73	15	16	13	44	73	88	73
Fighting in the street	T	13	11	18	42	70	9	8	11	28	47	70	58
Graffiti in the street	T	11	13	13	37	62	10	10	10	30	50	67	56
Smashing bottles in the street	T	10	8	12	30	50	6	7	13	26	43	56	47
Shoplifting	I	10	7	10	27	45	3	9	11	23	38	50	42
Checking people	T	7	7	9	23	38	6	11	7	24	40	47	39
Smashing windows in a derelict house	T	8	9	9	26	43	3	2	6	11	18	37	31
Gang fighting	I	5	9	9	23	38	2	2	7	11	18	34	28
Throwing stones at people	T	3	7	8	18	30	2	5	4	11	18	29	24
Damaging cars	I	4	2	8	14	23	5	6	4	15	25	29	24
Dialling 999 for a joke	I	4	3	5	12	20	4	5	8	17	28	29	24
Starting fires	S*	5	2	5	12	20	2	4	5	11	18	23	18
Stealing from home	I	2	4	3	9	15	2	4	7	13	22	22	18
Stealing petrol caps etc. off cars	I	4	0	4	8	13	1	5	6	12	20	20	17
Damaging road signs	T	4	2	1	7	12	4	5	2	11	18	18	15
Smashing a light on a lamp-post	T	4	4	3	11	18	1	0	3	4	7	15	13
Stealing from slot machines	I	2	0	3	5	8	0	5	2	7	12	12	10
Throwing stones at passing cars	I	3	1	5	9	15	0	1	0	1	2	10	8
Breaking and entering a shop, school, etc.	S	0	1	5	6	10	0	1	1	2	3	8	7
Smashing windows in an occupied house	I	1	3	0	4	7	0	0	2	2	3	6	5
Smashing glass in a 'phone box/bus shelter	T	0	1	2	3	5	1	0	1	2	3	5	4
Stealing from cars	S	0	2	2	4	7	0	0	0	0	0	4	3
Burglary, private house	S	1	0	0	1	2	0	0	0	0	0	1	1
Mugging	S	0	0	0	0	0	0	0	0	0	0	0	0

Seriousness: T = Trivial, I = Intermediate, S = Serious.
* " Starting fires " is classed as a serious offence, except when they are started on waste land railway embankments, etc. They are then classed " trivial ".

PARENTAL SUPERVISION: A NEGLECTED ASPECT OF DELINQUENCY

3. *The prevalence of misbehaviour outside school*

Table 3 shows the number and percentages of boys reporting various kinds of misbehaviour in the inner city, in the suburbs and overall. (Numbers are shown for each social handicap group.) The information is arranged in order of the number of boys who report individual items. The most trivial items are thus at the top of the list, but it can be seen that shoplifting (ranked as intermediate in nature of seriousness) was reported by 42 per cent. and is fifth in the list. Among offences rated as serious, " starting fires " was reported most frequently, though it is not clear how many boys engaged only in making bonfires on waste ground, which is classed as trivial, and how many set fire to buildings. The other offences classified as serious were reported by under 10 per cent. of boys; of these taking and driving cars without owners' consent and breaking and entering shops etc. were reported by 8 and 7 per cent. respectively. Overall, 14 per cent. of the boys reported no misbehaviour or delinquent act, 18 per cent. reported trivial acts only, 51 per cent. reported trivial and/or intermediate acts and 17 per cent. reported all three types of act, including serious acts.

An overall summary, classified by parental supervision and by social handicap, is given in Table 4.

TABLE 4

Self-reported misbehaviour (all boys) classified by seriousness of offence and (a) parental supervision, and (b) social handicap

(a)

	PARENTAL SUPERVISION							
	Strict		Intermediate		Lax		Total	
	n	%	n	%	n	%	n	%
No misbehaviour	7	29	7	12	3	8	17	14
Trivial	3	13	16	27	3	8	22	18
Intermediate	12	50	31	52	18	50	61	51
Serious	2	8	6	10	12	33	20	17
Total	24	100	60	100	36	100	120	100

(b)

	SOCIAL HANDICAP							
	Low		Moderate		Severe		Total	
	n	%	n	%	n	%	n	%
No misbehaviour	7	17	6	15	4	10	17	14
Trivial	6	15	8	20	8	20	22	18
Intermediate	23	58	20	50	18	45	61	51
Serious	4	10	6	15	10	25	20	17
Total	40	100	40	100	40	100	120	100

It is obvious that the percentage of boys reporting misbehaviour classified as of intermediate seriousness varies little with either parental supervision or with social handicap, being about half the boys in all groups. There is a trend for the proportion of boys reporting serious misbehaviour to increase with parental laxity and with social handicap, and a corresponding trend in the reverse direction for the percentage reporting no misbehaviour. The trend is statistically significant for parental supervision (chi-squared $=18.24$ with 6 d.f., $p < 0.01$) but not for social handicap (chi-squared $= 4.61$ with 6 d.f., chance expectation). Parental supervision thus seems to be more important than social handicap in determining self-reported misbehaviour.

HARRIETT WILSON

4. *Misbehaviour in school: the general picture*

The boys were also asked about 12 varieties of misbehaviour within school. These are listed in Table 5. (See section 5 for details on reliability.) The analysis of misbehaviour in the classroom reported by the boys, and classified by area, social handicap and parental supervision, is given in Table 6.

TABLE 5

The prevalence of misbehaviour within school: inner city and suburban samples

	INNER CITY					SUBURBAN ESTATES						
	SOCIAL HANDICAP					SOCIAL HANDICAP						
	Low	Mod.	Sev.	Total	%	Low	Mod.	Sev.	Total	%	Totals	%
Reprimand for fighting	17	18	17	52	87	14	17	19	50	83	102	85
Breaking school rules	16	17	15	48	80	16	17	19	52	87	100	83
Class dismissal	13	13	14	40	67	12	14	16	42	70	82	68
Lying to a teacher	14	12	10	36	60	7	11	13	31	52	67	56
Bullying	10	7	9	26	43	7	13	14	34	57	60	50
Cheeking a teacher	14	7	11	32	53	4	10	13	27	45	59	49
Scratching a desk	6	6	5	17	28	4	7	5	16	27	33	28
Stealing at school	2	2	7	11	18	1	8	8	17	28	28	23
Damaging school property	4	4	5	13	22	1	4	6	11	18	24	20
Truancy	3	3	6	12	20	1	1	10	12	20	24	20
Graffiti on walls	4	1	2	7	12	0	2	0	2	3	9	8
Swearing at a teacher	1	1	5	7	12	0	1	1	2	3	9	8

TABLE 6

Self-reported misbehaviour within school (eight items), classified by geographical area and
(a) parental supervision, and (b) social handicap

The average number of misbehaviours reported is given for each group, with the standard deviation in parentheses.

(a)	PARENTAL SUPERVISION		
	Strict	Intermediate	Lax
Inner city	3·20	3·60	4·50
	(1·60)	(1·72)	(2·09)
No of boys	10	30	20
Suburbs	2·29	3·23	4·75
	(1·79)	(1·63)	(1·25)
No. of boys	14	30	16

(b)	SOCIAL HANDICAP		
	Low	Moderate	Severe
Inner city	3·95	3·25	4·30
	(1·40)	(1·54)	(2·43)
No. of boys	20	20	20
Suburbs	2·10	3·60	4·55
	(1·61)	(1·28)	(1·60)
No. of boys	20	20	20

The analysis in that table is confined to the eight items used in the teacher's questionnaire: class dismissal, reprimand for fighting, punishment for breaking school rules, cheeking teacher, lying to a teacher, truancy, reprimand for stealing at school, swearing at a teacher. The table shows that

PARENTAL SUPERVISION: A NEGLECTED ASPECT OF DELINQUENCY

there is a general increase of reported misbehaviour by the boys with social handicap (aside from a small irregularity for the inner-city moderates), and also with increasing parental laxity.

On comparing classroom behaviour as reported by the boys in the inner city with that of the boys in the suburban schools, one finds very little difference, except that the boys of low social handicap in the suburbs report fewer misbehaviours than those in the inner city.

5. *Reliability of the self-reports*

Suspicion of the reliability of self-reports of misbehaviour is widespread, some believing that boys will attempt to conceal misbehaviour, leading to under-reporting, and others believing that boys will tend to boast and thus exaggerate. In the present study the reliability of the boys' reports can be checked in three ways: (i) comparison with police records; (ii) comparison with teachers' reports of within-school misbehaviour; and (iii) comparison with information obtained in the parental interviews.

(i) *Comparison with police records.* At age 10–11 few boys have police records but, in fact, there were 14 incidents involving 12 boys, eight in the inner city and four in the suburbs. There were three cautions, three convictions and eight under-age offences. All but one boy reported the offences.

(ii) *Comparison with teachers' reports.* Teachers' reports on eight items of within-school misbehaviour are analysed in Table 7, which is arranged in the same way as Table 6 for the boys' reports on the same items. Both show similar trends in number of items reported, the number increasing with greater parental laxity and social handicap. In every group the teachers report fewer items of misbehaviour than the boys, indicating that there is no overall concealment of misbehaviour on the part of the boys, though there

TABLE 7

Teacher-reported misbehaviour within school (same eight items as in Table 6), classified by geographical area and (a) parental supervision, and (b) social handicap.

The average number of misbehaviours reported per boy is given for each group, with the standard deviation in parentheses.

(a)	PARENTAL SUPERVISION		
	Strict	Intermediate	Lax
Inner city	2·80	2·87	4·40
	(2·44)	(2·20)	(2·18)
No. of boys	10	30	20
Suburban estates	0·79	2·43	3·69
	(1·21)	(1·93)	(1·79)
No. of boys	14	30	16

(b)	SOCIAL HANDICAP		
	Low	Moderate	Severe
Inner city	3·05	3·15	4·05
	(2·16)	(2·33)	(2·31)
No. of boys	20	20	20
Suburban estates	1·10	2·50	3·55
	(1·84)	(1·80)	(1·63)
No. of boys	20	20	20

HARRIETT WILSON

are one or two cases where it is highly probable that individual boys had adopted the technique of denying everything. In fact, examination of the individual records indicates that, in two schools, the teachers were concealing boys' misbehaviour; one school did not report any misbehaviour whatever, and the other reported only a single item on the part of one boy, though the boys themselves reported many. With these exceptions, the teachers' reports confirm the boys' general truthfulness.

The comparison between the boys' and the teachers' reports may be clearer in Table 8. The boys were arranged in nine groups; those who scored few (0–2) items of misbehaviour both on their own reports and on their teachers' reports; those with a low score on their own reports but a moderate number (3–5) on their teachers' reports; those with a low self-score but a high (6–8) teachers' score; those with a moderate self-score and a low teachers' score, and so on. For half the boys (49 per cent.) teachers' score and self-score agree; for 14 per cent. the teacher judges the boy more harshly than the boy judges himself; and for 37 per cent. the teacher judges the boy more leniently. It is interesting that the teachers regard more boys as misbehaving in the inner city than in the suburbs (chi-squared=7·98 with 2 d.f., p <0·02), but the boys do not show a significant difference in their self-ratings (chi-squared=1·08 with 2 d.f., chance expectation).

TABLE 8

Comparison of teachers' scores (number of items of misbehaviour reported) with boys' self-score

(a) Inner city

BOYS' SELF SCORE	TEACHERS' SCORE			
	0–2	3–5	6–8	Total
0–2	10	3	1	14
3–5	17	11	6	34
6–8	0	4	8	12
Total	27	18	15	60

(b) Suburbs

	0–2	3–5	6–8	Total
0–2	15	4	0	19
3–5	14	14	3	31
6–8	1	8	1	10
Total	30	26	1	60

(iii) *Comparison with parental interviews.* The parental interviews and the introductory part of the self-report interview gave comparable information on seven items: boy's preference for indoor or outdoor activities; boy's sociability; parents' reaction to boy's friends; rules about going out and coming home; boy's roaming and parents' finding; boy's clubs; boy's activities with father.

There was thus the possibility of seven disagreements in the statements of the boy and his parents but, in fact, serious discrepancies were rare. Over two-thirds (68 per cent.) showed one disagreement or none, most of the rest (29 per cent.) showed two or three, and only one boy had as many as five. The rarity of serious discrepancies gives further evidence of the reliability of the boys' self-report, though obviously there is more temptation to conceal misbehaviour than to give false information on items like the above.

PARENTAL SUPERVISION: A NEGLECTED ASPECT OF DELINQUENCY

Juvenile Delinquency

1. *Preliminary facts about the sample*

The total number of children of all ages in the two sub-samples is 703. However, for purposes of this research only children aged 10–17 are included. Among the 120 sample families the number was 595; of these 385 were boys and 210 were girls. The imbalance between the sexes is due to the method of sampling which prescribed a minimum of four children of whom one is a boy aged 10–11 and another an older brother.

There are significant differences in children's ages between the families resident in the inner city and in the suburban estates. These arise mainly on account of the smaller, younger families in the suburbs, who make up the moderately socially handicapped group. Consequently there are differences in the number of children under age 18 in each sub-sample. There are 204 boys and 98 girls in the inner city; 181 boys and 112 girls in the suburbs.

2. *The prevalence of juvenile delinquency*

The total number of boys aged 10–18 who were found to have been convicted or cautioned for serious offences was 47 in the inner city and 30 in the suburbs (20 per cent.). For girls the numbers were six and three respectively (4 per cent.). The numbers and distribution of offences are shown in Table 9.

TABLE 9

Delinquency charges resulting in convictions/cautions

	INNER CITY		SUBURBAN ESTATES	
	Boys	Girls	Boys	Girls
(1) Crimes of dishonesty:				
Theft*	77	6	17	3
Burglary*	50	2	12	—
Equipped to steal being a suspected person	—	—	—	—
Handling/receiving/ unlawful possession	3	—	1	—
Unauthorised taking of motor vehicles	6	—	5	—
Fraud, forgery, deception, etc.	—	—	1	—
(2) Aggressive crimes:				
Robbery	1	—	—	—
Malicious wounding, assault	1	—	2	—
(3) Damage to property:				
Criminal damage	3	—	6	—
(4) Sex offences:				
Unlawful sexual intercourse	1	—	—	—
Total	102	7	44	3

* Including attempts

As shown in Table 9, taking both the inner-city and suburban samples together, 77 boys had a total of 146 charges sustained against them, and nine girls had 10 charges, not counting offences (1) to (4) listed in Table 10.

HARRIETT WILSON

Other children from the sample families may have been found guilty or cautioned for minor offences only; these have not been recorded. The table shows that inner-city boys have a conviction/caution rate which is well over three times the rate of the suburban boys, and the rate of the inner-city girls is over twice that of the suburban girls. Recidivism and its relationship to social handicap and to parental supervision are discussed in section 3 (b).

Offences committed by delinquents which are *not* included in Table 9 or in the statistics of this section are shown in Table 10.

TABLE 10

Offences not included in Table 9 or in the statistics of this section

	INNER CITY		SUBURBS	
	Boys	Girls	Boys	Girls
(1) Offences " taken into consideration " or further charges	101	12	—	—
(2) Breaches of probation	12	—	4	—
(3) Minor motoring offences	25	—	11	—
(4) Drunk and disorderly, etc.	9	2	14	—
Total excluded offences	147	14	29	—

3. *Delinquency: trends and differences among boys*

(a) *Social handicap and parental supervision.* The distribution of families with and without delinquent boys is shown in Table 11 in relation to social handicap and parental supervision. This table shows clearly the close association between degree of social handicap and methods of parenting, with only three " lax " parents in the low SH group and only four " strict "

TABLE 11

Delinquent and non-delinquent families, social handicap and parental supervision

	PARENTAL SUPERVISION			
INNER CITY Social handicap:	Strict	Intermed.	Lax	Total
Low				
All families	3	15	2	20
Families with delinquent boys	1	3	1	5
Moderate				
All families	5	9	6	20
Families with delinquent boys	1	3	4	8
Severe				
All families	2	6	12	20
Families with delinquent boys	0	4	9	13
SUBURBS Social handicap:				
Low				
All families	7	12	1	20
Families with delinquent boys	0	5	0	5
Moderate				
All families	5	9	6	20
Families with delinquent boys	0	2	0	2
Severe				
All families	2	9	9	20
Families with delinquent boys	0	3	9	12

PARENTAL SUPERVISION: A NEGLECTED ASPECT OF DELINQUENCY

parents in the severe SH group, taking the inner-city and suburban samples together. The table also shows a trend for delinquent families to increase in number with decreasing parental supervision. In the inner city there are 10 " strict " families of whom two have delinquent boys; and there are 20 " lax " families of whom 14 have delinquent boys. In the suburbs there are 14 " strict " families, none of whom have delinquent boys, and 16 " lax " families of whom nine have delinquent boys. The latter, in fact, are all among the severely socially handicapped group.

However, the family as a unit is not an accurate measure for comparison because of variations in family size and in ages of their children. A more accurate measure of delinquency has been obtained by establishing the number of " boy-years at risk " (BYAR) or " girl-years at risk " (GYAR) for each family. For each boy or girl the number of years completed above age 10 and below age 18 was counted in order to reflect not only the number but also the ages of the children. Table 12 shows the number of boys at risk in each social handicap category, the number delinquent, boy-years at risk and the rate per 100 boy-years at risk.

TABLE 12

Delinquents: boy-years at risk, area and social handicap

| | SOCIAL HANDICAP | | | |
	Low	Moderate	Severe	Total
INNER CITY				
Boys at risk	61	76	67	204
Number delinquent	6	17	24	47
Boy-years at risk	254	344	285	883
Rate per 100 boy-years at risk	2·36	4·96	8·44	5·32
SUBURBS				
Boys at risk	58	52	71	181
Number delinquent	7	4	19	30
Boy-years at risk	250	167	296	713
Rate per 100 boy-years at risk	2·80	2·40	6·42	4·21
TOTALS				
Boys at risk	119	128	138	385
Number delinquent	13	21	43	77
Boy-years at risk	504	511	581	1596
Rate per 100 boy-years at risk	2·58	4·11	7·40	4·82

Although, at first sight, there appears to be a lower rate of delinquency in the suburban sample, this is not borne out when comparing the differences in terms of boy-years at risk. The two sub-samples do not differ significantly. (The values of chi-squared are 0·09, 1·77, 0·79 and 1·02 with 1 d.f. respectively, corresponding to chance expectation.)

However, although there is no significant difference in comparing the inner-city sample with the suburban sample, the increase of delinquency with increasing social handicap is significant. (The values of chi-squared with 2 d.f. are 5·92 for the suburbs, 9·43 for the inner city and 13·80 overall, corresponding to values of p of about 0·05, 0·01 and 0·001 respectively.) It should be remembered, nevertheless, that the existence of such a connection between delinquency and social handicap does not necessarily imply a

HARRIETT WILSON

direct causal relation; the relation could be indirect, through a variable correlated with both, and Table 11 suggests that this is parental supervision.

The relationship of parental supervision to delinquent boys is shown in Table 13. There are significant differences in the number of delinquents between the three parental supervision groups. The inner-city " strict " parents have produced only three delinquent boys (108 boy-years at risk), whereas the " intermediate " parents produced 17 delinquent boys (430 boy-years at risk) and " lax " parents have produced 27 delinquent boys (345 boy-years at risk)—nine times the number produced by strict parents, but boy-years at risk are only a little over three times as large. Similar patterns appear for the suburbs and the total.

TABLE 13

Delinquents: boy-years at risk, area and parental supervision

| | PARENTAL SUPERVISION | | | |
| | Strict | Intermed. | Lax | Total |
	0–1	2–3	4–7	
INNER CITY				
Boys at risk	31	100	73	204
Number delinquent	3	17	27	47
Boy-years at risk	108	430	345	883
Rate per 100 BYAR	2·78	3·95	7·83	5·32
SUBURBS				
Boys at risk	40	88	53	181
Number delinquent	0	17	13	30
Boy-years at risk	154	371	188	713
Rate per 100 BYAR	0	4·58	6·91	4·21
TOTALS				
Boys at risk	71	188	126	385
Number delinquent	3	34	40	77
Boy-years at risk	262	801	533	1596
Rate per 100 BYAR	1·15	4·24	7·50	4·82

(Variations with Parental Supervision Index: inner city: chi-squared$=6·90$ with 2 d.f., $p<0·05$; suburbs: chi-squared$=9·88$ with 2 d.f., $p<0·01$; total: chi-squared$=15·85$ with 2 d.f., $p<0·005$). There are no significant differences between the inner-city and suburban samples when allowance is made for differences in boy-years at risk.

(b) *Recidivism.* So far delinquency has been presented in terms of number of boys delinquent irrespective of the number of cautions or convictions obtained. This section presents the association of social handicap and parental supervision with those boys who have offended more than once. The total number of delinquent boys is 77 and, of these, 47 are single offenders and 30 are recidivists. Boys who offend repeatedly present more serious problems in terms of treatment and prognosis than boys who have only a single conviction. Are the recidivists to be found primarily in the more severely socially handicapped families and is there a relationship with parental supervision?

The distribution of recidivists is shown in Tables 14 and 15. In the first place, the suburban sample has too few recidivists to provide information which can be tested for significance. In the inner city, however, there is a

PARENTAL SUPERVISION: A NEGLECTED ASPECT OF DELINQUENCY

significant trend with social handicap (p<0·01) and similarly, taking both inner-city and suburban samples together, the social handicap trend is significant (p<0·005). In other words, recidivism increases with increasing degree of social handicap. Secondly, there is a trend with parental supervision but numbers in the suburban families are too small to test. In the inner city it reaches significance (p<0·01) and, taking inner city and suburbs together, it is highly significant (p<0·001). Thus, recidivism increases with increasing laxness.

TABLE 14

Recidivism: social handicap and area

Social Handicap:	Low	Moderate	Severe	Total
	1-2	3-4	5-11	
INNER CITY				
Boy-years at risk	254	344	285	883
Number of recidivists	0	9	12	21
Rate per 100 BYAR	0	2·62	4·21	2·38
SUBURBS				
Boy-years at risk	250	167	296	713
Number of recidivists	1	3	5	9
Rate per 100 BYAR	0·40	1·80	1·69	1·26
TOTAL				
Boy-years at risk	504	511	581	1596
Number of recidivists	1	12	17	30
Rate per 100 BYAR	0·20	2·35	2·93	1·88

TABLE 15

Recidivism: parental supervision and area

Parental Supervision:	Strict	Intermed.	Lax	Total
	0-1	3-4	4-7	
INNER CITY				
Boy-years at risk	108	430	345	883
Number of recidivists	0	6	15	21
Rate per 100 BYAR	0	1·40	4·35	2·38
SUBURBS				
Boy-years at risk	154	371	188	713
Number of recidivists	0	5	4	9
Rate per 100 BYAR	0	1·35	2·13	1·26
TOTAL				
Boy-years at risk	262	801	533	1596
Number of recidivists	0	11	19	30
Rate per 100 BYAR	0	1·37	3·56	1·88

(c) *Age of entry into delinquency.* The risk of a previously non-delinquent boy becoming delinquent varies considerably with the age of the boy; for a sample, comparable in many respects with the current severely socially handicapped group, it was found that 15 was the age at which the risk was greatest (Wilson, 1975). This result is confirmed by the present study. For the total sample (all social handicap groups and both inner-city and suburban estates) the numbers of non-delinquent boys at risk at various ages, the number becoming delinquent at each age and the percentage becoming delinquent at each age are as follows:

225

HARRIETT WILSON

TABLE 16
Age when first delinquent

Age (in years)	10	11	12	13	14	15	16	17	18
Not yet delinquent	335	258	219	182	158	128	101	88	68
No. first delinquent	8	8	14	8	10	14	7	8	2
% first delinquent	2·4	3·1	6·4	4·4	6·3	10·9	6·9	9·1	2·9

It will be seen that the rate of entry into delinquency rises from 2 per cent. at age of 10 to 11 per cent. at age 15 and then falls again, the average rate for ages 10–17 being 5·2 per cent. Figures for age 18 are given for comparison but are not taken into account in calculations, as they are not officially "juvenile". The rise and fall is not smooth, however, showing subsidiary peaks at ages 12 and 17. A similar variation is found for all sub-samples.

Following each boy through his years at risk from age 10 to his present age, we find that well over one-quarter have a police record by age 15 and well over one-third by age 17. Taking the severely socially handicapped boys only, the rate in the inner city is 55 per cent. by age 15; in the suburbs it is 35 per cent. (See Table 17, calculated as in Wilson, 1975.)

TABLE 17
Percentage delinquent before or during year of age

	10	11	12	13	14	15	16	17
INNER CITY								
Low	0	2	2	5	9	17	17	23
Moderate	3	6	14	16	19	31	35	42
Severe	5	14	28	36	45	55	62	62
Total	3	7	15	19	24	35	39	43
SUBURBAN ESTATES								
Low	2	2	5	5	12	15	23	23
Moderate	0	0	4	4	10	10	17	27
Severe	3	5	10	18	23	35	39	53
Total	2	3	7	10	16	23	29	36
ALL	2	5	11	15	21	29	34	40

(d) *Differences in offence patterns of the boys.* Table 19 shows considerable differences in offence patterns of the boys. Boys resident in the inner city had a total of 102 convictions or cautions; boys resident in the suburbs a total of 44 convictions or cautions. Taking into account the higher boy-years at risk in the inner city, the offence rate per 100 BYAR is 6·16 for suburban boys, but 11·33 for the inner-city boys, nearly twice as many (chi-squared = 12·54 with 1 d.f. p <0·001).

Again, taking all boys in the low SH category and all boys in the severe SH category, irrespective of area, it will be seen that the "lows" have, in all, 14 convictions or cautions, whereas the boys in the severe category have 88 convictions or cautions. Expressed in terms of an offence rate per 100 BYAR this gives 2·8 for the low SH group and 15·1 for the severe SH group (chi-squared = 40·25 with 1 d.f., p <0·0001).

PARENTAL SUPERVISION: A NEGLECTED ASPECT OF DELINQUENCY

4. *Delinquency, social handicap and parental supervision among girls*

The number of delinquent girls is too small to deserve detailed analysis; there were six girls in the inner city and three in the suburbs. In all but two cases the girls had engaged in shoplifting. Two of these girls were aged 12, and one of them repeated the offence aged 13. Two girls were aged 15, one 16 and one 17. There were also two convictions for burglary, both together with an older brother; one of the girls was 12, the other 14. In the inner city two girls belonged to families whose supervision was "intermediate" and four girls to families whose supervision was "lax". In the suburbs, one girl belonged to the "intermediate" supervision group and the other two, sisters, to a family whose parenting methods were very strict. They were the only offenders in that family (aged 15 and 16), both having been caught together in a shop when trying to take a pair of gloves.

5. *Parental offences*

(a) *Offence patterns related to social handicap*. An investigation of family patterns of offending must include a section on parents' offences. Are parents with police records—either singly or both—more likely to have delinquent children? Commonsense would suggest that this is likely.

Offences include assault, burglary, robbery, shoplifting, taking cars without owners' consent, other thefts, handling stolen goods, criminal damage, forgery and fraud. The many non-indictable offences, mainly traffic but also drunkenness, are not included.

Table 18 shows offending and non-offending parents by social handicap. The number of convictions for each parent is shown in two groups: those with no more than two convictions, and those with three or more.

It will be seen that rather more than one-third of the families have a parent with a police record, the proportion being higher in the inner city

TABLE 18

Parental offences and social handicap

Social handicap:	Low		Moderate		Severe		Total
No. of offences:	1-2	3+	1-2	3+	1-2	3+	
INNER CITY							
Offenders							
Fathers only	6	1	4	—	4	5	
Mothers only	1	—	1	—	—	—	25
Both	—	—	—	1	1	1	
Non-offenders	12		14		9		35
SUBURBAN ESTATES							
Offenders							
Fathers only	3	—	5	2	2	4	
Mothers only	—	—	—	—	3	—	20
Both	—	—	—	1	—	—	
Non-offenders	17		12		11		40
COMBINED AREAS							
Offenders	11		14		20		45
Non-offenders	29		26		20		75
Total	40		40		40		120

HARRIETT WILSON

(42 per cent.) than in the suburbs (33 per cent.). The difference is not, however, significant. There also appears to be a trend with social handicap. The proportion of parents with a police record for low SH is 28 per cent. and for severe SH is 50 per cent.; but this also is not statistically significant. It is of some interest that the majority of parents with three or more convictions are in the severely socially handicapped group with ten families, whereas the low SH group has only one and the moderate SH group four families. As the number of parents with three or more offences is only 15 in all—one-third of all offending parents—they are taken together with parents having one or two offences in the following section.

(b) *Offence patterns and parental supervision.* It appears that the parents who have police records exercise less parental supervision than non-offending parents. The distribution by Parental Supervision Index is as follows:

Parental Supervision Index:	0	1	2	3	4	5	6	7	Total
	Strict		Intermed.		Lax				
Offenders	—	5	13	8	4	5	4	6	45
Non-offenders	7	12	22	17	7	4	4	2	75

(Splitting into two groups PSI 0–3 and 4–7 gives chi-squared with Yates' correction and 1 d.f. = 4·23, $p < 0.05$).

Because of the significantly greater proportion of lax parents among offenders (42 per cent. as against 23 per cent. among non-offenders) one should expect a higher degree of delinquency, if for no other reason. Table 19 shows the distribution in the two areas of delinquent boys, number of convictions (including cautions) and recidivist boys for the three social handicap groups and parental offenders and non-offenders. Overall, parents who are offenders produce significantly more delinquents than non-offenders ($p < 0.005$), and more juvenile convictions ($p < 0.0001$). The same is true taking the inner city as a whole and the suburbs as a whole (inner city: $p < 0.05$ and $p < 0.001$; suburbs: $p < 0.05$ and $p < 0.001$). Again, taking all severely socially handicapped families, parents who are offenders produce significantly more delinquents ($p < 0.025$) and more juvenile convictions ($p < 0.0001$). (An interesting exception from this trend is the group of moderately socially handicapped families in the inner city, where non-offending parents provide more juvenile convictions (but not more offenders) than expected. This is entirely due to one very delinquent family whose parents have no police record.)

6. *The effects of parental supervision, social handicap, and parental criminality*

The evidence so far presented has shown that delinquency increases with parental laxness, with social handicap, and with parental criminality. One is led to ask: is it possible to separate the three effects and to assess their relative importance? The standard statistical techniques would be partial correlation coefficients and analysis of variance, but for the present data two problems arise:

(1) The grading of the three factors is qualitative (ordered nominal) rather

PARENTAL SUPERVISION: A NEGLECTED ASPECT OF DELINQUENCY

TABLE 19

Parental offenders and non-offenders

Social handicap group	Families	BYAR	Delinquents	Boys' convictions	Recidivists
INNER CITY					
Low					
Parental offenders	8	74	3	3	—
non-offenders	12	180	3	3	—
Moderate					
Parental offenders	6	53	1	1	—
non-offenders	14	291	16	33	9
Severe					
Parental offenders	11	159	18	46	8
non-offenders	9	126	6	16	4
Total					
Parental offenders	25	286	22	50	8
non-offenders	35	597	25	52	13
SUBURBS					
Low					
Parental offenders	3	54	2	2	—
non-offenders	17	196	5	6	2
Moderate					
Parental offenders	8	58	3	8	2
non-offenders	12	109	1	2	1
Severe					
Parental offenders	9	133	11	17	4
non-offenders	11	164	8	9	1
Total					
Parental offenders	20	232	16	27	6
non-offenders	40	482	14	17	4
TOTAL SAMPLE					
Lows					
Parental offenders	11	128	5	5	—
non-offenders	29	376	8	9	2
Moderates					
Parental offenders	14	111	4	9	2
non-offenders	26	400	17	35	10
Severes					
Parental offenders	20	292	29	63	14
non-offenders	20	290	14	25	5
Total sample					
Parental offenders	45	518	38	77	16
non-offenders	75	1079	39	69	17
TOTALS	120	1597	77	146	33

than quantitative, which makes an analysis based on partial correlation coefficients open to question.

(2) The numbers in certain classifications are small, to an extent that raises doubts about the use of analysis of variance.

One is therefore led to adopt a simple commonsense approach. Table 19 gives the number of delinquents per 100 boy-years at risk for (a) the three categories of parental supervision, (b) the three categories of social handicap, and (c) the two categories of parental criminality. It will be seen that the delinquent rate in lax families is over seven times that in strict families;

HARRIETT WILSON

the rate in severely socially handicapped families is just under three times that in families with low social handicap; and the rate in families with a police record of parental criminality is just under twice that in families with no police record. One thus concludes that parental supervision is the most important single factor in determining juvenile delinquency, and that social handicap is probably more important than parental criminality. The three hypotheses on page 211 are confirmed.

TABLE 20

Delinquent rate analysed by parental supervision, social handicap, and parental criminality

Factor	Delinquents per 100 BYAR	Ratio of rates of extremes
Parental supervision		
All strict (0–1)	1·11	7·2 : 1
All intermediate (2–3)	4·12	
All lax (4–7)	7·98	
Social handicap		
All low	2·58	2·9 : 1
All moderate	4·11	
All severe	7·39	
Parental criminality		
All with no record	3·66	2·0 : 1
All with record	7·16	

Summary

A. For the boys, comparisons of the inner-city families with the suburban families have shown the following:

1. The total number of boys aged 10–17, who had been cautioned or convicted for serious offences, was 47 in the inner city and 30 in the suburbs; this is 20 per cent. of the total.

2. Delinquency rates are higher in the inner city than in the suburbs, but this trend is not statistically significant.

3. There is a significant increase of delinquency with increasing degree of social handicap. Of the 40 families with severe social handicap 25 have delinquent boys.

4. There is also a significant increase of delinquency with increasing parental laxness. Of the 24 " strict " families three have delinquent boys; but of the 36 " lax " families 23 have delinquent boys.

5. Of the 77 delinquent boys 47 are single offenders and 30 are recidivists. The suburban sample has too few recidivists for statistical testing; in the inner city there is a significant trend with social handicap and also with parental supervision.

6. There is a higher rate of convictions and cautions in the inner city than in the suburbs, and the trend with social handicap and with parental supervision is significant overall.

PARENTAL SUPERVISION: A NEGLECTED ASPECT OF DELINQUENCY

7. The peak age of entry into delinquency is age 15, with subsidiary peaks at age 12 and 17.

8. Following each boy from age 10 to the age attained when records were inspected, over one-quarter of 15-year-olds, and well over one-third of 17-year-olds had a police record. Taking the severely socially handicapped boys only, 55 per cent. of 15-year-olds in the inner city and 35 per cent. in the suburbs had a police record, and the rates for 17-year-olds were 62 and 53 respectively.

B. Among girls the rate of delinquency is much lower than among boys, and it is not possible to make any useful generalisations.

C. More than one-third of the 120 families have a parent with a police record, the proportion being higher among inner-city families (42 per cent.) than in the suburbs (33 per cent.). There is also a trend with social handicap; among the low socially handicapped group the proportion of parents with a police record is 28 per cent. and among the severe socially handicapped group it is 50 per cent.

Parents who have a police record tend to exercise less parental supervision than parents who are non-offenders.

Parents who are offenders produced 7·3 delinquents per 100 boy-years at risk and non-offenders produced 3·6, half that rate. The sons of offenders have a higher conviction rate (including cautions) than the sons of non-offenders.

The contrasts between parents with and without police records are sharpest on comparing inner-city families as a whole, or the severely socially handicapped families as a whole.

D. The effect of parental supervision is more important than the effect of social handicap on juvenile behaviour in areas with high offender rates.

Conclusions

The preceding section attempted a statistical analysis of the association of methods of parenting and the behaviour patterns of children. It showed the likelihood of delinquency occurring when parental supervision is lax, but it did not attempt to show—and indeed the data would not have permitted it—that delinquency is inevitable in areas with high offender rates when parenting methods are lax. All that can be said is that it is probable. The present study was designed to test the findings of a previous study and to investigate whether there were exceptions to them under different conditions. The important variations were the inclusion of less deprived neighbourhoods and of less deprived families. The association of delinquency with laxness of parental supervision was confirmed, irrespective of place of residence and degree of social handicap. There was, however, a difference in relation to place of residence. Although the *offender* rate was not significantly related to neighbourhood, there was a noticeable difference in *offence* patterns: in the inner city there was a significantly higher rate of offences than in the suburbs.

HARRIETT WILSON

One can thus state with some confidence that parents who are lax in the supervision they give their children are highly likely to produce delinquents in areas that have high offender rates. Saying this, however, does not provide an answer to the question: " Why is this association highly likely?" Walker (1977), in an essay on the nature of explanation, asks what it is that makes people seek an explanation of any particular occurrence and suggests that " Almost always it is surprise: an encounter with something contrary to expectation ". In the context of our research findings the element of surprise is not contained in the nature of the findings as such, for one would consider them to be quite commonsense, but in the fact that so little attention has been paid to this factor in criminological studies. It is true that the Gluecks had employed some crude measures of the adequacy of maternal supervision as one of a number of indices which they hoped would form part of a theory explaining delinquency and crime in general. West and Farrington (1973, pp. 55–56) paid closer attention to parental supervision in a longitudinal study of a cohort of working-class school boys, and found that social workers' ratings of parental rules and " vigilance " showed an association with delinquency. However, in spite of this association, delinquents and non-delinquents did not differ significantly once family income or parental criminality were taken into account. As a result parental supervision was dropped from the analysis in favour of a general social handicap factor. West's comments on this decision are pertinent in the context of our findings: " It may be that in our study the parental supervision ratings were based on insufficiently precise criteria and hence subject to class bias. The findings illustrate yet again the extreme difficulty of distinguishing between aspects of family life that are in practice closely interlinked ". (*ibid.* p. 56).

The difficulty of distinguishing statistically between supervision and degree of social handicap has been an equally vexing problem in our study, and it is precisely for this reason that we will now proceed to a different kind of explanation of the processes that we believe to be at work in the generation of delinquency in high-crime areas. Walker refers to it as the " narrative kind " of explanation which " should take over part of the territory from scientific explanations, especially in the field of human behaviour ". Scientific explanations may tell us about necessary conditions for this or that kind of misbehaviour, but " it will be left to a narrative to tell how this *can* happen " (*ibid.* p. 141).

In homes where parents exercise supervision it is difficult for children to join in the delinquent activities of their peers as a regular entertainment, even though they may get away with an occasional escapade or they may be tempted to engage in occasional shoplifting. Strictly supervising parents tend to explain their attitude not just in prescriptive terms (" Don't do this and don't do that "), but primarily in terms of critical assessments of other children's behaviour of which they do not approve. In using the technique of labelling other people's children as bad these parents do not just indicate their disapproval of delinquent behaviour, but at the same time they personalise the problem. The child receives two messages: first, that certain forms of behaviour are undesirable, and secondly, that certain boys are not

PARENTAL SUPERVISION: A NEGLECTED ASPECT OF DELINQUENCY

behaving in a manner that would warrant closer acquaintance. The way of living of the delinquent boys is denigrated and simultaneously the position of the strictly supervised boy is elevated to a status which debars him from close contact with those who do not know their manners. The fact that adolescents in homes with a strict regime are relatively unaffected by delinquency indicates that the message is internalised. The technique of strict supervision of the younger child turns into self-imposed control; he prefers not to mix with boys whose behaviour he disdains and whose style of life has nothing in common with his own.

Methods which rely heavily on status-related values are handled more happily by people who have a degree of self-confidence and status-consciousness. To interpret the failings of others as personality inadequacies comes naturally to the minds of persons who strive to conquer their own tendencies to fail. But persons who are imbued with a sense of failure, that may be rooted in a memory of family failure, may have different motivations. Their experiences may have taught them to adopt a different attitude; they may have calculated the risks and rewards of offending and may have exploited opportunities that came their way. We found parents who had police records to be less communicative about their attitudes to delinquency or, if willing to discuss the matter, tending to blame other children. They tended to be more concerned about " getting in trouble " themselves through the delinquent behaviour of their children, and they believed that, with luck, they might not.

Parental methods were not always consciously formulated or even clearly recognised as in any way determining their children's conduct. This was particularly the case among severely socially handicapped families who tended to use techniques of child-rearing which they had always practised and from which they saw no reason to depart. Greater awareness was noticeable among families who had experienced changes of circumstances or environment and who had acquired the means to change their life-styles.

The hesitation, expressed in the first section of this paper, in establishing a causal relationship between parental supervision and delinquency stems from the justified suspicion that the findings may be exploited in corrective terms. It appears that not the children but the parents are to blame for delinquent behaviour. What is more, in the current state of knowledge about the ineffectiveness of various forms of treatment of offenders, it may be considered worthwhile to make the parents the focus of corrective programmes, either educative or punitive. Both are already subject to public discussion and the findings of our study might lend additional force to the argument supporting parental education or parental culpability. It is for that reason that we emphasise our disagreement with any attempts to use the material presented in this paper in such a manner.

The essential point of our findings is the very close association of lax parenting methods with severe social handicap. Lax parenting methods are often the result of chronic stress, situations arising from frequent or prolonged spells of unemployment, physical or mental disabilities among members of the family, and an often permanent condition of poverty (Wilson,

233

HARRIETT WILSON

1974). If these factors are ignored and parental laxness is seen instead as an "attitude" which can be shifted by education or by punitive measures, then our findings are being misinterpreted. It is the position of the most disadvantaged groups in society, and not the individual, which needs improvement in the first place.

There are, however, parents in less disadvantaged positions who are also employing lax methods of supervision. The problem in this kind of family is a different one. Many parents who are more consciously engaged in the upbringing of their children are strongly influenced by the current trends towards more permissive methods. The modern parent often sees himself or herself as an "enabler" whose main task is to develop an orientation towards the child's self-determination. The negative aspect of this movement lies in the failure to acknowledge the principle of reciprocity in parent-child relationships and the duty of the child to develop a responsible attitude towards others. This understanding of parental tasks, which equally affects educators, has led to a preoccupation with techniques of child-rearing methods at the expense of the objectives which should be the aim of the socialisation of children. The many young parents who have benefited from improved standards of living and have "shopped around" for new ways of handling their children in an endeavour to give them what they themselves never had in childhood are particularly at risk in adopting permissive methods of what they understand to be "child-centredness" without fully realising the dangers inherent in setting no limits to their children's choices. What is needed is a redefinition of the rights and responsibilities of parents and children in the light of current trends towards juvenile insubordination, but this is a long-term objective which should not be directed only at parents of delinquent children but which concerns the entire community.

REFERENCES

BALDWIN, J. (1974). "Problem housing estates—perception of tenants, city officials and criminologists", *Social and Economic Administration*, 8, 116-135.

BALDWIN, J. and BOTTOMS, A. E. (1976). *The Urban Criminal*; London: Tavistock Publications.

BELSON, W. A. (1968). "The extent of stealing by London boys and some of its origins," *Advancement of Science*, 25, No. 124, 171-184.

CLARK, J. P. and WENNINGER, E. P. (1962). "Socio-economic class and area as correlates of illegal behaviour among juveniles," *American Sociological Review*, 27, 826-834.

CLARKE, R. V. G. (1978) (ed.). *Tackling Vandalism*; Home Office Research Study, No. 47, London: HMSO.

FARRINGTON, D. P. (1973). "Self-reports of deviant behaviour: predictive and stable?" *Journal of Criminal Law and Criminology*, 64, 99-110.

GIBSON, H. B. (1967). "Self-reported delinquency among schoolboys and their attitudes to the police," *British Journal of Social and Clinical Psychology*, 6, 168-173.

PARENTAL SUPERVISION: A NEGLECTED ASPECT OF DELINQUENCY

GLADSTONE, F. J. (1978). In Clarke, R. V. G. *Tackling Vandalism*, Home Office Research Study, 47; London: HMSO.

HEAL, K. and PERRY, J. Unpublished research; Home Office Research Unit.

HOLTERMAN, SALLY (1975). " Areas of urban deprivation in Great Britain: an analysis of 1971 census data," Department of Environment, *Social Trends*, 6; London: HMSO.

HOOD, R. and SPARKS, R. (1970). *Key Issues in Criminology*; London: Weidenfeld and Nicholson.

McDONALD, L. (1969). *Social Class and Delinquency*; London: Faber and Faber.

NEWSON, J. and E. (1968). *Four Years Old in an Urban Community*; London: Allen and Unwin.

NEWSON, J. and E. (1976). *Seven Years Old in the Home Environment*; London: Allen and Unwin.

NEWSON, J. and E. (1977). *Perspectives on School at Seven Years Old*; London: Allen and Unwin.

PEARCE, D. and BRITTON, M. (1977). " The decline in births: some socio-economic aspects", *Population Trends*, No. 7; London: HMSO.

THE PLOWDEN REPORT (1967). Central Advisory Council for Education, *Children and their Primary Schools*; London: HMSO.

SHAPLAND, J. (1978). " Self-reported delinquency in boys aged 11 to 14 ", *British Journal of Criminology*, 18, 255–266.

WALKER, N. (1978). *Behaviour and Misbehaviour: Explanations and Non-explanations*; Oxford: Blackwell.

WEST, D. J. and FARRINGTON, D. P. (1973). *Who Becomes Delinquent?*; London: Heinemann.

WILSON, HARRIETT (1974). " Parenting in poverty", *British Journal of Social Work*, 4, 241–254.

WILSON, HARRIETT (1975). " Juvenile delinquency, parental criminality and social handicap", *British Journal of Criminology*, 15, 241–250.

WILSON, HARRIETT and HERBERT, G. W. (1974). " Social deprivation and performance at school", *Policy and Politics*, 3, 55–69.

WILSON, HARRIETT and HERBERT, G. W. (1978). *Parents and Children in the Inner City*; London: Routledge & Kegan Paul.

WILSON, SHEENA and BURBRIDGE, M. (1978). " An investigation of difficult to let housing", *Housing Review*, July–August.

Separations [12]

British Journal of Psychiatry (1988), **152**, 80-90

Social and Parenting Factors Affecting Criminal-Offence Rates
Findings from the Newcastle Thousand Family Study (1947–1980)

I. KOLVIN, F. J. W. MILLER, M. FLEETING and P. A. KOLVIN

A rare opportunity to study deprivation and criminality across generations arose from the follow-up of the families who participated in the Newcastle Thousand Family Survey. The data on these families had been preserved and it was possible, using criminal records, to examine longitudinally whether children who grew up in 'deprived' rather than 'non-deprived' families were more at risk of offending during later childhood and beyond. The results of this study suggest that this is indeed so.

The thousand family survey

The study commenced in 1947 when the families of all the 1142 infants, from 1132 families, born in the city between 1 May and 30 June, were enrolled in an observer study of the incidence and types of illness in the first year of life. (Spence *et al*, 1954; Miller *et al*, 1960, 1974).

Throughout the school years, 1952–1962, records of growth were collected, and school behaviour and achievement were documented. After 1962, the systematic visiting of all the families ceased, but certain items of data, such as selective education, entry to employment, and contact with the law, were collected. At the end of the first, fifth, tenth, and fifteenth years, there were extensive analyses of the data on all families remaining in the study. The data from the 15-year analysis form the basis of the third volume written about the survey (Miller *et al*, 1974), and of the present work.

Following Sir Keith Joseph's 'Cycle of Deprivation' Speech in 1972, it was suggested that the records of the Thousand Family Study might be used as a basis for a study of the 'transmission' of deprivation. A follow-up study was conducted between 1979 and 1981 (the findings of which are now in preparation), and as part of that study, the authors of this paper were granted access to the relevant criminal records for data relating to the 847 families still in the study in 1952. The reason for focusing on the 847 families was that, during the first 5 years, extensive social data had been collected, upon which our definition of deprivation depended. For this reason, these families constituted the baseline cohort for this study. Only any further attrition from this cohort is of consequence to the findings reported in this paper.

The 1979–1981 study

Criteria of deprivation

Data on family deprivation relating to the 'Red Spots'* first

---

*Because all documents pertaining to the above study were identified by a small red legal seal, the index children became widely and popularly called 'Red Spots' and the term is useful for descriptive purposes.

5 years of life were collected and have been described elsewhere (Miller *et al*, 1960). In the current follow-up study, six categories of family deprivation – details of which are reported elsewhere (Kolvin *et al*, 1983) – were employed. All children were given a score of 0 or 1 in each category and their scores were added to give a total deprivation rating as shown in Table I. Definitions of these criteria are available in previous publications (Kolvin *et al*, 1983; Miller *et al*, 1985).

Sub-samples of the families were then isolated for special study, with three main objectives: firstly, to compare a sample representative of *all* the deprived families with a sample in which there was no evidence of deprivation; secondly, in order to observe the effects of severe deprivation by identifying a multiply deprived group; thirdly, by categorising families by type of deprivation, to examine the effect of each type separately. The following shows how the sub-groups were defined and what percentage of the trial cohort fell into each. It is to be noted that there is an overlap which was unavoidable – mutually exclusive groups could not have satisfied the objectives listed above.

(a) Not deprived; families in which there was no evidence of deprivation (57%).

(b) Deprived group; families deprived in at least one respect (43%).

(c) Multiply deprived; families deprived in at least three respects (14%).

Hypotheses

The main hypotheses under investigation were that:

(i) Underprivileged family environments are associated with criminal behaviour during the school years and thereafter.

(ii) Specific criteria of deprivation are associated with different patterns of criminality so that certain indices of social and family deprivation will have more harmful influences than others.

(iii) The greater the number of criteria of deprivation in a family, the greater the risk of offending.

TABLE I

Numbers of families studied in 1952 and 1957 when their children were 5 and 10 years of age with deprivation according to the specified criteria at the 5th year

	Year/total n			
	1952/847		1957/812	
	n	Percentage	n	Percentage
(a) Degree of deprivation				
(i) Not deprived	482	57	477	59
(ii) Any deprivation (one or more criteria)	365	43	335	41
(iii) One or two criteria	249	29	229	28
(iv) Multiple deprivation (three or more criteria)	116	14	106	13
			(iii) and (iv) are included in (ii)	
(b) Type of deprivation				
(i) Marital instability	123	15	112	14
(ii) Parental illness	103	12	88	11
(iii) Poor domestic and physical care of the children and homes	107	13	98	12
(iv) Social dependency	148	17	130	16
(v) Overcrowding	158	19	148	18
(vi) Poor mothering ability	129	15	120	15

The present study

In 1952, as stated above, 847 of the original families remained in the survey. The main loss between 1947 and 1952 had been by removal from the city. In addition, 45 children had died and 11 had contracted out of the survey, but remained in the city. The nature of the study at that time precluded any attempt to retain links with those families who had moved from the city. A further 35 families moved by 1957, leaving 812 at the time of the 10th year of analysis.

In the subsequent study, during 1979–1981, of the transmission of deprivation in a random stratified sample of 296 index children (Red Spots), 96% of those who were alive were traced; any criminal records theoretically were accessible. It is to be noted that in this follow-up, efforts were also made to trace families from this cohort who had moved from the city between 1952 and 1962, as, if the full sample of 847 Red Spots as adults is used, without correction for losses, as the base population, then prevalence rates for offences are likely to be under-estimated. Furthermore, in the follow-up study, more Red Spots were lost to the base population from deprived families than from other families (Kolvin et al, 1983). Eventually, as we had deprivation data on our 847 families, it seemed sensible to use them as the base population when studying rates of offending and apply the appropriate correction factor. The latter was achieved by using as a notional denominator, when calculating offence rates, the 812 Red Spots still living in Newcastle in 1957. This is equivalent to 4% attrition, subject to the uneven distribution noted above. The details of the 812 families when the Red Spots were 10 years of age are given in Table I.

Results

(a) Contact with the Law –
findings reported in the previous study

The third report of the study (Miller et al, 1974) contained an account of the offences by index children up to 18½ years. By their 15th year, 67 had offended, increasing to 98 by their 17th birthdays and 126 at age 18½ (Table II). By their 17th birthday, 22% of boys had offended, nearly 4% having four or more offences (Table II). In contrast, only 2.4% of girls had offended by 15 years and 3.7% by 17 years. In the 1960s, offences committed before the age of 17 years gave rise either to cautions or were considered in the juvenile courts. The above-mentioned data were gathered from local police records.

From the official criminal records (CRO data), we also had information on convictions in adult life for 106 families. When the CRO data and the '1000 Family' records were cross-referenced, some discrepancies were noted – it was known that the former source contained information about both juvenile and adult convictions of Red Spots who had moved away, or offences committed away from the immediate locale of Newcastle. On the other hand, the CRO records would have been reduced by the process of 'weeding', which consists of deleting records of relatively minor offences and also records about cautioning prior to age 17. The '1000 Family' material had not been exposed to the process of 'weeding' and therefore probably provided a fuller account of offences up to the age of 18 years occurring within or near Newcastle. Combinations of data from these two sources provided a best estimate of lifetime offence rates, although this did not coincide precisely with official listings of delinquency or criminality. We grouped

KOLVIN ET AL

TABLE II
Delinquency: children appearing in court before 18½ years of age from 380 boys and 380 girls in Newcastle upon Tyne 1947–1965

	One				Two	Three	Four or more
	Boys		Girls				
	n	Percentage	n	Percentage	Boys	Boys	Boys
By 15th birthday	58	15	9	2.4	6.5%	3.2%	2.2%
By 17th birthday	83	22	14	3.7	9.5%	4.6%	3.7%
By 18½ years	105	28	21	5.5	13%	7.8%	5.3%

Only three girls had more than one appearance before November 1965.
Adapted from Miller *et al* (1974)

our data according to offences committed before and after the age of 15 years.

(b) Incidence of criminality based on Home Office–CRO records: males and females

The incidence of offences committed by the age of 33 years, based on information from Home Office criminal record data, was 13.1% (*n* = 106). This data was analysed according to the degree and type of deprivation in the families and shows that rates of criminality increase markedly with the degree of deprivation, with a more than four-fold increase from 6.3% (*n* = 30) for the non-deprived group to 29.2% (*n* = 31) for the multiply deprived group, with the rate for the deprived group with one or two criteria being 19.2% (*n* = 44). The rates for individuals subject to the six different types of deprivation also varied from 21% of those exposed to marital disruption to 33% for those from homes with poor domestic care and lack of cleanliness. The rate of offences for males and females proved very different, being five times higher in males. The above figures are unlikely to include offences committed during the school years, particularly cautions, which are expunged at 17 years, and other minor offences which, through the process of 'weeding', are deleted from the criminal records. Finally, an important question is the extent to which these findings were influenced by the inclusion of minor motoring offences in the records. Examination of the criminal record data indicates that, in Newcastle, over the 20-year period from 1962 to 1981, the contribution proved to be rather marginal – in only seven of the 106 cases was a motoring offence considered to be the principal offence. In every one of these seven cases there was another associated indictable offence.

(c) Incidence of offences derived from combining the two different sources of information ('1000 Families' and CRO data)

Having combined the two sources of information as described above, and excluding the non-indictable cycling/motoring offences – it is to be noted that these did not appear in the CRO records unless the person had an existing

criminal offence – we obtained an estimate of total offences in our 847 families (Table III). It is noteworthy that of the 35 Red Spots from the families who moved away from Newcastle between 1952 and 1957 no less than 14 (40%) had been convicted by the age of 32. We found this surprising and difficult to explain, as Osborn (1980) found that moving from London (i.e. away from a large city) led to a decrease in delinquency.

Of 83 persons offending prior to the minimum school leaving age of that period, three quarters went on to commit further offences after that age. In addition, a further 66 individuals appeared in the criminal records for the first time after the age of 15. This gives a total of 149 offenders – rates by the 15th birthday of 10.2%, after 15 and up to 33 years of age 15.9% and, finally, anytime up to 33 years, 18.3%.

At all ages, convictions were overwhelmingly of males. Thus, by the age of 33, more than one in every four males had offended, but only about one in twenty females. The proportions of males varied according to the degree of deprivation, ranging from one in six of males from non-deprived families, to six in ten of males from multiply-deprived families. However, some forms of deprivation appear to have stronger associations with the offences than others, running at about five in ten of families where there was marital disruption or parental illness to six in every ten families with lack of cleanliness and poor quality of mothering.

We thus ascertained the proportion of individuals in various deprived groups. Considering what proportion of offenders suffered deprivation in their early years, we see in Table III that about a fifth of the male delinquents experienced parental illness and marital disharmony in their homes, and about a third, overcrowding, social dependency, and poor mothering. It is interesting to note that the rates of such deprivations are at much higher levels for female offenders, running at about a half in the case of social dependency and about two fifths in the case of over-crowding and marital disruption.

Next, we looked to see whether there were differences in rates of deprivation for those who committed their first offence before the age of 15 as compared with those who committed their first offence after that age. Table IV

DEPRIVATION AFFECTING CRIMINAL OFFENCE RATES   83

TABLE III
Offence rates in the base cohort of 847 families (corrected for losses)[1]

Overall number of offenders from 812 males and females (five non-indictable motoring offences are included)		
By 15th birthday	83	(10.2%)
After 15th birthday	129	(15.9%)
Either	149	(18.3%)[2]
Offence rate (according to severity of deprivation and sex of offender)		
(a) All males	125 from 404	(30.9%)[3]
All females	24 from 408	(5.9%)[4]
(b) Males in non-deprived families	40 from 226	(17.7%)[5]
(c) Males from all deprived families	85 from 178	(47.8%)[6]
(d) Males in families with multiple deprivation [overlaps with (c)]	35 from 53	(66.0%)

Offence rate (according to type of deprivation – males only)		Deprivation suffered by offenders			
		Males ($n = 125$)		Females ($n = 24$)	
Non-deprived families	17.7%	—		—	
Deprived families showing:					
Marital disruption	52.8%	28	(22%)**	10	(42%)***
Parental illness	51.1%	23	(18%)*	7	(29%)**
Poor physical/domestic care	67.3%	33	(26%)***	7	(29%)*
Social dependency	59.4%	38	(30%)***	12	(50%)***
Overcrowding	55.8%	43	(34%)***	9	(38%)***
Poor quality mothering	60.9%	39	(31%)**	8	(33%)**

1. Deprivation was assessed in 1952 when the children were 5 years old.
Numbers of non-indictable motoring offences included: 2. five; 3. four; 4. one; 5. one; 6. three.
Significance of difference from non-offenders: *$P \leqslant 0.05$; **$P \leqslant 0.01$; ***$P \leqslant 0.001$.

TABLE IV
Proportions of 125 offenders from 279 males who experienced deprivation in early childhood

	Numbers of males (%)					
	Non offenders	First offences before 15 years	First offences after 15 years	Total	Chi-squared	P
With criteria of deprivation	279	67	58	404		
Breakdown of criteria						
Marital instability	25 (9.0)	20 (29.9)	8 (13.8)	53	21.4	<0.001
Parental illness	22 (7.9)	19 (28.4)	4 (6.9)	45	20.2	<0.001
Poor physical/domestic care of children/home	16 (5.7)	18 (26.9)	15 (25.9)	49	30.3	<0.001
Social dependency	26 (9.3)	24 (35.8)	14 (24.1)	64	25.3	<0.001
Overcrowding	34 (12.2)	25 (37.3)	18 (31.0)	77	27.1	<0.001
Poor mothering	25 (9.0)	18 (26.9)	21 (36.2)	64	30.8	<0.001

shows a number of interesting findings. Firstly, while those who committed their first offence after 15 had seldom been exposed to marital instability or parental illness in their pre-school years, those who committed their first offence before 15 had often had such experiences. Secondly, both groups had been exposed to significantly high rates of poor physical and domestic care and mothering ability as children, compared with those with no convictions. Thirdly, offenders experienced higher rates of social dependency and overcrowding in childhood than non-offenders, with the tendency for the effect to be stronger in the case of social dependency before 15 years than after.

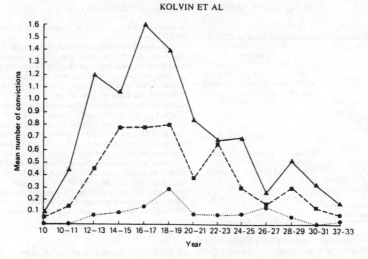

FIG. 1 Mean number of convictions at each age band for Red Spot males calculated in relation to the total population (*n* = 404).
▲ —— ▲ , multiply deprived (*n* = 53); ■ --- ■ , deprived (*n* = 178); ●···●, not deprived (*n* = 226).

(d) From youth to adulthood

Because the great majority of charges were brought against males, the rates for all males were not greatly different from the overall rates. It was found that nearly half of those charged after 15 years of age had already been charged before that age (52 out of 110 = 47%), and few of those who committed no offence after 15 years had committed an offence before (15 out of 294 = 5%). Males who were charged with offences before the age of 15 had a three in four chance of being charged again by the age of 33 years (52 out of 67 = 78%), but those who had not been charged by 15 years had only a one in six likelihood of being charged by 33 years (58 from 337 = 17%). It is to be noted that the above rates are estimates based on the notional denominator of 404 males.

(e) Female offenders

Only 24 females (5.9%) were charged with offences – a much lower incidence than for males: only 2% of girls in the non-deprived, but 9% in the deprived, and 15% in the multiply deprived groups. A steeper rise in the number of convictions as the level of deprivation increases was thus noted for girls (four and a half and seven times the non-deprived figure for the deprived and multiply deprived groups respectively), compared with boys (three and four times).

(f) Mean number of convictions in relation to age (males and criminal record data only)

The mean numbers of offences committed by males at each age to 33 years are set out in Fig. 1. The numbers have been calculated in relation to the degree of deprivation the individual experienced at 5 years of age. The picture is clear: the rates in pre-puberty (10 and 11 years) are low; then there is a steep rise through the teens (13–19) with the peak at 16–17 years. The rate then falls away, and at 32–33 years is almost as low as at the 10-year level. The three curves, representing each of the sample's sub-groups, soon diverge after age 10 but from 26–27 to 32–33 years they again converge. At every age band before 26 years those with multiple deprivation have the highest score, the deprived are intermediate, and the non-deprived the lowest. Each group has a small secondary peak between 26 and 29 years.

The differences in offence rates according to severity of deprivation give rise to a gradient not only of percentages of individuals who commit offences, but also of the mean number of offences for the whole of that population. After the age of 30 the mean number of offences committed in every group is very low.

(g) Analysis of data from Home Office Criminal records (males and females)

Since the official records have been subjected to 'weeding', the rate of offences over the period at risk based on such records should be regarded as minimal. Calculations were made from a notional population of 812 families, on the basis of 477 non-deprived individuals, 335 deprived, and 106 multiply deprived. For the principal offences of violence, sexual attacks, criminal damage, and fraud/forgery, the rates are all low, with the highest being a 3% rate of violence in the multiply deprived group. Only burglary, robbery, and theft (combined) show a gradient – mounting from 20 offences for the 477 non-deprived (= 4%) to 23 for the 106 multiply deprived families (= 22%).

TABLE V
Basic data concerning male convictions based on CRO data

	Families		
	Not deprived (n = 226)	All deprived (n = 178)	Multiply deprived (n = 53)
Number of males with criminal (CRO) records up to age of 32/33	27 (11.9%)	62 (34.8%)	27 (50.9%)
Number of offences			
1–5	20 (9%)	36 (20%)	14 (26%)
6–10	3 (1%)	9 (5%)	5 (9%)
11 or more	4 (2%)	17 (10%)	8 (15%)
Mean number of offences	0.7	2.9	5.1
Mean time incarcerated (in months)	7.9	13.9	20.9
Mean age in years at first court appearance	19.4	18.2	16.7

Known other offences, which are those additional to the principal offences, have been summed. There are some small increases in the percentage occurrence in the deprived over the non-deprived group – e.g. rates for the non-deprived, deprived, and multiply deprived groups are of 1%, 4%, and 8% respectively for criminal damage; and for taking and driving away 1%, 5%, and 10% respectively. However, none of the differences are significant except the item 'all other theft' where the rates are 3%, 13%, and 21% respectively. We also found that the multiply deprived group not only has a higher percentage of offences but also a higher percentage of repeated offences (see Table V).

These different offences were studied in relation to the six criteria of deprivation experienced in the early years of life. They were listed according to the highest and lowest rates of the different types of deprivation, and the following patterns emerged:

Offence	Highest percentage	Lowest percentage
Violence	Poor care/cleanliness of child and home	Parent illness
Criminal damage	Poor care/cleanliness of child and home	Parent illness
Fraud/ forgery	Social dependence	Parent illness
Theft	Poor care/cleanliness of child and home	Marital instability
Drink	Poor care/cleanliness of child and home	Over-crowding
Motoring	Poor care/cleanliness of child and home	Over-crowding

Despite what appear to be small differences between the groups with the highest and lowest rates, the findings suggest that poor care/cleanliness of child and home were the most powerful adverse influence in the family of origin, and parental illness and overcrowding were the least adverse – particularly in relation to different types of offences.

We examined a selection of offences for males, and these showed a more distinctive pattern. There was now a clear gradient of increase from non-deprived to multiply deprived on most offences, suggesting that all types increase in relation to the severity of deprivation in the family of origin. This was particularly true of theft. The pattern was confirmed by the characteristics of offences for males only (Table V) – this showed a steep increase in the mean number of convictions and mean time in custody, according to the degree of deprivation. There is also a decrease in the mean age at first Court appearance by more than 2 years from the non-deprived to the much deprived.

Finally, we used the profile approach developed by Gunn (Gunn & Robertson, 1976) to ascertain if any of the different types of deprivation were associated with a distinctive profile of offences. No such distinctions were found, except that high rates of theft and low rates of drug offences occurred broadly in all deprived groups.

(h) Family factors

(i) Some social factors and offending rates

The offence rates of the Red Spots in relation to occupational class of the fathers when the Red Spots were 5 years old were analysed. A close relationship was found between offence rates and lower occupational status, rising from 3% of those from social classes I and II, to 27% of those from social classes IV and V. The association is even stronger in the case of males only – 5% from occupational classes I and II, 26% from social class III, and 42% from social classes IV and V plus. Another way of looking at the data for both males and females is to look at non-offenders and offenders separately. Of the non-offenders, 12% came from occupational classes I and II, 55% from III, and 33% from the lowest occupational strata. The percentages for the offenders are 2%, 42%, and 56% respectively. The offenders tended to come from larger sibships, with a mean family size of 3.5 overall and 3.7 for males as compared with 2.6 overall and 2.5 for males who were not offenders. There was also more unemployment among the fathers of the offending groups.

(ii) Parental personality factors (Table VI)

Parental characteristics had been described and analysed in 1962, by which time the study team had known the families for 15 years and had long acquaintance of the dominant character traits of both the mothers and fathers of the Red Spot children. This present analysis showed that male offenders more often had parents who were characterised as 'ineffective', i.e. who did not cope with family matters, and they were also slightly more likely to have aggressive fathers, and less likely to have parents who were 'effective and kind'.

(i) Comment

Similar associations were described by Miller *et al* (1974) in relation to family factors, and juvenile delinquency

86   KOLVIN ET AL

TABLE VI

Predominant character traits of parents in relation to male Red Spots committing offences (assessed when subjects were aged 15 years)

Predominant characteristics of parents in relation to the care of children and the family	Non-criminal sons (n = 255)	Criminal sons (n = 111)
Effective and kind		
Father	123 (48%)	22 (20%)
Mother	90 (35%)	25 (23%)
Ineffective but kind		
Father	46 (18%)	31 (28%)
Mother	27 (11%)	38 (34%)
Aggressive		
Father	46 (18%)	32 (29%)
Mother	47 (18%)	18 (16%)
Anxious		
Father	5 (2%)	2 (2%)
Mother	71 (28%)	11 (10%)
Others (includes non-applicable)		
Father	35 (14%)	24 (22%)
Mother	20 (8%)	19 (17%)

The above data have not been corrected for losses.

defined as contact with the law. The present data reconfirms the well-known social origins of delinquency and criminality both in terms of poor occupational gradings of the breadwinner, unemployment, and large family size. But these are not the only origins – parental personalities also seem to play an important part.

Discussion

The Newcastle work is a longitudinal study and therefore has all the strengths of this design, but is also subject to a number of disadvantages. Thus it was not possible to study changes in the patterns of delinquency at different periods of time. An example of this is the relative increase in female delinquency over the last 25 years leading to an alteration in the male: female ratio for delinquency (Rutter & Giller, 1983). Furthermore, the longer the period covered by research, the greater the likelihood that results will reflect temporal changes occurring in a society which imposes limits on their analysis and interpretation. Rutter (1979) points to some of the difficulties: for example, alterations in law may entail certain behaviour moving in or out of the ambit of criminal law; criminal statistics are affected by the level of police activity: police treatment for offenders does

not remain constant; and the opportunity to commit crime is affected by social phenomena like the increase in the total number of self-service stores and motor vehicles. On the other hand, as the population of Red Spots is an age cohort, both the criminals and non-criminals were simultaneously exposed to the widespread changes in society, particularly the increase in frequency of criminal acts and the variations in police processing of delinquent acts which have occurred in the past 30 years.

Criminal records as a data source

In studying delinquency, it is axiomatic that a truer measure of delinquency will be obtained by relatively contemporaneous interviews than by a study of official records. Firstly, official records under-represent the true extent of criminal behaviour. Self-report surveys show that less than 15% of criminal acts result in police contact (West & Farrington, 1977). Even when police contact is made, the processing of the individual concerned may well vary according to the offender's age, sex, race, and previous record (Landau, 1981 – a study of 1603 police decisions on juveniles in London). Secondly, official-record studies fail to recognise the offence or conviction as merely one facet of a delinquent life-style. For example, the Cambridge study showed official delinquents at 18 to be almost uniformly at the socially deviant end of the spectrum with an excess of alcohol problems, driving offences, sexual experience, unemployment, poor family relationships, and anti-establishment attitudes (Farrington, 1979). It also needs to be borne in mind that while the majority of young people have committed delinquent acts, only a small minority enter the criminal records (Rutter & Giller, 1983).

Our work has been confined to the use of criminal records both to establish the incidence and the types of juvenile and adult indictable offences. We have examined each of the original records and have confirmed that in over 90% we are dealing with the most delinquent and serious criminal acts committed by the cohort over the years from 1957–1981. While we accept that there is much criminal behaviour which cannot be identified by surveys of criminal records, this latter method is free from the distortions which can occur in studies relying on self reports where there is a tendency to higher rates of non-response in delinquent populations (Rutter & Giller, 1983).

Prevalence rates

Another strength of the Newcastle research is that it comprised an entire birth cohort for a city, with delinquency data collected until the individuals were 32–33 years of age. It therefore constitutes one of a small number of longitudinal surveys of crime in this country and has provided a record of the prevalence of offending individuals from childhood to the age of 32–33 years. This period covers the main period of risk for new offences, for after the age of 33 years the rate declines.

As discussed above, Miller *et al* (1974) found that, considering the rates of offences up to the age of 15 years, then 17 years and, finally, 18½ years, for 760 individuals who had remained in the city, by the age of 18½, more than one in four of the boys had offended, but only about one in twenty of the girls (Table II).

We updated the figures to include adult criminality data and additional juvenile data, as described above.

Three quarters of delinquents offending before the minimum school-leaving age (15) of their time went on to commit further offences after that age. Sixty-six offended for the first time after the age of 15. From the total population of 847, 149 (10.2%) offended by their 15th birthday, 15.9% between 15–33 years, and 18.3% at any time up to 33 years (corrected for losses – see Table III). Both before and after 15 years of age the convictions were overwhelmingly due to offences commited by males; 31% of the men had been charged by the age of 33 but only 6% of the women.

It is noteworthy how closely the local rates, despite differences of definition and inclusion criteria, approximate the national prevalence rates of convictions of males born in 1953 of 31% up to the age of 28 and of females of 6% (Home Office, April 1985). The latter statistics take no account of convictions not included on the Home Office standard list – for instance, it excludes less serious motoring offences, drunkenness, prostitution, and persons cautioned by the police. To date, the best measure of juvenile criminality within one cohort is the Cambridge team's study of 411 boys aged 8–9 years taken from six state primary schools in a working-class area of London in 1961–1962. One in five of the group had been convicted as a juvenile, and nearly one in three by 24 years of age (West, 1982). Farrington (1981) estimated life-time prevalence by using official statistics based on a random sample showing estimated numbers of first convictions in each age group. He simply added the first-time conviction rate at each age group and concluded that about one third to one half of males acquire a criminal record during their lifetimes.

Despite following our cohort to 32–33 years of age, the rates fell short of Farrington's (1979, 1981)

estimates: he followed his cohort to only 24 years of age. One possible reason for the lower rates in Newcastle is that Farrington's conclusions are influenced by the working-class composition of the Cambridge cohort whereas the Newcastle population derived from a cohort of all births in the city over a defined period and this reduced the possibility of distortions. Further, the Newcastle research displays the often-reported relationship between occupational class of the family of origin and contact with the law.

The proportions of convictions for men ranged from one in six of men from families who were not deprived, to more than six in ten of men from families who were much deprived during their childhood. Some forms of deprivation appear to be more harmful than others. The risks were about five in ten in families where there was marital breakdown, parental illness, overcrowding , or social dependency; and about six in ten in families with defective cleanliness and poor quality of mothering – all suggesting that the quality of parental care is of fundamental importance.

The cardinal findings of the Newcastle research is the dramatic increase in the rates of delinquency and criminality in relation to the severity of deprivation in the family of origin. Some 60% of males coming from high-risk, much-deprived family backgrounds eventually end up with a criminal record. For females, the rates are very much lower, but the ratio of offences in the much deprived, as compared with criminality in the non-deprived, is much higher – four times higher in males but seven times higher in females.

Life-time trends

The Newcastle data demonstrates another aspect of life-time trends in relation to mean number of convictions (Fig. 1). There is a peak at about 16/17 to 18/19 years for the mean number of convictions, followed by a decline, with low rates at 32–33 years. Further, the mean number of convictions is closely tied to the severity of deprivation in childhood – the more severe the childhood deprivation, the earlier the offences are committed, and the higher the mean number of subsequent convictions, with a peak in late adolescence. A secondary peak occurred at about 28–29 years, but we do not know of any national or local circumstances which can explain this. These findings are consistent with West & Farrington (1973, 1977) who reported that whereas the peak age for first conviction was 14 years, 17 was the peak age for both the number of convictions and the number of individuals convicted.

Our findings support the notion of a group at high risk for criminality who commit their first offences while still at school. Almost eight in ten of the Newcastle males offending before 15 years of age committed further offences after leaving school, but only about one in six of those without offences before 15 years were subsequently offenders by 32–33 years of age. These findings are in line with other prospective surveys which report that a substantial proportion of youths convicted as juveniles subsequently have official contacts with the legal system as adults. For example, in the St Louis Study (Robins & O'Neil, 1958) 60% of juvenile delinquents had been arrested for subsequent non-traffic offences by 43 years of age. Similarly, McCord (1978) reported that 79% of 139 men convicted of offences in the Massachusetts Juvenile Court during 1933–1951 were reconvicted by 48 years of age. They also mirror the Cambridge findings of 61% of official juvenile delinquents being reconvicted as young adults and only 13% of those without convictions as juveniles being convicted as young adults (Farrington & West, 1979, 1981).

In summary, not only are children from much deprived backgrounds at higher risk for later delinquency and criminality, but as a group they are subject to many more convictions. Nevertheless, in adult life there is a marked fall in the frequency of criminal behaviour and, therefore, we can conclude that most juvenile delinquents do not become persistent offenders. In addition, few individuals commit offences for the first time in their late 20s.

Types of offences
(based on criminal record data for males)

It was found that all types of offences tended to increase in relation to the severity of deprivation and this was particularly true of theft. Furthermore, there did not appear to be any association between the type of offence and the nature of deprivation.

Previous research has demonstrated relatively high rates of adverse early-life experience in the backgrounds of delinquents, but we found that, for males, the rates are low, running from 18–34% for the different types of deprivation. In the case of females the rates are higher, running from 29–50%. Thus, while delinquency is a less frequent occurrence in females, where it does occur, deprivation appears to have a potent influence.

Next, marital instability and illness in parents are seldom associated with offences after the age of 15 years, but are relatively commonly associated with offences before that age. This suggests that the social origins of offences before and after 15 years differ in some important respects. Defective care of the child and home and poor mothering appear to have similar associations with offences at both ages. In addition, social dependency and overcrowding seem to be important in relation both to offences before and after 15 years, but more so in the latter than in the former.

Finally, while a high percentage, and at times the majority, of deprived males later commit offences (about 50–60%), only a minority of male delinquents have suffered early-life deprivations (18–34%).

Family mechanisms

All the types of deprivation we studied had significant correlations with criminality. First, there was a strong relationship between delinquency and severity of deprivation in the case of males. Second, there was a strong relationship between delinquency and the mother's poor care of the home and the child during the early years of life. Poor physical and domestic care of the child and home implies not only poor standards of care of the home and children, but also poor appreciation of the need for good-quality parenting in the early formative years, or the ability to organise, plan, or make wise provision for the future. In such circumstances, these mothers fail to provide guidance, direction, and supervision, and are poor models for imitation. These appear to be the most likely operative mechanisms. It is important to note that these two deprivations, namely, poor quality of parenting and poor standard of care of the home and the children, appear to have a much closer relationship with offending than do marital discord or breakdown. Nevertheless, it is likely that they act both separately and together to give rise to an atmosphere of family stress and general disorganisation and, for the child, a sense of lack of personal restraints (West & Farrington, 1973). It is tempting to suggest that these are the processes which lead to criminality. The work of McCord (1979) relating child-rearing antecedents to criminal behaviour in middle age is pertinent. The research demonstrates a significant link between early-life home atmosphere and adult criminality. Significant predictors which represented dimensions of child-rearing were parental conflict, supervision, and mother's affection. Predictors which reflected parental personality characteristics were aggressiveness, paternal deviance, and mother's self-confidence. All of these proved to be significant predictors of either property crimes or personal crimes, or both. Surprisingly, father's absence failed to distinguish non-criminals from criminals, and elsewhere, McCord (1982) comments that the focus should be turned from quantity of parenting to quality of parenting. The

DEPRIVATION AFFECTING CRIMINAL OFFENCE RATES   89

results of this latter important research are qualified by the nature of the population – all of whom were reared in congested urban areas in the USA during the 1930s and 1940s. Nonetheless, this work reinforces the view that family atmosphere during childhood has an important impact on subsequent behaviour. The Newcastle research deals with a total cohort and is, therefore, less subject to the limitations admitted by McCord, but suggests similar links between quality of care and mothering, and later criminality.

We have studied an index of social deprivation which is reflected by dependency on the social and welfare services. In our families, the rate of male criminality in those dependent on the social services was at least three times higher than in families without deprivation as we have defined it, but it is lower than in those with poor quality of parenting and poor care of the home and children. However, these three criteria of deprivation are significantly correlated with each other so that it is not easy to estimate the independent or relative contribution of each. Nevertheless, we hope to study these themes further by use of a more complex statistical model (multiple regression model). Again, it is tempting to speculate that one of the mechanisms leading to delinquency is a sense of freedom from personal restraints, as described by West & Farrington (1973), combined with a reaction to relative poverty.

The association with criminality proved stronger for deprivation than for occupational status of the parents, supporting the notion that criminality is a phenomenon which has significant origins in the extremes of family deprivation and dysfunction (Rutter & Giller, 1983). We have demonstrated the usual ecological correlation between neighbourhood variables and offender rates – the rates range from about one in six males in the more affluent wards to one in three in the poorest ward (this data will be re-examined in relation to ecological data collected by the social services). Furthermore, one of our criteria of deprivation at 5 years of age was overcrowding – there was a significantly higher rate of criminality in youths coming from overcrowded homes as compared with youths coming from homes in which there was none. We can advance all the usual explanations of the operative processes in terms of social meaning of such circumstances to the inhabitants of a disadvantaged neighbourhood – such as, lack of personal control over the social environment, lack to privacy, lack of sense of safety (Rutter & Giller, 1983). However, it is important to remember that overcrowding does not occur in isolation from other indices of deprivation, and poor social and economic circumstances (such as parental ill-health, poor care of the youth and the home, and

relatively poor parental control) are likely to act in concert to produce their effects.

Next, we have to consider whether the Newcastle research can add anything to the debate about the significance of a family variable such as family size: 17.3% of our male criminals, but only 3.4% of non-delinquents came from families with six or more children. These rates are very much lower than in the Cambridge study, suggesting a lower correlation of family size with delinquency when the data derives from a representative population. However, this lesser correlation does not detract from the close relationship of criminality with large families, and the latter with deprivation, causing circumstances in which children do not receive sufficient or adequate care.

Parental factors – criminality and personality

While we did not have data on criminality for the parents of Red Spots, we did have information about major defects of parental personality. These were based on judgements which were reached by a team of doctors and health visitors (community nurses) who had known the families over 10–15 years, and who had worked together during the years, 1947–1962, and measured deprivation (Miller *et al*, 1960, 1974). The results (Table VI) show the importance of the fathers' personality characteristics in relation to their sons' criminality and suggest that children of ineffective parents are at high risk of delinquency. Taken together, the findings again emphasise the importance of poor supervision, direction, and guidance of children in the genesis of delinquency.

Conclusion

In this study, we dealt with assessment of the relationship between social and family variables and offences against the law. The study was not designed to look at relevant current influences which are the object of interest of modern criminological research – such as differences of intake of troublesome boys into different secondary schools; perceptions of the consequence of offending; situational factors; and possible peer-group influences (Roff *et al*, 1972; Gath *et al*, 1977; Rutter *et al*, 1979). Even so, such factors are likely to be more common in the presence of adverse social and family circumstances, but the operative mechanisms remain unclear. Perhaps adverse social and family influences and parental attitudes make boys more vulnerable to such current environmental factors, or the effects of family influences may be mediated through individual characteristics in the boys – or there may be

90 KOLVIN ET AL

interactions between all these factors, but in different combinations in different delinquents. We are aware, however, that there are likely to be other interacting factors which may be as important as those we have mentioned. The latter theme will be explored in a subsequent paper.

Acknowledgements

This research was supported by a grant from the Department of Health and Social Security/Social Science Research Council, and by supplementary support from the Home Office, the City of Newcastle Priority Area Projects, the Rowntree Trust, the W. T. Grant Foundation and the J. Joffe Trust. We are grateful to Professor John Gunn for advice about criminal profiles.

References

FARRINGTON, D. P. (1979) Longitudinal research on crime and delinquency. In *Criminal Justice: An Annual Review of Research* (eds N. Morris & M. Tonry) vol. 1, pp. 289–348. Chicago and London: University of Chicago Press.
—— (1981) The prevalence of convictions. *British Journal of Criminology*, 21, 173–175.
—— & WEST, D. J. (1979) The Cambridge Study in Delinquent Development. In *An Empirical Basis for Primary Prevention: Prospective Longitudinal Research in Europe* (eds S. A. Mednick & A. E. Baert). New York: Oxford University Press.
—— & —— (1981) The Cambridge Study in Delinquent Development. In *Prospective Longitudinal Research* (eds S. A. Mednick & A. E. Baert) London: Oxford University Press.
GATH, D., COOPER, B., GATTONI, F. & ROCKETT, D. (1977) Child guidance and delinquency in a London borough. *Institute of Psychiatry, Maudsley Monographs No. 24*. London: Oxford University Press.
GUNN, J. & ROBERTSON, G. (1976) Drawing a criminal profile. *British Journal of Criminology*, 16,
HOME OFFICE (1985) *Home Office Statistical Bulletin ISSNO 143 6384*.
KOLVIN, I., MILLER, F. J. W., GARSIDE, R. F., WOLSTENHOLME, F. & GATZANIS, S. R. (1983) A longitudinal study of deprivation: life cycle changes in one generation – implications for the next generation. In *Epidemiology Approaches in Child Psychiatry II* (eds M. H. Schmidt & H. Remschmidt). Stuttgart and New York: G. Thieme Verlag.
LANDAU, S. F. (1981) Juveniles and the police. *British Journal of Criminology*, 21, 27–46.
MCCORD, J. (1978) A thirty year follow up of treatment effects. *American Psychologist*, 33, 284–289.
—— (1979) Some child-rearing antecedents of criminal behaviour in adult men. *Journal of Personality and Social Psychology*, 37, 1477–1486.
—— (1982) The relation between paternal absence and crime. In *Abnormal Offender, Delinquency, and the Criminal Justice System* (eds J. Gunn & D. P. Farrington). Chichester: Wiley.
MILLER, F. J. W., COURT, S. D. M., WALTON, W. S. & KNOX, E. G. (1960) *Growing up in Newcastle upon Tyne*. London: Oxford University Press.
——, ——, KNOX, E. G. & BRANDON, S. (1974) *The School Years in Newcastle upon Tyne*. London: Oxford University Press.
——, KOLVIN, I. & FELLS, H. (1985) Becoming deprived: a cross generation study based on the Newcastle upon Tyne 1000 Family Study. In *Longitudinal Studies in Child Psychology and Psychiatry* (ed. A. R. Nicol). Chichester: John Wiley and Sons.
OSBORN, S. G. (1980) Moving home, leaving London and delinquent trends. *British Journal of Criminology*, 20, 54–61.
ROBINS, L. & O'NEIL, P. (1958) Mortality and crime, problem children thirty years later. *American Sociological Review*, 23.
ROFF, M., SELLS, S. B. & GOLDEN, M. M. (1972) *Social Adjustment and Personality Development in Children*. Minneapolis: University of Minnesota Press.
RUTTER, M. (1979) *Changing Youth in a Changing Society*. London: Nuffield Provincial Hospitals Trust (1980), Cambridge, Massachusetts: Harvard University Press.
——, MAUGHAN, B., MORTIMORE, P., OUSTON, J. & SMITH, A. (1979) Fifteen thousand house: In *Secondary Schools and Their Effect on Children*. London: Open Books. Cambridge, Massachusetts: Harvard University Press.
—— & GILLER, H. (1983) Juvenile delinquency. In *Trends and Perspectives*. London: Penguin Education.
SPENCE, J. C., WALTON, W. S., MILLER, F. J. W. & COURT, S. D. M. (1954) *A Thousand Families in Newcastle upon Tyne*. Oxford University Press: London.
WEST D. J. (1982) *Delinquency: Its Roots, Careers and Prospects*. London: Heinemann.
—— & FARRINGTON, D. P. (1973) *Who Becomes Delinquent?* London: Heinemann.
—— & —— (1977) *The Delinquent Way of Life*. London: Heinemann.

*I. Kolvin, MD, FRCPsych, DipPsych, *Professor of Child and Adolescent Psychiatry, Nuffield Psychology and Psychiatry Unit and University of Newcastle upon Tyne*; F. J. W. Miller, FRCP, *Honorary Physician to Children's Department, Royal Victoria Infirmary*; M. Fleeting, MA, *Computer Scientist, Nuffield Psychology and Psychiatry Unit*; P. A. Kolvin, BA, *Barrister*

*Correspondence: *Nuffield Psychology and Psychiatry Unit (for Children and Young People), Fleming Memorial Hospital, Great North Road, Newcastle upon Tyne NE2 3AX*

[13]

The Cycle of Violence

CATHY SPATZ WIDOM

Despite widespread belief that violence begets violence, methodological problems substantially restrict knowledge of the long-term consequences of childhood victimization. Empirical evidence for this cycle of violence has been examined. Findings from a cohort study show that being abused or neglected as a child increases one's risk for delinquency, adult criminal behavior, and violent criminal behavior. However, the majority of abused and neglected children do not become delinquent, criminal, or violent. Caveats in interpreting these findings and their implications are discussed in this article.

THE SCHOLARLY LITERATURE ON FAMILY VIOLENCE HAS grown enormously during the last 20 years. One of the most pervasive claims that appears in both academic and popular writings refers to the cycle of violence: abused children become abusers and victims of violence become violent offenders. Over 25 years ago, in a brief clinical note entitled "Violence breeds violence—perhaps?" Curtis expressed the concern that abused and neglected children would "become tomorrow's murderers and perpetrators of other crimes of violence, if they survive" (1, p. 386).

Indeed, the notion of an intergenerational transmission of violence has become the premier developmental hypothesis in the field of abuse and neglect. In this article I review the current empirical status of this hypothesis, drawing on data from different disciplines—psychology, sociology, psychiatry, social work, and nursing; comment on methodological problems; and describe new research developments in the field. Although people maintain strong feelings about this topic, they ought to be aware of those aspects of the cycle of violence hypothesis that have received support and of areas where unresolved questions remain.

Literature Review

Researchers and professionals have used the phrases "cycle of violence" and "intergenerational transmission of violence" loosely to refer to assumptions or hypotheses about the consequences of abuse and neglect in relation to a number of different outcomes. Some writers refer exclusively to the hypothesized relation between abuse as a child and abuse as a parent (2). Others focus on the relations between child abuse and neglect and later delinquent, adult criminal, or violent behaviors.

Because there are difficult methodological problems confronting social science research, most investigations of child abuse have been criticized as methodologically flawed and limited in how the results can be generalized, their scientific validity, and ultimately their

Departments of Criminal Justice and Psychology, Indiana University, Bloomington, IN 47405.

policy relevance (3–5). There remains considerable debate about the definition of child abuse (6) and, consequently, much uncertainty about its prevalence. Even less is known about its effects. For children who have been abused or neglected, the immediate consequences may involve physical injuries or psychological trauma. In addition, the emotional and developmental scars of these children and those who witness severe family violence may persist. Furthermore, because many other events in the child's life may mediate the effects of child abuse or neglect, the long-term consequences of such childhood victimization are difficult to determine.

Abuse leads to abuse. In a recent review of empirical studies relevant to the intergenerational transmission of violence hypothesis, Widom (5) noted that there is surprisingly little empirical evidence to support the claim that abuse leads to abuse. Existing studies suggest that there is a higher likelihood of abuse by parents if the parents were themselves abused as children. Among abusing parents, estimates of a history of abuse range from a low of 7% (7) to a high of 70% (8). Among adults who were abused as children, between one-fifth and one-third abuse their own children (9, 10).

Many studies are methodologically weak and limited because of an overdependence on self-report and retrospective data, inadequate documentation of childhood abuse and neglect, and infrequent use of baseline data from control groups. In a comprehensive review of this literature, Kaufman and Zigler (2) concluded that the unqualified acceptance of the intergenerational transmission hypothesis—from abuse as a child to becoming an abusive parent—is unfounded.

Small-scale clinical reports. A number of frequently cited writings describe prior abuse in the family backgrounds of adolescents who attempted or succeeded in killing their parents (11), and of murderers (12), or of those charged with murder (13). These reports, offered as support for the cycle of violence, present provocative clinical accounts by astute observers; yet their own statistical usefulness is limited because of small sample sizes, weak sampling techniques, questionable accuracy of information, and lack of appropriate comparison groups.

As Monahan (14) argued, the most important piece of information researchers can have in the prediction of violence is the base rate of violent behavior in the population with which they are dealing. Particularly in the areas of abuse and neglect, there is a tendency to overemphasize individual case information at the expense of base rates. Appropriate control groups are necessary to assess the independent effects of early childhood victimization because many of the same family and demographic characteristics found in abusive home environments also relate to delinquency and later criminality (15). Without control groups to provide an estimate of such base rates, it is difficult to assess the magnitude of relationships.

In the United States, for example, groups with different demographic characteristics (males/females, blacks/whites, rural/urban) have different base rates of arrest for violent crimes (16). Thus, base rates—from the same general population of people at the same time period—must be taken into account in assessing the cycle of violence.

Delinquency. Another facet of the cycle of violence hypothesis refers to the relation between abuse and neglect and delinquency. The majority of studies that address this relation are retrospective ones (*17, 18*) in which the researcher typically asks delinquents about their early backgrounds. Estimates of abuse from these retrospective studies generally range from 9 to 29%. In prospective studies that follow up individuals who had been abused or neglected as children, the incidence of delinquency was between 10 and 17%. Of three prospective studies (*19–21*), two lacked control groups (nonabused comparisons). Most studies of delinquents report that the majority were not abused as children. In at least one study (*21*), rejected children had the highest rates of delinquency. However, without appropriate control groups and improved methodology, any conclusions remain highly ambiguous.

Violent behavior. Several studies involving delinquents (*18, 19, 22, 23*) and psychiatric patients (*24*) suggest that abuse and neglect are related to violent criminal behavior. However, findings are contradictory. Some provide strong support for the cycle of violence hypothesis; in others, abused and nonabused delinquents did not differ; and in at least one study, abused delinquents were less likely to engage in aggressive crimes later. Each of these studies has methodological problems, not the least of which is the universal lack of normal comparison groups providing baseline data. Furthermore, since existing studies focus primarily on violence among delinquents and adolescents, whether these childhood experiences have direct and lasting consequences for the commission of violent crimes into adulthood is unknown.

Aggressive behavior in young children. Another body of studies focuses on the relation between abuse, neglect, and aggressive behavior in young children. This work is based on experimental research and laboratory observations. Age groups vary, as do definitions of child abuse and outcome measures. However, these studies indicate with some consistency that abused children, as young as infants and toddlers, manifest significantly more aggressive and problematic behavior than nonabused or neglected children (*25*).

These studies also suggest the need to consider neglect as distinct from abuse, because in some reports (*26*) neglected children appeared more dysfunctional than those abused. With one exception (*21*), only these developmental psychology studies have systematically examined and reported differences between separate samples of abused and neglected children. By combining abused and neglected groups, or by studying only physically abused children, important differences in consequences may be obscured.

Observing violence. In addition to studies of children directly victimized, the indirect effects on children observing family violence have also been investigated in two types of studies. First, large-scale self-report surveys have found a modest, although fairly consistent, association between exposure to family violence and approval of violence or marital violence as an adult (*27*). Second, studies of the children of battered women suggest that observing abuse or extreme marital discord may be as harmful to the development of the child as physical abuse, although other factors might contribute to these findings (*28*).

Despite widespread belief in the intergenerational transmission of violence, methodological limitations substantially restrict our conclusions about the long-term consequences of early childhood victimization (*5*). The research described here was designed to overcome some of the methodological problems that have hindered the empirical documentation of the cycle of violence.

New Research Developments

During a 2-year research project, I examined a number of basic questions about the relationship between child abuse and neglect

and later violent criminal behavior. This research was designed to incorporate methodological improvements. These included a relatively unambiguous operational definition of abuse and neglect; a prospective design; separate abused and neglected groups; a large sample to allow for subgroup comparisons and to allow for conclusions with respect to violent criminal behavior; a control group matched as closely as possible for age, sex, race, and approximate social class background; and assessment of the long-term consequences of abuse and neglect beyond adolescence or juvenile court into adulthood.

The purpose of this project was to identify a large sample of substantiated and validated cases of child abuse and neglect from approximately 20 years ago, to establish a matched control group of nonabused children, and to determine the extent to which these individuals and the matched control group subsequently engaged in delinquent and adult criminal and violent behavior. At present, this research involves (and is limited to) the collection, tabulation, and analysis of official records (*29*).

The decision to use official arrest records for the dependent variable was made for several reasons. Arrest records are relatively easy to locate, and reasonably complete information on arrests in official records can be collected retrospectively (*30*). Results of self-report studies and research with the use of official records have been fairly consistent in terms of the correlates of crime (*31*). Although self-reports are basically reliable and valid for relatively minor offenses, more serious offenses are more efficiently revealed (and with fairly little bias) by some official data (*32*). Arrest records were also chosen because interviewing a large number of abused and neglected cases would be extremely costly. Compared to a good survey by interviewers, a register study such as the one described here tends to be much less expensive per case (*33*).

Design. This study is based on a standard design referred to as specialized cohorts (*33*) or observational cohorts (*34*). In a matched cohort design, both groups are free of the "disease" in question (violent or delinquent behavior) at the time they are chosen for the study and, because of matching, are assumed to differ only in the (risk) attribute to be examined (having experienced child abuse or neglect). Because it is not possible to randomly assign subjects to groups, the assumption of equivalency for the groups is an approximation.

In studies of the relation between child abuse and neglect and later delinquency or criminality, it is important to avoid ambiguity in the direction of causality of the events. Specifically, cases occur where delinquency precedes abuse or neglect in time and cases where delinquency itself may actually provoke the abuse or neglect of the child. Thus, to minimize this ambiguity and to maximize the likelihood that the temporal direction is clear (that is, abuse or neglect leading to delinquency or criminality), abuse and neglect cases were restricted to those in which children were less than 11 years of age at the time of the abuse or neglect.

In comparisons of delinquent or violent behavior, it is also difficult to judge what portion of the differences is due to the experience or factors under study and what portion is due to being labeled a delinquent or violent offender. My research does not totally avoid this problem, but by use of a prospective design, with data collection started at the point of abuse or neglect and before the onset of delinquency and violent behavior, the problem is minimized.

Abuse and neglect cases. All cases of physical and sexual abuse and neglect processed during the years 1967 through 1971 in the county juvenile court (situated in a metropolitan area in the Midwest) and validated and substantiated by the court were initially included. Abuse and neglect cases from the adult criminal courts were also included. In these cases, a criminal charge was filed against the adult defendant. During 1967 through 1971, there were 140 cases (physical and sexual abuse and neglect) processed in adult criminal court in which the victim was 11 years of age or less. After examining 2623 abuse and neglect petitions, a total of 908 cases were retained for this study (35).

Definitions. Physical abuse refers to cases in which an individual had "knowingly and willfully inflicted unnecessarily severe corporal punishment" or "unnecessary physical suffering" upon a child or children (for example, striking, punching, kicking, biting, throwing, or burning). Sexual abuse refers to a variety of charges, ranging from relatively nonspecific charges of "assault and battery with intent to gratify sexual desires" to more specific and detailed charges of "fondling and touching in an obscene manner," sodomy, and incest. Neglect refers to cases in which the court found a child to have no proper parent care or guardianship, to be destitute, homeless, or to be living in a physically dangerous environment. The neglect petition reflects the judgment that the behavior represents a serious omission by the parents—beyond acceptable community and professional standards at the time—to provide to children needed food, clothing, shelter, medical attention, and protection from hazardous conditions.

Matched control group. One of the critical elements of this research design is the establishment of a control group, matched as closely as possible on the basis of sex, age, race, and approximate family socioeconomic status during the time period under study (1967 through 1971). To accomplish this matching, the sample of abused and neglected cases was first divided into two groups on the basis of their age at the time of the abuse or neglect incidents: those under school age and those of school age (36).

Children who were under school age at the time of abuse or neglect were matched with children of the same sex, race, date of birth (± 1 week), and hospital of birth through the use of county birth record information. Of the 319 abused and neglected children under school age, there were matches for 229 (72%).

For children of school age, records of more than 100 elementary schools for the same time period were used to find matches with children of the same sex, race, date of birth (± 6 months), same class in same elementary school during the years 1967 through 1971, and home address, preferably within a five-block radius of the abused or neglected child. Out of 589 school-age children, there were matches for 438, representing about 74% of the group. Overall, there were 667 matches (73.7%) for the abused and neglected children (37).

This cohort design involves the assumption that the major difference between the abused and neglected group and the controls is in the abuse or neglect experience. Official records were checked to determine if the proposed control subject had been abused or neglected. If there was evidence that a control subject had been abused, then he or she was excluded from the control group. This situation occurred in 11 cases (38).

Demographic characteristics of the groups. Among the abused and neglected group, there are about equal numbers of males and females (49 versus 51%) and more whites than blacks (67 versus 31%). The mean age for the abused and neglected subjects is 25.69 years (SD = 3.53 years). The majority of the sample are currently between the ages of 20 and 30 years (85%), with about 10% under age 20 (the youngest is 16) and 5% older than 30 (the oldest is 32). The current age distribution of the sample indicates that our design has allowed sufficient time for most of the subjects to come to the attention of authorities for delinquent, adult criminal, and violent behavior (23, 39).

The controls are well matched to the abused and neglected subjects in terms of age, sex, and race. Controls are equally divided between males and females. The racial composition of the group is quite similar to that of the abused and neglected group, although slightly more controls are black (35%). Their mean age is 25.76 years (SD = 3.53 years; range, 16 to 33 years).

Data collection. Detailed information about the abuse or neglect incident and family composition and characteristics was obtained from the files of the juvenile court and probation department, the authority responsible for cases of abused, neglected, or dependent and delinquent children. Juvenile court and probation department records were also examined for the control subjects. Detailed delinquency and detention information was recorded for both groups. Adult criminal histories for all subjects were compiled from searches at three levels of law enforcement: local, state, and federal. Searches also extended to the Bureau of Motor Vehicles and (for all females) marriage license records to find social security numbers to assist in tracing subjects through criminal records.

The Cycle of Violence: Findings

Abused and neglected children have a higher likelihood of arrests for delinquency, adult criminality, and violent criminal behavior (40) than the matched controls. Table 1 presents the percentage of individuals in the abused and neglected and control groups who have official records for delinquency, adult criminality, and violent criminal behavior (41). In comparison to controls, abused and neglected children overall have more arrests as a juvenile (26 versus 17%), more arrests as an adult (29 versus 21%), and more arrests for any violent offense (11 versus 8%).

In addition to the extent of involvement, criminality is often described in terms of the number of offenses committed, the age at first arrest, and the repetitiveness (or chronicity) of a person's criminal activity. In comparison to controls, abused and neglected children as a group have a larger mean number of offenses (2.43 versus 1.41, $t = 4.49$, $P < 0.001$); an earlier mean age at first offense (16.48 versus 17.29, $t = 2.38$, $P < 0.05$); and a higher proportion of chronic offenders, that is, those charged with five or more offenses [17 versus 9%; x^2 (1) = 28.86, $P < 0.001$].

Differences related to demographic characteristics. To illustrate the independent effects of demographic characteristics, the results of separate analyses for sex and race are included in Table 1.

Sex. Males have higher rates of delinquency, adult criminality, and violent criminal behavior than females (Table 1). Within each sex, a history of abuse or neglect also significantly increases one's chances of having an official criminal record. Thus, despite the fact that women generally have lower rates of arrests for criminal behavior, abused or neglected females are significantly more likely to have an adult arrest (15.9%) than control females (9.0%), although the difference for females in these groups is not significant for violent crimes.

Race. Although blacks are statistically more likely to have official criminal records than whites (16), the same pattern exists across the abused and neglected and the control group for all three levels of criminal activity (delinquency, adult criminal, and violent criminal behavior). For blacks and whites, being abused or neglected increases the likelihood of having a criminal record as a juvenile and as an adult. However, for whites, being abused or neglected does not significantly increase the risk of an arrest for violent criminal behavior (42).

Age. Dividing our sample (ages 16 to 33 years) into four age groups of equal size, older subjects in both groups have higher frequencies of an adult criminal record than younger subjects [x^2 (3) = 36.17, $P < 0.001$] and of violent criminal behavior [x^2 (3) = 14.05, $P < 0.01$]. Although this finding may simply reflect the number of years available for the subjects to accumulate criminal records, it also illustrates the complexity of dealing with criminal behavior and the need to control for age.

Continuity. As seen so far, victims of early child abuse and neglect

162

differ from nonabused and nonneglected children on a number of indices of delinquency, adult criminality, and violent criminal behavior; however, not all aspects of criminal activity differentiate the groups. One example of such a similarity between the groups is provided by findings about the continuity between antisocial behavior as a juvenile and criminal behavior as an adult.

Of those with juvenile offenses, roughly the same proportion of abused and neglected children and controls go on to commit offenses as an adult (53 versus 50%). Similarly, of those with violent offenses as juveniles, approximately the same proportion go on to commit violence as an adult in the abused and neglected group (34.2%) as in the controls (36.8%). Thus, despite significant differences in the extent of involvement in criminal activity, nonabused and nonneglected subjects are just as likely as abused and neglected individuals to continue criminal activity once they have begun.

These findings are interesting in light of recent literature in criminology, particularly the current debates on criminal careers (*30, 43*). Although my findings indicate that officially recorded abuse and neglect increase one's likelihood of having an official criminal record and speed up the age at entrance into officially recorded delinquent activities, early childhood victimization does not appear to place one at increased risk for continuing in a life of crime. These findings reinforce the notion (*30*) that it is important to distinguish factors that may stimulate an individual to become involved in crime from the factors that affect whether the person continues or desists in a criminal career.

Does Violence Beget Violence?

In a direct test of the cycle of violence hypothesis, violent criminal behavior was examined as a function of the type of abuse or neglect experienced as a child. According to the cycle of violence hypothesis, individuals who experienced childhood physical abuse only should show higher levels of violence than individuals victimized by other

forms of abuse or neglect. Table 2 shows the percentage of subjects in each abuse group who have an arrest for any violent offense (*40*) (juvenile or adult record). As expected, victims of physical abuse had the highest level of arrests for violent criminal behavior, followed by victims of neglect. However, types of abuse and neglect are not distributed randomly in the sample across age, sex, and race groups, and thus bivariate analyses present an overly simplistic picture.

Need for multivariate models. Since sex, race, and age are independently related to differences in rates of violent criminal behavior, it is necessary to control for the effects of these factors in examining the hypothesized cycle of violence. Thus, data analysis and interpretation of these findings must incorporate and control for sample demographic characteristics.

One statistical technique for analyzing the influence of a set of explanatory variables on a "response" variable that takes a binary form is logistic regression or linear logistic response models. This technique models the log-odds of the presence or absence of a response as a linear function of the independent variable. Models were estimated with the use of iterative maximum likelihood methods (*44*), with any arrest for a violent crime as the response variable and race, sex, age, and group status (physical abuse, sexual abuse, neglect, and controls) as explanatory variables.

The estimated coefficients in the resulting fitted model for predicting the log-odds of an arrest for any violent crime are presented in Table 3. Group contrasts are with the control group, so that each pure type of abuse (omitting cases with more than one type of abuse) is compared to the control group, holding other factors constant. The results of this analysis indicate that, controlling for age, sex, and race, the physical abuse and neglect groups have a significantly higher likelihood of having an arrest for a violent offense than the controls (*45*). Thus, in the most direct and stringent test of the cycle of violence hypothesis, being physically abused as a child does increase one's propensity to commit further criminal violence. Although being neglected also increases one's likelihood of violent behavior, the type of abuse or neglect is not as powerful a predictor of violent criminal behavior as the demographic characteristics of sex, race, and age.

Caveats

My research was explicitly designed to examine the relation between abuse, neglect, and later violent behavior and to overcome methodological shortcomings in previous literature. However, this research has limitations because of its exclusive reliance on official records. Thus, one should be circumspect about these findings (*3, 4*) and not generalize inappropriately.

Much child abuse and neglect that occurs does not come to the attention of welfare departments, police, or courts. This fact especially applies to official data from the late 1960s and early 1970s, when it is generally believed that only a fraction of all maltreatment cases were reported. The abuse and neglect cases studied here are those in which agencies have intervened and those processed through the social service systems (*46*). These cases were dealt with before most states had adopted mandatory child abuse reporting laws and before the Federal Child Abuse Treatment and Prevention Act was passed.

Child abuse researchers have argued that there is bias in the labeling and reporting of child abuse cases and that lower income and minority groups are overrepresented in official reports of child abuse and neglect (*47*). The design discussed here does not generally include instances of abuse in higher level socioeconomic families in which such abuse may be more likely to be labeled an accident. On the other hand, national surveys of family violence have found that

Table 1. Extent of involvement in delinquency, adult criminality, or violent criminal behavior among abused and neglected (*n* = 908) and control (*n* = 667) groups. NS, not significant.

Demographic characteristic	Abused and neglected (%)	Controls (%)	χ^2	P
Juvenile record (delinquency)				
Overall	26.0	16.8	18.91	<0.001
Sex				
Male	33.2	22.2	11.38	<0.001
Female	19.1	11.4	8.66	<0.01
Race				
Black	37.9	19.3	21.29	<0.001
White	21.1	15.4	5.36	<0.05
Adult criminal record				
Overall	28.6	21.1	11.38	<0.001
Sex				
Male	42.0	33.2	6.18	<0.05
Female	15.9	9.0	8.16	<0.01
Race				
Black	39.0	26.2	9.46	<0.01
White	24.4	18.4	5.26	<0.05
Any violent criminal record				
Overall	11.2	7.9	4.68	<0.05
Sex				
Male	19.4	13.5	4.79	<0.05
Female	3.4	2.4	0.72	NS
Race				
Black	22.0	12.9	7.22	<0.01
White	6.5	5.3	0.70	NS

Table 2. Does violence breed violence? Any arrest for a violent offense as function of type of abuse [χ^2 (5) = 13.85, P = 0.02].

Abuse group	n	Arrest for any violent offense (%)
Physical only	76	15.8
Neglect	609	12.5
Physical and neglect	70	7.1
Sexual and other abuse	28	7.1
Sexual only	125	5.6
Controls	667	7.9

those with the lowest income are more likely to abuse their children (10). Even though most poor people do not abuse or neglect their children, there is a greater risk of abuse and neglect among the lowest income groups (48). Regardless, one cannot generalize from these findings to unreported cases of abuse and neglect, such as those cases handled unofficially by private medical doctors (4). Similarly, because of the exclusions (35), these findings are not generalizable to abused and neglected children who were adopted in early childhood.

Other potential biases may be introduced by relying on official records for exposure to abuse or neglect and criminality. Pagelow (49) suggested that the process of intervening and labeling abused and neglected children, disrupting their residence with their family, and stigmatizing the parents (who often received little or no assistance to improve), may create a self-fulfilling prophecy that can be difficult to resist or overcome. This implies that it is the official response to abuse, rather than the abuse itself, which begets later criminal behavior. On the basis of this reasoning, strong evidence for the long-term ill-effects of childhood victimization would be expected because the children in our abused and neglected sample were processed through the courts and presumably suffered all the negative effects associated with such a process.

On the other hand, because individuals in the control group could have been abused, but not officially reported as abused, the extent of the differences between the abused and neglected group and the controls might be suppressed. Thus, the findings here may represent an underestimate because the differences between the abused and neglected group and the control group may be smaller than would be the case for a "pure nonabused and nonneglected" control group.

In the case of the dependent variable, reliance on official arrest records for violent criminal behavior also represents an underestimate of potential violent behavior. These findings do not describe violent behavior, but rather violent criminal behavior. Whether these findings extend to violence in general, to spousal violence, and to violence directed at children is unknown at this time.

Therefore, it is important to locate and conduct a follow-up study with these individuals to determine the extent to which the abused and neglected subjects and the controls report having experienced child abuse or neglect and to determine the extent of delinquency, criminality, and violent criminal behavior not disclosed in official records. Eventually, further intergenerational transmission of violence to the offspring of these individuals (currently in their 20s and 30s) should be examined.

Conclusions and Implications

Early childhood victimization has demonstrable long-term consequences for delinquency, adult criminality, and violent criminal behavior. The results reported here provide strong support for the cycle of violence hypothesis. The experience of child abuse and neglect has a substantial impact even on individuals with otherwise little likelihood

of engaging in officially recorded criminal behavior. My findings are consistent with previous empirical data; however, there is now baseline data with which to assess the significance and magnitude of the association, and there is an assessment of the consequences of childhood victimization beyond adolescence into adulthood.

In a direct test of the violence breeds violence hypothesis, physical abuse as a child led significantly to later violent criminal behavior, when other relevant demographic variables such as age, sex, and race were held constant. However, being neglected as a child also showed a significant relation to later violent criminal behavior, and type of abuse was not as powerful a predictor of this behavior as demographic characteristics.

These findings indicate that abused and neglected children have significantly greater risk of becoming delinquents, criminals, and violent criminals. These findings do not show, however, that every abused or neglected child will become delinquent, criminal, or a violent criminal. The linkage between childhood victimization and later antisocial and violent behavior is far from certain, and the intergenerational transmission of violence is not inevitable. Although early child abuse and neglect place one at increased risk for official recorded delinquency, adult criminality, and violent criminal behavior, a large portion of abused or neglected children do not succumb. Twenty-six percent of child abuse and neglect victims had juvenile offenses; 74% did not. Eleven percent had an arrest for a violent criminal act, whereas almost 90% did not. These findings mean that prevention programs and intervention strategies aimed at buffering at-risk children play a potentially important role in the reduction of further violent criminal behavior.

In addition, alternative manifestations of the consequences of these early abusive experiences should be examined. For example, the effects of early abusive experiences may be manifested in different ways from those already discussed, in particular in withdrawal or self-destructive behavior (50). Thus, one possible explanation for the lack of a more substantial relation between childhood victimization and later delinquency, adult criminality, or violent criminal behavior may lie in more subtle indications of emotional damage such as depression, withdrawal, or more extreme behavior, as in suicide. Given the attrition that typically occurs in longitudinal studies, examination of cases lost because of early death would be particularly revealing. In some ways, studies that focus on violence and criminal behavior may be shortsighted.

Most likely, the long-term consequences of child abuse and neglect for females are manifest in more subtle ways. Abused and neglected females may be more prone to suffer depression and perhaps undergo psychiatric hospitalization as a consequence of these early childhood experiences, rather than direct their aggression "outwardly." Interpretation of results is also complicated because the type of abuse and neglect suffered by females and males differs (more females are sexually abused than males), which in turn may

Table 3. Predictors of any violent crime: coefficients from linear logistic response model. Likelihood ratio χ^2 (3) = 10.28, P = 0.016. Number of subjects was 1455.

Predictor variable	Coefficient	Z value*
Sex (male)	2.08	8.32
Race (black)	1.35	7.11
Age	0.11	3.67
Sexual abuse	0.54	1.20
Physical abuse	0.94	2.47
Neglect	0.53	2.65
Constant	−7.48	−0.84

*Z values are computed by dividing the coefficient by the standard error. Values of Z greater than 2.0 are regarded as statistically significant.

differentially affect the long-term consequences.

Abused and neglected children are generally at "high risk" for social problems. It is important to understand the potential protective factors that intervene in the child's development and to compare the development of those who succumb and those who are "resilient" and do not. Although one can speculate on why child abuse and neglect should have various outcomes, the substance of what is learned and the intervening linkages that transpire to produce aggression and violent criminal behavior are not well understood. For example, child abuse or neglect may not directly cause delinquency or violent criminal behavior. Rather, these outcomes may be an indirect by-product of these early abusive experiences. There are suggestions in the empirical literature about possible intervening variables (51). [A discussion of possible pathways and some of the potentially relevant variables is presented by Widom (5).] However, more research is needed to look at possible mediating variables that act to buffer or protect abused or neglected children from developmental deficits and later delinquent and adult criminal behavior. Studies must be undertaken to examine the role of what Garmezy (52) has called protective factors—dispositional attributes, environmental conditions, biological predispositions, and positive events— that act to mitigate against early negative experiences.

The scientific issue should not be the "box score" (the magnitude of the association between childhood victimization and later delinquent or criminal behavior), but rather the goal should be further knowledge of the processes involved (53). Research should be directed at understanding how these early experiences relate to later violent behavior, recognizing the likelihood of multiple pathways, and noting how possible protective factors act to buffer some children from the long-term negative effects of these early childhood experiences.

REFERENCES AND NOTES

1. G. C. Curtis, *Am. J. Psychiatry* 120, 386 (1963).
2. J. Kaufman and E. Zigler, *Am. J. Orthopsychiatry* 57, 186 (1987).
3. D. J. Besharov, *Child Abuse Negl.* 5, 383 (1981).
4. C. S. Widom, *Am. J. Orthopsychiatry* 58, 260 (1988).
5. ———, *Pathways to Criminal Violence*, N. Weiner and M. E. Wolfgang, Eds. (Sage, Newbury, CA, 1989).
6. The literature on child abuse and neglect encompasses several different phenomena: physical abuse, sexual abuse, neglect, severe physical punishment, and psychological maltreatment. Despite occasional references to the destructive impact of psychological abuse, the focus here is primarily on physical abuse and neglect. Excluded are medical reports that describe immediate or long-term physical consequences of early childhood trauma.
7. D. Gil, *Violence Against Children: Physical Child Abuse in the United States* (Harvard Univ. Press, Cambridge, MA, 1973).
8. B. Egeland and D. Jacobvitz, "Intergenerational continuity of parental abuse: Causes and consequences," presented at the conference on BioSocial Perspectives on Abuse and Neglect, York, ME, 1984.
9. L. R. Silver, C. C. Dublin, R. S. Lourie, *Am. J. Psychiatry* 126, 152 (1969); J. J. Spinetta and D. J. Rigler, *Psychol. Bull.* 77, 296 (1972); B. J. Steele and C. B. Pollock, in *The Battered Child*, R. E. Helfer and C. H. Kempe, Eds. (Univ. of Chicago Press, Chicago, 1974), pp. 103–147; R. S. Hunter and N. Kilstrom, *Am. J Psychiatry* 136, 1320 (1979); E. C. Herrenkohl, R. C. Herrenkohl, L. J. Toedter, in *The Dark Side of Families*, D. Finkelhor, R. J. Gelles, G. T. Hotaling, M. A. Straus, Eds. (Sage, Beverly Hills, CA, 1983), pp. 305–316.
10. M. Straus, R. Gelles, S. K. Steinmetz, *Behind Closed Doors: Violence in the American Family* (Anchor, Garden City, NY, 1980).
11. W. M. Easson and R. M. Steinhilber, *Arch. Gen. Psychiatry* 4, 27 (1961); E. Tanay, *Austr. N.Z.J. Psychiatry* 7, 263 (1973); C. H. King, *Am. J. Orthopsychiatry* 45, 134 (1975); I. B. Sendi and P. G. Blomgren, *Am. J. Psychiatry* 132, 423 (1975); J. M. Sorrells, *Crime Delin.* 23, 312 (1977).
12. J. W. Duncan and G. M. Duncan, *Am. J. Psychiatry* 127, 74 (1971); R. K. Ressler and A. W. Burgess, *FBI Law Enforc. Bull.* 54, 2 (1985).
13. M. Rosenbaum and B. Bennett, *Am. J. Psychiatry* 143, 367 (1986).
14. J *Monahan, Predicting Violent Behavior* (Sage, Newbury, CA, 1981).
15. W. H. Friedrich and A. J. Einbender, *J. Clin. Child Psychol.* 12, 244 (1983); R. Loeber and T. Dishion, *Psychol. Bull.* 94, 68 (1983); R. Loeber and M. Stouthamer-Loeber, in *Crime and Justice*, M. Tonry and N. Morris, Eds. (Univ. of Chicago Press, Chicago, 1986), vol. 7, pp. 219–339.
16. Department of Justice, *Crime in the United States—1985* (Government Printing Office, Washington, DC, 1986), pp. 166–67 and 182–184.
17. S. Glueck and E. Glueck, *Unraveling Juvenile Delinquency* (Cambridge Univ. Press, Cambridge, 1950); D. O. Lewis and S. S. Shanok, *Am. J. Psychiatry* 134, 1010 (1977); C. M. Mouzakitis, in *Exploring the Relationship Between Child Abuse and*

18. P. C. Kratcoski, *Child Welf.* 61, 435 (1982).
19. J. Alfaro, in *Exploring the Relationship Between Child Abuse and Delinquency*, R. J. Hunner and Y. E. Walker, Eds. (Allanheld, Osmun, Montclair, NJ, 1981), pp. 175–219.
20. F. G. Bolton, I. Reich, S. E. Gutierres, *J. Fam. Iss.* 2, 531 (1981).
21. J. McCord, *Child Abuse Negl.* 7, 265 (1983).
22. R. L. Jenkins, *Am. J. Psychiatry* 124, 1440 (1968); D. O. Lewis, S. S. Shanok, J. H. Pincus, G. H. Glaser, *J. Am. Acad. Child Psychiatry* 18, 307 (1979); S. Gutierres and J. A. Reich, *Child Welf.* 60, 89 (1981); M. Geller and L. Ford-Somma, *Violent Homes, Violent Children* (Report to National Center for Child Abuse and Neglect, Washington, DC, 1984); D. O. Lewis *et al.*, *Am. J. Psychiatry* 142, 1161 (1985).
23. E. Hartstone and K. V. Hansen, in *Violent Juvenile Offenders: An Anthology*, R. A. Mathias, Ed. (National Council on Crime and Delinquency, San Francisco, CA, 1984), pp. 83–112.
24. C. E. Climent and F. R. Ervin, *Arch. Gen. Psychiatry* 27, 621 (1972); H. T. Blount and T. A. Chandler, *Psychol. Rep.* 44, 1126 (1979); M. Monane, D. Leichter, D. O. Lewis, *J. Am. Acad. Child Psychiatry* 23, 653 (1984); R. E. Tarter, A. M. Hegedus, N. E. Winsten, A. I. Alterman, *ibid.*, p. 668.
25. T. J. Reidy, *J. Clin. Psychol.* 33, 1140 (1977); R. L. Burgess and R. D. Conger, *Child Dev.* 49, 1163 (1978); C. George and M. Main, *ibid.* 50, 306 (1979); E. M. Kinard, *Am J. Orthopsychiatry* 50, 686 (1980); R. M. Barahal, J. Waterman, H. P. Martin, *J. Consult. Clin. Psychol.* 49, 508 (1981); M. A. Perry, L. D. Doran, E. A. Wells, *J. Clin. Child Psychol.* 12, 320 (1983); D. A. Wolfe and M. D. Mosk, *J. Consult. Clin. Psychol.* 51, 702 (1983); D. M. Bousha and C. T. Twentyman, *J. Abnorm. Psychol.* 93, 106 (1984).
26. C. A. Rohrbeck and C. T. Twentyman, *J. Consult. Clin. Psychol.* 54, 231 (1986).
27. D. J. Owens and M. A. Straus, *Aggressive Behav.* 1, 193 (1975); D. Kalmuss, *J. Marriage Fam.* 46, 11 (1984); P. C. Kratcoski, *J. Adolesc.* 8, 145 (1985).
28. D. A. Wolfe, P. Jaffe, S. K. Wilson, L. Zak, *J. Consult. Clin. Psychol.* 53, 657 (1985); P. Jaffe, D. A. Wolfe, S. Wilson, L. Zak, *Am. J. Orthopsychiatry* 56, 142 (1986).
29. A complete description of the design of this study and details of the subject selection criteria are given by C. S. Widom (*Am. J. Orthopsychiatry*, in press).
30. A. Blumstein, J. Cohen, D. P. Farrington, *Criminology* 26, 1 (1988).
31. T. Hirschi, *Causes of Delinquency* (Univ. of California Press, Berkeley, 1969).
32. M. J. Hindelang, T. Hirschi, J. G. Weis, *Measuring Delinquency* (Sage, Beverly Hills, CA, 1981).
33. F. Schulsinger, S. A. Mednick, J. Knop, *Longitudinal Research: Methods and Uses in Behavioral Sciences* (Nijhoff, Boston, 1981).
34. J. M. Leventhal, *Child Abuse Negl.* 6, 113 (1982).
35. Excluded were juvenile court cases that represented: (i) adoption of the child as an infant (*n* = 322), (ii) "involuntary" neglect only (*n* = 319), (iii) placement only (*n* = 72), and (iv) cases of "failure to pay child support" (FTPCS) (*n* = 898). "Involuntary neglect" refers to cases in which the mother or other legal guardian is temporarily unable to provide for child (children) because of institutionalization in a girls' school, jail, prison, mental hospital, or medical facility. In FTPCS, there was no indication of neglect on the part of the caretaking parent. These cases represented a necessary step in seeking financial support from the noncustodial parent. There were 76 other exclusions, for the same and one additional reason (a morals charge against a mother with no evidence of abuse or neglect). Cases that involved adoption of an abused or neglected child were also excluded. Because of name changes concurrent with adoption and moves away from the county and state, the ability to locate official criminal histories for these individuals was seriously impaired. Thus, these 162 cases involving adoption were eliminated from the final sample. These findings, then, are not generalizable to adoptive cases of abused or neglected children.
36. Matching for social class is important in this study because it is theoretically plausible that any relation between child abuse or neglect and later delinquency or adult criminality is confounded or explained by social class differences. It is difficult to match exactly for social class because higher income families could live in lower social class neighborhoods and vice versa. The matching procedure used here is based on a broad definition of social class that includes neighborhoods in which children were reared and schools they attended. Similar procedures, with neighborhood school matches, have been used in studies of schizophrenics [for example, N. F. Watt, *J. Nerv. Ment. Dis.* 155, 42 (1972)] to match approximately for social class. Busing was not operational at this time, and students in elementary schools in this county were from small, socioeconomically homogeneous neighborhoods. After inspecting the home addresses of abused and neglected children and their matches, often the same street a few houses apart, it appeared as if the school matches might be closer than the birth record matches in terms of social class. To determine whether this matching procedure produced groups not evenly matched (hospital and school record matches), the analyses were repeated for the two subsets (abused and neglected children and their birth record matches and abused and neglected children and their school record matches), and they yielded essentially the same results. Although it would be surprising if social class had no effect on these results (arrest rates), given the matching procedure used here, there are good grounds for supposing that social class cannot explain all or possibly even most of the disparity in crime rates between the abused and neglected and the control groups.
37. The goal was to have a control group of approximately 700 subjects and to start with two matches (the second was backup in case the first was eliminated) for as many of the abused and neglected children as possible (up to 700). Non-matches occurred for a number of reasons. For matches through birth records, non-matches occurred in situations where the abused or neglected child was born outside the county or state or when date of birth information was missing. For school records,

non-matches occurred because class registers were unavailable because of the closing of the elementary school over the last 20 years or lack of adequate identifying information for the abused and neglected children.

38. An obvious limitation of this study is that the number in the control group who were actually abused, but not reported as such, is unknown. If the control group included subjects who had been officially reported as abused, at some earlier or later time period, this would jeopardize the design of the study. Thus, any child who had an official record of abuse or neglect was eliminated from the study, regardless of whether the abuse or neglect occurred before or after the time period of the study. An alternative was to include these subjects and treat them as a separate group in the analyses. However, because the number of these subjects was small ($n = 11$), this was not done.

39. M. E. Wolfgang, R. M. Figlio, T. Sellin, *Delinquency in a Birth Cohort* (Univ. of Chicago Press, Chicago, 1972); P. Strasburg, *Violent Delinquents* (Monarch, New York, 1978); D. Rojek and M. Erikson, *Criminology* 20, 5 (1982).

40. Violent crimes include arrests for robbery, assault, assault and battery, battery with injury, battery, aggravated assault, manslaughter/involuntary manslaughter/reckless homicide, murder/attempted murder, rape/sodomy, and robbery and burglary with injury.

41. A reanalysis of these findings was done, excluding abuse and neglect cases who did not have matches. Thus, the number of individuals in each group was 667. The results do not change with this smaller sample size. In cases where differences were significant, they became even more significant. In the few cases where differences were not significant, these results remained the same.

42. Because these findings are based on official records and official records overrepresent minority groups, the most obvious explanation for the higher rates of arrests for violent crimes among blacks would be the bias and discriminatory treatment by the criminal justice system. However, this explanation does not seem to explain the differences among blacks and the lack of difference for the whites, unless we postulate a "double jeopardy" theory. Another possible explanation is that parental violence is more severe among blacks than whites or that nonwhites are more physically abusive with their children and within their homes than whites; however, the data indicate that this is not the case. Among whites, approximately 20% suffered physical abuse, compared to less than 9% for blacks. Blacks suffered

more neglect, relative to whites in the sample.

43. M. Gottfredson and T. Hirschi, *Criminology* 26, 37 (1988).

44. R. J. Baker and J. A. Nelder, *The GLIM System, Release 3.77: Generalised Linear Interactive Modeling Manual* (Numerical Algorithms Group, Oxford, 1986).

45. Separate logit analyses were done by using different methods of dividing the abuse and neglect groups in addition to the one presented here, which is based on pure groups. In these analyses, the same pattern emerged, indicating the importance of physical abuse only and neglect. One exception was in replicating the logit analysis by using only those abused or neglected cases with matches. Here, in addition to physical abuse and neglect as significant predictors, sexual abuse only was also significant.

46. L. P. Groeneveld and J. M. Giovannoni, *Soc. Work Res. Abstr.* 13, 24 (1977).

47. R. J. Gelles, *Am. J. Orthopsychiatry* 45, 363 (1975); E. H. Newberger, R. B. Reed, J. H. Daniel, J. N. Hyde, M. Kotelchuck, *Pediatrics* 60, 178 (1977).

48. R. J. Gelles and C. P. Cornell, *Intimate Violence in Families* (Sage, Beverly Hills, CA 1985).

49. M. D. Pagelow, "Child abuse and delinquency: Are there connections between childhood violence and later deviant behavior?" Presented at the Tenth World Congress of the International Sociological Association, Mexico City, Mexico, 1982.

50. G. Bach-y-Rita and A. Veno, *Am. J. Psychiatry* 131, 1015 (1974); J. Kagan, *Daedalus (Boston)* 106, 33 (1977); H. P. Martin and P. Beezley, *Dev. Med. Child Neurol.* 19, 373 (1977); A. H. Green, *Am. J. Psychiatry* 135, 579 (1978).

51. A. Frodi and J. Smetana, *Child Abuse Negl.* 8, 459 (1984); M. A. Lynch and J. Roberts, *Consequences of Child Abuse* (Academic Press, London, 1982).

52. N. Garmezy, in *Further Explorations in Personality*, A. I. Robin, J. Aronoff, A. M. Barclay, R. A. Zucker, Eds. (Wiley, New York, 1981), pp. 196–269.

53. K. Heller, personal communication.

54. Supported in part by the National Institute of Justice grant 86-IJ-CX-0033, by Indiana University Biomedical Research grant S07 RR07031, and by a Talley Foundation grant w true the author was a visiting scholar in the Psychology Department at Harvard University, Cambridge, MA. I thank A. Ames, J. Lindsay, B. Rivera, and B. Tshanz for assistance with the data collection and B. Ross for assistance with the data analysis.

J. Child Psychol. Psychiat., Vol. 16, 1975, pp. 125 to 140. Pergamon Press. Printed in Great Britain.

ARRESTS AND DELINQUENCY IN TWO GENERATIONS: A STUDY OF BLACK URBAN FAMILIES AND THEIR CHILDREN

Lee N. Robins, Patricia A. West and Barbara L. Herjanic*

It is part of our folk wisdom that children resemble their parents in deviant behavior. As we say, "the apple does not fall far from the tree". Systematic evidence for the similarity of parents' and children's deviance dates at least from work in the 1920's by Burt (1925) and by Healy and Bronner (1926). Whether one looks at studies that take delinquent children as index cases and contrast their parents with the parents of non-delinquents, or whether one looks at studies that take criminals as the index cases and compare their offspring with those of non-criminal parents, the fact that deviance is linked across generations seems unanimously confirmed. What we know little about at this point is under what conditions this linkage occurs and whether there is a reflection in children of specific parents' behaviors or only a general tendency for deviance in one generation to be followed by some form of deviance in the next.

It is clear that there is not a simple invariate repetition of parental behaviors by children. While criminal parents tend to produce more than their share of disturbed children, some of their children appear normal and the disturbance in others is not always delinquency. Conversely, while delinquents seem to have "bad" parents more often than non-delinquents, many have apparently adequate parents and when the parent is not adequate, his problems may be something other than illegal acts. In the absence of perfect concordance between the behavior of parents and children, studying the conditions under which and the forms in which deviance in one generation is passed on to the next may provide suggestions as to how that transmission could be interrupted.

A study of the adopted children of criminals by Hutchings and Mednick (in press) suggests there are both genetic and environmental factors in the transmission of deviance, since children's criminality was related to criminality of both biological and adoptive parents. Unless the association with behavior of the adoptive parent was due entirely to selective adoptive placement of the offspring of criminals, this would suggest that the environment must have at the minimum a triggering effect for children with a genetic predisposition to deviance. Since removing all children of deviant parents to non-deviant homes would be both impractical and a gross invasion of parental rights, it would be useful to learn whether there were any natural childhood settings which seem to reduce the risk of deviance for the children of deviant parents in the hopes of fostering such countervalent forces.

*From the Department of Psychiatry, Washington University School of Medicine, 4940 Audubon Avenue, St. Louis, Missouri, 63110 U.S.A.

Accepted manuscript received 19 *June* 1974

125

Several years ago, the first author became interested in the possibility that the quality of the extended family might help to explain whether or not parents' deviant behavior was passed on to their children. It was likely that the extended family would play a larger role in the lives of children of deviant parents than of non-deviants, since inadequacies in the natural parents often required grandparents or aunts and uncles to step in as caretakers. To lay the groundwork for exploring the effect of the grandparents, we had asked the index subjects in a follow-up study of white adults, who were formerly child guidance clinic patients or normal control subjects chosen from school records, for the names and ages of their children. We already had considerable information about the grandparents of these children from the original clinic records, which contained information about their functioning as parents of the index patient cases. In addition, both patient and control cases were asked many questions about their parents in interview.

For 67 sons over age 18 and reared in our own city, we located school records and checked police records. We found, as we had expected, a relationship between the index cases' deviant behavior and their sons' failure to complete high school and delinquency (Robins and Lewis, 1966). And we also found a striking relationship between the sons' problems and reports of deviance in their grandparents, i.e. parents of our index cases. While this finding was consistent with the hypothesis that the behavior of the extended family might modify the child's outcome, the study had some important weaknesses. Only sons were studied; their number was small; and their parents were predominantly child guidance clinic patients who may not be representative of the general population of parents of deviant and non-deviant children. In addition, information about the non-index parent was limited to reports in interview by the spouse and such records concerning the index case as happened to refer to the spouse, and we had no information about his or her parents, i.e. the other set of grandparents.

The current study is an attempt to improve on the first one and to extend it to a normal black sample of children of both sexes. The design resembles that of the first study in that the starting point was a follow-up of children into adulthood and that, during the follow-up interview, these now adult males were asked for the names and ages of each of their children as well as for information about the behavior of their spouses and parents. In an extension of the design of the original study we also obtained the name and age of each child's mother, so that records for the non-index parent could be sought. Thus our information is somewhat more symmetrical than in the first study and covers paternal aunts and uncles as well as grandparents. The study is still in progress, but a first portion of it, to be reported here, has been completed.

METHOD

In 1965 and 1966, 223 out of 235 black men aged 30–36 who had been identified in St. Louis public elementary school records, were located and interviewed. In addition, their school records through high school were obtained as well as records from a number of other agencies, including the police and the juvenile court. To be eligible for the study, elementary school I.Q. records of 85 or higher were required. The sample was chosen so that in elementary school half appeared to be

A STUDY OF BLACK URBAN FAMILIES AND THEIR CHILDREN 127

living in intact families and half in broken homes, judging from the name of the guardian on the school records; half had moderate to severe truancy and/or academic retardation and half had less severe or no elementary school problems; half had guardians in the lowest socio-economic status (i.e. unemployed, domestics or un-skilled laborers) and half had guardians with jobs above that range. All had been born in St. Louis and had resided there at some time between 1959 and 1964 (i.e. after age 25). The sample selection criteria were devised for testing the effect of broken homes, school problems and social class on the black men's outcome. They have no direct relevance to this study of the offsprings' outcomes. However, it may be important to remember that the fathers came from the top half of the I.Q. range of black public school students of that era and that there were approximately twice as many from the higher socio-economic statuses as one would have found by chance.

When each man was interviewed, we asked him for names, birthdates, and sex of his children and for the names and ages of his children's mother(s). His answers enabled us to identify children and mothers in public records. We also asked whether he had any illegitimate children but did not pursue their names and their mothers' names if they were not volunteered. For all children, we asked which had lived with the father and with whom they had lived when they were not with him. To get a measure of the father's (the index subject's) own involvement with the extended family, we asked whether he kept in touch with his blood relatives and with his current or most recent wife's relatives.

Because the men were in their early thirties when interviewed, many of their children are still too young to know for certain whether they will graduate from high school or whether they will become juvenile delinquents. Therefore we are studying only those children who were 18 by 31 December 1973. There were 198 qualifying children reported in interviews with 101 men. For 145 of these children, we found records indicating that they had lived in St. Louis at some time. The current report deals with these 145 children and their families. They are the children of 76 men involved in 80 relationships with 79 women. (One of the mothers had children by two of the men in the sample. If this seems a remarkable coincidence, remember that the men were all about the same age, all attended the same public schools and lived in the same urban ghetto, which is really a small town within a large city.) The 53 children omitted either grew up outside of St. Louis, were illegitimate child-ren whose names had not been volunteered by the father, or were children whom we could not identify in records, often because the mother had remarried and the child was using the unknown step-father's name. Illegitimate children and those brought up in other men's households were included when they could be identified. Eleven (8 per cent) of the 145 children included were illegitimate and 7 (5 per cent) ap-peared in records under a last name other than that of their father.

Because the men were only 30–36 when interviewed in 1965 and 1966, for their children to have now reached the age of 18, they had to have been born by the time their fathers were approximately 25 yr of age. We were concerned that our age requirements, by selecting men who became fathers early, might have selected unusually deviant or unusually conforming fathers. However, there is no evidence that the fathers of these children differed in early deviance from men who had

128   LEE N. ROBINS, PATRICIA A. WEST AND BARBARA L. HERJANIC

no children or had them later in life (Table 1). Similar proportions had been held back and truanted in elementary school, had finished high school, and had been known to the juvenile authorities. Since excluding children born to fathers over age 25 does not seem to have biased our selection of their fathers, the results reported here would probably be representative of children of our total sample.

TABLE 1. FATHERS OF OFFSPRING STUDIED COMPARED WITH TOTAL PREVIOUS
GENERATION

	Fathers (76) (%)	Total sample from fathers' generation (235) (%)
Held back and truanted in elementary school	19	20
Finished high school	47	53
Had juvenile offense	31	29

For mothers and children, we sought school and juvenile court records. We often had first to obtain birth certificates to get precise dates of birth and early addresses with which to verify identities in school and police records. We also obtained the mothers' adult arrest records and updated the fathers' arrest records to the age at which his youngest child in the study was aged 17. The present report is based on police and juvenile records of both parents, police and juvenile court records of the offspring, and information about other relatives obtained through the father's interview and occasionally through records sought for the father which mentioned deviance of his parents or siblings. No attempt has been made to interview the children or their mothers. Because information about police records of fathers, mothers, and offspring are based entirely on official records, and not on interview data, there is no possibility that bias or halo effects on the part of the researchers has played a part in finding relationships between the police records of the two generations. Of course, it is entirely possible that the appearance of a record for the child may reflect bias on the part of a policeman or judge who happened to know that one or both parents had a record.

Delinquency in this study is defined as being known to the juvenile court or to the police before the age of 17 for a non-traffic offense. "Adult" arrests are non-traffic arrests at age 17 or later. The choice of age 17 as the cut-off point conforms to the Missouri law defining juveniles.

The present paper sets out to do three things:

(1) To learn whether there have been changes in delinquency patterns over a generation.

(2) To establish the extent and nature of the continuity between parents' arrest histories and their children's.

(3) To find other family characteristics that might protect children of arrested parents from repeating the parental pattern.

RESULTS

(1) *Changes in delinquency over a generation*

Surprisingly, in the light of the widespread reports of increases in juvenile delinquency over the last 20–30 yr, we found no change in the proportion known to the juvenile court or to the police before the age of 17 in the two generations (Table 2). The fathers had a juvenile delinquency rate of 31 per cent and their sons also had a delinquency rate of 31 per cent. Girls had a lower rate of delinquency, only 14 per cent, as had their mothers before them (16 per cent). (For this calculation, we omitted mothers whose school records showed they grew up outside the St. Louis area and thus were not at risk of arrest by the St. Louis police. All the fathers were reared in St. Louis.) These delinquency rates are higher than were rates in the earlier study of the white sons of patients and controls, of whom only 19 per cent had a juvenile offense. This probably reflects a difference in liability to arrest by race, rather than an increase in overall rates of delinquency in the intervening 9 yr between the two studies.

TABLE 2. JUVENILE DELINQUENCY IN TWO GENERATIONS (EXCLUDING TRAFFIC ARRESTS)

	Males		Females	
	N	Percent delinquent	N	Percent delinquent
Parents	(75)	31	(64)*	16
Offspring	(86)	31	(59)	14

*Mothers whose high school records showed them to have grown up outside of St. Louis are excluded since they would not have been at risk of being known to St. Louis police or juvenile courts. Since the fathers were all selected from St. Louis school records, they were by definition at risk of arrest in St. Louis.

In the current all-black sample, the ratio of male to female rates of delinquency was 2 : 1. This is a considerably lower ratio between the sexes than is usually reported (Lunden, 1964, Table 23).

Not only has the overall number of delinquents remained much the same between one generation and the next, but the frequency of offense types has also remained much the same (Table 3). The offenses in Table 3 for the fathers are based on the total sample rather than only on the fathers of these particular boys, to provide more stable estimates of the rates for specific offenses in the parent generation. As compared with the fathers' generation, the sons show a slight increase in auto theft, perhaps because there are more autos, and a slight increase in narcotics arrests. However, there is nothing like the tide of narcotic arrests that reports of a heroin epidemic in the late 1960's might have led us to expect. Indeed, among boys young enough to acquire a juvenile arrest for drugs after 1968, there was only a single case. In both generations the principal offense was theft.

Missouri juvenile court records are destroyed when the offender reaches age 21, but a card is kept indicating that he or she was known to the court. Since girls' referrals to juvenile court were often parent-initiated, rather than police-initiated, there was often no associated police report to explain the nature of the complaint. Thus we lack information in some cases about the charge against the mothers and the older daughters. We can note, however, an apparent small increase in the frequency of theft among girls, since this is an offense which comes to police attention. There is also a suggestion that girls may have become delinquent earlier in the younger generation. However, the small numbers make both observations questionable.

130   LEE N. ROBINS, PATRICIA A. WEST AND BARBARA L. HERJANIC

TABLE 3. HAS THE NATURE OF JUVENILE DELINQUENCY CHANGED?

	Father's generation (235) (%)	Sons (86) (%)	Mothers (79) (%)	Daughters (59) (%)
Delinquent	29	31	16	14
Age first offense				
Before 13	10	10	3	4
13–14	7	6	3	5
15–16	12	15	10	5
One offense	17*	12	9	8
Two offenses	7	7	4	2
Three or more	12	12	3	4
Nature of offense‡				
Theft	19	20	1	7
Peace disturbance	8	7	1	4
Vandalism	6	10	1	0
Injury	5	8	0	3
Weapons	5	7	0	2
Sex	4	5	1	0
Runaway	4	3	1	3
Auto theft	3	6	0	0
Incorrigible	1	3	5	5
Narcotics	†	3	0	0

*Adds to more than 29 per cent because arrests through age 17 are included.
†Less than 0·5 per cent.
‡Add to less than 16 per cent for mothers because court records are destroyed at age 21. Information about specific offenses comes only from police records for older generation.

(2) *The effect of parental arrest*

(a) *The transmission of delinquency between parents and children.* Figure 1 presents the association between the parents' delinquency and their child's. The left side of the figure takes the parent as the index case and looks at the frequency with which a parent produced one or more delinquent sons or daughters, given that he or she had at least one child of the appropriate sex. The right side of Fig. 1 takes the child as the index case and looks at the frequency with which he or she had a delinquent parent. Looking at the left side, we note that while delinquency in both the mother and father is associated with delinquency in their sons, there is a significant increase only for the mothers.

The chances of having at least one delinquent son or daughter increase, of course, with family size and thus an association between parental delinquency and large families might account for the relationship between parent's and children's delinquency. On the right hand side of Fig. 1, where results are presented from the child's point of view, family size is not confounded with parents' delinquency, since every child has exactly one father and mother. Delinquent offspring of both sexes tended to have delinquent mothers at a level well above chance. Delinquent boys also tended to have delinquent fathers, but the difference was not quite significant. For daughters there was no association between their own delinquency and delinquency in the father.

A STUDY OF BLACK URBAN FAMILIES AND THEIR CHILDREN 131

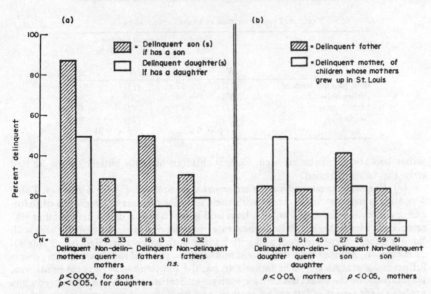

FIG. 1. Transmission of delinquency between generations. (a) From parent's point of view: risk of having a delinquent child. (b) From child's point of view: risk of having a delinquent parent.

Although delinquency in females is rare in both generations, the association between mothers' and daughters' delinquency was so strong that in parents of delinquent girls the 2 : 1 ratio of male to female delinquency in the overall sample is reversed to 1 : 2. The stronger effect of maternal than paternal delinquency on boys as well is shown by reduction of the male–female ratio of delinquency in the parents of delinquent boys to 1·6 : 1 while it is increased to 3 : 1 in the parents of non-delinquent boys.

(c) *Adult parental arrests.* It is sometimes thought that young black males are so vulnerable to arrest in U.S. cities and that their arrests are so random that one could neither expect to find many free of arrest records nor any meaningful correlates of their being arrested. In our sample, however, 38 per cent of the boys and 44 per cent of the girls had fathers who had had no significant arrests (i.e. not more than two arrests of any kind, no convictions, and no arrests for a felony). In addition, paternal arrests were strongly associated with the delinquency of their children (Table 4). Almost half of the boys with an arrested father were delinquent (45 per cent), compared with only 9 per cent of those whose father was not arrested. For girls, 24 per cent were delinquent when they had an arrested father and none was delinquent when the father had not been arrested.

For both sexes, having both parents arrested was associated with a higher risk than was having only one parent arrested. It is difficult to say whether this was an effect of the mother's arrest or an effect of a double dose of parental influence, irrespective of the parent's sex, because it was rare to have a mother arrested if the

132   LEE N. ROBINS, PATRICIA A. WEST AND BARBARA L. HERJANIC

TABLE 4. EFFECTS OF TWO PARENTS' ADULT ARRESTS

| | Percent delinquent among | | | |
| | Boys (86) | | Girls (59) | |
	N	(%)	N	(%)
Both parents arrested	(21)	57	(13)	31
Father only	(32)	38	(20)	20
Mother only	(7)	43	(2)	0
Neither	(26)	0	(24)	0
	$p < 0.001$		$p < 0.01$	

father had not also been arrested. Only 9 children had this pattern, while 52 had only the father arrested.

(c) *Comparing parental delinquency and arrests as predictors of offspring delinquency.* Table 5 compares parents' adult arrests with their juvenile offenses as predictors of delinquency in their offspring. For both boys and girls, having a delinquent mother was associated with a higher delinquency rate than having a delinquent father, with having either parent arrested, and with having both parents arrested (see Table 4). However, the number with delinquent mothers was so small that it was not a powerful predictor statistically. The father's arrest, the most common of these predictors, was statistically the most powerful for both sexes. Statistically, the two best predictors for boys were arrests of father and mother, and for girls, father's arrest and mother's delinquency. Putting these two predictors together (Table 6), it is possible to predict delinquency with about the same level of success for boys as for girls. Note that no boy or girl is delinquent in the absence of both predictors, and also note that both boys and girls are delinquent in only slightly over half the cases when both parental predictors are present.

TABLE 5. PARENTS' ARREST COMPARED WITH PARENTS' DELINQUENCY AS PREDICTORS OF CHILD'S DELINQUENCY

| | Percent delinquent among | | | |
| | Sons | | Daughters | |
	N	(%)	N	(%)
Father has adult arrest	(52)	44	(33)	23
None	(34)	12	(26)	0
	$p < 0.003$		$p < 0.02$	
Father is delinquent	(26)	46	(14)	14
Not	(60)	25	(45)	13
	$p < 0.05$		n.s.	
Mother has adult arrest	(31)	48	(15)	27
None	(55)	22	(44)	9
	$p < 0.02$		$p < 0.10$	
Mother is delinquent	(11)	64	(9)	44
Not	(66)	29	(44)	9
	$p < 0.05$		$p < 0.03$	

Taking boys and girls together, having two parents arrested was the strongest predictor of delinquency. Half (50 per cent) were delinquent with both parents arrested. If in addition the father had been a juvenile delinquent, the rate increased to 56 per cent; if the mother had been a delinquent, it increased to 60 per cent; and if both parents had been delinquent, it increased to 67 per cent. Thus even with both parents delinquent *and* arrested, 2 of the 6 children so affected were not themselves delinquent.

TABLE 6. TWO BEST PARENTAL PREDICTORS FOR BOYS AND GIRLS

			Proportion delinquent when			
Boys				Girls		
	N	(%)			N	(%)
Father and mother arrested	(21)	57	Father arrested and mother delinquent		(7)	57
One parent arrested	(41)	37	Father arrested, mother not delinquent		(25)	16
Neither parent arrested	(24)	0	Father not arrested		(21)	0
	$p < 0.001$				$p < 0.001$	
	$\varphi = 0.46$				$\varphi = 0.50$	

(3) *Behavior of members of the extended paternal family*

Since only about half of the children were delinquent even when they had both the better two parental predictors of delinquency, and only two-thirds when all 4 parental predictors were present, some factors other than the parents' infractions of the law must explain why some of these children became delinquent and others did not. To search for protective factors, we consulted information from the father's interview about the behavior of his parents and siblings. Antisocial behavior on the part of both paternal grandparents was associated with delinquency in the children, but there was little difference between one antisocial grandparent and neither (Table 7). When paternal aunts or uncles had been arrested, more children were delinquent. Delinquency was less powerfully related to paternal relatives' behavior than to parents' behavior.

TABLE 7. EXTENDED FAMILY AND CHILDREN'S DELINQUENCY

	Proportion delinquent among			
	Boys		Girls	
	N	(%)	N	(%)
Paternal grandparents antisocial				
Both	(6)	83	(6)	33
One	(40)	33	(26)	11
Neither	(40)	23	(28)	11
	$p < 0.02$		$p < 0.15$	
Paternal aunt or uncle arrested				
Yes	(42)	40	(25)	24
No	(38)	24	(30)	7
	$p < 0.10$		$p < 0.10$	

In our previous study of the offspring of white child guidance clinic patients and controls, we had found grandparents' behavior more strongly related to child-

134   LEE N. ROBINS, PATRICIA A. WEST AND BARBARA L. HERJANIC

ren's delinquency than we did parents' behavior (Table 8). We were puzzled by the strong relationship between the grandparent and grandchild's behavior in the earlier study, having expected the behavior of the parent to have a more direct effect. The current study supports our earlier expectation.

The difference in the results of the two studies may result from differences in the sources of data. Most of the information about grandparents in the first study came from psychiatric clinic records, made when the parent was about age 13 and grandparents in their late thirties or early forties. Information about grandparental deviance was being sought to explain the behavior of the parent, who had been referred for psychiatric or behavior problems. In the current study, grandparents were twenty years older at the time of data collection and the parent was not a patient. Since acting-out behavior often decreases with aging, any deviance the grandparents may have shown was more probably long past and recall of it less accurate, particularly since there was no motivation to recall it to explain the parents' behavior.

TABLE 8. THREE GENERATIONS: EFFECTS OF ANTISOCIAL GRANDPARENTS VS PARENTS
IN BLACKS AND WHITES

	White sons age 17 by 1959		Delinquency in Black sons age 17 by 1973		Black daughters age 17 by 1973	
	N	(%)	N	(%)	N	(%)
Overall rates	(67)	19	(86)	31	(59)	14
Either grandparent antisocial	(36)	33	(46)	39	(32)	16
Neither grandparent antisocial	(31)	3	(40)	23	(27)	11
Either parent antisocial	(28)	28	(63)	43	(35)	23
Neither parent antisocial	(39)	13	(23)	0	(24)	0

Failure to recall deviance long past should strengthen, rather than reduce, the relationship between grandparents' and their grandchildren's behavior if that relationship depends on the child's being exposed to a *current* example of the grandparents' deviance. But if the mode of effect was indirect—through the grandparents' influence on the parent—forgetting his past deviance should attenuate the relationship.

The relationship between grandparents' and grandchildren's deviance did appear to be more indirect than direct. It will be noted in Fig. 2 that the grandparents' behavior seemed to affect parents' arrests more than grandchildren's delinquency. In addition, when the two best parental predictors were held constant (parents' adult arrests for boys and fathers' arrest history plus mothers' delinquency for girls), the effect of the grandparents' behavior was no longer statistically significant. Thus we infer that the chief influence of the grandparental deviance was to produce antisocial parents who in turn influenced the child, rather than directly affecting the child himself. The effect of the parents on the child, when one controls on whether or not the grandparent was antisocial, remains strong ($p < 0.001$), indicating that the parent's behavior affects his child's whether or not he himself is the offspring of an antisocial parent.

A STUDY OF BLACK URBAN FAMILIES AND THEIR CHILDREN 135

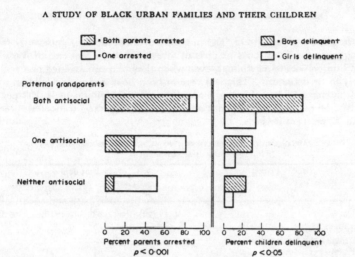

FIG. 2. Effect of antisocial paternal grandparents on parents' arrests and children's delinquency. Grandparents vs children, controlling on parent arrest: *n.s.* Parents vs children, controlling on antisocial grandparents: $p < 0.001$.

The grandparent's deviance had an additional indirect effect which we had not anticipated. Whenever both paternal grandparents were antisocial, not only were almost all of their sons arrested, but almost all of the sons' spouses as well. Thus children with antisocial grandparents were likely to have *two* arrested parents. When only one paternal grandparent was antisocial, there was also an increased but smaller risk of having both parents arrested.

Although we cannot show a statistically significant direct effect of grandparents' behavior on grandchildren's delinquency, the rare cases where both grandparents were antisocial have the highest rate of delinquency (83 per cent) among boys found with any combination of predictors, and a rate for girls (40 per cent) almost as high as when the mother was delinquent. The failure to find a statistically significant direct effect may be due only to the small number of children (11) with two antisocial grandparents.

Like the grandparent's effect, the effect of aunt's or uncle's arrest diminished when the parent's arrest was held constant, but the trend persisted. When a parent had been arrested but the paternal aunts and uncles were law-abiding, 37 per cent of boys and 17 per cent of girls were delinquent, compared with 50 per cent of boys and 30 per cent of girls when an aunt or uncle was also arrested.

(4) *Other family characteristics*

In addition to the behavior of grandparents and aunts and uncles, we examined other family characteristics that might protect the child from delinquency when both his parents had been arrested (Table 9). We examined the father's job level, which relatives lived in the child's city, broken marriages for parents and paternal aunts and uncles, education of paternal grandparents and paternal aunts and uncles, and

136   LEE N. ROBINS, PATRICIA A. WEST AND BARBARA L. HERJANIC

size of the child's sibling group. The only one of these factors significantly related
to delinquency for either boys or girls of arrested parents was size of the sibling
group. Children with fewer siblings, even when they had two arrested parents, were
less likely to be delinquent. This was true of both boys and girls. Children of two
arrested parents who had three or more siblings were delinquent in 100 per cent
of boys and 50 per cent of girls; with one or two siblings rates were 50 per cent for
boys and 22 per cent for girls.

TABLE 9. DELINQUENCY IN CHILDREN OF TWO ARRESTED PARENTS WITH VARYING
FAMILY CHARACTERISTICS

| | Percent delinquent | | | |
| | Boys | | Girls | |
	N	(%)	N	(%)
Total	(21)	69	(13)	31
Family characteristics				
Relatives in St. Louis				
Paternal grandmother	(14)	64	(11)	36
Paternal grandfather	(5)	100	(2)	100
Paternal uncle	(18)	67	(8)	38
Paternal aunt	(20)	65	(9)	44
High school graduation by relatives				
One or both paternal grandparents	(10)	60	(9)	33
Neither grandparent	(11)	73	(4)	25
Any aunt or uncle	(10)	80	(7)	43
All dropouts	(8)	50	(3)	33
Father's job				
Low	(13)	62	(10)	20
High	(8)	75	(3)	67
Marital stability				
Father's first marriage intact	(0)	—	(2)	0
remarried	(5)	80	(5)	20
divorced or separated	(15)	60	(6)	50
Paternal aunt and uncle				
unmarried or first marriage intact	(2)	100	(2)	0
divorced or separated	(17)	59	(8)	50
Number of siblings				
Two or less	(14)	50	(9)	22
Three or more	(7)	100	(4)	50

One reason having a large number of siblings might have led to delinquency is
that it increased the chance of having at least one delinquent sibling. Of children
with 1 or 2 siblings over 18, 25 per cent of boys and 31 per cent of girls had a delinquent sibling; of those with 3 or more siblings over 18, 58 per cent of boys and 50
per cent of girls had a delinquent sibling (Table 10). In both small and large families,
having a delinquent sibling was associated with being delinquent oneself. Brothers
of delinquents were delinquent in 69 per cent of cases in small families and 57 per
cent of cases in large families, compared with 21 per cent and 20 per cent respectively
when siblings were not delinquent. Sisters of delinquents were delinquent in 18 per
cent of cases in small families and 25 per cent of cases in large families, compared
with 8 per cent and 0 per cent respectively when siblings were not delinquent. While

there are too few large families in our sample to give us confidence in these results, it looks as though a principal mechanism through which large families encourage delinquency (see West, 1973), may be through increasing the risk of exposure to a delinquent sibling.

TABLE 10. FAMILY SIZE AND DELINQUENCY IN SIBLINGS OVER 18

	Proportion with at least one delinquent sibling			
	One or two siblings over 18		Three or four siblings over 18	
Boys	(51)	25%	(12)	58%
Girls	(35)	31	(8)	50

	Proportion delinquent when						
	One or more siblings delinquent				No siblings delinquent		
	One or two siblings over 17		Three or four siblings over 17		One or two siblings over 17		Three or four siblings over 17
Boys	(13)	69%	(7)	57%	(38)	21%	(5) 20%
Girls	(11)	18	(4)	25	(24)	8	(4) 0

DISCUSSION

Methods

This paper introduces a method for investigating the effect of parents' behavior on their children's behavior. We started with a life history interview with a cohort of men whose names had been selected from elementary school records, who were born and brought up in the same city in which they lived as adults, and who had children old enough to have passed through the age of risk for delinquency. We asked the men for their children's names, ages and the children's mothers' names. Armed with these, we located birth dates, school records and police and juvenile court records for fathers, mothers and children. After investigating the relationships between parents' and children's arrest records, we used information obtained at interviews with the fathers to attempt to learn what other family factors might be important in explaining the children's arrests.

Arrest records were chosen over interview data about arrests because they are relatively easy-to-locate objective measures. The cohort design using parents as index cases was chosen in preference to two other ways in which we might have sought the arrest records of two generations: (1) an area survey in which parents of children 18 yr or older would have been interviewed to obtain identifying data with which records for both generations could be sought, or (2) identifying a cohort from school or birth records, as we did, but asking about their parents rather than their children, and then proceeding in the same way we have in this study to locate records of both generations.

As compared with the area survey, the cohort study avoids a number of biases. In area surveys, deviants tend to be missed because they are away from home much of the time, have no fixed residence, or are currently in hospitals or jails. Those parents found at home might avoid mentioning children who are highly deviant. Any method which reduces the availability of deviant cases is obviously undesirable

138   LEE N. ROBINS, PATRICIA A. WEST AND BARBARA L. HERJANIC

when studying arrest histories. In our cohort study such biases against deviant parental cases were avoided by identifying the fathers in early school records, before they became deviant, and locating virtually all as adults even when in jail or hospitals. Biases against deviant cases of children were avoided by asking the fathers to identify their children at ages below which those children who eventually became delinquent had usually had their first arrest.

The second alternative, starting with a cohort of children rather than a cohort of parents, does not suffer from the problems of area surveys, but it would have created another problem. The parents of a cohort of children would have grown up in diverse geographical areas. This would have been even more the case for black parents than for whites, because of the large black migration from the rural south to northern cities in the last generation. As a result parents' records would have been hard to locate and less meaningful, since they would have resulted from unequal exposures to risk of arrest. In addition, children would have been less well informed about the birth dates, place of birth, and early addresses of their parents than parents were about their children's, which would have made the parents' positive identification in police records problematical.

The method we did choose required starting with parents who had a range of deviance. Just over half (58 per cent) of the fathers had had an adult police record and 31 per cent had had a delinquency record. Obviously it is not practical to start with parents who are likely to have a very low or very high rate of deviant behavior, since there will be few cases of the opposite type to permit contrasting the effects of deviance with no deviance. In our study, the low level of arrests (27 per cent) and delinquency (16 per cent) in mothers did hamper investigating the mother's effect.

Results

The rates of delinquency we found for boys (31 per cent) is considerably lower than the rate of 50 per cent reported by Wolfgang *et al.* (1972) for a black male school cohort in Philadelphia who reached the age of 18 by 1963. The difference may be largely accounted for by the fact that Pennsylvania law sets the upper age limit of juvenile status at 17, while Missouri law sets it at 16. But there may be other factors as well. Our sample selected fathers born in St. Louis, with I.Q.s of 85 or higher, and oversampled the higher occupations of the grandparents. These three decisions resulted in a sample of children from higher socio-economic statuses than the average black, since the fathers had been educated in urban schools, had good intellectual capacity, and had some family background advantage. This should not mislead the reader into thinking they were mostly middle class. The current occupations of index subjects (which included the fathers of these children) had a median Duncan socio-economic index score of 24, well below the national average of 36, but above the national average for blacks of 21 (Blau and Duncan, 1967, calculated from Table 6.3). The slightly high status of selected children may mean their rates of delinquency were somewhat below average. In Philadelphia, for instance, Wolfgang (1972) found that the delinquency rate dropped to 36 per cent for black boys from higher status families, a rate close enough to our 31 per cent to be explained by our lower cut off age.

It was surprising to find little change in delinquency rates over a generation in this cohort. To be sure, this was a short generation, since none of the fathers was more than 25 yr of age at the time that a child was born who could meet the age criteria for the study. Nonetheless this does raise questions in the light of widely reported rising delinquency rates. One wonders whether the national rise may not be almost entirely attributable to new groups, becoming at risk of delinquency rather than increases in rates in urban-born blacks, who were already at high risk. Migrants to the cities probably have much higher risks of arrest after arrival than they had had in the rual environments from which they came. In addition, middle class risks may have greatly increased, not only due to marijuana smoking and political demonstrations but because the police may be less likely to overlook delinquency in middle class children as the proportion of the middle class grows. It seems probable that special privilege can be extended to a group only when that group remains small.

We found parental arrests (as juveniles and adults) an extremely potent predictor of children's arrests, even in this high risk population of inner city black children. Parental arrest was as potent for girls as for boys. It has been commonly thought that delinquency, particularly in inner city areas, was chiefly a peer group phenomenon. These findings suggest that at best peer group pressure or imitation may be a necessary but not a sufficient condition to explain delinquency. Conforming parents apparently were able to innoculate their children against enticement into delinquent activities even in the high delinquency areas to which housing segregation confined most blacks.

While the effect of parents' arrests was very striking, explaining 50 per cent of the variance in both boys' and girls' delinquency, there was evidence that the child was not simply re-enacting his parent's behavior. The father's adult arrests were a more important predictor than his own delinquency, suggesting an environmental rather than a genetic effect. It will be possible in future papers to investigate whether amount of exposure to the arrested father was important, since many of these children, particularly those with arrested fathers, grew up in fatherless homes.

Arrests and delinquency in both parents seemed to make a difference in the behavior of children of both sexes. Therefore the mechanism of influence does not seem to be identification with the same-sex parent. However, the scarcity of arrested mothers makes estimates of the effect of the mother's arrests dubious. Future studies might well choose the mother rather than the father as the index parent, so that one could intentionally enrich the proportion of mothers with deviant histories. That plan, however, might result in a dearth of children without arrested fathers, since arrested women seldom have law-abiding mates.

Our efforts to do deviant case analysis, i.e. to find out why some children did not become delinquent even when they had two arrested parents, was not particularly successful. We found some evidence that the extended family in the persons of conforming paternal grandparents, aunts and uncles contributed to a child's chances of avoiding delinquency, but much of the effect appeared to be indirect, i.e. through influencing the parents' behavior. It is difficult to show an effect of any factors in addition to the parents' arrests in our relatively small sample when so much of the variance (50 per cent) was accounted for by parental arrest. A larger sample might make it possible to explore the effects of the extended family in more detail. We did note, however, a small effect not only of the extended family but also of

140   LEE N. ROBINS, PATRICIA A. WEST AND BARBARA L. HERJANIC

siblings' delinquency even when we restricted ourselves to children brought up by arrested parents.

The failure to show a large effect of the extended family means that our results so far have not produced clear-cut suggestions for intervention. Enlisting the services of conforming relatives would not seem a powerful enough method to overcome the effects of arrested parents. We plan next to relate school experience to delinquency for these children. Perhaps success in school will be a more powerful explanatory variable than conformity of relatives. If so, educational intervention may appear more clearly advantageous than mobilizing close relatives.

This study of black children has replicated some findings from our previous small study of sons of white child guidance clinic patients and matched controls. In both studies, we found that adult behavior of the parent was a more powerful predictor than his early delinquency. In both we also found that social class as reflected in the father's job made relatively little contribution when the deviance of the parent was taken into account.

In sum, the use of a parental cohort to identify and follow children through the age of risk of delinquency seems to be a feasible way to approach a difficult but important question: Under what conditions is parental deviance transmitted to children? We have yet to show that it produces a blueprint for intervening in that transmission.

SUMMARY

In interviews a cohort of 223 young black urban-born men were asked for names and ages of their children and the children's mothers. Police and juvenile court records were obtained for both parents and all offspring past the age of official designation as a juvenile—145 children of 76 men qualified. A comparison of juvenile records of parents and children showed similar rates and types of offenses. Parental arrest histories were powerful predictors of their children's delinquency. Other family characteristics that might modify the risks of delinquency in children of arrested parents were explored.

Acknowledgement—This paper was supported by U.S.P.H.S. Grants MH-18864 and MH-36598 (RSA).

REFERENCES

BLAU, P. M. and DUNCAN, O. D. (1967) *The American Occupational Structure*. Wiley, New York.
BURT, C. (1925) *The Young Delinquent*. Appleton & Co., New York.
HEALY, W. and BRONNER, A. F. (1926) *Delinquents and Criminals: Their Making and Unmaking*. Macmillan, New York.
HUTCHINGS, B. and MEDNICK, S. A. (In press) Registered criminality in the adoptive and biological parents of registered male criminal adoptees. In *Genetic Research in Psychiatry* (Edited by FIEVE, R., ROSENTHAL, D. and BRILL, H.). Johns Hopkins University Press, Baltimore.
LUNDEN, W. A. (1964) *Statistics on Delinquents and Delinquency*. Charles C Thomas, Springfield, Illinois.
ROBINS, L. N. and LEWIS, R. G. (1966) The role of the antisocial family in school completion and delinquency: a three generation study. *Soc. Q.* 7 (4), 500–514.
WEST, D. J. (1973) *Who Becomes Delinquent*. Heinemann, London.
WOLFGANG, M. E., FIGLIO, R. M. and SELLIN, T. (1972) *Delinquency in a Birth Cohort*. The University of Chicago Press, Chicago.

The Trasler Social Learning Theory

[15]

CRIMINALITY AND THE SOCIALISATION PROCESS*

By Prof. G. B. TRASLER   *Department of Psychology, University of Southampton*

The fact that criminologists from several disciplines are currently paying a great deal of attention to what is generally called 'the socialisation process' should occasion no surprise. Early students of crime, it is true, were inclined to believe that the marked reluctance to behave aggressively or to appropriate the property of others which characterises most men and women must be an inborn virtue; but the investigations of social anthropologists have shown that this is not so. The rules which define what is, and what is not, criminal behaviour are to a considerable extent peculiar to particular societies. However, to say that people learn not to behave criminally presents certain difficulties. Some writers (and for that matter most judges) have adopted a rather simple version of Thorndike's early view of punishment (which he later repudiated); they assume that the habit of stealing tends to be strengthened by satisfactory consequences, and can be stamped out by ensuring that the outcome of such behaviour is generally disagreeable. In its naïve form this assumption is clearly untenable; few of us, fortunately, have actually tried murder or burglary and sampled its unsatisfactory consequences—and on the other hand our central prisons are filled with recidivist thieves who have made a very poor living from their crimes. The effect-learning model was intended to apply to quite specific sequences of operant behaviour; what it has to say concerns changes in the frequency with which such actions will recur during a limited period of time. It is difficult to see how it could be made to account satisfactorily for the complex, pervasive and remarkably permanent results of the socialisation process.

A more promising alternative has been proposed by O. H. Mowrer, who has recently published a modified version of his two-factored theory of

learning.[1,2] The pivot of Mowrer's theory is the contention that in normal, well-socialised individuals impulses to behave criminally are reliably blocked by anxiety reactions (or, more precisely, transitory states of autonomic arousal) which have been acquired during childhood by a process of conditioning. The way in which this happens is most easily made clear by an example. Let us suppose that a small child who has suddenly lost patience with his mother lashes out with his feet. This action is likely to be followed by a punishment of some kind (or at least a rebuke) which upsets him. The sequence of events leaves, as a kind of by-product, a conditioned reaction; that is to say, the impulse which initiated the behaviour tends to become associated with the (unpleasant) state of arousal which immediately followed it. Once such an association has been firmly established (after perhaps half a dozen repetitions of the sequence) the recurrence of the impulse elicits an autonomic reaction which is sufficiently marked to block the behaviour. The child is still, on occasion, exasperated—but he does not kick. His mother will probably explain that 'he knows what will happen if he does it again', but according to Mowrer what inhibits the behaviour is not anticipation of the consequences which might ensue, but an involuntary resurgence of the distress which followed similar actions in the past.

This conception of social training has its origins in the laboratory study of passive avoidance behaviour. Its principal merit is simplicity; we are required to make no assumptions about processes of reasoning or choice, and indeed we should expect that on most occasions the conditioned reaction would operate sufficiently swiftly to deflect the individual from 'wrong' behaviour before he could become aware of a formed intention. It is not uncommon for those of us who frequent the criminal courts to hear a judge say to a rapist or to the author of grievous bodily harm: 'How could

* Paper read to Section J (Psychology) on August 28, 1964, at the Southampton Meeting of the British Association.

our society survive if we all yielded, as you have done, to our brutish impulses?'—but he would probably be extremely indignant if one were to accuse him of harbouring secret desires of this kind. Fortunately most of us are not obliged constantly to consider and to reject impulses to criminal behaviour; our social training has equipped us with what (by a rather loose analogy) might be termed 'a socio-perceptual set' which causes us to overlook opportunities for crime with a regularity that is quite heartbreaking to a seasoned criminal.

I mention this because it is relevant to the question of what it is that is learned during social training. Although Mowrer generally calls this 'anxiety', for the sake of brevity, he does not intend, I believe, that it should be thought of as merely an hypothetical construct, nor yet as a subjective experience. It is more accurately defined as 'a state . . . of autonomic, especially sympathetic, activation'*—and is therefore observable by standard laboratory methods. This is important because it means that most of the hypotheses about the nature of criminality which are derivable from the theory can be checked in a reasonably direct and rigorous fashion.

I want now to look rather more closely at what is implied by this theoretical scheme about the conditions that are necessary for effective social training. The first matter to be considered is the 'conditioning stimulus'. In avoidance behaviour this is always complex, and comprises perceptions of the external environment and also of internal stimuli—what are conventionally termed 'response-produced' stimuli. In the case of child training we may presume that these are mostly desires and intentions. Let us suppose, by way of example, that a mother finds her child filching money from her handbag. She may simply say, 'that's very naughty', and punish him; in this event the conditioning stimulus is virtually the whole medley of perceptions which immediately preceded the punishment—approaching the handbag, being curious, poking about in it, seeing money and experiencing the impulse to take it—and as it is so complex, it tends to be rather poorly defined, and at the same time highly specific to that particular situation. If the episode is repeated, the child will presumably develop a tendency to refrain from

taking money from his mother's handbag. But most parents are more explicit than this; they will say, 'it is naughty to take other people's money'—or, more elaborately, 'taking money like that is stealing, and stealing is very wrong'. Such remarks help the child to identify the relevant characteristics of the situation (for example, the intention to take the money) and to discriminate these from unimportant ones, such as the place from which it was taken. The more elaborate form of rebuke involves the further step of relating the child's action to a concept of much greater generality—the notion of stealing—and is an attempt to make use of the episode to implant an aversion to any action which the child recognises as stealing. Thus although the basis of the conditioned reaction is still an association between an impulse and the punishment-induced arousal which followed it on a particular occasion, language is employed to secure a high degree of generalisation.

There is a further consequence of this sort of parental behaviour which is important. As we have seen, training can only take place when the child spontaneously performs a forbidden act. By the rules of chance, specific behaviours like taking money from mother's handbag, filching sweets, or pilfering from a shop only happen occasionally. If they are treated as discrete events, training must necessarily take a long time. On the other hand, if behaviours classifiable as 'stealing' are clearly defined as such for the child, opportunities for driving home this general lesson will occur more often—he may well commit each of these three types of theft in the course of a day or two. We should also expect this procedure to facilitate transfer to novel situations, because the child will be strongly motivated to pay attention to those particular characteristics which distinguish stealing from non-stealing behaviour.

On the basis of this analysis we can identify two parameters of the socialisation process which are likely to have an important bearing upon its effectiveness. The first of these is the readiness of parents to use particular misdemeanours as opportunities for training. There is substantial evidence, from sociological studies, of wide variations in the extent to which this is done. Some parents take a long-term, serious view of their role, seeing it as the moulding of character; to them, childish pilfering is a grave matter because (as

* This definition is due to Mr. S. A. Barnett⁸ (p. 349).

they will tell you) if it is not corrected in good time the child will grow up to be a thief. Other parents take a more indulgent, custodial view, regarding petty pilfering as natural and blameless, because the child is 'not old enough to know any better'. Secondly, much will depend upon the extent to which the parents are able to recognise, and to explain to the child, the general principles involved in particular actions. There is some evidence that both of these variables have some correlation with socio-economic status, at least in contemporary Britain and in the United States. In his review of the American material Bronfenbrenner[4] suggests that the intention to train the child systematically is on the whole characteristic of middle-class and upper-working-class families; unskilled labourers and their wives, on the other hand, are more likely to regard parenthood more casually, punishing occasionally in order to abate an immediate nuisance without taking much thought for the long-term outcome of their actions.

It is only fair to point out that the reliability of much of the evidence upon which Bronfenbrenner's survey was based has been called in question by Lillian Robbins, who demonstrated that when parents are asked to recall how they brought up their children, their replies are likely to be seriously distorted in the direction of current fashions in child care.[5] However, this discovery is, on the whole, less damaging to those investigations which were concerned with attitudes to child rearing than to those which claimed to have identified class differences in practical methods of weaning, toilet-training, and the like.

The account of socialisation which I have outlined accords an important role to verbal explanations as an aid to discrimination, and particularly as a device for securing quite extensive generalisation of the avoidance reaction. Bernstein has proposed a most interesting distinction between two types of language which seems to be relevant here. The first, which he calls 'public' language, is comparatively crude and disjointed, and consists mainly of commands, questions and statements of fact; sentences are often incomplete and tend to be repetitive. Because of these defects, 'public' language is not adequate to convey subtle distinctions or abstract notions, though it works well enough for most ordinary purposes. On the other hand what is termed 'formal' language is more complex in structure and better adapted to the expression of abstract concepts; there is a greater emphasis upon the relations between events and the logical consequences of propositions. Bernstein suggests that while 'public' language is used to some extent by everyone, it is virtually the only means of communication in those social groups which comprise Class V of the Registrar-General's scheme—that is to say, the families of manual workers. In middle-class homes, on the other hand, and in those of skilled workers, considerable use is made of the more sophisticated 'formal' pattern of language.[6, 7] The implications of this argument for our problem are fairly clear; we should expect parents who are restricted to the use of 'public' language to be relatively unsuccessful as agents of socialisation. It is, of course, a fairly well-established fact that families in Class V do contribute a disproportionately large number of recruits to the ranks of the convicted.[8, 9] There is also some evidence that offenders as a group are conspicuously incompetent at tasks which demand verbal reasoning and the use of abstract concepts—that is to say, problems for which 'formal' language is necessary. Both of these observations are consonant with our argument, though neither, of course, can be said to support it. But it would certainly not be impossible to design an experiment to test these contentions.

I would like to turn next to the other primary element in the conditioning process—the unconditioned stimulus. In studies of child rearing methods it is usual to contrast love-oriented and punishment-oriented techniques of discipline—that is to say, those which rely upon the temporary withdrawal of parental approval as a sanction, distinguished from those based upon the infliction of pain or the withholding of treats. Love-oriented methods seem generally to be more effective in securing reliable conformity with parental standards—a fact which is commonly explained by reference to internalisation and the formation of guilt. I think there is a danger, however, that by concentrating upon the sanctions themselves we may overlook the wider patterns of social interaction into which they fit. Let us refer once more to our little model. The sanction, in this view of child training, is clearly a reinforcement in the Pavlovian sense—that is to say, a stimulus which elicits the response to be conditioned, which in this case is a state of autonomic arousal. But the parallel with laboratory studies of avoidance training is not quite as obvious as it appears. In animal experiments it is usual to employ as the unconditioned stimulus a severe electric shock, which is no doubt unpleasant for the animal, as well as causing a reaction of the sympathetic system. But the autonomic reaction is 'caused by' the shock, not the pain; admittedly stimuli which evoke marked sympathetic response are generally unpleasant, but that is not the same thing. The point of this observation becomes clear when we try to compare such experiments with punishment administered to a child. Here the method is not an electric shock, but a technique chosen for the fact that the pain which it causes is accompanied by a minimum of direct disturbance of bodily processes. I suspect that to achieve a degree of activation of the autonomic system comparable with that produced in the rat by a severe shock would demand a beating so painful as to be quite unacceptable to most parents.

If this contention is correct, it follows that physical punishments achieve their effect indirectly —that is to say, as secondary reinforcers. There can be no essential difference between a slap and a frown as disciplinary sanctions—a proposition with which many child psychologists would agree, I think. But we are left with two further questions: what is the primary unconditioned stimulus in child training?—and why, if they operate in the same fashion, should techniques of socialisation which employ physical punishment be less effective than love-oriented methods? I believe that the answer to the second question contains some clues to the first, so I would like to begin with that one.

Reliance upon love-oriented methods to the exclusion of all other forms of sanction and control is particularly characteristic of middle-class and upper working-class families. It forms part of a style of living which emphasises the internal cohesiveness of the family, and is generally pursued in suburban areas which are physically fragmented into household territories, each with its garden, its fences, and its gate. It is customary for families to 'keep themselves to themselves'; casual gossip and 'neighbouring' is frowned upon, and it is generally agreed that intimate matters concerning the family are not discussed outside it, except perhaps with a close friend. In this social pattern the period

of his life during which the child is wholly dependent upon his parents for affection and reassurance is quite long. Children do not, as a rule, establish close relationships with adults who are not members of the family, and contacts with age-peers develop late and are so restricted that they play a comparatively small part in the child's social experience until he starts school.

Parents who make considerable use of physical punishments are most frequently to be found in Social Class V; the father is generally an unskilled man, living in a high-density housing area. Here families live in close proximity to each other; 'neighbouring' and other casual contacts are encouraged by the physical arrangement of dwellings and by social custom. Children make extensive contacts outside the immediate family group at an early age. By the time they are two years old they recognise and are spoiled by 'aunties' in adjoining households; at three they are already making firm friendships with other children of their own age, and at the age of four they may spend quite a large proportion of the day in play-groups in the street, in other people's houses, or otherwise out of sight of their parents. In these circumstances parental disapproval is by no means the serious matter that it is in the middle-class culture; a scolded child simply runs next door to be comforted by an 'auntie', or wanders off with his friends, who are already a source of reassurance and support to him. In any case, as we have seen, systematic 'character training' is not usually an important aim of parents in this social stratum.

In attempting to distinguish between these two styles of family life I may have overstated the differences; the most that I would claim is that these are types which are unequally distributed between the social classes. But the point that I want particularly to make is that orthodox love-oriented techniques are to be found in their purest form in those social groups which maximise the duration and the exclusiveness of the child's dependency upon his parents; physical punishments tend to be used (and indeed they are the only available form of sanction) in sub-cultures in which the child is wholly dependent upon his parents for a much shorter time, and begins to find social satisfactions beyond the family particularly among his age-peers, while he is still quite young.

This argument takes us some way, I think, towards an answer to our question about the relative ineffectiveness of physical punishments: it is that they tend, for complex sociological reasons, to be employed in families which are not well organised for the training of children.* Our other question, you will remember, concerned the primary source of reinforcement in socialisation. The discussion in which we have just engaged suggests that the overt act of punishment—a rebuke or a slap—elicits anxiety because it is the signal that has, on past occasions, been followed by temporary deprivation of the satisfactions and reassurances of social intercourse. In a middle-class family, being out of favour implies a high degree of isolation; in a working-class family the child has alternative sources of satisfaction, so the change in his social environment that is signalled in this way is less drastic. But in order to relate this to our psychological model we have to explain why temporary deprivation of this kind should elicit anxiety. Some theorists have postulated the existence of a primary fear of isolation, arguing that punishment is effective because it has become associated with the onset of this fear. There are difficulties about this; it is hard to conceive of a basic drive of the kind that is proposed. Infants certainly seem, in some circumstances, to tolerate short periods of solitude without showing signs of distress.

Mowrer's revised theory offers an alternative explanation which does not oblige us to assume the existence of such a drive. It is based upon the notion of the 'safety signal'—a stimulus which, on previous occasions, has preceded the *termination* of some unpleasant state of affairs.[1] This seems to be roughly what we mean when we say that a child finds the presence of his parents 'reassuring'; there are a great many episodes in infancy when the appearance of the mother heralds the abatement of hunger or discomfort or fright, and it seems reasonable to assume that in course of time her smile and affectionate talk become safety signals in Mowrer's sense. Now the point about stimuli of this type is that their termination appears to

* This contention received some indirect support from the work of Jephcott and Carter in 'Radby',[10] in which a comparison was made between two streets of comparable working-class status, one of which yielded a much higher incidence of delinquency than the other.

function as a negative (or 'incremental') reinforcer; that is to say, when the safety signal is withdrawn this causes an unpleasant state of arousal —or, as we say, 'anxiety'. Indeed it has been demonstrated, in what appears to be a well-designed experiment, that avoidance behaviour in animals can be maintained for extended periods by this means.[11] It must be admitted that this explanation is as yet little more than speculation; there are a great many technical problems to be resolved, not the least of which is to identify the physiological processes involved. But this may well prove to be a fruitful line to investigate, and there seems to be no real difficulty about devising techniques for doing this.

I would like, finally, to mention two further consequences of the different styles of child training to which I referred earlier. Socialisation takes the form of a prolonged interaction between the individual, with his particular range of capacities and defects, and the social pressures which are brought to bear upon him. It follows that failure of socialisation, and thus criminality, may arise in several ways. Sometimes it is the consequence of grossly inadequate childhood training; in other cases, as Professor Eysenck will argue,[12] failure is to be blamed upon a constitutional defect which renders the individual unresponsive to his parents' efforts to socialise him. It seems likely that the majority of offenders fall somewhere between these extremes—they could have been trained by highly efficient techniques, but were actually brought up in families which were not particularly well organised for this task.[9]

This is a convenient distinction to draw, but we must remember that it gives a static view of a dynamic process. Some of the individual variables in the equation are not constitutional in the narrow sense, but are the product of prior learning. The example which I have particularly in mind concerns what might be called the 'characteristic patterns of dependency' that are established in early childhood. Socialisation is by no means wholly effected within the family; that some theorists write as if it were reflects, perhaps, the middle-class culture from which most psychologists are drawn. The children of unskilled workers, as we have seen, learn early to derive a substantial proportion of their social experiences and satisfactions from the peer-group. This has implications, of course, for the *content*

550   G. B. TRASLER

of socialisation—that is to say, for the definition and generalisation of conditioned aversions—and it has the further consequence of establishing a special sensitiveness to the approval and censure of age-peers, which contrasts with the responsiveness to adult criticism that is typical of the middle-class child. We may guess that the different habits of dependency which are formed in this way probably play an important part in shaping the child's response to later opportunities for social learning, particularly at school—and that they may help to determine how he will react to the authority of individuals and of social groups as he matures through adolescence to adulthood. If this is so, it is something which ought to be taken into account when we are planning new methods for the treatment of offenders, because it would follow from this reasoning that the majority of criminals, and probably a much higher proportion of those that are trainable, are likely to be a great deal more responsive to group pressures than to the influence of individual borstal housemasters or probation officers.[13]

It must, of course, be recognised that the social patterns we have been discussing are themselves subject to continuous change. There is reason to believe, for example, that the differences in styles of child rearing which once sharply divided the social classes are rapidly disappearing under the combined influences of increasing affluence and educational opportunity, changes in housing arrangements, and Dr. Spock; working-class parents are increasingly inclined to take their responsibilities seriously, and have the means to do so, while middle-class mothers have become more relaxed and permissive, and perhaps in a sense less effective as wielders of the unconditioned stimulus.[4] One would expect changes of this kind to have some effect, over the years, upon the criminal statistics; and indeed there is already some sign, in the United States[14] and perhaps in this country also,[15] that the incidence of delinquency is increasing more rapidly among the children of middle-class parents than in the much-disparaged Class V. But if these social transitions are a little inconvenient for our theory-building, rudely changing the nature of variables which we have just succeeded in pinning down, they also constitute an opportunity to check the validity of some of our most confident assumptions. This is one anxiety-arousing situation, I regret to say, in which avoidance is not possible.

REFERENCES

1. MOWRER, O. H. (1960a): *Learning Theory and Behaviour.* New York: Wiley.
2. MOWRER, O. H. (1960b): *Learning Theory and the Symbolic Processes.* New York: Wiley.
3. BARNETT, S. A. (1963): *A Study in Behaviour.* London: Methuen.
4. BRONFENBRENNER, U. (1958): In E. E. Maccoby, T. M. Newcomb & E. L. Hartley (eds.) *Readings in Social Psychology* (3rd edn.), pp. 400–24. New York: Holt.
5. ROBBINS, L. C. (1963): *J. abnorm. soc. Psychol.* **66**, 3, 261–70.
6. BERNSTEIN, B. (1959): *Brit. J. Sociol.* **X**, 4, 311–26.
7. BERNSTEIN, B. (1961): *Educ. Research,* **III**, 163–76.
8. GIBBENS, T. C. N. (1963): *Psychiatric Studies of Borstal Lads,* pp. 61–4. London: Oxford U.P.
9. TRASLER, G. B. (1960): *The Explanation of Criminality.* London: Routledge & Kegan Paul.
10. SPROTT, W. J. H., JEPHCOTT, A. P., & CARTER, M. P. (1954): *The Social Background of Delinquency.* Nottingham: The University.
11. MORSE, W. H., & HERRNSTEIN, R. J. (1956): *Amer. Psychol.* **11**, 430.
12. EYSENCK, H. J. (1964): *Advancement of Science,* **XX**, 90, 124–35.
13. TRASLER, G. B. (1964): *Cambridge Opinion,* **38**, 17–22.
14. *Juvenile Delinquency: Report of the Committee on the Judiciary, United States Senate* (87th Cong. 1st Sess., Report No. 169), pp. 1–3. Washington: U.S. Govt. Printing Office, 1961.
15. LITTLE, W. R., & NTSEKHE, V. R. (1959): *Brit. J. Delinq.* **X**, 130–5 (but see also GIBBENS, T. C. N., *op. cit.*).

Peer and Sibling Influences, Including Unpopularity

[16]

0091-4169/91/8202-360
THE JOURNAL OF CRIMINAL LAW & CRIMINOLOGY
Copyright © 1991 by Northwestern University, School of Law

Vol. 82, No. 2
Printed in U.S.A.

ADVANCING KNOWLEDGE ABOUT CO-OFFENDING: RESULTS FROM A PROSPECTIVE LONGITUDINAL SURVEY OF LONDON MALES

ALBERT J. REISS, JR.* AND DAVID P. FARRINGTON**

Perhaps the most frequently documented conclusion about delinquent behavior is that most offenses are committed with others rather than by persons acting alone. Breckenridge and Abbott[1] were perhaps the first to observe that not only are most delinquent offenses committed with others, but that even most youths who routinely offend alone are influenced by others. Because of this article's behavioral perspective, we refer to persons who act together in a crime as co-offenders and to their committing that crime as co-offending.[2] Co-offending is a universal pattern in all major forms of delinquency and characterizes offending patterns in countries with widely different cultural traditions such as Argentina,[3] Japan,[4] and India.[5]

Offending with others often is characterized as group offending, implying either that members act together as a unit or that individual offending is organized by group affiliation. When peer

---

* Department of Sociology, Yale University.
** Institute of Criminology, Cambridge University.

Acknowledgements: The data collection in the London longitudinal survey was funded by the Home Office. We are very grateful to Lynda Morley for extracting and computerizing the co-offending data from the Criminal Record office.

[1] *See* S. BRECKINRIDGE & E. ABBOTT, THE DELINQUENT CHILD AND THE HOME 34-35 (1917).

[2] *See* Reiss, *Understanding Changes in Crime Rates, in* INDICATORS OF CRIME AND JUSTICE: QUANTITATIVE STUDIES 11 (S. Fienberg & A. Reiss eds. 1980). *See also,* Reiss, *Co-offending Influences on Criminal Careers,* 2 CRIMINAL CAREERS AND CAREER CRIMINALS 121 (A. Blumstein, J. Cohen, J. Roth & C. Visher eds. 1986); Reiss, *Co-offending and Criminal Careers,* 10 CRIME AND JUSTICE: A REVIEW OF RESEARCH 117 (M. Tonry & N. Morris eds. 1988).

[3] *See* L. DEFLEUR, DELINQUENCY IN ARGENTINA: A STUDY OF CORDOBA'S YOUTH (1970).

[4] *See* Yokoyama, *Criminal Policy Against Thieves in Japan,* 1 KANGWEON L. REV. 191 (1985).

[5] *See* C. HARTJEN & S. PRIYADARSINI, DELINQUENCY IN INDIA: A COMPARATIVE ANALYSIS 58-61 (1984).

groups with a defined leadership are territorially organized and engage in a wide range of antisocial behavior, they are referred to as gangs[6]. Most of those who offend with others are not, however, members of large or highly structured groups.[7] Rather, most delinquent offenses are generally committed by two or three individuals who are only loosely associated with one another.[8] Lewis Yablonsky refers to loosely organized peer aggregates as near-groups.[9]

There is a substantial difference between the construct and measures of co-offending and the theoretical constructs and measures of association with delinquent peers, friends' involvement in delinquency,[10] or delinquent peer group bonding.[11] Measures of association with delinquent peers and of friends' involvement in delinquency usually indicate how many of one's friends engage in delinquent acts, and whether or not one is also delinquent; these measures, however, do not indicate whether delinquent friends are co-offenders in illegal acts. Professors Elliott, Huizinga and Menard also include whether one's friends encouraged law breaking in their measure of peer group involvement.[12] Their measure of delinquent peer group bonding is a measure of peer group involvement weighted by exposure to delinquent peers. These constructs and their measures differ from those for co-offending, which indicate the *actual* involvement of a person in illegal behavior with the same or different persons.

I. Co-offending in Criminal Careers

Three offending patterns characterize criminal careers. One type of offender always offends alone and can be said to have a *solo offending career*. Another type always offends with others and can be said to have a *co-offending career*. The third and most common type of offender engages in a *mixed solo and co-offending career*. From cross-sectional studies we know that solo offending is relatively uncom-

---

[6] F. Thrasher, The Gang 45-57 (1927). *See also,* W. Miller, Violence by Youth Gangs and Youth Groups as a Crime Problem in Major American Cities 8-10 (1975).

[7] *See* Klein & Crawford, *Groups, Gangs, and Cohesiveness,* 4 J. of Res. in Crime and Delinq. 142 (1967); Morash, *Gangs, Groups, and Delinquency,* 23 Brit. J. of Criminology 329 (1983).

[8] *See* Shaw & McKay, *Social Factors in Juvenile Delinquency,* 13 Report on the Causes of Crime, vol. 2, at 191-99 (1931); J. Short & F. Strodtbeck, Group Process and Gang Delinquency (1965).

[9] Yablonsky, *The Delinquent Gang as a Near-Group,* 7 Soc. Probs. 108 (1959).

[10] Friedman & Rosenbaum, *Social Control Theory: The Salience of Components by Age, Gender, and Type of Crime,* 4 J. of Quantitative Criminology 363, 369 (1988).

[11] D. Elliott, D. Huizinga & S. Menard, Multiple Problem Youth: Delinquency, Substance Abuse, and Mental Health Problems 143 (1989).

[12] *See id.*

mon at young ages and does not become the typical form of offending until the late teens or early twenties.[13] We also know that solo offending rises sharply at the peak age of juvenile offending, and becomes the dominant form of offending by the mid-twenties.[14] Moreover, the mean number of offenders that commit any particular offense declines with age. Offenses committed by three offenders become relatively uncommon after age twenty; those committed by four or more persons become infrequent at an earlier age, perhaps by age seventeen.[15]

These changes in the proportion of solo offending to co-offending are often cited to support the hypothesis that most criminal careers begin with a predominance of co-offending but that solo offenders are more likely to survive or persist in offending. Among the different reasons offered for their persistence are that persons who offend primarily alone are less likely to be apprehended through apprehension of a co-offender, that early on offenders calculate their financial gains as greater from solo offending, and that most offenders calculate the risk of capture when offending alone as minimal. Moreover, a deadly weapon may substitute for the threat and power of co-offenders in offenses such as robbery and assault.

Yet these changes are also consistent with hypotheses that there is either selective desistance of persons who primarily co-offend, or a shift from co-offending to solo offending as offenders grow older. Among the reasons for selective desistance of persons who have never offended alone are that they are reluctant to take the risks of solo offending, that they are more dependent on older peers who cease offending, that they are less likely to be selected by older co-offenders who increasingly turn to solo offending, or that an early apprehension deters them from further offending. The explanation for an age-related shift from co-offending to solo offending rests on the fact that many offenders commit a mix of offenses alone and with others. With experience, gradually those offenders who commit a mix of offenses alone and with others shift towards solo offending because they perceive lower risks of offending alone and a greater financial return in not having to share the proceeds of burglary or theft with others. Longitudinal data on offending careers are required to establish whether there are changing patterns of offending alone and with others with age or whether the selective at-

---

[13] R. HOOD & R. SPARKS, KEY ISSUES IN CRIMINOLOGY 87-89 (1970).
[14] *Id.*
[15] *Id.*

trition of those who offend primarily with others accounts for a preponderance of solo offending at later ages.

II. EXPLANATIONS OF CO-OFFENDING

Despite considerable documentation of co-offending in delinquent behavior, little about co-offending is explained by theories of delinquency. In this article we attempt to draw some of the theoretical implications that findings on co-offending have for theories of delinquency and criminality and to test these implications with data from a prospective longitudinal study of London males.[16] We focus particularly on the role of co-offending in induction to and desistance from delinquent and criminal careers.

Many theorists focus on the role of co-offending in the *onset* of delinquent behavior or the induction to a delinquent or criminal career. Edwin Sutherland's theory of differential association[17] is one of the few theories of delinquent and criminal behavior that offers an explanation for co-offending behavior. Although Sutherland's theory does not explain co-offending, it postulates that delinquent behavior is learned largely through association with patterns of delinquent behavior.[18] A major vehicle for learning is participation in delinquent behavior with others, i.e., co-offending. The theory is rarely tested and support for it rests largely on demonstrating that most delinquents associate with other delinquents and participate with them in delinquent activity. There is no adequate longitudinal test of the theory demonstrating that delinquent behavior is learned through contacts with the already delinquent.

A competing theory assumes that some individuals develop antisocial behavior patterns that predispose them to and eventually results in their delinquent conduct.[19] Their participation in delinquency with others is explained by a process whereby the like keep company. There is self-selection or mutual attraction of the like-minded, a companionate homophily, or a form of assortative mating.[20] One is likely to select as friends those who are like oneself: "birds of a feather flock together".[21] Empirical evidence of as-

---

16 *See* Farrington & West, *The Cambridge Study in Delinquent Development: A Long-Term Follow-Up of 411 London Males*, in CRIMINALITY: PERSONALITY, BEHAVIOR, AND LIFE HISTORY 115 (H. Kerner & G. Kaiser eds. 1990).

17 *See* E. SUTHERLAND & D. CRESSEY, CRIMINOLOGY 75-76 (9th ed. 1974).

18 *Id.* at 76.

19 *See* S. GLUECK & E. GLUECK, UNRAVELING JUVENILE DELINQUENCY 146-49, 163-64 (1950).

20 Merton, *Intermarriage and the Social Structure: Fact and Theory*, 4 PSYCHIATRY 361 (1941).

21 "So as far as delinquency is concerned, then, 'birds of a feather flock together'.

sociation in delinquent acts thus demonstrates merely the concomitance of behavior of two or more persons, whereas the effects of association must be demonstrated by a temporal sequence of behavior.[22]

Travis Hirschi's control theory is an alternative to both differential association and group selection theories.[23] Hirschi's control theory holds that a boy's stake in conformity affects his choice of friends rather than the other way around. Hirschi emphasizes "feathering rather than flocking."[24] Although there is a strong tendency for boys to have friends whose attitudes are congruent with their own, it is the stake in conformity that most affects choice of friends. A low stake in conformity leads to antisocial choices while a high stake leads to prosocial choices. Hirschi contends that even contact between persons with differing stakes in conformity rarely leads to delinquency.[25]

To test adequately which of these theories makes the correct deductions about the role of co-offending in delinquent and criminal behavior, data from a prospective longitudinal study are required. The study must temporally locate the onset of antisocial and delinquent conduct and measure each person's stake in conformity. The study must then demonstrate that delinquent conduct either develops largely apart from any social learning in association with other delinquents or correlatively that non-delinquents learn delinquency only through association with delinquents. Moreover, adoption of one of the competing theories will depend upon demonstrating that selection of friends or companions is based on homophily, especially with respect to conformity. None of these competing theories has been tested with data from a prospective longitudinal birth cohort design.[26]

III. RECRUITMENT INTO CRIMINAL CAREERS

Despite decades of research on offending, little is known about

---

This tendency is a much more fundamental fact in any analysis of causation than the theory that accidental differential association of non-delinquents with delinquents is the basic cause of crime." S. Glueck, *Theory and Fact in Criminology*, 7 BRIT. J. OF DELINQ. 92 (1956). *See also*, S. GLUECK & E. GLUECK, *supra* note 19, at 164.

[22] Reiss & Rhodes, *An Empirical Test of Differential Association Theory*, 1 J. OF RES. IN CRIME AND DELINQ. 5, 6 (1964).

[23] *See* T. HIRSCHI, CAUSES OF DELINQUENCY 16 (1969).

[24] *Id.* at 159.

[25] *Id.* at 157.

[26] Designs to test the theories are mainly cross-sectional comparisons based on retrospective data collection. The Gluecks used matched samples of delinquents and nondelinquents. *See* S. GLUECK & E. GLUECK, *supra* note 19.

how and why co-offenders are selected. There are several major theories about how delinquent careers begin through recruitment into co-offending.[27] Quite apart from initial recruitment into offending, however, there is a need to explain how co-offenders are selected for committing particular offenses. How does one account for the particular patterns of selection into co-offending?

One of the earliest explanations of initial recruitment is that family members play a major role in socializing young people into careers in crime. The classic sociological study of Clifford Shaw[28] emphasized the role of siblings in recruitment into co-offending and criminal careers. Other studies disclose that male delinquents come from larger families than do male non-delinquents of the same age and socioeconomic status.[29] There is evidence that these differences in family size are entirely due to an excess of brothers[30]. Yet parents and other relatives also are occasionally found as co-offenders. It is thus difficult to determine from most cross-sectional studies whether siblings are a major source of recruitment into co-offending, and especially whether older siblings recruit younger ones.

A second hypothesis is based on a more general explanation that accounts for the selection of co-participants in many activities: selection is based on propinquity, either opportunistically or through acquaintance. Thus, whether or not a family member initially recruited another into offending, one might expect from their co-habitation that family members would be a likely source of co-offenders. Similarly, offenders should disproportionally select one another to commit a particular offense if they live close to one another, given their greater opportunities for contact and communication. Because of the opportunistic nature of much juvenile offending, juveniles' search for co-offenders is likely to be limited to those encountered in their neighborhood or school community. As offenders age, however, their activities will more often take them outside of their community. With aging, therefore, one expects propinquity to be less important in the selection of co-offenders. We

---

27 E. SUTHERLAND & D. CRESSEY, *supra* note 17, at 71-93; C. SHAW, THE NATURAL HISTORY OF A DELINQUENT CAREER 226-27 (1931); Eynon & Reckless, *Companionship at Delinquency Onset*, 2 BRIT. J. OF CRIMINOLOGY 162 (1961).

28 C. SHAW, BROTHERS IN CRIME 3-89 (1938).

29 T. FERGUSON, THE YOUNG DELINQUENT IN HIS SOCIAL SETTING 57 (1952); D. WEST & D. FARRINGTON, WHO BECOMES DELINQUENT? 31-32 (1973); Blakeley, Stephenson & Nichol, *Social Factors in a Random Sample of Juvenile Delinquents and Controls*, 20 INT'L. J. OF SOC. PSYCHIATRY 203 (1974).

30 Jones, Offord & Abrams, *Brothers, Sisters, and Antisocial Behavior*, 136 BRIT. J. OF PSYCHIATRY 139 (1980).

shall test this hypothesis by examining the residence pattern of co-offenders.

A third major hypothesis is that people are recruited into criminal careers by close friends or peers who are much like them. Consequently, their pattern of co-offending is stable and persists over time. This explanation implies that an offender who recruits a person to co-offend will continue to select that co-offender and that the co-offender will also be a stable accomplice in his subsequent co-offending. There will be reciprocity in co-offending, once the relationship is established. At issue here is the homogeneity and stability of co-offending relationships and networks over time.[31] Accordingly, we shall examine similarities in the age, sex, race, and criminal experience of co-offenders, as well as the duration of relationships between the same co-offenders, and whether there is reciprocity in co-offending.

A competing hypothesis assumes the contrary—that juvenile offending networks and their delinquent peer relationships are relatively unstable and that for the most part juvenile networks are not linked to adult networks. Consequently, co-offenders will be quite close in age but their relationship will be short-lived. Other research supports the conclusion that most delinquents in a community are linked by their co-offending into one or more loosely structured networks.[32] Where there are a dozen or more persons in such networks, membership turnover is fairly high[33] and co-offender affiliations are of relatively short duration.[34] Delinquents thus appear to be linked in loosely structured networks of transitory relationships that facilitate their search for accomplices.[35] Accordingly, we shall examine the extent to which an offender commits offenses with the same people and the stability of co-offending relationships over time.

A fourth hypothesis is based on the fact that individuals in a network vary considerably in their individual rates of offending. Many of the high rate offenders have a large number of different co-offenders and move among networks to recruit accomplices; they

---

[31] Sarnecki, *Delinquent Networks in Sweden*, 6 J. OF QUANTITATIVE CRIMINOLOGY 31 (1990).

[32] J. SARNECKI, CRIMINALITY AND FRIEND RELATIONS: A STUDY OF JUVENILE CRIMINALITY IN A SWEDISH COMMUNITY 153 (D. Galarrage trans. 1984); G. SUTTLES, THE SOCIAL ORDER OF THE SLUM 166 (1968).

[33] Klein & Crawford, *Groups, Gangs, and Cohesiveness*, 4 J. OF RES. IN CRIME AND DELINQ. 142 (1967); Sarnecki, *supra* note 31.

[34] J. SARNECKI, *supra* note 32, at 140.

[35] Klein & Crawford, *supra* note 33; Sarnecki, *supra* note 31.

are designated as recruiters.[36] Recruiters ordinarily do not continue selecting the same person as a co-offender. According to the hypothesis, a substantial proportion of individuals are inducted into offending by a small number of these recruiters.[37] Because the accomplices of a recruiter differ from one offense to another, a recruiter should have a substantial number of different accomplices in a short period of time, given the recruiter's high individual rate of offending. Given also the relative difference in offending experience between recruiters and their accomplices, one would expect accomplices to be younger than their recruiter and more likely to be engaging in their first offense.

The behavior of both recruiters and co-offenders has important theoretical and practical implications for theories of deterrence and incapacitation. Considering the hypothesized role of recruiters in offending networks, it seems reasonable to conclude that, if one could identify and selectively incapacitate recruiters, then both the prevalence of offenders in a population and the incidence of offending would be affected. But, as Professor Reiss[38] points out, research on the effects on the crime rate of incapacitating offenders makes a false assumption that each offense in an individual's rate of offending is a single offender offense. The assumption that the number of crimes averted by incapacitation is equal to the individual's rate of offending (multiplied by the time of incapacitation) is clearly false when an offense has co-offenders. Just how many crimes are averted by incapacitation is a function of the replacement rate of incapacitated members, their rates of offending, and the deterrent effect of incapacitation on co-offenders who are not incapacitated. If the effect of a network member's incapacitation leads to recruitment of new members whose individual rates of offending exceed that of the incapacitated member, then incapacitation might increase the crime rate. Correlatively, if incapacitation has a deterrent effect on co-offenders, then it may actually reduce the crime rate by an amount greater than that of the offending rate of the incapacitated member. Thus, the size of an incapacitation effect depends upon the size of a co-offending network, the fluidity of its boundaries, the rate of replacement, and the deterrent effect on co-offenders who are not incapacitated. Accordingly, theories of both deterrence and incapacitation must take into account the effect of sanctions on co-offenders and the effect on recruitment and replacement of offend-

---

36 Reiss, *Co-offending and Criminal Careers, supra* note 2.

37 *Id.* at 149-50.

38 Reiss, *Understanding Changes in Crime Rates, supra* note 2, at 12-13.

ers in the network.[39]

Below we test some of these hypotheses using data from a prospective longitudinal study of offending by a cohort of London males followed up in the Cambridge Study in Delinquent Development.

IV. DESIGN OF THE CAMBRIDGE STUDY

A. DESCRIPTION OF THE SAMPLE AND SURVEY

The Cambridge Study in Delinquent Development is a prospective longitudinal survey of 411 boys. When first contacted in 1961-62, these boys were all living in a working class area of London, England. The vast majority of the sample (399 boys) were chosen by taking all the boys then aged eight or nine who were on the registers of six state primary schools within a one mile radius of the established research office. In addition, twelve boys from a local school for the educationally subnormal were included in the sample in an attempt to make it more representative of the population of boys living in the area.

The selected boys were almost all white. Only twelve, most of whom had one parent of West Indian origin, were black. The vast majority (90%) were being brought up by parents who had themselves been reared in the United Kingdom or Ireland. On the basis of their fathers' occupations, 94% could be described as working class (categories III, IV, or V on the Registrar General's scale of occupational prestige). The boys were therefore, overwhelmingly urban, working class whites of British origin.

Male or female psychologists interviewed and tested the boys in their schools when they were about eight, ten, and fourteen years old. Young male social science graduates interviewed them again in the research office at ages sixteen, eighteen, and twenty-one. Two last interviews, at ages twenty-five and thirty-two, were carried out in their homes. At age thirty-two, 367 of the 403 men still alive were personally interviewed, and a further eleven, mostly living abroad, completed questionnaires. Thus, data were obtained from 94% of the men still alive twenty-four years after the start of the survey.[40]

---

[39] *Id.* at 13-15.

[40] For more details of this survey, *see* Farrington & West, *supra* note 16. *See also* Farrington, *Later Adult Life Outcomes of Offenders and Non-Offenders, in* CHILDREN AT RISK: ASSESSMENT AND LONGITUDINAL RESEARCH 220 (M. Brambring, F. Losel & H. Skowronek eds. 1989); D. WEST, DELINQUENCY: ITS ROOTS, CAREERS, AND PROSPECTS (1982); D. WEST & D. FARRINGTON, *supra* note 29; D. WEST & D. FARRINGTON, THE DELINQUENT WAY OF LIFE (1977).

B. INFORMATION ON OFFENDING

As part of the survey, repeated searches were carried out in the central Criminal Record Office in London to try to locate the criminal conviction records of the men, their biological fathers and mothers, their full brothers and sisters, and (in recent years) of their wives and cohabitees. Convictions were only counted if they were for offenses normally recorded in the Criminal Record Office. This led to the exclusion of almost all motoring offenses, together with other minor crimes, such as public drunkenness and common (simple) assault. The most usual offenses included were thefts, burglaries, and unauthorized takings of motor vehicles.

Over one-third of the sample (153 males, or 37%) were convicted for offenses committed between ages ten and thirty two inclusive. In England and Wales, the minimum age of conviction is ten, and under the criminal law, a juvenile delinquent becomes an adult at seventeen. Conviction rates in this study were similar to arrest rates, because most arrests of the sample males between ages ten and thirty-two were followed by convictions. Because of delays between offenses and convictions sometimes exceeding one year, the dates of offenses were used to define ages of offending, rather than the dates of convictions. Because one criminal event could sometimes lead to several offenses, for example when a burglar was convicted both of burglary and of going equipped to steal, only the most serious offense per offending day was counted.

Between ages ten and thirty-two, the 153 convicted males in the sample accumulated a total of 613 convictions and committed a total of 683 offenses on different days (an average of 4.5 offenses each). These figures show that, in the majority of cases, each conviction was for only one offense.

Because the data on offending are derived from convictions at age ten and older, they do not permit as rigorous a test of the onset hypothesis as might self-report or other data on co-offending at earlier ages. For that reason we focus more on the recruitment and selection of co-offenders into criminal careers and their role in desistance.

C. INFORMATION ON CO-OFFENDING

The criminal records specified whether each person committed his offense with, or was convicted with, others. In the majority of cases, the records also specified the names and dates of birth of these co-offenders. All such co-offenders were searched for in the Criminal Record Office. Of 369 different co-offenders who were not either sample males or relatives (fathers, mothers, brothers, sisters, wives), the criminal records of 336 were found; the records confirmed that the person co-offended with the sample male.

In nine cases, there was no trace of the co-offender's record. In twelve cases, the co-offender's record was found, but it did not include the offense allegedly committed with the sample male. In ten cases the co-offender had been found not guilty of the offense allegedly committed with the sample male. These thirty-one persons were not counted as co-offenders, although they were specified as such in the criminal records of the original sample males. (Two other co-offenders were dead, according to the criminal records, and their files had been destroyed. These two were counted as co-offenders.)

Excluding the above thirty-one cases, the 683 offenses of the sample males involved a total of 616 co-offenders, or an average of 0.90 each. Since these figures are based on convicted offenders only, they probably underestimate the true degree of co-offending because the police may not have known about co-offenders in some cases and other co-offenders may not have been convicted. Of the 616 co-offenders, seventy-six were unidentified by the police, three were identified by name but not by date of birth, and two had since died, as explained above. This left 535 co-offenders whose complete criminal records were found, comprising 408 different persons.

In the vast majority of cases, all co-offenders were convicted for the same offense. However, in a few cases two people convicted together had committed different but related offenses arising from the same incident, for example burglary and receiving stolen goods. Co-offenders who were convicted for the same offense may not have been equally responsible. In some cases, the court may have been unable to establish who among the co-offenders was primarily responsible for an offense, and convicted all co-offenders of the offense even though only one actually committed it. Similarly, some offenses may have been facilitated more by accomplices than other offenses. For example, if co-offenders were all convicted of shoplifting, each may have facilitated the shoplifting by the others; this scenario seems less likely if each co-offender is convicted of carrying an offensive weapon.

V. FINDINGS

A. CO-OFFENDING IN CRIMINAL CAREERS

Earlier we noted that in previous studies aggregate cross-

Psychological Explanations of Crime

sectional data disclose that more of the offenses committed at later ages are committed alone; correlatively there is a decrease in co-offending, though most offender careers continue to show a mix of offenses committed alone and with others. As noted earlier, longitudinal data on offending careers are required to establish whether changes in individual career patterns of offending are due to aging, selective attrition, or/and survival. Such data are necessary to account for the increase in solo offending at later ages. We shall begin by examining how co-offending varies with age, including its variation with age of onset and length of criminal career. We will also inquire whether offending alone or with others in the *first* offense helps predict the future course of a criminal career. Finally, we shall examine whether any decrease in co-offending with age reflects either selective dropout or a change in offending patterns in individual careers with age.

1.   Change in Solo Offending with Age

We must first establish that aggregate data for the London sample show an increase in solo offending with age. Table 1 shows how the incidence of co-offending varied with age. In this and other tables, the co-offenders are *in addition* to the sample male. About half of the offenses (333, or 49%) committed by the males up to age thirty-two were committed alone. Very few offenses were committed by large numbers of offenders: four or more co-offenders were involved in twenty-two offenses (3%) and three co-offenders were involved in a further thirty-eight offenses (6%). The maximum number of verified co-offenders in one offense was ten.

The incidence of co-offending decreased with age[41] in the London sample (Table 1). The average number of co-offenders per offense decreased from 1.2 at ages ten to thirteen to 0.3 at ages twenty-nine to thirty-two and the percentage of offenses committed alone increased from 25% at ages ten to thirteen to 84% at ages twenty-nine to thirty-two. Over all age groups (ten to thirty-two), age was highly correlated with the average number of co-offenders ($r = -.84$; $p \leq 0.001$) and with the percentage of offenses committed alone ($r = +.92$; $p \leq 0.001$).

The decrease in the number of co-offenders with age has implications for the age-crime curve, which differs when plotted for of-

---

[41] The total age range was divided into periods according to English legal status: ten to thirteen (child); fourteen to sixteen (young person); seventeen to twenty (young adult); and twenty-one and older (adult). The first twelve years of the adult age range were divided into three equal four-year periods: twenty-one to twenty-four; twenty-five to twenty-eight; and twenty-nine to thirty-two.

TABLE 1

CHANGES IN CO-OFFENDING WITH AGE

Age	Number of Co-Offenders 0	1	2	3+	Total Offenses	Percent Alone	Average No. of Co-Offenders
10-13	15	25	13	7	60	25	1.2
14-16	60	39	32	23	154	39	1.2
17-20	108	74	37	22	241	45	1.0
21-24	57	27	11	5	100	57	0.7
25-28	44	13	12	1	70	63	0.6
29-32	49	5	2	2	58	84	0.3
Total	333	183	107	60	683	49	0.9

fenses rather than for offenders. The age-crime curve has great theoretical and empirical significance.[42] Two offenders committing one offense appear twice in the usual age-crime curve based on offenders. This same offense would appear only once in an age-crime curve based on offenses. Figure 1 shows the effect of adjusting the age-crime curve for the number of co-offenders. For example, twenty-eight offenses were committed by twenty-two different offenders aged thirteen. Taking account of the 411 sample males at risk of offending at this age, the offending rate was 6.8 offenses per 100 males.[43] The average number of co-offenders at this age was 1.4. Assuming that all co-offenders were of the same age, an offending rate of 6.8 per 100 converts into an offense rate of 2.8 per 100, in view of the average offending group size of 2.4.

Figure 1 shows that the *offense* curve peaked later than the *offender* curve (at age twenty in comparison with age seventeen). Later ages were relatively more important in the offense curve than in the offending curve. For example, the offending rate at ages ten to twelve (2.6) was similar to the offending rate at ages thirty-one to thirty-two (2.5). However, the average number of co-offenders in an offense at ages ten to twelve (2.1) was twice as great as at ages thirty-one to thirty-two (1.0) because none of the twenty offenses involved

[42] Blumstein, Cohen & Farrington, *Criminal Career Research: Its Value for Criminology*, 26 CRIMINOLOGY 1 (1988); Gottfredson & Hirschi, *Science, Public Policy, and the Career Paradigm*, 26 CRIMINOLOGY 37 (1988).

[43] Because of small numbers, some ages are combined as follows: ten to twelve; twenty-one to twenty-two; twenty-three to twenty-four; twenty-five to twenty-six; twenty-seven to twenty-eight; twenty-nine to thirty; and thirty-one to thirty-two. Lower frequencies at these ages reflect patterns of early onset in official records of delinquency and of desistance from offending in the adult years. The offending rate is based on the number of offenders, counting an offender more than once if he commits more than one offense. An offender rate could be calculated based on the number of different offenders. At age thirteen, this would be 5.4 offenders per 100 males.

FIGURE 1

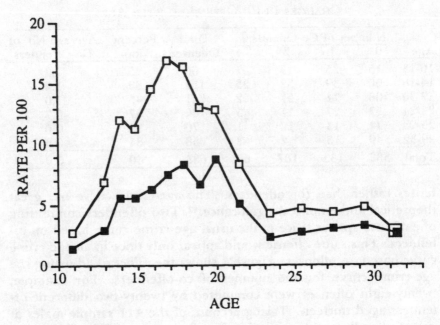

□— Offenders

■— Offenses

co-offenders. Hence, the offense rate at ages thirty-one to thirty-two (2.5) was twice as great as the offense rate at ages ten to twelve (1.3). It follows that unless the number of co-offenders is taken into account, the interpretation of the age-crime curve based on the offending curve can be misleading. For example, offending appears to be less common in the teenage years when the number of offenses is plotted rather than the number of offenders.

2. Variation in Co-offending with Type of Offense

Just as most theories do not render co-offending problematic, they also do not take variation in types of delinquent and criminal behavior into account. The theories generally treat all law violation equally, and most tests of a theory use an additive index of delinquency even when offenses vary in seriousness. Yet it is apparent that the extent of co-offending varies by type of offense. Table 2 shows how co-offending varied with different types of crimes in the London sample.

Burglary and robbery are especially likely to involve co-offenders. The average number of co-offenders was 1.4 in 119 bur-

TABLE 2

CO-OFFENDING IN DIFFERENT TYPES OF CRIMES

Crime Type	Total			Age 10-16			Age 17-32		
	Percent Alone	N	Mean No. Co-Offenders	Percent Alone	N	Mean No. Co-Offenders	Percent Alone	N	Mean No. Co-Offenders
Burglary, Robbery	29	136	1.3	25	56	1.6	31	80	1.2
Theft from MV*	32	38	1.1	17	18	1.3	45	20	0.9
Suspicion	33	30	1.0	29	14	1.4	38	16	0.8
Theft of MV*	43	108	0.9	37	38	1.1	46	70	0.7
Other Theft	45	107	0.9	38	39	1.1	49	68	0.8
Shoplifting	49	41	0.8	30	20	1.0	67	21	0.6
Fraud, Receiving	64	70	0.7	60	10	0.5	65	60	0.7
Violence	72	85	0.7	75	12	0.8	71	73	0.7
Other	76	68	0.4	57	7	0.7	79	61	0.4
Total	49	683	0.9	35	214	1.2	55	469	0.8

* MV = Motor Vehicle

glary offenses and 1.2 in seventeen robbery offenses committed by the London offenders. Theft from a motor vehicle, other theft, and offenses of suspicion (e.g., going equipped to steal, loitering with intent) were also slightly more likely to involve co-offenders than the average for all offenses. Some offense classifications, like "other theft" are too heterogeneous to warrant conclusions about co-offending. "Other theft," for example, includes the predominantly juvenile offense of theft from automatic machines (average co-offenders 1.1 in 17 offenses) and the predominantly adult offense of theft from employers (average 0.6 in 18). Offenses classed as violent have below average numbers of co-offenders: assault (0.8 in 43 offenses), threatening behavior (0.9 in 25), and possessing an offensive weapon (0.3 in 17). Other offenses least likely to involve co-offenders were fraud (average 0.7 in 40 offenses), receiving stolen goods (0.6 in 30), and the heterogeneous "other" category, which consisted of damage to property (0.9 in 22), driving while disqualified (0.0 in 21),[44] drug abuse (0.4 in 19), and sex offenses (0.2 in 6).

It is noteworthy that the three categories of offenses with the lowest rates of co-offending—violence, fraud/receiving, and other—were also the most likely to be committed at the older ages. Given that co-offending decreases with age, it might be expected that offense types committed at older ages would tend to be solo offenses. Table 2 disentangles age and offense type to some extent. Overall, the average number of co-offenders decreased from 1.2 in the juvenile years (ages ten to sixteen) to 0.8 in the adult years (ages seventeen to thirty-two). This decrease occurred within all offense types except fraud/receiving (where there were only ten offenses committed at ages ten to sixteen), a finding that is not surprising given the lesser opportunity for those two offenses in the juvenile ages. The decrease within all offense types suggests that the decrease in co-offending with age occurs independently of the changing pattern of offense types. Similarly, offense types with a high average number of co-offenders at the juvenile ages also tend to have a high number at the adult ages, and offense types with a low average number at the juvenile ages tend to have a low number at the adult ages. Consequently, we conclude that the relationship between co-offending and offense type is independent of age.

This was confirmed by a logit analysis[45] of Table 2, in which the number of crime types was collapsed into three groups of three.

---

44 The offense "driving while disqualified" is necessarily a solo offense.

45 *See generally* S. FIENBERG, THE ANALYSIS OF CROSS CLASSIFIED CATEGORICAL DATA (1980).

Crime type predicted the probability of committing offenses alone independently of age ($G^2 = 60.24$, 2 d.f., $p < 0.001$), and age was predictive independently of crime type ($G^2 = 7.41$, 1 d.f., $p < 0.01$).

3. Changes in Co-offending with Experience in Offending

Changes in co-offending with age, as already noted, can be explained by recourse to different hypothetical deductions. One deduction is that *experience* in committing crimes both alone and with others leads the individual offender to conclude that the risks and benefits of offending alone are most favorable. We have no decision measures for the London sample to test this predicted effect of experience. However, we can determine whether or not both aging and experience have effects on co-offending and solo offending by investigating whether there are changes in solo offending with the order of each conviction numbered from first to last—its serial number.

Table 3 shows how the average number of co-offenders varies with the serial number of the offense. In general, the incidence of co-offending stays relatively constant from the first to the eighth offense, but then declines for the later offenses. Almost certainly this is because offenses with higher serial numbers are committed at older ages. Table 3 also shows that the average number of co-offenders stays reasonably constant with the total number of offenses committed in a criminal career and with the age at first conviction (except for offenders first convicted at age twenty-one or older). The incidence of co-offending also stays relatively constant with career length, measured simply by the number of years between the first and last offenses. The decline in co-offending with the serial number of the offense suggests that experience in offending, both alone and with others, may explain some of the decline in co-offending with age. However, that the rate of co-offending remains relatively constant for up to eight offenses and then declines suggests that age may be more important than experience in explaining the decline in co-offending.

4. Co-offending in First Offenses

Some theories of delinquent and criminal behavior regard co-offending as the major means of recruitment into criminal activity. Moreover, the number of co-offenders involved in an offense is hypothesized to be greater in offenses by the young because they require peer support in risk taking. Because we lack self-report data about co-offending at early ages and are limited to convictions of

TABLE 3

CO-OFFENDING VERSUS SERIAL NUMBER OF OFFENSE, TOTAL NUMBER OF OFFENSES, AGE FIRST CONVICTED, AND CAREER LENGTH

Serial No. Offense	Co-Offenders Mean	N	Total No. Offenses	Co-Offenders Mean	N	Age First Convicted	Co-Offenders Mean	N	Career Length (years)	Co-Offenders Mean	N
1	1.0	153	1	0.8	49	10	1.0	72	0	0.7	55
2	1.1	104	2	1.0	60	11	1.1	69	1-2	1.2	36
3	1.1	74	3	1.0	45	12	0.6	49	3-4	1.1	69
4	0.8	59	4	0.8	32	13	1.1	92	5-6	1.1	40
5	0.9	51	5	0.9	55	14	1.1	78	7-8	1.1	62
6	1.2	40	6	1.1	48	15	0.8	125	9-10	0.7	40
7-8	0.9	61	7	1.1	21	16	0.9	57	11-12	1.2	48
9-10	0.5	46	8	1.0	40	17	1.0	56	13-14	0.9	69
11-12	0.7	35	9	1.2	18	18-20	0.9	48	15-16	0.8	179
13-15	0.6	30	10	0.5	40	21-32	0.4	37	17-19	0.8	33
16-20	0.5	30	11-14	0.9	110				20-22	0.8	52
			15-20	0.9	165						

those age ten or older, we are unable to test whether or not this hypothesis is correct. Taking convictions after age ten into account, the 153 first offenses were only slightly more likely to involve co-offenders than the remaining 530 offenses. The average number of co-offenders for the first offense is 1.0, versus 0.9 for later offenses.

Again, when addressing the issue of the role of experience in changes in patterns of co-offending with age, an important question is whether co-offending or solo offending in the first offense helps in predicting the future criminal career. Table 4 shows that those who committed their first offense alone tend to commit fewer offenses on average (3.6) than those whose first offense was committed with one (average 5.0) or two or more (average 5.1) other offenders. Similarly, those whose first offense was alone were less likely to recidivate (be reconvicted) than the remainder (60% recidivism, as opposed to 73% and 74% respectively for those with one, or two or more co-offenders).

The major problem in interpreting these figures is that the total number of offenses and the probability of recidivism decreased markedly with the age at first conviction. Table 4 shows how the total number of offenses and the percentage of recidivists varies with the number of co-offenders in the first offense, while controlling for age at first conviction. It can be seen that, at ages ten to thirteen and seventeen to twenty, those who committed their first offense alone also committed the lowest number of total offenses. However, at ages fourteen to sixteen, those who committed their first offense alone committed the highest number of offenses. Hence, there is no consistent tendency for solo offending in the first offense to be associated with few total offenses for all ages at first conviction. A logit analysis of Table 4 confirmed that neither solo nor co-offending predicted the probability of recidivism independently of age.

Table 5 uses transition matrices to investigate whether solo or co-offending in one conviction predicts recidivism and either solo or co-offending in the next conviction. For example, 79% of the twenty-four offenders who were first convicted of a solo offense at age ten to sixteen recidivated, in comparison with 87% of sixty-one offenders who first co-offended. Of those convicted a second time, 53% who committed the first offense alone were also alone on the second offense. In comparison, 62% of those who were with others in the first offense were also with others in the second offense.[46]

---

[46] This analysis was based on successive *convictions*, not successive offenses, because two offenses leading to the same conviction often had the same number of co-offenders,

TABLE 4

NUMBER OF CO-OFFENDERS IN THE FIRST OFFENSE VERSUS LATER CRIMINAL CAREERS

| Age at First Offense | Number of Co-Offenders | | | | | | | | | | | | Total | | |
| | 0 | | | 1 | | | 2 or more | | | | | | | | |
	Mean No. Offenses	N	Percent Recidivist	Mean No. Offenses	N	Percent Recidivist	Mean No. Offenses	N	Percent Recidivist				Mean No. Offenses	N	Percent Recidivist
10-13	7.0	7	86	8.1	16	100	8.6	12	83				8.1	35	91
14-16	5.8	17	82	5.4	14	86	4.5	19	79				5.2	50	82
17-20	2.3	21	67	2.4	14	43	2.9	8	75				2.4	43	60
21-32	1.5	17	18	1.6	5	40	1.0	3	0				1.5	25	20
Total	3.6	62	60	5.0	49	73	5.1	42	74				4.5	153	68

TABLE 5
CO-OFFENDING IN ONE OFFENSE VERSUS RECIDIVISM AND CO-OFFENDING IN THE NEXT

Serial No. of Offense	Ages 10-16				Ages 17-32				Total			
	Recidivate Percent	N	Alone Next Time Percent	N	Recidivate Percent	N	Alone Next Time Percent	N	Recidivate Percent	N	Alone Next Time Percent	N
1-alone	79	24	53	19	42	38	56	16	56	62	54	35
1-with others	87	61	38	53	47	30	50	14	74	91	40	67
2-alone	93	14	46	13	59	32	58	19	70	46	53	32
2-with others	91	23	14	21	61	33	30	20	73	56	22	41
3-alone	100	6	33	6	65	20	62	13	73	26	53	19
3-with others	83	18	40	15	76	29	59	22	79	47	51	37
4-alone	100	8	50	8	62	21	69	13	72	29	62	21
4-with others	100	7	14	7	85	20	59	17	89	27	46	24

Offenders tend to specialize in either solo or co-offending. The probabilities of recidivism given in Table 5 are always less for offenses committed alone than for offenses committed with others, except after a second or later juvenile offense, when recidivism rates are very high and numbers are small. Therefore, there is a tendency for solo offenders to desist rather than persist. However, a logit analysis showed that neither solo nor co-offending predicted recidivism independently of age and serial number of offense. Interestingly, these variables had a significant three way interaction ($G^2 = 3.86$, 1 d.f., $p < 0.05$).

The probability of a solo offense following another solo offense is always greater than the probability of a co-offender offense being followed by a solo offense (except after the third juvenile offense, when the numbers are very small). A logit analysis showed that age ($G^2 = 7.20$, 1 d.f., $p < 0.01$) and solo or co-offending ($G^2 = 5.38$, 1 d.f., $p < 0.025$) independently predicted solo or co-offending in the next offense, but that serial number did not.

An important question is whether sample males who commit their first offenses with more criminally experienced co-offenders are likely to have more extensive criminal careers than those who commit their first offenses with other first offenders. In fact, there was no relationship between having criminally experienced co-offenders in the first offense and the future criminal career. The forty males who committed first offenses with other first offenders averaged 5.4 offenses each in their criminal careers, in comparison with 5.2 for the forty-two who committed first offenses with at least one co-offender who was more criminally experienced. Even for first offenses at ages ten to thirteen, the differences were very small—8.7 offenses for fifteen sample males with first co-offenders versus 9.0 for eleven sample males with more experienced co-offenders.

Interestingly, however, the co-offenders among the sample males themselves have, on the average, much higher individual rates of offending than the sample males themselves. Whereas the 153 convicted sample males amassed a total of 683 offenses, or an average of 4.5 offenses each, the 408 different co-offenders amassed a total of 3,622 offenses, or 8.9 each. Moreover, whereas none of the sample males amassed more than twenty offenses, 12% of the co-offenders (48 of the 408) each had more than this number of offenses. Conversely, whereas 32% of sample males (49 of the 153)

---

partly because the conviction was often for a connected series of offenses committed close together.

had only one offense, this was true of only 11% of the co-offenders (45 of the 408).

5. *Explaining the Decrease in Co-offending with Age*

Co-offending may decrease with age because of changes in the population of offenders (e.g., if co-offenders tend to desist while solo offenders tend to persist) or because of behavioral changes within offenders (i.e., if any given offender becomes more likely to offend alone with age). We have shown that there is no tendency for solo offenders in general to persist. Another way of investigating this issue is to study changes within the criminal careers of persistent offenders. We classified twenty-two of the sample males as the most persistent offenders because each committed at least ten offenses. In the aggregate these twenty-two offenders (5% of the sample) committed 46% of all offenses—315 of 683 offenses.

Table 6 shows some characteristics of the twenty-two most persistent offenders. Most of their criminal careers were characterized by approximately equal numbers of solo and co-offending offenses. Fifty-two percent of the total crimes committed by persistent offenders were committed alone. One person (case 290) was exclusively a solo offender, one (case 590) was a predominantly solo offender, and two (cases 181 and 560) were predominantly co-offenders.

Table 7 shows that the average number of co-offenders of these twenty-two persistent offenders decreased markedly with age, as did the co-offending of more occasional offenders. Over all ages from ten to thirty-two, the correlation between age and the average number of co-offenders was very similar for those with ten-plus offenses ($-.69$) and those with one to nine offenses ($-.68$). Similar results were obtained when the definition of persistent offenders was widened to encompass the forty offenders with six or more offenses, who accounted for 442 (65%) of the 683 offenses. Over all ages, the correlation between age and the average number of co-offenders was very similar for those with six-plus offenses ($-.73$) and those with one-five offenses ($-.72$; all correlations $p < 0.001$). One could thus conclude that the decrease in co-offending with age is not caused by the persistence of solo offenders and/or the dropping out of co-offenders, but instead reflects changes within individual criminal careers.

In another investigation of the decrease of co-offending with age, the average number of co-offenders per offense in the first half of each persistent offender's criminal career was compared with the average number in the second half. For the twenty-two most persis-

TABLE 6

Characteristics Associated with 22 Persistent Offenders

Persistent Offender	No. Offenses	Percent Alone	No. Co-Offenders	No. Known	No. 1st Offenders	Serial No. Lower	No. Different Co-Offenders	No. Repeated
052	17	53	18	6	2	1	5	1
114	12	42	11	11	3	7	10	1
181	12	17	17	15	1	7	4	11
252	12	67	5	5	0	2	4	1
281	10	40	10	3	2	1	3	0
290	10	100	0	0	0	0	2	0
301	10	60	6	4	1	0	0	0
310	16	31	26	23	1	9	4	8
341	20	45	22	22	8	15	15	5
383	10	70	3	3	1	0	17	0
402	16	63	7	6	0	1	3	1
411	18	50	14	11	0	1	5	0
522	12	42	17	8	2	4	11	2
541	12	50	10	10	6	5	6	1
560	11	9	15	15	2	12	9	3
590	12	83	8	8	2	4	12	0
743	19	42	19	19	10	18	8	5
763	19	63	8	8	0	0	14	1
781	13	62	7	3	0	3	7	0
851	20	55	14	12	5	7	3	0
882	20	50	16	11	3	10	12	2
892	14	71	6	5	2	1	9	2
Total	315	52	259	205	51	112	162	43

TABLE 7

CHANGES IN CO-OFFENDING WITH AGE FOR PERSISTENT OFFENDERS

	Mean Number of Co-Offenders							
	10+ Offenses		1-9 Offenses		6+ Offenses		1-5 Offenses	
Age	Mean	N	Mean	N	Mean	N	Mean	N
10-13	1.3	32	1.2	28	1.2	42	1.2	18
14-16	1.1	70	1.2	84	1.1	105	1.3	49
17-20	0.8	120	1.1	121	0.9	157	1.0	84
21-24	0.6	41	0.8	59	0.7	59	0.6	41
25-28	0.5	28	0.6	42	0.5	38	0.6	32
29-32	0.2	24	0.4	34	0.4	41	0.1	17
Total	0.8	315	1.0	368	0.9	442	0.9	241

tent offenders, this average decreased in sixteen cases and increased in only four (Wilcoxon $T=41$, $N=20$, $p \leq 0.01$; the average was the same in the remaining two cases). For the forty offenders with six or more offenses, this average decreased in twenty-seven cases and increased in nine (with four the same: Wilcoxon $T=159$, $N=36$, $p \leq 0.005$). These results again show changes within individual criminal careers.

VI. RECRUITMENT INTO OFFENDING AND SELECTION OF CO-OFFENDERS

The prospective design of the Cambridge Study in Delinquent Development permits a partial examination of various hypotheses about recruitment into delinquent and later criminal careers and the selection of co-offenders.

A. ROLE OF RECRUITERS IN CO-OFFENDING

Any criminal network has a small number of high rate offenders who persist in offending over a fairly long period of time. The first hypothesis is that some of these persisters function as recruiters into offending, either by recruitment of "innocent" persons to a first offense or by recruitment of prior offenders into recidivism. Recruiters are a subset of persistent offenders who are identified by the fact that they commit crimes with a large number of different co-offenders, most of whom are less experienced in crime than the recruiter and some of whom are initially recruited into offending.

The twenty-two offenders identified as persistent in the London sample are shown in Table 6. Over all, there was no marked tendency to offend with less experienced co-offenders, since the average serial number of the offense of the co-offender was lower than that of the persistent offender in only about one-half of the cases (112 out of 205, or 55%). Nonetheless, six of the twenty-two persistent offenders—numbers 114, 341, 560, 743, 851, and 882 in Table 6—can be identified as recruiters in that they displayed a marked tendency to offend with less experienced offenders. A majority of their co-offenders were either first offenders or among those committing an offense whose serial number was below that of the persistent offender. In total, sixty-nine of their ninety co-offenders were less experienced. The most common offense in these sixty-nine cases was burglary (26) followed by theft of vehicles (14). Furthermore, these six persistent offenders accounted for 68% of the co-offenders (35 of 51) committing their first offense. Again, the most common offense in these thirty-five cases was burglary (15), followed by theft of vehicles (6). It is therefore plausible to classify these persistent offenders as "recruiters." Were these proportions to hold for a current population of offenders, it seems feasible to select these offenders from a population of high rate offenders for special treatment since, as recruiters, they appear to have a substantial impact on the prevalence rate of offenders in the population.

B. SELECTION OF FAMILY MEMBERS AS CO-OFFENDERS

One hypothesis explaining recruitment into delinquency is that older family members recruit younger ones into delinquent behavior.[47] A corollary is that co-habitation facilitates the opportunistic selection of one's co-offenders. The 408 different co-offenders included thirty-five males who were also part of the original sample (two of whom were also brothers), 323 unrelated males, thirteen unrelated females, twenty-four brothers, four sisters, four fathers, one mother, and four wives. This distribution of the co-offending pairs makes abundantly clear that the selection of co-offenders, whether as a juvenile or later as an adult, is largely limited to males. Offending with females was infrequent; only 5% of the co-offenders (22 of the 408) were female. Nonetheless, 41% of the twenty-two female co-offenders were family members, either a mother, wife or sister. By comparison only eight percent of the male co-offenders (30 of the 386) were either fathers or brothers. Quite clearly, when males select[48] a female co-offender, it is far more likely to be a family member than when they select a male co-offender.

The likelihood of co-offending with brothers depends, of

---

[47] Clearly this explanation fails to account for how the older family member became delinquent or criminal.

[48] The term "select" may mislead since the data do not permit us to determine whether the selection is made by a primary offender or rather by mutual selection.

course, on whether a sample male has brothers. About two-thirds of convicted sample males (105, or 69%) had one or more brothers. Table 8 shows how the probability of co-offending with a brother varied according to the difference in age between the brother and

TABLE 8
CO-OFFENDING WITH BROTHERS

Age of Brother vs. Sample Male		No. Brothers	No. Co-Offending	Percent
8+	years older	21	2	10
6-8	years older	19	1	5
4-6	years older	27	2	7
2-4	years older	31	1	3
0-2	years older	24	4	17
0-2	years younger	29	5	17
2-4	years younger	28	6	21
4-6	years younger	26	1	4
6-8	years younger	20	1	5
8+	years younger	27	0	0
Total Older		122	10	8
Total Younger		130	13	10
Total		252	23	9

the sample male. For example, convicted sample males had a total of twenty-one brothers who were at least eight years older than they, and only two of these brothers were co-offenders.

Co-offending of sample males with their brothers was most likely to occur when the brothers were close in age: zero to two years older (17%), zero to two years younger (17%), or two to four years younger (21%). Co-offending was significantly more likely for those with brothers in these age ranges than for the remainder ($\chi^2 = 12.7$, 1 d.f., $p < 0.001$). Overall, 23 out of 252 full brothers who survived at least to the age of criminal responsibility (10) were co-offenders (9%), and the probability of co-offending was similar for older and younger brothers.[49]

The difference in age between a sample male and his brother was related to the number of brothers that a sample male had. Of the 252 brothers, 99 were in families where the sample male had one or two brothers (70 sample males), eighty-two were in families with three or four brothers (25 sample males), and seventy-one were

---

[49] The number of co-offending brothers is twenty-three here because two co-offending brothers who were also sample males were added to the twenty-four other co-offending brothers, but three co-offending brothers of sample males were deleted because they co-offended with a sample male who was not *their* brother.

in families with five or more brothers (10 sample males). Co-offending with brothers was most common where a sample male had three or four brothers (16 out of 82, or 20%), and especially in this case with brothers who were up to two years older or up to four years younger (12 out of 32, or 38%).

Lacking information on the number of males in the London population who might be considered eligible for selection as co-offenders, we are unable to calculate the exact probability that one would randomly select a related person as compared with an unrelated person as a co-offender. Given the orders of magnitude in comparing the selection of brothers from the total number of eligible brothers and the random selection of a male from the population of all eligible males, excluding brothers, it is apparent that there is a selection bias towards brothers.

C.   PROPINQUITY IN SELECTING CO-OFFENDERS

Our third hypothesis is that offenders disproportionally select one another to co-offend if they live in close proximity. The effect of propinquity on selection of co-offenders is expected to be greater for younger than older offenders. The measure of propinquity used to test this hypothesis is to compare the location of offenses with those of their offenders.

English criminal records almost always include the location of the offense and usually include as well the current addresses of all offenders. In this study, the majority of locations of offenses and addresses of offenders were in London. These were coded according to their location in London postal districts. The codes placed locations to the nearest mile. Of the 679 offenses whose locations were recorded, 43% (294) were committed in the immediate study area of seven postal districts where the sample males were living at age eight. Another 39% (262) were committed in one of the other 112 London postal districts. Twelve percent (83) were committed in the Home Counties surrounding London, and 6% (40) were committed elsewhere.

The addresses for 556 offenses were recorded for the sample males up to age thirty-two. At the time of the offense, 57% (317) of the sample males lived in the original study area and 31% (171) elsewhere in London. Another 8% (46) lived in the Home Counties and 4% (22) elsewhere in the United Kingdom. The probability of a convicted sample male living in the study area decreased with age—from 79% at ages ten to thirteen to 42% at ages twenty-nine to thirty-two. The offense was most likely to involve co-offenders when the sample male was living in the study area (55%), in comparison with 49% of offenses committed by sample males living in other London postal districts, 39% by sample males lived in the Home Counties, and 27% when sample males lived elsewhere. The average number of co-offenders was 1.0 for sample males in the study area, 0.9 for those in other London postal districts, 0.6 for those in the Home Counties, and 0.4 for those elsewhere.

One problem in interpreting these figures is determining to what extent the decreasing incidence of co-offending outside London reflects increasing mobility with the increasing average age of offenders. Very few convicted sample males aged ten to sixteen (only 6) lived outside London. For offenses at ages seventeen to twenty, the average number of co-offenders was 1.0 for the 178 males living in London (in the study area or other postal districts) and 0.6 for the twenty-seven living elsewhere. At twenty-one to thirty-two, the average number of co-offenders was 0.6 for the 172 males living in London and 0.3 for the thirty-five living elsewhere. Therefore, the tendency for offenses committed in London to involve more co-offenders held independently of the age of the offender.

In the 535 sample male/co-offender combinations, 47% (252) of the offenses were located in the study area and 35% (189) in other London postal districts. There were 13% (72) in the Home Counties, and 4% (22) elsewhere. Almost two-thirds (64%) of the sample male addresses (277 cases) were located in the study area and an additional 29% (128) in other London postal districts, 6% (24) in the Home Counties, and 2% (7) elsewhere. Correlatively, 62% (289) of the co-offenders' addresses were in the study area, 30% (140) in other London postal districts, 6% (29) in the Home Counties, and 2% (10) elsewhere.

Table 9 shows the distances between locations of offenses and addresses of sample males and of co-offenders. The data show that sample males and co-offenders tended to commit offenses close to where they were living. In about half of the cases (46% for sample males and 52% for co-offenders), the offense was committed in the same postal district or within about one mile of the person's address. These percentages underestimate proximity, since some of the offenses and offenders outside London would also have been close to each other.

Table 9 also shows that addresses of sample males were very close to addresses of co-offenders. In 60% of cases, the two addresses were either within the same postal district or within about one mile of each other. Although not shown in Table 9, restricting

TABLE 9

MILE DISTANCES BETWEEN LOCATIONS OF OFFENSES, ADDRESSES OF
SAMPLE MALES, AND ADDRESSES OF CO-OFFENDERS

Distance	Offense to Sample Male		Offense to Co-Offender		Sample Male to Co-Offender	
	Percent	N	Percent	N	Percent	N
Same District	29	126	29	136	46	185
1 mile	17	75	23	104	14	57
2 miles	15	66	11	50	14	56
3 miles	6	25	7	34	4	15
4-5 miles	7	31	6	29	6	22
6+ miles	6	27	4	18	4	15
Outside London	20	86	20	94	12	48
Total	100	436	100	465	100	398

the analysis to offenses committed in London, the percentage of
cases where the two addresses were within the same postal district
or within one mile decreased with the age of the sample male from
100% at ages ten to thirteen to 53% at ages twenty-one to thirty-
two. Although it is clear, then, that propinquity in the selection of
co-offenders declines with age, at all ages a sizeable proportion of
all co-offenders in any offense reside in fairly close proximity to each
other and to the location of the offense.

1. Stability of Co-Offending Relationships

There are competing hypotheses concerning the stability of
networks of offenders and of relationships among co-offenders.
One hypothesis assumes that homophily dominates the selection of
co-offenders and contributes to long-term stability in co-offending
relationships and their networks. It also leads to a separation of juvenile from adult offender networks. A competing hypothesis assumes the contrary, that while the networks of offenders are fairly
homogeneous in composition, they are loosely structured so that relationships among network members are unstable with a resulting
high turnover in the co-offenders of any individual offender. We
shall examine first the extent to which homophily dominates selection of co-offenders and then turn to examine the extent to which
co-offending relationships and networks are stable.

2. Homophily in Co-Offender Selection and Network Structure.

a. Age

Complete criminal records were obtained for the 535 co-offenders, comprising 408 different persons. Table 10 is based on the 535 possible comparisons between the ages of sample males and their co-offenders. It can be seen that co-offenders tended to be very close in age to sample males for offenses committed under age twenty-one.

TABLE 10

DIFFERENCE IN AGE BETWEEN SAMPLE MALE AND CO-OFFENDER

Age Difference	Age of Sample Male					
	10-13	14-16	17-20	21-24	25-32	Total
Co-Offender Younger By:						
5+ years	0	0	0	4	14	18
4 years	0	0	5	3	2	10
3 years	0	7	9	10	3	29
2 years	2	7	29	7	2	47
1 year	8	34	34	4	2	82
Same Age	28	51	49	4	0	132
Co-Offender Older By:						
1 year	11	22	33	7	0	73
2 years	12	13	9	3	0	37
3 years	8	2	7	4	0	21
4 years	1	7	8	2	1	19
5-10 years	0	0	16	10	5	31
11+ years	0	3	14	10	9	36
Total	70	146	213	68	38	535

When the sample male was aged ten to thirteen, co-offenders were the same age or only one year younger or older in 67% of cases (47 out of 70). The comparable figure was 73% at ages fourteen to sixteen (107 out of 146), and 54% at ages seventeen to twenty (116 out of 213). In contrast, co-offenders differed in age by five years or more in 74% of cases (28 out of 38) when the sample male's age was twenty-five to thirty-two. No sample males aged ten to thirteen were convicted with an adult co-offender (aged 17 or over), whereas this was true of 19% (29 out of 146) of the sample males aged fourteen to sixteen. Conversely, 21% (45 out of 213) of the sample males who were seventeen to twenty were convicted with a juvenile co-offender; only one older sample male was convicted with a juvenile co-offender. Hence, a juvenile committed an offense with an adult in only 75 of the 535 co-offending pairs (14%). There is, it appears, substantial separation of juvenile from adult networks in the selection of co-offenders.

There was a slight (non-significant) tendency for co-offenders to be older than sample males (217 cases) rather than younger

(186). This difference in age was particularly marked (and significant, $p < 0.05$) for the sample male's first offense, when fifty-eight co-offenders were older and only thirty-four younger (and forty-two the same age). For all subsequent offenses of the sample males, co-offenders were equally likely to be older or younger; 159 co-offenders were older, 152 younger, and ninety of the same age.

Age homophily is evident in the selection of co-offenders. Table 11 shows that the sample males are similar to their co-offenders in age, serial number of the offense, age at first conviction, and total number of offenses. For example, when the sample male was convicted for his first offense, in the majority of cases his co-offender was also convicted for a first offense (74 out of 134, or 55%). All correlations between sample males and co-offenders are significant: $r = .57$ for age; .44 for serial number; .31 for total number of offenses; and .21 for age at first conviction; all $p \leq 0.001$), providing evidence for homophily in selection.

b. Ethnic Status

As previously noted, the London sample was homogeneous in composition, with all but three percent being white. Only twelve of the sample males were blacks of West Indian or African origin; eight of these twelve were convicted of offenses. Limited by the small numbers of sample blacks and the preponderance of sample whites (both in the sample and in Greater London), we examined whether sample males and co-offenders tended also to be similar in ethnic status. Not surprisingly, blacks were less likely than whites to have a co-offender of the same ethnic status. The eight convicted black sample males had a total of twenty-seven known co-offenders, ten of whom were recorded as black (37%). The criminal records, however, did not always indicate race. Bearing in mind that three of the eight convicted sample blacks were not identified as blacks in the criminal records, it would be reasonable to conclude that a majority of those co-offending with blacks were probably also black. By contrast, the 145 white sample males who were convicted of crimes had a total of 508 known co-offenders, only fifteen (3%) of whom were recorded as black. Thus, while there is considerable ethnic homophily in the selection of co-offenders, it seems reasonable to conclude that it is also a function of the relative distribution of whites and blacks in the London population.

c. Stability of Co-Offender Relationships

The stability of relationships among co-offenders is not easily

TABLE 11
COMPARISONS BETWEEN SAMPLE MALES AND CO-OFFENDERS

Sample Male	Age Co-Offenders Mean	N	Sample Male	Serial No. of Offense Co-Offenders Mean	N	Sample Male	Age First Convicted Co-Offenders Mean	N	Sample Male	Total No. of Offenses Co-Offenders Mean	N
10-13	12.8	70	1	2.5	134	10	14.4	62	1	5.4	29
14-16	15.6	146	2	3.2	103	11	12.8	71	2	5.0	59
17-20	20.4	213	3	3.9	67	12	13.7	23	3	7.7	41
21-24	24.9	68	4	5.6	44	13	15.8	86	4	9.0	21
25-28	26.3	21	5	4.8	38	14	15.5	72	5	11.0	44
29-32	33.0	17	6-7	4.6	62	15	15.5	82	6-7	6.7	74
			8-10	5.8	44	16	16.0	45	8-10	8.9	70
			11-14	11.5	26	17	16.7	55	11-14	9.1	78
			15-20	10.8	17	18-20	17.2	28	15-20	14.6	119
						21-32	18.4	11			

ascertained, given that some offenders commit only one or two offenses that occur within a short interval of time. One way to address the problem is to examine the stability of relationships of persistent offenders with co-offenders. As described earlier, there were twenty-two offenders who were considered persistent because they committed at least ten offenses.

Co-offending pairs and triplets were generally short-lived among the persistent offenders in the London sample. Persistent offenders had a total of 205 co-offenders whose complete criminal histories were found. Only forty-three of these were repeat co-offenders. On the average, then, committing offenses repeatedly with the same person was unusual. The time interval between the first and last offense committed together was one year or more for only nine co-offending pairs. Three of these involved brothers. The longest interval between the first and last offense for a co-offending pair was five years four months out of a possible interval of approximately twenty-two years. Interestingly, none of these nine cases involved two co-offenders in continuing residential proximity. Furthermore, only two of the nine cases concerned continuing commission of the same offense (burglary), although five of these nine co-offending pairs committed at least one burglary together.

VII. CONCLUSIONS

Most theories are concerned with the onset of delinquent and criminal behavior and not with continuation of or desistance from criminal conduct. With a few exceptions, causal theories do not take into account the fact that co-offending is an integral aspect of much criminal activity. This paper has explored some of the dimensions of co-offending behavior and their potential relevance for theories about criminal conduct. Longitudinal data from the Cambridge Study in Delinquent Development were used to test inferences from contemporary theories about delinquent and criminal careers.

It has long been known that there are changes in co-offending with age, but our findings indicate that the incidence of co-offending decreases with age primarily because individual offenders change and become less likely to offend with others rather than because of selective attrition of co-offenders or persistence of those who offend primarily alone. As males age, they are more likely to offend alone, though most males continue to commit some offenses with others. Exclusive solo offending or exclusive co-offending behavior is uncommon at all ages, though there is a significant tendency for specialization in either solo or co-offending. Studies of the most persistent offenders showed that they had approximately equal numbers of solo and co-offending offenses. The likelihood of recidivism is slightly less after offenses committed alone than with co-offenders. Hence, knowing that an offense is committed alone or with others may help in predicting the future course of the offender's criminal career. When the age-crime curve is corrected to take account of co-offending, the peak age is shifted upwards (from seventeen to twenty), and offending at older ages becomes proportionally more important.

Most theories do not take variation in types of delinquent and criminal behavior into account. The London data show that co-offending varies with offense type and is especially important for the offenses of burglary and robbery. Further research is required to establish why certain types of offenses are more or less conducive to co-offending. Co-offenders tend to be similar in age, sex, race, and criminal experience. It was rare for sample males to offend with fathers, mothers, sisters, wives, or unrelated females. The likelihood of offending with a brother was greatest when a brother was close in age to the sample male. Most sample males and their co-offenders tended to live close to each other and tended to commit offenses close to where they lived. Further research is required to investigate whether opportunity factors (e.g. physical proximity) drive co-offending or whether people who have already decided to offend select associates from those who are readily available.

The selection of co-offenders takes place within networks which appear to be open systems that are relatively restricted in their age range. In the selection of co-offenders, there is substantial separation of juvenile from adult networks of offenders. According to other studies, the composition of these networks is relatively unstable. There is high turnover in co-offending relationships with most lasting for only relatively short periods of time. Persistent offenders particularly tend to commit offenses with different people, so that their co-offending pairings tend to be short-lived.

There is evidence that a small proportion of the offenders with high individual rates of offending recruit different co-offenders for each offense. Six of the twenty-two most persistent offenders seemed to be recruiters, since they tended to offend with less experienced co-offenders and with those committing first offenses. In the context of recruitment, the most common offense was burglary, followed by vehicle theft. Recruiters may substantially affect the prevalence of offenders in a population since they recruit at the margin. Because they can be identified by their behavior, some criminal justice interventions could well be focused on these recruiters. Selective incapacitation of recruiters, for example, might have a substantial impact upon the prevalence of offenders and, because of their high individual rates of offending, also reduce the incidence rate significantly.

We regard this paper as an exploration in the development and testing of theory about the role of co-offending in delinquent and criminal behavior. Unfortunately, the main longitudinal data set available for testing theories is comprised of a relatively small and homogenous population of males. Most of our analyses, therefore, are based on small numbers. Moreover, the measures of offending were limited to official convictions. Future studies should measure co-offending using self-reports as well as official records and should seek to establish the criminal careers of co-offenders in order to investigate co-offending networks more thoroughly. At a minimum, official agencies should routinely collect and publish information about co-offenders.

Because of the design and measurement limitations of the London study, we caution against regarding the analyses presented here as definitive. We hope, however, that they will show what kinds of analyses can be carried out to help advance knowledge about co-offending. Studies of co-offending in the past have been hindered by the lack of information about co-offenders in official records or self-reports. Our hope is that this article will persuade criminologists of the importance of collecting information about and investigating co-offending, and that other researchers will seek to replicate our methods using longitudinal data with larger samples. Finally, we have pointed to a few policy implications of the findings on co-offending to emphasize the importance of co-offending behavior for determining crime policy as well as for theory testing.

[17]

Journal of Abnormal Child Psychology, Vol. 12, No. 1, 1984, pp. 111-126

Childhood Aggression and Social Adjustment as Antecedents of Delinquency[1]

James D. Roff[2]
Eastern Michigan University

Robert D. Wirt
New School for Social Research

A sample of 2,453 grade school children were followed into young adulthood through record sources. Teacher interviews provided information about low-peer-status children that was assessed in relation to subsequent delinquency for both sexes and young adult criminality for males. A multivariate design evaluated the joint effects of social class, a measure of family disturbance, and childhood problem behavior factors as antecedents of delinquency. Childhood aggression emerged as the most prominent antecedent factor for males but not for females. Social class and family disturbance were associated with aggression but did not have significant direct effects on delinquency. Aggression was related to severity of delinquency. Dispositional status, reflecting severity, was the best indicator of which delinquent males would have adult criminal records. A causal model is presented.

Investigation of the antecedents of delinquency has shifted from an emphasis on the prediction of delinquency, a formidable task, to the specification of causal models. The latter approach requires that the

Manuscript received in final form July 18, 1983.
[1]The study was supported by a grant from the Scottish Rite Schizophrenia Research Program, N.M.J., U.S.A. Portions of the study were presented at the Life History Research conference in Monterey, California, 1981. The authors wish to thank June White, Cindy Hanson, and Ned Worell for their help in conducting this research. Data for this research was originally gathered by Merrill Roff. Follow-up data were contributed by Ronald Peek, Donald Bamber, Charles Watson, Shiela Makie, William S. Ward, Edward S. Posey, Chris Hemlabs, and Harriet Barnes.
[2]Address all correspondence to James D. Roff, Department of Psychology, Eastern Michigan University, Ypsilanti, Michigan 48197.

relevant variables be known and that hypotheses about relationships among variables be generated and ultimately tested. Given this orientation, modest but stable relationships, while of small predictive value, can assume theoretical importance. For example, lower social class indices have been related to increased rates of delinquency, although even this statement has been qualified (Clark & Wenninger, 1962; Reiss & Rhodes, 1961). With a more sophisticated model, it becomes apparent that this relationship is mediated by intervening child and family variables to the point where social class has little independent predictive value when considered with other appropriate variables (Robins, 1978). Still, social class is related to these intervening variables and needs to be included in the model.

The domains that need to be measured, suggested by previous research, include childhood aggression, social adjustment, school achievement, family conflict and neglect, and predelinquent behavior such as truancy, stealing, and running away, as well as a measure of delinquency-inhibiting behavior (Glueck & Glueck, 1950; Havighurst, Bowman, Liddle, Matthews, & Pierce, 1962; McCord & McCord, 1959; Robins, 1966; West & Farrington, 1973; Wirt & Briggs, 1959). Additional domains could be added but these appear most promising. In fact, childhood aggressive behavior in middle childhood has emerged as the most important indicator of increased risk for delinquency among males (Eron & Huesmann, 1983; Eron, Walder, Huesmann, & Lefkowitz, 1974; Farrington, 1978; Havinghurst et al., 1962). Moreover, ratings of childhood aggression in males have been related to delinquency within levels of social class and levels of intelligence (Conger & Miller, 1966). More serious delinquency as indicated by crimes of violence has been associated with prior ratings of aggressive behavior (Farrington, 1978). Ratings of aggression by teachers or peers have displayed considerable stability from childhood for both sexes (Eron et al., 1974; Olweus, 1979). Although social class measures would be expected to be related to ratings of aggression, there are studies where no significant relationship was found (Olweus, 1980) or where the relationship was in the opposite direction from that expected (Eron et al., 1974). Since most samples have included only males, the longitudinal relationship of aggression to delinquency for females remains less certain.

Peer rejection as a measure of childhood social adjustment has been associated with an increased risk for delinquency in both sexes (Roff, 1972). Poor social adjustment does not appear to be specific to delinquency in that it has been found to be a precursor for a wide range of young adult maladjustment (Roff, 1970). Although there are exceptions (Olweus, 1974), low peer status and aggressive behavior should be significantly correlated. The conjunction of peer rejection and aggression should indicate significantly elevated risk for delinquency.

Path analysis provides a method for assessing the relative effect of these variables when considered together in a causal model (Kenny, 1979; Spaeth, 1975). The present study focuses on the contribution of aggression to the development of delinquency in the context of peer rejection. Specific questions addressed include the following:

1. What is the extent of the relationship between childhood aggression and later delinquency for children who have been rejected by their peers? What impact do other childhood and family variables have on this relationship? What moderating effects are produced by sex and social class?
2. How specific is aggression to delinquency when compared to other outcomes and to other antecedents such as peer rejection?
3. What is the relationship of childhood aggression to severity of delinquency and subsequent young adult criminal offenses among delinquents?

Answers to these specific questions can contribute to the further specification of a developmental model of delinquency.

METHOD

In the early 1960's, peer status information was collected for approximately 17,000 third-through sixth-grade students in two midwestern cities. All public schools were included in one city and half the public schools in the second city. Peer status was determined by sociometric ratings by same-sex classmates within each classroom. A peer status score was computed for each subject by subtracting the number of liked-least choices from the number of liked-most choices, with the resulting total converted to a standardized score.

Semistructured teacher interviews were conducted, at that time, for the least popular boy and girl in each classroom, the most popular boy or girl, and a middle peer choice child of the opposite sex from the most popular child in the class. These interviews were designed to elicit from the teacher more specific information about the child, information relevant to the child's social adjustment. This subsample of 2,453 grade school children with teacher interview information available was followed through record sources into the young adult period (for further details about the original sample, see Roff, Sells, & Golden, 1972).

Schools were divided into four social class quartiles in the first city, while only schools from the two lowest quartiles were included in the second city. Social class was determined by the income and educational levels for the census tracts included in each school district. Each subject was assigned the social class of his/her school, which, at the time, drew from a relatively homogenous neighborhood. Social class was coded to make lower scores indicate lower social class. Throughout the article, social class will be used to designate what is social class of school or neighborhood. Race has not been included as a separate variable since schools were not allowed, by state law in the early 1960's, to collect this information about individual students. Approximately 4% of the school population in these cities was black.

A search of juvenile records provided a measure of delinquent outcome. Delinquency was defined as the opening of a formal juvenile record that indicated a juvenile court referral. Most, but not all, were adjudicated delinquent. This outcome variable was scored as a dichotomous variable, present or absent. In addition, delinquent males from city 1 were grouped in three categories reflecting increasing severity of delinquency: nonconfined-probation only ($N = 63$), confined-county home ($N = 18$), and confined-state training school ($N = 19$). State Bureau of Investigation records revealed which male subjects had committed adult criminal offenses between the ages of 18 and 24-27. Female subjects were not checked through this source due to the small numbers found in preliminary efforts. Hospital and outpatient clinic records indicated which subjects had mental health treatment as adolescents or young adults. State, county, VA, and university records were obtained for this purpose. Subjects who migrated out of the state were not followed.

For low-peer-status children ($N = 1,127$), teacher interview information was analyzed to identify specific problem behavior associated with peer rejection. Analysis of the typed transcripts of teacher interviews began with the abstracting and coding of problem behavior using a 41-item checklist. After elimination of low frequency items (items checked for less than 5% of the sample), the 24 remaining items were intercorrelated and the correlation matrix factor analyzed. Eight factors had eigenvalues greater than 1.0 and accounted for 53.9% of the variance. Only the first four factors have been presented in Table I since the remaining four factors were defined by two items or less, were less consistent when each sex was analyzed separately, or were not found when an oblique rotation was used. Furthermore, these factors were not significantly related to delinquency. The first four factors accounted for 34.3% of the total variance and 78.6% of the variance accounted for by the eight factors. Table I gives the items with loadings greater than .30 for the first four orthogonal factors (varimax rotation) with both sexes combined. Factors very similar to the first four appeared when each sex was analyzed separately and when an oblique rotation was used (the highest correlation among the four factors was .12). The first factor, including aggressiveness and rebelliousness, was expected to be related to

Table I. Factor Loadings on Childhood Factors for both Sexes
Combined (N = 1,127)[a]

Childhood variables	Factors			
	1	2	3	4
Rebellious-classroom	.67			
Rebellious-playground	.76			
Physical aggression	.62			
Verbal aggression	.52			
Lack of remorse	.43			
Hyperactive, restless		.52		
Excitable		.51		
Anxious, nervous		.65		
Nervous mannerisms		.53		
Poor school achievement			.84	
Low IQ mentioned			.54	
Specific learning disability			.31	
Poor attention				.40
Apathy, indifference				.86
Seclusive, avoidant				.31

[a] Only loadings greater than .30 have been included.

subsequent delinquency, particularly in the context of peer rejection. The second factor reflected anxiety expressed in terms of excitability and restlessness. The third factor indicated poor school achievement and limited scholastic ability in the judgment of the classroom teacher. The fourth suggested a motivational deficit involving apathy and indifference primarily with regard to classroom activities.

Factor coefficients were computed to provide weights for each of the variables defining each factor in Table I. Factor scale scores were obtained for each subject. Assessment of reliability, in the form of interrater agreement for a subset of 50 cases, yielded coefficients of .78, .66, .63, and .69 for the four factor scales. Internal consistency for the scales as measured by Cronbach's alpha was .74, .63, .52, and .41, respectively (N = 1,097).

A predelinquent scale was constructed from four variables not included in the factor analysis due to low frequencies (stealing in school, stealing in the community, trouble with the law, and running away from home) and two variables (lying and truancy) that were included but did not have high loadings on any of the first four factors. These rationally selected variables, although individually of low frequency, might be combined to form a scale related to delinquency. Assessment of interrater reliability, in the manner previously mentioned, produced a correlation of .93 (N = 50) for the predelinquent scale. Cronbach's alpha was a modest .42 for this scale (N = 1,127).

Information about the family was abstracted if provided by the teacher interview. A global rating of severity of family disturbance was made on a 5-point scale, with higher scores reflecting greater disturbance. Interrater reliability for this family variable was low ($r = .54$, $N = 50$).

Middle peer choice males were investigated but, as expected, problem behavior was much less frequently mentioned for this group compared to the low-peer-choice subjects. For this reason, a similar analysis was not undertaken for middle- or high-choice subjects.

Data were analyzed by using path analysis to examine the joint effects, for each sex, of the childhood problem behavior factors, the predelinquent scale, the family variable, and social class of school as antecedents of delinquency and young adult criminality for males. The mental health treatment contact variable and a record of welfare (for city 2 subjects only) provided an opportunity to assess the specificity of the relationships suggested by the path analysis for delinquency.

RESULTS

Table II provides the delinquency rates for males by social class quartiles for three levels of peer status. The combination of low peer status and lowest social class produced the highest rate of delinquency (46.3%). Individuals in this cell were approximately nine times more likely to be delinquent than males in the cells defined by highest social class and either middle or high peer status. For the total male sample with teacher interviews, 26.3% became delinquent. The multiple correlation for peer status and social class as predictors of delinquency was significant ($R = .28$, $p < .01$). Individual regression coefficients for peer status and social class were significant ($t = 7.4$, 7.1, $p < .01$). Peer status and social class were not significant predictors of adult criminality when delinquent-non-delinquent status was included as a predictor.

Table II. Percent Delinquent by Social Class and Peer Status for Males

Peer status	Social class				Total	N
	1	2	3	4		
Low	46.3	34.7	29.3	17.7	35.3	605
Mid	34.0	18.3	20.0	4.9	22.3	296
High	23.4	10.1	9.4	5.6	13.6	323
Total	37.2	24.5	21.6	11.5		
N	414	429	190	191		1,224

Table III. Percent Delinquent by Social Class and Peer Status for Females

| Peer status | Social class quartiles | | | | Total | N |
	1	2	3	4		
Low	15.0	11.3	7.1	2.1	10.3	609
Mid	16.7	6.6	1.9	0.0	8.2	330
High	8.2	2.9	0.0	0.0	3.8	289
Total	13.9	8.0	4.0	1.0	8.2	
N	411	423	201	193		1,228

Table III presents parallel information for females. A similar pattern was found but in the context of a lower overall delinquency rate (8.2%). The multiple correlation of peer status and social class with delinquency was significant ($R = .19$, $p < .01$). Individual regression coefficients for peer status and social class were also significant ($t = 3.4, 6.0$, $p < .01$).

For low-peer-status males, aggressive problem behavior in grade school, as measured by factor 1, was significantly correlated with delinquency ($r = .30$, $p < .01$). Table IV gives the correlations for all variables with delinquency and adult criminality for males. For a sample of this size ($N = 557$) a correlation of .11 is significant at the .01 level (two-tailed test).

For low-peer-status females, severity of family disturbance was the best single predictor of delinquency (see Table IV). Aggression (factor 1) was related to delinquency ($r = .13$, $p < .01$). Information about adult criminal offenses was not obtained for females.

Table V shows the relationship between childhood aggressiveness and delinquency within each social class quartile by sex. There was less variability in both predictor and criterion for social class 4 (high) males and for social class 3 and 4 females. Only within the lowest social class was a significant relationship found between factor 1 scale scores and delinquency for females ($r = .20$, $p < .05$).

The path analysis in Figure 1 shows the significant paths from aggression (factor 1) and the predelinquent scale to delinquency for low-peer-status males. Social class and the severity of family disturbance rating contributed to these childhood variables, but not directly to delinquent outcome. Standardized beta coefficients were computed using the entire variable set, but only the variables with significant beta coefficients have been included in Figure 1. Beta coefficients for variables not included in Figure 1 can be found in Table IV. The multiple correlation for all predictors with delinquency was .40 and with adult criminality .44. With delinquency removed as a predictor, the remaining variables had a

Table IV. Correlations and Beta Coefficients for Predictors of Delinquency and Adult Criminality

	Males		Females	
	β	r	β	r
Delinquency				
Aggression	.25[b]	.30[b]	.08	.13[b]
Anxious	−.03	−.01	−.03	−.02
School achievement	.08	.10[a]	.01	.06
Apathy	.07	.09[a]	.11[a]	.14[b]
Predelinquent	.18[b]	.25[b]	.04	.11[b]
Family-severity	.07	.17[b]	.12[b]	.17[b]
Social class	−.08	−.18[b]	−.09[a]	−.15[b]
Adult criminality				
Delinquency	.34[b]	.41[b]		
Aggression	.12[b]	.24[b]		
Anxious	−.04	−.02		
School achievement	.06	.09[a]		
Apathy	.03	.02		
Predelinquent	.03	.16[b]		
Family-severity	.06	.15[b]		
Social class	−.04	−.14[b]		

R (Delinquency) = .40, $F(7, 549)$ = 14.6 R (Delinquency) = .25, $F(7, 550)$ = 5.4
R (Adult criminality) = .44, $F(8, 548)$ = 16.4

[a] $p < .05$.
[b] $p < .01$.

Table V. Correlations Between Childhood Aggression Factor Scale Scores and Delinquency Within Social Class Quartiles

	Social class					Total low peer sample
			Males			
Low	1	2	3	4	High	
	.29[b]	.29[b]	.36[b]	.17		.30[b]
N	184	199	87	92		562
			Females			
Low	1	2	3	4	High	
	.20[a]	−.02	.09	−.06		.13[b]
N	181	193	96	95		565

[a] $p < .05$.
[b] $p < .01$.

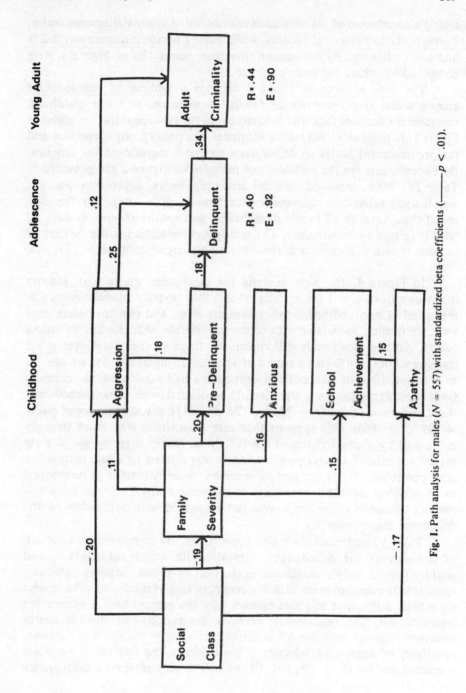

Fig. I. Path analysis for males ($N = 557$) with standardized beta coefficients (———— $p < .01$).

multiple correlation of .31 with adult criminality. Among delinquent males, 32.4% had adult criminal records, while among nondelinquents ony 3.2% had adult offenses. By convention, the error terms (E) in Figure 1 were computed by taking the square root of $1-R^2$.

The path analysis in Figure 2 displays a pattern of relationships among social class, severity of family disturbance, and the childhood variables for females that was comparable to the relationships for males in Figure 1. In contrast to the results for males, the paths from aggression and the predelinquent scales to delinquency were not significant for females. Beta coefficients for the variables not included in Figure 2 are provided in Table IV. When included with the other predictors, aggression was not significantly related to delinquency for females ($\beta = .08$). For females, social class, severity of family disturbance, and apathy (factor 4) were all weakly related to delinquency. The multiple correlation for the full set of predictors with delinquency as the criterion was significant ($R = .25, p < .01$).

In Figure 3, the path analysis for delinquent males with teacher interviews from city 1 ($N = 100$) reveals that severity of delinquency as measured by nonconfined, confined-county level, and confined-state level was significantly associated with continued trouble with the law as young adults. Among those male delinquents confined at the state level (state training school), 58% had a record of an adult criminal offense by age 25. In contrast, 19% of nonconfined delinquents had adult criminal records. Childhood aggression was significantly associated with nonconfined-confined delinquent status ($r = .27, \beta = .29, p < .01$) but social class was not ($r = .05, \beta = .06$). This suggests that case disposition was more strongly influenced by characteristics of the individual rather than by social class bias. Poor school achievement (factor 3) was related to adult criminality after controlling for severity of delinquency. Apathy (factor 4) functioned as an inhibitor of adult criminality in the same context. Social class and severity of family disturbance were not associated with aggression among delinquent males from city 1.

Table VI addresses the issue of specificity. By comparing the pattern of correlations for delinquency, mental health treatment contact, and welfare (city 2 only), childhood aggression in males appears relatively specific to the development of delinquency. In fact, if those individuals who were both delinquent and had contact with the mental health system are partialed out, the relationship between aggression and mental health treatment contact in Table VI is further reduced ($r = .05$). For females, specificity of aggressive behavior is less evident. The full set of variables predicted welfare ($R = .29, p < .01$) as well as they predicted delinquency

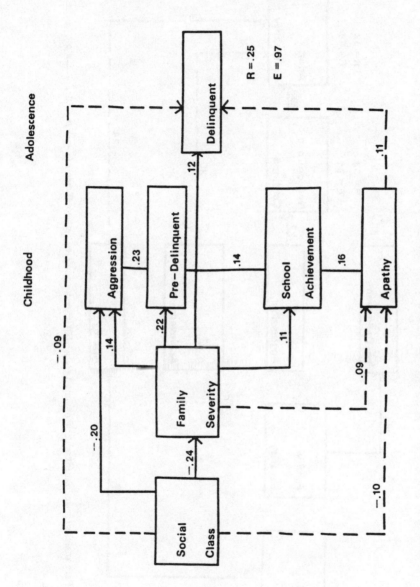

Fig. 2. Path analysis for females ($N = 558$) with standardized beta coefficients (– – – $p < .05$, ——— $p < .01$).

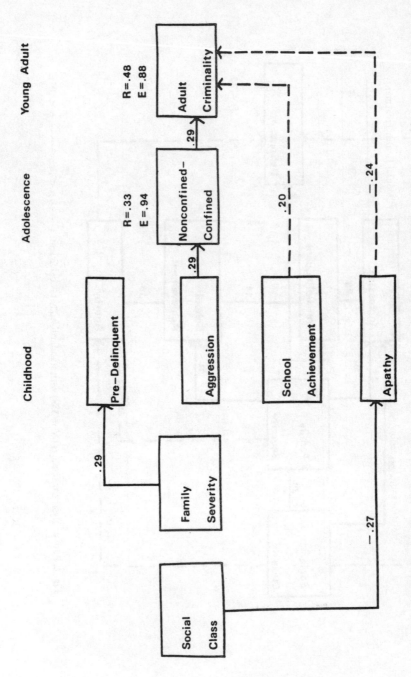

Fig. 3. Path analysis for delinquent males from city 1 ($N = 100$) with standardized beta coefficients (– – – – $p < .05$, ——— $p < .01$).

Table VI. Correlations for Aggression, Social Class, and Peer Status with Delinquency, Mental Health Treatment, and Welfare

	Males			Females		
	Aggression	Social class	N	Aggression	Social class	N
Low-peer-status subsample						
Peer status						
Delinquency	.30b	-.18b	562	.13b	-.15b	565
Mental health treatment	.08	-.03	562	.07	-.02	565
Welfare (city 2 only)	.03	-.06	205	.14c	-.13	197
Total peer interview sample						
Peer status						
Delinquency	.21b	-.20b	1224	.09b	-.17b	1228
Mental health treatment	.17b	-.04	1224	.10b	-.02	1228
Welfare (city 2 only)	.14b	-.08	449	.10a	-.13b	446

[a] $p < .05$.
[b] $p < .01$.
[c] $t = 1.97$, $p = .05$.

for females and better than they predicted welfare for males. Welfare was the one outcome that was more frequent for females (17.5%) than for males (7.3%). Social class followed the pattern of relationships for aggression. The social class variable was limited to two quartiles in city 2, which reduces the correlations of social class with welfare in Table VI. Peer status, in contrast, served as a more general predisposing factor for the outcome variables in Table VI.

DISCUSSION

The model suggested for males indicates the importance of childhood aggression, in the context of peer rejection, as an antecedent of delinquency. Social class and the family variable functioned as antecedents of aggression in Figure 1, although the causal ordering assumed can be questioned. Studies that measure aggression and find it unrelated to social class or peer status would appear to measure something different. In this study, the negative reaction of peers to the behavior qualifies the type of aggression assessed (similar to the Skinnerian concept of an operant defined by contingencies). An additional qualification involves characteristics of the sample. The school systems that provided the subjects contained relatively few minority students. As a result, it is an open question to what extent the findings can be generalized to urban areas differing markedly in racial composition.

Sex differences highlight the problem of prediction for females. It might be noted that correlation coefficients are directly influenced by base rates. The differences between lowest social class males and females for the correlation between aggression and delinquency was solely due to base rate differences. Other sex differences were in excess of base rate diferences alone. While aggression was relatively specific to delinquency for males, it was related to both delinquency and welfare status for females. This suggests that conditions similar to those leading to delinquency in males may lead to welfare status in females. Severity of family disturbance, as a global rating, proved to be relatively nonspecific in terms of childhood problem behaviors, although it was associated most strongly with the predelinquent scale for both sexes. Peer status had relatively nonspecific effects with regard to outcomes for both sexes. The similar relationships for social class, severity of family disturbance, and peer status across sexes served as a form of replication.

In evaluating the model presented in Figure 1, the modest proportion of variance accounted for suggests possible improvement. Three sources of improvement include (1) better measurement of existing variables, (2) addition of new childhood and family variables, and (3) addition of adolescent variables more proximal to the criterion. Clearly, a more reliable family variable would be desirable, as would a more objective measure of school achievement. A differentiated set of family variables might produce greater specificity. The results of other longitudinal studies suggest that additional variables from middle childhood would not improve prediction dramatically, in that the distance in time between predictors and criterion introduces certain limitations. The greatest improvement would be aticipated if more proximal adolescent variables were included. Related to this point, aggression for fifth- and sixth-grade males was more highly correlated with delinquency ($r = .35$) than was the same measure for third- and fourth- grade males ($r = .23$). Since aggression, peer status, and school achievement would all be expected to possess considerable stability, later assessment of these variables should be related to the earlier measures but function as better predictors of outcome.

The results do show a recurring pattern where variables significantly related to an intervening variable make little, if any, direct contribution to a criterion. This pattern was found for peer status and social class in relation to delinquency and then adult criminality, social class and severity of family disturbance in relation to aggression and then delinquency, aggression in relation to delinquency and then adult criminality, and aggression in relation to severity of delinquency and then adult criminality. This pattern gives added emphasis to the importance of including appropriate intervening variables in the model. When intervening variables were not included (high-peer-status males) or did not produce significant paths (aggression for females), social class assumed more importance as a predictor.

The model presented can be seen as a preliminary effort that suggests the extent of specific relationships that can be tested in future research. Further elaboration of the model requires the integration of findings from intensive cross-sectional studies of family socialization and social conditions as associated with childhood aggression and the delineation of factors that contribute to the stability of aggressive problem behavior. One result of the shift in emphasis from aggression as a predictor of delinquency to the development of a causal model has been a shift from delinquency to aggression as the construct of primary interest.

REFERENCES

Clark, J. P., & Wenninger, E. P. (1962). Socioeconomic class and area as correlates of illegal behavior among juveniles. *American Sociological Review, 27,* 826-834.

Conger, J. J., & Miller, W. C. (1966). *Personality, social class and delinquency.* New York: Wiley.

Eron, L. D., & Huesmann, L. R. (1983, April). *Stability of aggressive behavior.* Paper presented at the meeting of the Society for Research in Child Development, Detroit.

Eron, L. D., Walder, L. O., Huesmann, L. R., & Lefkowitz, M. M. (1974). The convergence of laboratory and field studies of the development of aggression (pp. 213-246). In J. DeWit & W. W. Hartup (Eds.), *Determinants and origins of aggressive behavior.* The Hague: Mouton.

Farrington, D. P. (1978). The family background of aggressive youths. In L. Hersov, M. Berger, & D. Shaffer (Eds.), *Aggressive and antisocial behaviour in childhood and adolescence* (pp. 73-94). Oxford: Pergamon.

Glueck, S., & Glueck, E. (1950). *Unraveling juvenile delinquency.* Cambridge: Harvard University Press.

Havighurst, R. J., Bowman, P. H., Liddle, G. P., Mathews, C. V., & Pierce, J. V. (1962). *Growing up in River City.* New York: Wiley.

Kenny, D. A. (1979). *Correlation and causality.* New York: Wiley.

McCord, W., & McCord, J. (1959). *Origins of crime.* New York: Columbia University Press.

Olweus, D. (1974). Personality factors and aggression: With special reference to violence within the peer group. In J. DeWit & W. W. Hartup (Eds.), *Determinants and origins of aggressive behavior* (pp. 535-565). The Hague: Mouton.

Olweus, D. (1979). Stability of aggressive reaction patterns in males: A review. *Psychological Bulletin, 86,* 852-875.

Olweus, D. (1980). Familial and temperamental determinants of aggressive behavior in adolescent boys: A causal analysis. *Developmental Psychology, 16,* 644-660.

Reiss, A. J., & Rhodes, A. L. (1961). Delinquency and social class structure. *American Sociological Review, 26,* 720-732.

Robins, L. N. (1966). *Deviant children grown up.* Baltimore: Williams & Wilkins.

Robins, L. N. (1978). Sturdy childhood predictors of adult antisocial behaviour: Replications from longitudinal studies. *Psychological Medicine, 8,* 611-622.

Roff, M. (1970). Some life history factors in relation to various types of adult maladjustment. In M. Roff & D. F. Ricks (Eds.), *Life history research in psychopathology* (Vol. 1, pp. 265-287). Minneapolis: University of Minnesota Press.

Roff, M. (1972). A two-factor approach to juvenile delinquency and the later histories of juvenile delinquents. In M. Roff, L. N. Robins, & M. Pollack (Eds.), *Life history research in psychopathology* (Vol. 2, pp. 77-101). Minneapolis: University of Minnesota Press.

Roff, M., Sells, S. B., & Golden M. (1972). *Social Adjustment and Personality Development in children.* Minneapolis: University of Minnesota Press.

Spaeth, J. L. (1975). Path analysis. In D. J. Amick & H. J. Walberg (Eds.), *Introductory multivariate analysis* (pp, 53-89). Berkeley: McCutchan.

West, D. J., & Farrington, D. P. (1973). *Who becomes delinquent?* London: Heinemann.

Wirt, R. D., & Briggs, P. F. (1959). Personality and environmental factors in the development of delinquency. *Psychological Monographs, 73*(15, Whole No. 485).

[18]

Brit. J. Psychiat. (1980), **136**, 139–145

Brothers, Sisters and Antisocial Behaviour

MARSHALL B. JONES, DAVID R. OFFORD and NOLA ABRAMS

SUMMARY The brothers of 73 delinquent boys were found themselves to be more antisocial than the brothers of 73 matched control boys. Further, the average antisocial score of the probands' brothers increased with the number of brothers in the family, holding the number of sisters constant, and decreased with the number of sisters, holding the number of brothers constant. These results are interpreted in terms of male potentiation and female suppression of antisocial behaviour in boys. Results are also reported for 59 pairs of matched delinquent and control girls and their siblings.

Delinquent boys have been found repeatedly to come from larger sibships than non-delinquent boys of the same age and social background (Ferguson, 1952; Miller *et al*, 1974; West and Farrington, 1973; Blakely *et al*, 1974). The same is true of boys who, while antisocial, have not been adjudicated as delinquent (Rutter, Tizard and Whitmore, 1970; West and Farrington, 1977). Several of the reasons advanced to explain this finding may be grouped together under the heading of 'inadequate family resources'. For example, Rutter and Madge (1976, pp. 211–212) mention overcrowding, poor nutrition, reduced parental supervision, and increased stress on the mother as possible mediating mechanisms for the sibship size effect. All of these factors depend in part on a common underlying fact: The same adults working with the same income and other material assets cannot give as much of their attention, time, or money to an individual child when the family is large as they could if it were smaller.

Robins, West and Herjanic (1975) propose a very different explanation. They suggest that contagion is a key aetiological factor in antisocial behaviour. That is, when one boy in a family becomes antisocial, the probability that others will be affected is increased. The more boys there are in a family the more likely it is that at least one will be antisocial. Hence, boys in large families are more likely to be at increased risk for antisocial behaviour (through association with an already affected brother) than boys in smaller families. The result is that large families have disproportionately more antisocial boys than small ones.

The present paper began with the usual finding, that is, larger sibship size among delinquent probands than among non-delinquent control boys (Offord, Allen and Abrams, 1978). After the original report was already in press, it was observed that this difference was due entirely to an excess of brothers; probands and controls did not differ in number of sisters.

We than directed our attention to the probands' brothers, who had also been studied as to antisocial behaviour; and it was here that the main results to be reported in this paper were found. Data will be presented for the brothers and sisters of both male and female probands.

Method

Male probands

The subjects consisted of all boys placed on probation to the Probation and After-Care Services from the Juvenile Court of Ottawa-Carleton between 1 November, 1972 and 15 November, 1973 and who had attended the Ottawa Public School system for at least four of their first eight years of schooling.

Seventy-nine boys met the criteria for inclusion in the study. The families of 73 of the 79 were located and agreed to participate. The 6 non-participating families did not differ significantly from the 73 participating families on any of the variables available to us from the Juvenile Court records, namely, age, socio-economic class level (Pineo and Porter, 1967), sibship size, reason for and age at first court appearance, and number of times on probation.

For each proband a control was selected and matched for age (within six months,) school performance (a similar record of repeating a grade or special class placement), IQ (within five points), and socio-economic class (within one level). In addition, the control must have been seen by the school personnel as *not* being a behaviour problem in the school setting and must not have appeared in Juvenile Court.

The parents or guardians of each participating family, both experimental and control, were interviewed. The interviews lasted one and a half to two hours and were carried out by persons, usually college graduates, especially trained for the purpose. In addition to demographic and other data, extensive information was collected concerning each proband and control and all siblings, including age of onset, duration, number and kinds of antisocial symptoms. The symptoms covered were an enlarged version of the list developed by Robins (1966). Inter-rater agreement in excess of 90 per cent was established for the antisocial rating, that is, number of symptoms. More detail as to the matching criteria, symptoms covered, etc. can be found in Offord, Allen and Abrams (1978).

Female probands

The subjects consisted of girls placed on probation to their parents or to the Probation and After-Care Services by the Juvenile Court of Ottawa-Carleton between July, 1972 and January, 1975 and who had been attending schools in the Ottawa region at the time they were placed on probation. Since both English and French schools were contained in this region, a further stipulation for entry into the sample was that the girls had attended English-speaking schools for the majority of their school years. The purpose of this stipulation was to ensure that differences within the sample were

not due to English versus French cultural background.

Sixty-five girls met the criteria for inclusion in the study. The families of 59 of the 65 girls were located and agreed to participate. Participating and non-participating families did not differ on any of the variables available to us, the same ones already listed in connection with the male probands. For each proband a control was selected and matched in the way already described for the male probands; and the same information was collected from the parents or guardians on all probands, controls, and siblings. Further information is available in Offord, Abrams, Allen and Poushinsky (in press).

Results

Male probands, family size

The original result was that the probands came from larger sibships than their controls (Offord, Allen and Abrams, 1978). The 73 probands had a total of 203 'siblings', including under this term not only all full brothers and sisters but also any other person less than 18 living in the home, whereas the 73 controls had 154 such siblings. The difference in mean number of siblings, 2.78 versus 2.11, was significant at the .02 level by a paired t-test ($t = 2.43$).

The biological siblings, however, included 29 persons who were dead at the time of the proband's first court appearance. Twenty-five of these 29 cases were relatives of the probands and only four of the controls. This difference was itself significant at the .001 level ($\chi^2 = 14.12$). That is, the probands were more likely to have dead full brothers or sisters than the controls.

The results for the remaining siblings, 178 belonging to the probands' families and 150 to the controls', appear in Table I. Two of the probands' siblings were of unknown sex. The distribution by sex of the remaining 326 siblings among proband and control families yields a value of χ^2 equal to 6.80, $P < .01$. The probands have significantly more brothers than the controls.

Table II presents a breakdown of this result by sibship size. For all sizes of sibship the probands have more brothers than sisters, whereas controls with 3, 4, or 7 sibs have more brothers

TABLE I

Siblings of the 73 delinquent probands and their controls, by sex. All persons under 18 living in the home are counted as siblings

Group	Index	Brothers	Sisters	Unknown	Total
Probands	73	112	64	2	178
Controls	73	73	77	0	150

TABLE II

Number of brothers and number of sisters in delinquent proband and control families by sibship size, excluding the index case

	Probands			Controls		
Sibship size	N	Brothers	Sisters	N	Brothers	Sisters
0	9	0	0	13	0	0
1	11	8	3	14	2	12
2	23	29	17	22	21	23
3	12	21	14*	11	17	16
4	11	25	18*	8	20	12
5	4	13	7	4	8	12
6	1	4	2			
7	1	6	1	1	5	2
8	1	6	2			
	73	112	64	73	73	77

* There was one sib of unknown sex in sibships of size 3 and similarly in sibships of size 4.

but controls with 1, 2, or 5 sibs have more sisters.

Male probands, brothers' antisocial behavior

Strictly speaking, the results in Tables I and II do not rule out an interpretation of the family size association in terms of inadequate family resources. It could be that boys are more of a drain on those resources than girls. Hence, families with more boys may in fact have 'less to go around' than families with fewer boys, even though the total number of children is the same. One way to examine this possibility is to study antisocial behaviour in the probands' *brothers* as a function of the number of brothers and the number of sisters in the family.

Table III presents the results. Each individual antisocial score is displayed. Of the 73 probands 19 had no brothers. Two others could not be included because antisocial scores were not available for the siblings. One proband had four brothers (with antisocial scores of 0, 0, 1, and 8) and four sisters. Since no other sibship contained either four brothers or four sisters, this one

contributed no information to the analysis and is not, therefore, included. The scores for the remaining 93 brothers are all presented.

Significance in Table III was evaluated by means of partial rank correlation (Kendall, 1948). Across the rows the count S was obtained by adding '1' every time one boy had both more brothers and a higher antisocial score than another boy. When one boy had fewer brothers and a higher antisocial score than another boy, '1' was subtracted. If two boys came from families of the same size or had identical antisocial scores, '0' was added. The value of S is presented for each row. The variance of S, that is, the standard error squared, was then calculated as described by Kendall, making corrections for ties, for each row. These values are also presented in Table III. The overall value of S, +197 for the rows, was then divided by the square root of the overall variance of S (Jones, 1957). The result in this case is a normal deviate of 2.34, P < .02. Hence, the antisocial scores of the probands' brothers tend

142   BROTHERS, SISTERS AND ANTISOCIAL BEHAVIOR

TABLE III

Antisocial scores for the brothers of the 73 male probands

Number of sisters	Number of brothers				N	S	Var S
	1	2	3	5			
0	0 0 1 4 7 8	0, 1 0, 2 1, 2 1, 2 0, 4 4, 6 2, 13 8, 9 9, 12	4, 5, 12		27	+52	1,545.6
1	0 0 1 1 1 2 3 5 6	0, 1 1, 1 0, 3 1, 3 1, 5 1, 6 6, 7	1, 1, 2 2, 2, 4 2, 2, 4 1, 1, 16		35	+54	4,060.9
2	0 0 0 1	0, 0 0, 2	0, 1, 2 0, 0, 3 0, 2, 4 4, 4, 8	1, 1, 2, 3, 4	25	+89	1,462.5
3	2 3 12		2, 4, 14		6	+ 2	20.4
N	22	36	30	5	93	ΣS = +197	ΣVar S = 7,089
S	+10	+133	+37	0	—	ΣS = +180	—
Var S	1,063.1	4,218.4	2,602.2	0	—	—	ΣVar S = 7,883.7

to increase across the rows, that is, holding the number of sisters constant.

Down the columns '1' was added every time one boy had *fewer* sisters and a higher antisocial score than another boy. Conversely, '1' was subtracted every time one boy had more sisters and a higher antisocial score than another boy. Ties were handled the same way as across the rows. Significance was then determined as already described. The normal deviate for the columns is $z = 2.03$, $P < .05$. Hence, the antisocial scores of the probands' brothers tend to decrease with increasing numbers of sisters, holding the number of brothers constant.

Male probands, other results

As others, for example Robins, West and Herjanic (1975), have also reported, the antisocial scores of the probands' brothers were significantly greater than the antisocial scores of the controls' brothers. Significance was evaluated by means of the Mann-Whitney U test (Siegel, 1956), resulting in a normal deviate equal to 3.57, $P < .001$.

The sisters of the male probands, however, were not more antisocial than the sisters of the controls. In this case the Mann-Whitney U test resulted in a normal deviate of 1.06.

The analyses in Table III were also carried

out for the controls' brothers, the controls themselves, the probands' sisters, and the controls' sisters. No significant or near-significant results were obtained in any of these analyses.

The partial rank correlation between the proband's and his brothers' antisocial scores, calculated within sibships of the same size and composition by sex, was positive but not significant, $z = 1.00$.

Female probands, all results

The 59 female probands and their like-numbered controls had respective totals of 146 and 133 boys and girls living with them in their homes. This difference is not significant; and the distribution is not significant either. When the proband is female, there is no disturbance in family size or composition.

Both the brothers and the sisters of the female probands have more antisocial symptoms than their control counterparts. The Mann-Whitney U test yields normal deviates of 3.72 and 2.98 for the brothers and sisters respectively, both significant at the .01 level. This result is a departure from the pattern for male probands where only the brothers had more antisocial symptoms and not the sisters.

Antisocial behavior as a function of the number of brothers and number of sisters was analyzed in the same ways for the female proband and control sibships as it was for the male proband and control sibships. No significant or near-significant results were obtained.

Discussion

The main finding in the present study is the way antisocial behavior in the brothers of male delinquents varies as a function of male or female predominance in the sibship. Our subjects, therefore, are the brothers of male delinquents, not the delinquents themselves. Furthermore, only 13 of the 93 brothers studied in this report had ever appeared in court; and in these 13 cases much of the behavior on which the antisocial ratings were based took place before the boys' court appearances. Hence, the antisocial behavior under study was largely undetected, that is, not adjudicated.

In a recent paper, Clarke and Softley (1975) claim that undetected delinquency is not re-

lated to the ratio of boys to girls in a family. 'Self-reported delinquency scores at the ages of either 14–15 or 16–17 were available for this group', write the two authors (p. 251), 'and it was found that the overall ratio of 100 brothers to 100 sisters did not vary with seriousness of self-reported delinquency'. Clarke and Softley are referring here not to their own work but to a longitudinal study by West and Farrington (1973) of 411 boys living in one particular area of London. The task we now take up is to show that, carefully examined, the West and Farrington data do not contradict our own.

First, we know nothing about the reported non-relationship beyond the sentence already quoted. We do not know, for example, whether dead siblings were excluded. Nor do we know if half-siblings or unrelated children living in the home were included. The latter point is especially important since the inclusion of other children than full sibs can make a considerable difference in the results.

Second, as West and Farrington (1977) have subsequently made clear themselves, self-reported delinquency is liable to be minimized by some subjects and exaggerated by others. For some types of offence the proportion giving an accurate account may be small indeed. Where the offence involves violence against persons, for example, West and Farrington (1977, p. 24) find that only 13.3 per cent of the boys give an account that agrees with the official records. Furthermore, it is not known which boys tend to exaggerate and which to minimize their antisocial behavior. Since boys are not expected to be completely free of antisocial behavior, it could be that those with little antisocial behavior exaggerate what they do whereas those with a great deal minimize it. Such an effect, if it existed, would obscure the true differences in antisocial behavior among boys, thereby making the demonstration of any systematic relationship less likely.

Third, the result reported by Clarke and Softley does not, apparently, control for number of sisters; and this is essential if male potentiation of antisocial behavior is to be shown. A family with many boys tends also to be a family with many girls. As we have seen, however, the presence of many sisters tends to suppress anti-

144   BROTHERS, SISTERS AND ANTISOCIAL BEHAVIOR

social behaviour in the boys. To isolate the effect of many boys in the family the number of sisters must be held constant.

Fourth and last, the West and Farrington sample was not as a whole an especially high-risk group. No potentiating effect was found in our data either for controls or the brothers of controls. The main reason was an insufficiency of antisocial behaviour altogether. In order for an effect on antisocial behaviour to be shown one must work in a population that has a substantial amount of it.

We conclude, therefore, that our main result is not contradicted by the West and Farrington data or, as far as we know, by any other finding in the literature.

The present study supports the contention, most clearly stated by Robins, West and Herjanic (1975), that male predominance in the sibship favours the development of antisocial behaviour in boys. There are, however, two major amendments. First, Robins *et al* use a 'contagion' model in formulating their hypothesis. 'It looks', they write (p. 137) 'as though a principal mechanism through which large families encourage delinquency may be through increasing the risk of exposure to a delinquent sibling'. The amendment is that the interaction among boys may develop toward delinquency even though no boy in the sibship is delinquent at the start. The process is not so much contagion, in which one boy communicates his delinquency to others, as it is interaction, in which the boys respond to one another in ways that tend to realize the potentials for antisocial behaviour inherent in all of us. We call this process *male potentiation* of antisocial behaviour.

The second amendment is, of course, the role of girls and women. The mere presence of females is certainly not sufficient to suppress antisocial behaviour in males, as is clear from studies of street gangs (Cloward and Ohlin, 1970). The girls in our study are sisters and therefore present in the family on terms of approximate equality with their brothers. The hypothesis that girls and women suppress antisocial behaviour in males must be carefully limited. It holds or, better, we claim that it holds only where the girls or women stand roughly on a par with their male counterparts.

Finally, a word is in order concerning the female probands and their siblings. Delinquent children tend strongly to be male. Furthermore, the rates of *undetected* antisocial behaviour seems also to differ in the two sexes; girls are much less prone to it than boys (Gold, 1966; Short and Nye, 1956; Williams and Gold, 1972). These findings are at least largely explained by the different socialization programs for the two sexes. Antisocial behaviour, especially in its more aggressive and violent forms, is socially suppressed more consistently and with fewer qualifications in girls than it is in boys. Both statistically and socially, delinquency in girls is more extreme than it is in boys. Therefore, the forces making for deviance must be stronger in a girl's case than they are for the average boy delinquent.

The present results are consistent with this view of girl delinquency. First, when the proband is female, her siblings of *both* sexes are more antisocial than their control counterparts, whereas the sisters of male probands are no more antisocial than the sisters of control boys. Second, although antisocial behaviour is present with sufficient frequency to show an effect if one existed, there is no evidence of male potentiation or female suppression among either the brothers or the sisters of girl delinquents. In these families it appears that the *same* forces which produced antisocial behaviour in the proband are also active with respect to her siblings. The result is a general tendnecy toward antisocial behaviour, sufficiently strong to mask the potentiating or suppressing effects of male or female predominance in the sibship.

References

BLAKELY, R., STEPHENSON, P. S. & NICHOL, H. (1974) Social factors in a random sample of juvenile delinquents and controls. *International Journal of Social Psychiatry*, 20, 203–17.

CLARKE, R. V. G. & SÖFTLEY, P. (1975) The male: female ratio among the siblings of delinquents. *British Journal of Psychiatry*, 126, 249–51.

CLOWARD, R. A. & OHLIN, L. E. (1970) *Delinquency and Opportunity*. New York: Free Press.

FERGUSON, T. (1952) *The Young Delinquent in his Social Setting*. London: Oxford University Press.

GOLD, M. (1966) Undetected delinquent behaviour. *Journal of Research in Crime and Delinquency*, 3, 27–46.

MARSHALL B. JONES, DAVID R. OFFORD AND NOLA ABRAMS   145

JONES, M. B. (1957) An addition to Schaeffer and Levitt's 'Kendall's Tau'. *Psychological Bulletin*, 54, 159–60.

KENDALL, M. G. (1948) *Rank Correlation Methods*, p. 43. London: Charles Griffin.

MILLER, F. J. W., COURT, S. D. M., KNOX, E. G. & BRANDON, S. (1974) *The School Years in Newcastle upon Tyne*. London: Oxford University Press.

OFFORD, D. R., ABRAMS, N., ALLEN, N. & POUSHINSKY, B. A. (in press) Broken homes, parental psychiatric illness and female delinquency. *American Journal of Orthopsychiatry*.

—— ALLEN, N. & ABRAMS, N. (1978) Parental psychiatric illness, broken homes, and delinquency. *Journal of the American Academy of Child Psychiatry*, 17, 224–38.

PINEO, P. C. & PORTER, J. (1967) Occupational prestige in Canada. *Canadian Review of Sociology and Anthropology*, 4, 24–40.

ROBINS, L. N. (1966) *Deviant Children Grown Up*. Baltimore: Williams and Wilkins.

—— WEST, P. A. & HERJANIC, B. L. (1975) Arrests and delinquency in two generations: a study of black urban families and their children. *Journal of Child Psychology and Psychiatry*, 16, 125–40.

RUTTER, M. & MADGE, N. (1976) *Cycles of Disadvantage*. London: Heinemann.

—— TIZARD, J. & WHITMORE, K. (1970) *Education, Health and Behaviour*. London: Longman.

SHORT, J. F. & NYE, F. I. (1958) Extent of unrecorded juvenile delinquency: tentative conclusions. *Journal of Criminal Law, Criminology and Police Science*, 49, 296–302.

SIEGEL, S. (1956) *Nonparametric Statistics for the Behavioral Sciences*, Pp. 116–126. New York: McGraw-Hill.

WEST, D. J. & FARRINGTON, D. P. (1973) *Who Becomes Delinquent?* London: Heinemann.

—— —— (1977) *The Delinquent Way of Life*. New York: Crane Russak.

WILLIAMS, J. R. & GOLD, M. (1972) From delinquent behaviour to official delinquency. *Social Problems*, 20, 209–29.

Marshall B. Jones, Ph.D., *Professor, Department of Behavioral Science, The Pennyslvania State University College of Medicine, Hershey, Pennsylvania 17033, USA,*

David R. Offord, M.D., *Professor, Department of Psychiatry, McMaster University Medical Center, Hamilton, Ontario L8N 3L6, Canada,*

Nola Abrams, *Research Assistant, Department of Psychiatry, Royal Ottawa Hospital, Ottawa, Ontario K1Z 7K4, Canada*

This research was supported in part by National Health Grant No. 605-7-764 from the Department of National Health and Welfare, Canada.

(*Received 17 April; revised 15 May 1979*)

School Influences

[19]

J. Child Psychol. Psychiat. Vol. 26, No. 3, pp. 349–368, 1985.
Printed in Great Britain.

0021-9630/85 $3.00 + 0.00
Pergamon Press Ltd.
© 1985 Association for Child Psychology and Psychiatry.

FAMILY AND SCHOOL INFLUENCES ON BEHAVIOURAL DEVELOPMENT

MICHAEL RUTTER

Department of Child and Adolescent Psychiatry, Institute of Psychiatry, London

Abstract—Research findings are reviewed with respect to possible family and school influences on behavioural development, but with special reference to socially disapproved conduct. The hypothesis that statistical associations between environmental variables and children's disorders represent causal connections is considered in terms of the three main alternatives—hereditary influences, the effect of children on their parents, and the operation of some third variable. It is concluded that each has some validity but that nevertheless there are true environmental effects. The mechanisms underlying their operation are discussed with respect to parental criminality, family discord, weak family relationships, ineffective discipline, and peer group influences. Individual differences in response to adversity are discussed in terms of age, sex, temperament, genetic factors, coping processes, patterning of stressors, compensatory good experiences and catalytic factors. The various ways in which environmental effects may persist over time are considered in terms of linkages within the environment as well as within the child. It is concluded that long-term effects are far from independent from intervening circumstances.

Keywords: Behavioural development, individual differences, continuities/discontinuities in development

INTRODUCTION

NUMEROUS studies have shown that children with various kinds of behavioural problems tend to come from homes or schools that are disadvantaged or deviant in some respect (see reviews by Hinde, 1980; Rutter, 1981a, 1982, 1984a; Rutter & Madge, 1976; Rutter & Giller, 1983). As a result it has come to be widely accepted that family difficulties—as reflected in such factors as broken homes, child neglect or marital discord—cause children to have psychiatric disorders. But what evidence is there that family, school and community environments do truly influence children's behaviour? And, insofar as they do, which aspects of the environment matter? Do the effects vary according to the child's age and personal qualities? To what extent do such environmental influences persist and how far are the ill-effects reversible? What mechanisms are involved in the developmental continuities and discontinuities associated with the long-term sequelae of serious adversities in childhood? It is only through answers to questions such as these that the crude statistical associations between family (or school) deviance or disadvantage and child disorder can be translated into any theoretical or practical concepts of how environmental factors may influence the course of psychosocial development. In this selective overview of a

Requests for reprints to: Prof. M. Rutter, Department of Child and Adolescent Psychiatry, Institute of Psychiatry, De Crespigny Park, Denmark Hill, London SE5 8AF, U.K.

Accepted manuscript received 23 February 1984

350   M. RUTTER

very large topic, therefore, these are the matters to which particular attention is paid. The focus is strictly on behaviour rather than cognition, and within the behavioural domain on extreme variations or deviant outcomes in terms of socially disapproved conduct rather than on variations within the normal range.

ALTERNATIVE EXPLANATIONS

The first question of whether the statistical associations between environmental variables and children's disorders represent causal connections requires an examination of three main alternatives: (a) that the associations represent hereditary rather than environmental influences; (b) that the main effect is from the child to the family rather than a unidirectional parental influence on the children; and (c) that both the family (or school) characteristics and the children's disorders are due to some third variable, such as social disadvantage or physical hazards in the environment.

Genetic transmission

The suggestion that the associations reflect genetic rather than experiential factors constitutes a very real possibility. The question needs to be tackled by means of several different research strategies.

Animal studies. Firstly, environmental effects may be examined directly by means of experiments in which the circumstances of rearing are deliberately altered. For obvious ethical reasons, usually this can be done only in animals. Nevertheless, the findings are clear-cut in showing that marked changes in the environment do indeed have important effects on psychological development (Rutter, 1981a). In these studies we know that the effects were environmental rather than genetic because of the experimental conditions.

Heritability estimates. A second approach is provided by heritability estimates. The findings show that in no case is the genetic determination of psychological attributes so strong that there is no room for environmental effects (McGuffin & Gottesman, 1984; Shields, 1980). Heritability estimates are also useful in showing differences between attributes in the extent of the environmental contribution. For example, it is clear that although genetic factors play some part in juvenile delinquency, environmental factors predominate (Rutter & Giller, 1983). On the other hand, it seems that hereditary influences may be more influential in the case of criminal behaviour that is associated with personality disturbance and that persists from childhood into the adult years.

But, family resemblances also provide another important datum—the extent to which the environmental influences operate within or between families (Rowe & Plomin, 1981). If children in the same family tend to be similar in their characteristics the implication is that they share the most important environmental influences and hence that the crucial factors are likely to be those that affect the family as a whole. This is very much the situation with respect to juvenile delinquency and conduct disorders where it is common for several children in the family to show similar behaviour. The expectation that follows from this observation is that the families of delinquents are likely to differ markedly from the families of non-delinquents in the overall environments they provide for the children. As we shall see, that is indeed what has been found.

In contrast, if brothers and sisters tend to be dissimilar in their attributes, the implication is that the environmental influences are likely to be ones that impinge differently on each member of the family. That is what seems to be the case with personality features and possibly also emotional disturbance (Loehlin & Nichols, 1976; Scarr, Webber, Weinberg & Wittig, 1981). The suggestion, here, is that it will be factors such as ordinal position, or differential treatment by parents, or stresses specific to the individual, or extra-familial influences that will be most important. But systematic differences between families according to the personality characteristics of the children are not to be expected. In other words, heritability data not only provide some estimate of the overall importance of family influences as determinants of individual differences under the environmental conditions studied, but also provide pointers as to the likelihood that such influences operate in much the same way on all children in the family. The findings suggest that with conduct disturbances to a substantial extent they do, whereas with emotional disturbances and personality features usually they do not.

Rearing in biological and adoptive homes compared. A further variant of the same strategy consists in the comparison of children from similar biological backgrounds according to whether or not they were reared by their biological parents or were adopted in infancy. The findings suggest that when the biological background is seriously deviant or disadvantaged, children who are adopted have a better outcome than those who remain with their biological parents (Bohman & Sigvardsson, 1980; Rutter & Madge, 1976; Rutter & Giller, 1983; Scarr, 1981; Scarr & Weinberg, 1983). Genetic factors still play a part in determining individual differences in behaviour and attainment, but the superior environment of the adoptive homes seemed to result in a general raising of the outcome for the group as a whole. However, it should be added that the evidence regarding the 'protective' effects of adoption is much stronger with respect to intelligence than it is for behaviour. Regrettably, there is a singular paucity of data on the benefits or otherwise of adoption in terms of non-cognitive outcome measures.

Characteristics of adoptive homes. The adoption paradigm, of course, may be used in a second way to examine environmental effects—through the determination of associations between adoptive family characteristics and disorder in the children. Provided selective placement effects can be excluded or controlled for, any such associations must represent environmental influences of one sort or another. This design has been used surprisingly rarely with respect to children's conduct disturbance. There is some evidence of associations between adoptive family characteristics (such as social class, divorce and parental mental disorder) and the children's behaviour and adjustment but the findings are too fragmentary for firm conclusions (Bohman, 1970; Cadoret & Cain, 1980; Mednick, Moffitt, Pollock, Talovic, Gabrielli & Van Dusen, 1983; Raynor, 1980).

Rearing effects after 'controlling' for genetic factors. An alternative strategy is provided by the use of designs that seek to 'control' for possible genetic effects. For example, in our study of children in families with a mentally ill parent we found that marital

352   M. RUTTER

discord was associated with conduct disturbance in the children even within a
subgroup, all of whom had a parent with a life-long personality disorder (Quinton &
Rutter, 1984a). Similarly, among institution-reared girls the outcome in adult life
was worse for those who experienced disrupted parenting in early childhood even
after account had been taken of deviance and disorder in the biological parents
(Quinton & Rutter, 1984b). Of course, it was not possible in either study entirely
to rule out the possibility that disrupted parenting or marital discord represented
some unmeasured genetic variable. On the other hand, this could not apply to Roy's
(1983) finding that hyperactivity was more frequent in institution-reared children
than in family-fostered children in spite of the fact that the biological backgrounds of
the two groups were closely comparable.

Change of environment. Environmental effects may be studied more directly through
the consequences of *changes* in the environment. Two rather different examples of this
research strategy may be given. Firstly, evidence of the importance of the social
group comes from investigations of the effects of a total change in the non-familial
environment. For example, West (1982) in his prospective study of London boys
found that delinquent activities tended to diminish following a move to somewhere
outside London (a change not explicable in terms of the boys' or the families' prior
characteristics as measured). These, and other, findings suggest that young people's
delinquent activities are influenced by the social group in which they find themselves.

Secondly, it has been found that changes in family circumstances are also associated with effects on the children's behaviour. For example, my colleagues and I
(Rutter, 1971) investigated children, all of whom had been separated from their
parents as a result of family discord or family problems. Within this group, who
had experienced severe early family stress, a change for the better, in terms of a
return to harmony or at least a cessation of open discord, was associated with a
marked reduction in the risk of conduct disturbance. Similarly, it has been shown by
Hetherington, Cox & Cox (1982) and by Wallerstein & Kelly (1980) that whether or
not disorders in the children of divorcing parents diminished was a function of whether
or not divorce improved family relationships. When the divorce brought harmony,
the children's problems tended to improve, but when parental discord and difficulties
continued so, too, the children's disorders tended to persist. Other studies (Rutter &
Giller, 1983) have given rise to similar findings most of which point to environmental
effects associated with changes in the quality of family relationships. However, in
some circumstances children's disturbed behaviour acquires self-perpetuating qualities
that cause it to persist in spite of alterations in family circumstances (Quinton &
Rutter, 1984a; Richman, Stevenson & Graham, 1982).

This design, of course, has even greater power if the effects of changes can be studied
in relation to family environments that involve no genetic linkage. Yarrow & Klein
(1980) used this strategy with respect to infant behaviour in their study of transfers
from foster to adoptive homes but the method has yet to be used to investigate
influences on conduct disturbance in older children.

Non-familial environments. The final strategy for disentangling genetic and environmental effects concerns the study of non-familial environments. There is now a
substantial literature showing major differences in the behaviour of children according
to the characteristics of the institutional environment in which they find themselves.

Thus, studies of institutions for delinquents, such as probation hostels or correctional schools, have shown large differences between them in rates of absconding and reconviction (Rutter & Giller, 1983). Broadly speaking, the 'successful' institutions were characterized by a combination of firmness, warmth, harmony, high expectations, good discipline and a practical approach to training. Similarly, other studies (Rutter, 1983b) have shown that secondary schools vary greatly in a host of different measures of pupil success. Furthermore, these differences in outcome have been shown to be systematically associated with the qualities of the schools as social organizations.

Obviously, in these institutional studies, there can be no question of genetic transmission in the ordinary sense, in that the staff and pupils have no biological relationship. The consistent association between the characteristics of the institution and the behaviour of the pupils strongly suggests a causal connection that represents an environmental effect. The query here is of a different kind—in which direction does the causal arrow run? Did the institution shape the children's behaviour or, rather, did the qualities of the children make the institution what it was? Of course, that question also arises with the family associations, and we need to consider the various ways in which the problem of how to determine the direction of causation may be tackled.

Child effects on the environment

As with genetic transmission, the first question is whether there is any evidence in favour of the alternative explanation, that is, is there any reason to suppose that children can have effects on how adults behave? This question was first raised in a systematic fashion by Yarrow (1963) with respect to parent–child interaction in foster families, by Thomas, Chess & Birch (1968) in relation to child temperament, and by Bell (1968, 1974) through his reanalysis of the direction of effects in studies of socialization. Since Bell's critique, evidence has accumulated to show that there are important child effects (Bell & Harper, 1977; Belsky & Tolan, 1981; Lerner & Spanier, 1978; Lewis & Rosenblum, 1974; Maccoby & Martin, 1983; Rutter, 1977), although it has to be added that our knowledge on these effects remains rudimentary. Nevertheless, there is no doubt that they exist and the question is whether or not they account for the observed associations between environmental variables and child disorder.

Input differences to schools. That issue may be considered in terms of the research strategies used in studying possible school effects. The question of whether the school affected the children, or, rather, whether the children shaped the functioning of the school may be tackled by determining the timing and patterning of the associations between school characteristics and pupil behaviour or attainments. If the schools influenced the pupils, the correlations should be weak at the time of school entry but strong at the time of school leaving. Conversely, if the pupil characteristics shaped teacher behaviour the reverse should occur, that is the strongest association should be with the intake measures. In our own study (Maughan, Mortimore, Ouston & Rutter, 1980) the former proved to be the case. Thus, for example, the school measures correlated 0.39 with the children's behaviour at intake but 0.92 with that at the end of secondary schooling (both correlations, of course, refer to differences between schools rather than to those between children). The findings on timing and patterning provide strong circumstantial evidence of a causal effect of the school on the child. That is not to say that the reverse does not also occur (almost certainly it does) but it appears there is a true influence on the child stemming from characteristics of the school environment.

Timing and patterning of associations in families. Much the same issues arise with respect to the associations with family variables. Did family discord cause the child to develop behavioural problems or did the presence of a difficult child in the family lead to quarrelling and discord? Did harsh and inconsistent punishment cause the boy to be aggressive or was it that the parents were led to take extreme measures just because the boy's disruptive behaviour failed to respond to more ordinary methods of discipline? Again, there are reasons for supposing that both may occur. For example, Patterson (1982) found that aggressive boys were indeed less responsive than other boys to disciplinary measures; Gardner (1977) showed experimentally that autistic children elicited different patterns of interaction from the adults with whom they were placed. So how may we determine how far and in what circumstances the family factors influence the child rather than vice-versa?

Of course, the matter is clear-cut in the case of the many family variables that could not have been caused by the child. Thus, it is obvious that such variables as being the oldest child, having a younger sib born, or being bereaved could not conceivably have resulted from the child's behaviour. In other cases, the fact that the family factors antedated the child's disturbance makes the direction of causation equally clear. This would be so, for example, with many instances of parental criminality or mental disorder and, equally, it would apply in many cases of marital discord. But, often, it is difficult to be at all sure about the timing. For example, prospective longitudinal studies of high-risk populations—such as the West & Farrington (1973, 1977) study of working class London boys—have been able to obtain parental measures before the children became delinquent. But we know that many of the boys showed difficult and troublesome behaviour when they were younger—some years before they appeared in court.

There is no easy way out of this dilemma and often there has to be a reliance on an interpretation of the overall pattern, together with an assessment of which causal process is more likely. Perhaps the situation where this problem arises most obviously concerns the associations between conduct disorder in boys on the one hand and family discord, poor parental supervision and inefficient discipline on the other. A key feature here is that in such families it is usual for several sons to show behavioural disturbance. As already noted, genetic factors do not seem to play a major role in these disorders and hence there is no ready explanation of why so many of the children should show problems if the association with family discord stemmed from the children's behaviour. Rather, it is more plausible that the association stemmed from a general effect of the family on the children resulting from problems in the parents. But this suggestion demands some explanation of why the parents should show such severe difficulties in parenting and in marital relationships. Is it possible to predict these difficulties in advance of the children's birth? Empirical findings show that to some extent it is.

For example, our own study following London children into early adult life (Quinton & Rutter, 1984b; Rutter, Quinton & Liddle, 1983) provides relevant

FAMILY AND SCHOOL INFLUENCES ON BEHAVIOURAL DEVELOPMENT   355

data. It was found that those who experienced severe adversities in their own child-
hoods were the ones most likely to grow up to show difficulties in many aspects of
adult functioning, including marked problems in parenting. People's experiences of
rearing when they were young were important determinants of their own qualities as
parents when they reached adulthood, as also found by Kruk and Wolkind (1982;
Wolkind & Kruk, 1984). Other studies, too, provide limited evidence that characteristics of parents, as assessed prior to the children's birth, predict aspects of parental
behaviour (Maccoby & Martin, 1983).

Association with some third variable

The third main alternative to family effects to be considered is that both the
parents' behaviour and that of the children are due to some third variable. Thus,
one might postulate that the association between parental criminality and delinquency
in the sons or that between marital discord and aggressive behaviour in the children
are due, not to any causal link between the two, but rather to the fact that both are
caused by some other influence such as poverty or poor housing. Of course, this is
a possibility that must be borne in mind in any study of hypothesized causal influences,
and analyses to investigate the matter were undertaken in all the research considered
so far. The results show that it is most unlikely that the family links are an artifact
of some broader environmental variable. The associations are remarkably similar in
all socio-cultural groups (Robins, 1978; Rutter & Giller, 1983). Of course, that is
not to argue that social disadvantage has no effects on behaviour; obviously, it does.
Research findings strongly suggest that the styles and qualities of parenting are
much influenced by the social context and by the presence of stressors and of emotional
support (Belsky, 1981; Belsky, Robins & Gamble, 1984; Bronfenbrenner, 1979;
Crnic, Greenberg, Ragozin, Robinson & Basham, 1983; Quinton & Rutter, 1984b).
The point being made is the narrower one that the consequences of social disadvantage are not sufficient to explain or account for those family effects that are
found in all sectors of society.

Conclusions on environmental effects. We may conclude that the three main types of
alternative explanation all have some validity. There are genetic effects, children do
influence parents, and family functioning is modified by the broader socio-cultural
environment. Nevertheless, these fail to account for all family and school effects.
Accordingly, it may be inferred that there is good evidence of environmental influences
on behaviour stemming from experiences both within and outside the home. We need
to consider now the evidence that might indicate which mechanisms and processes
are involved.

MECHANISMS AND PROCESSES

In that connection I shall largely concentrate on those aspect of family functioning
found to be associated with conduct disorders and delinquency. Five may be picked
out for more detailed consideration (Rutter & Giller, 1983): criminality in the
parents, intra-familial discord, weak family relationships, ineffective discipline and
peer group influences. These variables cover a wide range and it is necessary to ask
which are the crucial dimensions. This is particularly important because the five

features overlap greatly. We need to search for means to 'pull apart' variables that ordinarily tend to go together. The procedures may be illustrated by taking just a few specific examples.

Broken homes and family discord

At one time, much emphasis was placed on the supposed importance of broken homes as a cause of delinquency. The notion was that it was the fact of family break-up that was damaging. The idea seemed plausible in that broken homes were indeed statistically associated with delinquency. But what alternative explanations should be considered? One obvious contender is the presence of family discord and quarrelling (Rutter, 1971, 1982). To differentiate the two it is necessary first to split broken homes into those where discord was a prominent feature and those where it was not. Divorce and separation constituted causes that met the first criterion and parental death met the second. Several large-scale studies have data that differentiate these two causes of a broken home; the findings of all of them are agreed in showing that whereas divorce/separation is strongly associated with delinquency, death is only very weakly so. It seems that perhaps discord is more important than break-up *per se*. But if that were so, it should follow that discord in unbroken homes should also lead to delinquency. It has been found that it does. It might also be predicted that temporary separations should predispose to conduct disorders if they arose as a result of discord but not if they occurred for other reasons. Again that has been confirmed. Also, if discord is indeed a causal factor it might be expected that a reduction in discord should be followed by a diminution in the risk of conduct disturbance. Once more, empirical findings show this to be so. We may conclude that the relevant mechanism is likely to involve discordant relationships rather than break-up *per se*.

Weak family relationships

Weak family relationships have also been found to be associated with delinquency. The possible importance of personal relationships is shown by the finding that a good relationship with one parent has an ameliorating effect even in the presence of general family discord (Rutter, 1971; Rutter *et al.*, 1983). However, discord and weak relationships so often accompany one another that it is difficult to separate their effects. When this is the situation, it is necessary to seek special circumstances where this is not the case. Rearing from infancy in a good quality group Home or other institution with multiple changing caretakers provides the nearest approach. Because of the frequent changes in parent-figure and because of the more 'professional' approach to child-rearing, children are less likely to form close bonds and attachments with their caretakers in this setting than if they were brought up in a nuclear family. On the other hand, usually such institutions are not particularly discordant and quarrelsome environments. So the question is what happens to young people reared in that way? Data on that point are limited but they are consistent in showing that conduct disorders are much increased in frequency among children reared from infancy in an institutional setting (Quinton & Rutter, 1984b; Roy, 1983; Rutter *et al.*, 1983; Wolkind, 1974; Yule & Raynes, 1972). Accordingly, it appears that weak family relationships are important in their own right quite apart from their association with discord.

Supervision and discipline

But it is necessary also to consider some of the specific influences that shape particular behaviours—the role of adult supervision and discipline. At one time, attention was focused on the use of specific practices, on the severity of discipline, and on matters of consistency (Becker, 1964). But it became clear that these were not the most relevant dimensions and the focus has shifted in recent years (Maccoby & Martin, 1983). It is not yet certain how the findings are best conceptualized, but Patterson (1982) plausibly suggests four dimensions as likely to be most important: (a) the lack of 'house rules' (so that there are no clear expectations of what children may and may not do); (b) lack of parental monitoring of the child's behaviour (so that the parents are not adequately informed about his acts or emotions and hence are not in a good position to respond appropriately); (c) lack of effective contingencies (so that parents nag and shout but do not follow through with any disciplinary plan, and do not respond with an adequate differentiation between praise for prosocial and punishment for antisocial activities); and (d) a lack of techniques for dealing with family crises or problems (so that conflicts lead to tension and dispute but do not result in resolution). The pointers, then, are that we need to focus on an awareness of what children are doing, the process of disciplinary management (including problem-solving methods), and the efficiency of the techniques used.

However, also, the evidence suggests that the socio-emotional context of the discipline (i.e. the pre-existing parent–child relationship and the affective quality of the disciplinary interaction) is at least as important as the particular procedures used. In addition, it appears that key elements in discipline are as likely to be in the parental practices that serve to prevent disruptive behaviour as in any steps taken after the event.

Models of behaviour

So far, most of the dimensions considered have been concerned with one or other aspect of control (either internal or external). But it is clear that control concepts, on their own, provide an inadequate explanation for the specific form or content of children's behaviour (Hirschi, 1969; Elliott, Ageton & Cantor, 1979). In that connection, we need to turn to the role of parental criminality and of peer group influences. Doubtless, they exert their effects through several different means, including those considered already. But, in addition, we need to add the dimension of modelling. Both delinquent peers and criminal parents provide a model of aggression and of antisocial attitudes. Their behaviour constitutes something to be copied and identified with by the children, as well as a setting in which delinquent solutions to problems are regarded as acceptable, or at least to be tolerated. The same applies with delinquent siblings—a possible reason for delinquency being more frequent in boys from large families (Offord, 1982).

To summarize the findings on conduct disorder, it appears that the operative mechanisms probably include emotionally discordant patterns of social interaction, weak family relationships, inefficient supervision and discipline, and deviant models of behaviour. It should be noted that these mechanisms probably apply as much to school influences (Rutter, 1983b) as to family effects.

INDIVIDUAL DIFFERENCES IN RESPONSE TO ADVERSITY

With all these family influences the evidence has been consistent in showing the marked variation in outcomes following even the most extreme adverse experiences. Some children succumb with the development of disorder, but others escape showing resilience in the face of adversity (Garmezy, 1981; Garmezy & Nuechterlein, 1972; Garmezy & Tellegen, 1984; Rutter, 1979; Werner & Smith, 1982). The possible reasons for this individual variation need to be considered.

Age-dependent susceptibilities

The first question that arises with respect to any developmental function is whether or not there are developmentally determined age-specific susceptibilities (Rutter, 1981a, b). Of course, the issue here is not whether adverse effects are generally greater at one age period than another (it would be absurd to assume that all adversities operate in the same way), but rather whether particular environmental influences vary in their effects according to children's social, emotional and intellectual maturity. It seems that some do.

Thus, the effects of age have been found to be particularly marked in the case of hospital admission, where the age period of greatest risk has proved to be about 6 months to 4 years (Rutter, 1981a).

The effects on selective attachments also seem to be largely restricted to the first few years of life. The pattern of social disinhibition and indiscriminate friendships that is seen in some institution-reared children applies to those admitted in the first 2 years of life and not to those admitted in later childhood (Wolkind, 1974).

Bereavement, in contrast, seems more likely to lead to severe grief reactions in adolescence than in earlier childhood (van Eerdewegh, Bieri, Parrilla & Clayton, 1982; Rutter, 1981b).

Sex differences

The sex of children has been found to influence their response to various family stressors and adversities. In general, it has been found that boys are more vulnerable than girls (Rutter, 1970, 1982). This is most evident with respect to family discord, disharmony and disruption but also it has been observed with other environmental factors.

Temperamental factors

Quite apart from sex and age differences, it is evident that children vary greatly in their temperamental styles, that is in their characteristic mode of behaviour and in the manner in which they respond to differing situations (Plomin, 1983; Porter & Collins, 1982). These temperamental styles have been found to be associated with differences in children's responses to various forms of stress and adversity.

Genetic factors

Genetically determined vulnerabilities may also play a role. Although data on the point are decidedly limited, there is some evidence from studies of fostered or adopted children to suggest that genetic factors associated with delinquency or conduct disturbance may operate, in part, through creating an increased vulnerability to adverse environmental influences (Cloninger, Bohman & Sigvardsson, 1981; Crowe, 1974; Hutchings & Mednick, 1974).

FAMILY AND SCHOOL INFLUENCES ON BEHAVIOURAL DEVELOPMENT   359

Coping processes

Many such hazards require some reaction or response from the child. Accordingly, it might be thought that the outcome would be influenced by what he does about the stress situation—that is by the coping process (Rutter, 1981b). It is obvious that some coping processes could increase the risk of maladaptation or disorder whereas others could improve adaptation and reduce the risks of a deviant outcome. The notion of effective and ineffective coping is a very plausible one. Unfortunately, we lack good data on what differentiates effective and ineffective mechanisms.

Patterning and multiplicity of stressors

The persistence of ill-effects following stress or adversity depends to a substantial extent on whether or not the environmental hazards continue to impinge on the child. However, there is evidence that the patterning and multiplicity of stressors at any one time is also important (Rutter, 1979, 1981a, b). Thus, the presence of chronic psychosocial adversity makes it more likely that a child will suffer ill-effects from acute stressors. There are interactive effects between psychosocial adversities so that the presence of one potentiates the effect of a second or third (Rutter, 1979, 1983a).

Compensatory good experiences

Another sort of interaction has also been proposed—the balance between pleasant and unpleasant events (Lazarus, Cohen, Folkman, Kanner & Schaefer, 1980). The notion is that the presence of happy experiences, to some extent, can provide a buffer that reduces the impact of unhappy ones. Thus, the shielding influence of a good relationship in the midst of discord and disharmony has been mentioned already. In addition, good experiences at school can, perhaps, do something to compensate for difficulties at home (Quinton & Rutter, 1984b; Rutter, 1979). Success and a sense of self-esteem are important elements in growing up and factors that enhance a person's feelings of their own worth may prove protective. But, again, we lack evidence on the extent to which good experiences can compensate for bad ones.

Catalytic factors

Finally, I need to mention the possibility of 'catalytic' factors. The concept is one of those factors that are largely inert on their own, but, when combined with environmental stresses or hazards, either increase their effect (so-called 'vulnerability' factors), or decrease their impact (so-called 'protective' factors). For example, the presence of a supportive social network and of a cohesive social group are thought to operate in that fashion (Henderson, 1981; Rutter, 1981a, b; Werner & Smith, 1982).

It is clear, then, that any explanation for individual differences in children's response to stress and adversity must include both factors in the child and in his environment, although we do not know their relative importance.

PERSISTENCE OF ENVIRONMENTAL EFFECTS

Up to this point, the effects of family and school influences have been considered without explicit reference to any time frame. Some years ago it was commonly assumed that the effects of serious family adversity or deprivation in early childhood were very long-lasting and very difficult to reverse. However, research findings over the last decade or so have cast increasing doubt on that view (Clarke & Clarke, 1976; Rutter, 1981a) and we need to consider now the extent to which ill-effects persist and, more especially, the factors that determine persistence or non-persistence.

If we are to examine the persistence of effects we must focus attention on that small subgroup of children who experience severe early neglect, deprivation or disadvantage but who then experience a major change of environment followed by a normal pattern of upbringing thereafter.

Apart from single case studies of children rescued in middle childhood from cruel isolated rearing in cupboards and attics (Skuse, 1984), studies of late adoption are about the only examples we have of this phenomenon (Rutter, 1981a). The findings are consistent in showing very substantial recovery in most cases.

It is clear that environmental improvements in middle or late childhood can do much to reverse the ill-effects of early neglect, discord and deprivation. The effects of early bad experiences are not necessarily enduring and to a substantial extent the ill-effects are reversible provided that the environmental change is sufficiently great and that the later environment is sufficiently positive and beneficial. Interestingly, our own data from a follow-up into the mid-1920s of institution-reared girls showed very clearly that this effect extends right into adult life. The findings indicated that a stable harmonious marriage to a non-deviant spouse served to nullify the ill-effects of seriously adverse experiences in childhood (Quinton & Rutter, 1984b). Environmental factors continue to exert their effects well after physical maturity is reached. But just as 'bad' early experiences can be 'neutralized' to a substantial extent by good experiences in later life, so also the converse applies. A good home in the early years does not prevent damage from psychosocial stresses in adolescence. To a substantial extent, whether or not sequelae are enduring is dependent on continuities of experiences and on chain reactions.

However, other considerations must be added before the picture can be regarded as at all complete. There is the possibility that certain experiences have to occur during the early years for social development to proceed normally (Rutter, 1981a). Although the original notion of fixed and absolute 'critical periods' in development has had to be largely abandoned, the concept of 'sensitive periods' during which environmental influences have a particularly marked effect has some validity (Bateson, 1979, 1983). The generally favored candidate for this effect concerns the initial formation of selective attachments. It has been suggested by Bowlby (1969) that these first bonds must develop during the first two years or so if normal social relationships are to be possible later. The evidence to test that hypothesis is quite meagre but the few available data from studies of late-adopted children (Tizard & Hodges, 1978) are interesting and informative. Two main findings require emphasis. Firstly, even children adopted after the age of four years can develop bonds with their adoptive parents. To that extent, either the 'sensitive period' notion is wrong or it extends to a later age than usually supposed. But secondly, in spite of this development of parent–child bonds at age 4 to 6 years, the late-adopted children showed the same social and attentional problems in school as did those who remained in the institution. The implication is that, although attachments can still develop for the first time after infancy, nevertheless, to some extent fully normal social development may be dependent on bonding having taken place at an early age.

The findings are provocative in two respects: first, in their implication of a sensitive period for the optimal development of social relationships; and second, in the implication that the effects may persist into at least middle childhood in spite of a reduced change in family circumstances. Nevertheless, we should be wary about any mechanistic assumptions that the long-term effects of social experiences in the infancy period are independent of later happenings. To begin with, Tizard's data on late adopted children extend only to age 8 years and we do not know whether the findings in later childhood or adolescence would be different. The available evidence from other studies of late adopted children (Triseliotis & Russell, 1984) is inadequate for the resolution of that issue. However, the results of experimental primate studies of total social isolation in infancy may be relevant. On the one hand, the gross social anomalies of these isolation-reared animals persisted into adult life with little evidence of spontaneous recovery (Ruppenthal, Arling, Harlow, Sackett & Suomi, 1976). On the other hand, a variety of experiences in adolescence and adulthood resulted in a surprising degree of recovery of effective social functioning (Novak, 1979). Human data pertinent to this problem are very limited but they point to the same conclusions. Thus, our own study of institution-reared girls showed both: (1) that disrupted parenting in the early years was predictive of adult functioning; and (2) that the quality of marital relationships in adult life hugely modified the effects of these early experiences (Quinton & Rutter, 1984b). A more detailed analysis of the findings was informative in throwing light on the likely mechanisms involved. It was found that disrupted parenting had effects on the children's behaviour but also it was influential in terms of increasing the likelihood of other later adversities. Together these served to influence the circumstances in adolescence in which the choice of marriage partner took place. As a result, girls who suffered poor early social experiences were more likely than other girls to make an unsatisfactory marriage to a deviant man from a similarly disadvantaged background. To a very large extent, the persistent effects of disrupted parenting in infancy were a consequence of that linkage. However, if by good luck the marriage turned out well, the effects of childhood experiences were washed out.

The implication is that we need to re-think our concepts of the ways in which life experiences influence socio-behavioural development. Developmental theories that postulate a 'structure' of personality that is established during the course of the developmental process do not fit the empirical findings. Equally, however, behaviourist theories that conceptualize effects entirely in terms of the here-and-now without the need to invoke developmental considerations are inconsistent with the evidence. Constancy of behaviour over periods of several years is decidedly unusual. Similarly, the effects of early experiences cannot be considered without reference to the effects of later experiences. On the other hand, continuities in development, as well as discontinuities, are very striking. Evidence on the mechanisms that underlie both is very limited but we should consider what little is known on the processes that may be operative (Rutter, 1984b).

362   M. RUTTER

DEVELOPMENTAL CONTINUITIES AND DISCONTINUITIES

Selection of environments

As already noted, one important source of continuities is the linkage between different environments. Thus, in our follow-up study into adult life, institutional rearing made it more likely that the women would marry a deviant spouse (Quinton & Rutter, 1984b; Rutter *et al.*, 1983). Similarly, the conditions of upbringing played a part in determining whether the women experienced poor social conditions in adult life, then seriatim social circumstances influenced the women's social functioning. Or, again, institution-reared girls who left the institution to return to discordant families were more likely than other girls to have babies in their 'teens; teenage pregnancy, in turn, was then associated with an increased risk of a poor social outcome. Brown, Harris & Bifulco (1984) have described a closely comparable chain of circumstances in the findings from their latest study of depressed women. The environments change but the experience of one sort of 'bad' environment makes it more likely that the individual will go on to experience other sorts of 'bad' environment.

Opportunities

A further mechanism leading to continuities concerns the effects stemming from the opening up or closing down of opportunities. For example, in our study of inner London secondary schools (Rutter, Maughan, Mortimore, Ouston & Smith, 1979), we found powerful effects of the school environment on pupil behaviour and attainments while the children were still at school. We found no direct effects of schooling on the young people's employment one year after school-leaving but there were most important indirect effects as a result of the earlier school influences (Gray, Smith & Rutter, 1980). The school influence on exam qualifications opened up or closed down employment opportunities and in this way produced more lasting chain effects.

Effects on the environment

A third type of linkage over time is provided by the effects of family or school experiences on the environment. For example, Dunn & Kendrick (1982) showed marked behavioural reactions in first born children following the birth of a sibling. This new event introduced an important element of discontinuity but there were linkages with the past and with the future. The mother's previous style of parenting had an effect on how children reacted, but also the arrival of a sibling altered the overall pattern of family interaction. In this way a supposedly 'acute' event had 'chronic' circumstances; as a result the quality of the first born's relationship with his sibling showed a remarkable level of consistency over several years. Perhaps, too, such a changed pattern of family interaction may constitute part of the explanation for the surprisingly lasting effects of recurrent hospital admission (Douglas, 1975; Quinton & Rutter, 1976). Thus, Hinde's experimental studies with rhesus monkeys showed that the long-term effects of brief separation experiences were largely dependent on the extent to which the separation served to disturb and increase tensions in the mother–infant relationship (Hinde & McGinnis, 1977).

Vulnerability, resilience and coping skills

Another mechanism concerns so-called 'sensitization' and 'steeling' effects (Rutter, 1981b). Early events may operate by altering sensitivities to stress or in modifying styles of coping which then protect from, or predispose towards, disorder in later life only in the presence of later stress events (Rutter, 1981b). The suggestion, then, is not that there is any direct persistence of good or ill-effects but rather that patterns of response are established that influence the way the individual reacts to some later stress or adversity. If the pattern is one that increases the harm from later stress it is termed a 'sensitization' effect. Conversely, if it decreases the harm it is spoken of as 'steeling'. The literature contains several examples of both these effects. For example, it seems that the experience of one unpleasant separation may render the individual more likely to be affected adversely by later stressful separations. Conversely, a happy separation experience may prove protective. Similarly, we found that adversities in childhood rendered individuals less resilient in the presence of stresses in adult life (Quinton & Rutter, 1984b; Rutter *et al.*, 1983). There seems little doubt that early events may protect from or predispose towards later disorder through 'sensitization' or 'steeling' effects, but we lack any adequate understanding of how these effects come about, or what determines whether they are protective or damaging.

Habits, attitudes and self-concepts

Alternatively, childhood experiences may have persisting effects as a result of influences on habits, attitudes and self-esteem. Children's self-concepts include feelings of self-esteem, of self-efficacy or ability to control one's destiny, and of ego-resiliency (Harter, 1983). Findings are very limited on the role of these features as mediating mechanisms or modulating influences in children's response to life experiences; nevertheless, several types of findings suggest that they may play a significant role. Thus, it is a commonplace observation that 'problem' parents both fail to plan their lives and also feel unable to control what happens to them (Rutter & Madge, 1976; Tonge, James & Hillam, 1975). We do not know how that feeling of impotency arises but it seems probable that, to a substantial extent, their continuing family difficulties stem from these attitudes and concepts. Thus, for example, we found that institution-reared girls tend to marry on impulse to escape from an unhappy situation, their lack of 'planning' for marriage much increased the likelihood that they would make an unsatisfactory marriage (Quinton & Rutter, 1984b). On the other hand, the girls who experienced good experiences and success of some kind at school (in any aspect of life) were significantly more likely to 'plan' marriage and choose a husband for positive qualities—perhaps because their school success had given them a self-image of people who could control their destinies. Similarly, there is evidence that the taking of a boy to Court for theft, and hence his public 'labelling' as a delinquent, serves to increase the likelihood that he will persist in delinquent activities (Rutter & Giller, 1983). It is probable, too, that some of the school effects on pupils' attainments and behaviour stem from influences on habits, attitudes and self-concepts, as well as from more direct effects on learning (Rutter, 1984b).

364   M. RUTTER

'Sleeper' effects

There has been some controversy in the literature on whether or not there are 'sleeper effects' due to 'dormant change' in the organism arising as a result of early life experiences (Clarke & Clarke, 1981, 1982; Seitz, 1981). As already discussed, there is no doubt that there can be delayed effects in the sense of changes in functioning that are causally linked with earlier experiences but yet which do not become manifest in that form until sometime later. However, the concept of 'dormant change' does not seem to be a particularly helpful one in that it does not specify the mechanism involved. Although certainly much has still to be learned regarding the processes involved in long-term effects, it seems probable that usually they are mediated by either some form of immediate effect on the individual (as on habits, attitudes or sensitivities) or some impact on later environment (as with the opening up or closing down of opportunities) or some form of transactional effect involving both.

CONCLUSIONS

These few suggested mechanisms by no means exhaust the possibilities. However, they suffice to make the point that the concept of continuity in development implies meaningful links over the course of time and not a lack of change. The processes involve linkages within the environment as well as within the child. It should be added that even the few available findings point strongly to the poverty of prevailing theories on the nature of psychosocial development and especially on the ways in which it may be influenced by environmental circumstances. We have come to appreciate that there is a crucial difference between risk *indicators* and causal *mechanisms*. As I noted, research findings have served to increase our understanding of the latter. Thus, we have moved from concepts of broken homes, to family discord, to coercive family processes. But still we lack knowledge on exactly how those operate, on which developmental processes are affected, and on the ways in which developmental continuities and discontinuities arise. The findings on family and school influences on behavioural development have done much to clarify the issues but if further progress is to be made it will be necesary to improve both our theoretical concepts and our methods of statistical analysis. If the complex patterns of interaction and of indirect linkage are to be translated into meaningful concepts of developmental processes, it will be crucial to use analytic methods that are designed for the task. These postulated interactions are by no means synonymous with statistical interaction effects in conventional multivariate analyses (see Rutter, 1983a) and we must adapt our methods to ensure that they truly test the concepts in question.

In conclusion, it is apparent that there are important family and school influences on behavioural development. The effects are sizable but they vary markedly across individuals and according to the ecological context; moreover, they are transactional, rather than unidirectional, in nature. The evidence runs counter to the view that early experiences irrevocably change personality development (Rutter, 1981a) and also runs counter to the suggestion that any single process is involved (Sackett, 1982); nevertheless, in some circumstances the indirect effects may be quite long-lasting. Even so, such long-term effects are far from independent from intervening circumstances. Rather, the continuities stem from a multitude of links over time (Rutter *et al.*, 1983). Because each link is incomplete, subject to marked individual variation and open to modification, recurrent opportunities to break the chain continue right into adult life.

REFERENCES

Bateson, P. (1979). How do sensitive periods arise and what are they for? *Animal Behavior*, 27, 470–486.

Bateson, P. (1983). The interpretation of sensitive periods. In A. Oliverio & M. Zappella (Eds), *The behavior of human infants* (pp. 57–70). New York: Plenum Press.

Becker, W. C. (1964). Consequences of different kinds of parental discipline. In M. L. Hoffman & L. W. Hoffman (Eds), *Review of child development research*, Vol. 1 (pp. 169–208). New York: Russell Sage Foundation.

Bell, R. W. (1968). A reinterpretation of the direction of effects in studies of socialization. *Psychological Review*, 75, 81–95.

Bell, R. W. (1974). Contributions of human infants to care-giving and social interaction. In M. Lewis & L. A. Rosenblum (Eds), *The effects of the infant on its caregiver*. New York: Wiley.

Bell, R. W. & Harper, L. V. (Eds) (1977). *Child effects on adults*. Hillsdale, NJ: Erlbaum.

Belsky, J. (1981). Early human experience: a family perspective. *Developmental Psychology*, 17, 3–23.

Belsky, J. & Tolan, W. (1981). Infants as producers of their own development: an ecological perspective. In R. Lerner & N. Busch-Rossnagel (Eds), *Individuals as producers of their development: a life-span perspective*. New York: Academic Press.

Belsky, J., Robins, J. & Gamble, W. (1984). The determinants of parental competence: toward a contextual theory. In M. Lewis (Ed.), *Beyond the dyad*. New York: Plenum Press.

Bohman, M. (1970). *Adopted children and their families*. Stockholm: Prosprion.

Bohman, M. & Sigvardsson, S. (1980). Negative social heritage. *Adoption and Fostering*, 5, 25–31.

Bowlby, J. (1969). *Attachment and loss: I. Attachment*. London: Hogarth Press.

Bronfenbrenner, U. (1979). *The ecology of human development: experiments by nature and design*. Cambridge, MA: Harvard University Press.

Brown, G., Harris, T. O. & Bifulco, A. (1984). Long-term effect of early loss of parent. In M. Rutter, C. Izard & P. Read (Eds), *Depression in childhood: developmental perspectives*. New York: Guilford Press (in press).

Cadoret, R. J. & Cain, C. (1980). Sex differences in predictors of antisocial behavior in adoptees. *Archives of General Psychiatry*, 37, 561–563.

Clarke, A. M. & Clarke, A. D. B. (1976). *Early experience: myth and evidence*. London: Open Books.

Clarke, A. D. B. & Clarke, A. M. (1981). 'Sleeper effects' in development: fact or artifact? *Developmental Review*, 1, 344–360.

Clarke, A. M. & Clarke, A. D. B. (1982). Intervention and sleeper effects: a reply to Victoria Seitz. *Developmental Review*, 2, 76–86.

Cloninger, C. R., Bohman, M. & Sigvardsson, S. (1981). Inheritance of alcohol abuse: cross-fostering analysis of adopted men. *Archives of General Psychiatry*, 38, 861–868.

Crnic, K. A., Greenberg, M. T., Ragozin, A. S., Robinson, N. M. & Basham, R. B. (1983). Effects of stress and social support on mothers and premature and full-term infants. *Child Development*, 54, 209–217.

Crowe, R. R. (1974). An adoption study of antisocial personality. *Archives of General Psychiatry*, 31, 785–791.

Douglas, J. W. B. (1975). Early hospital admissions and later disturbances of behaviour and learning. *Developmental Medicine and Child Neurology*, 17, 456–480.

Dunn, J. & Kendrick, C. (1982). *Siblings: love, envy, and understanding*. Cambridge, MA: Harvard University Press.

Elliott, D. S., Ageton, S. S. & Canter, R. J. (1979). An integrated theoretical perspective on delinquent behavior. *Journal of Research into Crime and Delinquency*, 16, 3–27.

Gardner, J. (1977). Three aspects of childhood autism: mother–child interactions, autonomic responsivity, and cognitive functioning. PhD Thesis, University of Leicester.

366   M. RUTTER

Garmezy, N. (1981). Children under stress: perspectives on antecedents and correlates of vulnerability and resistance to psychopathology. In A. I. Rabin, J. Aronoff, A. M. Barclay & R. A. Zucker (Eds), *Further explorations in personality*. New York: Wiley Interscience.

Garmezy, N. & Nuechterlein, K. (1972). Invulnerable children: the fact and fiction of competence and disadvantage. *American Journal of Orthopsychiatry*, **42**, 328–329 (Abstract).

Garmezy, N. & Tellegen, A. (1984). Studies of stress-resistant children: methods, variables and preliminary findings. In F. Morrison, C. Lord & D. Keating (Eds), *Applied developmental psychology*, Vol. 1, (pp. 231–287). New York: Academic Press.

Gray, G., Smith, A. & Rutter, M. (1980). School attendance and the first year of employment. In L. Hersov & I. Berg (Eds), *Out of school: modern perspectives in truancy and school refusal* (pp. 343–370). Chichester: Wiley.

Harter, S. (1983). Developmental perspectives on the self system. In E. M. Hetherington (Ed.), *Socialization, personality and Social development*, Vol. 4, *Mussen's handbook of child psychology*, Vol. 4 (pp. 275–385). New York: Wiley.

Henderson, S. (1981). Social relationships, adversity and neurosis: an analysis of prospective observations. *British Journal of Psychiatry*, **138**, 391–398.

Hetherington, E. M., Cox, M. & Cox, R. (1982). Effects of divorce on parents and children. In M. Lamb (Ed.), *Nontraditional families* (pp. 233–288). Hillsdale, NJ: Erlbaum.

Hinde, R. A. (1980). Family influences. In M. Rutter (Ed.), *Scientific foundations of developmental psychiatry* (pp. 47–66). London: Heinemann Medical.

Hinde, R. A. & McGinnis, L. (1977). Some factors influencing the effect of temporary mother–infant separation: some experiments with rhesus monkeys. *Psychological Medicine*, **7**, 197–212.

Hirschi, T. (1969). *Causes of delinquency*. Berkeley: University of California Press.

Hutchings, B. & Mednick, S. A. (1974). Registered criminality in the adoptive and biological parents of registered male adoptees. In S. A. Mednick *et al.* (Eds), *Genetics, environment and psychopathology* (pp. 215–227). Amsterdam: North-Holland.

Kruk, S. & Wolkind, S. N. (1982). A longitudinal study of single mothers and their children. In N. Madge (Ed.), *Families at risk* (pp. 119–140). London: Heinemann Educational.

Lazarus, R. S., Cohen, J. B., Folkman, S., Kanner, A. & Schaefer, C. (1980). Psychological stress and adaptation: some unresolved issues. In H. Selye (Ed.), *Guide to stress research*. New York: Van Nostrand Reinhold.

Lerner, R. M. & Spanier, G. B. (Eds) (1978). *Child influence on marital and family interaction: a life span perspective*. New York: Academic Press.

Lewis, M. & Rosenblum, L. A. (Eds) (1974). *The effect of the infant on its caregiver*. New York: Wiley.

Loehlin, J. C. & Nichols, R. C. (1976). *Heredity, environment and personality: a study of 850 sets of twins*. Austin: University of Texas Press.

Maccoby, E. E. & Martin, J. (1983). Socialization in the context of the family: parent–child interaction. In E. M. Hetherington (Ed.), *Socialization, personality and social development*, Vol. 4, *Mussen's handbook of child psychology* (4th edition) (pp. 1–101). New York: Wiley.

Maughan, B., Mortimore, P., Ouston, J. & Rutter, M. (1980). Fifteen thousand hours: a reply to Heath and Clifford. *Oxford Review of Education*, **6**, 289–303.

McGuffin, P. & Gottesman, I. I. (1984). Genetic influences on normal and abnormal development. In M Rutter & L. Hersov (Eds), *Child and adolescent psychiatry: modern approaches* (2nd edition). Oxford: Blackwell Scientific (in press).

Mednick, S. A., Moffitt, T. E., Pollock, V., Talovic, S., Gabrielli, W. F. & Van Dusen, K. T. (1983). The interitance of human deviance. In D. Magnusson & V. Allen (Eds), *Human development: an interactional perspective* (pp. 221–242). New York: Academic Press.

Novak, M. A. (1979). Social recovery of monkeys isolated for the first year of life: II. Long term assessment. *Developmental Psychology*, **15**, 50–61.

Offord, D. R. (1982). Family backgrounds of male and female delinquent. In J. Gunn & D. P. Farrington (Eds), *Abnormal offenders, delinquency, and the criminal justice system* (pp. 129–151). Chichester: Wiley.

Patterson, G. R. (1982). *Coercive family process*. Eugene, Oregon: Castalia Publ. Co.

Plomin, R. (1983). Childhood temperament. In B. B. Lahey & A. E. Kazdin (Eds), *Advances in clinical child psychology*, Vol. 6 (pp. 45–92). New York: Plenum Press.

Porter, R. & Collins, G. M. (Eds) (1982). *Temperamental differences in infants and young children*. Ciba Foundation Symposium 89. London: Pitman Books.

Quinton, D. & Rutter, M. (1976). Early hospital admissions and later disturbances of behaviour: an attempted replication of Douglas' findings. *Developmental Medicine and Child Neurology*, **18**, 447–459.

Quinton, D. & Rutter, M. (1984a). Family pathology and child disorder: a four year prospective study. In A. R. Nicol (Ed.), *Longitudinal studies in child psychology and psychiatry: practical lessons from research experience.* Chichester: Wiley (1985).

Quinton, D. & Rutter, M. (1984b). Parenting behaviour of mothers raised 'in care'. In A. R. Nicol (Ed.), *Longitudinal studies in child psychology and psychiatry: practical lessons from research experience.* Chichester: Wiley (in press).

Raynor, L. (1980). *The adopted child comes of age.* London: Allen & Unwin.

Richman, N., Stevenson, J. & Graham, P. J. (1982). *Preschool to school: a behavioural study.* London: Academic Press.

Robins, L. (1978). Sturdy childhood predictors of adult antisocial behaviour: replications from longitudinal studies. *Psychological Medicine,* 8, 611–622.

Rowe, D. C. & Plomin, R. (1981). The importance of nonshared (E_1) environmental influences in behavioural development. *Developmental Psychology,* 17, 517–531.

Roy, P. (1983). Is continuity enough?: Substitute care and socialization. Paper presented at the Spring Scientific Meeting, Child and Adolescent Psychiatry Specialist Section, Royal College of Psychiatrists, London, March.

Ruppenthal, G. C., Arling, G. L., Harlow, H. F., Sackett, G. P. & Suomi, S. J. (1976). A 10-year perspective of motherless–mother monkey behavior. *Journal of Abnormal Psychology,* 85, 341–349.

Rutter, M. (1970). Sex differences in children's responses to family stress. In E. J. Anthony & C. Koupernik (Eds), *The child in his family* (pp. 165–196). New York: Wiley.

Rutter, M. (1971). Parent–child separation: psychological effects on the children. *Journal of Child Psychology and Psychiatry,* 12, 233–260.

Rutter, M. (1977). Individual differences. In M. Rutter & L. Hersov (Eds), *Child psychiatry: modern approaches* (pp. 3–21). Oxford: Blackwell Scientific.

Rutter, M. (1979). Protective factors in children's responses to stress and disadvantage. In M. W. Kent & J. E. Rolf (Eds), *Primary prevention of psychopathology,* Vol. 3, *Social competence in children* (pp. 49–74). Hanover, NH: University Press of New England.

Rutter, M. (1981a). *Maternal deprivation reassessed* (2nd edition). Harmondsworth, Middlesex: Penguin.

Rutter, M. (1981b). Stress, coping and development: some issues and some questions. *Journal of Child Psychology and Psychiatry,* 22, 323–356.

Rutter, M. (1982). Epidemiological–longitudinal approaches to the study of development. In W. A. Collins (Ed.), *The concept of development.* Minnesota Symposia on Child Psychology, Vol. 15 (pp. 105–144). Hillsdale, NJ: Erlbaum.

Rutter, M. (1983a). Statistical and personal interactions: facets and perspectives. In D. Magnusson & V. Allen (Eds), *Human development: an interactional perspective* (pp. 295–319). New York: Academic Press.

Rutter, M. (1983b). School effects on pupil progress: research findings and policy implications. *Child Development,* 54, 1–29.

Rutter, M. (1984a). Family and school influences: meanings, mechanisms and implications. In A. R. Nicol (Ed.), *Longitudinal studies in child psychology and psychiatry; practical lessons from research experience.* Chichester: Wiley (in press).

Rutter, M. (1984b). Continuities and discontinuities in socio-emotional development: empirical and conceptual perspectives. In R. Emde & R. Harmon (Eds), *Continuities and discontinuities in development.* New York: Plenum Press.

Rutter, M. & Giller, H. (1983). *Juvenile delinquency: trends and perspectives.* Harmondsworth, Middlesex: Penguin.

Rutter, M. & Madge, N. (1976). *Cycles of disadvantage.* London: Heinemann Educational.

Rutter, M., Maughan, B., Mortimore, P., Ouston, J. & Smith, A. (1979). *Fifteen thousand hours: secondary schools and their effects on children.* London: Open Books; Cambridge, MA: Harvard University Press.

Rutter, M., Quinton, D. & Liddle, C. (1983). Parenting in two generations: looking backwards and looking forwards. In N. Madge (Ed.), *Families at risk* (pp. 60–98). London: Heinemann Educational.

Sackett, G. P. (1982). Can single processes explain effects of postnatal influences on primate development. In R. N. Emde & R. J. Harmon (Eds), *The development of attachment and affiliative systems* (pp. 3–12). New York: Plenum Press.

Scarr, S. (Ed.) (1981). *Race, social class and individual differences in IQ.* Hillsdale, NJ: Lawrence Erlbaum.

Scarr, S. & Weinberg, R. A. (1983). The Minnesota adoption studies: genetic differences and malleability. *Child Development*, 54, 260–267.

Scarr, S., Webber, P. L., Weinberg, R. A. & Wittig, M. A. (1981). Personality resemblance among adolescents and their parents in biologically related and adoptive families. *Journal of Personality and Social Psychology*, 40, 885–898.

Seitz, V. (1981). Intervention and sleeper effects: a reply to Clarke and Clarke. *Developmental Review*, 1, 361–373.

Shields, J. (1980). Genetics and mental development. In M. Rutter (Ed.), *Scientific foundations of developmental psychiatry* (pp. 8–24). London: Heinemann Medical.

Skuse, D. (1984). Extreme deprivation in early childhood: II. Therapeutic issues and a comparative review. *Journal of Child Psychology and Psychiatry*, 25, 543–572.

Thomas, A., Chess, S. & Birch, H. G. (1968). *Temperament and behavior disorders in children*. New York: University Press.

Tizard, B. & Hodges, J. (1978). The effect of early institutional rearing on the development of eight-year-old children. *Journal of Child Psychology and Psychiatry*, 19, 99–118.

Tonge, W. L., James, D. S. & Hillam, S. M. (1975). *Families without hope: a controlled study of 33 problem families*. British Journal of Psychiatry Special Publication No. 11.

Triseliotis, J. & Russell, J. (1984). *Hard to place: the outcome of adoption and residential care of children*. London: Heinemann Educational.

van Eerdewegh, M. M., Bieri, M. D., Parrilla, R. H. & Clayton, P. J. (1982). The bereaved child. *British Journal of Psychiatry*, 140, 23–29.

Wallerstein, J. S. & Kelly, J. B. (1980). *Surviving the break up: how children and parents cope with divorce*. New York: Basic Books.

Werner, E. E. & Smith, R. S. (1982). *Vulnerable, but invincible: a longitudinal study of resilient children and youth*. New York: McGraw-Hill.

West, D. J. (1982). *Delinquency: its roots, careers and prospects*. London: Heinemann Educational.

West, D. J. & Farrington, D. P. (1973). *Who becomes delinquent?* London: Heinemann Educational.

West, D. J. & Farrington, D. P. (1977). *The delinquent way of life*. London: Heinemann Educational.

Wolkind, S. (1974). The components of "affectionless psychopathy" in institutionalized children. *Journal of Child Psychology and Psychiatry*, 15, 215–220.

Wolkind, S. N. & Kruk, S. (1984). From child to parent: early separation and the adoption to motherhood. In A. R. Nicol (Ed.), *Longitudinal studies in child psychology and psychiatry: practical lessons from research experience*. Chichester: Wiley (in press).

Yarrow, L. J. (1963). Dimensions of maternal care. *Merrill-Palmer Quarterly of Behavior and Development*, 9, 101–114.

Yarrow, L. J. & Klein, R. P. (1980). Environmental discontinuity associated with transition from foster to adoptive homes. *International Journal of Behavioral Development*, 3, 311–322.

Yule, W. & Raynes, N. V. (1972). Behavioural characteristics of children in residential care in relation to indices of separation. *Journal of Child Psychology and Psychiatry*, 13, 149–258.

Situational Influences

[20]

Ronald V. Clarke and Derek B. Cornish

Modeling Offenders' Decisions: A Framework for Research and Policy

ABSTRACT

Developments in a number of academic disciplines—the sociology of deviance, criminology, economics, psychology—suggest that it is useful to see criminal behavior not as the result of psychologically and socially determined dispositions to offend, but as the outcome of the offender's broadly rational choices and decisions. This perspective provides a basis for devising models of criminal behavior that (1) offer frameworks within which to locate existing research, (2) suggest directions for new research, (3) facilitate analysis of existing policy, and (4) help to identify potentially fruitful policy initiatives. Such models need not offer comprehensive explanations; they may be limited and incomplete, yet still be "good enough" to achieve these important policy and research purposes. To meet this criterion they need to be specific to particular forms of crime, and they need separately to describe both the processes of involvement in crime and the decisions surrounding the commission of the offense itself. Developing models that are crime specific and that take due account of rationality will also demand more knowledge about the ways in which offenders process and evaluate relevant information. Such a decision perspective appears to have most immediate payoff for crime control efforts aimed at reducing criminal opportunity.

Most theories about criminal behavior have tended to ignore the offender's decision making—the conscious thought processes that give purpose to and justify conduct, and the underlying cognitive mechanisms by which information about the world is selected, attended to, and processed. The source of this neglect is the apparent conflict between

Ronald Clarke was until recently Head of the Home Office Research and Planning Unit and is now Professor of Criminal Justice, Temple University. Derek Cornish is Lecturer in Psychology in the Department of Social Science and Administration, London School of Economics.

decision-making concepts and the prevailing determinism of most criminological theories. Whether framed in terms of social or psychological factors, these theories have traditionally been concerned to explain the criminal dispositions of particular individuals or groups. More recently, faced with the need to explain not just the genesis of people's involvement in crime but also the occurrence of particular criminal acts, greater attention has been paid by theory to the immediate environmental context of offending. But the resulting accounts of criminal behavior have still tended to suggest deterministic models in which the criminal appears as a relatively passive figure; thus he or she is seen either as prey to internal or external forces outside personal control, or as the battlefield upon which these forces resolve their struggle for the control of behavioral outcomes.

A number of developments, however, have combined to question the adequacy of explanations or models of offending that do not take account of the offender's perceptions and thought processes. Interest in the criminal's view of his world—characteristic of the "Chicago School" of sociology—revived during the early 1960s within the sociology of deviance that was beginning to stress the importance of developing an understanding of the offender's perspective. In mainstream criminology a similar revival of interest was also fueled by the apparent failure of the rehabilitative ideal—and hence, many argued, of deterministic approaches to criminological explanation. Disenchantment with treatment also shifted attention and resources to other means of crime control, such as incapacitation, deterrence, and environmental approaches to crime prevention; and it became apparent that offenders' perceptions might be salient to the success of these alternatives. As a result, interest grew in the 1970s in ecological studies of criminal activity, in criminal life histories, in cohort studies of criminal careers, and in offenders' accounts of how they went about their activities. At the same time, other academic disciplines such as economics and psychology were exploring, and in some cases applying to criminological problems, concepts and models of information processing and decision making.

Despite the vigor with which these diverse developments have been pursued, little serious attempt has been made to synthesize them; in particular, no concerted attempt has been made to draw out their implications for thinking about crime control policies. This may not be surprising given that most sociologists of deviance—whose theoretical concerns most directly corresponded to those of criminologists—had repudiated criminology's crime control goals (see Sparks 1980). And the antideterministic rhetoric that accompanied the explorations of deviancy sociologists, to say nothing of the ideological climate within which their studies tended to be conducted, further limited the impact both of methodologies and findings on mainstream criminology.

This essay reviews these developments primarily from the standpoint of their possible contribution to crime control policies. This might seem unnecessarily and even harmfully restrictive, but a narrowing of focus can sometimes be an advantage in policy-relevant research. When describing the long-term development of the Home Office Research Unit's program of crime control research, we have argued (Clarke and Cornish 1983) that simple and parsimonious accounts of criminal behavior—such as those provided by dispositional or situational theories—can have considerable heuristic value. They do not have to be "complete" explanations of criminal conduct, but only ones "good enough" to accommodate existing research and to suggest new directions for empirical enquiry or crime control policy. As soon as they no longer serve these ends they should be modified or discarded. We illustrated our argument by tracing the successive development of (i) dispositional theories "good enough" to guide research into treatment effectiveness; (ii) "environmental/learning" theories that accounted for the principal findings of the treatment research (that under the powerful influence of the contemporary environment the effects of intervention tend to dissipate rapidly); (iii) "situational" accounts that were developed from the environmental/learning perspective in order to guide the direction of research into crime prevention; and (iv) rudimentary "choice" theories that were developed to provide a means of understanding crime displacement (which is often the result of situational crime prevention measures).

It is with the enhancement and refinement of rational choice models of crime, made necessary by the recent growth of research interest documented below, that this essay is concerned. Section I documents the convergence of interest among a variety of academic disciplines—the sociology of deviance, criminology, economics, and cognitive psychology—upon a conception of crime as the outcome of rational choices and decisions. A brief and selective review is undertaken of each discipline's major contributions to the notion of crime as the outcome of rational choices—the intention being to provide a flavor of each approach and a summary of what seem to be its main limitations. Section II outlines the main requirements of decision models, temporarily "good enough" to explain the processes of criminal involvement (initial involvement, continuance, and desistance) and the occurrence of criminal events. In essence, these models are flowchart diagrams that identify the main decision points and set out the groups of factors bearing upon the decisions made. For reasons that we discuss, decision models need to be specific to particular kinds of crime, and we have chosen to illustrate the construction of such models with the example of residential burglary. In conclusion, Section III discusses the implications of the decision models for ways of thinking about crime control policies and associated research efforts.

I. Relevant Concepts

The following discussion of research relevant to the rationality of offending is couched in the form of brief reviews—and even briefer critiques—of the contributions made by each of the disciplines concerned. The reviews are intended to illustrate the confluence of interest in rationality and to provide the material for the synthesis of concepts and findings attempted in Section II.

A. *Sociology of Deviance*

In contrast to most earlier sociological formulations, the "deviancy theories" that were developed in the 1960s explicitly emphasized the cultural relativity of definitions of delinquency, the relationship between social control and the distribution of political and economic power in society, and the need to appreciate the meaning of deviance from the actor's perspective. Of greater relevance for our purposes, these theories also explicitly rejected deterministic and pathological explanations of crime in favor of those emphasizing its purposive, rational, and mundane aspects (see Taylor, Walton, and Young 1973; Box 1981)—concerns also shared by much previous oral history research (Bennett 1981). For example, Taylor et al. asserted that ". . . a social theory must have reference to men's teleology—their purposes, their beliefs and the context in which they act out these purposes and beliefs. . . . Thus men rob banks because they believe they may enrich themselves, not because something biologically propels them through the door . . ." (p. 61).

A substantial body of ethnographic work illustrates and supports many of the tenets of deviancy sociology. The following examples relate to the rational, largely nonpathological, and commonplace nature of much crime and illustrate how it is accommodated in the individual's day-to-day life:

i) Howard Becker's (1963) observation—based on his studies of marijuana use among jazz musicians in the 1950s—that deviants frequently see their conduct as a rational and obvious response to the pressures and opportunities of their particular circumstances. They may come to this position in a series of rationalizing "private conversations" in which they reconcile public and private morality. To justify their conduct, they may make use of "techniques of neutralization" (Matza 1964; Sheley 1980) such as: "everyone else does it"; "I am only borrowing it"; "he shouldn't have started it," and so on.

ii) Evidence from the life histories of individual offenders that criminal involvement is frequently initiated by relatives, friends, or acquaintances, and hence that the drift into crime is seen as unremarkable and almost natural (Samuel 1981); that legal and illegal ways of earning a living are not necessarily in conflict and may even be complementary (Klockars 1974; Prus and Irini 1980; Maguire 1982); that offenders frequently develop an increasingly more sophisticated and businesslike approach to crime (Shover 1972); and that certain forms of crime, such as bank robbery or truck hijacking, provide both the excitement and the large sums of money that are requirements of "life in the fast lane" (Gibbs and Shelly 1982).

iii) Documentation from participant-observation research that in many (if not most) occupational groups, such as waiters (Henry 1978), bread roundsmen (Ditton 1977), and dockworkers (Mars 1974), pilfering and cheating are commonplace and are largely accepted by managers and workers alike as legitimate perquisites. Indeed, as Denzin (1977) suggests in his case study of the American liquor industry, illegal activity may be routine, institutionalized, and essential to the satisfactory performance of the industry.

iv) Evidence that offenders may decide that the risks of continued criminal behavior are not justified by the rewards: among Parker's (1974) group of adolescents many gave up shoplifting and opportunistic theft of car radios when, as a consequence of increased police activity, some of their number were apprehended and placed in custody. West's (1978) study of the careers of young thieves provides similar evidence of the rational nature of decisions to desist.

v) Matza's (1964) observation that much delinquency is "episodic"— that individuals choose to engage in delinquency at certain times but not at others; that "manufacture of excitement" provides the reason for much adolescent delinquency; and that much offending is of a petty, everyday, even "mundane" character. Similarly, Humphreys's (1970) findings showed that even behavior commonly viewed as pathological—casual homosexual encounters in public lavatories—often represents clearly encapsulated episodes within essentially normal heterosexual and "respectable" life-styles.

vi) The observation made by Cohen (1972) in his study of clashes between groups of "mods" and "rockers" and by Marsh, Rosser, and Harre (1978) in their studies of football hooliganism, that much of the "uncontrollable" violence between rival gangs of youths is highly ritualized; it rarely causes serious injury and is calculated to produce maximum effect upon onlookers.

vii) Evidence from interviews with offenders convicted of serious violence (Athens 1980; Felson and Steadman 1983) that many apparently unpremeditated or impulsive acts of violence are in fact the result of intentions formed during a sequence of confrontations between offender and victim immediately prior to the incident or sometimes even days or weeks beforehand.

While deviancy theory has generated a mass of suggestive data on the perspectives, attitudes, and life-styles of offenders, its limitations in terms of the crime control orientation of this discussion stem from three of its fundamental premises—the deliberate eschewal of the test of immediate practical or policy relevance, the belief that individuals are in a position to provide comprehensive and valid accounts of the reasons for their behavior, and the rejection of more quantitative and controlled methods of data collection. The end result is that although the ideas produced may provide valuable insights and hypotheses, their validity and generalizability are frequently suspect.

B. Criminology

The past two decades have seen a great expansion of criminological research—largely the result of direct funding by governments—and a marked change in the topics investigated. General disillusion with the rehabilitative ideal and criticisms of the determinism of mainstream criminology, especially in Britain, meant that credence was once more given to "classical" views about crime that emphasized the offender's own responsibility for his conduct. This has been reflected in the reaffirmation of the importance of such sentencing principles as just desert and due process for juvenile offenders, as well as an increased interest in deterrent sentencing and incapacitation. And in response to the same disappointment with rehabilitation, criminologists began to explore methods of prevention focused not upon the offender's inner personality but on the immediate circumstances surrounding the offense. Improved understanding was sought about the rewards of crime, the relationship between criminal opportunities and crime, and the ways in which crime becomes part of the offender's everyday life. Some of the themes of these new lines of research can be grouped together as follows:

i) The findings of *longitudinal cohort studies* (e.g., Wolfgang, Figlio, and Sellin 1972; Petersilia 1980; West 1982) that, while large proportions of boys in any age group may commit acts of delinquency, most even of the more persistent offenders appear to desist from crime as they reach their late teens or twenties. This may be because they decide that continued criminality is incompatible with the demands of holding a full-time job or settling down to marriage and a family (see Greenberg 1977; Trasler 1979)—or for some it may represent a shift from "street crime" to occupational deviance.

ii) Recent research in the *ecological* tradition that has inferred from the distribution of particular crimes that offenders make rational choices. For example, on the basis of findings that it is the homes on the borderlines of affluent districts that are at most risk of burglary, Brantingham and Brantingham (1975) suggested that burglars preying on such districts will select the nearest of the suitable targets because escape may be easier and because they prefer to operate where they feel least conspicuous. Similar considerations of reducing risk and effort, minimizing inconvenience, and trading on familiarity explain other findings about the ecology of crime, such as that juvenile offenders seldom stray far from their immediate neighborhoods (e.g., Downes 1966); that crimes tend to be committed en route between an offender's place of residence and his habitual place of work or leisure (Rengert and Wasilchick 1980); that offenses tend to cluster along main roads (Fink 1969; Luedtke and Associates 1970; Wilcox 1974); that neighborhoods with easily understandable "grid" layouts tend to have higher rates of victimization than those with more "organic" street layouts, that is, with winding avenues, culs-de-sac, or crescents (Bevis and Nutter 1977); and that offenders' "images of the city"—their familiarity with its different parts or their perception of the differential ease or rewards of offending—correspond with observed crime patterns (Carter and Hill 1979).

iii) *Crime-specific* studies of burglary (Scarr 1973; Reppetto 1974; Waller and Okihiro 1978; Walsh 1980; Maguire 1982; Winchester and Jackson 1982), vandalism (Ley and Cybrinwsky 1974; Clarke 1978), and shoplifting (Walsh 1978), which have shown that the vulnerability of particular targets can be explained largely on the basis of factors such as ease of opportunity, low risk, and high gain. For example, Winchester and Jackson (1982) found in their study of burglary in Southeast England that the most important factors determining victimization were the apparent rewards, the chances that the house was occupied, and the siting of the building, which either facilitated or restricted access. Thus they found that houses standing in their own grounds were much more likely to be burglarized than ones in the middle of a terrace. Waller and Okihiro (1978) and Reppetto (1974) found that apartment blocks given protection by a doorman had particularly low levels of burglary. Shoplifters are more likely to operate in large self-service stores where it is easy to steal, and which provide a more impersonal target (Walsh 1978). As for vandalism, the targets are more likely to be public property such as telephone kiosks or bus shelters (Sturman 1978) or private property that has been abandoned or left in a state of disrepair (Ley and Cybrinwsky 1974). In other words, vandals appear to choose targets that are afforded less protection or (perhaps) where repair will not cause individual owners too much hardship.

iv) These findings from crime-specific studies about target vulnerability are complemented by information obtained from offenders themselves. For example, *interviews* with convicted burglars by Reppetto (1974), Waller and Okihiro (1978), Walsh (1980), Maguire (1982), and Bennett and Wright (1983, 1984) confirm that, the decision having been made about the locality in which to commit burglary, the choice of the particular house is made on judgments of the likelihood of its being occupied and the difficulty of entering without being seen. And interviews with muggers (Lejeune 1977) have shown that victims are chosen as being unlikely to resist while yielding an acceptable payoff.

v) Studies of the *opportunity structure* for crime have shown that fluctuations in levels of offending reflect the supply of available opportunities. This has been demonstrated for auto crime by Wilkins (1964), Gould (1969), and Mansfield, Gould, and Namenwirth (1974) and for residential burglary by Cohen and Felson (1979). The latter mounted a persuasive case for regarding increases in burglary as the outcome of the increased portability of electronic goods and of an increase in numbers of unoccupied houses as more women go out to work.

vi) *Crime prevention experiments* have shown for a wide variety of offenses (including vandalism, car theft, football hooliganism, aircraft hijacking, and theft or robbery on public transport) that reducing opportunities or increasing risks through environmental management and design can achieve reductions in the incidence of crime (see Clarke 1983). In many cases offenders appear to decide that the risks and effort of offending are no longer worthwhile. For example, few of the motorists prevented from using illegal "slugs" in a particular district of New York by the installation of redesigned meters are likely to have parked their cars in some other more distant place so as to save a few pennies (Decker 1972). In other cases, reduction of opportunities has simply displaced the attention of offenders to some other time, place, or target of crime (see Reppetto 1976). For instance, the introduction of steering-column locks on all new cars from 1971 onward did not produce the expected immediate reduction of car thefts in England and Wales—because most car theft is for temporary use, offenders simply turned their attention to unprotected pre-1971 models (Mayhew et al. 1976).

These various strands of research provide much useful information about offenders' decision making, but they have been pursued too much in isolation from each other and without the benefit of a coherent theoretical perspective. The decision-making concepts employed have been derived from common sense or culled from the unsystematic accounts of offenders. In consequence the relevance of the research for policy is limited. For example, the concept of displacement—of central importance for policy-making—has not been disassociated from its theoretical origins as the outcome of powerful internal drives toward criminality. This has meant that much, perhaps undue, skepticism has been expressed about the value of situational crime prevention. But it is not difficult to see how displacement could be accommodated within a decision-making framework (i.e., as the outcome of choices and decisions made by the offender in the face of changed circumstances) and how this might give a better basis for advocating the reduction of criminal opportunities.

C. Economics

As with recent work in the sociology of deviance and criminology, developments in the economic analysis of criminal behavior have tended to revive some of the concerns of classical criminology. Located in the utilitarian tradition of Beccaria and Bentham, these approaches argue that individuals, whether criminal or not, share in common the properties of being active, rational decision makers who respond to incentives and deterrents. In Gary Becker's words, "a useful theory of criminal behavior can dispense with special theories of anomie, psychological inadequacies, or inheritance of special traits and simply extend the economist's usual analysis of choice" (1968, p. 170).

In contrast to classical economic and criminological theories, however, the new economic formulations take account of the existence and influence of a restricted number of potential individual differences (see Ehrlich's [1979] discussion of the role of "preferences" and Cook's [1980] discussion of subjective evaluation). The economists' emphasis on the importance of the concepts of rewards and costs and their associated probabilities has much in common with the accounts of behavioral psychology. Where economic models depart radically from behavioral ones is in their stress on the importance of the concept of choice.

To chart the various economic models of criminal behavior and the econometric studies to which these models have given rise is outside the purpose of this brief review (but see Palmer 1977; Orsagh and Witte 1981; Freeman 1983; Orsagh 1983; Pyle 1983), as is the extension of economists' interests into the fields of resource allocation by law enforcement agencies (Pyle 1983) or the development of complex mathematical models to study criminal justice decision making (Garber, Klepper, and Nagin 1983; Klepper, Nagin, and Tierney 1983). The relevance of economic models of rational choice to the present discussion may be summarized as follows:

i) Whatever their current limitations, economic models of criminal decision making effectively demystify and routinize criminal activity. Crime is assumed a priori to involve rational calculation and is viewed essentially as an economic transaction or a question of occupational choice—a view compatible with many of the recent sociological and criminological studies of crime as work (e.g., Letkemann 1973; Inciardi 1975; Akerstrom 1983; Waldo 1983). In the same way, phenomena such as displacement or recidivism can be provided with economic rationales as alternatives to explanations that emphasize offender pathology (see, e.g., Furlong and Mehay's [1981] econometric study of crime spillover).

ii) Such economic models are currently extending their analysis beyond crimes motivated predominantly by financial gain. Thus, attempts are being made to find room for nonpecuniary gains as a component of expected utilities (through their translation into monetary equivalents) and to suggest models for so-called expressive crimes—

such as those involving violence to the person (Ehrlich 1979)—which emphasize their responsiveness to incentives and deterrents.

iii) Economic models suggest that law enforcement agencies are justified in proceeding on the basis that criminals are deterrable; thus they both provide some grounds for optimism and suggest a range of factors (beyond traditional deterrence theory's preoccupation with certainty and severity of punishment) which might be manipulated in the interests of crime control. These include, for example, the potential rewards of crime and the degree of effort required. Similarly, exploration of the relationship between unemployment and crime (Orsagh and Witte 1981; Freeman 1983) also provides some economic rationale for rehabilitative programs designed to improve offenders' prospects of legitimate work.

Despite the welcome rigor these contributions have brought to criminological theorizing and to the evaluation of policy, there are a number of problems that for the purposes of the current discussion limit the usefulness of existing economic models of criminal decision making. A variety of economic models have recently been proposed (e.g., Heineke 1978; Orsagh and Witte 1981), which recognize the need to include individual differences, but they have generated little empirically based micro analysis of individual criminal behavior. Some attempts to study such models using individual-level data have recently been made (e.g., Witte 1980; Ghali 1982). But it remains the case that, as Manski (1978) pointed out, economic modelers seem largely unaware of the growing empirical data on criminal behavior from other disciplines; they continue to produce theoretical accounts of individual choice behavior which "are too idealized and abstract from too much of the criminal decision problem to serve as useful bases for empirical work" (p. 90). Where empirical investigations are undertaken they tend to be macro analyses using aggregated crime data; and the interaction between micro analysis (uninformed by empirical data) and macro analysis (using imperfect and inadequate data, and uninformed by relevant information about the bases of individual criminal decision making) may be impoverishing both efforts.

These criticisms suggest that current economic models have yet to achieve satisfactory accounts of the bases upon which individual criminals actually make choices, and that they may also underplay individual differences in information-processing capacities and strategies (Cook 1980). The question whether the increasingly sophisticated empirical research on deterrence using aggregated data provides a valid means of monitoring the effectiveness of criminal justice policy lies outside this discussion (but see Pyle 1983). So far as the development and evaluation of more specific crime prevention and control policies in relation to particular offenders and offenses is concerned, however, it may be that this requires the investigation of actual decision processes rather than the further elaboration, in isolation, of a priori models. In this connection it is interesting to note that, as a result of their review of empirical economic studies using aggregate and individual-level data, Orsagh and Witte (1981) remarked that the relationship between economic viability and crime might vary with the type of crime and the individual involved. Such comments indicate the pressing need for further empirical data, such as those provided by Holzman's (1983) study of labor force participation among robbers and burglars, to clarify these issues and to encourage the construction of narrow-band empirically informed models.

D. *Cognitive Psychology*

With the few exceptions noted below, a considerable body of recent psychological research on information processing and decision making has passed largely unnoticed by criminologists. The impetus for this work, which itself contributed to criminological theory, should be briefly mentioned. During the 1960s, many psychologists were becoming disenchanted with the concepts of personality traits and predispositions as determinants of behavior; more attractive was the suggestion of radical behaviorism that the most important influences in relation to criminal behavior (reinforcements and punishments) lay outside the organism. This approach, which has some similarity to economic theories of crime, emphasized the importance not only of incentives and deterrents but also of current situational cues and opportunities. This latter emphasis became a primary influence on British studies of situational crime prevention (Mayhew et al. 1976), the further development of which drew attention to the need for a fuller understanding of criminal decisions (see Clarke and Cornish 1983).

Within academic psychology, the reaction during the last decade against the environmental determinism of radical behaviorism has led to an increasing recognition of the important role played by cognitive processes. This can be seen in the development of more sophisticated "social learning" theories (Bandura 1969, 1977) that stressed additional mechanisms of learning, such as imitation (which required the assumption of symbolic mediational cognitive processes), and reintroduced person variables in the guise of cognitive competencies and capacities (Mischel 1973, 1979). Several attempts to apply selected social learning concepts to an analysis of criminal behavior have been made (e.g., Akers 1977; Feldman 1977; Conger 1978).

It is not in respect of social learning theory alone, however, that developments of direct relevance to an understanding of criminal decision making have occurred. Studies of the professional judgments of clinicians and similar personnel concerning risky decision making, and of information-processing strategies in decision making, provide their relevant insights and analogies. The contributions itemized below relate as much to the methods and concepts as to substantive findings in this area:

i) Psychological studies of professional judgments made in clinical and similar settings have for a long while suggested that even experts often handle information in less than perfectly rational or efficient ways (Meehl 1954; Wilkins and Chandler 1965; Wiggins 1973).

ii) These findings received further support from early studies of risky decision making (see Kozielecki [1982] for a review) which suggested that people did not always behave in accordance with economic models of the rational, efficient decision maker—they frequently failed to make decisions that were objectively the "best" (Cornish 1978). An attempt to apply one such model (the subjective expected utility model) to an experimental study of the factors involved in juveniles' decisions about committing hypothetical crimes is reported by Cimler and Beach (1981).

iii) Some of the reasons for the failure of a priori models to explain decision making were identified by Slovic and Lichtenstein (1968). They suggested that real-life decision makers might be led to pay selective attention to certain risk dimensions over others by reason of their "importance-beliefs"—notions derived from past experience, logical analysis of the decision task, or even quite irrational fears and prejudices.

iv) These conclusions led naturally to an increased emphasis upon information-processing models and strategies in relation to real-life decision making (see Cornish [1978] on gambling; Carroll [1982] on criminal behavior). "Process tracing"—a technique for studying decision making as it actually occurs in natural settings by asking subjects to think aloud about the decision task (Kleinmuntz 1968)—has recently been applied to the investigation of offending decisions by Carroll and Herz (1981) and Bennett and Wright (1983).

v) Payne (1980) has suggested that more attention should be paid to the characteristics of the decision maker as information processor and their effect on the handling of choice problems. Warr and Knapper's (1968) model for person perception emphasizes the effects on information processing of the perceiver's stable personal characteristics, of ephemeral moods, previous experiences, and expectations, and of the decision rules employed by the decision maker's "processing centre." Crucial to the operations involved might be Slovic and Lichtenstein's "importance-beliefs," Cook's (1980) "standing decisions," and the wider concept of "knowledge structures" used by Nisbett and Ross (1980).

vi) An emphasis on decision rules suggested that inferential "rules-of-thumb" are universally employed in order to enable decision making to proceed rapidly and effectively. Some of these judgmental heuristics (Tversky and Kahneman 1974; Kahneman, Slovic, and Tversky 1982) can lead to error: for example, too much attention may be paid to information that is readily available or recently presented, and inductive rules may be too quickly formulated on the basis of unrepresentative data.

vii) Finally, it appears that the riskiness of an individual's decisions may vary according to whether the decision is made alone, or as a group member. Early studies had suggested that group decision making tended to be more "risky"; hence the phenomenon was termed "risky-shift" (Pruitt 1971). Recent reviews (Myers and Lamm 1976), however, suggest a more complex picture in which group decisions may also become more cautious under certain conditions.

The facts that people do not always make the most "rational" decisions, that they may pay undue attention to less important information, that they employ shortcuts in the processing of information, and that group decisions may be different from individual ones are all clearly relevant to an understanding of criminal decision making. But cognitive psychology is still at an early stage in its development and the topics studied so far are not necessarily those that best illuminate criminal decision making. For example, there has been perhaps too much concentration upon bias and error in information processing (see Nisbett and Ross 1980), whereas, in fact, the judgmental heuristics involved usually enable individuals to cope economically and swiftly with very complex tasks (Bruner, Goodnow, and Austin 1956)—a process Simon

(1983) has termed "bounded rationality." And there are some other basic issues, perhaps of particular relevance to crime control policies, which have scarcely been addressed by the discipline. These include the extent to which cognitive strategies are produced consciously or unconsciously, the degree to which they are under the individual's own control, whether they indicate a predisposition to process information in a certain manner or merely a preference for doing so, and the extent to which individuals differ in their information-processing capacities and competencies.

Finally, of special relevance to the present discussion, the question has not properly been considered whether those individuals who habitually make criminal decisions think in different ways from other people. This, in fact, is the claim made by Yochelson and Samenow (1976) on the basis of detailed clinical interviews with 240 criminals, most of whom had been detained in hospital as a result of being found guilty by reason of insanity. Yochelson and Samenow believe that criminals *choose* specific thinking patterns—of which they identify fifty-two characteristic modes including suspiciousness, self-seeking, manipulativeness, impulsiveness, concrete and compartmentalized thinking, and excitement or sensation seeking—which inevitably lead to crime. Such thought patterns, while internally logical, consistent, and hence "rational" to the offender, may be regarded as both irresponsible and irrational by the noncriminal.

Many methodological criticisms have been made of Yochelson and Samenow's work (e.g., Burchard 1977; Jacoby 1977; Nietzel 1979; Sarbin 1979; Vold 1979), but it remains true that the thinking patterns identified have much in common with many of the concepts reviewed above, that is, with individual information-processing styles and strategies and with motivational and cognitive biases. Moreover, they reflect themes commonly encountered in criminal life histories (Hampson 1982) such as the offender's preoccupation with maintaining "machismo" and with "techniques of neutralization." This further reinforces the point that a full (and policy-relevant) understanding of the processes of criminal decision making will not be gained through studies of "normal" decision making alone.

II. Models of Criminal Decision Making

Even allowing for some selective perception on our part, we believe that the material in Section I demonstrates that during the past decade there has been a notable confluence of interest in the rational choice, nondeterministic view of crime. This is a natural perspective for law and economics, but it has also achieved wide currency in criminology's other parent disciplines—sociology and psychology—as well as within the different schools of criminology itself. That the shift is part of a broader intellectual movement is suggested by the increasing popularity of economic and rational choice analyses of behaviors other than crime. Why there should be this movement at the present time and what social forces and events might be implicated is difficult to say, but cross-fertilization of ideas between different groups of people working on similar problems always occurs, and certain individuals have deliberately applied the same theoretical perspective to a variety of different problems. For instance, Gary Becker (1968) pioneered his economic analyses of crime when dealing with the economics of discrimination and has since extended his method to choice of marriage partner (Becker 1973, 1974).

Despite the shift of interest described above, there has been little attempt to construct a synthesis—within a rational choice framework—of the concepts and findings provided by the various approaches. As an illustration of the value of such a synthesis, it is worth making brief reference to the approach adopted by one of us in a review of the research on the determinants of gambling behavior (Cornish 1978). While not adopting so explicit a decision-making orientation, the review made similar use of concepts from sociology, psychology, and economics as a basis for analyzing existing control measures and for suggesting future directions for policy and research. It recognized, first, the importance of rational though not exclusively economic considerations when explaining a behavior commonly regarded as being pathologically motivated; second, the need to treat gambling, not as a unitary form of behavior, but as a collection of disparate behaviors each with their own distinctive features; third, and as a corollary, the need to pay close attention to situational factors relating to the gambling "event"; fourth, the need to develop explanations of gambling behavior which would make specific reference to factors determining, respectively, likelihood and degree of involvement; fifth, the role of learning in the development of heavy involvement in certain forms of gambling; and last, the scope for both exploiting and controlling gambling behavior through manipulation of people's information-processing activities.

The models of crime presented below also offer a way of synthesizing a diverse range of concepts and findings for the purpose of guiding policy and research, but they are developed within the context of much more explicit decision making. They are not models in which relationships are expressed either in mathematical terms (as in, e.g., economic models) or in the form of testable propositions (see, e.g., Brantingham and Brantingham's [1978] model of target selection). Nor are they even "decision trees" that attempt to model the successive steps in a complex decision process (see Walsh [1980] for an example relating to burglary). Rather, they are schematic representations of the key decision points in criminal behavior and of the various social, psychological, and environmental factors bearing on the decisions reached. Our models resemble most closely the kind of flow diagrams frequently employed to represent complex social processes—for example, the explanatory models for fear of crime developed by Skogan and Maxfield (1981) and for victimization proneness by Hindelang, Gottfredson, and Garofalo (1978).

The models, which need to be separately developed for each specific form of crime, are not theories in themselves but rather the blueprints for theory. They owe much to early attempts to model aspects of criminal decision making by Brantingham and Brantingham (1978), Brown and Altman (1981), and Walsh (1978, 1980). But these earlier models were largely confined to just one of the criminal decision processes—target selection—and they also depended upon a commonsense explication of the likely decision steps taken by the "rational" criminal. Our models are concerned not just with the decision to commit a particular crime, but also with decisions relating to criminal "readiness" or involvement in crime; and they also take some account of the recent psychological research on cognitive processing.

This research is still at a relatively early stage, and as yet there is only a comparatively small body of criminological data relevant to decision making upon which to draw. Any attempt to develop decision models of crime must at this stage be tentative. Thus our aim is only to provide models that are at present "good enough" to accommodate existing knowledge and to guide research and policy initiatives. Even such "good enough" models, however, have to meet the criticism that they assume too much rationality on the part of the offender. But as the review in Section I has indicated, rationality must be conceived of in broad terms. For instance, even if the choices made or the decision processes themselves are not optimal ones, they may make sense to the offender and represent his best efforts at optimizing outcomes. Moreover, expressive as well as economic goals can, of course, be characterized as rational. And lastly, even where the motivation appears to have a pathological component, many of the subsequent planning and decision-making activities (such as choice of victims or targets) may be rational.

A. Modeling Criminal Involvement and Criminal Events

There is a fundamental distinction to be made between explaining the involvement of particular individuals in crime and explaining the occurrence of criminal events. Most criminological theorists have been preoccupied with the former problem and have neglected the latter. They have sought to elucidate the social and psychological variables underlying criminal dispositions, on the apparent assumption that this is all that is needed to explain the commission of crime itself. But the existence of a suitably motivated individual goes only part of the way to explaining the occurrence of a criminal event—a host of immediately precipitating, situational factors must also be taken into account. And a further distinction that must be recognized by theorists concerns the various stages of criminal involvement—initial involvement, continuance, and desistance. That these separate stages of involvement may require different explanatory theories, employing a range of different variables, has been made clear by the findings of recent research into criminal careers (see Farrington 1979; Petersilia 1980).

The distinctions between event and involvement have to be maintained when translating traditional perspectives into decision terms. It may be that the concepts of choice or decision are more readily translatable and more fruitful in relation to continuance and desistance than to initial involvement, but to some extent this may depend on the particular offense under consideration. For some offenses, such as shoplifting or certain acts of vandalism, it might be easier to regard the first offense as determined by the multiplicity of factors identified in existing criminological theory and as committed more or less unthinkingly, that is, without a close knowledge or consideration of the implications. But however much people may be propelled by predisposing factors to the point where crime becomes a realistic course of action, it may still be legitimate (or, at least, useful) to see them as having a choice about whether to become involved. Once the offense is committed, however, the individual acquires direct knowledge about the consequences and implications of that behavior; and this knowledge becomes much more salient to future decisions about continuance or desistance. It may also provide the background of experience to render initial involvement in another crime a considered choice (see Walsh's [1980] discussion of burglary as a training ground for other crimes).

B. The Need for Models to Be Crime Specific

The discussion above has anticipated another important requirement of decision models of crime: whether of involvement or of event, these must be specific to particular kinds of crime. Recent preoccupation with offender pathology and the desire to construct general statements about crime, deviancy, and rule breaking have consistently diverted attention from the important differences between types of crime—the people committing them, the nature of the motivations involved, and the behaviors required. Whatever the purposes and merits of academic generalization, it is essential for policy goals that these important distinctions be maintained. And, moreover, it will usually be necessary to make even finer distinctions between crimes than those provided by legal categories. For instance, it will not usually be sufficient to develop models for a broad legal category such as burglary (Reppetto 1976). Rather it will be necessary to differentiate at least between commercial and residential burglary (as has already been done in a number of studies) and perhaps even between different kinds of residential and commercial burglaries. For example, burglary in public housing projects will be a quite different problem from burglary in affluent commuter areas, or from burglary in multioccupancy inner-city dwellings. And the same is obviously true of many other crimes, such as vandalism, robbery, rape, and fraud. The degree of specificity required will usually demand close attention to situational factors, especially in event models.

The emphasis on specificity, however, should not be taken as contradicting the fact, established in research on criminal careers, that particular individuals may be involved in a variety of criminal activities. But their involvement in separate activities does not necessarily derive from the same sources, though *in practice* the separate processes of involvement in different crimes may be interrelated. This means that in explaining a particular individual's pattern of criminal activity it may be necessary to draw upon a variety of specific models and perhaps to describe the links between them. However, this is a matter for those interested in the etiology of individual criminality and in related policies—such as rehabilitation and incapacitation—focused upon the individual offender. Whether they be specialists or generalists, our own interest in offenders is primarily restricted to occasions when they are involved in the offense under consideration. This is because each form of crime is likely to require specific remedies and, by shifting the focus from offender to offense, a range of neglected options is likely to be brought into the policy arena. All our models reflect this focus of interest and our purpose below is to lay out their formal requirements.

C. *The Example of Residential Burglary*

We have chosen below to illustrate the construction of decision models of crime through the example of residential burglary in a middle-class suburb. Although it might have made more interesting reading to have selected a less obviously instrumental offense, our choice in the end was made for reasons of convenience: knowledge about this offense is relatively well advanced and we have been involved in some of the recently completed research (Clarke and Hope, in press). This work suggests that the offenders involved are generally rather older and more experienced than those operating in public housing estates, but less sophisticated than those preying on much wealthier residences. Since decision models are for us primarily intended to make criminological theorizing of greater relevance to crime control policies, we believe that practical considerations should play a large part in determining the specificity of the model: the offense modeled should be as specific as current knowledge allows, while at the same time sufficiently common or serious to justify the development of special preventive policies.

In the following pages we will present four models—one concerned with the criminal event and the others with the three stages of criminal involvement—since the decision processes for each model are quite different. It may not always be necessary for policy purposes to model all four processes; indeed, as said above, decisions about which models to develop, and at what level of detail, ought to be governed by policy goals. Our present aim is primarily didactic: first, to set out the models in order to identify the links between them; second, to locate and to give some hint of the ways in which existing criminological data might be interpreted within a decision framework; and third, to illustrate how, through development and examination of the models, the most fruitful points of intervention in the criminal decision process might be identified. As our purpose is not to develop fully elaborated decision models of residential burglary, but only to demonstrate their feasibility, we shall not usually indicate where they draw upon empirical findings (which in any case have been mentioned above) and where they rely upon our own armchair theorizing.

One obvious implication of the need for specificity is that the configuration of the models may vary significantly among different kinds of crime. For instance, models involving offenses which appear to depend primarily upon "presented" opportunities (e.g., shoplifting, Carroll and Herz [1981]) will probably be simpler than those (such as residential burglary) involving opportunities that must be "sought" (see Maguire 1980). And these in turn will be simpler than those involving offenses where the opportunities are created or planned (e.g., bank robberies).

D. Initial Involvement

Figure 1 represents the process of initial involvement in residential burglary in a middle-class suburb. There are two important decision points: the first (box 7) is the individual's recognition of his "readiness" to commit this particular offense in order to satisfy certain of his needs for money, goods, or excitement. Readiness involves rather more than receptiveness: it implies that the individual has actually contemplated this form of crime as a solution to his needs and has decided that under the right circumstances he would commit the offense. In reaching this decision he will have evaluated other ways of satisfying his needs and this evaluation will naturally be heavily influenced by his previous learning and experience—his moral code, his view of the kind of person he is, his personal and vicarious experiences of crime, and the degree to which he can plan and exercise foresight. These variables in turn are related to various historical and contemporaneous background factors—psychological, familial, and sociodemographic (box 1). It is with the influence of these background factors that traditional criminology has been preoccupied; they have been seen to determine the values, attitudes, and personality traits that dispose the individual to crime. In a decision-making context, however, these background influences are less directly criminogenic; instead they have an orienting function— exposing people to particular problems and particular opportunities and leading them to perceive and evaluate these in particular (criminal) ways. Moreover, the contribution of background factors to the final decision to commit crime would be much moderated by situational and transitory influences; and for certain sorts of crime (e.g., computer fraud) the individual's background might be of much less relevance than his immediate situation.

The second decision (box 8), actually to commit a burglary, is pre-cipitated by some chance event. The individual may suddenly need

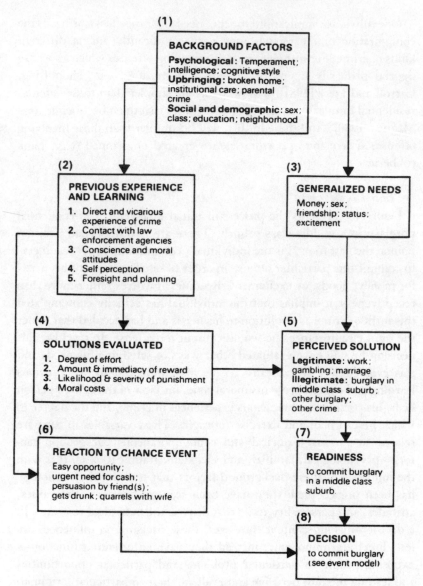

FIG. 1.—Initial involvement model (example: burglary in a middle-class suburb)

money, he may have been drinking with associates who suggest committing a burglary (for many offenses, especially those committed by juveniles, immediate pressure from the peer group is important), or he may perceive an easy opportunity for the offense during the course of his routine activities. In real life, of course, the two decision points may

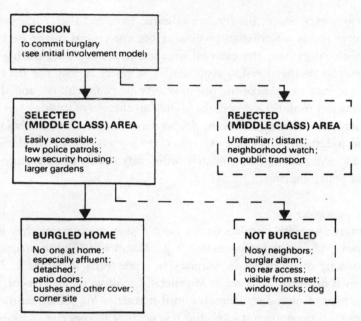

FIG. 2.—Event model (example: burglary in a middle-class suburb)

occur almost simultaneously and the chance event may not only pre-cipitate the decision to burgle, but may also play a part in the percep-tion and evaluation of solutions to generalized needs.

E. The Criminal Event

Figure 2 depicts the further sequence of decision making that leads to the burglar selecting a particular house. As mentioned above, for some other crimes the sequence will be much lengthier; and the less specific the offense being modeled, the more numerous the alternative choices. For example, should a more general model of burglary be required, a wider range of areas and housing types would have to be included (see Brantingham and Brantingham 1978). In the present case, however, there may be little choice of area in which to work, and in time this decision (and perhaps elements of later decisions) may become routine.

This is, of course, an idealized picture of the burglar's decision mak-ing. Where the formal complexity of the decision task is laid out in detail, as in Walsh's (1978, 1980) work, there may be a temptation to assume that it entails equally complex decision making. In real life, however, only patchy and inaccurate information will be available. Under these uncertain circumstances the offender's perceptions, his previous experience, his fund of criminal lore, and the characteristic features of his information processing become crucial to the decision reached. Moreover, the external situation itself may alter during the time span of the decision sequence. The result is that the decision process may be telescoped, planning may be rudimentary, and there may be last-minute (and perhaps ill-judged) changes of mind. Even this account may overemphasize the deliberative element, since alcohol may cloud judgment. Only research into these aspects of criminal decision making will provide event models sufficiently detailed and accurate to assist policy-making.

F. Continuance

Interviews with burglars have shown that in many cases they may commit hundreds of offenses (see, e.g., Maguire 1982); the process of continuing involvement in burglary is represented in figure 3. It is assumed here that, as a result of generally positive reinforcement, the frequency of offending increases until it reaches (or subsequently reduces to) some optimum level. But it is possible to conceive of more or less intermittent patterns of involvement for some individuals; and intermittent patterns may be more common for other types of offenses (e.g., those for which ready opportunities occur less frequently). It is unlikely that each time the offender sets out to commit an offense he will actively consider the alternatives, though this will sometimes be necessary as a result of a change in his circumstances or in the conditions under which his burglaries have to be committed. (These possibilities are discussed in more detail in regard to the "desistance" model of fig. 4.)

More important to represent in the continuing involvement model are the gradually changing conditions and personal circumstances that confirm the offender in his readiness to commit burglary. The diagram summarizes three categories of relevant variables. The first concerns an increase in professionalism: pride in improved skills and knowledge; successive reductions of risk and an improvement in haul through planning and careful selection of targets; and the acquisition of reliable fencing contacts. The second reflects some concomitant changes in lifestyle: a recognition of increased financial dependence on burglary; a choice of legitimate work to facilitate burglary; enjoyment of "life in the fast lane"; the devaluation of ordinary work; and the development of excuses and justifications for criminal behavior. Third, there will be changes in the offender's network of peers and associates and his rela-

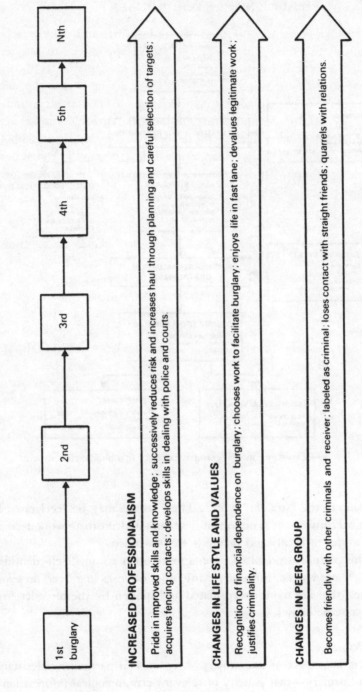

Increasing frequency of burglary (due to success) till personal optimum selected

1st burglary → 2nd → 3rd → 4th → 5th → Nth

INCREASED PROFESSIONALISM

Pride in improved skills and knowledge; successively reduces risk and increases haul through planning and careful selection of targets; acquires fencing contacts; develops skills in dealing with police and courts.

CHANGES IN LIFE STYLE AND VALUES

Recognition of financial dependence on burglary; chooses work to facilitate burglary; enjoys life in fast lane; devalues legitimate work; justifies criminality.

CHANGES IN PEER GROUP

Becomes friendly with other criminals and receiver; labeled as criminal; loses contact with straight friends; quarrels with relations.

Fig. 3.— Continuing involvement model (example: burglary in a middle-class suburb)

172   Ronald V. Clarke and Derek B. Cornish

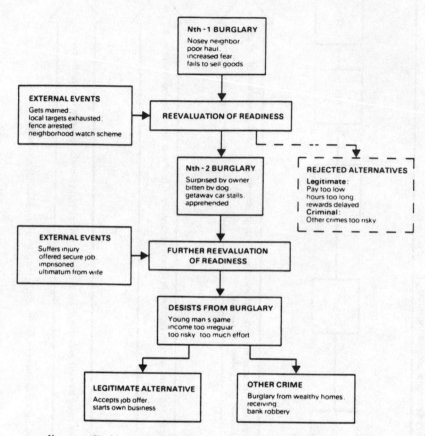

FIG. 4.—Desistance model (example: burglary in a middle-class suburb)

tionship to the "straight" world. These trends may be accelerated by criminal convictions as opportunities to obtain legitimate work decrease and as ties to family and relations are weakened.

This picture is premised upon a more open criminal self-identification. There will be, however, many other offenses (e.g., certain sexual crimes) that are more encapsulated and hidden by the offender from everyone he knows.

G. Desistance

It is in respect of the subject of figure 4 in particular—desistance from burglary—that paucity of relevant criminological information is especially evident. While the work of, for example, Parker (1974), Greenberg (1977), West (1978), Trasler (1979), Maguire (1982), and

West (1982) provides some understanding of the process of desistance, empirical data, whether relating to groups or individuals and in respect of particular sorts of crime, are very scanty. Nevertheless, there is sufficient information to provide in figure 4 an illustration of the offender's decision processes as he begins a renewed evaluation of alternatives to burglary. This follows aversive experiences during the course of offending and changes in his personal circumstances (age, marital status, financial requirements) and the neighborhood and community context in which he operates (changes of policing, depletion of potential targets). These result in his abandoning burglary in favor of some alternative solution either legitimate or criminal. While desistance may imply the cessation of all criminal activity, in other cases it may simply represent displacement to some other target (commercial premises rather than houses) or to another form of crime. Desistance is, in any case, not necessarily permanent and may simply be part of a continuing process of lulls in the offending of persistent criminals (West 1963) or even, perhaps, of a more casual drifting in and out of particular crimes.

H. Some General Observations

The decision models illustrated above should be seen as temporary, incomplete, and subject to continual revision as fresh research becomes available. Even now they could probably be improved by the explicit specification of linkages within and between models. Moreover, accepting the "good enough" criterion governing their development, they are still open to two general criticisms. On the one hand, it might be argued that the benefits of a decision approach have been oversold by selecting a crime such as burglary, which has clear instrumental goals and requires planning and foresight. However, the decision elements in many other forms of crime—such as fraud or traffic offenses (see Brown [1981] for the latter)—may be even more salient. And, as our earlier review suggests, a decision approach is applicable to all forms of crime, even apparently impulsive or irrational ones. On the other hand, considering the aptness of residential burglary for treatment in decision terms, one might have expected the resulting models to be better articulated and less dependent upon anecdotal evidence. Moreover, given the amount of further empirical data required to make even the burglary models adequate, can it be realistic to suggest that such models have to be developed for all the different kinds of crime? The answer must be that since the models are intended to assist policy-making, pragmatic considerations should be preeminent: the harm caused by the particular crime under consideration must be considered sufficient to justify the investment in research.

III. Conclusions

During the course of this discussion a number of deficiencies in current criminological theorizing have been identified. Many of these flow from two underlying assumptions: that offenders are different from other people and that crime is a unitary phenomenon. Hence, the preoccupation with the issue of initial involvement in crime and the failure to develop explanations for specific kinds of offending. Moreover, explanatory theories have characteristically been confined to a limited selection of variables derived from one or another of criminology's contributory disciplines; and none of the dominant theories has taken adequate account of situational variables. A decision-making approach, however, stresses the rational elements in criminal behavior and requires explanations to be specific to particular forms of crime. It also demands that attention be paid to the crucial distinction between criminal involvement (at its various stages) and criminal events. By doing so it provides a framework that can accommodate the full range of potentially relevant variables (including situational ones) and the various competing but partial theories.

A. Policy

These advantages for explanation also hold for analysis of policy. Instead of defining the search for effective policy in terms of coping with broad problems such as juvenile delinquency or the rise in crime, the decision models encourage a policy focus upon the specific crimes, such as school vandalism, joy riding, rape by strangers, and pub violence, which may be giving rise to the broader concerns. Breaking down larger problems into more clearly defined constituent parts usually affords a greater prospect of effective action. But the distinctions between crimes need to be finer, not only than those of existing theory (e.g., between instrumental and expressive offenses, or between predatory and violent offenses) but also than those provided by legal categories. In addition, the more comprehensive view of the determinants of crime provided by the interlocking decision models of involvement and event identifies a broader range of both policy options and possible points for intervention. Options can then be prioritized in relation to the specific offense under consideration in terms of practicality, immediacy of effect, and cost effectiveness. For example, the appropriate involvement and event models for joy riding (theft of vehicles for personal use) might suggest a variety of measures, including increased leisure provision for juveniles at risk, community service for convicted offenders, "lock-your-car" campaigns, and the provision of better public transport. The most cost-effective method might turn out to be the improvement of vehicle security, since the assumption of rationality underlying the decision perspective supports measures that either increase (or seem to the offender to increase) the costs and effort of offending or decrease the rewards. The costs of this improved security would need to be carefully assessed; they should be weighed against the costs of the offense—these latter being broadly defined to include personal inconvenience and waste of police time—and any possible costs incurred by displacement.

Both the crime-specific focus for policy and the decision perspective are likely to favor more narrowly defined situational or deterrent measures by, for example, enabling the limits of displacement to be more clearly specified. While there is much unrealized potential for such measures (see Clarke 1983), there are dangers in going too far down this road. For example, different crime problems are sometimes concentrated together in the same localities and this may suggest coordinated action. It may also be the case that the best chance of apprehending individuals involved in certain particularly vicious criminal behavior—multiple rapes, for instance—lies in crackdowns on certain other offenses such as "curb crawling" or "cruising" by men in automobiles looking for prostitutes.

This latter point relates directly to the issue how far offenders are generalists rather than specialists, which is at the heart of questions about the policy value of the decision models. There is certainly evidence from the criminal careers research cited above that many of the most recidivist offenders are generalists. But it is not entirely clear to what extent they may specialize in certain forms of crime at particular times. It seems likely that the more closely offenses are defined, the more they will be found to be committed by characteristic offender types. Thus children involved in vandalism of schools may be different from those who assault teachers or, indeed, who vandalize other targets. To the extent that their special characteristics, in particular the motives and reasons underlying their conduct, can be identified and described, it may be possible to suggest more carefully tailored forms of intervention. Catchall interventions for loosely defined offender groups are unlikely to achieve their objectives.

176   Ronald V. Clarke and Derek B. Cornish

There are other ways in which the decision approach helps to account for the limited effectiveness of current treatment efforts. Programs tend to pay too much attention to modifying the influence of
"disposing" variables and in doing so take too little account of the
posttreatment environment, including the offender's current social and
economic situation, the role of chance events, and the specific opportunities open to him for crime. To be successful, treatment must take
more account of these contemporaneous influences. Where the pressures and inducements are primarily economic, the measures needed
are ones likely to increase the attractions and possibilities of conformity,
such as programs that give the offender new skills or ways of earning a
living. These programs must be based not only on a more careful
analysis of the particular needs and circumstances of the target group,
but also of the market for labor: it may be, for example, that work
programs are of limited effectiveness for those already in work or for
those able to earn considerably more money by illegitimate means.

As for incapacitation, the relevance of decision models lies in the fact
that they demand a detailed understanding of continuance and desistance. In particular more needs to be known about offenders' reasons
for switching crimes or for engaging in a variety of different crimes at a
particular time. Knowledge of this kind will help to determine the
feasibility of identifying suitable target groups for containment.

B. Research

The decision approach suggests three important directions for research: the mounting of further crime-specific studies, the devotion of
more attention to the offender's perspective when criminal careers are
studied, and the elucidation of decision processes at the point of offending. Some notable examples of crime-specific research have been
quoted in this essay. But there is much more scope for work of this
kind, particularly if, as our analysis seems to require, finer distinctions
between crimes are adopted. As for offenders' perspectives on their
careers, examples of the sorts of information needed have already been
given. A question of central importance concerns the part played in
desistance by changes in personal circumstances as compared with being arrested and sentenced. For example, an understanding of the impact of law enforcement and criminal justice systems will require study
of the offenders' sources of information and the way in which the
information is evaluated. It cannot be assumed that offenders' views of

the system and its measures bear a close relation to those of policymakers. It will be important to ask, for example, whether the official information is reaching its targets, whether the message is consistent, and whether it is believed. The need to understand the processing of information is also salient to modeling decision processes at the point of offending. More knowledge is needed, in particular, about the heuristic devices employed in assessing costs and payoffs, about how anxieties concerning the morality of the act and the risk of apprehension are dealt with (e.g., through shutoff mechanisms and techniques of neutralization) and about the effect of alcohol (see Bennett and Wright, in press), of anger, or, indeed, of other emotions.

Getting the questions right will help to determine the appropriate methodologies, and our preceding discussion has illustrated the wealth of available techniques to acquire the necessary information—participant observation, retrospective interviews, experimental studies of decision making, ecological mapping, crime site surveys, and "process tracing" in vivo or by using films and photographs. For some offenses, such as residential burglary, there may already be enough data to attempt a detailed simulation of the decision process.

Each of these methods makes certain theoretical assumptions and has its characteristic limitations. For example, the use of interviews and introspection to investigate criminal decision making may reveal more about people's post hoc commonsense or self-serving explanations for their behavior than about either the processes involved or the factors actually taken into account (Nisbett and Wilson 1977). Again, it should not be assumed that decision making in the real world can be easily simulated in the laboratory (see Ebbesen and Konecni 1980). Given the complexities of the issues and the dearth of information, triangulation of methods is essential, though any technique that enables criminal choices to be studied as they occur in naturalistic settings (see Payne's [1980] advocacy of process tracing) may be especially valuable.

The separation in the discussion above among theoretical formulations, policy, and research is, of course, artificial. In successful policy-relevant programs of research, there must be a dynamic interplay among theories, empirical studies, and policy implications. In particular, ongoing research should have a powerful feed-back effect upon the construction of models. And the impact of decision modeling on the structure of research is every bit as important as the policy applications discussed above.

C. Final Remarks

In conclusion, two general points seem worth emphasizing. First, the models have been developed primarily for the limited purposes of improving crime control policies and developing policy-relevant research. Such models have only to be "good enough"; they may not necessarily be the most appropriate or satisfactory for more comprehensive explanations of criminal behavior—though it seems likely that a decision approach might provide a useful starting point even for academic purposes. For example, Box (1981) has developed a sophisticated initial involvement model, based on control theory, which contains decision elements; while Glaser's (1979) more general "differential anticipation" theory incorporates elements of a decision approach within a hybrid involvement-event framework.

Second, decision models of crime might appear to imply the sort of "soft" determinism or modified classicism advocated by Matza (1964), namely, that while choices may be constrained, some leeway to choose still exists. And a criminology that makes use of such voluntaristic concepts might seem to have foresaken its traditional determinism.

A fuller discussion of this issue is beyond the scope of this essay (but see Glaser 1976; Schafer 1976). It is possible, however, to take a more pragmatic stance: while it is true that the concept of choice is likely to prove useful for generating and providing a framework for decision-making data, the resulting information supplies as many clues about determinants of behavior as it does about reasons and motives. This, in turn, enables both voluntaristic and deterministic models of offending to be elaborated further; it may be too soon, for example, to discount the sophisticated noncognitive accounts suggested by radical behaviorism (Skinner 1964, 1978). Perhaps, as Glaser (1976) implies, voluntaristic and deterministic assumptions are always best regarded as alternative heuristic devices for generating and organizing data. Under such circumstances it would not be surprising if the usefulness of their respective contributions to the task in hand—the more effective control of crime—appeared to vary from time to time. We believe, then, that decision-making concepts can be used for the purposes of constructing "good enough" theories without necessarily being firmly committed to a particular position in the free will/determinism debate—or to any consequential implications for crime control (Cressey 1979) or criminal justice (Norrie 1983). Indeed, the resulting policies remain, as before, the outcome of an uneasy blend of deterministic and neoclassical assumptions.

REFERENCES

Akers, Ronald L. 1977. *Deviant Behavior: A Social Learning Approach.* 2d ed. Belmont, Calif.: Wadsworth.

Åkerström, Malin. 1983. *Crooks and Squares.* Lund, Sweden: Studentlitteratur.

Athens, Lonnie. 1980. *Violent Criminal Acts and Actors: A Symbolic Interactionist Study.* London: Routledge & Kegan Paul.

Bandura, Albert. 1969. *Principles of Behavior Modification.* New York: Holt, Rinehart & Winston.

——. 1977. *Social Learning Theory.* Englewood Cliffs, N.J.: Prentice-Hall.

Becker, Gary S. 1968. "Crime and Punishment: An Economic Approach." *Journal of Political Economy* 76:169–217.

——. 1973. "A Theory of Marriage: Part One." *Journal of Political Economy* 81(4):813–46.

——. 1974. "A Theory of Marriage: Part Two." *Journal of Political Economy* 82(2):11–26.

Becker, Howard S. 1963. *Outsiders.* New York: Free Press.

Bennett, J. 1981. *Oral History and Delinquency.* Chicago: University of Chicago Press.

Bennett, Trevor H., and Richard Wright. 1983. *Constraints and Inducements to Crime: The Property Offender's Perspective.* Mimeographed. Cambridge: Cambridge University, Institute of Criminology.

——. 1984. "What the Burglar Saw." *New Society* (February 2), pp. 162–63.

——. In press. "The Relationship between Alcohol Use and Burglary." *British Journal of Addictions.*

Bevis, C., and J. B. Nutter. 1977. "Changing Street Layouts to Reduce Residential Burglary." Paper presented at the annual meeting of the American Society of Criminology, Atlanta, November.

Box, Stephen. 1981. *Deviance, Reality and Society.* London: Holt, Rinehart & Winston.

Brantingham, Paul J., and Patricia L. Brantingham. 1975. "The Spatial Patterning of Burglary." *Howard Journal of Penology and Crime Prevention* 14:11–24.

——. 1978. "A Theoretical Model of Crime Site Selection." In *Crime, Law and Sanctions*, edited by Marvin D. Krohn and Ronald L. Akers. Beverly Hills, Calif.: Sage.

Brown, B. B., and I. Altman. 1981. "Territoriality and Residential Crime: A Conceptual Framework." In *Environmental Criminology*, edited by Paul J. Brantingham and Patricia L. Brantingham. Beverly Hills, Calif.: Sage.

Brown, Ivan D. 1981. "The Traffic Offence as a Rational Decision." In *Psychology in Legal Contexts: Applications and Limitations*, edited by Sally M. A. Lloyd-Bostock. London: Macmillan.

Bruner, Jerome S., Jacqueline J. Goodnow, and George A. Austin. 1956. *A Study of Thinking.* New York: Wiley.

Burchard, John D. 1977. "Review of Yochelson and Samenow's *The Criminal Personality*, vol. 1." *Contemporary Psychology* 22(6):442–43.

Carroll, John S. 1982. "Committing a Crime: The Offender's Decision." In *The*

180   Ronald V. Clarke and Derek B. Cornish

Criminal Justice System: A Social-psychological Analysis, edited by Vladimir J. Konecni and Ebbe B. Ebbesen. Oxford: Freeman.

Carroll, John S., and E. J. Herz. 1981. "Criminal Thought Processes in Shoplifting." Paper presented at the annual meeting of the American Society of Criminology, Washington, D.C., November.

Carter, Ronald L., and Kim Q. Hill. 1979. *The Criminal's Image of the City*. New York: Pergamon.

Cimler, Edward, and Lee Roy Beach. 1981. "Factors Involved in Juveniles' Decisions about Crime." *Criminal Justice and Behavior* 8:275–86.

Clarke, Ronald V., ed. 1978. *Tackling Vandalism*. Home Office Research Study, no. 47. London: HMSO.

————. 1983. "Situational Crime Prevention: Its Theoretical Basis and Practice Scope." In *Crime and Justice: An Annual Review of Research*, vol. 4, edited by Michael Tonry and Norval Morris. Chicago: University of Chicago Press.

Clarke, Ronald V., and Derek B. Cornish. 1983. *Crime Control in Britain: A Review of Policy Research*. Albany: State University of New York Press.

Clarke, Ronald V., and Tim Hope. In press. *Coping with Burglary: Research Perspectives on Policy*. Boston: Kluwer-Nijhoff.

Cohen, Lawrence E., and Marcus Felson. 1979. "Social Change and Crime Rates Trends: A Routine Activity Approach." *American Sociological Review* 44:588–608.

Cohen, Stan. 1972. *Folk Devils and Moral Panics: The Creation of the Mods and Rockers*. London: MacGibbon & Kee.

Conger, Rand D. 1978. "From Social Learning to Criminal Behavior." In *Crime, Law and Sanctions*, edited by Marvin D. Krohn and Ronald L. Akers. Beverly Hills, Calif.: Sage.

Cook, Philip J. 1980. "Research in Criminal Deterrence: Laying the Groundwork for the Second Decade." In *Crime and Justice: An Annual Review of Research*, vol. 2, edited by Norval Morris and Michael Tonry. Chicago: University of Chicago Press.

Cornish, Derek B. 1978. *Gambling: A Review of the Literature and Its Implications for Policy and Research*. Home Office Research Study, no. 42. London: HMSO.

Cressey, Donald R. 1979. "Criminological Theory, Social Science and the Repression of Crime." In *Criminology: New Concerns*, edited by Edward Sagarin. Beverly Hills, Calif.: Sage.

Decker, John F. 1972. "Curbside Deterrence: An Analysis of the Effect of a Slug Rejector Device, Coin View Window and Warning Labels on Slug Usage in New York City Parking Meters." *Criminology* (August), pp. 127–42.

Denzin, Norman K. 1977. "Notes on the Criminogenic Hypothesis: A Case Study of the American Liquor Industry." *American Sociological Review* 42:905–20.

Ditton, Jason. 1977. *Part-Time Crime: An Ethnography of Fiddling and Pilferage*. London: Macmillan.

Downes, David. 1966. *The Delinquent Solution*. London: Routledge & Kegan Paul.

Ebbesen, Ebbe B., and Vladimir J. Konecni. 1980. "On the External Validity of Decision-making Research: What Do We Know about Decisions in the Real World?" In *Cognitive Processes in Choice and Decision Behavior*, edited by Thomas S. Walsten. Hillside, N.J.: Erlbaum.

Ehrlich, Isaac. 1979. "The Economic Approach to Crime: A Preliminary Assessment." In *Criminology Review Yearbook*, vol. 1, edited by Sheldon L. Messinger and Egon Bittner. Beverly Hills, Calif.: Sage.

Farrington, David P. 1979. "Longitudinal Research on Crime and Delinquency." In *Crime and Justice: An Annual Review of Research*, vol. 1, edited by Norval Morris and Michael Tonry. Chicago: University of Chicago Press.

Feldman, M. Phillip. 1977. *Criminal Behaviour: A Psychological Analysis*. London and New York: Wiley.

Felson, Richard B., and Henry J. Steadman. 1983. "Situational Factors in Disputes Leading to Criminal Violence." *Criminology* 21:59–74.

Fink, G. 1969. "Einsbruchstatorte vornehmlich an Einfallstrassen?" *Kriminalistik* 23:358–60.

Freeman, Richard B. 1983. "Crime and Unemployment." In *Crime and Public Policy*, edited by James Q. Wilson. San Francisco: Institute of Contemporary Studies Press.

Furlong, W. J., and S. L. Mehay. 1981. "Urban Law Enforcement in Canada. An Empirical Analysis." *Canadian Journal of Economics* 14(1):44–57.

Garber, Steven, Steven Klepper, and David Nagin. 1983. "The Role of Extralegal Factors in Determining Criminal Case Disposition." In *Research on Sentencing: The Search for Reform*, vol. 2, edited by Alfred Blumstein, Jacqueline Cohen, Susan E. Martin, and Michael H. Tonry. Washington, D.C.: National Academy Press.

Ghali, Moheb A. 1982. "The Choice of Crime: An Empirical Analysis of Juveniles' Criminal Choice." *Journal of Criminal Justice* 10:433–42.

Gibbs, John J., and Peggy L. Shelly. 1982. "Life in the Fast Lane: A Retrospective View by Commercial Thieves." *Journal of Research in Crime and Delinquency* 19:299–330.

Glaser, Daniel. 1976. "The Compatibility of Free Will and Determinism in Criminology: Comments on an Alleged Problem." *Journal of Criminal Law and Criminology* 67:487–90.

———. 1979. "A Review of Crime-Causation Theory and Its Application." In *Crime and Justice: An Annual Review of Research*, vol. 1, edited by Norval Morris and Michael Tonry. Chicago: University of Chicago Press.

Gould, Leroy C. 1969. "The Changing Structure of Property Crime in an Affluent Society." *Social Forces* 48:50–59.

Greenberg, D. F. 1977. "Delinquency and the Age Structure of Society." *Contemporary Crises* 1:189–223.

Hampson, Sarah E. 1982. *The Construction of Personality: An Introduction*. London: Routledge & Kegan Paul.

Heineke, J. M. 1978. "Economic Models of Criminal Behaviour: An Overview." In *Economic Models of Criminal Behaviour*, edited by J. M. Heineke. New York: North-Holland.

Henry, Stuart. 1978. *The Hidden Economy*. London: Martin Robertson.

182   Ronald V. Clarke and Derek B. Cornish

Hindelang, Michael J., Michael R. Gottfredson, and James Garofalo. 1978. *Victims of Personal Crime: An Empirical Foundation for a Theory of Personal Victimization.* Cambridge, Mass.: Ballinger.

Holzman, Harold R. 1983. "The Serious Habitual Property Offender as 'Moonlighter.' " *Journal of Criminal Law and Criminology* 73(4):1774–92.

Humphreys, Laud. 1970. *Tearoom Trade: Impersonal Sex in Public Places.* Chicago: Aldine.

Inciardi, James, A. 1975. *Careers in Crime.* Chicago: Rand McNally.

Jacoby, Joseph E. 1977. "Review of Yochelson and Samenow's *The Criminal Personality*, vol. 1." *Journal of Criminal Law and Criminology* 68:314–15.

Kahneman, Daniel, Paul Slovic, and Amos Tversky. 1982. *Judgment under Uncertainty: Heuristics and Biases.* New York: Cambridge University Press.

Kleinmuntz, Benjamin. 1968. "The Processing of Clinical Information by Man and Machine." In *Formal Representation of Human Judgment*, edited by Benjamin Kleinmuntz. New York: Wiley.

Klepper, Steven, Daniel Nagin, and Luke-Jon Tierney. 1983. "Discrimination in the Criminal Justice System: A Critical Appraisal of the Literature." In *Research on Sentencing: The Search for Reform*, vol. 2, edited by Alfred Blumstein, Jacqueline Cohen, Susan E. Martin, and Michael H. Tonry. Washington, D.C.: National Academy Press.

Klockars, Carl B. 1974. *The Professional Fence.* London: Tavistock.

Kozielecki, J. 1982. *Psychological Decision Theory.* Boston: Reidel.

Lejeune, Robert. 1977. "The Management of a Mugging." *Urban Life* 6(2):123–48.

Letkemann, P. 1973. *Crime as Work.* Englewood Cliffs, N.J.: Prentice-Hall.

Ley, David, and R. Cybrinwsky. 1974. "The Spatial Ecology of Stripped Cars." *Environment and Behaviour* 6:53–67.

Luedtke, Gerald, and Associates. 1970. *Crime and the Physical City: Neighborhood Design and Techniques for Crime Reduction.* Springfield, Va.: National Technical Information Service.

Maguire, Mike. 1980. "Burglary as Opportunity." *Research Bulletin* no. 10, pp. 6–9. London: Home Office Research Unit.

Maguire, Mike, in collaboration with Trevor Bennett. 1982. *Burglary in a Dwelling.* London: Heinemann.

Mansfield, Roger, Leroy C. Gould, and J. Zvi Namenwirth. 1974. "A Socioeconomic Model for the Prediction of Societal Rates of Property Theft." *Social Forces* 52:462–72.

Manski, Charles F. 1978. "Prospects for Inference on Deterrence through Empirical Analysis of Individual Criminal Behaviour." In *Economic Models of Criminal Behavior*, edited by J. M. Heineke. New York: North-Holland.

Mars, Gerald. 1974. "Dock Pilferage." In *Deviance and Social Control*, edited by Paul Rock and Mary McIntosh. London: Tavistock.

Marsh, Peter, Elizabeth Rosser, and Ron Harre. 1978. *The Rules of Disorder.* London: Routledge & Kegan Paul.

Matza, David. 1964. *Delinquency and Drift.* New York: Wiley.

Mayhew, Patricia M., Ronald V. G. Clarke, Andrew Sturman, and J. Michael Hough. 1976. *Crime as Opportunity.* Home Office Research Study no. 34. London: HMSO.

Meehl, Paul E. 1954. *Clinical versus Statistical Prediction: A Theoretical Analysis and a Review of the Evidence*. Minneapolis: University of Minnesota Press.

Mischel, Walter. 1973. "Toward a Cognitive Social Learning Reconceptualisation of Personality." *Psychological Review* 80:252–83.

———. 1979. "On the Interface of Cognition and Personality: Beyond the Person-Situation Debate." *American Psychologist* 34:740–54.

Myers, David G., and Helmut Lamm. 1976. "The Group Polarization Phenomenon." *Psychological Bulletin* 83:602–27.

Nietzel, Michael T. 1979. *Crime and Its Modification: A Social Learning Perspective*. New York: Pergamon.

Nisbett, Richard, and Lee Ross. 1980. *Human Inference: Strategies and Shortcomings of Social Judgment*. Englewood Cliffs, N.J.: Prentice-Hall.

Nisbett, R. E., and T. Wilson. 1977. "Telling More Than We Can Know: Verbal Reports on Mental Processes." *Psychological Review* 84:231–59.

Norrie, Alan. 1983. "Freewill, Determinism and Criminal Justice." *Legal Studies* 3(1):60–73.

Orsagh, Thomas. 1983. "Is There a Place for Economics in Criminology and Criminal Justice?" *Journal of Criminal Justice* 99(5):391–401.

Orsagh, Thomas, and Ann Dryden Witte. 1981. "Economic Status and Crime: Implications for Offender Rehabilitation." *Journal of Criminal Law and Criminology* 72(3):1055–71.

Palmer, J. 1977. "Economic Analyses of the Deterrent Effect of Punishment: A Review." *Journal of Research in Crime and Delinquency* 14:4–21.

Parker, Howard J. 1974. *View from the Boys: A Sociology of Down-Town Adolescents*. Newton Abbot, England: David & Charles.

Payne, J. 1980. "Information Processing Theory: Some Concepts and Methods Applied to Decision Research." In *Cognitive Processes in Choice and Decision Behavior*, edited by Thomas Wallsten. Hillsdale, N.J.: Erlbaum.

Petersilia, Joan. 1980. "Criminal Career Research: A Review of Recent Evidence." In *Crime and Justice: An Annual Review of Research*, vol. 2, edited by Michael Tonry and Norval Morris. Chicago: University of Chicago Press.

Pruitt, D. G. 1971. "Choice Shifts in Group Discussion: An Introductory Review." *Journal of Personality and Social Psychology* 20:339–60.

Prus, Robert C. and S. Irini. 1980. *Hookers, Rounders and Desk Clerks: The Social Organization of the Hotel Community*. Toronto: Sage.

Pyle, David J. 1983. *The Economics of Crime and Law Enforcement*. London: Macmillan.

Rengert, George F., and J. Wasilchick. 1980. "Residential Burglary: The Awareness and Use of Extended Space." Paper presented at the annual meeting of the American Society of Criminology, San Francisco, November.

Reppetto, Thomas A. 1974. *Residential Crime*. Cambridge, Mass.: Ballinger.

———. 1976. "Crime Prevention and the Displacement Phenomenon." *Crime and Delinquency* 22:166–77.

Samuel, Raphael. 1981. *East End Underworld: Chapters in the Life of Arthur Harding*. London: Routledge & Kegan Paul.

Sarbin, Theodore R. 1979. "Review of Yochelson and Samenow's *The Criminal Personality*, vol. 1." *Crime and Delinquency* 25(3):392–96.

184   Ronald V. Clarke and Derek B. Cornish

Scarr, Harry A. 1973. *Patterns of Burglary*. For the U.S. Department of Justice. Washington, D.C.: Government Printing Office.

Schafer, Stephen. 1976. "The Problem of Free Will in Criminology." *Journal of Criminal Law and Criminology* 67:481–85.

Sheley, Joseph F. 1980. "Is Neutralisation Necessary for Criminal Behaviour?" *Deviant Behaviour* 2:49–72.

Shover, N. 1972. "Structures and Careers in Burglary." *Journal of Criminal Law, Criminology and Police Science* 63:540–49.

Simon, Herbert A. 1983. *Reasoning in Human Affairs*. Oxford: Blackwell.

Skinner, Frederick B. 1964. "Behaviorism at Fifty." In *Behaviorism and Phenomenology*, edited by T. W. Wann. Chicago: University of Chicago Press.

———. 1978. *Reflections on Behaviorism and Society*. Englewood Cliffs, N.J.: Prentice-Hall.

Skogan, Wesley G., and Michael G. Maxfield. 1981. *Coping with Crime: Individual and Neighborhood Reactions*. Beverly Hills, Calif.: Sage.

Slovic, P., and S. Lichtenstein. 1968. "The Relative Importance of Probabilities and Payoffs in Risk-Taking." *Journal of Experimental Psychology Monograph*, vol. 78, no. 3, pt. 2.

Sparks, Richard F. 1980. "A Critique of Marxist Criminology." In *Crime and Justice: An Annual Review of Research*, vol. 2, edited by Norval Morris and Michael Tonry. Chicago: University of Chicago Press.

Sturman, Andrew. 1978. "Measuring Vandalism in a City Suburb." In *Tackling Vandalism*, edited by Ronald V. G. Clarke. Home Office Research Study no. 47. London: HMSO.

Taylor, Ian, Paul Walton, and Jock Young. 1973. *The New Criminology*. London: Routledge & Kegan Paul.

Trasler, Gordon B. 1979. "Delinquency, Recidivism, and Desistance." *British Journal of Criminology* 19:314–22.

Tversky, A., and D. Kahneman. 1974. "Judgment under Uncertainty: Heuristics and Biases." *Science* 185:1124–31.

Vold, George B. 1979. *Theoretical Criminology*. 2d ed. New York: Oxford University Press.

Waldo, Gordon P., ed. 1983. *Career Criminals*. Beverly Hills, Calif.: Sage.

Waller, Irvin, and Norman Okihiro. 1978. *Burglary: The Victim and the Public*. Toronto: University of Toronto Press.

Walsh, Dermot P. 1978. *Shoplifting: Controlling a Major Crime*. London: Macmillan.

———. 1980. *Break-Ins: Burglary from Private Houses*. London: Constable.

Warr, P. B., and C. Knapper. 1968. *The Perception of People and Events*. Chichester: Wiley.

West, Donald J. 1963. *The Habitual Prisoner*. London: Macmillan.

———. 1982. *Delinquency: Its Roots, Careers and Prospects*. London: Heinemann.

West, W. Gordon. 1978. "The Short Term Careers of Serious Thieves." *Canadian Journal of Criminology* 20:169–90.

Wiggins, Jerry S. 1973. *Personality and Prediction: Principles of Personality Assessment*. Reading, Mass.: Addison-Wesley.

Wilcox, S. 1974. "The Geography of Robbery." In *The Pattern and Control of Robbery*, edited by Floyd Feeney and A. Weir. Davis: University of California Press.

Wilkins, Leslie T. 1964. *Social Deviance*. London: Tavistock.

Wilkins, Leslie T., and Ann Chandler. 1965. "Confidence and Competence in Decision Making." *British Journal of Criminology* 5:22–35.

Winchester, Stuart, and Hilary Jackson. 1982. *Residential Burglary: The Limits of Prevention*. Home Office Research Study no. 74. London: HMSO.

Witte, Ann Dryden. 1980. "Estimating the Economic Model of Crime with Individual Data." *Quarterly Journal of Economics* 94:57–84.

Wolfgang, Marvin E., Robert M. Figlio, and Thorsten Sellin. 1972. *Delinquency in a Birth Cohort*. Chicago: University of Chicago Press.

Yochelson, S., and S. E. Samenow. 1976. *The Criminal Personality*. 2 vols. New York: Aronson.

Name Index